Medieval Manuscripts for Mass and Office
A guide to their organization and terminology

Many books discuss the theology and doctrine of the medieval liturgy: there is no dearth of information on the history of the liturgy, the structure and development of individual services, and there is much discussion of specific texts, chants, and services. No book, at least in English, has struggled with the difficulties of finding texts, chants, or other material in the liturgical manuscripts themselves, until the publication of *Medieval Manuscripts for Mass and Office* in 1982.

Encompassing a period of several centuries, ca 1200–1500, this book provides solutions for such endeavours. Although by this period the basic order and content of liturgical books were more or less standardized, there existed hundreds of different methods of dealing with the internal organization and the actual writing of the texts and chants on the page. Generalization becomes problematic; the use of any single source as a typical example for more than local detail is impossible.

Taking for granted the user's ability to read medieval scripts, and some codicological knowledge, Hughes begins with the elementary material without which the user could not proceed. He describes the liturgical year, season, day, service, and the form of individual items such as responsory or lesson, and mentions the many variants in terminology that are to be found in the sources. The presentation of individual text and chant is discussed, with an emphasis on the organization of the individual column, line, and letter. Hughes examines the hitherto unexplored means by which a hierarchy of initial and capital letters and their colours are used by the scribes and how this hierarchy can provide a means by which the modern researcher can navigate through the manuscripts. Also described in great detail are the structure and contents of Breviaries, Missals, and the corresponding books with music. This new edition updates the bibliography and the new preface by Hughes presents his recent thoughts about terminology and methods of liturgical abbreviation.

ANDREW HUGHES is University Professor and Professor of the Centre for Medieval Studies and Faculty of Music at the University of Toronto. He is the author of several books including *A Bibliography of Medieval Music: The Sixth Liberal Art* (Toronto, 1974) and *Late Medieval Liturgical Offices: Resources for Electronic Research* (Pontifical Institute for Medieval Studies, 1994).

The Ranworth Antiphonal, f 1, Advent Sunday (see page 311)

ANDREW HUGHES

Medieval Manuscripts for Mass and Office: A guide to their organization and terminology

UNIVERSITY OF TORONTO PRESS
Toronto Buffalo London

Toronto Buffalo London
Printed in Canada
Reprinted in 2019
First paperback edition 1995
ISBN 0-8020-5467-6 (cloth)
ISBN 978-0-8020-7669-4 (paper)

Printed on acid-free paper

Canadian Cataloguing in Publication Data

Hughes, Andrew, 1937–
Medieval manuscripts for mass and office

Bibliography: p. 382
Includes index.
ISBN 0-8020-5467-6 (bound) ISBN 0-8020-7669-6 (pbk.)

1. Liturgics – History – Sources. 2. Liturgies, Early Christian – History – Sources. 3. Liturgies – Manuscripts – History. 4. Liturgies – Manuscripts – Terminology. 5. Manuscripts, Latin (Medieval and modern). I. Title.

BV185.H83 264′.00902 C81-094453-7

Contents

8/Office Books 160

9/Lent and Easter Week 245

APPENDICES

INDICES

Acknowledgments

This book has been nearly fifteen years in the research, writing, re-writing, and final production. During that period so many people have assisted me that it is impossible to list them all by name. Numerous graduate and undergraduate students have helped me as research assistants: I thank them all, and in particular Joanna Dutka and Rudi Schnitzler, now both professors in Canadian universities. The assessors of this book, who remain anonymous to me, offered several useful suggestions and were generous in their evaluations; Professor John Brückmann was especially encouraging. Scores of librarians throughout North America and Europe gave unstintingly of their time and expertise: Kathleen McMorrow, the librarian of the Faculty of Music, University of Toronto, graciously allowed me special privileges in the borrowing of books and microfilms for the final production stages. Jack Branker and Karen Hendrick of the Photoduplication Department of the Robarts Library, University of Toronto, did splendid work to produce the photographs from films and slides which were often several generations removed from the originals: any lack of quality in the reproductions must be attributed to my lack of ability as a photographer or to the worn state of heavily used microfilms. Jim Grier helped to compile the Bibliography, and made useful additions and revisions.

One of the assessors spoke of the nightmare the typesetters would have in the printing of this book, with its complex tables and many changes of typeface. For conventional typesetting, the nightmare would have been real. In fact, the setting was done almost entirely under my supervision by three typists entering the text directly into the terminal of a typesetting computer. It took some three or four weeks. All the typists worked long hours in order to complete the input before one of the deadlines: to Lynn West and Daniel Neff, both of the Opera School of the Faculty of Music, many thanks; to Elizabeth Brickenden especial thanks for her loyal and hard work. If any bassoons have crept into the text, it is entirely Elizabeth's fault: for every other blemish I am responsible. The tabular material was prepared by Howarth and Smith, the professional typesetters. Even this material, however, was proof-read and changed as necessary at the terminal by the typists, just as was the normal text. I must thank Phil Bellamy, of

Howarth and Smith, for steering the work through the typesetting computer, and Ian McLean, also of Howarth and Smith, for his careful work on the tabular material and for coping with the special intricacies of the Ordo in section **741.**

Carol Derk, Diane Droste, Edward English, Maurice Esses, John French, and Lynn Sampson assisted with the proof-reading. Lorraine Ourom gave me a great deal of her time, and took on the extra task of copy-editing the typescript in addition to her usual work: Collette Copeland did much of the drudgery of the copy-editing. Many others at the University of Toronto Press were of invaluable assistance. I thank them all.

Publication of this book has been made possible by grants from the Canadian Federation for the Humanities, using funds provided by the Social Sciences and Humanities Research Council of Canada, and from the Subsidized Publications funds of University of Toronto Press.

Andrew Hughes
Vigilia Nativitatis 1980
Toronto

Preface

1 This book originated to fill a practical need. It is to introduce students of the later middle ages to the manuscripts of the liturgy. Even for the person able to read the script and abbreviations of the period, working with liturgical books is difficult, and acquiring the necessary skills and experience even more so. The difficulty stems, I believe, from three principal factors which are outlined in the introduction. My purpose is to show the reader how liturgical books are organized and how they may be used for research: it is not to write yet another elementary introduction to the liturgy. Nevertheless, the person who lives the day-by-day Latin liturgy, and the scholar who knows that the Lauds antiphons are very stable from era to era and place to place, may gain little from the first part of the book, where essential preliminary information is presented. But I hesitate to characterize even that information as elementary because, seeking to avoid the superficial survey and the broad generalization and using numerous published descriptions as well as many manuscripts, I have tried to show discrepancies, variants, alternatives, exceptions, and modifications. Much of the first part, up to chapter 5 but excluding chapter 3, summarizes material to be found in previously published books. There are so many publications that it may be several years before the reader realizes, as I eventually came to realize, that not one describes in more than an elementary way how the liturgical services are arranged in the manuscripts and how their texts, music, and rubrics are presented on the page. The organization, content, layout, and writing of liturgical manuscripts are so varied, in fact, that the generalizations by which complex topics can be made comprehensible are hardly possible.

The variability is in the presentation of detail. Just as the general shape of the liturgy and the order of services is consistent, so is the overall organization of the liturgical book: the difficulties lie in the exceptions, in the variants from season to season, from church to church, and from century to century, and in the alternative methods of presentation. Hence the emphasis in the first part of the book on differences separating use from use. Such differences may help us to localize and to date the sources. Much of the book therefore consists of factual description, often in the form of 'And next there follows ...'

This approach has been very difficult to avoid, and, if thereby the book has become tedious to read from cover to cover, I hope that its value as a reference book for specific occasions will not be lessened. In particular there is a certain amount of repetition. The information of the first part had to be recalled as individual manuscripts were described in the second. I was tempted to consolidate the two parts into one single section: in place of repetition there would then have been endless qualifications, exceptions, clauses and subclauses, and notes, which would have obscured the principle in a mass of detail. Essential repetitions from part to part have been allowed to stand. Repetitions from smaller section to section also seemed unavoidable, especially if sections were to be more or less self-contained. If the same material may appear in four or five different forms and in different contexts in as many different places in the liturgical books, then in the descriptions of those places the material recurs and the same things have to be said about it. Instructions concerning the ordinary of the Mass, for example, may occur in the Temporale of Graduals or of Missals and Noted Missals, requiring a reference when each book is described, or in the Ordo misse, or in the Kyriale, requiring two additional references. Wherever possible, I have tried to eliminate obtrusive repetition by using cross-references or by presenting figures or typographical 'facsimiles' to demonstrate the visual format of the original.

2 For manuscript sources I have used a great many which were to hand on microfilm, taking into account the fact that many users of liturgical books of the middle ages can do so only by way of films; these were often available because of some importance other than that they were liturgical books. Many, for example, contain particularly interesting decorations, or have polyphonic music on flyleaves. Hundreds of other manuscripts were investigated in personal trips to European and North American libraries when I was engaged on other research. The selection of sources was, then, quite arbitrary, but as balanced as possible. I have included only books directly relevant to Mass and offices; Breviaries and Antiphonals, Missals and Graduals, and the smaller 'books' which are usually included within those compendia. Many others are necessary in order to gain a complete picture of any one rite. The decision to eliminate Processionals, Pontificals, Ordinals, Manuals, and others was made on the basis of availability, the already increasing length of this study, and on the belief that once the principles of the main books are understood, it becomes easy to use the others.

3 Several matters of style and presentation need comment. To facilitate references and to avoid the extra stage required for the production of a conventional index, I have numbered the paragraphs; those of the preface take single digits; the introduction begins with **10**, chapters 1, 2, ... 9 begin respectively with **100, 200, ... 900**; Appendices I-IX begin with **1000-9000** respectively. Occasionally several short paragraphs stand under a single number. Whenever a boldface number appears in this book, including the Index, it refers to the bold number which stands at the margin in the indentation for paragraphs. On the other hand, numbers in normal type following a letter, eg, M7, A22, refer to the manuscript sources listed at the end of the book. There is a potential ambiguity: A22 may mean ms A22 or (mostly in diagrams and formulas) 'twenty-two antiphons.' The context and the normal use of 'ms' or 'source' will make the meaning clear.

Immediately after this preface are lists showing the numerous abbreviations used in the book. The algebraic strings resulting from an excess of abbreviations are graceless and difficult to read. Nevertheless, without such shortening many of the figures would have been impossibly large, and extra repetition would have crept into many sections. Furthermore, the difficulty of digesting in one's mind a serpentine and endless paragraph such as immediately follows would usually force the reader to evolve for himself a written formula such as that shown afterwards.

On this feast, the items recorded for Matins are the invitatory and hymn, both given in incipit only. In the first nocturn, there are three antiphons, given complete, and the incipit of the dialogue, followed by the three lessons given complete. The first two responsories appear in incipit only, and the third is complete. In the second nocturn, all three antiphons and the dialogue are given in incipit: the three lessons are complete, as are responsories four and six, although responsory five appears only as an incipit. In the third nocturn the three antiphons and dialogue are given in incipit: all three lessons are complete and all three responsories, seven to nine, are given in incipit.

Although this example is of course tendentious, services will often have to be described in similar detail. The alternative 'notation' may seem just as indigestible but it is much more concise and, once the reader has acquired a familiarity with the abbreviations, it has the advantage of demonstrating the patterns more clearly. We could use:

On this feast, Matins is presented as follows:

ih AAAd LrLrLR aaad LRLrLR aaad LrLrLr.

Even more concisely:

ih A3d LrLrLR a3d LRLrLR a3d (Lr)3.

We need to evolve convenient tools for comparing liturgical manuscripts and collating their contents in a form which is immediately striking: some condensed way of recording the contents is therefore suggested here. Despite the usefulness of these formulas, I have tried to avoid over-using them in the running text.

Certain words which some authors begin with a capital letter are here not printed in this way. In particular the genre names lack capitals: names of the books retain the capital. Thus, the gradual chant is found in the Gradual. Incipits of texts receive the customary capital. Thus, the alleluia chant of Mass is distinct from the textual Alleluia which is appended to many chants during Easter. The consistent use of italics proved difficult to maintain. In general I have used them for a first reference to a foreign term such as *prosa* and thereafter to accept it as an Anglicized word not needing the typographical differentiation. The exemplification of rubrics and incipits within them has also been the cause of some difficulty: normally the rubric has been printed in italic, to indicate the original red script, and the black incipit in normal type. Occasionally, however, it has been necessary to reverse that principle. No ambiguity, I think, will result. Wherever confusion might result I have explained the methods, special abbreviations, and signs.

Preface to the Paperback Edition

I have taken the opportunity in this new edition to correct typographical errors, and to clarify a few confusing matters, especially in the Figures. Otherwise, it has not been possible to make substantial changes to the text, and in general it has not been necessary. I should have liked to meet one reviewer's wish: to do for manuscripts existing before the twelfth century what I attempted to do for those appearing after that date. Such an enterprise would, however, require considerable time with sources that are often quite different in structure, if not in content, and would be effective only with several more facsimiles. For some understanding of the most important of the earlier sources, I direct the reader to Hesbert's *Corpus antiphonalium officii*, a detailed and comprehensive inventory of a dozen secular and monastic sources, from which some sense of their structure can be assembled.

Several publications that address the issues of liturgical abbreviation, terminology, and manuscript structure and design have been added to the bibliography. I have also briefly appended my own recent thoughts about terminology (immediately below), and methods of liturgical abbreviation (in a supplement to the Abbreviations): the need for establishing some consistency in both areas seems more urgent now that computers and databases have become so important to research in the humanities. Following Appendix I, on page 280, is a brief but important note about the Kalendar dates of saints' feastdays.

TERMINOLOGY

One of the purposes of this text is to identify and categorize as many variants of terminology as possible, taking into account only the texts and chants of the services themselves. In the more general sense, ecclesiastical terminology remains a problem: what is Use, rite, ceremonial, or liturgy itself? What are the terms for administrative structures and procedures of the church?

These matters have been well addressed by John Harper in his book *The Forms and Orders of Western Liturgy* ... (1991), which presents more simply and in a wider context some of the material to be found in exhausting detail in this book. Assessing Harper's book for publication, I referred to it as a book I wished I had written.

It has become clear, too, that English terms for smaller elements of the liturgy need to be much more carefully used. Unambiguous definitions are probably not possible, and in some cases it may be necessary to surround with cumbersome qualifications an otherwise simple word that in the context of the original sources may be clear. Three words that have given particular problems or created misunderstandings since the first edition appeared are text, chant, and office.

Texts and chants

Texts in the liturgy are performed in one of four ways: silently, in a spoken voice, sung to a (reciting) tone, or sung to a melodic chant. Rarely is there any difficulty in distinguishing among these categories. My own preference for the way the words text and chant should be used is implicit in the preceding sentence: text refers to the words, and chant to the plainsong. Others prefer to use the word chant to refer to texts that are sung to plainsong (synonym: plainchant), regardless of whether the music is actually present or even known. To refer to 'chant' when no music is present or mentioned, however, is misleading. Moreover, to allow an unambiguous description of a text separated from its music, it would be necessary to resort to the inelegant and tautologous 'a chant without its plainchant' or to 'a chant without its music.' Nevertheless, the issue is not quite so clear: we *should* distinguish between texts that are sung and those that are not, and the simple word 'text' is not adequate for that purpose. We must either use as many words and qualifications as are necessary to be quite explicit, or we must coin some new terms.

Cryptographers use the term 'cleartext' to refer to a text before it is encrypted. Surely, for a discipline as complex as liturgical studies, we should anticipate the need for new terms of a similar kind where it is necessary to be precise. For the four categories mentioned above, I would suggest *silenttext, spokentext, intonedtext,* and *sungtext*; for the most part, identification of the genre will obviate the need for these somewhat cumbersome neologisms. The last is the simplest to accept, and takes care of the most contentious ambiguity, distinguishing between texts sung to melodic plainsongs and all others.

I have already begun consistently to use the term *chantword* to refer to a single word of text together with the chant that accompanies it (see 'Chantwords ...' in the supplement to the Bibliography). By extension, *chanttext* would refer to the whole text of a genre with its plainsong; *sungtext* could then signify the text of any item sung to plainsong without necessarily implying that the music was present. Many may prefer to be explicitly accurate: 'an antiphon text' or 'an antiphon plainchant,' or 'the text and chant of a hymn.'

Office and historia

At least three uses for the word office are current. All are correct and can be justified by medieval usage. Various meanings attach to the word depending on the interests of the user, and are presumably understood by the user. But not necessarily by the audience. In some circumstances it will be appropriate to use office to refer to the whole matter of the feastday: all of its various texts, chants, and gestures. Alternatively, it can refer only to the office hours of the feastday, or only to Mass. On other occasions, the term is implicitly used to refer to the lessons and prayers, the *intonedtexts.* Other scholars interested in the parts of the feastday that are sung to plainsongs may use the word to mean the *sungtexts.*

Of the two terms, *officium* and *historia* are not clearly defined or unambiguously used in the Middle Ages: for both of these terms the meanings are as varied as are those for the English word 'office,' although *historia* (in the later Middle Ages, at least) probably refers more usually to the *sungtexts* rather than to the *intonedtexts* or the office as a whole. Tempting though it may be, to try to impose on these normal words a rigid meaning would be impossible.

For the office as a whole – texts, chants, gestures, processions, censing, and so on – the word *rite* (with a lowercase letter) would serve (the distinction is set out clearly in Harper, p. 13): 'the rites of Christmas Day' (as distinct from the Roman Rite) is unambiguous and unexceptional. For the office as a collection of all its texts, or its *sungtexts*, or its *intonedtexts*, the matter is not so simple, short of adjectival or parenthetical appendages. To refer to all of the texts without distinguishing among their categories, the word *formularies* could be used, a more or less conventional and probably unexceptional usage. But it will still need to be attached to the word 'office' or 'Mass.' For the other options I see no convenient alternative other than to add to the words 'office' or 'Mass' the precise texts that are intended: 'the office hours (*sungtexts*) for Thomas of Canterbury,' or 'the *sungtexts* of the office for ...,' or 'the antiphons and responsories of ...'

Fortunately, such inelegant constructions may be avoided when the context is apparent: in a volume concerned only with the *sungtexts* of the office hours (as is my recent book *LMLO*) a more casual terminology may be acceptable.

Some addenda to the first edition

In the interests of a comprehensive listing of terminology and liturgical usage as it appears in the original sources, I here provide a brief list of matters, mostly words, that do not appear in the first edition. I have not systematically collected new material, and the additions are thus mercifully few. Since it was not possible to add these to the body of the book or to the index, readers may wish to make a suitable notation next to the relevant sections or in the index. Some points set out below are little more than undocumented and unresearched issues that came to my attention in the course of other, quite different work: some of these would provide excellent material for detailed study.

- *additiones* a term referring to suffrages after Lauds (Austria, Innsbruck, University Library, ms 351)
- *apparitio* Epiphany
- homily: was the homily after the Gospel at Matins announced by name? References to it, for example, *Omelia sancti Gregorii*, are normally in rubrics. Yet the edition, *Divine Office*, prints this text in black, perhaps reflecting modern practice.
- Matins in which all antiphons are together and all responsories together, instead of alternating in nocturns: this arrangement is characteristic of Beneventan and Carthusian manuscripts (for Benevento, see Kelly, *The Beneventan Chant*; for Carthusian, see, for example, Cambridge, Fitzwilliam Museum, ms 371)
- *memoria* can refer to a full proper service or to an isolated suffrage or prayer

- *ps* although apparently referring to *psalmus,* this abbreviation is often used before the repetenda of responsories (see, for example, several Avignon office manuscripts).
- Sarum: some evidence suggests that the liturgy of this Use was made artificially consistent by deliberate rearrangement and editing.
- Vespers: According to the Benedictine rule, Vespers has four antiphons. In the introduction to *Analecta Hymnica* (vol 5, pp. 10–11) Dreves sets out the number of antiphons used by various orders: Cistercians 4; Franciscans and Benedictines 5; Dominicans 1 (and Cistercians are said to have a single antiphon at Lauds, and proper antiphons for each of the little hours). Although aware of this problem for a number of years, I have not pursued the issue in documentary sources, and have come to no clear conclusion in casual investigation of the liturgical books themselves. Clearly there is some confusion, probably arising from the method by which the proper items are distributed in the sources. The possibilities for such confusion and how the confusion might be resolved are precisely what this book tries to present: where there is a single antiphon, presumably proper, are the others supplied from the Common? How many?
- *victatorium, vitatorium* these terms for the invitatory are somewhat more common than **218**n36 leads the reader to suppose: Beaune, bibl. municipale ms 26; Clermont-Ferrand, bibl. mun. ms 842; Montserrat, monastic library ms 880; and other sources. The invitatory is often special in ways other than its form or the Psalter used for its text: it occurs only in a few of the eight modes; in regularly rhymed offices it is often in Classical metres or prose rather than accentual poetry; in Paris, bibl. nat. ms 12036, only the invitatories are fully noted. See also Vatican, bibl. apost. ms Barb. lat. 408.

Abbreviations

4 In order to reduce the cumbersome nature of some of the discussions, and to make many of the figures possible, I have abbreviated the different genres and items of the services to a single letter, normally the letter with which the usual name begins, or to a symbol. Where texts are concerned, the lower case letter is used to indicate that only an incipit of the item occurs. Services, seasons, and sections of books are also shortened to their initial letter, and different type-styles have been used to distinguish these abbreviations. The following styles of type occur:

roman – used for genres other than those in boldface, for seasons, and (preceded by 'ms' or 'source') for referring to sources;
boldface – used for the sung items of Mass;
script – used for services (where possible these will be spelt in full in normal type);
sans serif – used for sections of books.

Despite the adoption of various type-styles, some letters in the same style still refer to more than one item: **G**, for example, stands for both the Gloria and the gradual. Where the context and knowledge to be gained from this book are not sufficient to eliminate the ambiguity, clarification will be included in the text. Letters-followed-by-numerals represent the original sources and are preceded by the word 'source' or 'ms'. The abbreviations are separated according to their meaning (type-style) in the following lists; in each list they are in alphabetical order. Frequently in the captions to the figures within the book, unusual abbreviations will be expanded as a reminder to the reader of their meaning.

I have tried to avoid using abbreviations within the running text when they are not necessary: their justification appears in the preface. Here it remains to explain how the abbreviations are combined to present services in concise formulas: a numeral following the abbreviation specifies the number of repetitions of that item which are consecutive at that point in the service; a numeral following parentheses shows the number of repetitions of the items within the parentheses. Thus Ap stands for an antiphon with its psalm-incipit, Ap3 for a single antiphon covering three psalms shown in incipit, (Ap)3 for three antiphons each with its own psalm-incipit. Different services will be separated by a slash / where necessary, sometimes with a reference to the abbreviation for (or full name of) the service. Often the presence of certain genres identifies the service sufficiently: only Vespers, for example, ends with the Magnificat M, or with the Magnificat and prayer, MO.

Bibliographical references are sometimes by short titles, or by citations such as Frere (1901), or by the occasional abbreviation: all of these are explained in the bibliography.

Supplement to the Paperback Edition

The decisions about the nature and style of liturgical abbreviations for the first edition were made before the ubiquitous availability of computers had made research simultaneously more complex and more simple. In the intervening years, I have devoted a major part of my activities to the computerization of liturgical research, and to the indexing of texts and chants by means of databases and other computer programs, particularly with the repertory of late medieval offices. This venture has come to fruition in the publication of my recent volumes under the siglum *LMLO* (see the supplement to the Bibliography).

Reliance on and the limitations imposed by the use of the computer has forced some changes to the abbreviation system developed for the first edition of this book. More details regarding these constraints are in *LMLO.* In particular, the method by which identical letters are distinguished in the present volume – by the use of distinct typefaces – proved impossible to preserve (and indeed, unsatisfactory in many respects). To distinguish different typefaces in a computer text requires the addition of cumbersome and intrusive codes that complicate indexing and printing. Moreover, using different typefaces makes it impossible to use these abbreviations in handwritten notes, where a chief benefit is to be gained.

I am still convinced – now even more so – of the need for abbreviation and concise methods of recording liturgical phenomena. *LMLO* sets out a system, more complete than but to a large extent using and extending the one laid out here. In place of different typefaces, various symbols are used as prefixes and suffixes to distinguish the various categories of abbreviations separated into the six lists below. Such a scheme also makes it possible to remove some of the ambiguities (e.g., C for both Credo and communion chant) of the system used here. It also makes possible the use of mnemonic letters in place of the typographic and not always meaningful symbols of List 1f.

Details of the new schemes cannot be presented here. The following outlines some of the chief characteristics:

- the principal difference in the abbreviations are in (1) List 1a, where E now represents the Gospel antiphons (*ad Evangelium*) previously recorded as M, B, and N; and (2) in an expansion of Lists 1b and 1c with additional genres and services, including W for second vespers, E for Eucharistic propers, and O for the Ordinary of Mass;

- to distinguish ambiguities, for example, A for antiphon and A for Agnus, the service letter must precede the abbreviation for a genre;
- services, genres, and the number of the genre within a service are now associated with the equals sign in a formulation generalized as SGN. In narrative text, where no ambiguity arises, the letters and numbers of SGN alone may suffice, as with MR9 for Matins responsory 9. Elsewhere and in cases of ambiguity =SGN may be preferred: for example, the Agnus at Mass would be =OA, the fourth antiphon at Vespers =VA4. For descriptions of services, the formulation S=GNGN ... is useful: the hypothetical matins service laid out on page xiii would now appear as M=ih.A3d{LrLrLR}.a3d{LRLrLR}.a3d{Lr}3;
- various prefixes to the =SGN codes may identify the liturgical season, and suffixes may identify other details such as the feria of a week or the musical mode of the chant. Generally, these prefixes and suffixes are designed to be self-explanatory, and yet (for the most part) to allow sorting in the correct liturgical order: for example, 1=Adv.2=LA4.5c for the fourth antiphon of Lauds in the second week of Advent, in mode 5 ending on c;
- sections of book identified in List 1e and one or two items from List 1f are now associated with the numeral 2 and a hyphen. This allows the sectional arrangement of books (as described in **749–751** and **889–897**) to be clearly distinguished (and isolated by computer processes if necessary) from other similar formulas: 2-TKPSC or 2-TKPCS.

For a few purposes in this text, for example, distinguishing the antiphons for *Benedictus* from *Magnificat* and *Nunc dimittis* (all now designated as E), the new schemes would themselves be unsatisfactory. In any case, to change the schemes running throughout this text would have required revisions far more extensive than was possible. The new schemes are therefore not implemented here.

Symbols

LIST 1a

A antiphon
B Benedictus or the Benedictus antiphon
C chapter
D dialogue or preces (see also □ in list 1f below). The versicle of a dialogue will end with ':' (or ... if incomplete), and the response or its incipit will then be shown. See *D*.
D the liturgical greeting, *Dominicus vobiscum: Et cum ...*
E epistle
G gospel
H hymn
I invitatory
K canticle, lesser or major
L lesson, reading (may be a chapter, epistle, or gospel or homily, but normally refers to the lessons at Matins)
M Magnificat or Magnificat antiphon
N Nunc dimittis or Nunc dimittis antiphon
O oratio, collect, secret, post-communion, etc (ie, any prayer)
Ø great O antiphons
P psalm
Ps used for a specific psalm, followed by a number
R responsory
V verse, of a responsory, gradual, or alleluia, etc: the versicle and response of a dialogue are abbreviated under D

LIST 1b

Mass chants

A Agnus *or* alleluia
B Benedicamus Domino
C Credo *or* communion chant
G Gloria *or* gradual
H Hymnus trium puerorum
I Ite missa est *or* introit
K Kyrie
O offertory chant
S sanctus
T tract
V verse of a gradual or alleluia

LIST 1c
Service or action

$\mathcal{C}$	Compline	$\mathcal{S}$	Sext
$\mathcal{H}$	Hours	~	sprinkling of holy water
$\mathcal{L}$	Lauds	$\mathcal{T}$	Terce
$\mathcal{M}$	Matins	~	thurification, ie, censing
$\mathcal{N}$	Nones	$\mathcal{V}$	Vespers ($\mathcal{V}_1$ $\mathcal{V}_2$ for first and second Vespers)
$\mathcal{P}$	Prime		

LIST 1d
Season or feast

Adv	Advent	Nat	Nativity (Christmas)
Asc	Ascension	Pas	Pascha (Easter)
CX	Corpus Christi	Pen	Pentecost (Whitsun)
Epi	Epiphany	QT	Quatuor Tempora (Ember days)
L	Quinquagesima	Tri	Trinity
LX	Sexagesima	XL	Quadragesima (Lent)
LXX	Septuagesima		

LIST 1e
Section of a book

A	Aspersion (see ~ in list 1f)
C	Common of saints
D	Dedication feast
H	Hymnal
I	Invitatorium
K	Kalendar
O	Ordo
Ø	Ordinary of the Mass, Kyriale
P	Psalter
R	general rubric (a major section of a book: for incidental rubrics see = and ≠ in list 1f below)
S	Sanctorale
T	Temporale
V	Votive services, to the Virgin (see ⊕ in list 1f below)
W	Votive services in general

LIST 1f

- ✠ benediction (text, including *Deo gratias* and *Benedicamus Domino*, or action)
- → procession
- ~ distribution, as of ashes or palms, censing (thurification), or aspersion
- † office or Mass of the Dead
- ⊕ memorial or suffrage, and general votive services, including V of list 1e above
- ● doxology
- • doxology incipit
- ⊥ Tonary
- = incidental rubric
- ≠ incidental rubric with incipits
- □ a substantial section of preces
- ○ abbreviations within ○ or ⊂⊃ etc represent material gathered into stocks
- ■ miscellaneous additions
- * this symbol is used, by modern convention, to show where the solo incipit of a chant ends

MANUSCRIPTS OR PRINTED SOURCES

The sources or manuscripts which are referred to by abbreviations such as source A1 or ms B1 are listed and described on pages 390 to 408.

Introduction

10 'The history of medieval liturgy must be treated as one of the main sources of western culture.'[1] This judgment, by eminent contemporary liturgists, must be endorsed by all who deal with the medieval world. Christian civilization and devotion were based on and inspired by the liturgy: the development of chivalry and ethics to some extent stems from the 12th-century growth of Marian worship. 'The clergy . . . absorbed all the functions of a literary class'[2] since the arts of drawing, writing, and painting were confined almost exclusively to liturgical books prepared by clerics, and since medieval writers examined the principles of thought, language, speech, and grammar through the exegesis of liturgical texts. The influence of the Franciscans on poetry, at least in England, has been widely explored; largely unknown is the influence of truly liturgical poetry in such genres as the *prosa* and rhymed office. Education began with the Psalter, and readings and chants were carried into daily life to inspire love songs and epics:[3] computation, formula, and calculation derive from work with problems of the calendar. From the need to explain and summarize the increasing complexity of the services, the principles of organization, abstraction, and generalization were worked out. Whether cloistered or not, man ordered his day by the services and the church bell signalling them, and his year by the succession of church feasts, and he examined all his actions and related them to his religion. It is surprising therefore that no serious effort has so far been made to present in simple terms to the student of the medieval period the basic information he needs in order to examine for himself and to understand the liturgical background as transmitted in the primary sources, the manuscripts.

11 Liturgical studies must start from the texts. Facts about gesture, ceremonial, actions, vestments, and other such matters, although important as secondary and perhaps corroborative evidence, can tell us little about the character and development of a rite that is not better obtained by studying the texts themselves. This is certainly the view of Vogel,[4] resulting in his adoption of liturgical manuscripts as the fundamental sources of knowledge. He means quite strictly those books which contain what was actually said and sung in the services in a regular and repeated manner, extending this definition only to include certain Ordines which, by listing incipits, give essential information about the order and presence or absence of items at certain times. Excluded are such publications as exegetical tracts, sermons, and commentaries on liturgical matters, athough these, and especially the last, may provide information about ceremonial, action, and methods of performance, as well as rules for adapting service because of coincident feasts.

But, as Vogel states elsewhere, there appears to be 'une certaine désaffection des médiévistes pour les documents du culte chrétien ...'[5] He continues with a reference to the difficulties often experienced in orienting oneself in the discipline of liturgical studies. The primary difficulty, for the beginner and often for the more experienced researcher, seems to me to lie in the difficulty of orienting oneself in the manuscripts. With such skill learned, the business of orientation within the discipline should follow more easily. Difficulties with the use of liturgical manuscripts derive principally from three interrelated factors, and from a combination of the first two which amounts almost to a separate factor in itself.

12 First, by ordering our year according to a secular calendar of months and weeks, we have become ignorant of the church year upon which any understanding of the liturgy and its sources must be based. Second, the Reformation of the 16th century and the more recent enactments of the Roman church have made the Latin service something of a rarity so that students do not have the benefit of the modern ritual as a starting point. Third, even for the trained medievalist, the organization and paleographical format of the liturgical manuscript may present severe problems, most of which are exacerbated when the study must be done, as is frequently the case, from microfilm or other black-and-white reproductions. Familiarity with the Kalendar,[6] the structure of the services, and with the detailed arrangement of the manuscripts is an essential before any truly liturgical studies can be undertaken. Expertise in the first two does not necessarily make the liturgical book comprehensible since the first element, the Kalendar, constantly modifies the way in which the second, the order of the services themselves, is presented in the books. Thus, even if the user thoroughly knows the detailed internal structure of a service he will never find that service presented in that way in the sources because, to choose only three examples, items which are repeated in fact are not repeated in writing; or various items are distributed between various books so that no one book is complete without the others; or a particular item, instead of being listed as it appears in the service throughout a season, may be given in a stock of such items appearing only at the beginning of the season or perhaps quite separately elsewhere. These and other variable factors are combined in different ways according to the season, the day, and perhaps even according to the hour. A fourth element must therefore be added, to lie third in the sequence of essential prerequisites to liturgical study: Kalendar, service, variability, manuscript organization.

13 Information on the first two may be obtained from any number of books: discussion of the latter pair is almost non-existent. This book is designed to fill the gap, and thus chapter 3, dealing with the problems of variability, and chapter 6 to the end, describing numerous medieval manuscripts, form the most important sections. The preceding and intervening chapters, discussing the Kalendar and the structure of the services, will appear unnecessary since information on these topics has so frequently been presented. Apart from the desirability of including this material within the same covers, these chapters are present for another reason. To cull the facts from previously published material would require the perusal of a multitude of books, some designed not to inform on this particular subject but to introduce the reader to the history of the church, to its dogma, or to the religious and spiritual significance of the texts, or to some other special aspect, each viewing the matter from a different perspective, none viewing it as a prerequisite to the study of the primary manuscripts. In most general descriptions of the Kalendar and the services there is, furthermore, the natural tendency to use the Latin liturgy as established by the 16th-century enactments of the Council of Trent. Thus a standard and modern terminology is likely to be used. Sexagesima Sunday will probably be so named, in English or in Latin (*Dominica in sexagesima*), so that the appearance in a medieval manuscript of *Dominica secunda in septuagesima* or even *Dominica octava post Epiphaniam*, both of which refer to that day, may hinder the inexperienced student for a considerable time. In addition, many authors assume that the reader is already familiar with some sort of church year. Unfortunately, even though Christmas and Easter still provide some landmarks, the organization of our secular year by months rather than by church festivals has caused our knowledge of the latter method of temporal order to fall into disuse. Conscious reflection that Easter is a movable feast and Christmas is not reminds us that somewhere in the year there must be an adjustment to account for the extra or missing weeks. The absence in secular life of any special observance on prominent feasts which we all know, such as Ascension and Pentecost, and the emphasis on Sunday as the special day, make it difficult for the inexperienced to remember that feasts may fall on weekdays. Hence, the novice may be considerably confused to discover in a manuscript that feria vi (Friday) follows immediately after the feast of Ascension. The present chapter on the Kalendar, then, is given in order to alert the user to the ambiguities and alternatives of terminology and to give him sufficient flexibility that the medieval manuscript no longer presents such formidable difficulties in this respect.

14 Publications describing the structure of the services, like those discussing the Kalendar, are often written with a different purpose and just as frequently assume a great deal of knowledge, often beginning from the modern services. I know of no text which gives the information necessary for the student to fill in the details of the services throughout the year: none explains in sufficient detail so that the beginner has some landmarks to guide him through the bewildering, although usually logical, maze of unparagraphed text and rubrics. None explains, for instance, what the word *Per.* at the end of a prayer, or *Tu.* at the end of a reading, may mean: ignorance of such apparently elementary matters, astonishing perhaps to many, is common. Too often, moreover, the modern scholar of the medieval liturgy states or implies that the practice of the middle ages must have been so-and-so because that is the way it is done nowadays (that is, before Vatican II, 1962-5). This reliance on tradition rather than on evidence documented in contemporary sources surely stems from the very difficulty of finding the latter in many instances: much of liturgical practice was so much a part of everyday custom, known to all, that it did not need to be explained or prescribed, or, therefore, written down. When such evidence does exist it is often in quite unexpected places, either in a book which is not strictly liturgical at all, or incidentally in some passing rubric buried within the liturgical book: the expenditure of effort tracing such evidence, if possible at all in North America, is not worthwhile for most needs. One quite basic matter may be cited, and will be discussed at more length later. Although easy to document the antiphonal performance of psalms, it is extremely hard to discover clear information stating whether the choirs alternate on half-verses, or on complete verses. Virtual silence on such a fundamental matter is surprising. I cannot claim to have searched all, or even many, Customaries, Ordinals, and other such books, where such information may occur, but books of this kind tend to concern themselves with practices which are special to a particular place rather than universal. So far as is possible here, I have tried to find medieval evidence where necessary, and have tried to avoid the tendency to make from particular evidence statements which are general in nature. The middle ages is a series of periods in which inconsistency and lack of standardization was the rule, universality the exception.

15 Inconsistency is epitomized in the ways in which the same service will vary throughout the year. The variability of items in all services is described by using qualifying terms such as proper, common, ferial, ordinary, or seasonal – words which have such limited meanings for the modern reader that their use for qualifying the medieval liturgy may be questioned. The whole matter of proper versus common has previously been told much too simply, if at all: nevertheless, the terms must be retained because of the force of centuries of tradition. One example may be cited of the way in which special kinds of variability can cause one to doubt one's senses or, worse, to doubt the accuracy of other scholars. Mass on the Day of Great Scrutiny, the Wednesday of the fourth week of Lent, is said to have two graduals and a tract:[7] examination of that day in manuscripts will disclose only the two graduals except in a few sources which do give the opening words of the tract. Having gone to manuscript after original manuscript to 'make sure of the facts,' one is now tempted to revise the statement: 'Mass on the Day of Great Scrutiny normally has two graduals, which in rare cases may be followed by a tract; the statement made by X is therefore incorrect.' Only an examination of the Mass of Ash Wednesday, four weeks and many pages earlier, discloses that its tract is to be repeated on all Mondays, Wednesdays, and Fridays of Lent, and is thus indeed to be sung on the day in question. Here, then, an item common not to the whole year, nor to a season, nor to a week, but common to Mondays, Wednesdays, and Fridays in Lent has caused a problem. To the expert already familiar with such intricacies, this kind of difficulty may seem to be simple of solution and, alerted once to such a situation, the attentive scholar should not be similarly misled on a second occasion. But the liturgy is bursting with such traps. A fairly detailed description of the kinds of repetition and the kinds of change which normally take place may help to show the reader where and how such traps occur: I have tried to alleviate the tedium of minutely factual reporting by means of figures and diagrams.

16 The reader must always bear in mind the inconsistency of the middle ages, and this applies to the element of variability in another way: the kind of variability itself may change from source to source. Thus what is proper then common at certain points in one manuscript may be common then proper at the same points in another. Nevertheless, by and large such differences between sources and between uses do not appear to be great, nor are they difficult to follow once the basic principles are mastered. Despite the relative uniformity in this matter, for describing the principles it seemed necessary to use a single and easily accessible source against which the others may be compared. Convenience rather than any liturgical preference dictated the choice and, unless there is a note to the contrary, the published Sarum (Salisbury) Breviary and Missal are cited.[8] For the former book I have used the edition originally printed in 1531 and, occasionally, another printed in 1555. It may be that these prints and the few others used here have been included under the term 'manuscripts' where the word 'sources' should have appeared. Some of the other books printed more recently, such as the Sarum Missal (published in 1861 and another in 1916), are editions of manuscripts, as were the books printed early in the 16th century. The Roman Missal printed in 1474,[9] which is more central to the practices of the later middle ages and to subsequent use, has also been used as a standard: the Sarum books, however, are more convenient in many ways as a basis from which to draw comparisons. The English use of Sarum in the middle ages, far from being provincial, was 'not only universally admired, it was perhaps the most widespread of any.'[10] Moreover, it is the only use of the middle ages, including Roman, Franciscan, Dominican, and Benedictine, for which the majority of liturgical books have been recently published, in either facsimile or edition. The Missal, Breviary, Gradual, Antiphonal, Tonary, Ordinal, Customary, and Manual are all accessible in indexed and well-presented modern editions. Monastic, that is Benedictine, use is well represented by the edition of the Breviary of Hyde Abbey,[11] the introduction to which has one of the best descriptions of the office hours and how they differ in secular and monastic rites. Franciscan and Dominican practices, although of enormous importance for the codification and standardization of the later medieval liturgy, are not represented in modern editions (apart from those books, no doubt differing little, actually used by the two orders in recent times). The reforms of the former order and many of the books transmitting its rituals are described in detail by Van Dijk,[12] who relates them to the incipient standardization of the Roman practices: the earliest books of the Dominicans, also produced in the

13th century, have frequently been described,[13] although none edited from the originals. Because of the relative uniformity of Franciscan and Dominican practices, at least from the early 14th century, manuscripts from these orders have not generally been compared with each other here: secular in format, representative sources of each have been included with the other secular sources.

17 Printed editions with spacing, paragraphs, running heads to indicate the liturgical date, and various type-styles to distinguish rubrics and texts, are probably the best intermediary between the basic knowledge so far described and its application to an actual manuscript, and can enable the user to learn, by thorough page-by-page collation, the format of his manuscript. A second stage might be the use of published facsimilies which have indices of texts with their liturgical occasions,[14] or which have running heads printed above the facsimiles.[15] But the use of such aids can only be a temporary crutch, and eventually the user will have to come to his own conclusions about how the very different layout of a manuscript can be handled without assistance of this sort. The features described in this book are also crutches of a kind, but they are inherent in the sources themselves and were surely understood and used by the original readers.

Finally, we arrive at the manuscripts. My purpose here is to provide some visual clues to the structure of liturgical manuscripts. Work can then proceed until the familiarity with texts, and the knowledge of what should occur where, makes the visual organization merely a complement to quicker methods of orientation. Much has been published on the illumination and decoration of manuscripts, very little on the relation of the initial to the structure of the book or to the item it begins. The problems are not purely paleographic, although the layout of liturgical manuscripts does present peculiarities to be examined later. Apart from having the ability to read the scripts and abbreviations, which must be taken for granted here, the user of a Missal, or Breviary, or Gradual must know what to expect, and herein lies the origin of many errors and misunderstandings. Since in most cases the knowledge must come from the manuscripts themselves, few scholars nowadays are familiar enough with the Latin liturgy to be able to identify texts and their liturgical occasions instantly. Yet such a skill, fundamentally a matter of memory, is of the greatest assistance in working with service books of all kinds.

Music

18 If it is true that liturgical studies must start from the texts, then it must be acknowledged that music is an essential component of most of those studies. Of the texts used in the liturgy, at least half of the different categories, and the same proportion of the items used on any one day, are sung to music ranging from the simple chant to the very elaborate. Many of the remaining texts are sung to some form of more or less elaborate musical recitation in which there are passages which may be distinctive and informative. Only those items such as prayers and dialogues which are either not sung at all or are sung to a monotone pitch throughout offer little or no help to the scholar seeking musical evidence. With the majority of liturgical texts therefore (although perhaps not with those which are most frequently studied) there may well be additional information to be gained from an examination of the music. For the non-musician, reluctance to work in this specialized field perhaps results from a feeling of inadequacy with respect to 'musicianship' or 'musicality.' No one knows how these concepts relate, if at all, to the medieval period and the application of modern beliefs about them is clearly to be avoided: work with the musical aspects consists of down-to-earth physical observation as much as does work with the scripts, and similarly may be treated as an exercise in symbol-recognition. Certainly to be stressed is the importance of liturgical knowledge for many kinds of musical research, and of musical knowledge for most liturgical study.

Medieval music is overwhelmingly liturgical. One of the important tasks for scholars is the identification of texts set to music or of plainsongs used as the basis for compositions. For various reasons, indices of incipits and of melodies are not usually much help in this process (see **612, 8001**), and until the liturgy can be more easily explored the discovery of crucial information often remains a matter of chance.[16] Unfortunately, it is still possible for editors to misinterpret the meaning of *novem lectionum* or to think that *sequentia* announcing the continuation of the gospel reading at Mass is the musical *sequentia* more properly called *prosa* which may occur in the same place.[17] An example not of error but of confusion resulting from ignorance may be cited with respect to the *Vespro della beata Vergine* of 1610, by Monteverdi: most editors of this work have 'run into difficulties ... because of insufficient attention to these [liturgical] matters.'[18] The exact contents and correct order of the items within the work can be determined only by a study of the practice regarding Marian Vespers in the composer's time. A similar study of the Roman or Sarum services of the early 16th century is essential for a full understanding of the transition from Catholic to Lutheran or Anglican services, and to appreciate the origin of such important musical forms as the anthem, chorale, and oratorio. It is commonly said, for example, that Evensong is modelled on Vespers, although such a statement is merely a loose approximation: the same is true of the generalization usually made about Luther's changes to the Mass.

19 Matters of performance practice can sometimes be settled, or at least more correctly approached, through a consideration of the liturgical setting. The solo or choral performance of polyphonic items may be cited: fundamentally important features of this kind can be deduced for polyphony of the Notre Dame school of about 1200, or for polyphony from major manuscripts such as the source of Easter processional music, British Library Egerton 3307,[19] or even for isolated compositions.[20] Such items as these are, in any case, usually incomplete in the polyphonic source and the full rendering can be obtained only through the addition of plainsong at the correct points, determined from the plainsong manuscripts themselves. To choose a more contemporary instance, Stravinsky's Mass (1948) follows proper liturgical procedure by omitting from the setting the priest's solo intonations of Gloria and Credo: professional choirs only too often make nonsense of these texts by failing to draw a suitable intonation from a liturgical source.

Some knowledge of liturgical use also helps us to understand how composers' attitudes have changed through the centuries. The earliest composers emphasize sequences, *prose*, a para-liturgical form not truly part of the ritual but added to it, and, until the St Martial school of about 1100, composers still preferred to set non-ritual items such as devotional songs. The position of such items within the liturgy can be determined in some instances by the inclusion within the setting of 'cues': a *conductum* (spelt thus) setting in the Calixtinus manuscript of the mid-12th century, for example, must serve as a processional piece before the gospel at Mass because it is preceded by a setting of the words *Lector lege . . . Jube domne*[21] with which the reader requests the celebrant's blessing in Mass. Through the 12th century we may see composers beginning to set solo items from the liturgy itself, especially responsorial forms such as gradual and alleluia and responsory. In the 13th century, a period of great upheaval in liturgical matters and in the organization of liturgical books, the setting of liturgical texts to part-music fades in importance, and when it revives, in the 14th and 15th centuries, musicians are more interested in setting the choral items of the services, the ordinary of the Mass, and devotional pieces such as antiphons which may or may not find a regular place in the established ritual. In the late 15th and 16th century yet other parts of the liturgy attract the attention of composers, particularly psalms, readings, and even versicles and responses or prayers normally reserved for spoken or intoned performance. The composition of Preces, especially by Anglican musicians, may be cited. Lamentations, elaborate readings from Holy Week, were very popular in the 16th century, and here the inclusion of a special termination, not part of the biblical text or the usual *Tu autem* formula with which Matins lessons normally end, has often caused bewilderment, especially among those not aware in the first place of such formulas.

20 Finally, to return to the 7th and 8th centuries, the earliest liturgical manuscripts, textual or musical, probably represent the written-down versions of orally-transmitted material.[22] Comparison of different versions may illuminate how words and music are transmitted by such a method: the middle ages may in fact be a storehouse of information on this subject for the ethnomusicologist or anthropologist.

The other side of the musico-liturgical coin may be revealed, to demonstrate some of the possible ways in which musical evidence may be used by the liturgical scholar. As has already been implied, most such evidence derives in the first place from a visual examination producing factual results rather than from an aural, aesthetic, and therefore ambiguous, examination requiring musicianship. The notation of plainsongs is probably the most immediately useful factor; by the later middle ages at least it is describable just as accurately as are script and decoration, although there remain some matters whose precise significance is not understood. Like script and decoration too, and perhaps in a few cases more accurately than either, the notation can identify provenance and date. In some cases it may even help to identify the cleric for whom a manuscript was destined: the careful and unusually complete presentation of reciting tones, visually grouped to clarify the declamation of the syllables, for example, suggests that the cleric who performed such items was the intended user of the book, as is the case with certain sources of the 14th-century English coronation which seem to have been prepared for the archbishop or abbot.[23]

21 Incidental variants in the musical melody, which can be ascertained even from an uncomprehending visual collation of the notation, are just as significant in liturgical study as are variants in the text and may reinforce or set in doubt conclusions derived from the texts alone. The methods of comparison and 'textual' analysis are much the same, although complicated by several extra dimensions such as the spacing of the notes vis-à-vis syllables, the use of several apparently equal alternatives for many of the symbols, and the difficulty of distinguishing error from legitimate variant (see **612, 8001**). I am practically certain from other research in progress that it is possible by this means to draw conclusions about sources which are copied from each other or through intermediaries, or which are unrelated, and perhaps even to identify the styles of certain ateliers. Apart from refining, correcting, or endorsing evidence provided by the texts, occasionally the plainsongs may supply evidence obtainable in no other way. In the case of English manuscripts transmitting the office of Thomas Becket, for instance, there are notational or melodic variants which seem peculiar to either Sarum or York or another local use, and sometimes this information canot be gained from any other evidence. Similar information about provenance or intended destination may be deduced from the changing association between texts and melodies: within the large repertory of hymns and sequences in particular, the same text may be set to several different tunes or one tune may be used for different texts. Completely different melodies are not uncommon in the standard repertory: one text in the Becket office has two melodies, one of which seems to be English, the other perhaps French. The same is true of one antiphon in an office of the conception of the Virgin. The antiphon *Unxerunt Salomonem* has several tunes dependent on century and geography. Failure to recognize such musical differences or even to consider them can lead to erroneous conclusions.

It would seem feasible to compile lists of musical variants alone from which it would be possible immediately to distinguish between major uses, orders, and perhaps individual institutions, as well as eras. The task would be enormous.

22 Differences between musical styles, also ascertainable from visual inspection of the notation, are easy to identify in most cases. As will be shown later, certain musical styles tend to be related to kinds of genre so that identification of the former can help with the identification of the latter. A responsory and verse may be distinguished from a versicle and response or from an antiphon which happens to have a verse. In this respect I have particularly in mind the Mandatum service of Maundy Thursday, where the naming of items may be haphazard and a musical definition may enable a more precise terminology to be used. Nevertheless, as has been stressed numerous times already, the middle ages is not necessarily consistent, even in its use of musical styles, and we should probably not force consistency onto its forms.

Paradigms

23 It is easiest to describe variants against an acceptable and widely accepted standard. This is where the existing descriptions of the services, especially those which are concise, tend to be misleading. There is no standard service of Matins, or ferial Mass, or whatever, in the middle ages, and the variants are from source to source, century to century, season to season, week to week. What then can be accepted as the recognized normal ritual, what as variants from the normal, what as accretions?

In its two thousand years, a good many centuries of which are moderately well documented, the liturgy has not remained static: additional texts, substitute texts, occasional texts, flow in and out of use, making it difficult to establish either a basic order of liturgical practice or the sequence or presence of texts within that order. During the 13th century, however, and mainly consequent upon the foundation and different requirements of the mendicant orders, especially the Franciscans, a reform and gradual standardization of the liturgy and its books originated at the papal court in Rome.[24] No one single reference book, from which all others were copied, seems to have resulted: it is not yet clear, how consistent are later Franciscan books, but the Breviary and Antiphonal of the order, *secundum ordinem curie Romane*, were sent to the twenty provinces in 1230. The Dominicans, following cosely in the steps of their less learned brothers, produced a *summa* of Dominican practice in the form of a comprehensive manuscript authorized in Paris in the 1260's and copied for the use of the master-general, from which all further copies were supposed to be made.[26] Although they have not been systematically identified and collated, Dominican books from that time are probably more consistent than those of any other single use.

24 The reforms and codifications seem to have been chiefly concerned with ritual actions and the order of the services, that is, with the establishment of a Ordinal, and only secondarily with the overgrowth of additional texts and services which had characterized the previous centuries. The result was a clearer establishment of a universal ritual, so that we can state that a certain order of services is to be expected, and that certain items within the services are normal, and that certain items are additional accretions. This general standardization makes the publications of paradigms less objectionable, provided that suitable caveats are appended. The texts within the services remain flexible to a great extent, even though we may be sure that an invitatory or a hymn is to be expected; the tunes remained variable from use to use; numerous accretions of different kinds in different places were retained. It is still possible and indeed essential to speak of uses although the number of distinctly different forms is certainly less than it was earlier in the middle ages. The main uses of importance in the later centuries are:[27] Benedictine, Cistercian, and other monastic rites; Franciscan-Roman, Dominican, and other regular rites; secular rites. Of the secular uses, many have yet to be identified and their differences noted: only the English rites of Sarum, York, and Hereford have been investigated to any extent. Paris has been virtually unexplored, although Chartres, Rouen, Lyons, and Lille have been examined. The Ambrosian rite of Milan has been discussed quite extensively. A number of publications are concerned with the rites of Scandinavia and Germany, but the remainder of Europe is still virtually unknown. Only in the 16th century, with the reforms of the Council of Trent, were local variant and accretions of all kinds eliminated, creating a moderately uniform Missal and Breviary for the whole of Europe.

25 Before the 13th century, then, the liturgy is fraught with great variability and uncertainty of order and of precise text as well as with extreme problems of documentation. Subsequent to the 16th century there are few radical differences. The intervening centuries – the 13th to the 15th – lavishly supplied with manuscripts, offer challenges of both kind and quantity. Moreover, they are unquestionably of most general use to the scholar who is not particularly concerned with origins.

The difficulties and dangers of presenting paradigms of the services are obvious. Yet such formulas are necessary. I hope that the later chapters of this book, which deal with the way services are presented in numerous manuscripts, will help to loosen the rigidity of the skeletons in the earlier chapters. In every case, the skeleton must be clothed with the flesh of more precise information. Thus, if one wishes to state that a particular service was conducted in a specific manner, the precise date and year, together with a precise place, ought to be appended. In many cases this is, of course, not possible, and fortunately such exact detail is rarely necessary.

Terminology

26 An awkward problem in any field, terminology is at its most cumbersome in liturgy. Exact definitions are often impossible and, in good medieval fashion, the meaning of a word as well as its spelling may change with each appearance. I cannot claim to have been entirely consistent in the matter of spelling, especially in the matter of classical as opposed to medieval practices, and do not think the fact troublesome: I have, however, tried to be reasonably consistent as to the meaning which attaches to each word. In quotations, of course, the usage of the original document determines the meaning(s). Ambiguities and variant meanings are noted when terms are introduced.

In most cases, Latin has been retained in quotations simply because it is the language of the originals. Even with a minimum knowledge, the student can understand most liturgical instructions: here it is not usually necessary to understand the texts themselves. There are certain occasions where the original terminology can be made more precise in translation: *antiphona*, for instance, is normally translated quite satisfactorily as antiphon, but in certain contexts it may be more precisely rendered as votive or devotional antiphon. The qualification distinguishes the antiphon without a psalm from the normal psalm-antiphon. Votive antiphons are used to venerate the Virgin or a saint in contexts outside the set services. Names of seasons and days have normally been translated into English, except where there is no equivalent. Some names, with no precise equivalents in English and equally cumbersome in both languages, have been paraphrased. The feasts of Ascension, Pentecost, Trinity, and Corpus Christi, which sometimes need to be discussed together, may be called 'the spring feasts' even though Corpus Christi sometimes falls in summer.

I have tried to use terms as precisely as possible. Distinctions such as those between ecclesiastical and liturgical, between biblical and sacred, are important.

History

27 To study the history and origins of the material is a lifetime's work in itself, and I refer to such information only when it illuminates the practices of the period under discussion. Nevertheless, in order to place in a historical context some of the additions and accretions referred to in subsequent chapters, I present the following briefest outline of church history.

Christianity grew out of the Jewish religion and in the first centuries interaction between the two was common, the ceremonies and rituals changing considerably. Illegal in this period, the new religion began with services which were essentially private and, as far as the minimal evidence allows us to judge, lacking uniformity. From the 4th century, with the legalizing of Christianity and the consequent adoption of public services, more standardization of ceremony had to be introduced. To the readings, prayers, and recitation of psalms which had predominated in the ritual taken from the Jews, there were added certain non-scriptural texts such as hymns; the construction of large churches prompted choral rather than solo singing of psalms. During the 4th century and continuing the separation of public and private worship, the Christian society began to split formally into secular and monastic communities, the former concerning themselves with pastoral ministry and attending to the everyday spiritual needs of the people, the latter with seclusion from everyday life and a constant round of devotion to God. The secular churches naturally emphasized the public offices and seem to have looked with disfavour upon any newly composed non-scriptural poetry; moreover, until the establishment of professional bodies of singers, the kind of devotional music sung must have been very restricted. The monastic communities, on the other hand, reaching a pinnacle of organization and codification with the work of St Benedict, ca 530, developed the full round of services throughout the day, welcomed and preserved non-scriptural items, and had resident choral bodies, to put their musical abilities on a high level.

28 The different attitudes and practices continued until perhaps the 6th century when, under the influence of the basilican monks of St Peter's, Rome, the secular liturgy began to adopt monastic customs to a large degree. The first codification of general liturgical practice, which was attempted by Pope Gregory the Great, ca 600, is of immense importance in this respect. At this time many additions were made to the Roman Liturgy from monastic and Byzantine examples, more or less establishing the services as we now know them. This first series of additions, forming the basic liturgy, was not completed until the 11th century, however, since a few isolated items such as the Credo were very slow to appear in Roman practice. Meanwhile a whole new series of additions had encroached on the fundamental offices and became an inessential, massive, and disturbing imposition onto the underlying services.

29 As the Roman services gradually solidified in the 7th to 12th centuries, the main centre of liturgical development, as well as of learning and literature and music in general, shifted to Gaul where the renaissance of the 9th century provided the impetus for the writing of much new sacred poetry which was added to the normal items of the liturgy in the form of tropes. This trend was to increase, maintain a flourishing life, and survive until the 16th century. Charlemagne's attempt in the 9th century to impose an empire-wide liturgy failed, but in the process of drawing from Roman, Byzantine, English, and Gallican rituals, texts, and chants, he certainly laid the foundation for what is now called, erroneously, Gregorian chant.[28] French monasticism, and especially the reforms of the Benedictine monastery of Cluny in the 10th century, played an important role in making the liturgy even more elaborate with textual and musical additions. In addition to the newly inserted texts, there were also complete new services. The desire for devotion to particular saints and an increasingly fervent veneration of the Virgin Mary led to the creation of numerous memorial or commemorative services for the Virgin, for the Dead, for All Saints, etc, and to the creation of a duplicate set of offices and Masses modelled on the fundamental series. Memorials were said in addition to the normal round: a duplicate office would usually replace the normal services on one of the weekdays. At the same time, smaller services consisting of prayers and psalms and commemorating secular persons such as benefactors or monarchs were added. The purpose of the church, the worship of our Lord, was in serious danger of being swamped by extra-liturgical accretions. Besides services within the day, the addition of feast days themselves, celebrating individual saints, mushroomed in the centuries from 800 to 1500. The special services for these days may in theory have been intended for performance in addition to the regular offices, either on the same day or in the case of a real collision between important festivals on successive days. But in practice the performance of new feasts soon came to replace the normal services. Thus the proper purpose of the liturgy was changed in favour of special devotions directed not at God but at individual saints.

Although subjected to constant criticism from various quarters, such accretions remained a standard part of liturgical practice all over Europe, with the exception of the rites of certain monastic and regular orders to be mentioned, until the 16th century. They produced a system which is enormously more complicated than modern liturgical practice can even suggest. Evidently a day so full of devotion could have been accomplished most easily in monastic circumstances, although many extra services did creep into secular uses.

30 In the course of the 12th century the emphasis moved back to Rome despite the importance of Cîteaux, and monastic practices of the preceding centuries were adopted, at least in part: hymns were finally introduced, together with most of the other accretions. Opposing the tendency toward proliferation of ornament and service, however, the Cistercian monks began a reform designed to strip the services of many of their unnecessary texts, chants, and memorials. The austerity of worship which came to be characteristic of the Cistercians was a necessary first step towards the reforms instituted by the mendicant orders of the following century. For that century, the 13th, saw the rise of religious groups which were to play a fundamental role in the firm establishment of the Roman service, specifying more precisely those parts which were basic and those which were inessential accretions. St Francis and St Dominic founded orders of regular monks, not bound to houses but itinerant. Still expected to recite the daily offices, at least to themselves, clergy who travelled could not carry with them the paraphernalia required for all the accretions: indeed they were not supposed to own books at all. The peculiar needs of these two mendicant orders, then, forced upon the Roman curia a reorganization of liturgical practices, and this resulted in an even stricter codification of customs and rituals. Outside the Franciscan, Dominican, and Cistercian orders, however, most of the accretions remained in force in many secular establishments as well as in monasteries until the 16th century, when the pressures of the Reformation caused the church to try to return to the original liturgy shorn of its inessental overgrowth. Of course, the authorities at that time did not know, any more than we do now, what the original liturgy was, but we may assume that the intention was to restore to their rightful significance the fundamental services worshipping God rather than those petitioning saints.

This book will be concerned with the practices in force during and after the Franciscan and Dominican reforms of the 13th century and before the 16th century, and how these practices may be discovered from the liturgical books of the period.

MEDIEVAL MANUSCRIPTS FOR MASS AND OFFICE

1

The Liturgical Time

THE YEAR

100 A ritual which is to be used daily and for year after year must have both variety and repetition. A statement of what is repeated or varied and where those repetitions and variations occur could be presented, although cumbersomely, in a simple list of the complete practices day by day throughout the year. The services, their texts, music, and ritual differ on each day of the week, Sunday being more elaborate than the weekdays. Such daily changes would not invalidate our day-by-day list, since Sundays always fall on Sundays. But many special feasts, Christmas Day for example, fall upon an invariable date. These occasions have their own special and more elaborate texts and music. They will fall on a different day of the week as the years progress and in one year their special features may have to be adapted and mingled with the daily ritual for Sunday, in another year with the ritual for Wednesday. The adaptation of a normal Wednesday, for example, is quite familiar to us when we go to special Christmas services on that day. A comprehensive list adapting the feasts of fixed date to all seven days of the week, made more complex by the irregularity of leap years, is evidently out of the question for practical purposes. To increase the complexity, another variable occurs. For reasons which we need not discuss, the date of the main feast of the church is itself variable. Easter Sunday, the day which commemorates the resurrection, may fall on any one of thirty-five different dates: this too is familiar in everyday life. Since the resurrection, with the incarnation at Christmas, is the main event around which the whole of Christian life is built, so Easter Sunday is the day around which the most important part of the church year is ordered: the six weeks of Lent, before Easter, and the whole of the Easter season always vary their position within the church year in the same way as does Easter Sunday. For Masses, but not for other services, all of the relatively unimportant Sundays of summer vary similarly. The date of Easter must therefore be established before any details of the yearly variations can be elucidated. Liturgical books thus conventionally begin with a Kalendar from which, by means of formulas, the date of Easter Sunday can be determined. The method by which this is done will be examined, together with other information contained in the Kalendar, in appendix I. The constant concern with the mathematics of the yearly calendar and of the heavenly spheres, the sun and moon especially, is one reason for the emphasis placed on arithmetic and astronomy in the system of medieval education. Within the Quadrivium, the close connection of music with both of these subjects in the middle ages hardly needs stressing; neither does its intimate connection with the liturgy.[1]

101 The year is organized in two periods. One is based around the incarnation, the fixed-date festival of Christmas, whose services may occur on any one of the seven days of the week; the other is based around the movable feast of the resurrection, Easter, whose services may fall on any one of thirty-five dates. Figure 1.1 shows the year from Advent to Advent, horizontally. Thirty-five years, one for each possible date of Easter including leap years, have been arranged so that successive Easter Sundays fall on consecutive dates of the year, a convenient sequence which nevers occurs in practice. Advent Sunday, shown by the dotted line, may fall on any of the seven dates from 27 November to 3 December. Occurring on the former date at the beginning and top of the diagram, it falls on 29 November a year later, at the top right-hand corner. The 'serrations' show its movement within the seven days. The feast of St Andrew, 30 November, may therefore fall before Advent, after Advent Sunday, or on that day. The season of Advent extends up to Christmas and, including Advent Sunday but not Christmas Day itself, always has four Sundays. As with any feast of fixed date, Christmas Day and Epiphany, 6 January, may occur on any day of the week. In the 'season' after Epiphany there is always at least one Sunday, together with its six weekdays, and separating that Sunday from Epiphany may be any number of weekdays from none to six (in the latter case, Epiphany would itself fall on a Sunday). This period, consisting thus of seven to thirteen days, is represented in figure 1.1 by the blank parallelograms.

At this point, and as it were grinding against the 'serrations' of the seven-day variations, the period variable by thirty-five days 'meets' the weeks after Epiphany. If Easter falls on 22, 23, or 24 March, the earliest dates possible, this period directly follows the first complete week (Sunday to Saturday) after Epiphany, as shown at (1) in figure 1.1. When Easter is very late, the period cannot follow directly and a hiatus occurs. According to the date of Easter any number from one to five extra weeks, distinguished in figure 1.1, have to be added. The major part of the year, beginning two and a half weeks before Lent, continuing through that season, past Easter Sunday, through Easter time up to Trinity Sunday, contains the most important and often the most ancient services that the church celebrates. Following Trinity Sunday is the summer, a season almost devoid of important festivals, because of the medieval preoccupation with the harvest. At least twenty-two and at most twenty-seven Sundays follow Trinity.[2] When Easter is very late, on 24 or 25 April, Advent Sunday of the next liturgical year follows directly after the twenty-second Sunday, as at (2) in figure 1.1. Otherwise, one to five extra weeks occur which complement the extra weeks after Epiphany and whose ritual is often drawn from that period. Liturgical adjustments for these extra weeks of summer occur at the end of the season

FIGURE 1.1
The calendar year (showing the arrangement as Easter moves)

Parallelograms represent complete weeks, triangles incomplete weeks.

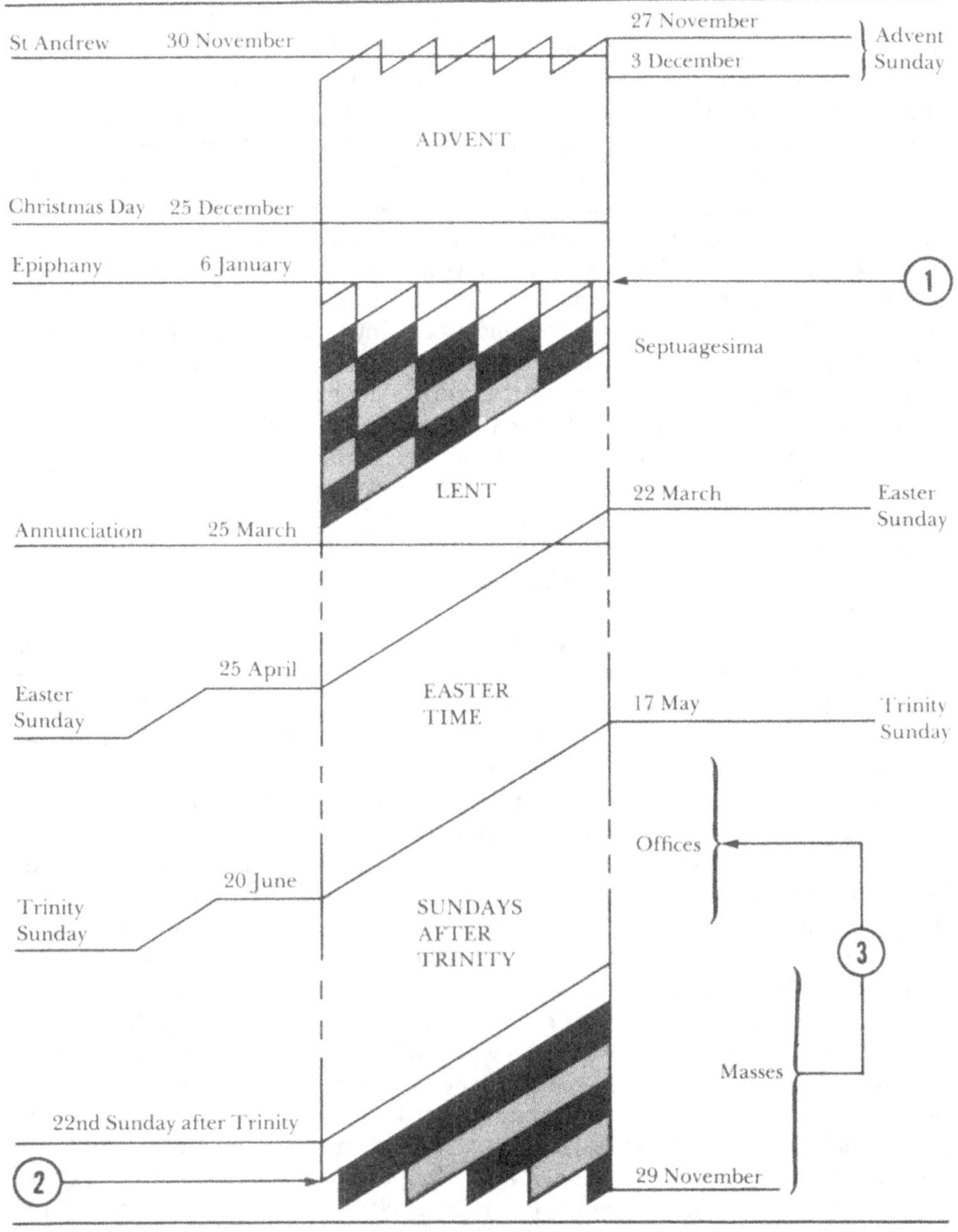

1 Quinquagesima directly follows the first complete week (Sunday to Saturday) after Epiphany.
2 Advent Sunday directly follows the twenty-second Sunday after Trinity.
3 The extra weeks are placed at the end of the summer for Masses, and after Trinity Sunday for the offices.

for Masses, and near its beginning for the offices: see (3) in figure 1.1, and sections **726, 835, 871**.

102 In the earliest days of Christianity the only services required were those devoted to our Lord, commemorating the important times of his life. The round of such services is therefore known as the Temporale [Domini nostri Jesu Christe], 'the Time of our Lord'. Conventionally, the liturgical year begins with Advent, but this practice was not universal in the earlier middle ages and reminders of alternative practices sometimes occur.[3] In chronological order, then, the important occasions are (1) the preparation for Christ's coming, (2) his birth, (3) his circumcision, (4) the manifestation to the Gentiles, or the adoration of the Magi, called Epiphany, (5) his forty-day fast, (6) his entry into Jerusalem along roads strewn with palms, (7) the Last Supper, (8) the betrayal and crucifixion, (9) his resurrection, (10) his ascent into heaven, (11) the descent of the Holy Ghost. These special events form the feasts or main seasons of the Temporale, and all are quite familiar, although their Latin names may not be in current use: (1) *Adventus*, (2) *Nativitas*, (3) *Circumcisio*, (4) *Epiphania*, (5) *Jejunium*, literally a 'fast,' infrequently used because there are other ways of referring to the days of Lent, (6) *Dominica in ramis palmarum* 'Palm Sunday,' (7) & (8) the *triduum*, that is, the three days preceding Easter Sunday: *Cena domini* 'the Feast of our Lord' or 'Maundy Thursday,' and *Parasceve* 'Good Friday,' and *sabbatum sanctum*[4] 'Holy Saturday,' (9) *Dominica resurrectionis*, (10) *Ascensio*, (11) *Pentecostes* 'Whitsunday.'

Sunday, *dominica*, is not usually referred to by the term *dies*, 'a day,' except in the case of Easter Sunday itself, where *in die resurrectionis* is commonly found. Feasts such as Christmas and Ascension are usually named *die nativitatis, die ascensionis*, or *in die* . . . The former, using the ablative of *dies*, is presumably an abbreviation of the latter phrase. An elementary knowledge of Latin or Greek makes self-evident the names for most liturgical occasions and further explanation will be presented only where necessary.

103 The individual feast days mentioned above have their own special and proper services which are naturally more elaborate than those of other days in the year, when Christ is remembered in more general ways. Nevertheless, to some extent each day has its own proper texts, ceremonial, and music, even though repetition from week to week may occur. The special, variable material for feasts and for everyday use is referred to as *Proprium de Tempore*, 'the Proper of the Time.' Certain minor elements which are common to many days or to all days will be examined in detail later. Feast days are preceded by their eve, and in most cases are followed by an octave. As with so many liturgical terms, in the later middle ages it is difficult to attach a precise and invariable meaning to the term used for 'eve,' namely *vigilia*. Even though its origin in the night-long vigil beginning on the evening before the feast is clear and the same limitation of time continues to apply on most occasions, the word *vigilia* can also refer to the complete day preceding the feast and also to its vigil beginning on the evening before. This is true, for example, of the day before Christmas and that before Pentecost and such 'eves' are characterized by many proper texts for all their services, from first to second Vespers. The extent of the *vigilia* can be

FIGURE 1.2
The main seasons and feasts of the temporale

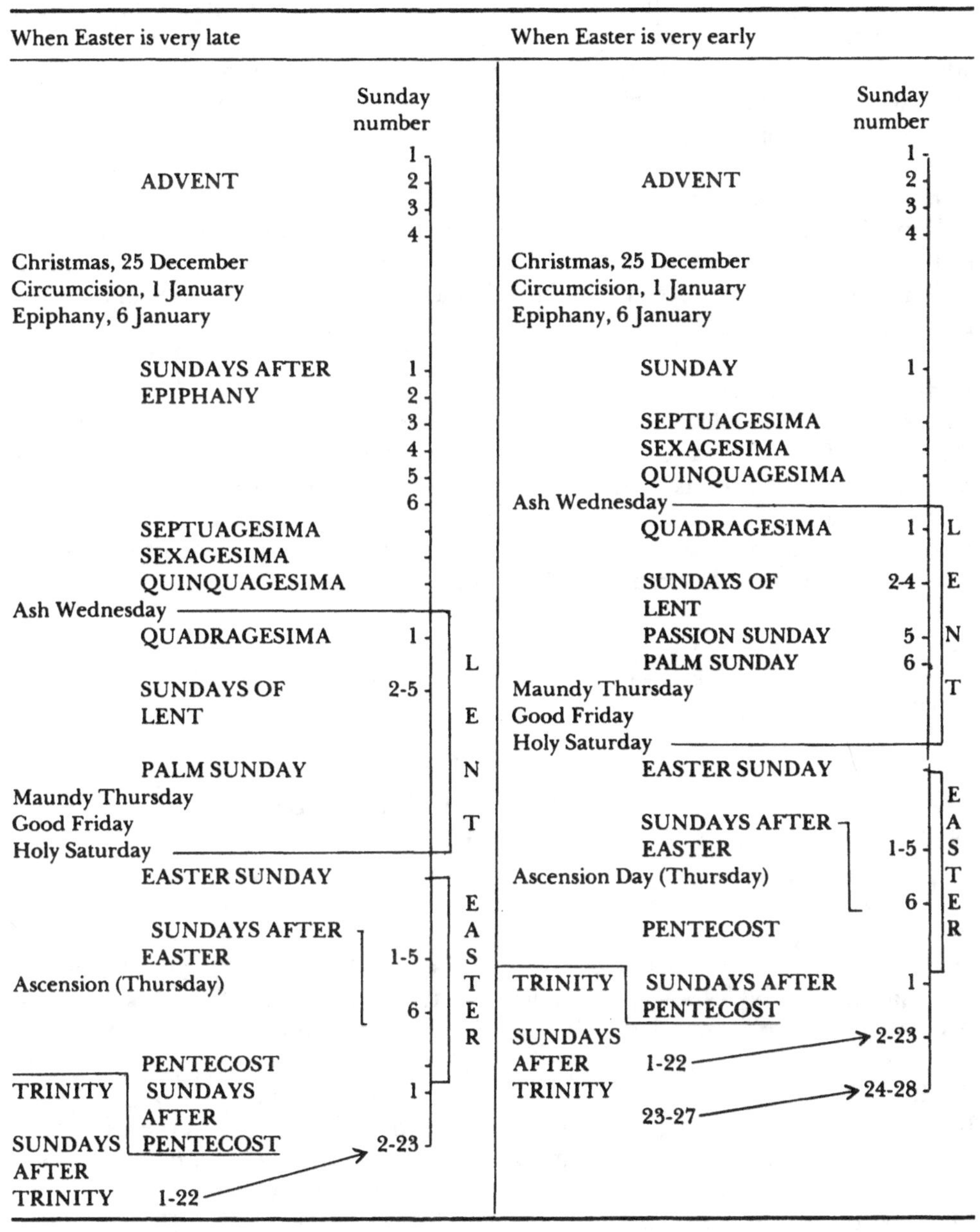

determined from the context. The latter term octave, refers to the same day one week later[5] as well as to the intervening days. In Latin, the meanings are distinguished by preposition and case: *infra octavas* or *infra octavam, in octavis* or *in octava* 'within the eight days,' *post octavas* or *octavam* 'after the eight days' or 'after the eighth day,' and *in octavam* 'on the eighth day.' The occurrence of octaves affects the naming of certain Sundays, as we shall see. We can now itemize the sequence of the Temporale and give names to many days of the year. Figure 1.2 presents the material schematically and introduces one additional feast of the Temporale. It shows the two extreme versions of the year, when Easter is very early and very late: either diagram may be followed in the subsequent discussion.

Temporale and Sanctorale

Henceforth, without special warning, the word Temporale will refer to the round of services through the year, and also to the book or section of a book in which they are written down. Similarly, Sanctorale will refer to the services for the saints and to the place where they are written down.

Advent and Christmas

104 Advent always has four Sundays, henceforth Advent 1, 2, 3, 4.[6] Christmas Day always falls after, and its Eve may fall on, the fourth Sunday. In the latter case, with Advent 4 on its latest possible date, the Sunday ceremonial will have to adapted to allow for the rituals of Christmas Eve. Furthermore, in this case the Sunday after Epiphany is on its earliest possible date and only one other Sunday intervenes between Christmas and Epiphany:

December	January
24 Advent 4 and Christmas Eve	1 Circumcision
25 Christmas Day	2
26	3
27	4
28	5 Vigil of Epiphany
29	6 Epiphany
30	7 Epiphany 1 Sunday
31 Sunday	

Since Christmas Eve can fall on six other days of the week, this situation is unusual and in all other cases there are two intervening Sundays between Advent 4 and Epiphany 1. Christmas, Circumcision, and Epiphany, feasts of fixed date, may fall on these Sundays.

This chapter is concerned with occasions commemorating Christ. Nevertheless, we must introduce some feasts venerating saints. In the early days of the church the number of saints was so few that a separate book gathering their feasts was not needed and the details of their services were included with the services of the Temporale in chronological order. Even when a Sanctorale was evolved, the feasts of saints occurring in the days after Christmas and commemorating events from the earliest days of Christianity were often retained in the Temporale.[7] Their celebration within the complex octave of Christmas, and the constant adaptation caused by the further superimposition of a movable Sunday ceremonial, made lengthy and detailed instructions necessary. Some more organized and universal uses from the later middle ages, the Cistercians and Dominicans in particular but not the Franciscans nor the Roman curia, prefer to place these feasts in the Sanctorale.[8] But to remove these saints' feasts from the Temporale into another book or section of a book made it necessary each year to combine two physically separated sequences of feasts for the same few days. Most uses retain the traditional arrangement. Even though a separate Sanctorale had appeared as early as the 8th century in the Gradual of Monza and in early Breviaries of the 10th and 11th centuries,[9] the services for one saint canonized in 1173 were nevertheless added to the Temporale and retained in that position where the other Christmas saints were also thus retained. The services of Thomas of Canterbury occur on 29 December, within the octave of Christmas.[10] In many liturgical books, therefore, the section devoted to the Temporale of Christmas includes these feasts:

December
25 Christmas Day
26 St Stephen, protomartyr
27 St John, apostle
28 Holy Innocents, remembering the massacre of the children after Christmas
29 St Thomas of Canterbury
30 *sexta die post nativitatem*
31 St Silvester, bishop of Rome, d. 335, and the Vigil of Circumcision

January
1 Circumcision
2-4 octaves of Stephen, John, and the Innocents
5 Vigil of Epiphany, with a memorial to St Thomas
6 Epiphany

The phrase *sexta die*, for a day which may be Sunday, should be observed.

Epiphany to Palm Sunday

105 One Sunday, Epiphany 1, with its complete week, always follows Epiphany. If Epiphany itself is a Sunday, Epiphany 1 is the following Sunday, the octave, and there are two complete weeks from Epiphany to Septuagesima. When Epiphany is not on a Sunday, Epiphany 1 falls within the octave and is therefore sometimes called *Dominica infra octavas Epiphanie*. In the event of Easter being late there are up to five extra weeks between Epiphany 1 and Septuagesima Sunday: *Dominica (2-6) post Epiphaniam*, now referred to as Epiphany 2-6. An alternative terminology sometimes found is *Dominica (1-5) post octavas Epiphanie*. As with other days where the name can be expressed in several equally correct ways, the usage of the source in question must be ascertained. This period, and the Sunday which begins it, is also known as the season, or Sunday, *Domine ne in ira* from the incipit of the first responsory of the first Sunday, Epiphany 2.

Moreover, if the period contains no extra Sundays, or one or two, it may be referred to as *tempus breve*, if three, *tempus equale*, if four or five, *tempus prolixum*.[11] The following Sunday, sometimes called the sixth Sunday [after the octave] of Epiphany, is Septuagesima Sunday, so called because it falls within seventy days but more than sixty days before Easter. The next Sunday is within sixty, Sexagesima, the next within fifty, Quinquagesima. Septuagesima, Sexagesima, and Quinquagesima are in fact short seasons within which the Sunday occurs. The correct terminology is therefore *Dominica infra Septuagesimam*, etc. Sexagesima and Quinquagesima are sometimes referred to as first and second Sundays within Septuagesima. Falling within forty days of Easter (excluding Sundays) the next Sunday is Quadragesima or *Dominica 1 in Quadragesima*, henceforth XL 1 (these seasons are often abbreviated to LXX, LX, L, and XL in the sources and will often be so written here). Some items such as alleluias appear inconsistently between Septuagesima and Lent since, when the latter period was extended backwards **(902)**, they were sometimes replaced with penitential items such as tracts. The season of Quadragesima extends to Easter and has five ordinary Sundays, XL 1-5, of which the first may be known as *in albis*,[13] the fourth as *Letare*, and the fifth as *Dominica in passione*, Passion Sunday. Palm Sunday, *Dominica in ramis palmarum*, follows. This season of Lent with its forty weekdays (that is, not Sundays) commemorates Christ's fast.

Holy Week and Easter

106 The week preceding Easter Day, Holy Week or *Hebdomada sancta* or *major*, is very special, remembering as it does Christ's last days. Maundy Thursday, Good Friday, and Holy Saturday have already been mentioned and their services will be examined in more detail in chapter 9. After Easter Day is a season of rejoicing to celebrate the resurrection, the season of Easter time, *tempus paschale*, which extends from Easter Sunday to the Saturday after Pentecost, inclusive.[14] The season has seven Sundays, the first six being either Sundays after Easter, *Dominica (1-6) post Pascham*, or the octave of Easter and five Sundays after the octave. The octave itself may be called *Dominica in albis depositis* or, confusing it with XL 1, *Dominica in albis*: an alternative name is *Quasimodo*.[15] The Sunday, Pascha 6, falls within the octave of Ascension Day (Thursday) and is sometimes called *Dominica infra octavas ascensionis*. The name Pentecost, given to the seventh Sunday, derives from its position as the fiftieth day after Easter.

Trinity and the summer

107 The remaining Sundays of the year may be numbered after Pentecost, for example, *Dominica 21 post Pentecosten*, Pentecost 21, in which case there will be at least twenty-three or if Easter is early at most twenty-eight. However, made obligatory in 1334 but certainly celebrated much earlier in some places was the feast of Trinity Sunday, a week after Pentecost.[16] Some sources therefore number the remaining Sundays after Trinity. Pentecost 21 will then be the same as Trinity 20, and so forth. According to Fr. Dominique Delalande, *Le Graduel des*

Prêcheurs (Paris, 1949) page 282, in *later* Dominican sources Sundays are numbered after the octave of Trinity. Even after Trinity was established some sources still preserve the numbering after Pentecost so that there are several alternatives:

Pen.	Pen.	Pen.	Pen.
Tri.	Tri.	Tri. = oct. Pen.	Tri.
Pen. 2	Tri. 1	1 post oct. Pen.	Tri. oct.
Pen. 3	Tri. 2	2 post oct. Pen.	1 post Tri. oct.
Pen. 19	Tri. 18	18 post oct. Pen.	17 post Tri. oct.

In the last case, there appear to be four Sundays where there are in fact only three: the services for the octave of Pentecost, displaced by those of Trinity, have been retained in the source. The effect of the insertion of Trinity on the disposition of the services in the summer has not, as far as I know, been carefully examined. Frequent general statements occur, such as the one that the Mass for the octave of Pentecost was shifted to the next free weekday, the usual procedure when two Masses coincided. But the sources are inconsistent in their handling of the difficulty. As will be seen in a later chapter, the sources are also often confused and inaccurate about the numbering of the Sundays, especially later in the season. The only safe method of finding the correct number is to count from Pentecost.

The presence of Trinity may be used as one piece of evidence for dating a source after 1334. Another feast of the Temporale added during these weeks was Corpus Christi. Celebrated at least in Liège from about 1246, it was authorized for universal use by 1264.[17] The Thursday after Trinity is set aside for the feast, and the following Sunday may therefore be referred to as *Dominica infra octavas Corporis Christi.* Some examples of the manner in which this feast disturbs the arrangement of services will be presented.[18] Divided into several short periods, the weeks of the summer are frequently known by names which derive from either the Matins responsory with which they begin or the book of the Bible from which the daily readings are drawn. The arrangement of these periods will be examined in detail later.

Trinity 1: *Deus omnium* (R) or 'Kings,' *Liber regum*
1st Sunday after 28 July: *In principio* (R) or 'Wisdom,' *Liber sapientie*
1st Sunday after 28 August: *Si bona* (R) or 'Job'
1st Sunday after 11 September: *Peto Domine* (R) or 'Tobias'
1st Sunday after 20 September: *Adonay* (R) or 'Judith'[19]
1st Sunday after 27 September: *Adaperiat* (R) or 'Machabees'
1st Sunday after 28 October: *Vidi Dominum* (R) or 'Ezechiel'

It is evident from the above table that after the first Sunday of Trinity all subsequent Sundays vary in date by up to seven days: Trinity 1 will of course vary by up to thirty-five, according to the date of Easter. As far as the offices are concerned, the return from a variation of thirty-five days to one of seven days takes place by adjusting the number of weeks in the first season of the summer, *Deus omnium.* For Masses, the adjustment takes place at the end of the summer, after Trinity 22, where extra weeks are inserted as necessary. The introit therefore supplies the name for Sundays of this period only in the case of the first Sunday after Trinity, which in addition to the names derived from the offices may be called *Domine in tua*. The parallelism between offices and Mass which holds true for most of the year is dislocated during the summer.

108 Throughout the year, therefore, there is considerable ambiguity in the naming of Sundays and seasons. The presence of octaves or the insertion of a new feast may result in some alternatives, and the choice of introit or responsory or an important action of the time may provide others. Which of the names is chosen is of no importance and the manuscripts are inconsistent: such information, however, may provide corroborative evidence for assigning a source to a certain family or use. Appendix II gives a list of the most common names.

The ferias and fasts

109 The term feria refers to any day of the week, including Sunday: *Dominica*, however, is normally used for Sunday instead of feria i.[20] Monday is therefore feria ii and so on through the week. Normally Saturday too is given a special name, *sabbatum*, although feria vii is occasionally found.[21] The liturgical week, then, begins with *Dominica*, continues through ferias ii-vi, ending with *sabbatum*.[22] Feria thus comes to accept the special meaning of 'weekday' in distinction to Sunday, and eventually the even more special meaning of 'weekday' in distinction to Sundays and feast days: Ascension Day, for example, although on a Thursday is not generally referred to as a feria. The sources are again not consistent, and the older meaning of 'weekday' in opposition only to Sunday does occur sometimes: 'if a feast of nine lessons occurs on a certain feria of Lent.'[23] Henceforth, except when quoting the sources or for special reasons, feria will be accepted as an English term meaning 'a day which is neither a Sunday nor a feast.' Also, feria vii will be used rather than sabbatum. The difference between feria and dies, observed in the sources, must be closely preserved.[24] For example, since Epiphany is a feast of fixed date, the days within its octave may include a Sunday and cannot be referred to as ferias. Compare *feria secunda infra octavas Trinitatis* with *die secunda infra octavas Epiphanie*. Although many have their own proper texts and ritual, especially during Lent, the ferias which have really important services in the Temporale are quite few. Such services have to be itemized in the liturgical books, of course, and the manner in which this is done will provide much material later: here we are concerned with those which have special names.

110 Apart from the great fast of Lent, three ferias are set aside for fasting and penitence in each of the four seasons: these days thus receive the name *Quatuor tempora* or, in old-fashioned English terminology, the Quarter tense. I shall refer to them as Ember days. They are the Wednesday, Friday, and Saturday in the third week of Advent, in the first week of Lent, in the week after Pentecost, and in the week following 14 September (which may be any week from Trinity 12-17).[25] In the books their full names might be *feria quarta* (or *sexta* or *sabbatum*) *quatuor tempora Adventus Domini* (or *Quadragesime*, etc) although it is not usually necessary to state the season. In addition to these fasting days, the Monday, Tuesday, and Wednesday preceding Ascension Day are set aside for special supplication and penitence and are called Rogation Days, *feria secunda in rogationibus*, etc: the Sunday preceding them, Pascha 5, is therefore sometimes called Rogation Sunday. Associated with Rogation time are the greater Litany and special processions. The beginning of the great fast of Lent is also marked with a special day, *Caput jejunii*, which falls on a Wednesday, the fortieth weekday before Easter. The traditional association of penitence with sackcloth and ashes results in the alternative name, *feria (quarta) cinerum*, 'day of ashes,' whence Ash Wednesday – compare also the English name 'Ember days' for the Quatuor tempora fasts – and the following Thursday, Friday, and Saturday are known in Latin as ferias *post cinerum*. The three days preceding Easter, the triduum, are occasionally called ferias in the manuscripts although they are in fact feasts with very special services and each with its own name, already noted.

In a discussion of the year no other ferias need to be singled out, even though in the books others may be itemized. The ferias of Advent, for example, serve as models for the whole year and may be presented in some detail. Ferias of the fourth week in Advent which may coincide with Christmas Eve are given at some length and *die vi nativitatis*, being an isolated day in a series of feasts, may be itemized. Similarly the days after Epiphany, because of their complexity, and many ferias of Lent, because of their solemnity. Certain ferias in every week of the year may have votive services assigned to them. The votive office, usually a fairly complete imitation of all the major services of any day, is commemorative in nature and may be performed at any time rather than being assigned to a particular date. It was common, especially in monasteries, for the votive office of the Dead, or to all Saints, or to the Virgin to be said every day in addition to or in place of the regular services.[26] In other cases, the commemorative office of the Virgin was normally assigned to Saturday, that of the Holy Cross to Friday, and so forth. To other ferias may be assigned commemorative offices of patron or local saints.[27]

111 The Temporale, then, as a name applied to the liturgical year includes all that has been mentioned so far except, strictly, the feasts of the saints around Christmas. As a part of a liturgical book, the Temporale includes these feasts where they are retained in that position, and in the later middle ages is usually the first part of the book after the Kalendar. It is always presented in chronological order beginning with Advent. Familiarity with the names of the days and an ability to read the rubrics will enable the reader to discover what part of the year he is examining. This task will often be made easier by a consideration of the initials, an aspect to be taken up when the books themselves are described.

THE DAY

The offices

112 The main order of the Temporale has been fixed since the earliest days of Christianity. For even longer the basic arrangement of services within each day has been used, since it derives directly from Jewish practices. The public offices of the Synagogue were at sunrise and sunset: between them, during the day, were hours set aside for private meditation and reflection and, during the night, nocturnal vigils.[28] Two kinds of division in the services thus occur, between public and private offices, and between nocturnal and diurnal offices. Both divisions are important and remain in the church services even today. A similar pattern was taken over by the early Christians and has undergone only slight modification.[29] In the early centuries it seems that the course was as follows. To some extent, every day, but certainly every Sunday, was a commemoration of Christ's death and resurrection: the vigil service was thus preserved, especially on Saturday night, to remember the Holy Saturday watch over Christ's body. Beginning with the sunset service at which the lamps, *lucerne*, were lit,[30] the vigil continued through the night (in theory), and ended with the approach of daylight, *matutinus* and the sunrise office. The nocturnal group therefore came to have three parts with the names *lucernaria*, *vigilie*, and *matutine* (or *laudes matutinales*). The hours of private prayer, required of all the faithful, began to be organized into prayer sessions conducted in small groups which later developed into monastic communities. In the 4th century the church took control of these sessions. At first there seem to have been only three per day, perhaps commemorating the condemnation of Christ, which took place about the third hour of daylight, *tertia hora*, his crucifixion, *sexta hora*, and his death, *nona hora*. In the 4th and 5th centuries the monastic communities, separating themselves from secular Christian society, preserved both nocturnal and diurnal services whereas the churches, which served the ordinary public, preserved only the nocturnal course, chiefly the morning and evening offices. The next few centuries were to be concerned with the full establishment of the monastic round of devotions and the beginnings of Rules which would codify ritual and ceremonial practice as well as monastic behaviour in general. Soon two more services were added to the three hours of private devotion. These were at the *prima hora*, introduced ca 382 apparently because the interval between the *laudes matutinales* and the prayers at the *tertia hora* was so long that the monks remained in bed,[31] and at the completion, *completorium*, of the day. The latter came after the *lucernaria* service and before the monks went to bed, and the new office probably grew out of the final blessings before sleep. Whatever its precise origin, it split the first nocturnal service from the vigils. Such a split had already occurred in any case through the intervention of hours of sleep so that the vigils were not night-long but began soon after midnight. The insertion of the new service helped to push the *lucernaria* back into the late afternoon so that they came to be regarded as part of the diurnal rather than the nocturnal course.[32]

113 This timetable was recognized and endorsed in the West by St Benedict in his Rule, written ca 500-50 for the monks of Monte Cassino.[33] The Rule was later adopted all over Europe. Later versions sometimes elaborate and modify Benedict's timetable in minor ways and, especially, extra services and local variants began to creep in, but we may safely generalize about the usual order of the services. The course came to be known by several names, the Office Hours, Canonical Hours, Divine Office,[34] *opus Dei*, etc. Henceforth I shall use the term 'hours' or 'offices.'

The names of the nocturnal offices changed, either by the time of St Benedict or later, although occasionally there are hints of the earlier terminology. Probably because the service occurred earlier in the evening than was originally the case,[35] Benedict calls *lucernaria* by the word *vespertina*,[36] which later becomes *vespere*, usually but not always[37] in the plural, whence Vespers. Benedict still refers to *vigilie*, but this later becomes *nocturna*, or *nocturne*,[38] for obvious reasons, and later still it becomes *matutine*, for reasons which are not easy to document.[39] An exception to this is the *vigilie mortuorum*, 'the vigils of the dead,' which because of its accurate reflection of the original purpose preserves the original term. Since *vigilie* had usually become *matutine*, the original *matutine* or *laudes matutinales* at daybreak also changed its names, to *laudes*, which is usually said to derive from the opening words of psalms 148 and 150, prominently used in the service. The changing of names, and especially the earlier use of *matutine* for what we now call Lauds, can cause confusion, although by the later middle ages the present-day sequence of hours and names was quite firmly established. Figure 1.3 (p 16) summarizes the development.

114 Another change came about, partly through the introduction of the service at the end of the day, after the first nocturnal service. Because the first nocturnal hour began the overnight vigil for the following day, it originally began that day's series of services. The insertion of the new service closing the day had two effects: it pushed the first nocturnal hour earlier, and it also actually ended the day so that the earlier service lost its association with the nocturnal group and therefore with the ceremonies of the following day, and gradually came to be regarded as part of the diurnal group.[40] By the later middle ages, then, the normal liturgical day began at midnight or soon after, with Matins, and ended with Compline and sleep. However, Easter Sunday and by analogy all Sundays, and then by imitation all important feast days, retained the nightly vigils preceding the day itself and thus came to have two Vespers services and two of Compline, the first of which begin before midnight. This overspill into the preceding day required an adjustment of Vespers and Compline of that day. The latter service so rarely has proper texts that we need not consider it further. Mostly affecting Vespers, therefore, the modification consisted in replacing the texts and music of that service with texts and music proper to the Sunday or feast. First Vespers is the more important of the two Vespers services and indeed some lesser feasts give proper texts and chants for only that service, second Vespers being largely said from the common texts of the normal day superseded elsewhere by the feast. Thus we have two principal kinds of liturgical day in the later middle ages, the ferial and the Sunday or festal, as in figure 1.4 (p 17).

FIGURE 1.3
The liturgical day (offices)

earliest Christian services	by the time of St Benedict	through the middle ages	late middle ages: ferias only
vesperalia or *lucernaria*			
MIDNIGHT	MIDNIGHT		MIDNIGHT
vigilie	*vigilie – nocturne – matutine*		Matins
matutine or *laudes matutinales*	*matutine* or *laudes matutinales*	*laudes*	Lauds
Ad			
primam horam	*prima*		Prime
tertiam horam	*tertia*		Terce
sextam horam	*sexta*		Sext
nonam horam	*nona*		Nones
	lucernaria or *vespere*	*vespere*	Vespers
	completorium		Compline
MIDNIGHT	MIDNIGHT		MIDNIGHT

Although proper texts and celebrations often begin with first Vespers, in liturgical books the rubric announcing the feast to which they are proper may occur between Compline and Matins, where the day begins according to ferial practice and clock time. We shall examine later the nature of the adjustments necessitated, for example, by the coincidence of first Vespers of one feast with second Vespers of another feast on the preceding day. But let us note here that when a movable feast falls on the date of a different fixed feast, the two are said to 'occur'; when they fall on consecutive days they are said to 'concur,' and second Vespers of the earlier feast would occur with first Vespers of the other[41], as in figure 1.5. Apart from special cases such as those of Holy Week, the ferias of the Temporale adopt the ferial round of services. Saturday, since it precedes the two-Vespers Sunday, normally has no Vespers service (**427**). Sundays and the feasts of the Temporale adopt the festal round.

Mass and Chapter

115 We now need to see where Mass and some other ceremonies occur during the course of the day. The time of day at which the services were held differs: the *horarium* for winter and summer was designed to accommodate the length of the days and nights. Moreover, the number of accretions to the services differed from era to era and from place to place. The precise hour is not of much

FIGURE 1.4
Festal and ferial offices

Festal services are printed in capitals, ferial in lower case.

ferias	Sunday or major feast	lesser feast
. . .	. . .	. . .
Sext	Sext	Sext
Nones	Nones	Nones
Vespers	FIRST VESPERS	FIRST VESPERS
Compline	Compline	Compline
MIDNIGHT	MIDNIGHT	MIDNIGHT
Matins	MATINS	MATINS
Lauds	LAUDS	LAUDS
Prime to Nones	PRIME to NONES	PRIME to NONES
Vespers	SECOND VESPERS	second Vespers
Compline	COMPLINE	Compline
MIDNIGHT	MIDNIGHT	MIDNIGHT
Matins	Matins	Matins

FIGURE 1.5
Feasts which concur

Second Vespers of the earlier feast would normally be replaced by propers of first Vespers of the feast.

. . . FIRST VESPERS COMPLINE	
MIDNIGHT	
MATINS, LAUDS PRIME to NONES SECOND VESPERS COMPLINE	FIRST VESPERS COMPLINE
MIDNIGHT	
	MATINS . . .

FIGURE 1.6
The liturgical day (complete)

ferias	fasts	Sundays	double feasts
		Vespers	Vespers
		Compline	Compline
Matins	Matins	Matins	Matins
Lauds	Lauds	Lauds	Lauds
Prime	Prime	Prime	Prime
Chapter	Chapter	Chapter	Chapter
		✠	✠
		Aspersion	Terce
Terce	Terce	Terce	Aspersion
Sext	Sext	Mass	Mass
Mass	Nones	Sext	Sext
Nones	Mass	Nones	Nones
Vespers	Vespers	Vespers	Vespers
Compline	Compline	Compline	Compline

concern for our purposes. However, we should know that on Sundays and feasts the principal Mass of the day was said after Terce whereas on ferias it was said after Sext, about mid-morning or noon; on fasts it was after Nones.[42] Even this is not invariable; the information is not always easy to find, and often has to be worked out from a study of the particular day in question.[43] On Sundays Mass was preceded by the blessing of the salt and water and by a procession, each with its own little ceremony and sometimes occurring at different times. The 13th-century Ordinal of Sarum, for example, says: 'On all Sundays the blessing of salt and water occurs after Chapter . . . On ordinary Sundays they are blessed in choir and sprinkled before Terce: on double feasts and on Palm Sunday they are sprinkled after Terce.'[44] On the other hand, the New Sarum Ordinal dating from the mid-14th century, specifically mentioning the change, says: 'On all Sundays the blessing of salt and water occurs after Prime and Chapter at the choir-step . . . On double feasts they are blessed outside choir, privately[45] before some altar, and are sprinkled after Sext. But until recently, according to the old Ordinal, they were sprinkled after Terce and Sext was said after Mass.'[46] Such are the minor variants in detail we constantly discover once we start probing beyond the main outlines of the Temporale and the basic sequence of services.

116 The other daily occurrence, at least in the monastery and other collegiate establishments, was the Chapter meeting or *capitulum*, which partook of the nature of a service in some respects. The same variability in position as with the principal Mass occurs, although the duty was usually fulfilled after Prime on Sundays and feasts, after Terce on ferias.[47] Often associated with the Chapter meeting was a morning Mass or Chapter Mass, which preceded it.[48] The daily round of services or business meetings is summarized in figure 1.6.

Beyond what has been said it is increasingly difficult to decide what are the essential parts of the Temporale round of services and what are accretions to that round, and to decide how far the private prayers said before and after some of the services are to be considered separate brief services of their own when they become extended and organized, or how far some of the processions, the number and extent of which depend to a great extent on the geography of the church and its grounds, should be regarded as normal and usual. The significance and organization of such ceremonies, which some may describe as para-liturgical, will be considered when we discuss the internal structure of the services. Before leaving the basic liturgical year in its overall aspect, however, we need briefly to mention some other ceremonies which occur on special days or are sufficiently universal to be inseparable from the daily devotions.

Other ceremonies

117 Advent is unremarkable. Its Ember days, like those of the three other seasons, have no major alterations or additions of services. Christmas Day, of course, is special. Apart from processions whose number and times are variable according to location it has three Masses, the first said after Matins and often known as *missa in gallicantu*, 'at cock-crow.' After Lauds is the dawn Mass, *in aurora*, and after Terce as usual the principal Mass, *magna missa*. The last was preceded by a procession even when the day was not Sunday, although the occurrence of Sunday could affect the time of the procession.[49]

On Ash Wednesday the ashes are blessed with prayers, dialogues, chants and processions, usually after Sext or Nones and preceding Mass. Similarly on Palm Sunday the procession preceding Mass is considerably extended, beyond the blessing and sprinkling of Holy Water, with the blessing and distribution of the palms and with readings and chants interrupting the procession at several stations, or places where halts are made. The first three weekdays of Holy Week are unexceptional. In the early middle ages Maundy Thursday, Good Friday, and Holy Saturday seem to have had none of the hours from Prime to Vespers, inclusive, at least as public or communal services: some sources require them to be said *privatim* or *secreto*.[50] By the later middle ages the little hours had been added as normal diurnal services at least on Thursday and Friday, and Vespers was curiously entangled with the end of Mass, celebrated after Nones, so that both Mass and Vespers finish simultaneously. On Maundy Thursday, this Mass service was preceded by an elaborate procession with the penitents and accompanied by readings and prayers. Later in the evening, after the meal, the church altars were washed with water and wine and then an additional service was held in the Chapter house. This latter was the *Mandatum*,[51] or foot-washing ceremony, sometimes called *pedilavium*. Compline was then said *privatim*. Good Friday has no extra services or processions, but the combined Mass and Vespers ceremonial is highly special. The little hours on Holy Saturday were still suppressed, being said *privatim*, and the following Vespers and Mass service represents the Easter vigil and is preceded by a very long and complex ceremony involving many readings and prayers, the blessing of the New Fire and the Paschal candle and the Font, and several processions including the sevenfold and fivefold Litanies. The annual service of baptism was also performed at this time so that the new Christians could participate in the joys of Easter Sunday. The main differences about the last three days of Holy Week, then, are the partial suppression of the little hours, the combination of Mass and Vespers and the extension of that combined service by extremely elaborate processions and other ceremonies beforehand and the addition of the *Mandatum* afterwards on Thursday.

118 Although Easter Sunday normally has additional processions, it is distinguished rather by the splendour of its ceremonial than by any additional services. Mass is at the usual time for Sundays, after Terce. The Rogation Days after Pascha 5, too, are distinguished only by the extent of their processions before Mass, which, being ferial, is celebrated after Sext. The procession includes the greater Litany.

We may summarize the liturgical day by concluding that the *opus Dei*, the hours, run their course throughout the year without major variant in order or time. Additional celebrations are most often in the form of some processions preceding the principal Mass of the day, sometimes with a little hour intervening between the procession and Mass. Mass itself was said at several different times of day, after Terce, Sext, or Nones, depending on the solemnity of the occasion: Christmas Day has three Masses. Allowing for the varying times of Mass, the daily order is very stable. Unfortunately, the imposition of the feasts of fixed date celebrating the saints disturbs the Temporale in greater or lesser degree according to the number of saints' days which have to be included. In the late middle ages there was often a large number, and in the period we are considering many other accretions to the daily round further complicated the services. The Sanctorale and accretions will be set aside so that we can examine in detail the internal structure of the services of the Temporale. Prior to describing this structure and in order to avoid irrelevant explanation and to use a maximum of unambiguous proper names, the textual and musical forms will be analyzed, followed by an examination of how they tend to vary or to remain unchanged from day to day and season to season.

2

The Textual and Musical Forms

200 The elements of liturgical devotion are quite simple, the two most important being prayer and readings of scripture. Additions consist principally of conventional formulas for introducing and ending each of these elements and the insertion at specific points of meditations on the preceding item. In these latter places music, with its ineffable qualities of emotional and spiritual intensity, plays an important role.

Prayers

201 Prayer was of two kinds, private and communal, the latter carried out in an organized framework which we call a church service. It is this kind that we are chiefly concerned with, although there are still times, specifically during the consecration of the Host at Mass, when private prayer may be used: the priest says the consecration prayers *privatim* or *secreto*, in a low voice, while the congregation prays silently.[1] We have already seen examples of the hours said *privatim*. Although by the late middle ages the terms *oratio* and *collecta* are used indiscriminately to refer to prayers, the former term will generally be used here.[2] A few special prayers must be singled out.

The Lord's Prayer, the *Paternoster* or *oratio Dominica*, is said at many places during the services, either by the priest or by the whole choir or congregation, and the last clauses frequently take the form of a dialogue. Easily confused with the *oratio Dominica*, nowadays or in the middle ages, is the *oratio dominicalis*, which strictly refers to the Sunday prayer lasting through the week but which by analogy seems to refer sometimes to any prayer proper to 'the day' and repeated throughout its services and through its octave. The *Ave Maria* or *Salutatio angelica* seems to have been a prayer more of private devotion than of liturgical rule and, although it may appear in certain places within the services, these will differ from use to use: it has no fixed occasion. What we now know as the general confession is a sequence of three prayers, the *Confiteor*, *Misereatur*, and *Absolutionem*, said after Prime and Compline and during the preparation for Mass and sometimes involving a complicated alternation between priest and congregation referred to as *preces*, a term nearly always found in the plural.

More will be said of preces in the relevant positions. A whole series of mostly invariable prayers, some said *secreto* and now called secrets, occurs at Mass before the consecration of the Host. These fall into three groups which are continuous, and all are said by the priest as he prepares and consecrates the Host: the Oblation or Offertory prayers, the Preface prayers, the Canon prayers. As we shall see, the Sanctus and Agnus are amongst these and are the only ones to be taken up by the choir with moderately elaborate music, the others (when not said *secreto*) being recited or intoned by the priest to set musical formulas, mostly of one note. Finally we may mention a prayer used only on Holy Saturday during the Easter Vigil: this is the *Exultet iam angelica*, sung by one of the celebrants to a very special and ancient reciting melody.

Most prayers, especially the communal ones with their established texts, have introductory and closing formulas: the priest's *Oremus* and congregational *Amen* are the two most obvious, and other common closing phrases are *per omnia secula seculorum, Amen* and *per Christum Dominum nostrum.* Opening conventions often consist of such phrases as *Presta* (or *Concede*, or *Excita*, or *Da*), *quesumus, omnipotens* (or *sempiterne*) *Deus* . . . *ut* . . . Such opening and closing formulas are often rendered in abbreviation in the liturgical books, the letters PQOD beginning the text, or the word *per* occurring by itself at the end. In these cases the full phrase has to be known, or sought elsewhere, and often it is almost impossible to determine whether, for example, *per omnia* . . . or *per Christum* . . . should be used, if the source is not more specific than *per* . . . Appendix VI gives some rules for terminations.

Readings

202 Known under the general heading of *lectiones*, readings were in the earliest days presumably drawn entirely from the Bible, but through the middle ages other writings were introduced so that the source might be scripture or a sermon of a notable Christian figure such as a Pope or a Church Father, or a Homily or a Gloss by a similar writer. Eventually, accounts of saints' lives and their deeds were used as special readings for the relevant celebration: often such biographies were inaccurate, even apocryphal, and the term *legenda*, originally used like *lectio* to mean any reading, came to have its pejorative meaning of fabulous. This meaning seems to be no earlier than the 16th century. Although the word *lectio* or *legenda* includes the whole group, *sermo, homilia* (or *omelia*), *expositio* and similar terms were also used for the relevant kind of reading. Several words distinguished different types of scriptural readings and *epistola, evangelium*, and *passio* should need no further comment. *Historia* was conventionally used for readings drawn from the Old Testament, and was later applied also to newly composed saints' biographies,[3] and since Old Testament *lectiones* formed a prominent part of the Matins service, the term is sometimes used to refer to the whole service. The word *capitulum* is also used for a miscellaneous reading from scripture and should not be confused with 'chapter': the meaning is of course 'heading' and most *capitula* are very short, a matter of one or two sentences.

Various formulas for beginning and ending readings may be used in some cases, and are usually abbreviated as are the prayer formulas. Opening phrases seem concerned with establishing a time, such as *In illo tempore* for gospel passages, *In diebus illis* for Old Testament passages, *Ante diem festum* for a reading of Good Friday, *Cum natus esset* for one of Epiphany. As we shall see, readings for consecutive days or weeks were originally drawn from consecutive passages of the same book. The first of such readings may be introduced by the word *Initium* and subsequent readings by the work *sequentia*. With regard to the latter word, we shall notice a position where a dangerous ambiguity lies in wait for the unwary or the uninformed.

Psalmody[4]

203 Out of the different ways in which psalms were recited grow the two chief methods of performing the musical items of the liturgy. We are not here investigating the musical qualities but simply the formal divisions of the text between celebrant, or some soloist, and congregation, or later some trained body of singers.

Most important in this respect is a distinction between solo and choral performance based solely on a practical consideration. Choirs cannot easily begin simultaneously on a unanimous pitch. It is therefore necessary for all items, even though fully choral, to begin with an intonation sung by a soloist. Although sometimes called an incipit, *intonatio* is its more proper name. Many simpler items, such as versicles and responses, are already announced by a single singer. Manuscripts do not often indicate very clearly, if at all, the extent of the intonation, although some careful and precise books, especially those of Dominican use, may place a small incise, or stroke, on the musical stave. Modern editions may use an asterisk or similar sign. The information may sometimes be found in a rubric or an Ordinal.

Psalms

204 Psalms are different from most of the other scriptural writings in that they are poetic. Their structure is well known: short verses or stichs, that is, single lines, are each divided into hemistichs in which the thought of the first is paralleled in the second. The following is an example: *Ps 33 (Revised Standard Version)/Ps 32 (Vulgate)*[5]

Exsultate justi in Domino; *rectus decet collaudatio.*	Rejoice in the Lord, o you righteous! Praise befits the upright.
Confitemini Domino in cithara; *in psalterio decem chor-* *darum psallite illi.*	Praise the Lord with the lyre, make melody to Him with the harp of ten strings.
Cantate ei canticum novum; *bene psallite ei in* *vociferatione.*	Sing to Him a new song, play skilfully on the strings with loud shouts.

As with the prayers and readings already described, the recitation was often brought to a close with a formula. Each of the five books into which the Psalter is divided in the Vulgate ends with a pre-Christian 'doxology,' usually based on the words *Benedictus Dominus.*[6] Since they were Old Testament and thus Jewish, all the psalms had to be made specifically Christian, and a new doxology formed the standard closing phrase, said by the congregation at the end of each psalm. Known as the lesser doxology, it is the *Gloria Patri et Filio et Spiritui sancto* which emphasises the Holy Trinity.[7]

Canticles

205 This same doxology was appended to the three major canticles even though they do not need to be made orthodox (since they are taken from the New Testament) and to the other canticles which, like the psalms, are usually drawn from the Old Testament. Although none of the canticles are psalms, they are poems of the same literary genre, they are performed like psalms, and are frequently introduced by the abbreviation Ps, for *psalmus*, in medieval sources. Accompanied by 'refrains' in exactly the same way as psalms, their verses are performed antiphonally (see **214-16**), as psalm verses are in similar circumstances. As a genre they are called *cantica* (sing. *canticum*). The three major canticles, the *Magnificat, Benedictus,* and *Nunc dimittis*, with texts from the gospel of the evangelist Luke, are more usually called *evangelia*, a term which must not be confused with the readings known as *Evangelia*. These three items are regularly sung near the end of Vespers, Lauds, and Compline respectively. There are fourteen lesser canticles, of Old Testament origin. All are sung at Lauds, one for each day of the week with alternatives for Lent. Monastic rites have numerous additional canticles, drawn from various literary sources, for use in the third nocturn of Matins.

Direct psalmody

206 In the earliest days of Christianity the psalms were recited, either said or sung by a soloist and at a later period by soloists, while the congregation listened.[8] This kind of performance, with no alternation of performers, is not widely used in the public services of the later middle ages, at least for the recitation of psalms. The tract, consisting in one of its forms of numerous psalm or psalm-like verses sung by a soloist at penitential Masses, is virtually the only important item performed in direct psalmody. The recitation of psalms by a single person such as the priest in his preparation for Mass, or by the monk in his private prayers, is also direct psalmody. Even though the former occasion will be specified in the rubrics for the official preparation for Mass, both occasions are private rather than public and official in nature. The line between the two is sometimes difficult to draw. Direct psalmody is illustrated in figure 2.2a (**216**).

Refrains

207 Whether the psalm is performed by a soloist or chorally, within the context of a service it is accompanied by a refrain. Refrains, which are more usually known by specific technical names to be mentioned below, are always sung by the whole group, in the earliest days including the congregation. Sometimes the group would repeat the verse just sung by the soloist, as in figure 2.2b, in which case it need learn no extra material; or it may respond with the second half of the verse after the soloist sings the first half, as in figure 2.2c, in which case it must know the psalm texts.

Ps 135, *Confitemini Domino,* is one of a group of psalms known as refrain psalms because the second half of the verse is identical each time:

4 *Qui facit mirabilia magna solus, quoniam in eternum misericordia eius.*
5 *Qui fecit celos in intellectu, quoniam . . .*
6 *Qui firmavit terram super aquas, quoniam . . .*

208 As well as responding in these simple ways, in the earliest days of Christianity the congregation used to respond with a refrain independent of the psalm, often a short phrase such as *Amen, Amen, Amen,* or 'O God unmovable.'[9] Such refrains may have been sung at the end of the psalm or after each verse, as in figure 2.2d. The simplest version of this form, where the refrain is very brief, occurs only in the Litany of the later middle ages and none of the text is from the psalms:

Sancte Paule	*ora pro nobis*
Sancte Andrea	*ora pro nobis*
. . .	
Sancti Johannes et Paule	*orate pro nobis*
etc.	

The practice of choral repetition of whole verses, or of choral performance of the second hemistich to the solo performance of the first, did not survive into later medieval times, although a good many Reformation churches adopted such methods. The refrain which was quite independent of a psalm fell into disfavour, at least until the institution of new feasts and the canonization of new saints necessitated the composition of new, non-biblical texts. To provide a text for the increasingly elaborate musical chant of the refrain, the standard procedure in the central liturgical repertory was to paraphrase key verses of the psalm to which the refrain belongs. Originally such paraphrase refrains would have been sung only in association with the psalm from which they are drawn; soon, however, the complexity of liturgical requirements would have made it impossible to observe this principle. There is now no sign other than the textual relationship that a particular refrain belongs to one psalm rather than another. Moreover, the paraphrase often conflates verses of different psalms:

Psalm 37	introit
22 *Ne derelinquas me Domine*	*Ne derelinquas me Domine*
Deus discesseris a me	*Deus meus, ne discedas a me:*
23 *Intende in adiutorium meum*	*intende in adiutorium meum*
Domine Deus salutis mee	*Domine virtus salutis mee*

Psalm 139
8 *Domine Domine virtus salutis mee*

As in this refrain, an introit,[10] the paraphrase often involves only minor changes of a word or two or an inversion of sentences. A more varied refrain is the first antiphon for Matins of the Common of Confessors,[11] drawn from the first verses of the Psalter:

Psalm 1.1-2	
Beatus vir qui non abiit in consilio impiorum, et in via peccatorum non stetit, et in cathedra pestilentie non sedit; sed in lege Domini voluntas eius, et in lege eius meditabitur die ac nocte.	*Beatus vir, qui in lege Domini meditatur; voluntas eius permanet die ac nocte, et omnia quecumque faciet, semper prosperabuntur.*

The following genres, to be described in more detail later, are in fact the refrains to psalms or canticles: alleluias, antiphons, communions, graduals, introits, invitatories, offertories, responsories. By the later middle ages, the psalm verses have been entirely eliminated in some of these genres, making it difficult to assign them to either of the categories of chant which must now be introduced. The two categories differ first in the manner in which the psalm or the psalm verse is performed.

Responsorial psalmody

209 Because the choral body, congregation or trained *schola*, responds to the solo recitation of the psalm this type of performance is called responsorial. The singing of the whole psalm with choral interjections of a refrain after every verse resulted in a very long item, and with the increasing standardization of the services and the constant accretions to them, some form of shortening eventually had to occur. One method of abbreviation results in responsorial psalmody: the number of psalm verses sung by the soloist was reduced, until only a single verse remained; concurrently the congregational refrain became more complex. The latter development could take place only in monastic communities in the earliest days, because until the establishment of the *schola cantorum* in Rome and similar professional bodies elsewhere, monasteries were the only places to have any sort of a trained body of singers capable of singing a complex melodic refrain. Responsorial psalmody is therefore in essence a monastic form, and it occurs chiefly in the nocturnal office of Matins. When a single verse remains, the form is that of figure 2.2e abbreviated from 2.2d. The single verse is not necessarily the first verse of the psalm. The choral refrain is retained both before and after this verse, resulting in an RVR pattern, where R stands for refrain (it will later stand for responsory, one proper name for the refrain) and V for verse. In time, but only for certain responsorial forms, another abbreviation was carried out, in this case to the repeat of the refrain: instead of singing the complete refrain, the choir would take it up from a point somewhere in its course. Apart from the Litany, eight items in the liturgy, all sung, can be regarded as responsorial according to the above criteria. Of these, five lost or modified some of the responsorial features and nowadays may not be thought of as responsorial: introits, invitatories, communions, offertories, and tracts will be examined in a later section. The different ways in which responsories, graduals, and alleluias took up the various methods of abbreviation will be explained forthwith. Each of these items, and perhaps also the other five, may be called a responsory, although it is common to find the term *responsorium* or its abbreviation only for responsories themselves and for graduals in manuscripts of certain areas. Strictly speaking the term responsory applies only to the refrain and does not include the solo verses, which are so labelled. Commonly, no distinction is made between these different shades of meaning and none is usually required: where necessary the separate sections will be called refrain and verse.

210 The responsory, the responsorial item chiefly found in Matins, is also known in English as respond or response. I do not like the first alternative, and shall reserve the second for the congregational reply to a versicle in certain dialogues to be discussed. The refrain of the responsory is conventionally shortened in some way when it is said after the verse. Taken up from some mid-point and sometimes called a *repetenda*, the shortened text, lacking its first words, frequently does not make good sense, a fact which has been deplored. Abbreviation of this kind was practised as early as the 9th century.[12] The last responsory of each nocturn at Matins ends with a doxology, sometimes referred to as a verse. Lacking the final phrase, from *sicut erat* . . ., a feature which seems to be a survival of the earlier form of the lesser doxology (see **204**), this 'verse' is otherwise identical with the doxology of psalms.[13] The presence of a doxology, or of other verses as in the example below, usually results in a further abbreviation of the refrain for its third appearance, and yet more for its fourth. Rubrics normally clarify the structure. Manuscripts do not necessarily indicate the points from which abbreviated repeats begin, although an incise on the musical stave and a capital letter in the text usually appear. The precise place of the repetenda may otherwise be determined by the cue word(s) given at the end of each verse. The standard form of a simple responsory without additional verses or doxology then is R*§V§;[14] here the * marks the end of the solo intonation (this method is a modern convention) and the § marks the beginning of the repetenda (various ways, or none at all, are used in modern editions). Several responsories are shown with their music, as in an Antiphonal or Noted Breviary, in plates 14a-f; in column 3 of 14b, for example, is the responsory *Aspiciebam* with its verse *Potestas* and repetenda *Et datum*. The cue word *Ad* of the repetenda after the doxology of another responsory appears in plate 27c. The majority of the examples in the plates are of great responsories, *responsoria prolixa*, as in plates 22 (with the chant) and 1 (without the chant): simpler and shorter versions of this form are the short responsories, *responsoria brevia*. Fig. 2.1 illustrates the general form of the responsory.

FIGURE 2.1
The form of the responsory

* shows the end of the solo incipit.
§ shows the point at which the repetenda begins.

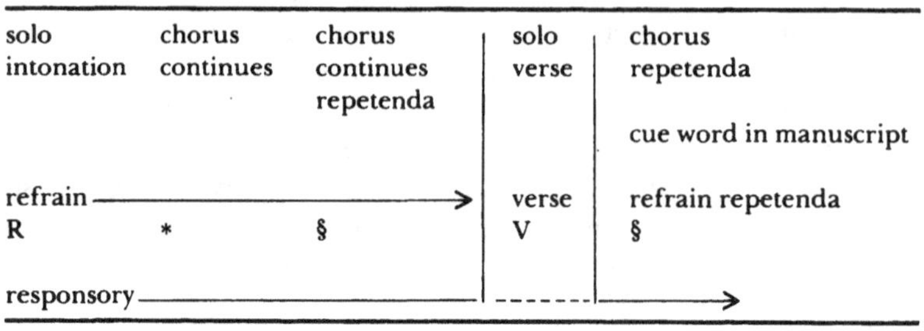

solo intonation	chorus continues	chorus continues repetenda	solo verse	chorus repetenda cue word in manuscript
refrain ————	————	————→	verse	refrain repetenda
R	*	§	V	§
responsory ————	————	————	- - - - - - -	————→

211 A few special responsories retain hints of the earlier form with many psalm verses since they have several solo verses, after each of which the refrain is repeated, usually with progressive abbreviation. The office of the Dead, because it preserves some of the character of the original nocturnal vigil and is very ancient, has features of this kind: the final responsory at Matins, *Libera me Domine de morte*, has several verses and a gradually shortened refrain. Rather than quoting *Libera me*, I give here the first responsory of Advent Sunday Matins, which has a similar form and which includes the doxology even though it is the first responsory of the nocturn. I include the rubrics translated from the 13th-century Sarum Antiphonal: they recur, unchanged except for additional detail, in the Sarum Breviary of 1531.[15] The extent of the solo intonation is not made precise in either of these books.

Three boys in surplices at the choir-step begin the responsory:

Aspiciens a longe ecce video Dei potentiam venientem, et nebulam totam terram tegentem. § Ite obviam ei, et dicite: † Nuntia nobis si tu es ipse ‡ qui regnaturus es # in populo Israel. •

Beholding from afar, lo, I see the coming power of God, and a cloud covering the whole earth. Go to meet him, saying: 'Tell us if you are the one who will rule over the people of Israel.'

One boy sings the verse:

Quique terrigene et filii hominum, simul in unum dives et pauper,

All you men of earth and sons of men, both rich and poor,

Chorus: § Ite . . .	Go . . .
All repetitions are said to the end of the refrain. One boy sings the verse:	
Qui regis Israel, intende, qui deducis velut ovem Joseph.	You who rule Israel, guide us, as Joseph leads the sheep:
Chorus: † Nuntia . . .	'Tell us . . .'
One boy sings the verse:	
Excita Domine potentiam tuam et veni, ut salvos facias nos.	Arouse thy power, o Lord, and come to make us saved,
Chorus: ‡ qui . . .	who will . . .
The three boys say the verse:	
Gloria Patri et Filio et Spiritui Sancto.	Glory be to the Father, the Son and the Holy Ghost,
Chorus: # in popu . . .	over the people . . .
During the Gloria Patri *the choir remains standing.*[16] *The same three boys begin the responsory again and it is sung through* (percantetur) *by the choir.*	

In this example, the progressive abbreviation of the refrain is so arranged that the text does make good sense. Wagner cites a slightly different arrangement, also making sense, from the 11th Ordo Romanus.[17] Plate 14b shows this chant in a French manuscript.

Responsory texts are drawn principally from the historical books of the Bible or from sacred literature of the early Christian era rather than from the psalms. As Apel points out,[18] they are therefore not strictly psalmodic.

212 Graduals are somewhat simpler since there is hardly ever more than one verse,[19] there is never a doxology, and the refrain is never shortened although it may be omitted. In this responsorial item, called *responsorium grad[u]ale* from the common practice of singing it at the pulpit at the choir-step (*gradus chori*), the choir nowadays takes the last word or two of the solo verse. Wagner cites a rubric from the *Ritus servandi in cantu missae* and an English manuscript of the 15th century where this practice is documented, and claims that it is of late medieval origin.[20] The reason for this procedure, and evidence from the middle ages confirming it, is elusive. Was it the normal practice in every performance or only when the refrain was not repeated after the verse? In the latter circumstance, some form of choral termination may have been felt necessary to balance the opening choral refrain. Complete absence of the gradual refrain after the verse, the ultimate in abbreviation, means that there is no choral reply and it is thought that one result may have ben the change from the name *responsorium (graduale)* to *graduale*.[21] Omission of the refrain is clearly documented in certain contexts, such as when another chant immediately follows the gradual.[22] As with the shortening of the responsory refrain, this omission may damage the sense of the text.[23] Unlike responsories, graduals mostly draw the text of both refrain and verse from the psalms.[24] The scheme of a gradual, then is **G*VG*** or **G*(V** with choral termination). Plates 4b and 16 show graduals with chants; in the latter the abbreviation is R for *responsorium gradale*. Plate 13 shows the gradual *Excita Domine* with its verse *Qui regis* in a Missal, without the chant.

213 The alleluia of Mass became responsorial only after it was the custom to include a solo verse. At what period the verses were added is not certain, although it seems to have taken place between ca 550 and ca 750.[25] Again as Apel correctly points out, since there was originally no verse, the origin cannot have been psalmodic, nor can the ultimate form have been achieved by abbreviation from a more complete psalm. The normal structure by the later middle ages is, like the responsory and gradual, fundamentally **A*VA*** with a solo intonation and choral continuation. In this refrain the word *alleluia* may be distributed between **A** and * in various ways, or repeated for each. The complicating factor is the normal presence in later medieval sources of a *(p)neuma* or melismatic extension of the final *-a* of *alleluia*. Often called a *jubilus*, this extension may appear at the end of either or both of the * sections and sometimes at the end of the solo verse **V** as well. There are numerous musical, rubrical, and liturgical problems regarding the *neuma* which remain unsolved. It is this melismatic extension which most authorities regard as the place where the sequence, a most important musical and textual trope, originated.[26] Plate 7c shows the *Alleluia* V. *Pascha nostrum* with an alternative verse *Epulemur* (for Vespers), followed by a sequence.

Antiphonal psalmody

214 Responsorial and direct psalmody depends on the solo performance of the psalm. Antiphonal psalmody depends on choral performance, a method which Batiffol suggests may have resulted from the establishment of Christianity as a legal religion, the consequent building of public basilicas to hold large congregations, and the further consequent necessity that the psalms should be more forceful in volume.[27] However, choral performance was a regular feature of worship in the Jewish Temple[28] and its use in the Christian church was probably as much a result of tradition; Batiffol's suggestion may provide only a reason for its rapid development. The structure of the psalm texts themselves, with their half-verse parallelism, and the architectural layout of the places where choirs sang in the middle ages, in two opposing ranks called *decani* and *cantoris* from the traditional location of the Dean's and Cantor's seats, lent itself ideally to a performance in which two choirs alternated. Antiphonal singing of this kind is so traditional and commonplace that evidence giving the solution to a basic problem is difficult to find. Did the choirs alternate every half-verse, or every whole verse? It seems more commonly to have been the latter.[29] Rules for the use of Sarum include two passages which refer to alternation every whole verse.[30] In the first, the *punctum* is the end of the verse, where the other half of the choir takes over, and the *metrum* is the cadence at the half-verse, where the half-choir breathes:

Psalmodiam non nimis trahantur: punctum nullus teneat sed cito dimittat. Post metrum bonam pausam faciamus.

In the second passage, the performance of a specific item is made quite clear:

In die Pasche ad vesperas . . . primum Alleluya incipiant rectores chori; deinde chorus ex parte decani primum versum psalmi totum dicat cum Alleluya: deinde chorus ex parte cantoris totum alium versum psalmi cum Alleluya canant: et sic alternatim totum psalmum canant; et in fine psalmi tota antiphona a toto choro cantetur.

According to Van Dijk, this passage derives from St Bernard's rules for Cistercians: he cites numerous passages from Dominican, Franciscan, and Augustinian rules to demonstrate alternation of whole verses.[31] Similarly difficult is ascertaining whether the doxology was performed in a manner continuing the antiphonal performance for its half or whole verses, as the case may be, or whether the half-choirs joined together for this text. Certainly they seem to have sung the refrain together, although it is hard to find evidence as clear as in the second passage cited above. At some time during the early middle ages the refrain became an integral part of the antiphonal performance, perhaps in imitation of the same principle as it applied to the solo singing of psalms. The psalm was now sung by alternating half-choirs, the refrain by the whole choir after every verse.[32] The refrain, beginning with a solo intonation, was also sung by the whole choir before the psalm. Proving too long, this kind of piece was abbreviated in a different manner from that by which responsorial psalmody was shortened: in antiphonal psalmody the repetitions of the refrain were eliminated, leaving the whole psalm intact. The scheme

R 1 R 2 R 3 R 4 etc . . . R . . . ,
in which the numbers refer to psalm verses, was abbreviated to

R 1 2 3 4 . . . R.
See figure 2.2g & h. Where there is a doxology, the refrain is usually retained both before and after that 'verse.'

215 Because of its association with the antiphonal singing of two half-choirs in the psalm the refrain itself unfortunately received the name antiphon. The method of performance and the genre must not be confused. Antiphons are not performed antiphonally. It is customary to speak of the psalm being sung 'under' the antiphon or, conversely, of the antiphon as 'covering' the psalm. As with responsorial forms, some items of the liturgy preserve remnants of the earlier practice by retaining the refrain, or antiphon, after all or after many of the psalm verses. The invitatory, if we wish to categorize it as antiphonal rather than responsorial, is one example (see **218**); the 'processional' chant for the sprinkling of water before Sunday Mass may be performed similarly.[33] The canticle *Nunc dimittis* with the antiphon *Lumen ad revelationem* for Purification is sung with full choral antiphony and a repeated refrain. Just as the basic scheme of the responsorial type of psalmody has some later modifications, so too with the antiphonal. One change, a further shortening, is the omission of the choral completion of the antiphon after the solo intonation, before the psalm. In this case, the soloist may continue with the first half-verse of the psalm, the second half being taken up by his side of the choir and antiphonal performance continuing from the second verse. The structure is therefore as follows, where the lower case 'a' is used to represent the incipit rather than the whole of the antiphon (A), and where x and y represent the two halves of the choir:

a	1½	1½	2	3	4 . . .	A*	doxology	A*
solo		choir						
		x	y	x	y	x	x y	x
						y		y

At * the usual practice was probably to have the soloist re-intone the antiphon. It was common in certain services to combine psalms, especially the shorter ones, into a single text. When sung thus, only a single doxology and antiphon occurs and we may speak of '(three) psalms under a single antiphon.' The earliest antiphon texts are paraphrases of psalm verses and other biblical passages, and later are drawn from many different literary sources.

216 The different types of psalmody are of such basic importance and are so often confused that I have thought it useful to give a figure summarizing and contrasting the three types and their development. From figure 2.2 we may obtain some idea of how the responsorial refrain of d), by adopting the length, textual style, and complexity of one of the other two types of responsorial psalmody, b) or c), may have grown in elaboration from a single word to a lengthy phrase itself resembling a psalm verse. Present-day methods of performance are often not those of the middle ages: type c), common nowadays, is not to my knowledge practised in the later medieval period, although of course one cannot generalize about the whole of Europe over two or three centuries in such matters. Performance b) is similarly unknown to me. Performances as in a), d), and g) were still in use on certain occasions, but e) and h) must be regarded as normal.

In present usage the terms responsorial and antiphonal have acquired the meaning of 'musically elaborate' and 'musically simple', referring to stylistic characteristics of the chants. Statistically, this commonly accepted interpretation is valid and it will be used here, with due caution, but the generalization is often incorrect: some responsories are quite simple, many antiphons are musically very complex. Each of these terms, then, may relate to a form, a method of performance, or to a musical style: their contexts must be carefully considered.

FIGURE 2.2
Psalmody and methods of performance

Numbers are psalm verses: a & b represent half-verses. Material in Roman type is sung by soloists; material in **bold** type is sung by the **choir**. Ref. = refrain. ‡ denotes sections abbreviated in later revisions.

DIRECT PSALMODY	a)		1		2		3 . . .		n		chorus may end with some formula such as *Amen* or *Alleluia*
RESPONSORIAL PSALMODY	b)		1	**1**	2	**2**	3	**3**	n	**n**	not used in middle ages
	c)		1a	**1b**	2a	**2b**	3a	**3b**	na	**nb**	
	d)	[**Ref.**]	1	**Ref.**	2	**Ref.**	3	**Ref.**	n	**Ref.**	cf Litany
					abbreviated to						
	e)					**Ref.**	n	**Ref.**‡			the basic form of the responsory (RVR), gradual (**GVG**), and alleluia (**AVA**)
ANTIPHONAL PSALMODY	f)		**1a**	**1b**	**2a**	**2b**	**3a**	**3b**	**na**	**nb**	alternating half-choirs
	g)	[**Ref.**]	**1a**	**1b Ref.**	**2a**	**2b Ref.**	**3a**	**3b Ref.**	**na nb**	**Ref.**	refrain by whole choir
					abbreviated to						
	h)	‡**Ref.**	**1a**	**1b**	**2a**	**2b**	**3a**	**3b**	**na nb**	**Ref.**	the basic form of psalm and antiphon (APA)

Independent antiphons

217 Independent antiphons are usually quite elaborate as to musical style. Originating as a refrain to a psalm, the antiphon ought to be used only in that context. But gradually, and especially as the system of extra-ritual devotions increased, certain devotional texts and chants quite independent of psalms were composed and these too were called antiphons. Moreover, a few psalm-antiphons were divorced from their association with the psalm in order to be used as separate items for devotional purposes. Antiphon, then, includes both psalm-antiphons and devotional (or votive) antiphons, the latter being later and freer compositions when they are not identical textually and musically with the former, The four famous Marian antiphons, *Alma redemptoris mater, Regina celi, Salve regina,* and *Ave regina* are devotional items with no connection with a psalm. On the other hand, *Nesciens mater* is a psalm-antiphon sometimes used independently. Furthermore, certain processional items in various kinds of form may be called antiphons. In fact, the terminology for processional texts and chants is not at all precise, the same item being referred to as antiphon or responsory or even hymn in different sources.[34] Even when the antiphonal or responsorial method of performance seems clear, the musical style and sometimes the source of the actual melody in another liturgical position may speak against the obvious designation.

Invitatory, aspersion, introit, offertory, communion

218 An important item which is responsorial in its method of performance yet more like an antiphon in its musical style and liturgical function is the invitatory. Details of its performance vary from feast to feast but it is quite clear from the sources studied that the psalm verses are sung by soloist(s) and the refrain is choral.[35] Despite these responsorial characteristics, the function of the whole item as an introductory piece like the introit and the simpler melodic style of its refrain normally result in the latter being called an antiphon. Moreover, the complete psalm is sung, as in a psalm and antiphon. The psalm text is not that of the Vulgate, but from an earlier translation the proper name for which varies from author to author.[36] In place of the eleven verses of the Vulgate text there are five long sections beginning respectively *Venite, exultemus* . . . *Quoniam Deus* . . . *Quoniam ipsius* . . . *Hodie* . . . *Quadraginta*: the invitatory antiphon is sung after each. This item alone, with its characteristically displayed five parts, forms the basis for a small section within a complete Antiphonal (**624**). Plate 12 shows two of the invitatory tones.

Also antiphonal in musical style and by name but responsorial in its method of performance is the music which accompanies the aspersion preceding Mass. The 'refrain' is either *Asperges me Domine* . . . or, for Easter time, *Vidi aquam* . . . Each of these 'antiphons' has only one psalm verse, for *Asperges* the first of Ps 50 from which the *Asperges* text itself is drawn, and for *Vidi* the first of Ps 117 or 105 or 106 (all identical), the *Vidi* text being drawn from Ezechiel 47, 1 & 9. We have already established that a reduction in the number of psalm verses is characteristic of responsorial psalmody: the solo performance of the psalm verses here [37] and the shortening of the refrain on its repetition after the verse are also features which distinguish responsorial from antiphonal performance. To call these items responsories, however, would invalidate tradition and all printed indices. The term antiphon is suitable only because it describes perfectly the melodic style of the chants and the setting of the texts to the music. In the Sarum Ordinal the psalm verse of *Asperges* is sung in two halves separated and followed by the complete refrain: the refrain is shortened after the doxology.[38] On the other hand the Roman Missal of 1474 lists only the first half of the verse, a common enough abbreviation which may still imply the complete verse, and it does not repeat the antiphon other than after the doxology.[39] No doubt many other variations in form and performance could be recorded. Plate 24 shows this item.

219 The introit, the introductory item for Mass, is even more clearly antiphonal in form as well as style, like the offertory and communion, two other proper chants of the Mass.[40] All are characterized by a reduction of the number of psalm verses said in an otherwise normal psalm-antiphon structure. Because of its length, the entrance procession in papal churches probably used the whole psalm: elsewhere, and occurring at different places at different times, the number of verses was reduced as necessary, and the shorter version remained customary.[41] If the procession or other ceremonies remained unfinished at the time the doxology was sung, it seems to have been the custom to sing a few extra psalm verses followed again by the refrain so that in a complete performance of the introit the doxology may appear in the middle of the piece rather than at the end. Such extra verses were called *versus ad repetendum* or *repetenda*.[42] But unlike responsorial items where the verse is so called and therefore preceded with an abbreviation such as V, the introit conventionally has its verse preceded by the word or abbreviation *psalmus*, Ps, or Ꝑ .[43] Apel says that nothing is known of the medieval method of performance:[44] the most extensive rubric I know from the later middle ages is cited by Wagner[45] from an English book and occurring with minor differences in other English sources of about the same time. It merely states that the following scheme is normal, without specifying which parts are solo and which choral: **I V I ● I**. The absence of information regarding the participation of solo and choir is surprising since this source is specific about gradual, alleluia, and tract. There would certainly have been a solo intonation. I know of no late medieval source which even hints at *versus ad repetendum* after the doxology. Plate 8 illustrates the introit *Reminiscere* with the abbreviation for *officium*, and Ps *Ad te Domine*, in a Missal: in a manuscript with music it may appear as in plate 24. Here the verse *Vias tuas* of the Advent Sunday introit *Ad te levavi* has the music of the psalm-tone. In the offertory and communion the psalm verses have normally disappeared by the late middle ages, leaving what appears to be an independent antiphon, and reminders of the original verses occur only in certain items.[46] Plates 3e and 8 illustrate both chants, in a Gradual and Missal respectively.

Tracts and the hymnus trium puerorum

220 The small number of medieval tracts in the oldest group all consist of a series of psalm verses. Some later tracts have verses drawn from other books of the Bible. Of the three common terms by which they are introduced in the manuscripts, *tractus, responsorium*, and occasionally *graduale*, only the first survives into common later medieval use.[47] The last two terms, and certain features of one group of tracts, have led to the suggestion that this group may have originated as graduals with several verses and choral refrains, of which the latter fell away. The ornate musical style of most tracts also relates them more closely to responsorial psalmody than to antiphonal. There are different methods of performance and once again English manuscripts which are distinguished by their lavish rubrics give us the most useful information. The tract *Qui regis*, from the Ember days of Advent, for example, is sung by two soloists: 'two clerics . . . at the choir-step [*gradum chori*] sing together this whole complete [*totum et integrum*] tract.'[48] It has three verses and no refrain, and is thus direct psalmody in its clearest form. *De necessitatibus*, from the Ember days of Lent, also has three verses and no refrain, and the choral and antiphonal performance is stressed in a rubric before and after the chant: 'the choir alternatim says the tract *De* . . . and this tract is sung alternatim by the whole choir.'[49] With these types we could speak of direct tracts (as in direct psalms) or antiphonal tracts. Musically speaking, all tracts fall into one of two groups, and within each group all tracts are 'closely bound together by the use of identical thematic material'[50] which is presented in different order and varied as necessary. There are thus only two basic melodies.

221 Often called tracts in the sources are three other chants which occur after the tracts on the Ember Saturdays of Advent, Lent, and September: these are, respectively, *Benedictus es Domine*, and *Benedictus es in firmamento*, and *Omnipotentem semper*.[51] Pentecost Ember days lack the item. The first two are consecutive sections from the canticle of the three boys thrown into the furnace, from the book of Daniel, and each is sometimes referred to as the *hymnus trium puerorum*, or *laus puerorum*, or *canticum*. Another common term for these two, deriving from the word with which almost all verses begin, is *benedictio(nes)*. *Omnipotentem semper* is not scriptural and was written in poetic form by Walafrid Strabo in the 9th century. Each text has a different chant and none resembles either of the two melodies used for tracts. Moreover, each is responsorial in performance, unlike tracts. The only justification for the medieval habit of referring to them as tracts is therefore their liturgical position following tracts. Since their literary character, method of performance, and musical chants are quite unlike those of hymns, there is as little justification for the use of the word hymn in modern books: even if the medieval liturgist had distinguished strictly between *ambrosianus* for hymn and *hymnus* for these items, which he did not, that distinction has certainly disappeared nowadays. The most suitable way of referring to them seems to be as responsorial canticles, but a neologism of this kind is unlikely to supplant the traditional terms. All three are responsorial, but in slightly different ways. Separating readings, they are in a position normally occupied by responsorial items. They are characterized by numerous verses sung by a soloist, after each of which there is a choral refrain which may change as the piece progresses. The first refrain is a choral repetition of the first solo verse. The precise arrangements shown below may vary from source to source. Subscript symbols specify the number of the verse or half-verse, and superscript the number of the refrain or half-refrain: sometimes, as stated, verse and refrain are identical (=). *Benedictus es in firmamento* has two refrains.

$$V_1 = R^1\ V_2\ R^2\ V_3\ R^2 \ldots V_n\ R^2\ V_1 = R^1$$

Benedictus es Domine has three refrains, the last two appearing later and the first involving only half the first solo verse.

$$V_{1a\ 1b} = R^{1a\ 1b}\ V_2\ R^{1b}\ V_3\ R^{1b} \ldots V_n\ R^2\ V_{n+1}\ R^2\ \mathrm{Dox}\ R^3\ \mathrm{Dox}\ R^3\ V_{1a}\ R^{1b}$$

Omnipotens semper has two refrains, alternating strictly, and the second is the second half of the first.[52]

$$V_{1a\ 1b} = R^{1a\ 1b}\ V_2\ R^{1a\ 1b}\ V_3\ R^{1b}\ V_4\ R^{1a\ 1b} \ldots$$

Plates 3c-d show the hymnus *Benedictus es Domine* and the tract *Qui regis* in a manuscript with music: plate 13, columns two and four, shows them in a Missal, without the chant.

Although the main characteristics of the true hymn, to be discussed in the next section, are considerably different, it should be noted that some hymns, especially when used for processions, alternate solo verses with a choral refrain which is identical with the first verse: this repetition for the refrain and the type of performance make the processional hymn similar (in these respects only) to the *hymnus*. Otherwise the musical and textual characteristics are quite unrelated.

Hymns and sequences

222 Hymns fall into the class of accretions, since they are not of biblical origin and do not form a part of the original Roman liturgy. However, they were retained when other accretions were, by and large, excised in the 16th century and, together with some forms not always known under the title of hymn but of the same kind of origin, they have such a standard position in the services that they can hardly be recognized as accretions. The composition of newly-written Christian poetry flourished in the second to fourth centuries and such pieces were given the name *psalmi idiotici*, a title which would have to be paraphrased in translation as 'non-biblical sacred poetry of recent composition in the general style of psalms.'[53] Most of this poetry was banished by the church, but a few pieces survived, and the hymns in particular were retained in monastic usage and later passed back into the secular Roman liturgy. The earliest hymns were 'roughly speaking' quantitative, later styles were accentual and rhymed:[54] numerous stanzas were performed to the same simple melody. The association, correct or incorrect, of St Ambrose with the composition of some of these texts led to the term *ambrosiani*, which is still occasionally used even much later. References to the method of performing hymns in the late middle ages are difficult to find, and we assume that either a fully choral performance or an antiphonal rendering for alternatim choirs on alternate stanzas was the practice.[55] Some processional chants are called hymns, and correspond with the textual and musical criteria outlined above, but their stanzas are explicitly performed by soloists at a station on the processional route. Here the word stanze, literally from *stare* 'to stand,' betrays the processional origin. Between each stanza the choir sings a refrain to the same tune whose words are usually those of the first solo stanza. The responsorial character of this kind of hymn has already been mentioned. Plates 1 and 14 show several hymns, such as *Eterne rerum* and *Nunc sancte nobis*: the complete texts are given. In manuscripts with the chant the first stanza will have the music, followed by the other stanzas: occasionally these too are supplied, unnecessarily, with music.

223 The *Gloria in excelsis Deo* is also a hymn and is sometimes called the *hymnus angelicus* because its opening words are those of the angels announcing the birth of Christ (Luke 2:14), and sometimes the greater doxology, a term of much more recent origin used by analogy with the lesser doxology, the *Gloria Patri*. The text is more psalmodic than the texts of true hymns since it does not rhyme, nor is it metrical. Like the *Te Deum* of slightly later date, it was originally one of the *psalmi idiotici* and intended for an office service.[56] The *Te Deum* too may be referred to as a hymn although it is more psalmodic in style: it is sometimes called *psalmus*.[57] Just as the hymns themselves were adopted by the Roman office only after a long period during which the monasteries preserved them, so too with the *Gloria in excelsis* and *Te Deum*. In this sense they must be regarded as accretions. Instructions for the performance of *Gloria* and *Te Deum* are likewise difficult to trace; although the former seems to have been choral throughout (after an intonation by the priest), the latter may have been fully choral or antiphonally choral.[58] By analogy with the psalms, all the *psalmi idiotici*, including the *Gloria* and *Te Deum*, have doxologies.[59] Hymns have various alternative doxologies; *Gloria* and *Te Deum* have invariable verses built into the end of the text.

Like the hymn, but centuries later, the sequence arose in monastic circumstances and spread to secular uses. Originally intended as an extension to the alleluia, it was regarded as a trope rather than as an official part of the liturgy and in the reforms of the Council of Trent almost all sequences were removed, as were all of the other tropes. Unlike other tropes, the sequence does commonly appear in liturgical manuscripts of the later middle ages and must therefore be included here. The texts of sequences are of course newly composed and by the later middle ages are metrical, stanzaic and rhymed. Unlike the hymn, however, the melody changes from stanza to stanza. After a solo intonation, the stanzas would probably have been performed antiphonally. When the chant, which changes with subsequent stanzas, is not given in the sources, the text is hard to distinguish from that of a hymn.

Creeds[60]

224 A creed is commonly known as *symbolum*, 'a token' or 'warrant of belief,' from the Greek. The so-called Nicene creed, *Credo in unum Deum*, whose text first appears at the Council of Chalcedon (451) was only later considered to be a statement of beliefs compiled at Nicea (325). Its early use was restricted to those about to be baptized and it was established as part of the Mass of the Roman rite only in the 11th century: it thus has the character of an accretion but, like the hymns, it was not excised. Nevertheless, evidence of its very late insertion into the standard Roman ritual is to be seen in its continued omission from the ferial Mass and its relegation to a special place in the liturgical books (**712, 736-7**). The whole text, in the Mass, must be said by everybody. Thus, except for the opening intonation which is sung by the priest, it is sung chorally throughout.[61] The Athanasian creed, *Quicunque vult*, consists of forty rhythmical sentences originally for private and non-liturgical use. It was probably composed (not by Athanasius) somewhere in Gaul in the 5th or 6th century, used in the German liturgy by the 9th, and was disseminated to northern Europe in the succeeding centuries. The date of its adoption by Rome is uncertain. Performed as one of the 'psalms' at Prime on Sundays, it is sung antiphonally by tradition: I know of no medieval evidence. The Apostles' creed, *Credo in Deum*, was the Roman pre-baptismal profession of faith and seems to have been current by the 4th century. It is not used as a regular part of any service.

Kyrie, Sanctus, Agnus

225 All three of these items are repetitive in form and all are very ancient. Kyrie and Agnus have three invocations (each of which may be subdivided in the Kyrie) and consist of repeated acclamations. As such they are closely related to and almost certainly derived from the similar type of acclamation in the processional Litany: indeed, even nowadays, the major Litanies of the church retain the words *Kyrie eleison* at the beginning and end, and *Agnus Dei* at the end. The presence of the Kyrie at the beginning of Mass may thus be a remnant of a stational procession before Mass: the Agnus was perhaps taken over from the same processional words. Both items are sung chorally throughout, unless they are troped. The Sanctus has a similar set of acclamations, chorally sung, but it is in essence the continuation of a prayer. Forming the last part of the Preface prayer *Vere dignum* it completes the sense of the preceding word *dicentes*, '. . . saying: Holy, Holy . . .' and in theory brings the Preface of the Mass to an end (plate 23). In practice, the Sanctus in continued by the choir after the priest has begun the prayers of the Canon (see **511**). The Benedictus, or second section of the Sanctus, may even be delayed until the elevation of the Host, and there is some evidence for regarding the two sections as independent pieces.[62]

Dialogues, benedictions, preces

226 I have already mentioned opening formulas such as *Oremus* and special introductions and closes to readings and prayers. Doxologies serve the same sort of function for closing psalms, psalm-like texts, and hymns. A more general formula, which focuses attention and denotes an important point in the service is the liturgical greeting, *Dominus vobiscum*, and its reply, *Et cum spiritu tuo*.[63] I shall identify the relevant places where it occurs. A similar specific purpose is served by the benediction or blessing, which may amount to an extensive formula. The shortest and simplest are those which precede or follow important items such as lessons, or the services themselves. Usually some sort of versicle and response is involved: in the case of benediction preceding the lesson, the reader asks the officiant to bless him, *Jube domne*[64] *benedicere*, and the officiant replies with another sentence; in the case of the blessing after services, the officiant opens with *Benedicamus Domino* or *Ite missa est*, to which the congregation replies *Deo gratias*. The Latin terminology for such forms may be, for example, *versiculus* and *responsio*. Although convenient, these terms and the English versicle and response have sometimes led to confusion with response, for responsory, and verse (*responsorium, versus*). Where possible I shall avoid confusion by using a more precise word such as benediction (abbreviated to the sign used in the sources ✠), often leaving it to the reader to discover whether a dialogue of the verse and response type is involved. In the subsequent illustrations of the structure of the services the problem cannot always be avoided, however, and the abbreviation D will be used. *D* stands for the liturgical greeting and its response.

An extended series of versicles and responses, or of versicles without responses, often mingled with other forms such as prayers and the recitation of psalms and said after or between services, is usually known by the term preces (plate 2b). The general confession, mentioned earlier (**201**), usually forms part of the preces. Commemorations and memorials have a similar scheme, typically consisting of a dialogue, an antiphon, and a prayer when they are said outside the framework of a service, and of a prayer alone when they are said within. Preces are conventionally said after Prime, the longer form of memorial is said after Vespers or Lauds, and the shorter form (the prayer alone) appears after the daily collect within Mass or Lauds or Vespers.

Musical styles and liturgical contexts

227 Before proceeding to the internal shape of the services it may help to have a preliminary idea of how the forms I have just described relate to each other and to their liturgical function and to see roughly how the services are varied in terms of action or meditation, in terms of narrative serving to instruct the congregation or of congregational affirmation, in terms of effect, function, and the pace with which the service moves, and in terms of musical style. Also, having seen the elements from which the liturgy is constructed, let us see how they can be placed in larger blocks. The liturgy is too complex for the description to be comprehensive, and only the most obvious features can be mentioned. We shall be interested to a large extent in the emphasis placed on the words, with which the examination may begin.

The words and their meaning are obviously of primary importance in anything that constitutes an affirmation or acclamation or whenever some form of edification is intended. In the Credo, the Gloria, psalms, and the Paternoster, choral or congregational participation is of the essence and unanimity of affirmation or praise is the intention. During the performance of these items nothing else of importance is taking place to detract from the communal devotion. During readings, homilies, sermons, or such items as the Preface, all are passive, receiving moral enlightenment. To follow such spiritual uplifting with active participation would destroy the effect of the reading and, with the notable exception of the gospel, a period of meditation follows. The words have been heard, now they should be pondered. Further words would be unsuitable. Music, however, is an ideal medium through which to be uplifted again, and after readings occur the most elaborate musical styles, to be found mainly in the responsorial forms. Here, then, we have the first combination of elements: readings are normally followed by responsorial chants. The latter are not textless, but their words are usually, at least in the original intention, a reinforcement of the subject matter of the reading. Such additional commentaries in the form of musical elaborations are analogous to the tradition of glossing, of commentaries on psalms and such literature, with which the middle ages is littered. The words of responsorial chants are often relatively unimportant, their message having been stated in the reading: the music can therefore increase in complexity. Moreover, the emphasis on the solo performer of responsorial items perhaps results from the desire to continue the solo reading; the music of the solo verse of responsories is a highly ornamented reciting tone. The choir may be seated during the solo verses, in a passive, receptive attitude.[65] Nevertheless, when the time comes for the choir to sing the refrains, its role is usually one of considerable action, demanding musical virtuosity: in a curious reversal of what is normal, the choir must sing chant which is more elaborate and difficult than that of the trained soloist.

228 Briefly, the musical characteristics of responsorial chants are these. There are many more musical notes than syllables of text so that frequently a single syllable may be stretched over numerous notes: it then becomes virtually unintelligible in relation to the adjacent syllables. The musical notation is complex and characteristic, and the syllables of text are widely separated on the page, making these chants quite easy to recognize. In addition, responsorial chants are longer than other chants and sometimes involve repetitions of short segments of music, especially when there are no syllables. The methods of construction, unification, and variety are therefore primarily musical rather than textual. Melodically, responsorial items tend to use a wide range of notes within a short distance and to be ornamental in style. Referring principally to the relation between the number of notes and the number of syllables, the term 'melismatic' describes the style concisely. Because the church objected strenuously to the seductive potential of pure music without words, the alleluia, whose refrain has only those four syllables, caused St Augustine some heart-searching.[66] Plates 3, 14, and 16 show the notational style of melismatic chants.

A responsorial chant follows each major reading except the gospel at Mass; responsories follow the Matins lessons; gradual and alleluia follow the epistle at Mass. The invitatory, although responsorial in performance, does not follow a reading and is not musically elaborate. With several readings, each with its responsory, a few conventional blessings, opening and closing formulas, and some versicles and responses placed together, we already have a major part of the services complete: to form the offices we have to add only a group of psalms and their antiphons.

229 Where the words must be heard and understood by all, as in solo readings and blessings and other formulas, the musical style has to be simple, that is, basically one note to a syllable and recited on a single pitch. The reciting tones for dialogues are shown in the left-hand column of the frontispiece. The tone for the chapter is in the right-hand column. Since the psalms were originally sung by a soloist, and soloists have always had the tendency to display virtuosity, the development of verses which retained their solo performance was in the direction of increasing elaboration, as we have seen with the verses of responsorial items. On the other hand, the adoption by the choir of psalm recitation necessitated the preservation, or development, of the 'syllabic' style. The term is inadequate because it says nothing of the melodic character: we should perhaps cumbersomely say 'intoned recitation.' The Gloria and Credo, for example, are also 'syllabic'; while traces of intoned recitation can be found underlying some of their melodies they are certainly not sung to a single pitch. In these two items we have words which must not be obscured by elaborate music, but which need not have the same qualities of audibility, since all are singing them. They are therefore syllabic and melodic. The Gloria was from the first a congregational item: in the pontifical services of Rome, however, where the congregation was likely to be small, the trained *schola* sang it (except for the priest's intonation) and its musical style consequently became more complex.[67] Antiphons, not having the same derivation from solo performance as the psalm verses, do not at all resemble psalms musically despite their close connection with them. Neither is the import of their words quite so significant as in Gloria and Credo and they may therefore show qualities of increased musical emphasis. But the proximity of the psalm antiphon to its psalm limits the exuberance and the music is generally of the type which has one, two, or a few notes to a syllable with a moderately elaborate melodic line. Antiphons, then, are generally shorter than responsorial items, with only a few notes (often only one note) to a syllable, so that their notation is simpler. Repetition of musical phrases rarely occurs and the melodic movement, in both detail and overall layout, tends to be restrained. Referring again principally to the relation between number of notes and number of syllables, the term 'neumatic' is sometimes applied. Plates 3e, 17, 18b, and 27a-c show the notational style of neumatic chants.

230 While we cannot put together any other items to form larger sections, as we can with readings and responsorial chants, and with psalms and antiphons, we can associate certain other items with particular kinds of activity. Where physical action occurs the musical style cannot be complex and tends to be neumatic. There are some exceptions, especially in processional items, which tend to be elaborate. On the other hand many processional chants, or chants once associated with processions, are very simple. We may note here such items as the Kyrie, the Litanies, and two items which are later accretions, the sequence and the conductus. In some places the body of singers is passive while the celebrant or some other group is active: the Sanctus and Agnus are sung during the priest's prayers and acts of consecration.[68] These two items have repetitive texts and quite simple music so that there is little distraction from the solemnity of the actions. Offertory and communion, although they have nowadays lost their precise significance, were evidently thought of at one time as accompanying the congregation's actions and presumably had as many verses as was necessary. No important words conflict with the performance of these chants, and their original association with psalms determined the character of the musical style, which is neumatic and similar to that of other antiphons. Plate 3e shows both offertory and communion.

231 There is therefore a precise, delicate, and aesthetically beautiful relationship between the emphasis placed on the audibility of the words and the musical style to which they are sung, also between communal action or inaction and the musical style. With some overlapping we may fit these variables into four kinds of 'texture' in the services which may roughly be called 'narrative,' 'meditative,' 'affirmative,' and 'active,' dividing the last into action which is carried out by all simultaneously, as in processions, and action carried out by the celebrant while the rest are passive. The four textures are alternated to provide contrast and variety and are linked by blessings and other formulas as well as by direct dialogue between celebrant and assistant, or between celebrant and choir, in the form of versicles and responses. Certain items belong together, reading with responsory, psalm with antiphon (although each may occur independently), prayer with preces and dialogues. We must also consider the alternation between solo and choir, between choir and choir, and dialogues formed from various combinations of these. We must consider the origins of the texts: if biblical, whether they are Old or New Testament; if non-biblical, whether they are in the form of explanatory comment or merely recounting true or false legend. We have a wealth of material and of different aspects from which to regard the liturgical whole. Some of these aspects we shall consider in detail. The broad outlines presented in this book can give little idea of the subtlety with which the forms are constructed within themselves, textually and musically, or of the methods by which part of the daily ritual may be linked, textually or musically, with another in a different context.

3

Proper and Common[1]

300 In order to understand how the liturgical book is organized and what sections it contains, we must first know in some detail three matters concerning the services: (a) what the normal structure of each service is, (b) when items normally occurring are not said at all, and (c) on what occasions the normal items change their texts and, in manuscripts with music, their chants. The normal structure (that is, the order and arrangement of items which is in force for the majority of the year) is almost without exception identical from secular source to source or use to use: monastic rites, agreeing within each use, differ from each other only in minor respects, and from secular uses also in relatively small and consistent ways. Matins is the service in which monastic practice is significantly different from secular.

The occasions on which items change their texts are likewise fairly consistent in broad principle, and depend largely on the importance of the day or season. Thus, unimportant days, especially of summer and the weeks after Epiphany, are likely to share texts. More important seasons may differ from each other by using different texts common within each season. Feasts and important Sundays will adopt texts which are mostly proper to the day and to no other. The range is thus from the text common to every day of the year to the one proper to only a single service, with every intervening gradation, and with schemes of alternations and interlocking ranging from the simple to the complex. Details of repetitions and changes probably vary from source to source, at least where different uses are concerned, and any generalization must be inaccurate. Most complicated and variable are the offices, since they are seven in number, each often changing in some respect each day: Mass, which is frequently used for the whole of the following week with little change, is relatively simple. When no other sources are mentioned the discussion of these matters is based tacitly on the Sarum Breviary of 1531, on recent editions of the medieval Sarum Missal, and on the Roman Missal of 1474.

301 If it is not possible in this book to make a detailed comparison of one use with another, it is necessary at least to examine the kinds of repetition and text-sharing which occur. My intention is to make as systematic as possible what is done without much conscious thought by every person who uses liturgical books habitually for worship: it is also to define precisely the way terms will be used so that exact descriptions can be made of arrangements which the worshipper does not need to express mathematically. Only by such rigorous description can the practice of one manuscript be compared with that of another. For it is not a simple matter of common as opposed to proper, which are the two terms by which the nature of a text is most usually described: a common-sense use of those two terms in their everyday meaning will often be sufficient, but frequently qualifications will be necessary. Sometimes more accurate words will have to be used. There is a small number of other standard terms, such as ferial, but no comprehensive lexicon to describe all situations, and very few, if any, of the terms are without exceptions since the meaning of one tends to overlap the meaning of the next: an item may be proper in one context and simultaneously common in another. Although everyday words can be adapted, occasionally it has been necessary to coin terms and I have tried to make these comprehensible without a dictionary. I have also attempted to preserve the conventional terms where possible even though without qualification they are often misleading or ambiguous.

Probably the most difficult single term is 'ferial.' As a noun, feria properly or originally referred to every day of the week including Sunday, but has come to mean the weekdays excluding Sunday. It was in this latter and usual modern sense that I decided to use it (**109, 304**). But as an adjective or adverb ferial(ly) may or may not even in the modern sense involve Sunday, according to context. Thus, there are ferial antiphons for each day of the week, including Sunday. This ambiguity we must preserve, and whether or not Sunday is included can usually be made clear.

302 Now let us examine the meaning of proper and common. An item used on only one day in the year is certainly proper to that day: an item used on two separate days is proper to each and common to both. What do we say of an item that is used on seven separate days? Where is the line between proper and common? Ferial partakes of both proper and common since it means, for instance, proper to Tuesday and common to all Tuesdays. The clearest meaning of proper must be 'special to one day and that day only.' Thus a text may be proper to Christmas Day. We must surely take the day as the convenient unit, and if a text is proper to Christmas Day but common to Vespers, Matins and Lauds of that day, we surely have to say that in so many words or, if necessary, by means of abbreviations: proper to Nat $\mathcal{V}_1$ $\mathcal{M}$ $\mathcal{L}$. We may extend 'special to one day' to 'a limited number of separate days' and clearly say that a text is proper to all the Sundays of Easter time with the implication that it is never used elsewhere: common, with the same limitation, would carry the same meaning but without the implication. While it may be logical, and in some rare cases necessary, to apply proper to 'a number of consecutive days,' as with a text proper to Easter week (that is, common to all the days of that week and no other), it is probably undesirable. Where a number of consecutive days, relating only to the Temporale, is concerned, let us prefer the term 'seasonal' with the name of the season appended, or the terms 'weekly,' 'two-weekly,'[2] etc, again with the implication of 'common to that season or week but to no other.' Proper, then, always implies the exclusion of any time other than what is specified.

PROPER *special to one day only: to a small number of separate days: rarely, to a small number of consecutive days (but here 'seasonal' or 'weekly' is preferred).*

SEASONAL *the season will be liturgical rather than by secular calendar: the text proper to the season specified and to no other is used for every day of that season, unless a proper is given.* The word 'seasonal' may be replaced by the name of the season, for example, the Lenten introit.

WEEKLY *the Sunday or festal proper is used on all the subsequent days of the week or octave and nowhere else.*

303 The clearest meaning of common must be 'common to every day on which an item is used.' The Magnificat canticle, for example, is a common text, but its antiphon is not. Here we may take the whole year as the basis, remembering that certain texts common to the whole year may occasionally be omitted altogether or that some service may be said only at irregular intervals. Unless qualified by a season or in some other way, common shall refer to every occurrence of the item within the year. The phrase 'common to Advent' would appear to duplicate 'Advent seasonal' except that it does not carry the implication of 'and nowhere else,' so that if the same text were used throughout Advent and Easter we could refer to 'common to Advent and Easter seasons' with the meaning of every day within each of those times. Within the principles used here, the same text cannot be Advent seasonal and Easter seasonal. We may extend 'common to every day' to 'common to a large number of days, not necessarily consecutive' provided we specify the character of the days, for example, common to all fasts or to all feasts. Common to all Masses or to all Vespers would carry the same meaning.

COMMON *to every day of the year on which an item is said or, with qualification, to every day of the season: to a large number of days or services of specified character.*

304 We need now to examine some special cases of frequent occurrence and indeed of basic importance, most of which involve some modification or combination of proper and common. To express them with sufficient qualifying words would be cumbersome. The following list is largely self-explanatory.[3]

1) Common to all days *with the same name*:
   a. including Sundays: FERIAL
   b. excluding Sundays: FERIAL, with a nearby reference to Dominical;
2) Common to all Sundays, when necessary to distinguish it from a weekday text: DOMINICAL;
3) Common to a group of Sundays, but not ferial: DOMINICAL, with a nearby reference to a season or to some other qualification;

4) Common to all days *regardless of name*:
   a. including Sunday: COMMON, SEASONAL, or WEEKLY as defined above,
   b. excluding Sunday: DAILY, usually with a reference to a season,
   c. excluding isolated days provided with propers: GENERAL;
5) proper to each Sunday: DOMINICAL (PROPER).

Most noticeable here is the confusion regarding ferial: in standard usage it refers to both 1a and 1b and it is nearly always clear from the context which is in question. The nearby reference to or exclusion of Sundays, for example, informs the reader that ferial must relate only to weekdays. It is normal for the weekdays to use ferial texts and for Sundays to use propers (a sentence which *per se* illustrates the principle of the preceding sentence) and although I do not know of any instance in which ferias have propers and Sundays have ferial texts a term for Sunday-ferial as opposed to feria-ferial may be needed: I have coined Dominical. Sometimes when the Sundays have propers, all the ferias regardless of name have a common text for which 'daily' seems to be suitable: when the Sunday too has that text, common, seasonal or weekly seems correct. 1b and 4b above represent incomplete weeks to which a Sunday must be added. In double-barrelled descriptions of this kind it will be clearer to place the unqualified part of the pair before the qualified part, so that the adjective refers only to the latter:

1b and 2 – ferial and Dominical
1b and 3 – ferial and (Easter) Dominical
1b and 5 – ferial and Dominical proper

Situations under 4b would replace ferial here with daily.

Further complicating the situation of a Sunday service containing proper items where the weekdays do not is the peculiarity of Sunday or festal Vespers. Instead of one service beginning the week or octave with proper items, two services, first and second Vespers, occur. Thus, where the Sunday and ferias may produce double-barrelled descriptions such as those above, for Vespers we may need triple-barrelled phrases such as seasonal common (Vespers 1) and Dominical proper (Vespers 2) and ferial. Unique to Vespers, these arrangements are described in more detail when that service is discussed (**427-9** and figure 4.9).

305 Two other kinds of arrangement are worth singling out. Sunday or festal items may be repeated in sequence throughout the week or octave with as many rotations as necessary to fill the week, thus:

Sunday	items 1 2 3 4		Thursday	item 4
Monday	item 1		Friday	item 1
Tuesday	item 2		Saturday	item 2
Wednesday	item 3			

Referred to in the sources as *per ordinem*, this arrangement may be described as 'in (numerical) order.' This may be regular, involving only the items of the first day, or it may include a few ferial items to replace items of the first day, as frequently happens with the Matins responsories, or it may be irregular but following the same principle (**419-22, 428**). Special days falling within a 'numerical' sequence, as is the case with Ember days, simply interrupt the distribution:

Advent 3: a b c / *ii*: a / *iii*: b / *iv (QT)*: a b c / *v*: c . . .

If such an interruption were to cause the following Sunday to fall in a similar within-the-sequence position, the sequence of the following week would normally begin afresh. Such arrangements are often not noted very clearly, since their performance is often a matter of daily habit, and are difficult for the researcher to ascertain. Repetitions of Sunday items tend to take place in threes, because of the three nocturns, whose versicles, responsories, and benedictions are usually distributed in order: interruptions in the Temporale also tend to occur in threes, as with the Ember days, or on feria v, as with Ascension and Corpus Christi, in which case there are three clear ferias beforehand for the sequence to be completed.

306 Similar but on a larger scale and less frequent in occurrence is the distribution of a group of propers over the following days in a regular or irregular, but certainly fixed, manner. Here we may refer to the eight or nine days following Ascension, when frequently the Ascension Day propers are used for the Sunday within the octave and on the octave, and the propers for the day after Ascension recur on the following Monday, those for the next day on the following Tuesday. A suitable and immediately comprehensible term is not easy to find: 'set distribution' is perhaps the least objectionable. In the case of Ascension and its octave, a certain confusion may arise by the appearance within the octave of an apparent proper which is in fact only the isolated reappearance of one of the Easter seasonal texts temporarily submerged by the Ascension propers: the introit and collect of the two isolated days after the octave of Ascension may be cited. The ferial and proper antiphons of Matins during these days are itemized below.

Pascha 5	one proper antiphon, in one nocturn
ii-iv	Easter ferial antiphons
Ascension (v)	three propers, in one nocturn
vi	three propers, in one nocturn
vii	three propers, in one nocturn
Pascha 6	as Ascension Day (v)
ii	as feria vi
iii	as feria vii
iv	as feria vi
Ascension Octave (v)	as Ascension Day (v)
vi	Easter ferial
vii	Easter ferial

Other more haphazard forms of recurrence are to be found, and the Ascension period supplies several examples. In general, the term 'interlocking' may be used to describe the kind of arrangement whose precise details will need exact description or presentation in tabular form. Figure 4.9a, section **428**, showing the distribution of Vespers items in the days following Ascension, may be studied.

307 ORDINARY Although this term is restricted to items of the Mass, it could well have had some convenient application to the offices. Its definition is easy to frame: it refers to the common items or texts of Mass. With a few exceptions this includes all the prayers of the Preface and Canon, the preces and benedictions, all those prayers which are invariable, as well as the six sung texts, Kyrie, Gloria, Credo, Sanctus, Agnus, and dismissal formula. The last of these has two forms and may be considered 'seasonal': the texts of the others are by and large invariable and only in this state are they strictly ordinary:[4] the addition of tropes renders them proper. Since the melody of these items varies through the year, they should be referred to as 'ordinary with the chant proper to . . . .'

In chapters 4 and 5 the proper and common nature of parts of the offices and Mass, respectively, will be examined by investigating individual items. Leading up to the actual method of presentation in liturgical books, chapter 6 will consolidate the earlier material by showing the proper and common nature more from the point of view of the day, week, or season.

308 STOCK Sometimes the distribution of certain items is left to the discretion of some official such as the precentor. Sometimes a numerical or set distribution is required but cannot be prescribed exactly because the period over which the distribution occurs is variable, as after Epiphany and Trinity. In such cases the items may be presented in lists written down at a convenient point, usually before the first item is needed. Such lists or stocks are also often the result of merging earlier books section by section rather than in an order determined by practical use.

4

The Offices

400 Unless otherwise stated in the following discussions of the offices, the Temporale is in its simplest condition, that is, without feasts of the saints, special feasts of the Temporale itself, and special days such as the fasting days. Any one of these events may cause a modification of the principles to be outlined.

The psalms

401 The main purpose of the offices is the recitation of the psalms. To this end the psalms are distributed within the offices over the seven days of the week so that the full course is said every week of the year, at least in theory. Although the total number of psalms is the same, the present numbering of them in the Authorized Version is not the same as that used in the Roman Breviary, which adopts the medieval numbering, since the former follows later Hebrew sources than were used for the Vulgate. The concordance in figure 4.1 shows the differences. I shall henceforth use the numbering of the Vulgate. Between the two versions the number of verses sometimes differs because of a rearrangement of the 'paragraphs,' although there is no difference in wording: the twenty-one verses of Ps 9, for example, are only twenty in the Authorized Version because the former includes the 'title' of the psalm as a verse. Other differences in the kind of medieval Psalter used are irrelevant here and will be pursued later (**873-5**).

402 The precise distribution of the psalms over the offices has differed from time to time, especially during the middle ages, and also from use to use, and the exact details must be sought from the relevant Psalter or Breviary. St Benedict himself laid the foundation for a certain amount of variability even within monastic orders: 'But we strongly recommend, if this arrangement of the psalms [just described] be displeasing to anyone, that he arrange them otherwise, as shall seem better to him; provided always that he take care that the psalter with its full hundred and fifty psalms be chanted every week and begun afresh every Sunday at Matins.'[1] Benedict also mentioned the principle which has always been used of dividing the longer psalms into sections and, conversely,

FIGURE 4.1
The numbering of the psalms

Vulgate	Auth. Ver.	Vulgate	Auth. Ver.
1-8	1-8	114	116:1-9
		115	116:10-end
9:1-21	9		
9:22-end	10	116-145	117-146
10-112	11-113	146	147:1-11
		147	147:12-end
113:1-8	114		
113:9-end	115	148-150	148-150

placing two short psalms together: '. . . let the longer psalms [at Vespers] . . . be divided, namely, the hundred and thirty-eighth, the hundred and forty-third, and the hundred and forty-fourth. But the hundred and sixteenth psalm, being short, shall be joined to the hundred and fifteenth.'[2] Psalm 118, for instance, was divided into twenty-two sections which corresponded with the stanza division noted with Hebrew letters in the Vulgate:[3] in medieval sources this sometimes appears as eleven sections each with two stanzas. Figure 4.2 shows two different ways of distributing the psalms, that implied by St Benedict and basically preserved in monastic uses, and that given in the Sarum Breviary of 1531 and representing the majority of secular uses. Although the details vary, several general principles emerge. The 150 psalms are split into two groups, 1-108 for the nocturnal hours, mostly at Matins, and 109-150 for diurnal use, mostly at Vespers. They are said by and large in numerical order through the week but some are 'removed' for use at other hours. Standard throughout the ages has been the position of Ps 94, *Venite exsultemus*, used as the invitatory psalm at the beginning of Matins, the first official psalm of the day. Similarly common to the two distributions shown is the use of the long psalm 118 at the little hours, mainly on Sundays, of Pss 50, 62, 66, 148-150 (148 and 150 being the *Laudate* psalms) at Lauds, of Pss 4, 90, 133 at Compline. It will be clear from figure 4.2 that in monastic and secular use the main sequential, numerical distribution lies in Matins and Vespers while the other hours use much repetition throughout the week. The chief differences are that Benedict, curiously, in view of his 'begun afresh every Sunday at Matins,' begins the sequence with Prime of Monday and has twelve psalms every day at Matins and four at Vespers, whereas the Sarum Breviary has eighteen at Sunday Matins, twelve on the other days, and five every day at Vespers. Other ways in which monastic uses differ from secular will be presented later. Since St Benedict is not specific as to which psalms are to be subdivided at Matins, in this figure the longer ones have been chosen. For both monastic and secular distributions there may be minor variants within the year.

FIGURE 4.2
The cursus of psalms

Italic numbers indicate monastic usage; the others secular usage. Compare figure 8.18. Where there is no entry or dash the entry to the left is repeated through the rest of the week (but the entry under Monday monastic Vespers takes two lines to fit into the column).

	Sun.	Mon.	Tues.	Wed.	Thurs.	Fri.	Sat.
M	*3 & 94*						
A	*20-31*	*32-44*[a]	*45-58*[b]	*59-72*[c]	*73-84*[d]	*85-100*[e]	*101-8*[f]
T							
	94						
	1-20[g]	26-37	38-51[h]	52-67[i]	68-79	80-96[j]	97-108
L	*66 & 50*						
A	*117, 62*	*5, 35*	*42, 56*	*63, 64*	*87, 89*	*75, 91*	*142*[k]
U	*148-150*						
D							
S	92	50					
	99	5	42	64	89	142	91
	62 & 66						
	148-150						
P	*118*[l]	*1,2,6*	*7-9*[m]	*9*[n]*-11*	*12-14*	*15-17*[o]	*17*[p] *19*
R							
I	21-25[q]	–	–	–	–	–	–
M	53						
E	117	–	–	–	–	–	–
	118[l]						
	120	–	–	–	–	–	–
T	*118*[r]	*118*[r]	*119-121*				
S	*118*[r]	*118*[r]	*122-124*				
N	*118*[r]	*118*[r]	*125-127*				
T	118[s]						
S	118[s]						
N	118[s]						
V	*109-112*	*113-116*[t]					
E		*&128*	*129-132*	*134-137*	*138*[u]*-140*	*141-144*[v]	*144*[w] *147*
S							
P	109-113	114-120	121-125	126-130	131-136[x]	137-141	143-147
C	*4 & 90 & 133*						
O							
M	4 & 30[y] *& 90 & 133*						
P							

NOTES

a: 35 & 42 omitted, 36 in two sections; b: 50 & 56 om.; c: 62-64 & 66 om., 67 & 68 each in two sections; d: 75 om., 77 in two sections; e: 87 & 89-91 & 94 om., 88 in two sections; f: 103-106 all in two sections; g: 4 om.; h: 42 & 50 om.; i: 53, 62, 64, 66 om.; j: 89-92 & 94 om.; k: Benedict says the first part of the Canticle serves as the psalm here; l: four sections; m: first part of 9; n: second part of 9; o: first part of 17; p: second part of 17; q: only on certain Sundays of the year; r: three sections; s: six sections; t: 115 & 116 as one psalm; u: 138 in two sections; v: 142 om., 143 in two sections, first part of 144; w: second part of 144; x: 133 om.; y: first part only.

Deus in adiutorium

403 That the versicle *Deus in adiutorium* . . . and its response were said before each of the hours was apparently so much taken for granted that a statement to that effect is difficult to find. In the Sarum Psalter of 1531, under *Ante horas diei*, there is no mention of the dialogue. The Breviary refers to it only before Matins and not before the other hours of Advent Sunday: rubrics for the Sunday are, however, quite incomplete in the 1531 edition.[4] In various places in the Customary of Sarum it is implied before some of the hours.[5] The Old Ordinal shows it before Vespers and Compline, but nowhere else. Only in a single source of the New Ordinal is there a clear statement:[6]

> *Deinde dicat sacerdos executor officii voce extensa hoc modo; quod dum dicat signet se signo crucis.* Deus in adiutorium meum intende. *Et chorus respondeat hoc modo:* Domine ad adiuvandum me festina. *Et procedendo*: Gloria Patri . . . seculorum. Amen. Alleluia. *Et sciendum est quod iste predictus ordo dicendi tenendus est in omnibus horas fere per totum annum: et dicitur fere, quia in tribus feriis proximus ante Pascha et in ebdomada pasche et in die animarum ad matutinas et ad omnes alias horas non dicitur* Deus in adiutorium . . . etc.

This does not fully agree with the instructions in the Customary:[7]

> *De modo dicendi* Deus in adiutorium *ad vesperas et ad alias horas*: Deus in adiutorium meum intende. Domine ad adiuvandum me festina. Gloria Patri . . . seculorum. Amen. Alleluia. Laus tibi Domine, rex eterne glorie.

In the Psalter, before Lauds, the dialogue is shown after the versicle and response proper to Lauds, and the sentences beginning *Laus tibi* are cited as an alternative, *pro temporis diversitate*, to the *Alleluia*.[8] No doubt similar discrepancies are common in other uses and other books: the true nature of the dialogue as common or seasonal and its presence before all or only some of the hours must be sought in individual cases from rubrics and Ordinals.

MATINS

404 The secular organization will be described first. Betraying the origin of the service as a nocturnal vigil, the heart of Matins is the nocturn, which consists of psalms and antiphons followed by readings and responsories: the psalm section is ended with brief preces, the readings are preceded by blessings. The number of nocturns varies from one to three according to the rank of the day, and each nocturn is similar. Preceding the first nocturn are preces, the invitatory, and usually a hymn;[9] following the last nocturn on Sundays and certain feasts during certain seasons is the Te Deum. Basically, then, the arrangement is:

brief preces		D
invitatory		I
hymn		H
	versicle and response	D
each of 1, 2, or 3 nocturns	psalms and antiphons	(Ap)
	brief preces	D
	benedictions, lessons, and responsories	(✠LR)3
Te Deum		

Within the nocturns the number of psalms differs, depending on the number of nocturns as well as the rank of the day. The number of antiphons and doxologies also differs, but not necessarily in the same way as the psalms; several psalms may be sung under one antiphon and doxology, or each psalm may have its own. The number of readings, however, is constant, always three within each nocturn, each leading to a responsory; at least the third responsory of each nocturn has the doxology.[10] In certain rites of the earlier middle ages, the Te Deum seems to have replaced the last responsory; conversely, and frequent in the later middle ages, when the Te Deum is not said the last responsory of the last nocturn may be repeated and this practice is sometimes referred to as 'doubling,' the responsory being sung *dupliciter*.[11]

405 Matins in monastic uses varies in a number of minor details. The following outline is summarized from Tolhurst's excellent description of Benedictine practice, which may be taken as typical.[12] After the opening preces but before the invitatory, Ps 3 is sung without an antiphon: it is thus one of the few examples of direct psalmody. The first two nocturns always have six psalms, unlike secular uses where the number differs, and the third nocturn has three canticles. There may be one antiphon for each psalm, or one antiphon covering all six psalms: the three canticles are covered by one antiphon. The number of lessons within the nocturns also differs. In full offices with three nocturns for Sundays and major feasts each nocturn has four lessons, each with its benediction and responsory. Moreover, after the Te Deum following the twelfth lesson and responsory is another reading, of a gospel with the usual formulas which accompany such texts. The hymn *Te decet laus* (according to Benedict), a benediction, and the daily collect close the service. A shorter monastic form of Matins with two nocturns is ordered for weekdays. Both nocturns have the six psalms and antiphons as usual. In winter the first nocturn has three readings and responsories instead of the normal four, in summer only one of each; the second, regardless of season, has only a very short chapter, which may be an epistle, without a responsory. Closing ceremonies are less elaborate.

406 The typical forms of secular and monastic Matins are given schematically in figure 4.3: variants through the year, or of different rites, will be examined later. The abbreviations in the figure, although self-explanatory if the outline of items has been understood from the text, are listed in section **4**. The secular festal arrangement shown in figure 4.3 has all three nocturns and is therefore a feast 'of nine lessons' *novem lectionum*, but numerous feasts are 'of three lessons' *trium lectionum*, having only a single nocturn. Similar terminology for monastic feasts, *duodecim lectionum*, is sometimes found. This classification, expressed by abbreviations (ix lc, iii lc, and xii lc), is normally added to the Kalendar. All Sundays in both monastic and secular uses have the full complement of nocturns except Easter Sunday and often the Sundays and ferias of Easter time (including Pentecost Sunday) which have a shortened form of one nocturn in secular, and the form of winter ferias in monastic, uses.[13] This abbreviation is thought to result from the lengthy overnight vigil preceding Easter Day, in which it was difficult to perform the full Matins service.

FIGURE 4.3
Secular and monastic matins

The less obvious abbreviations are: D, dialogues, *preces*; *D*, the liturgical greeting; K, canticle. (P4A)3 means, for example, four psalms and an antiphon, then four psalms and an antiphon, then four psalms and an antiphon.

	preliminary items	nocturns§		concluding items
Secular				
Sundays	D IHD	(P4A)3	D (✠LR)3	
(9 lessons)		(P4A)3	D (✠LR)3	
		(P4A)3	D (✠LR)3	Te Deum or 9th R doubled
feasts	D IHD	(PA)3	D (✠LR)3	
(9 lessons)		(PA)3	D (✠LR)3	
		(PA)3	D (✠LR)3	Te Deum or 9th R doubled
ferias	D IHD	(P2A)6	D (✠LR)3	–
(3 lessons)				
Monastic				
Sundays and	D Ps3 IH	(PA)6	D (✠LR)4	
feasts		(PA)6	D (✠LR)4	
(12 lessons)		K3A	D (✠LR)4	Te Deum *DGH✠O*
winter ferias	D Ps3 IH	‡(PA)6	D (✠LR)3	
(3 lessons)		P6A	C	D Litany *DO*
summer ferias	D Ps3 Ps94 H	‡(PA)6	D ✠LR	
(1 lesson)		P6A	C	D Litany *DO*

‡ (PA)6 or P6A in either nocturn.
§ In later, more detailed work, nocturn three will need expressing more precisely as ✠GLR (✠LR)2 or 3 in order to show the brief gospel passage introducing the seventh (or ninth monastic) lesson.

The preliminary items

407 Exactly where the service begins is not always clear and the extent of the opening preces is not standard, a flexibility which probably owes its origin to the fact that the monks proceeded directly from the dorter to the church and that some of the prayers and sentences may have been said before leaving the dorter. The Sarum Psalter of 1531[14] lists the prayers to be used before the hours, including *Aperi, Domine, os meum,* clearly based on Ps 50:17, followed by the Lord's Prayer, *Ave Maria,* and the Apostles' creed, then the invitatory psalm. The corresponding Breviary is more precise about Matins: '*The priest says*: Pater noster, Ave Maria. *Then he begins the service in this way*: Domine labia mea aperies [Ps 50:17]. *The chorus replies*: Et os meum annuntiabit laudem tuam. *The priest immediately [says]*: Deus in adiutorium meum intende. (*The chorus replies*): Domine ad adiuvandum me festina. Gloria Patri . . . [Ps 69:2].'[15] Precise instructions for the performance of the invitatory follow. The Paternoster and the psalm verse

Domine labia ... Et os ... appear to be standard elements: the psalm verses *Deus in adiutorium ... Domine ...*, although usual before all the other hours, do not always appear before Matins.[16] Different forms of these preces would have to be sought in the relevant books; it seems unlikely that any major variants would occur. Nor does it seem likely that their form would vary during the year, although they are totally omitted, as are the invitatory and hymn, on the triduum, for example: rubrics on the day in question would so indicate. Excluding such omissions, then, the preces are common texts.

408 The invitatory psalm is surely standard to all uses throughout the middle ages and, again excluding omissions, is common. Its antiphon is not common and varies in a way which is probably more complex than that of most items. The feasts of the Temporale, Christmas Day and its vigil, Ascension, and Corpus Christi, and the *Quatuor tempora* of Advent (but not of the other seasons) have proper invitatory antiphons which supersede others on those days and during and on the octave of those feasts. The same is true of the invitatories for the saints after Christmas. Many Sundays, those of Advent and Lent in particular, have proper texts, but during Easter time and the summer the antiphon tends to be Dominical, common to a group of Sundays such as those within one historia. The extra Sundays after Epiphany, if any, adopt in anticipation the antiphon of Septuagesima. For ferias there are both daily and ferial texts: every feria of Advent except the Ember days, for example, has the same daily text, and others may occur for the six days following Epiphany and Easter, for Easter time, and for part of Lent. The remainder of Epiphany, and of Lent, and all the summer ferias generally seem to use the six ferial texts, of which there is one for each weekday. On the triduum the invitatory is omitted altogether.[17] On the day of Epiphany secular sources generally omit the invitatory although monastic sources have it.[18] Tolhurst states that in a later monastic abridgement of the practice described in Benedict's rule the invitatory was omitted on summer ferias, being replaced by the invitatory psalm sung antiphonally by the choir:[19] in the monastic manuscripts studied many summer ferias clearly still have the invitatory, with its antiphon given in incipit, and since omission in a manuscript may often imply repetition, the actual distribution is difficult to ascertain precisely. The appearance of the invitatory antiphon in liturgical books, therefore, will be irregular.

409 Whereas the invitatory and its variable antiphon are surely present in all uses throughout the middle ages, the same is not always true of the Matins hymn: St Benedict mentions it but Amalarius (9th century) does not.[20] In the earlier centuries we may explain the presence or absence as the difference between monastic and secular practice, described respectively by Benedict and Amalarius. However, the hymn found its way into Roman secular use gradually, and none of the sources used for this book, from the later medieval period, fails to include the item. But, like the invitatory, it is conventionally omitted on Epiphany day, on the triduum, and unlike the invitatory also on Easter Sunday and during Easter week.[21] Otherwise it is mainly seasonal, the same for Sundays and ferias within each season: Advent, Christmas, Epiphany, most of Easter time, and the summer each have a seasonal text superseded of course by the propers of feasts or saints. During Lent, the text changes every two weeks. Seven ferial hymns, one for each day of the week including Sunday, are provided for the weeks after the octave of Epiphany up to the first Sunday of Lent. The doxology is variable and for hymns in metres other than the usual Iambic dimeter it is usually included with the hymn verses:[22] the various versions of *Pange lingua*, for Corpus Christi and other times of the year, may be cited. Otherwise only the incipit of the doxology may be included and the complete text must be sought elsewhere, in a rubric for example. For Iambic hymns there is no doxology for Advent; from Christmas up to 2 February (Purification) it is *Gloria tibi*, with a variant for Epiphany week, thence to Easter it is *Presta pater*. From Easter to Ascension it is another variant of *Gloria tibi*, and *Presta pater* is used again up to the beginning of summer. Except in places where the hymn text is given in full, information about the exact distribution of the doxologies is often not easy to find, being buried in rubrics or in Ordinals. Although many texts seem to be universal for certain times of year, some of the seasonal and proper hymns vary from source to source, and even within a season the texts for Vespers, Matins, Lauds, or the other hours may exchange amongst themselves. The standard doxology texts also appear to interchange quite freely from hymn to hymn and season to season. Moreover, the same hymn text may have several different tunes, each suitable for a particular period: this further complicates the distribution of hymns and the description of them as proper or common, as well as the way they appear in liturgical books.

410 Hymns are conventionally followed by a versicle and response. In most uses this probably varies with the office, as well as with the season, but these two sentences are so often given only in incipit or are left out completely that it is impossible to generalize.[23] The same is true of the versicles and responses which occur in the nocturns of Matins, which precede Lauds, or which appear in various other places: all of these as well as those which follow hymns share a common stock of texts distributed or repeated over the various services. The pursuit of differences between individual uses would be very laborious, and is not necessary here: it is one of a number of features which may help to place a manuscript within a certain use or order. What information is easily available will be mentioned when necessary. In the schemata of section **406**, no versicle is shown after the Matins hymns in monastic uses, where one does occur in secular uses: this seems to be the most reasonable conclusion derived from confusing and conflicting evidence of secondary and original sources.[24]

The nocturns: psalmody and preces

411 Apart from the different number of psalms and antiphons on Sundays, feasts and ferias in secular and monastic uses, already observed, there are no peculiarities, additions, or omissions to be noted. The distribution of common texts and the methods by which they are superseded by propers of the Temporale are as follows. For each weekday the correct number of antiphons is assigned and, according to the table of typical arrangements in section **402**, secular uses have thirty-six (six for each feria), monastic uses have thirty-six or

FIGURE 4.4
Matins in the octave of Ascension

The figure shows the sequence of antiphons at Matins in the Sarum Breviary throughout the week.

feast	feria	
ASC DAY (= Pas 5, v)		three propers, in one nocturn
	vi	three propers, in one nocturn
	vii	three propers, in one nocturn
Pascha 6		as Ascension Day
	ii	as vi above
	iii	as vii above
	iv	as vi above
Ascension octave	v	as Ascension Day
	vi, vii	revert to the Easter ferial text of one proper, in one nocturn

six (six or one for each feria). These ferial antiphons are used during Advent, Epiphany, Lent, and summer in conjunction with the correct number of antiphons for Sundays: nine in secular uses (three for each nocturn), thirteen in monastic (six for nocturns 1 & 2, and one for the canticles in the third nocturn). The actual numbers are a theoretical prescription only and may differ from source to source. Frequently, for example, in place of nine, twenty-seven may be given so that there are nine seasonal Dominical antiphons for Advent, nine others for Epiphany, nine more for the summer:[25] the presence of eighteen antiphons would imply some other seasonal distribution for the Sunday texts.[26] The thirteen prescribed for monastic use may be reduced to seven when there are two psalms under each antiphon instead of a single psalm (and the canticles) under each. Thus, a monastic Breviary of Erfurt has the following arrangement for Sundays:[27]

(P2A)3:	Pss 20 & 21, 22 & 23, 24 & 25,	and	3 antiphons;
(P2A)3:	Pss 26 & 27, 28 & 29, 30 & 31,	and	3 antiphons;
K3A:	three canticles,	and	1 antiphon;
			7 antiphons.

Easter time has seasonal texts. Easter day and its octave share proper antiphons, usually three in a single nocturn, and subsequent Easter Sundays share a single proper antiphon in a single nocturn. Ferias of Easter, with one antiphon in a single nocturn, have a single text, commonly *Alleluya, alleluya, alleluya, resurrexit Dominus sicut dixit vobis*, of which is used whole, in part, or varied.

412 A full complement of propers occurs on the usual feasts, Christmas, Epiphany, the triduum, Trinity, and Corpus Christi, which usually have nine antiphons (or monastically twelve), and Passion, Palm, Easter and Pentecost Sundays where the three nocturns are reduced to one nocturn (of secular format in monastic uses) usually with three antiphons. These propers are sometimes distributed over the octaves in different manners. The sixth day after

FIGURE 4.5
The numerical distribution of Trinity and Corpus Christi antiphons

		antiphons									
TRINITY		1	2	3	4	5	6	7	8	9	Trinity texts
feria	ii	1	2	3							
	iii	4	5	6							
	iv	7	8	9							
	(v, vi, vii originally repeating ii, iii, iv)										
CX	v	1	2	3	4	5	6	7	8	9	Corpus Christi texts
	vi	1	2	3							
	vii	4	5	6							
SUNDAY		1	2	3	4	5	6	7	8	9	
	ii	7	8	9							
	iii	1	2	3							
	iv	4	5	6							
octave		1	2	3	4	5	6	7	8	9	

Christmas, free of propers, repeats the Christmas antiphons: Circumcision may repeat some of them with other propers of its own: the vigil of Epiphany may repeat many of the Circumcision propers. A similar mixture, repeating the propers of the day with an occasional substitution characterizes the octave of Epiphany. The octave of Ascension is especially interesting since nine propers (all originally belonging to Ascension Day itself, perhaps) are ordered over the days following the feasts. The Sarum Breviary has the arrangement shown in figure 4.4. Note how feria vi and sabbatum, the last two days of Easter time, revert to the ferial text of the season. Trinity and Corpus Christi, on both of which feasts the three nocturn service returns, distribute the nine propers of secular use numerically: the octave of the latter feast and the intervening Sunday repeat all nine propers. The intervention of Corpus Christi made it impossible to continue the numerical distribution of Trinity antiphons beyond Wednesday (figure 4.5). In monastic sources, which return to the normal three nocturns on Ascension Day rather than Trinity, the proper antiphons for these feasts are not repeated through their octaves, at least in the sources studied: ferias of this time adopt the Easter ferial texts.

413 After the psalms and antiphons, a versicle and response and a Paternoster are the common elements.[28] The Sarum Breviary has an additional prayer, the *Ave Maria*, after the Pater, said to be a blunder although it occurs clearly in the Temporale and in the 14th-century New Ordinal:[29] the instructions are very precise.

V. Ex Sion species decoris eius.
R. Deus noster manifeste veniet.
Then the Pater noster *and* Ave Maria *are said by the whole choir, privatim. And note that the* Pater noster . . . *in Sarum Use is never begun by the priest in an audible voice except at Mass . . ., and after the priest says audibly* Et ne nos inducas in tentationem, *the choir replies* Sed libera nos a malo.

Differences in detail from this arrangement, as for instance on Maundy Thursday, when the sentences *Et ne nos* . . . and *Sed libera* and the following benediction are omitted,[30] will be found under the relevant day. The versicle and response are variable, but for the less important times of the year an underlying ferial and common Dominical series ocurs, consisting of three Dominical and six ferial texts, superseded only by the versicles proper to high feasts and seasons. More important seasons are characterized by the numerical distribution of the three proper Sunday or festal texts over the following octave or season. Advent, for example, has only three texts, one for each nocturn on the first Sunday, which are then used over and over again in order for the single text of each feria and repeated on subsequent Sundays. The Christmas season, including Christmas Eve, has its proper texts distributed as follows:

Vigil (one proper)	a	Circumcision	b c e
Nativity (three)	b c d	Vigil Epiphany	e
die vi	b	(if Sunday)	b c d

The triduum each have proper texts, and during the Easter season two ferial texts very similar to each other alternate more or less regularly.

In France and Rome there was a short absolution after the versicle and response:[31] we shall see this in some Franciscan manusripts (**852**).

The nocturns: benedictions and readings

414 Although the benediction in each case precedes the reading, its character often depends on the kind of lesson, and a description will be delayed. The three readings in each nocturn are three sections of the same *legenda*: this accounts for such apparent anomalies as the rubric to the first lesson of feria ii, Advent 1: *legenda ii* . . . *lectio i*.[32] It is certainly the first lesson of Matins and of the day, *lectio 1*. But it is the second reading from the book of Isaiah, *legenda ii*, the first having taken place in the first nocturn of Advent Sunday, the preceding day. All three lessons of the nocturn, or at least of the first nocturn, are regarded as a single *legenda*. Apparently, however, this term was reserved for a reading from the Bible, and thus is not applicable to second and third nocturns. Where there is more than one nocturn, each usually has a reading of a different character, although within the nocturn all lessons are of the same kind.

415 The first kind of reading is direct recitation of the Bible, lessons from which are begun immediately after the benediction, without reference to their specific origin. Certain books are appointed to various seasons of the year, each book to be read in the correct order in continuous sequence throughout the season. When the book is one of the Prophets each lesson ends with the phrase *Hec dixit Dominus Deus, convertimini ad me, et salvi eritis*, often abbreviated to *Hec* or *Hec dixit* in the sources. Otherwise, unless specifically stated to the contrary, every lesson ends with the phrase *Tu autem Domine miserere nostri*, abbreviated *Tu* or *Tu autem*. The opening and closing formulas differ in particular on the triduum. A second kind of reading used during the Temporale is the sermon, a moral, didactic commentary on the spiritual meaning of the day or season written by one of the great church writers such as St Gregory or St Augustine, sometimes unidentified, or unknown. Sermons too are begun without a title and end with *Tu* . . . A third kind is the homily, *omelia*. Also written by a notable church figure, it is a commentary on a short passage from one of the four Evangelists and a more specific title is *Expositio* or *Expositio evangelii*. Before the first lesson of the nocturn but after the benediction, the reader announces the text on which the homily is based (*Lectio sancti evangelii secundum Mattheum xxi*, for example) then in every case he begins with the conventional words *In illo tempore* and then reads the sentences from the gospel. Having announced the title and source of the homily or stated some phrase such as *Omelia ex diversis tractibus* he then intones the homily itself. Lessons two and three of the nocturn continue the homily without additional formula but, as usual, every lesson begins with the benediction and ends *Tu autem* . . . In the earliest centuries both sermons and homilies were probably extemporised. Other kinds of reading, lives of saints and the like, occur only for the relevant celebrations and do not form a part of the Temporale, except for those saints around Christmas.

416 In the Temporale in general all days with three nocturns assign to the first a reading, to the second a sermon, to the third a homily. The reading of nocturn one is, with a few exceptions to be mentioned, drawn from the Old Testament: Isaiah in Advent; Genesis, Exodus and Jeremiah from Septuagesima through Lent so that the days preceding Easter are characterized by the Lamentations of Jeremiah. The summer Sundays are served by several books, which give their names to the weeks covered. They are the historical parts of the Bible: Historia Regum (Kings); Historia Sapientie (Wisdom, although, rather than the book of Wisdom, it is Ecclesiastes that is read here);[33] Job; Thobie; Judith; Machabeorum; Ezechielis. Only the extra Sundays after Epiphany, the erratic insertion of which would disturb the regular succession of readings, use passages drawn from the New Testament, from the Epistles of Paul. Certain feasts, some added later like Trinity Sunday and Corpus Christi and their octaves, and others like the first Sunday in Lent and some lesser Sundays have sermons (rather than scripture) relevant to the day or season even in the first nocturn and continued in the second, which is normally devoted to such readings. Conversely, instead of sermons in the second nocturn, the extra Sundays after Epiphany and the Sundays of summer, because of their indeterminate character, continue the scriptural readings begun in their first nocturn, such as the Epistles of Paul after Epiphany and the historical books in summer. The second nocturn of Maundy Thursday and Good Friday differ, too, in that they use Expositions on psalms rather than sermons. Also providing the only exceptions in their third nocturn, these two days use epistles rather than homilies. Otherwise, every day with three nocturns relies on the *Expositio evangelii*, the homily, in the last nocturn.

417 Old Testament readings cease during the Easter season, and are mostly replaced, at the beginning of this period of single nocturn services, by homilies preceded as usual by the gospel sentences upon which they are based: the purely symbolic Christological significance of the Old Testament is replaced by the fulfillment of the prefiguration, the essence of Christianity in the gospels, Christs' resurrection. Later in Easter, readings are from the Apocalypse or the letter of St James the apostle. The Easter season, in this context, includes all Sundays, feasts, ferias, vigils, and the Rogation days, from Easter Day to the week after Pentecost. Similarly, vigils and fasts outside Easter time have homilies in their single nocturn. That nocturn on such days, then, takes the form of the third nocturn of Sundays. The single nocturn of ferias other than those mentioned is equivalent to the first nocturn of Sundays, continuing the reading begun in the first nocturn of the preceding Sunday, Old Testament through the summer and before Easter, New Testament after Easter. The ferias of the extra weeks after Epiphany continue the readings set by their Sundays, using epistles. Apart from the brief passages which form the basis for the homily, gospels are read at Matins only in the two Genealogies and in monastic rites: after the twelfth responsory, and after the Te Deum when it is sung, part of a gospel is read in monastic liturgies. On Christmas Day this is the Genealogy according to Matthew (1:1-16), the *Liber generationis*. This same Genealogy is sung as an additional lesson in secular uses, also on Christmas Day but before the Te Deum in this case: secular liturgies provide for a second Genealogy, that of Luke (3:23-38), to be sung before the Te Deum on Epiphany. In order to stress the importance of these gospel readings, after the benediction the liturgical greeting *Dominus vobiscum* ... is used to introduce them, followed by the usual opening for gospels *Initium* (or *sequentia*) *sancti evangelii secundum* ... Epistles are read at the second nocturn of monastic ferias, in the extra weeks of Epiphany, and on the ferias of Easter time.

418 Every single lesson has a benediction, requested by the reader with the invariable words *Jube Domine* (or *Domne*) *benedicere* (plate 25).[34] The Temporale has only a few texts used over and over again, and each group is associated with a particular kind of lesson. The benedictions often appear all together in a list, for example at the end of the Psalter, perhaps with a set of complex rubrics about their distribution. In order to illustrate how such a list may be made out in the middle ages, I translate here part of the Sarum Customary, omitting everything not relevant to the Temporale and replacing the actual text of the benediction with a number:[35]

Whenever there are nine lessons, throughout the whole year, these six benedictions are said at Matins ... They are also said on feasts of three lessons without a homily ... and in and on octaves, and on ferias of Easter time, according to their order in the nocturns. In nocturn I these three are said: 1 2 3; in nocturn II these three: 4 5 6; in nocturn III, before a homily on or a reading of Mark 7a, Matthew 7b, Luke 7c, John 7d. When there is not a homily [in the third nocturn] then at the seventh lesson say this benediction: 7e; for the eighth lesson ... : 8. However, when the first lesson [of the third nocturn] is a homily, the benediction for the second will [also] be 8 ... For the ninth leson: 9a, except from Trinity to Advent (however, the feast of Corpus Christi and its octave ... still use 9a).[36] But whenever there are only three lessons in the Temporale and they are a homily, then 9a is the third benediction. From Trinity to Advent, on Sundays, the ninth benediction is: 9b. On all ferias outside Easter time without a homily, these three benedictions are said: 10 11 12.

FIGURE 4.6
The numerical distribution of Matins responsories (this figure shows a common secular scheme)

Sunday	a b c	d e f	g h i	[j ferial]
ii	a b c			
iii		d e f		
iv			g h j	
v-vii	as ii-iv			

Because of its condensed form this appears extravagantly complex, and indeed it takes some effort to deduce the correct practice: the reader may care to exercise his ingenuity in translating the above rubrics into a table. Regarding the tenth lesson of Christmas and Epiphany Matins, the Genealogies, we need note only that since they are gospels (Matthew and Luke, respectively) benedictions 7b and 7c will be used. Monastic benedictions have not been easy to find in the sources available: the one Benedictine manuscript to contain them certainly has a prescription much simpler than that quoted above: four are given for each nocturn, with the rubric

when a regular office has only a single lesson, the first benediction is said: when there are three lessons the two following it are added. On ferias when a homily is read, the three last benedictions of the third nocturn are recited.[37]

The nocturns: responsories and Te Deum

419 The nine responsories of Sundays and feasts are normally distributed numerically, three by three, through the week following the day. Most Sundays and feasts, including each day of the triduum, have nine proper texts; many of the fasts and vigils as well as the single nocturn feasts of Easter time, and a few other days such as those preceding the triduum, have three proper texts. Occasionally not every one of the nine is strictly proper. The fourth, fifth, and sixth responsories of XL 1, for instance, are identical with the three propers of the preceding Ash Wednesday. The precise numerical distribution and interruptions of that sequence are extremely complex and can best be illustrated in diagrams, but a few general remarks are possible. The last responsory of each nocturn is often rather special, and this is even more true of the last responsory of the last nocturn, the ninth (or twelfth, in monastic sources): tropes are frequently to be found here, for example. Singling out the ninth, we observe that it may be replaced in the numerical distribution by an alternative, usually noted immediately afterwards as though it were a tenth responsory. This alternative is the ferial responsory. In a normal distribution it will be the third responsory of Wednesday and Saturday, where the ninth would otherwise have occurred (figure 4.6). Occasionally the third and sixth may be replaced in this way. On special occasions, such as the last weeks of Lent, when the doxology is also omitted, the last responsory in each nocturn may be repeated. During the Christmas season, Circumcision has eight propers and the ninth is drawn from the ninth of Christmas Day: the second week of Lent has three 'ninth'

FIGURE 4.7
The numerical distribution of monastic responsories
(this figure shows the scheme of Advent at Hyde Abbey, ms B39)

Sunday	a b c d	e f g h	i j k l
ii-iii	b g h	i k l	
iv-v	b g h	i k l	
vi	b g h		
vii	a Marian service replaces the Temporale		

responsories, the first for Sunday, the first alternative for Wednesday, the second for Saturday. Later we shall be noting the special treatment of the final responsory in the Easter nocturns, and of the ninth in the summer Sunday nocturns. Monastic distribution is similarly numerical but where ferias have only three responsories each, amounting to eighteen in the week, the twelve of Sunday cannot be repeated completely: there may be one and a half 'statements' of all twelve, or the last responsory of each Sunday nocturn may be omitted.[38]

420 *Aspiciens a longe,* the very first responsory of the year, is especially elaborate and has been described (**211**): as with the ninth on this day, it is not used for the ferias. Since the numerical distribution is thus thrown two short in a secular use, two ferial responsories may be noted after the ninth on the Sunday. Exemplifying the different arrangements which may be found are two monastic manuscripts which, although partly changing their order, have eleven of the twelve Advent responsories in common. Both are Benedictine. The 15th-century Breviary of Bursfeld specifies the responsories *per ordinem* for feria ii of Advent and gives no further information, nor any ferial texts to substitute for *Aspiciens* or any other responsory.[39] On the other hand, the 13th-century Breviary of Hyde Abbey eliminates *Aspiciens* from the ferial round as well as five others whose texts are Marian rather than Advent in character[40] (figure 4.7). Lending its name to the day and the season, *Domine ne in ira* is the first responsory of Epiphany 2. Every responsory of this Sunday and the following week is proper, the numerical distribution being suspended, but the texts are repeated ferially from week to week for as many extra weeks as are present.

421 During the opening weeks of Easter time, where only a single nocturn usually occurs, the last responsory of Easter Day may provide a refrain for the whole season, or the three responsories of Easter form an alternating refrain, with other recurrences complicating the whole scheme. As usual, English uses seem to prefer intricate patterns, and we may compare the Sarum and Hereford Breviaries with a 15th-century Breviary of Krakow[41] (figure 4.8). In this figure capital letters represent texts different from those represented by lower case letters, and although the stock of texts is more or less common to all repertories, a letter representing a text in one column will not necessarily represent the same text in another column: the letters are merely intended to show where repetitions occur within columns. At ¶ in the Sarum books it is unclear what the distribution is to be: on feria ii of the second week the rubric referring to texts

FIGURE 4.8
The distribution of responsories at Easter time

Capital letters represent texts different from those of lower case letters. Although the stock of texts is more or less common to all repertories, a letter representing a text in one column will not necessarily represent the same text in another column: the letters are merely to show where repetitions occur within columns. For ¶ ‡ see the text, paragraph **421**, where more details are given.

	Sarum			Hereford			Krakow		
Easter Sunday	abc			abc			abc		
ii-iv	dec	fgc	hic	dea	fgb	hic	def	ghi	jkl
v-vii	djc	fkc	hlc	jka	lmb	noc	*as ii-iv*		
Pas 1	*as prev. week*			pqa			*as prev. week*		
ii-iv	mno	pqr	stu	rst	uvw	xyz	mno	pqr	stu
v-vii	*as ii-iv*			ABC	rst	‡	vwx	yzA	nop
Pas 2	mnc			pqb			*as prev. week*		
ii-vii	¶			*as prev. week*			*as prev. week*		
Pas 3	*as prev. week*			pqc			*as prev. week*		
ii-iv	¶			*as prev. week*			BCD	EFG	HIJ
v-vii							BCD	EFG	IJH
Pas 4	vwc			DEa			*as prev. week*		
ii-iv	xyz	ABC	DEF	FGH	IJK	LMN	BCD	EFG	JHI
v-vii	GHI	JKL	MNO	OPQ	FRS	GOP	BCD	EFG	HIJ
Pas 5	*as prev. week*			DEb			*as prev. week*		
ii-iv	*as prev. week*			*as prev. week*			BCD	EFG	IJH

m-u states that they should be said *alternis vicibus* until the fourth Sunday: on the other hand, a rubric at feria ii of the third week states that the responsories are as in the preceding week.[42] At ‡ the Saturday Matins is replaced by the services to the Virgin. A few additional subtleties may be noted. Text b in Hereford represents a responsory with two verses, which are to be used alternately as the responsory appears in the distribution: the continual rotation of HIJ in Krakow averts strict repetition. Other refinements may be observed, and every source studied seems to provide a different set: uses are not consistent even within themselves. The Krakow arrangement here, with its more frequent repetition and simpler scheme, is somewhat more typical than that of the English sources. Monastic distributions, too, seem in general to repeat directly rather than to use 'refrain' items and arabesques of the kind illustrated.

422 The weeks of summer time have a simpler rotation. The nine responsories of Trinity Sunday are used in continuous sequence as the ninth responsory of all the subsequent Sundays up to Advent, provided that the Sunday immediately preceding Advent uses the ninth of Trinity as the ninth of the Sunday. Each historia therefore provides eight propers which are common to all Sundays of the historia and which are distributed *per ordinem* or *successive* over the ferias. Normally two or three ferial responsories are given for each historia, and these are supposed to be fit in 'here and there, as convenient and necessary' to correct dislocations caused by the interpolation of saints' feasts. One of the ferial responsories is to be used in place of the ninth, the one drawn from Trinity Sunday.

After the Sunday responsories in the manuscripts, there may be several ferial responsories. In this position, too, any items of the same kind which are required for processions during the week will probably be listed. After the last responsory sung in the service, Matins is over, at least in secular uses, unless the Te Deum is said.[43] This hymn is invariable and therefore common to all its occasions. To specify accurately and briefly what these are is probably impossible because of the different practices of individual rites: it is said only when the Gloria is included at Mass since, like the Gloria, it is a hymn of joy. It is thus omitted during Advent and Lent, although there are exceptions, and it is not sung on ferias or lesser feasts.[44] Harrison's statement is perhaps the best: the Te Deum is sung 'on Sundays and most feasts, except in Advent and Lent.'[45] Many authorities state, or at least imply, that all the hours are closed with the versicle *Benedicamus Domino*, to which the choir replies *Deo gratias*; as far as I can discover from the original manuscripts, this is true of Matins only when Lauds does not immediately follow (see **423**). In monastic uses, on Sundays and feasts (but not on the triduum), Matins is extended by a reading, hymn, and prayer. The reading, a gospel, is introduced with the liturgical greeting and the usual opening formula and repeats the sentence stated at the beginning of the ninth lesson and upon which the homily is based, continuing that verse with the following verses of the gospel. The invariable hymn *Te decet laus*, sung next, is succeeded by a prayer which is proper on the important Sundays and feasts, but which is otherwise a repetition of the general collect of the day. Memorials are frequently added here. Of this point in the service, Benedict says 'the blessing having been given let them begin Lauds,'[46] a prescription which would seem to imply the final versicles mentioned above: on the other hand he fails to mention the versicle with which Lauds begins.

LAUDS

423 Matins is sometimes followed so closely by Lauds that the two are almost a single service [47] and when there are only one or two items in Lauds which need to be noted in the sources they may often be appended to the last item of Matins without further comment or new heading:[48] this is in any case true of the versicle and response which precede Lauds. The service is much simpler than Matins. The opening preces may, the Sarum Psalter suggests,[49] include the Paternoster, *Ave Maria*, and Apostles' creed: it is difficult to see how these could fit into a service more or less continuous after Matins. The opening versicle and response, the invariable *Deus in adiutorium* with its response, and a doxology are always present. Basically seasonal, the first versicle and response is occasionally replaced by an alternative when the proper seasonal sentences have been used earlier, for example, as one of the benedictions for the lessons of Matins. The main feasts and their octaves have propers and, as usual, the triduum omits the sentences (and the other preces) altogether. Somewhat oddly, Christmas Eve has versicle and response proper to itself alone. A common Dominical text and one daily text are provided for the weeks after Epiphany and for the summer.

424 The psalms of course are assigned in the manner described earlier for the normal cursus: apart from seasonal substitutions in some rites, only the second psalm and the lesser canticle change, the former ferially and the latter ferially with seven Lenten alternatives. There are therefore fourteen lesser canticles.[50] I shall consider the canticles as psalms, and combined psalms as one psalm. Each of the psalms has its own antiphon and, except for the canticle, its own doxology: alternatively, all five psalms are sung under a single antiphon and doxology. There are thus either five antiphons or a single one for the service as it has been described so far. Most Sundays and feasts have five proper antiphons, occasionally the first of these being used for the single antiphon through the following week, as at Epiphany, Easter, Ascension, etc. The Sundays of Easter time have either five, which are those of Easter Sunday, or one, which is the first of that day, and after Easter week itself there is one text common to all ferias: *Alleluya, alleluya.* In the third week of Advent and in Holy Week, each weekday has five proper antiphons; elsewhere weekdays use ferial texts. These ferial antiphons are accompanied by five Dominical antiphons which are used when no proper is supplied, that is, during the usual periods after Epiphany and in the summer: however, all five Dominical texts are used only at the beginning of each new period and otherwise only the first is sung.[51] In this last contingency Sunday Lauds will be less elaborate, with only a single antiphon, than the ferial Lauds, which each have their five ferial antiphons.

425 The chapter, which has no opening formula, is short and may be drawn from either the Old or the New Testament. To end it, the choir says *Deo gratias.* Most Sundays and feasts repeat the chapter of first Vespers and this reading is often used for the whole week, but Advent, Lent and Easter each have a single ferial chapter unrelated to the changing Sunday texts. The triduum and Easter week have no chapter. One Dominical and one daily chapter serve days not provided with propers. Between monastic and secular uses the sole difference at Lauds is the presence at this point in monastic rites of a short responsory, the proper and common distribution of which seems to be quite variable. There is of course a set of ferial texts, and the feasts and the Sundays of Lent often have a proper responsory which is presumably repeated for the following ferias. Advent and Easter, however, usually seem to have either a seasonal text or a seasonal Dominical and a daily text. The hymn, versicle, and response which follow change with the seasons in almost the same way as the opening versicle, but are omitted from Easter week as well as the triduum. The summer, like the other seasons, has only one hymn, but the weeks after Epiphany up to Lent have seven texts, one for each day of the week. These ferial hymns have a common doxology, although this final verse is otherwise proper to each seasonal text.

426 The antiphon to the gospel canticle *Benedictus Dominus Deus* is very special, and almost every day has its own proper text, often very long. Occasionally the octave, or the Sunday within the octave will repeat the antiphon of the day itself; occasionally the antiphons from first Vespers will be used in order throughout the following week; and occasionally a choice of three or four antiphons for the Benedictus at Lauds and the Magnificat at Vespers will be written down at the end of the Sunday services. Because there is a proper Benedictus antiphon for each Sunday, even during the periods for which normally no propers are supplied, there are only six ferial texts.

As with Matins, it is difficult to determine exactly where the service ends, although here we may be sure there was a blessing of some kind. In addition there was usually a prayer or some extra preces and even whole psalms before the blessing, and such accretions were made the whole year round with a few exceptions such as the Ember days of Advent, and Christmas Eve.[52] Even without such additional preces, often after the prayer were memorials, of the Virgin, of the day superseded by a feast, or of a feast during its octave. The only items to occur without fail, however, are the liturgical greeting, *Dominus vobiscum*, followed by a prayer, and a repetition of the greeting to introduce the final invariable blessing *Benedicamus Domino*, to which the choir responds *Deo gratias*. The prayer is often proper, but usually a repetition of the prayer in first Vespers, the collect of the day. Except in Lent, when Sundays and ferias have proper texts, the prayer of the first Sunday of a season provides the texts for the ferias of that season, even when the text changes for later Sundays.

The service can be summarized as follows:

D P5●A
or   } C[R]HD B *DO*✠
D (P●A)5

The correct psalms for both monastic and secular uses can be determined from figure 4.2 (**402**).

VESPERS

427 Ending also with a major canticle, using the Magnificat for the Benedictus in the above diagram, Vespers closely resembles Lauds in its structure, and a good many of its items such as the reading, hymn, versicle and response, and of course the collect of the day, are often common to the two services. Sometimes the psalm antiphon is common or the antiphons for the Lauds Benedictus and Vespers Magnificat are interchangeable or drawn from the same stock. The essential differences are these: (a) the opening versicle, *Deus in adiutorium*, omitted as usual on the triduum, is replaced during Easter week with a nine-fold Kyrie; (b) after the chapter there may be a short or sometimes a great responsory. It is present or absent not according to whether the use is monastic or secular, but according to the time of the year. Omitted on lesser days, this item does not appear at all in the modern liturgy.[53]

As pointed out earlier, Sundays and feasts have two Vespers services, the first occurring on the vigil. If the vigil is not itself a feast but is a normal day, as is usually the case in the Temporale, its Vespers is for the most part simply superseded by the items proper to the ensuing feast. First Vespers of Sunday, for example, supersedes the Saturday office and the items for the service are often written down after the heading or rubric which announces the Sunday: alternatively, the rubric may announce *In vigilia* . . . before Vespers. In any case, the previous day, usually a Saturday, will appear to end in liturgical books with Nones or, as normally happens later on in the year, with an even earlier office of the day when the later ones have become so repetitious that they need not be recorded at all. Compline, occurring after Vespers, hardly ever needs recording and therefore rarely appears: the nature of Compline as a Saturday or Sunday service must be deferred for the moment. A Sunday assumption of the Saturday Vespers is not always the case, as the frequent rubric about Saturday Vespers *quando de Dominica agitur* or the reference to the service as Vespers of Saturday indicates, and the office is occasionally distinguished by nothing of the following Sunday. Saturday Vespers appear only before less important Sundays, as during the summer. Following other Temporale feasts such as Christmas, Epiphany, and Ascension, both Saturay and Sunday Vespers may be superseded by items proper to the feast within whose octave the days fall.

First Vespers, *prime vespere*, is the more important of the two services, and hints of its extra solemnity may be seen when items of first Vespers are proper and the corresponding items of second Vespers are not. The earlier service may have five psalm-antiphons when at the later one all five psalms are sung under a single antiphon: Vespers of Trinity and Corpus Christi may be cited.

428 In addition to knowing how the individual items of Vespers vary or remain the same throughout the year, therefore, we also need to have some idea of how and when first Vespers differs from second. Some modification of the categories of proper and common is necessary since, instead of six ferias, in this case there are five, with two Dominical items, the first of which replaces feria vii. Further, since first Vespers more often has the proper Sunday material its texts will receive the description Dominical, even though it occurs on the Saturday. With these differences in mind, we may establish a set of 'patterns' for Vespers and a figure showing where these patterns occur for each item. An explanation of this in running text could give only the most general indications and remain readable: a comprehensive tabular reduction of a single use would be impracticably complex. What follows is an attempt to provide a general picture with as much detail as can be included, and it should not be used as evidence of any particular practice. The categories of common and proper are listed below, preceded by the abbreviations which make figure 4.9 possible: the order of their appearance does not indicate the frequency of their use. The abbreviations, listed alphabetically, represent the 'elements' of 'properness' and 'commonness' relevant to Vespers 1 & 2 ($\mathcal{V}_1$ $\mathcal{V}_2$) and the other days:

1 Vespers 1 is proper, and different from Vespers 2 and the other days,

2 Vespers 2 is proper, different from Vespers 1 and the other days,

12 Vespers 1 is not the same as Vespers 2, and both are different from the other days,

D Vespers 1 of several successive Sundays have a common (Dominical) text, different from Vespers 2 and the other days,

f ferial, in its usual sense, excluding Vespers 1 or 2 or both if these are mentioned,
o the item is omitted,
p the item is proper every day, excluding Vespers 1 and 2 if they are mentioned,
s seasonal, excluding Vespers 1 and 2 if they are mentioned,
V Vespers 1 is the same as 2, different from the other days,
w weekly, in the usual sense (ie, $\mathcal{V}_1 = \mathcal{V}_2 =$ daily),
X interlocking; see the following paragraphs,
Z items drawn from stock.

FIGURE 4.9
Proper and common at Vespers

Each column represents a genre: within the figure letters and numbers stand for specific types of properness and commonness as described in the text (**428-9**). Weekly (w) texts change each week: otherwise, common texts change only when the symbol changes or is repeated.

genre:	P	A	C	R	H	D	M	O
ADV	f	f	12s	1s‡	s	s	p‡	w
NAT	1s	1s	12	X	1s	X		12
CIRC			V					V
EPI & foll.			w	12o	w	w	pZ	1w
Epi octave			V	1o	12	12	p	V
Epi 1-5	f	f	Ds		f	Ds	D2f	w
LXX-LX			V				12Z	
L							p	
CJ, v, vi								p
XL 1-2			Vs	1s	s	s		Vp
XL 3				1w	s			
XL 4				1w				
XL 5			12	1w	s	s		
XL 6			V	X				
v, vi	-	-	o	o	o	o	//	¶
PAS	1w	s	•	•		ow	p	p
PAS 1-5	f		Dw	o	Ds	s	12Z	w
ASC	X	X	X	12o	s	s	X	X
PEN	f	1w	1w		1w	w	p	p
TRI	1f	1w	1w		w		12	w
CX	1f	1w	w		1w		X	
Tri 1	f	f	Ds	1o	Ds	Ds		
Tri 2-Adv				o			Z2f	

‡ A change in the seasonal text of the responsory begins sometime in the third week, dependent on the day on which begin the Great Os, a stock of antiphons from which the Magnificat antiphon is drawn in third and fourth week: see text.
- Five propers on feria v, repeated on feria vi.
// The proper of feria v repeated on vi.
¶ The text of feria vi repeats that of feria iv.
• The Vespers service of Easter week is a special service, described in the text.

FIGURE 4.9a
Proper and common at Vespers of Ascension time

Here, the proper texts of Ascension are placed in circles. They are repeated every time the hyphen crosses the line which extends from the circle: where that line is dotted, the proper texts are interrupted by seasonal and proper texts of Easter time. Vespers 2 of Ascension, for example, has five proper psalms and one proper antiphon repeated until the ferias after Pascha 6, and then again at Vespers 2 of the octave of Ascension.

genre:	P	A	C	R	H	D	M	O
Easter time	f	s	D w	o	s	s	p	w
Asc Vespers 1			(p)	(p)			(p)	p
Vespers 2	(5)	(1)		p			(p)	(p)
feria vi				o			p	
Pas 6 Vespers 1				o			p	
Vespers 2				o			(p)	(p)
ferias	f	f		o			p	
Asc oct Vespers 1								
Vespers 2				o				
feria vi	f	f		o				

Each of these types of properness or commonness applies particularly to certain genres or in certain seasons. The following list summarizes their distribution, with further details.

p *proper daily*
Magnificat
except when drawn from stock (as with the Great Os; days in the octave of Epi; ferias from Epi 2 to LX and from Pas 1 to Asc; $\mathcal{V}_1$ from Tri 2 to Adv)
or numerical (as on ferias of Tri and CX, drawn from psalm-antiphons of $\mathcal{V}_1$ in order)
see also under D2f and Z2f.
Collect (Christmas $\mathcal{V}_1$ and $\mathcal{V}_2$; Ash Wednesday and Thursday and Friday; triduum to Pas 1; Pentecost week)

w *weekly*
Chapter (Epi; CX)
Versicle (Pentecost; Tri; CX)
Collect (Adv; Epi 2 to Ash Wednesday; Pas 2 to Asc; Tri; CX to Adv)

s *seasonal*
Antiphons (Easter; one antiphon for the season)
Hymn (Adv; Epi; XL 1-2, 3-4, 5-6; Asc)
Versicle (Adv; Epi; XL 1-4, 5-6; Pas 2 to Asc; Asc)

f *ferial*
Psalms (except under 1f, 1s)
Antiphons (except under s, 1s, 1w)
Hymn (Epi 2 to XL)

1w — $\mathcal{V}_1$ *and weekly*
Antiphons (Pentecost, with one proper for $\mathcal{V}_1$, another proper for $\mathcal{V}_2$ continued through the week; Tri and CX, each with five propers in $\mathcal{V}_1$ and one in $\mathcal{V}_2$ continued through the week or octave)
Chapter (Pen; Tri)
Responsory (Lent)
Hymn (Pen; CX)
Collect (Epi)

1s — $\mathcal{V}_1$ *and seasonal*
Psalms (Christmas to the octave of Epi, $\mathcal{V}_1$ having five proper psalms, $\mathcal{V}_2$ having five which are seasonal unless superseded)
Antiphons (as under Psalms)
Responsory (Adv; Lent)
Hymn (Christmas to Circumcision)

1f — $\mathcal{V}_1$ *and ferial*
Psalms (Tri; CX; each of these feasts has five proper psalms for $\mathcal{V}_1$, and the ferial psalms for $\mathcal{V}_2$ and the days of the octave)

1o — $\mathcal{V}_1$ *the item is omitted in other Vespers throughout the week.*
Responsory (Epi to Lent)

Dw — *Dominical common* ($\mathcal{V}_1$) *and* $\mathcal{V}_2$ = *weekly*
Chapter (Easter time)

Ds — *Dominical common* ($\mathcal{V}_1$) *and* $\mathcal{V}_2$ = *seasonal*
Chapter (Epi 1 to LXX; summer, using the texts from Epi 1)
Hymn (Easter time; summer)
Versicle (Epi 1 to XL; summer, using the texts from Epi 1)

12 — $\mathcal{V}_1$ *and* $\mathcal{V}_2$
In figure 4.9, this situation occurs in two circumstances: (a) when the other days continue using a seasonal text which has already been established, as with the chapter of XL 5, (b) when the other days are superseded by the propers of saints, as after Christmas and the octave of Epiphany.

12s — $\mathcal{V}_1$ *and* $\mathcal{V}_2$ *and seasonal*
Chapter (Adv)

12o — $\mathcal{V}_1$ *and* $\mathcal{V}_2$ *the item is omitted elsewhere*
Responsory (Asc; Pen; Tri; CX)

D2f — *Dominical common* ($\mathcal{V}_1$) *and* $\mathcal{V}_2$ *and ferial*
Magnificat (Epi 1-5)

Z2f — $\mathcal{V}_1$ *from stock and* $\mathcal{V}_2$ *and ferial*
Magnificat (Tri 2 to Adv)

V — $\mathcal{V}_1 = \mathcal{V}_2$ As 12 above.

Vp — $\mathcal{V}_1 = \mathcal{V}_2$ *and proper daily*
Collect (XL to the triduum)

Vs — $\mathcal{V}_1 = \mathcal{V}_2$ *and seasonal*
Chapter (LXX-XL 6 iv, the seasonal text deriving from $\mathcal{V}_2$ of Epi 1 and extending back to that service; within this period XL 5 has 12 rather than V)

X *interlocking*
occurs at several times of the year and may involve rather simple patterns, as with the responsory of $\mathcal{V}_1$ of Circumcision, which repeats the item of $\mathcal{V}_2$ of Christmas. On the other hand the patterns of all items around Ascension are very complex: Figure 4.9a illustrates the kind of procedure.

Figures 4.9 and 4.9a show how the genres use these categories through the year; the former is not to scale, the proper feasts taking more space, for example, than Advent or the summer.

429 The collect is the only item which is almost always common to both Vespers, since it is 'of the day' or 'week,' and except in Lent it is mostly of the week. The hymn, versicle, and responsory are largely seasonal, but even here for long periods of the year first Vespers has its own seasonal text different from the seasonal text of other Vespers. The responsory, psalms and antiphons are nearly always different at each Vespers of Sunday, and this is true of the chapter outside Lent. Chapter and responsory change for most Sundays, although the latter is omitted during much of the year: the item at Second Vespers often provides the text common to the ferias of the following week or weeks. Psalms and antiphons are mostly ferial, except for the important feasts: the Magnificat antiphon is almost always proper. In several periods of the year, however, the Magnificat antiphon is drawn from a stock: this is so for the ferial Magnificats after Epiphany, and during Easter, and of the Saturday or first Vespers Magnificats during the summer. On the ferias before Christmas the Magnificat antiphons are drawn from the Great Os, a group of antiphons, usually seven in number but sometimes as many as twelve,[54] whose long and elaborate texts beginning with the word 'O' are all set to the same basic melody. These are distributed over a certain number of ferias preceding Christmas, but owing to the intervention of festal propers they may have to begin earlier in some years than in others. An earliest or latest date is usually set out in rubrics.[55] The common responsory of Advent changes its text only after the Great Os have begun. Figure 4.9 shows that, on occasions, second Vespers is more important than first since it rather than the earlier service has the proper item; principally true during the weeks of summer or after Epiphany, this situation indicates that first Vespers has reverted to its status as a ferial Vespers of Saturday because of the lesser importance of the Sunday.

Finally, with regard to Vespers in general, we may obseve that the chapter is mostly drawn from the New Testament except during Advent, and there is no sequence of readings. The chapter of second Vespers is frequently the same as that of Lauds or less frequently one of the lesser hours. During Lent, the collect on ferias is often the same as the *oratio super populum* at Mass on the same day (**515**).

430 Vespers of the days preceding Easter are quite special and are treated in the discussion of Holy Week (**911, 922, 932**). Vespers of Easter Week are also different and may be described here. Second Vespers of Easter Sunday and Vespers on the ferias of the following week omit certain items, replacing them with others. In place of the opening versicle is a ninefold Kyrie sung to one of the standard Kyrie chants.[56] The psalms are reduced to three, all sung under the single Easter antiphon, *Alleluia*. Then follows the gradual *Hec dies* with a different verse for each of the ensuing ferias, then an alleluia with a similarly changing verse. These two items are performed in the same manner as at Mass, and even by the same singers.[57] After the weekly versicle and response the service continues in a normal fashion with the Magnificat antiphon and the collect proper to the day. In this combination of office and Mass we may see a continuation of the Holy Week practice of singing Mass and Vespers simultaneously, but the intermingling of the two is here much less complex.

COMPLINE

431 Except for the days before and after Easter Day, not included in the descriptions which follow, the service changes little during the year, and only a few of its items are truly proper, the variable ones being mainly seasonal, through octaves of feasts or through two 'seasons' in Lent. The two opening versicles and responses, *Converte nos . . . Et averte . . .* and *Deus in adiutorium . . . Domine . . .*, do not change although the concluding doxology has an alternative for use *pro temporis diversitate*.[58] The four psalms are always ferial, sung under a single antiphon. The antiphon is proper only for Christmas and its Eve and otherwise ferial or seasonal (the 'seasons' may consist of a few days, as after Christmas, or weeks, as in Lent). Common to the whole year is the chapter, Jer. xiv, and it is followed by a responsory only during Lent, when there are two texts, the first with a doxology and sung to XL 5, the other without a doxology thence to Maundy Thursday. Omitted during Easter week, the hymn is entirely seasonal – Advent, the summer and the weeks after Epiphany sharing *Te lucis ante terminum*, Christmas and Pentecost sharing *Salvator mundi*, and four other hymns serving the remainder of the year. On the first three ferias of Pentecost week the sequence, *Alma chorus Domini*, replaces the hymn. *Custodi nos . . . Ut pupillam . . .* is the yearly versicle. Like the antiphons for the other major canticles, the antiphon to the canticle *Nunc dimittis* is the most variable part of the service although only the Vigil of Christmas has a truly proper text, unique to that day. About a dozen other seasonal texts are distributed over the year in much the same manner as has been described for the other seasonal texts. Noteworthy is the form of the antiphon for the third and fourth weeks of Lent, one 'season,' and of the antiphon from the fifth week to Maundy Thursday, another 'season'; each has three verses when sung on Saturdays, Sundays, and some feasts. On its return, the antiphon is abbreviated in a way similar to that of the responsorial refrain. Since the verses are sung by soloists, the method of performance also approximates that of the responsory.[59] The liturgical greeting, *Oremus*, and collect (*Illumina quesumus*), the second liturgical greeting and *Benedicamus* formula are invariable, although dispersed amongst numerous other preces and memorials. These accretions are by and large common through the year, and probably variable from source to source.

432 Since the service changes only at certain times during the year and is otherwise unaffected by propers it is noted only a few times, on Advent Sunday, Christmas Eve, Christmas Day, and so on. In fact, all the variants are sometimes recorded comprehensively in the Psalter, together with the ferial psalms, in a series of perhaps twenty separate services for the Temporale. Very little changes with the superimposition of feasts: the canticle antiphon or the psalm antiphon may be proper, or one of the seasonal hymns used also for double feasts, for example, may be sung out of its usual place. During Easter week, certain items are replaced by others and the order of service changes a little. Of the opening versicles, only *Deus in adiutorium* is said. To replace the ferial Ps 90, omitted, the canticle *Nunc dimittis* is moved from its place to join the other ferial psalms. All are then sung under the single Easter antiphon, *Alleluia*. As in Vespers, the gradual of Easter Mass occurs next, its refrain and the verse remaining the same throughout the week: *Hec dies* ... V. *In resurrectione tua*. The collect is common to the week, but different from the collect common to the remainder of the year.

Finally, we may note that, despite its position after first Vespers on Sundays, the service does not take on any characteristics of the Sunday except on the Vigil of Easter. After first Vespers of feasts, however, some items may be proper to the feast.

THE LITTLE HOURS

433 As with the other hours these offices, sometimes referred to as the services *ad cursum*, consist fundamentally of psalms followed by a reading, the whole introduced and closed by versicles and prayers. Prime is somewhat more complex than Terce, Sext, or Nones because its psalms are changeable, and its yearly hymn, *Iam lucis ortu*, has seasonal melodies. Terce has a similar complexity with its hymn, *Nunc sancte nobis*: replaced by *Veni creator spiritus* in the first half of Pentecost week, *Nunc sancte* returns during the second half but with the *Veni creator* melody.[60] The original tune returns on Trinity Sunday. These hymns, and *Rector potens* (Sext) and *Rerum Deus* (Nones), are as usual omitted on the triduum and during Easter week.

The distribution and variation of the psalms, which are usually sung in groups terminated with a doxology, can be determined from figure 4.2. In secular use the groups may be:

Sunday Prime
Pss 21 & 22, 23 & 24, 25 & 53, 117 & 118a (or 92 & 118a), 118b
ferias at Prime
Pss 53 & 118a & 118b

Terce, Sext, and Nones place a doxology after all three psalms or sections of 118. From Christmas to the octave of Epiphany in the Sarum Breviary there appears to be only one psalm, Ps 53, for Prime whether festal, Dominical, or ferial, This is surely an abbreviation for the full ferial group: elsewhere, when it is quite clear that all nine Dominical psalms are said, only the first is sometimes noted.[61] This kind of abbreviated setting-down is common when ferial or seasonal texts are concerned. During the Easter season, all Sundays and feasts have the simple ferial office: only Easter Sunday itself has an addition, specially noted,[62] of Ps 117 between 53 and 118. At Prime the three ferial or nine Dominical psalms, and at the other offices the three psalms or sections of Ps 118, are all sung under a single antiphon. On Sundays from Advent to Epiphany and on the Temporale feasts this antiphon is drawn from Lauds, Prime repeating the first, Terce the second, Sext the third, and Nones usually the fifth, occasionally the fourth[63] antiphon of the earlier service. The Easter Day antiphons, common to all Sundays of Easter, are similarly drawn from Lauds, Nones using the fourth. For other Sundays a Dominical common text is provided for each office,[64] and five seasonal antiphons for the ferias.[65] On the three days of the triduum all of these offices have the antiphon *Christus factus est.* Following the psalms and their antiphon at Prime is another item referred to as a psalm, the Athanasian creed (**224**), *Quicunque vult,* with its own antiphon. Apart from the triduum and Easter week, where it is replaced by special items, it is said every day of the year in the Sarum rite, though not in all other uses: often it was said only on Sundays. All the instructions for the changing of the antiphon are given on Advent Sunday:[66] summarized for the Temporale, they state that whenever nine psalms are said the antiphon is *Te Deum Patrem*, and on all other Sundays and feasts it is *Te iure laudant,* for all ferias it is *Gloria tibi Trinitas* except the week following Pentecost (*Gratias tibi Deus*) and Trinity, on which last occasion the *Quicunque* 'psalm' is included under the antiphon belonging to the preceding true psalms.

434 In all these hours the chapter and choral response, *Deo gratias*, follows,[67] except on the triduum and during Easter week. Prime is somewhat simpler than the other three services because it has only three different readings, distributed on (i) Sundays and feasts, (ii) ferias of Advent, Epiphany, and summer, (iii) the remaining ferias. The other three offices also have readings common to many days when there is no proper, as follows: (i) Sundays and feasts, (ii) ferias of Advent, (iii) the other ferias, including Epiphany and summer. Most Sundays, however, have a proper chapter: at Terce this is usually the same as the chapter at Lauds, and the following services, Sext and Nones, usually continue with subsequent verses of the book from which the chapter is drawn. As already noted, the Lauds chapter is sometimes itself drawn from first Vespers and repeated at second Vespers. Ferias of Lent have fortnightly chapters, but the sequence of readings is not preserved from Terce to Nones. Excluding Easter week, the chapters of Easter time are weekly: the chapter of Ascension and Corpus Christi is also used during their octaves. For Pentecost and Trinity the situation is slightly more complex: figure 4.10 illustrates the arrangement, as well as how the readings are sequential. Trinity is unorthodox in that only the chapter of Terce is proper, the chapters of Sext and Nones being the Dominical texts continued through the summer. After the intrusion of Corpus Christi the ferial texts of summer also take over.

FIGURE 4.10
The chapters of the Little Hours: Pentecost and Trinity

For Prime, see the text (**434**).

	Terce	Sext	Nones
PEN	Acts 2.1 (drawn from Lauds and Vespers)	2.2	2.3
feria ii	Acts 2.2 (drawn from Sext of Pen)	2.3 (from Nones of Pen)	2.4
	This order of chapters . . . serves for the whole week		
TRI	Rom. 11.33	1 Jo. 7	Eph. 4.5
ferias repeat the Dominical chapters			

435 The *responsorium breve*, short responsory, follows. As with some of the other items this is handled similarly in Terce, Sext and Nones, but Prime has a special case. The responsory for Prime has a common refrain, *Jesu Christe* . . ., with or without Alleluia according to season, with four different verses assigned to different seasons. The Sarum Psalter is confusing at this point since it lists three or four of the verses when explaining their proper occasions.[68] The Breviary clarifies the situation, referring to the correct verse when necessary. Basically the verse *Qui sedes ad dexteram Patris* is common, with four variants, one each for Christmas (up to Purification), Corpus Christi,[69] Epiphany week, and Easter time. The short responsory is omitted on the triduum.

In the other hours, the confusion between responsory and response is illustrated in its worst form. At Terce of Advent Sunday, for example, the Breviary has:[70]

Clericus dicat responsorium: Veni ad liberandum nos, Domine Deus virtutum. *Chorus idem repetat. Clericus dicat versum*: Et ostende . . .
Chorus: Domine Deus virtutum. *Clericus*: Gloria Patri . . .
Chorus: Veni ad liberandum nos, Domine Deus virtutum. §
Clericus dicat versum: Timebunt gentes nomen tuum, Domine. *Chorus respondeat sub eodem tono*: Et omnes reges terre gloriam tuam.
Hic ordo servetur in omnibus responsoriis cum suis versibus super horis dicendis per totum annum extra XL . . .

In this passage, the short responsory ends at §. The following verse and response are what I have referred to as versicle and response. In the rubric, *versibus* and *responsoriis*, being plural, must refer to both responsory and verse and versicle and response. The precise wording should be noted: it is the *ordo* which is common *per totum annum*, not the texts themselves. The use of *responsorium* and *versus* to refer to both the R.V. and V.R., as the abbreviations may appear in Breviaries, also appears in the rubric *capitula, responsoria, et versus sicut in die nativitatis*, which occurs on die vi and Circumcision, after Christmas. On several occasions in the little hours, the same texts are interchangeable in these items. And of course the same texts are used for responsories, versicles, even antiphons in other offices of the day. One of the common ways in which the texts of these items exchange concerns the repetition of the versicle and response as the responsory and verse of the following office. This does not apply to the music, of course. Thus, the V & R of Terce become respectively the R & V of Sext, the V & R of Sext become respectively the R & V of Nones. This occurs on the feasts of the Temporale, the Sundays of Easter, and on the Vigil of Christmas. A similar order is not observed at other times of the year, either Sunday or ferial. Occasionally, however, there are more complex interchanges: at Terce the versicle and response of Epiphany 1 reverse their order to become the verse and responsory respectively of the following ferias, while the versicle and response of those ferias, keeping the order of their texts, become the responsory and verse of Septuagesima Sunday. Many of these items recur at other offices, as mentioned, and the borrowings are too complex to be listed. But we may notice that the versicle and response are sometimes borrowed sequentially from the nocturns of Matins: for example, on the first Sunday of Lent, the V & R of Terce/Sext/Nones repeat the V & R of nocturn 1/2/3 at Matins. More frequently, however, the versicle and response of Terce uses that of nocturn 2, Sext draws from nocturn 3, and Nones has a new text. Trinity and Corpus Christi exemplify this arrangement.

436 Written presentation in Breviaries of this already complex interlacing may lead to further confusion. When these offices become so repetitive that only incipits need to be indicated, instead of showing the first word of each of the four 'sentences,' the abbreviation is itself abbreviated, thus:[71]

R. Benedicam	
V. Semper	R. Benedicam
V. Dominus regit	V. Dominus regit
R. In loco	

or R. Benedicam V. Dominus regit.

This appears to be a single responsory and verse rather than two separate items. Furthermore, occasionally the word *versus*, 'sentences,' alone seems to refer to versicle and response: on the first Sunday of Lent, for example, the rubric after Vespers reads: *Supradictus ordo versuum hujus Dominice ad utrasque Vesperas, et ad Matutinas, et ad alias horas servetur usque ad Passionem Domini, tam in feriis quam in Dominicis.*[72] The rubric for Easter Sunday is: *Hic ordo hujus diei, scilicet hymnorum et versiculorum, ad omnes horas servetur quotidie usque ad Ascensionem Domini, tam in feriis quam in Dominicis.*[73] Another feature which suggests that the responsory, its verse, the versicle, and its response may be considered as a single item is the fact that their variations throughout the year are almost identical. This is true of all three offices, but the text is of course different for each office. For this reason we may discuss the sequence of propers and commons of both these items together. In Advent and from Pascha 1 to Ascension the texts are seasonal. The

FIGURE 4.11
The exchange and re-use of responsory and dialogue texts

Letters in the headings stand for the genres responsory, verse, and dialogue with its versicle and response. Letters in the body of the figure do not stand for genres but represent texts: where the letter is repeated, the text is repeated. Where there is no letter, the text is proper, or ferial, or seasonal, and is not involved in the interlacings.

	Terce				Sext				Nones			
	R	V	D		R	V	D		R	V	D	
V.NAT	a[‡]	b	c	d	c	d	e	f	e	f	a	b
NAT			g	h	g	h	i	j	i	j	k[§]	l
EPI 1			m	n			o	p			q	r
ferias	n	m	s	t			o	p			q	r
LXX	s	t					o	p	q	r		
XL 1			A[//]	B			C[¶]	D			E[‡‡]	F
TRI			G[§§]	H	G	H	I[////]	J	I	J		

‡ Drawn from the single nocturn of Matins.
§ Drawn from Lauds.
// Drawn from nocturn 1 of Matins.
¶ Drawn from nocturn 2 of Matins.
‡‡ Drawn from nocturn 3 of Matins.
§§ Drawn from nocturn 2 of Matins.
//// Drawn from nocturn 3 of Matins.

Sundays from Epiphany to Lent and during the summer have a Dominical, and the ferias a ferial text for each item. Other periods mostly have weekly or short seasonal texts, and as usual the days from Maundy Thursday to the Saturday of Easter week have special services in which the responsory is not included. Figure 4.11 shows how the interchange and variation works in certain parts of the year.
437 At Prime the invariable versicle and response *Exurge Domine . . . Et libera . . .* and a collect end the service. The latter, with the customary dialogue and final benediction, usually falls within the body of a series of preces which normally follow. Four different texts for the collect are given,[74] with rubrics indicating their occasions, and separating double feasts from lesser feasts, ferias, and Sundays and from other feasts and *profestis*,[75] and distinguishing between feasts on which the choir is ruled,[76] all of these occasions being outside Easter week. This specification implies that Prime is not considered in the phrase *ad omnes horas* which occurs in the rubric controlling the collect of Terce, Sext, and Nones. Normally the prayer for these offices is the *oratio dominicalis* of Lauds, which is anticipated in first Vespers: . . . *semper oratio que dicitur ad Matutinas [*sc. *Laudes] dicitur ad III. VI. et IX.* (or *ad omnes horas*), *et ad secundas Vesperas*.[77] The subsequent exceptions refer to the fact that occasionally the Lauds collect, or the collect of first Vespers, is not the *oratio dominicalis*: in the former case, as on the days between Ash Wednesday and the first Sunday of Lent, and on and after

important feasts such as Ascension and Christmas, the hours repeat the Lauds prayer, which is proper to the occasion, rather than the *oratio dominicalis*; in the other case, repeating the Lauds text, as usual, repeats the *oratio dominicalis*.

In most of their items apart from the psalms, then, the little hours repeat material drawn from earlier offices. Most noticeable are the antiphons, drawn sequentially from Lauds. The collect is normally that of the week, the *oratio dominicalis*. The chapter of Terce, also often drawn from Lauds, is continued in Sext and Nones, just as Ps 118 is continued in the later services. Most confusing is the intricate interweaving and exchange of the responsory, verse, versicle, and response texts, for which the terminology of the rubrics is exceptionally ambiguous. As with Prime, the other lesser hours are normally followed by extensive accretions in the form of preces or other kinds of memorial, which obscure the later items of the services.

5

Mass

500 For most purposes except learning about the presentation of the service in manuscripts, Jungmann's comprehensive study of the Mass cannot be bettered.[1] Eliminating the minutiae of his historical detail and his emphasis on the development of the service, I have tried to isolate what is necessary to understand how the Missal and Gradual are organized. In its internal variety encompassing a much wider range of forms than any of the offices, the Mass is much less variable in the order and number of those forms. Whereas the number of nocturns at Matins and their internal structure can differ widely, and the number of antiphons at Lauds can vary, the overall structure of Mass remains almost the same throughout the year, and the proper or common nature of its constitutents is relatively simple. The chief reason for the wider range of forms in Mass is that it consists essentially of an office, with all the forms pertaining to offices, followed by an entirely different kind of service. Like the office hours, the first half of Mass is of Jewish origin and is sometimes called the Synaxis or Fore-Mass, whereas the second half is of definitely Christian origin. This latter half, with its commemoration of the Last Supper, gradually came to overshadow the preceding part because of its direct relationship to Christian events and the names given to it eventually came to stand for the service as a whole. Many terms are in use at various times and different areas,[2] only two having remained current, and others having retained more specialized meanings. Of *Eucharistia, Anaphora, sacrificium, oblatio, offerre, sacrum, Dominicum summum officium, actio, synaxis, missa*, etc, only the first and last would now be recognized by laymen. Normally, Mass or *missa* will be preferred here, but what this term includes at different periods is somewhat ambiguous;[3] in our study of contemporary sources other terms will occur in quotations. *Oblatio* and *actio* have preserved their original reference to the central act of consecration.

For important Masses most variable items are usually proper. Masses on less important ferias not only omit certain items but may repeat items from earlier services. A section will describe special Masses in which all or part of the service is unlike the standard format. Subject to confirmation in a particular Missal or

Gradual, all Sundays (but less strictly so for the Sundays of summer and after Epiphany), all ferias of Easter and Pentecost weeks, and all feasts of the Temporale have proper Masses, Christmas Day having its usual three proper Masses and a proper for its octave. The sixth day after Christmas takes the Sunday office, which is otherwise obscured by the proper Masses of the Christmas saints: the propers for the extra Sundays after Epiphany may be sung on earlier ferias without feasts, if the time is short.[4] Christmas Eve has a proper, but the vigils of Easter and Pentecost have Masses of a special kind. All fasting days during the year, including almost every feria in Lent, the Ember days, and Rogation days, have propers. To put this more simply, the shorter ferial Mass occurs only during the less important seasons, from the second week of Easter (excluding Pentecost week) through Advent up to the beginning of Lent. From these generalities it should not be taken that every variable item is always proper on every occasion mentioned, although the exceptions are rather infrequent.

MASS ON SUNDAYS, FEASTS, AND FASTS

The Fore-Mass

501 Originally an independent service, sometimes even celebrated in a different church,[5] this part was from the earliest time characterized by readings and prayers. Its non-Eucharistic character enabled the not-yet-baptized members of the community to participate, and we sometimes find the term Mass of the Catechumens instead of Fore-Mass or Synaxis. In the early middle ages the precise shape of the service may have been influenced by the development of the offices which it so much resembled, and to the readings and chants which form its nucleus were firmly attached other elements of a different kind. We may compare it in particular with Matins, whose structure of preces, introductory psalmody (invitatory psalm and refrain), hymn, psalmody, readings and responsories is reflected in Mass: preces, psalmody (introit and antiphon), Kyrie, hymn (for example, the Gloria), collect, readings and responsories. The Fore-Mass differs in that it has a Kyrie, probably a remnant of an opening Litany procession, and a collect, and omits the lengthy psalmody before the readings. I do not intend to suggest that any derivation from Matins ever occurred, and one may just as easily compare some of the other hours in which the collect, for example, does appear.

The preparation ceremonies

502 Consisting of several distinct parts, and sometimes interrupted by Terce, these ceremonies are at some periods extremely elaborate. There are basically three sections: the blessing of the salt and water; the sprinkling of them, which in certain churches involves a procession; the immediate preparation and entrance ceremonies beginning the Mass itself.

Performed only on Sundays, the service of blessing and sprinkling, apart from one seasonal item, consists of texts which are invariable and thus common, or ordinary, but since they occur only on Sundays they are noted separately from the other items of the ordinary of Mass. The blessing of the salt and water, the mixing of them, and the subsequent sprinkling of the main or only altar and of the priest's assistants takes place to the accompaniment of versicles and responses, prayers, and one sung text. The opening prayers are the two exorcisms, *Exorcizo te creatura salis* (or *aque)* . . . , which each have the termination proper to exorcisms, alternating with the two other prayers, *Immensam clementiam* and *Deus qui ad salutem*, followed by the mixing formula *Commixtio salis et aque* and another prayer, *Deus invicte*. At this point (the completion of the blessing), Terce may interrupt the ceremony (**115-16**), which continues, after Terce or immediately, with the sprinkling, at which *Asperges me* is sung: replaced by *Vidi aquam*[6] during Easter, it is the only part of these rituals which is not common. The character of *Asperges* and *Vidi* as responsorial in form and method of performance, although antiphonal in musical style and by usual name, has been mentioned (**218**). After *Asperges* or *Vidi*, there are several versicles and responses and a final prayer, *Exaudi nos Domine*. If Terce was not said earlier, it occurs at this point and there follows, in certain circumstances on Sundays and important feasts, a procession. Most commonly for the purpose of sprinkling side altars, this takes place only in large churches: parish churches, for example, have only a main altar and the procession is not needed. After the processional entrance into the church (not into the chancel), the preces immediately preceding Mass are said while the priest prepares himself. Where there is no procession and Terce has been delayed until the sprinkling was completed, Mass would follow immediately upon Terce, the celebrant and other clergy already being in choir. In such a case the first items of Mass are sometimes omitted and the service begins after the entrance ceremonies.[7] Indeed, in the high middle ages Mass frequently or conventionally began with the Gloria.[8]

The opening preces

503 These are a great deal longer and more elaborate than those before any of the hours and are associated with the vesting of the priest and his assistants in the vestry. During the late middle ages they were elaborated wtih many accretions so that they really became a little hour in themselves[9] and certain parts of them underwent development in the monastic offices before being introduced into the Mass.[10] Although called the *preparatio misse*, these preces also constitute an accompaniment to the entrance ceremonies and Ps 42, *Iudica me* (with its relevant fourth verse, *Introibo ad altare Dei*) said as part of the preces, served as an accompaniment to the procession on the way to the altar, rather than the introit, despite the latter's name. Subject to much variation and especially addition, the preparation opens with versicles and responses followed by Ps 42 said, rather than intoned, with its fourth verse as an antiphon, also spoken. The arrangement of this psalm and antiphon is very similar to that of normal antiphonal psalmody except that often the two halves of the antiphon are treated as a versicle and response.[11] As the psalm is said, the priest and his ministers move to the altar, where the confession and absolution, *Confiteor* . . . *Misereatur* . . . *Absolutionem* (or *Indulgentiam* . . .) are said in a semi-dialogue form.

More versicles and responses lead the two final prayers, *Aufer a nobis* and *Oramus te, Domine*. At some time during these sacerdotal preces the choir will usually have started the sung introit, the exact time for beginning the item dependent on a number of features such as the distance from sacristy to altar. Even the Kyrie may be started before the preparation preces are completed.[12] All items in the preparation are strictly common, invariable throughout the year both musically and textually, and will therefore be listed only once in the Missal or Ordinal or some other relevant place. Moreover, the confession and absolution series may receive only a reference, the precise method of performing them having been explained with their appearance in Compline or Prime.

The introit to collect

504 The original relationship of these four disparate items – introit, Kyrie, Gloria, collect – to each other is not entirely clear, nor is the date or chronology of their addition to and final establishment as the first major items of Mass. The introit, *introitus, ingressa, officium*, apparently stems from the papal ceremonial in the large Roman basilicas of the early middle ages, and after the establishment of a fully trained *schola cantorum*: in that setting it was concluded by a prayer.[13] The exact point of beginning the piece is often not clear and is variable throughout the middle ages. It is certain that the introit lost its processional character very quickly.[14] Before the introduction of the introit the processional function may have been fulfilled by a Litany which, since it usually ends services rather than opens them,[15] may have been the final drawing to a close of the preceding hour or of a blessing ceremony such as the blessing of the font on Holy Saturday or the Vigil of Pentecost,[16] or even the close of the preparation ceremonies themselves. In any case the Litany refrain, or at least its final petitions, was almost always some form of *Kyrie eleison, Christe eleison*. It seems likely that the processional nature, and therefore the repeated petitions, of the Litany disappeared, being usurped by the introit, whose own processional function in turn disappeared. Litany processions were commonly terminated by congregational songs or hymns, and popular prayers. Such may be the origin of the Gloria, the *hymnus angelicus*,[17] which was originally present between the Kyrie and collect only by way of exception, and even today is omitted from certain Masses. Whether or not the collect, which follows, represents the original post-introit or post-Litany prayer – a point irrelevant here – it is the climax of the opening ceremonies, the *oratio prima* or *oratio diei*, and is the first place where the priest addresses the congregation aloud. To focus the attention, therefore, the liturgical greeting precedes it. Unlike the other Mass prayers, this collect often introduces the thought of the particular day into the petition and is therefore sometimes known as a prayer of relative predication:[18] such a prayer is of course proper. Jungmann points to the balanced structure of this collect, seeing in it the last remnants of the oratorical art. Up to the 10th or 11th centuries it was common, especially in Gallican rites, to multiply the number of prayers said here, and we may see occasional reminders of this practice even in the later middle ages. This was the conventional place for memorials. Other kinds of addition sometimes occur, especially in services of consecration or ordination such as Masses for the coronation of kings or popes. Of these the *laudes gallicane* are probably the best known.[19]

The introit and collect, present in all Masses of the type under discussion, are proper to the week or octave. Only the introit is subject to the occasional exception, when less important Sundays share texts or borrow them from other seasons. What may appear to be exceptions for the collect are in reality ferial repetitions of the Sunday text in weeks which are otherwise complicated by proper texts on ferias (**412**). As far as their texts are concerned and if they are not troped, Kyrie and Gloria are ordinary,[20] but during Advent and from Septuagesima to Easter Sunday the latter is said only on two days, Maundy Thursday[21] and Holy Saturday.[22]

The readings, responsorial chants, and Credo

505 Forming the core of the once independent office-like service, the readings and their associated chants have changed somewhat during the ages and still retain a variability to remind us of their earlier structure. Originally with three readings, from the Old Testament, an epistle, and a gospel, separated by two musical items,[23] this part of Mass now has only two, with both musical items between them, the Old Testament lesson having been dropped. Special Masses still preserve vestiges of the older form. That the readings were once considered as continuous, in the sense of the Matins readings we have already examined (**414-17**), may still be ascertained from the sequence of epistles in particular, and from the use of the formula *Initium* (or *sequentia*) *sancti evangelii secundum* . . . to indicate the beginning or continuation of a gospel. The *sequentia* preceding the gospel in this manner must not be confused with the *sequentia*, or sequence, which (since it is appended to an alleluia) also precedes the gospel. The first reading, normally part of an epistle, occasionally part of Acts, is drawn from the Old Testament only on fasts, including the ferias of Lent, these being likely to retain the older stratum. Begun without an address to the people, and without a blessing, the lesson's first words are nevertheless in the nature of a formula; the statement of the source of the reading, then *Fratres* . . . or *Carissimi* (*Karissimi* in many manuscripts) . . . for the epistles, *In diebus illis* . . . for Acts and some of the Old Testament passages, *Hec dicit Dominus Deus* for other Old Testament readings. At the end the choir replies *Deo gratias*.

506 Normally, two musical items follow. Usually said to be gradual and alleluia, this is the combination used over a longer period of the year, and therefore in numerically more Masses, than any other combination. Gradual and alleluia are the normal components during Easter week, except for the Saturday, which has two alleluias (the verse of the first is the verse of the gradual sung on the preceding days). Otherwise the only period in which such a combination is used, to wit, from Trinity Sunday through Advent to Septuagesima, is the less important part of the year. Moreover, on the six Ember days which occur in this period, the alleluia is omitted or replaced by one or more other readings and graduals, its expression of joy obviously being not suitable for times of penitence. Also for this reason, the alleluia was not sung, or rather was not introduced, from Septuagesima through Lent to Easter. Here the combination is gradual followed by tract on Sundays, Ash Wednesday, and ferias ii, iv, and vi of Lent. Most of the other ferias of this period, supplied with proper Masses, have only the gradual; a few have special Masses and Holy Saturday has an alleluia followed by a tract. From the Saturday of Easter week to the Friday after Pentecost, the gradual is replaced by an alleluia, so that the combination is alleluia followed by a second alleluia, even though some manuscripts continue to indicate the first with the abbreviation Gr.[24] This duplication of alleluias is true even of the Ember days of Pentecost (but the Saturday has a special Mass); Rogation days have only a single alleluia. After discussing the special Masses, I give a table (figure 5.3) to show the arrangement of readings and chants throughout the year, including the periods just discussed. Here I shall summarize by stating that three main combinations are to be found: alleluia-alleluia during Easter time but not Easter week; gradual-tract, or gradual only, in Lent and other times of penitence; gradual-alleluia in Easter week and the remainder of the year. The responsorial nature of gradual and alleluia we have already discussed, and it remains to observe only that various accretions, of which we need remember only the sequence, took place in the area of the alleluia.[25]

507 After these musical items a deacon says the prayer *Munda cor meum* and turning to the priest requests the blessing with the usual formula, *Jube Domne benedicere*, and receives it, *Dominus sit in corde tuo*. The deacon then carries the gospel book to the pulpit, a movement which sometimes seems to have developed into a procession accompanied with music.[26] In its usual position to announce items of central importance, the liturgical greeting precedes the gospel itself. To the reader's formal announcement of the source of the reading, *Initium* . . . or *sequentia* . . ., the choir responds *Gloria tibi Domine*,[27] and beginning in almost all cases with the words *In illo tempore* the gospel is intoned. Various additions, of which some have been dropped, took place after the gospel. The most important is the homily, or what we might call the sermon, an explanation of or gloss upon the gospel. Musical items and other prayers were sometimes added.[28] In the absence of additions, the Credo is begun without further ceremony.

508 The prayers, benediction, and versicles of this part of Mass are all ordinary and invariable and are present in all normal Masses. The Credo is also ordinary, as far as its text is concerned, but usually it is said only on Sundays, double feasts, and through the octaves of Christmas, Easter, and the high feasts of the Temporale.[29] Gospel and epistle (or its Old Testament replacement) are almost without exception proper. So too are the alleluias, when they are said, apart from some Sundays after Epiphany, which have a seasonal text, and the second alleluia of Masses in the week after Pentecost. When the gradual is said, it too is usually proper but only during the important part of the year, and most of the summer Sundays borrow their texts largely from the ferias of Lent. Sundays after Epiphany have a seasonal text. During Easter week the verse is proper and the refrain is weekly. Moreover, there are occasional repetitions even during the main part of the year, especially before and after fasting seasons: for example, the gradual for the Monday of the first week of Lent recurs as the second gradual on the following Ember Saturday, the gradual for Tuesday recurs as the third gradual for the Saturday, the gradual for Wednesday recurs on the following Sunday, and the fourth gradual on the Saturday recurs on the Friday and Saturday of the September Ember days and for the fifth Sunday after Trinity. Thus graduals (which as we have seen may be related to tracts) repeat themselves, especially in the older services of the fasting days, more often than do the alleluias, newer items probably composed after the church year had been established. The tract too is mainly proper to the days on which it is said, the only large-scale exception being the tract for Ash Wednesday, which is common to all subsequent ferias ii, iv, and vi up to Easter, unless a proper text is noted.

At the end of the Fore-Mass, hints of its original function may occasionally be found. The dismissal of the catechumens, for instance, no longer finds a place,[30] nor does the general prayer of the church, the *oratio communis*, although a vestige of the latter remains in the liturgical greeting and *Oremus* which survive, without a prayer, in many sources.[31] Musical items were sometimes inserted here.

The Eucharist

Offertory and oblation prayers

509 Originally only to accompany the procession and offering of gifts, the *oblata*, the offertory chant, *offertorium* or *offerenda*, was made variable in length with differing numbers of verses. These had mostly disappeared by the 13th century. However, the silence during the priest's actions following the offering gradually lost its significance and the chant was extended through the actions right up to the Preface. The actions concerning the offerings are the priest's preparation of the altar,[32] the presentation and receiving of the gifts, the priest's offering of them to Christ and the request for Christ's blessing. The priest then washes his hands, requests those present to pray for him, to which his ministers reply, and says a silent prayer, the secret or *oratio super oblata*.[33] In the early middle ages this sequence of payers and petitions was often very extended and even in the later middle ages the structure was not entirely uniform, such items as *Veni creator spiritus* and *Veni sancte spiritus* being added to reinforce the request for Christ's blessing. In many ways the ritual anticipates the central and most important part of Mass, the Canon, which soon follows and it was often called the Little Canon.[34] By the late 15th century, Roman usage was obviously more or less identical with the practices used since that time and I list the prayers here from the Missal of 1474[35] together with those of the Sarum Missal.[36] Although they differ sharply, the main outlines of the priest's offering in a spirit of humility is clear in both, as is his cleansing and his request to be prayed for, and the reply:

Roman Missal	*Sarum Missal*
Suscipe sancte pater . . . offero	Suscipe sancta Trinitas . . . offero
Deus qui	
Offerimus tibi	
In spiritu humilitatis	
Veni sanctificator	(Veni creator spiritus)
Per intercessum	
Incensum illud	
Dirigatur	Dirigatur
Ascendat in	
Lavabo	Munda me
Suscipe sancta Trinitas . . . offerimus	In spiritu humilitatis
Orate [pro me], fratres	Orate, fratres
reply: Suscipiat Dominus	Spiritus sancti
SECRET	SECRET

All the prayers up to the secret are, within their respectives uses, ordinary, and invariable. The secret itself is almost always proper, even after Epiphany and during the summer, although the wording and thought on many days is very similar, and there are occasional exact repetitions. The offertory chant and text is usually spoken of as a proper item, but this is true only during the important parts of the year: most Sundays of Epiphany have a seasonal text and summer offertories are mostly drawn from Lent. The Pentecost week texts, too, are mainly drawn from elsewhere, as are a few texts of Lent, and even Advent and Easter time. The secret, said silently, ends with a conventional formula, the last and even more conventional words of which and the final Amen are sung aloud to a reciting tone: *Per omnia secula seculorum: Amen*. This formula is nearly always included visually within the Preface and therefore is sometimes thought of as beginning the Preface.[37]

The Preface

510 The Preface in fact begins with the second of these dialogues:

Per omnia secula seculorum: Amen
Dominus vobiscum: Et cum spiritu tuo
Sursum corda: Habemus ad Dominum
Gratias agamus Domino Deo nostro: Dignum et justum est

These invariable versicles are sung aloud, like the termination of the secret, and it is difficult to perceive that in the middle of these intoned sentences there is an important end and a new beginning, even though clearly emphasized by *Amen* and the liturgical greeting, respectively (see **739-40**). The prayer following the versicles is said silently up to its end, and is variable in a unique fashion: a standard general text is given at some relevant place, probably under the heading *Prefatio generalis* which also includes the preceding versicles. Consisting of several phrases, the variable part of the prayer begins with the words *Vere dignum* and ends with the word *dicentes*. These are invariable and are always

present, so that the proper sentences can always be identified by the opening words, which are in practice usually abbreviated to the symbol ⊕ (plate 10). Within the body of the text, a few, many, or all of the phrases may vary, but only those which differ from the general text are written down, the beginning of the variation being noted by a repetition of the last words of the general text to be used, the end of the variation being noted by a cue to the place where the general text is taken up again. Thus, most variations use the general text to the words . . . *eterne Deus* and differ therefrom, and these will appear as:
⊕ *eterne Deus*, followed by the variant: sometimes ⊕ is omitted.[38] Plate 23 shows the symbol combined with the E of *eterne*. If the variant rejoins the general text at the phrase *Per quem majestatem*, the cue *Per quem* will end the variant. These proper sentences, which are mostly insertions into the standard texts, are called embolisms.[39] From the words which cue in and cue out the embolisms the proper text can be assembled. The general Preface text, excluding embolisms, is common to all days not having a proper variant, and in the later middle ages Sundays did not normally have propers but used the same text as the ferias.[40] Propers may occur as follows: weekly for Christmas, Epiphany, Easter time, Ascension and Pentecost, seasonal for Lent and the summer.

511 This part of the Preface is not complete by itself, and its invariable final word, *dicentes*: 'saying:', leads to an invariable conclusion. Now usually thought of as a separate item, the conclusion is the Sanctus (plate 23). Textually ordinary unless troped, the Sanctus now has a whole repertory of proper chants, mostly more elaborate than the chant of the Preface itself and, to distinguish it further from the *Vere dignum*, the Sanctus is now performed by the choir. Originally the chant was a continuation of the common Preface melody,[41] but even so the Sanctus seems from the earliest days to have been congregational.[42] With several structural divisions and repetitions in its text, the Sanctus has tended to become split into sections, a tendency further enhanced by the chant's adopted function as an accompaniment to the ensuing Canon, which may be thought of in two sections. It seems certain that the Benedictus, or more correctly the Osanna-Benedictus-Osanna, was a later addition to the Sanctus.[43] During the later middle ages the custom grew up of allowing the often elaborate chant of the Sanctus to be extended over the Canon, which consists of priest's actions and prayers said silently, in order to provide some audible interest. The commonest arrangement was perhaps the singing of the Sanctus and the first Osanna over the Canon prayers up to the consecration, and the Benedictus and second Osanna during the prayers after that solemn moment: the text of the latter part, emphasizing 'he who comes in the name of the Lord,' would symbolize the change of the bread and wine into Christ's body and blood. The break between the two halves at the moment of consecration probably gave rise to the prevalent separation of the Sanctus into two movements. Sometimes, however, it appears that non-ritual musical items were introduced after the consecration, such accretions being called Salutations, in which case the whole Sanctus would be completed before the consecration.[44] Before the Santus is completed, then, but after he has said the text to himself, the priest will have begun the Canon.

The Canon, Embolism, and Communion cycle

512 These three sections, which often appear in liturgical books to be one large unit under the heading 'Canon', are clearly separated by the formulaic endings, Nos 16 and 19 of the table below: *Per omnia . . . Amen.* Just as the end of the secret appears visually to belong to the Preface, because both are accompanied with musical chants and staves (**739-40**), so here there appears to be no break in the sequence. In these sections, the oldest parts of the Eucharist,[45] there are some thirty prayers, many of which are little more than sentences, and preces. Almost all are said silently by the priest as he prepares the bread and wine for communion. Other than the occasional combination of some consecutive items into one longer prayer, the arrangement and texts of this part of Mass have changed little and do not vary greatly from use to use. I propose simply to list the incipits together with a brief indication of the prayer's function:

THE CANON

1	*Te igitur*	(plea for acceptance of gifts and offerings)
2	*Memento Domine*	(remembrance of the living)
3	*Communicantes*	(reinforcement of No 2)
4	*Hanc igitur*	(similar to No 1)
5	*Quam oblationem*	(plea for the final hallowing of the earthly gift 'that it may become the body and blood')
6	*Qui pridie*	
7	*HOC EST ENIM CORPUS MEUM*	(consecration prayer)
8	*Simili modo*	(consecration prayer)
9	*HIC EST ENIM CALIX SANGUINIS*	(consecration prayer)
10	*Unde et memores*	(interpretation of the mystery)
11	*Supra que propitio*	(further pleas for acceptance of offerings, with references to the sacrifice of Abel,
12	*Supplices te*	and Abraham's sacrifice)
13	*Memento etiam*	(remembrance of the dead)
14	*Nobis quoque*	(remembrance of ourselves)
15	*Per quem hec omnia*	(doxologies and prayers concluding the post-consecration ritual)
16	*Per omnia . . . Amen.*	

THE EMBOLISM

17	*Preceptis*	
18	*Pater noster . . . libera nos quesumus*	(the last petition taken up again for emphasis)
19	*Per omnia . . . Amen.* (*preces in prostratione*)	

THE COMMUNION CYCLE

20 *Pax Domini*	(prayer for peace)
21 *Fiat commixtio*	(the commingling of bread and wine)
22 *Agnus Dei qui tollis*	
23 *Domine Jesu Christe qui*	(prayers for peace)
24 *Pax tecum*	
25 *Domine Jesu Christe Fili*	(beginning of the communion rituals)
26 *Perceptio corporis*	(unworthiness of priest)
27 *Panem celestem*	(his acceptance of the body on the paten)
28 *Domine non sum dignus*	(his unworthiness)
29 *Corpus Domini nostri*	(his acceptance of the body itself)
30 *Quid retribuam*	(his acceptance of the chalice)
31 *Sanguis Domini*	(his acceptance of the blood)
32 *Quod ore sumpsimus*	(cleansing and arranging vessels after his communion)
33 *Corpus tuum*	

All of these items are ordinary except Nos 3 and 4, *Communicantes* and *Hanc igitur*, for which proper sentences always beginning with the same words are usually listed with the proper Prefaces, but under a separate heading such as *Infra actionem* or *Infra canonem*, 'within the Canon (as opposed to the Preface).' *Communicantes* is usually proper when the Preface is, *Hanc igitur* less often so. Often only the varying part of the text is noted, with the abbreviation *etc* to direct the reader to the remainder of the general prayer. Apart from announcing the particular mystery of the day to which it is proper, *Communicantes* in the middle ages frequently includes topical or local additions from which date and origin of the source can sometimes be deduced. The same is true of Nos 13 and 14, *Memento etiam* and *Nobis quoque*, where remembrance of local benefactors or patrons may be included, although apart from such accretions these two prayers are invariable. Numerous accretions in the form of other prayers took place adjacent to No 13, *Memento etiam*, and the other remembrance prayer, No 2, *Memento Domine*. Between the Embolism and the Communion cycle it was customary on the ferias of Lent and some other fasting days to insert a whole set of *preces in prostratione*.

513 Despite prohibitions, accretions in the form of the Salutations already mentioned were made after the Elevation of the Host, Nos 7 and 9, and after the Paternoster and sometimes after the Agnus as well. The Paternoster was said by everybody, although probably silently at least until the final petition. Hymns and antiphons for peace may have followed. Peace was emphasized too in the final invocation of the Agnus, *dona nobis pacem*, words which were probably added because of the postion of the item adjacent to the *Pax* prayers. Originally associated with the fraction ritual, which was rendered superfluous in the 9th or 10th century by the use of unleavened bread,[46] the Agnus came to be used as an accompaniment to the priest's communion (Nos 25-31). Thus it provided, like the Sanctus, some musical interest during this silent time. Also like the Sanctus, it was sometimes extended by further Salutations.[47] Whether it was lengthened in this way, or by troping, or by the repetition of the invocations as often as necessary, or by the insertion of special prayers or musical items between the invocations, the Agnus was made to extend over the silent period so that the communion chant was a direct sequel, lending the Agnus a special importance which appears to have been deliberately sought. Its performance by the choir with a true melody rather than a recitation formula aids this end: although the text is ordinary when untroped, the melody is variable.

Before the 13th century the invariable part of the Mass often ended with the Agnus, the later prayers or *benedictiones super populum* being variable, and we have noted the accumulation of prayers and songs after the Agnus: Nos 25 and 26 were particularly susceptible to such reinforcement. Nos 32 and 33 may be said during or even after the communion chant according to whether the act of communion is finished or not. Although these sections of the Mass are invariable, apart from the exceptions mentioned above, there may be differences and extensions, or changes in order in manuscripts of different uses.

Communion to dismissal

514 For various reasons, such as the lack of opportunity to confess frequently, communion of the faithful took place only rarely in the late middle ages, the Lateran Council of 1215 denoting Easter Day as the only obligatory time for common folk, although in monasteries Sunday communion was probably continued.[48] Instead of communion, praise and reverence and viewing of the Sacrament, in the form of Salutations at the Elevation for example, took its place. Originally intended to accompany the communion of the people, the communion chant had as many psalm verses as necessary, or other items were added.[49] With the infrequency of popular communion, this function was obscured and the verses were dropped, leaving only the antiphon and changing the character of the piece to that of a thanksgiving after communion and resulting as we shall see in a change in the position of the chant. When the abbreviation of the chant and the alteration in order had taken place, communion of the people was then either silent, as always on Good Friday and Holy Saturday, or accompanied by extra-ritual musical additions, sometimes even in the vernacular.[50] Alternatively, and particularly at the end of Holy Week, a part of an office such as Sext or Vespers was inserted so that the office closed simultaneously with the dismissal formula at Mass.[51] This gives rise to a very distinctive combination of Mass and office services, which I shall examine in the section on Holy Week.

515 When the communion chant accompanied the act of communion by the people it had to occur before prayers Nos 32 and 33 of the preceding section, since these are clearly post-communion texts: *Quod ore sumpsimus* . . . 'What we have received with our mouth' and *Corpus tuum* . . . 'Thy body which I have received . . .' Moreover the cleansing of the vessels and hands takes place during these prayers. As a result of their position they took the name *orationes post* *communionem*. With the reduction of the chant to a thanksgiving rather than an accompaniment, it changed its place in the order, so that by the late middle ages the sequence of items was: No 32 *Quod ore*, No 33 *Corpus tuum*, communion chant. But a further post-communion prayer remained in its position after the chant, probably because it was variable rather than common, as with the preceding prayers. This prayer also kept the name *oratio post communionem* which the other two tended to lose. Confusion may still arise from the similarity of *post communionem* for 'after the act . . .' and 'after the chant of communion.' Referred to also as *oratio ad complendum* or *complenda* from its erstwhile function as a concluding prayer, it was preceded by the liturgical greeting and *Oremus* to enhance its importance. In some eras there was a profusion of items after the communion, mostly prayers but also sometimes canticles and antiphons.[52] By the late middle ages only a vestige of these additions remains during Lent, when the final prayer is followed by an *oratio super populum* which was usually said also at Vespers.[53] In the sources used for this book, the normal order of items after the invariable Canon and Communion cycle was: communion chant, liturgical greeting, *oratio post communionem*, *oratio super populum* (during Lent), and the dismissal.

Both communion chant and post-communion prayers are almost entirely proper, with only a few repeats, mainly between the summer and earlier fasting days. The dismissal formula is ordinary, but there are two versions. The joyful *Ite missa est* from which the word *missa* originates, with its reply *Deo gratias*, said by priest and choir respectively, is used on days when the Gloria is said, that is, during Christmas, Epiphany, Easter and summer. When Mass is continued immediately by another service, as on Christmas Day, and during the times of year when the Gloria is not said, the dismissal is *Benedicamus Domino* answered also by *Deo gratias*. Although textually these two formulas may be considered ordinary to their own 'seasons,' their melodies are variable. The reply *Deo gratias* does not immediately follow its 'cue,' being delayed by the ceremonies after Mass.

Ceremonies after Mass

516 Although the service is officially finished,[54] by the 13th century an extra prayer, a last blessing, and a final reading had accrued, and often a large number of other items such as antiphons, canticles, and hymns. Only the prayer, blessing, and additional reading appear consistently. All are ordinary: the prayer is *Placeat tibi*, the blessing is *In nomine Patris et Filii et Spiritus Sancti. Amen* (although it may be more complex at pontifical Masses), the reading is the prologue to the gospel of St John, a passage with a prayer-like quality. The congregational *Deo gratias* is delayed until the completion of these items.

FERIAL MASSES

517 There are proper Masses, by and large, only for the ferias of Lent and other fasting days. For other ferias the Mass of the preceding Sunday is repeated, with a few minor changes to be outlined below. Since complete repetition of this kind results in a total absence of material written down on the days in question, some liturgical books appear to have no ferial Masses, and most modern and medieval texts seem to assume that the reader will know as a matter too obvious to need stating that ferial Masses repeat Sunday Masses. In fact, this assumption is made only in modern texts, although the relevant passages in medieval books are hard to find, often hidden in lengthy rubrics or in Ordinals which do not contain the texts themselves. Here is a selection of such rubrics, from which references to methods of performance, dress, incensing, and other matters have been excluded to leave only the material relating to the texts and the order of saying them:

The aforesaid method and order of service [that for Mass on Advent Sunday] is used on all ferias and feasts and on and within octaves, when the choir is not ruled, with this exception, that . . . the priest and his ministers enter to perform the service at the beginning of the introit of the Mass [on Advent Sunday they enter after the doxology of the introit: there follow some comments on the manner of performing gradual and alleluia].[55]

When there is a ferial Mass on the feria [and not a festal Mass] or when it is a Sunday Mass said on a feria [see below], neither the *Gloria* nor the *Ite* are said: nor are they said on vigils of the saints or of feasts of the Temporale except the vigils of Easter and Pentecost.[56]

From Septuagesima to Easter, the alleluia is not said at Mass, and for the whole of Lent on all Mondays, Wednesdays, and Fridays the tract is said as on the first Sunday of Lent [unless a proper is given]. On the other ferias up to Maundy Thursday and on all vigils except those of Sunday and during Easter time, only the gradual and its verse are said.[57]

From *Domine ne in ira* to Maundy Thursday and from *Deus omnium* to Christmas Eve, the following preces are said at daily Mass or Mass on feasts of three lessons, on and within octaves, when the choir is not ruled: after the *Per omnia* and before *Pax Domini* [prayers 19 and 20 of the table in section **512**] the chorus, prostrate, says . . . the whole psalm *Deus venerunt* with the *Gloria Patri*, and the psalms *Deus misereatur* and *Domine in virtute* similarly. Then the antiphon *Tua est potentia* is said, [followed by] *Kyrie eleison, Christe eleison, Kyrie eleison. Pater noster*. And all this is said without music . . . Then the priest intones *Et ne nos* [and many other versicles and several prayers].[58]

On ferias within Advent, and from *Domine ne in ira* up to Quadragesima and from *Deus omnium* to Advent, only five collects are said at Mass. From Lent to Maundy Thursday, seven, and in Easter time and on commemorations of the Virgin, only three.[59]

518 From these statements we may deduce that the method and order of ferial Masses, with the exceptions to be noted, is the same as that of Advent Sunday, but we have to generalize Advent Sunday to 'the preceding Sunday.' The celebration of a feast or a votive Mass or a Sunday Mass on a feria automatically supersedes the normal ferial service. The first two of these circumstances need no further comment: the performance of a Sunday Mass on a feria, an apparent contradiction, takes place when the Sunday Mass cannot be said (a) because a feast falls on the Sunday, superseding it, or (b) when the Sunday does not exist, as after Epiphany when the time is short. Such Sunday Masses are usually said on ferias after, but may occasionally take place on ferias preceding the Sunday.[60]

Ferial Masses, whether repetitions of the Sunday Mass or truly proper, are different in the following ways: (i) neither the Gloria nor the Ite are said, the latter being replaced by the Benedicamus, (ii) from the statements about when the Credo *is* said, we may deduce that it too is omitted, (iii) the number of prayers after the collect is limited, and changes according to season. The greatest difference, however, is in (iv) the *preces in prostratione*, a whole series of psalms, an antiphon, versicles and prayers, said on ferias which do not have a festal character, that is, every feria except those of Christmas, Epiphany, and Easter, and the triduum. No relics of these additions seem to have survived in modern times,[61] nor even in the Roman Missal of 1474.

Occasionally during the middle ages the Sunday texts are replaced during the week by others, although this practice seems rare. Proper epistles and gospels may be listed for ferias iv, vi, and vii of Advent, Epiphany to Lent, but not during the summer. These Wednesdays, Fridays, and Saturdays are the days of fasting during Ember weeks, but the presence of propers is not restricted to these weeks. Additions rather than changes sometimes occur:

Then the offertory *Ad te Domine* [of Advent Sunday] is said. The two following verses are sung on ferias, the first on one day, the second on another, but never on Sunday. It is done similarly within Septuagesima.[62]

MASSES WITH EXTRA LESSONS

Within the service

519 A few days of the Temporale have Masses which differ because they have more than the usual number of lessons. Excluding Masses on the triduum, described in the section on Holy Week, there are ten such days, all fasts: the Wednesdays and Saturdays (but not the Fridays) of all four Ember weeks, the Wednesday of the fourth week of Lent, also called the Day of Great Scrutiny because on this day the catechumens are examined for admission to baptism,[63] and the Wednesday of Holy Week, because of its proximity to the triduum.

Before considering these in detail let us recall the normal arrangement of the Fore-Mass during the different periods of the year, excluding the special days (figure 5.1). In this figure, observe the nucleus consisting of *DO*L followed by chant(s). Of the ten exceptions to this arrangement, six are Wednesdays, four are Saturdays, the former being special by the presence of one extra lesson, the latter with five extra lessons. Together with each extra lesson goes a versicle and prayer preceding, and a chant following: DOL chant. This group of four items I shall refer to as a lesson-unit. Within the Fore-Mass of ferias the extra lesson-unit or units occur as in figure 5.2. The last lesson-unit here is always the normal one of Mass, and its prayer (O) is therefore equivalent to the collect of a normal

FIGURE 5.1
The Fore-Mass in different seasons

Bold letters refer to the sung items of the Mass.

introit, Kyrie, (Gloria), greeting, prayer, followed by:

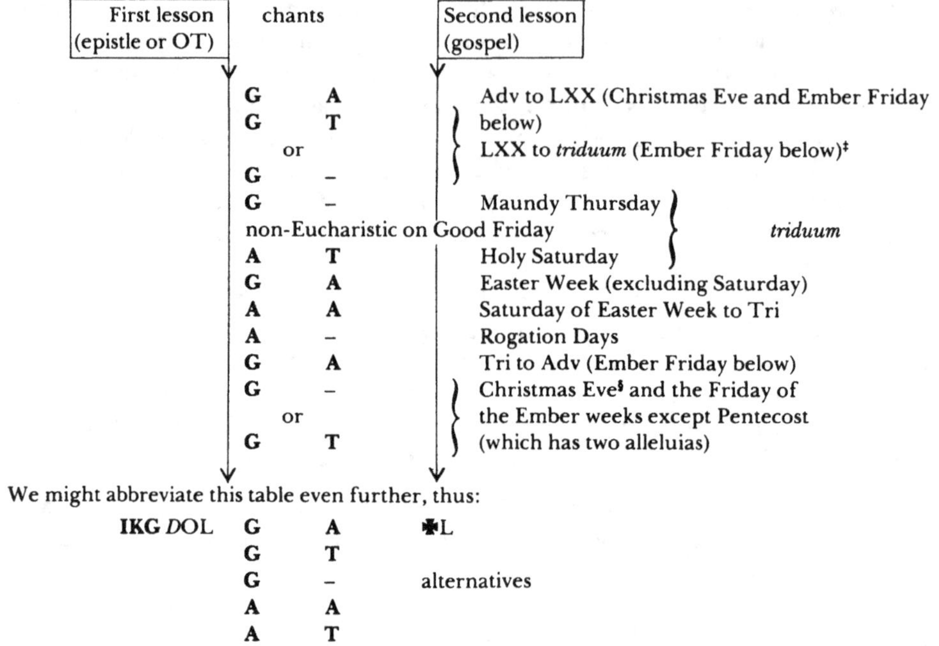

‡ Ferias ii, iv, and vi of each week have the tract *Domine ne secundum* or *De necessitatibus* after the **GT** or **G–**. This tract is repeated from earlier in the year, and the repetitions are often specified only by a rubric on the first appearance of the tract. The absence of even an incipit thereafter can be very misleading. On the Friday Ember day of Lent, for example, only one Missal (NM5) out of fifteen Mass books studied had the incipit of the tract immediately after the gradual: one Gradual (G8) had a second gradual. The MR49 and MS cols 136-7, 142, 150, 156, 162, etc are explicit.

§ An alleluia is often given for Christmas Eve in the manuscripts, with or without the rubric that it is for use only when the day is a Sunday.

Mass and will usually be the *oratio diei*; as such it is preceded by the liturgical greeting (*D*) as usual. All other units except those of the Wednesday and Saturday after Pentecost, where the single word *Oremus* is used, begin with the invariable versicles *Oremus. Flectamus genua. Levate*,[64] and the prayer is therefore more properly an *oratio* than a *collecta*. Each of the prayers is proper. Every reading, except for the fifth of Saturdays, and all graduals and alleluia verses are proper. The Saturday lessons, including the one common to all four Saturdays, are from the Prophets and are so termed in the sources: *Prophetia prima ... secunda ...* for first and second lesson, etc. There seem originally to have been twelve lessons on each of these Saturdays (there still are on Holy

FIGURE 5.2
The lessons of the Fore-Mass: ferias

Bold letters refer to the sung items of the Mass. Superscript o and n refer to lessons from the Old and New Testament, respectively.

the ferias	the lessons, and the surrounding items
Adv 3 QT iv, XL 4 iv, LXX QT iv (Wednesdays)	**IK** DOL^{o} **G** *DOL*^{o} **G** (XL 4 iv also has a **T**[‡]) ✠L^{n}
XL 1 QT iv, XL 6 iv (Wednesdays)	**IK** DOL^{o} **G** *DOL*^{o} **T** ✠L^{n}
Pen QT iv (Wednesday)	**IK** DOL^{n} **A** **Gloria** *DOL*^{n} **A** ✠L^{n}
Pen QT vii (Saturday)	**IK** DOL^{o} **A** DOL^{o} **A** DOL^{o} **A** DOL^{o} **A** DOL^{o} **A** **Gloria** *DOL*^{n} **T** ✠L^{n}
Adv 3 QT vii, XL 1 QT vii, LXX QT vii (Saturdays)	**IK** DOL^{o} **G** DOL^{o} **G** DOL^{o} **G** DOL^{o} **G** DOL^{o} **H** *DOL*^{n} **T** ✠L^{n}

‡ Cf note ‡ in figure 5.1: of the same fifteen Mass books only two (M5, NM5) showed the incipit of the tract after the two graduals.

Saturday), and some manuscripts preserve the heading *Sabbato in xii lectionibus*, but what the lessons were and why they were reduced seems obscure.[65]

520 The chants of the additional lesson-units are all graduals except (a) after Pentecost, when the alleluia supersedes everything, and (b) on the three remaining Ember Saturdays, which for the fifth additional unit share the versions of the hymnus (**221**). These performances of the hymnus follow the lesson common to all these Saturdays, to which reference has just been made. Relating from the book of Daniel the story of the three young Hebrews thrown into the furnace, and ending with the word *dicentes*, 'saying,' it leads, through that connective word, to the alleluia on the Saturday after Pentecost and to the hymnus, the hymn of the three boys, on the three other Saturdays. The hymnus itself is a paraphrase of the lesson. The chant of the 'normal' unit is either gradual, alleluia or tract as the diagram illustrates.

Before the service

521 Although the Holy Saturday Mass falls into the category described here, its ceremonies before Mass are very extended, including the blessing of the font and of the Paschal candle, as well as extra lessons. For this reason its description will be delayed (**929-32**). In keeping with the trend for the whole of Easter time to be modelled partly on the ceremonies for Easter itself, the vigil of Pentecost imitates the vigil of Easter, Holy Saturday, and therefore it, too, has ceremonies for the blessing of the font. This action occurs with prayers and extra lessons added before the Mass begins, and as with the additional lessons already discussed passages from the Prophets are read within lesson-units. The units are not quite so consistent in their structure, and the order of individual items within the unit is different. Here the lesson is followed by the prayer and there are no versicles other than the priest's *Oremus*. Some but not all of the units include a tract placed as usual after the lesson between it and the prayer: *Prophetia primus* (tract) *Oremus* prayer.

On the vigil of Pentecost there normally seem to be six units, only three with tracts, although the number differs from source to source. All lessons and tracts are taken from the Holy Saturday service, not necessarily in the same order, since the latter has twelve such units. All the prayers are different. Afterwards, if the blessing of the font is to take place (and if there is no font the blessing and the procession may be omitted), the tract *Sicut cervus* accompanies the movement to the font, where the liturgical greeting is given, followed by the usual kind of collect and the prayers of benediction.[66] Whether or not this blessing is carried out, the Mass itself now begins, replacing the introit with a Litany during which the schola enters the choir. After the *Kyrie eleison* which ends the Litany, the Kyrie of Mass is begun.[67] While this is being sung, the priest and ministers enter, having said the *Confiteor* and *Absolutionem* in the vestry.

Lessons: summary

522 Figure 5.3 summarizes the number, but not the order, of lessons and chants throughout the year: the number of additional lessons and chants may vary from source to source.

FIGURE 5.3
Readings and chants in the Fore-Mass

A, alleluia; **G**, gradual; **H**, hymnus trium puerorum; **L**, lesson (epistle or gospel, etc); **T**, tract. The numerals represent the number of lessons, graduals, etc.

	lessons before Mass		lessons preceding those of a normal Mass					normal Mass			
	L	**T**	**L**	**G**	**A**	**H**	**T**	**L**	**G**	**A**	**T**
ADV to LXX								2	1	1	–
Adv 3 QT iv			1	1	–	–	–	2	1	–	–
vi								2	1	–	–
vii			5	4	–	1	–	2	–	–	1
LXX to Maundy Thursday								2	1	–	(1)
XL 1 QT iv			1	1	–	–	–	2	–	–	1
vi								2	1	–	1
vii			5	4	–	1	–	2	–	–	1
XL 4 iv			1	1	–	–	–	2	1	–	1
XL 6 iv			1	1	–	–	–	2	–	–	1
Good Friday	4	2			non-Eucharistic						
Holy Saturday	12	4						2	–	1	1
EASTER SUNDAY to Friday								2	1	1	–
SATURDAY to TRINITY								2	–	2	–
Rogation Days								2	–	1	–
Vig. Pen	6	4						2	–	1	1
Pen QT iv			1	–	1	–	–	2	–	1	–
vi								2	–	2	–
vii			5	–	5	–	–	2	–	–	1
TRI to ADV								2	1	1	–
Sept. QT iv			1	1	–	–	–	2	1	–	–
vi								2	1	–	–
vii			5	4	–	1	–	2	–	–	1

6

Liturgical Books: Content and Format

600 The following section, the chief purpose for this book and to which all that precedes is merely factual information, concerns the organization, format, and structure of the liturgical manuscript. The first requirement is naturally that the student be able to read the scripts fluently: the development of the paleographical skills for reading texts and their abbreviations is beyond the scope of this study and henceforth expertise in this area must be taken for granted. Making the liturgical manuscript infinitely easier to use is a knowledge of the services sufficient to enable the immediate identification of such and such a text with such and such a day or season: such knowledge is not taken for granted since, until the sources can be read with ease, the acquisition of such information is extremely difficult.

Manuscripts can much more easily be read in the original than on microfilm. This is especially true of liturgical books, whose organization frequently depends on colour. Rubrics, one of the chief keys to orientation within the book, are as their names suggest usually red. They do not immediately leap to the eye in black and white, although the use of a filter in the photography will render them grey. Often the red paint used for them has flaked off or has been rubbed bare so that on film this chief aid to the book may be virtually invisible. In initial letters, the colour and size of which are a second key to orientation, reds and blues will be little distinct from black on a film. Based partly on microfilms of manuscripts acquired by me or by libraries for other purposes, discussions in this book will usually have to ignore colour. Appendix IV is devoted to the colour schemes observed and recorded from a few of the hundreds of manuscripts studied in the original. Descriptions here will otherwise contain no information not also available to the user of black and white microfilm.

601 Medieval manuscripts do not, as a rule, rely on visual spacing for the identification of sections. The liturgical manuscript is no exception. Normally every inch of the writing space is taken up with script, and the separation of items is made visible by colour and by initial letters. Various conventions, loosely applied, make the analysis both easier and in some ways more difficult. One convention, for example, dictates that any item with an initial of a certain size is so placed on the writing space that the initial appears at the beginning of the line: if there are obvious reasons for this, they need not concern us. This convention, once the particular scheme of the source has been analysed, may be of use simply in the numerical sense. For instance, in Advent in many Graduals, the seventh initial of more than a certain size will be that of the tract on Saturday of the third week (see the analysis of Graduals below, section **704**). This convention, on the other hand, can create difficulty. In order to use every bit of the writing space, scribes did not leave blank the ends of lines incomplete because of insufficient text. There was thus the problem of linking the end of a brief turnover, not enough for a complete line, with an initial required at the beginning of a new line. The turnover, when combined with other similar problems such as the need to incorporate an incipit or an identifying abbreviation such as R[esponsorium] as well, can cause severe problems of organization. It is important to remember in this connection that our deeply ingrained habit of reading from left to right and from top to bottom sequentially is sometimes a hindrance. Consider the following section from a Gradual at Stralsund (the dotted lines represent musical notation):[1]

....
cum benedicta tu in mulieribus et benedictus fructus ven
H.....................................*nativitatis*................ ....
Hodie scietis quia veniet *In vigilia* Ecce virgo tris tui *Cō*
....
dominus

This might be printed nowadays in the following form, which makes the sequence immediately apparent to us (music dots omitted here):[2]

cum benedicta tu in mulieribus et benedictus fructus ventris tui.
Comm. Ecce virgo, etc.

IN VIGILIA NATIVITATIS
Hodie scietis quia veniet dominus . . .

From this example, we may draw several helpful hints. Short turnovers are often written at the end of the next line, as they are sometimes even nowadays in poetry. The text of the next item, running towards the turnover, may or may not be separated from it by a rubric, or a manuscript stroke like a bar-line, by a paraph sign (such as ¶ , as in plate 11), or by some other means. Rubrics are frequently used to fill out incomplete text lines, announcing the next item or service or feast. They often read upwards if long enough to take up more than single line of some 'left-over' space, but too short to fill a complete line. Where the initial must stand at the margin and there is no space left in the preceding line, the rubric usually stands at the end of the line begun by the initial, separated from the text running towards it only by colour.

Here are some other examples:

Exurge quare obdormis Domine exurge et ne *mica. inlxma. officū*

Appearing at the top of the leaf,[3] this incomprehensible rubric involves the incorrect end of a word which begins on the previous page (*Dominica*), an abbreviation for the season (*in sexagesima*) and for the item (*officium*).

[orien]tibus adorate dominum. *In* Alleluia *octava*

Dicit do*Cō*.minus

These two examples present little difficulty.[4] The following is more confused:[5]

Ve qui dicitis malum bonum *leccō* cantate veniet. Et *v*[a]

The *cantate veniet*, written just a little smaller than what precedes, is the end of the responsory verse and the *Et*, also smaller, is the cue for the repetenda; the identification of the fifth lesson is split up as shown. Often in a manuscript giving the music, and as in the first example cited, the rubric occupies the space normally taken by the notation: lacking colour on a film, then, a rubric may be identified sometimes by this means:

Sometimes the initial begins the text of the lower text-and-music pair, as in the first diagram: the upper pair then completes the previous item. On the other hand, the initial may lead to the upper pair, as in the second diagram, and what follows the rubric is the text and music of a turnover ending the preceding item: the lower pair continues the item begun after the initial. In these two cases and in the very first example cited it may be very difficult to separate, on a film, the text of the item from the lower line of the rubric. Occasionally, as in the *orientibus* and *Dicit* examples above, the rubric may be written between the syllables of text when they are widely separated because of the musical style, and the appearance may be that of a continuous word. Rubrics are rarely in the margins unless they are later additions.

602 Another basic feature of manuscript organization, and a possible cause of some of the preceding characteristics, concerns the division of the page into columns. Some manuscripts adopt the two-column format, others the long-line method. Apart from the fact that the one or the other may help to identify a particular 'school' of manuscript production, the difference between the two is of little concern here. The former method may have been used because it alleviated the problem of the turnover: shorter lines may more easily be filled with the odd word or two left over, so that awkward interpolations do not occur so often. Without describing particular sources in some detail, a task which will occupy later sections, it is impossible to be more precise about the positioning of rubrics, turnovers, genre abbreviations, and other pieces of information, but the practice from source to source seems in its general principles to be fairly consistent. A detailed study of the organization, layout, and order of writing of liturgical books is needed. Hints about the order in which the various elements were added will appear in the course of this chapter.

Capital letters and initials

603 The characteristics of capital letters and initials are important for determining the position and genre in liturgical manuscripts and, as with the format just described, the principles used seem to be fairly consistent throughout the later middle ages. Nevertheless, an accurate and detailed study needs to be undertaken.[6] Descriptions of the style of initial or decoration, and technical names such as historiation, or flourished Lombards, and the like, will not find a place here. Such decorations are certainly related to the size and importance of a capital letter but the matter can be investigated, to lay a ground for later work, without the use of specialized knowledge of decorative styles. A terminology is needed, and the first but not the only criterion is that of size.

Henceforth the word initial, which will apply to letters at the margin such as the one beginning this sentence, must be carefully distinguished from the word capital. This sentence begins with a capital letter, which may appear anywhere within the writing space. Each of these words will acquire more precise and specialized meanings.

604 To be quite precise we may refer to letters which begin statements, texts, or important words by sizes, using a number to specify the number of lines of normal script into which the letter fits: it must be noted immediately, however, that the sizes ought to be relative within a single source rather than absolute. The most common liturgical initial, for example, occupies two lines of script (size 2) but in source G7 it spans two musical staves as well as their lines of text. Idiosyncracies need to be recorded. It will also be convenient to have names:

(1) Size 1 I shall refer to by the unqualified word 'capital.' This letter does not extend appreciably into the space below or above the line of letters, is normally not coloured, nor highlighted,[7] nor washed with colour. It occurs wherever it is required, and does not demand to be placed at the beginning of the next line. The frontispiece has many, such as the O of the first word *Dominica* (a special case following an initial), and the P five lines below it, the A in the same line as the P, and the E two lines below.

(1+) Size 1+, or the 'large capital,' extends into the space above the line of letters. It may be coloured, and if it is not it is usually highlighted. Like the capital, the large capital does not demand a new line, and occurs wherever it is required. None occurs in the frontispiece. Plate 1e has several, such as the Q, N, C (almost in the gutter), P, O, and P in column two of the left-hand leaf.

(1 + 1) In some sources, especially those with plainsong, another capital which I

shall call the 'extended capital' is distinctly larger than the previously described letter, extending well into the musical stave. It is usually not coloured, and it may have a highlight. Unlike the other capitals it normally appears at the margin. This letter or in its absence the size 1+ capital is often hard to distinguish from the smallest initial, which may be lesser in some quality (not necessarily size) than the size 2 initial to be described below. Plate 3 has several. At the foot of column two of plate 14b is a size 1 capital for *Nuntia*, a large capital (size 1+) for *Tollite*, and, above, an extended capital for *Qui*. The distinction here is between repetenda, verse, and responsory, respectively.

605 All capital letters are fundamentally 'calligraphic.' That is, they are the work of the scribe rather than of an artist, and consist only of penwork sometimes with a highlight. They will be entered by the scribe when he writes the text. This is not the case with the larger letters. It is possible, however, that the plain initial, size 2, when it is calligraphic (and thus lesser than the normal size 2), was added by the scribe as he wrote. On plates 17 & 22, for example, are numerous large letters occupying a complete text-line and stave, but which appear calligraphic and lesser than the full initial. The distinction between the L, D, and N at the left-hand margin of plate 22d and the L and Q within the text is very plain.

(2), or (1 + 1) This letter occupies two lines of text and usually the space above the upper line of text, and thus is called size 2, or an 'initial.' In the case of a manuscript with music, it extends from the line of text to the top of the musical stave accompanying that text, that is, one line of text and one stave (1 + 1). The plain initial, not necessarily completely undecorated but certainly calligraphic rather than artistic, occurs in some sources in certain circumstaces. The normal initial of this size, probably the most common initial in a liturgical book, is decorated, usually with black filigree penwork, foliage, etc, and is coloured in some of its area with red, or blue, sometimes gold or silver, and may be highlighted with a third colour. Because of its still relatively small size, it is rarely historiated or inhabited (that is, containing real pictures) although occasionally faces are later inscribed into the framework. A large capital letter usually follows it for the second letter of the word, a convention which is frequently observed even in modern printing. Requiring spaces to be left in the two text lines or in the line and stave, the initial letter is almost always placed within the ruling of the column or page, at the margin. Exceptions do occur, where the letter is in the margin,[8] or where the letter is run on within the course of the line, as with the D in the middle of column two, left-hand leaf, of plate 17. These exceptions are sometimes difficult to explain when the organization of the manuscript layout is considered. Advance planning seems to have been necessary, the scribe merely leaving space in his text, with a tiny cue-letter to indicate to the artist which letter to insert. We must distinguish here between 'at the margin' and 'in the margin.' In the latter case, rare, no spaces in the text lines need to be left. The letters I and J, and the ascenders or descenders of letters such as P and L, are always in the margin, beyond the left-hand edge of script, even when the convention is 'at the margin': the latter terminology will include these apparent exceptions. In addition, the size of these letters does not really conform to the principle established earlier. An initial I or J or L which is clearly equivalent to size 2 usually extends for more than two lines of text: the loop of the P will occupy the square left blank in two lines of text while its descender may extend two or three more lines downwards, outside the writing area.[9] When such letters or extensions occur in the gutter margin, they may be difficult to see, especially on a microfilm of a tightly bound book. Examples may be seen in many of the plates in appendix IX; plates 1, 8, 9, 13, and 14 have several.

606 In certain circumstances it is not possible to insert a required initial. Where two such initials occur on consecutive lines of text, one must be sacrificed: this rarely happens because the initial is normally used only for quite substantial texts. Similarly a size 2 initial is usually replaced with a smaller one on the lowest line of the page where it would otherwise extend into the lower margin. Some exceptions may be observed.[10] The letter I once again adapts itself somewhat differently, being broken and bent around the corner in these circumstaces, so that its lower half lies horizontally under the lowest line (plate 21). On the other hand, capitals in the top line may occasionally be extended upwards into the top margin even though they may thereby be made into initials and their size may be inconsistent.[11] The 2-line initial normally begins the text continued in the upper of the two lines (**601**). In some sources, especially when the initial is in rather than at the margin, the size of this most frequent letter may be three or even four lines although it will still be referred to as a size 2 initial, if necessary as size 2 (4): such a letter may begin any one of the three or four lines of text.

Larger initials will be so called, often with a figure in parentheses to indicate the number of lines. They extend from three or four lines to the whole page and are used to denote the major landmarks of a manuscript, and are always the product of the artist rather than the scribe. As we shall see, there seems usually to be no hierarchy within the larger initials themselves.

607 Although size has been chosen, and rightly so, as the first criterion of a letter's importance, it is by no means the only one. First, only the upward size of the letter has been considered with the assumption that letters except those mentioned are more or less square in outline. At least one source used for this book increases the width of the letter to stress its importance.[12] Plates 7a-b show the different versions of an E and H. Colour is the second criterion by which a letter must be judged. Gold leaf may raise the status of a size 2 initial, as with the letter which begins *Zelus domus tue* (the first antiphon at Matins of Maundy Thursday) in a Breviary from the Abbey of Bec.[13] As already stated, colour will usually have to be ignored here, for the sake of users of black and white microfilms. The colour schemes of certain sections of several manuscripts, examined in the original for precisely this purpose, will be described in appendix IV. Even on a film, however, it is possible to observe differences between black and grey. Black usually represents blue or black, the two being virtually indistinguishable, and grey represents red. Fortunately, the initial is normally red or blue and the two colours tend to alternate. The difference between a plain or calligraphic black initial and one coloured blue must be based on the amount of decoration that is used, and this is generally a safe guide. Just as the successive initials will tend to alternate betwen red and blue, so the larger capital, when it is used for successive verses of sequences of hymns or psalms, or any other item with multiple short verses, will alternate similarly. This conjunction of alternating colour, black/grey or blue/red, taken with the length of the item, makes such genres easy to identify. The alternation of colour, as with all the criteria discussed here, will be related to other specific circumstances in the following chapters.

608 For a number of genres with which an opening formula is used, the actual letter appearing as an initial may be some clue. Most obvious in this respect are the epistle and gospel at Mass, and the prayer, all of which normally begin with an initial. Epistles frequently begin with the formula whose first word is either *Fratres* or *Karissime/Carissime*: the latter form of the second word is rare and the K, since it too is otherwise rare, makes the genre easy to identify. The Kyrie is the only other item which begins with the letter, but this genre usually appears in quite another section of the book (plate 5 shows the K in a Litany). Gospels almost invariably begin with *In illo tempore* or *In diebus*, but the identifying letter is often lost in a tightly bound margin. Moreover, almost any other genre may begin with the letter. The initial which begins the prayer is more variable, but the following five words, three letters, are common: *Da . . .*, *Dominus . . .*, *Deus . . .*, *Presta . . .*, *Omnipotens . . .* Special instances such as the series of solemn prayers on Good Friday, all beginning with the initial O (plates 18a & b), or the series of great O antiphons of Advent, will be mentioned later. The large capital, being buried within the writing space, is more difficult to see quickly, athough in the original the highlight helps. A few letters may be singled out. All begin rubrics which specify days or feasts, and the large capital is the letter normally used for rubrics. Common are: *In . . .*, *Dominica . . .*, *Sancti . . .*, *Feria . . .* (plates 1, 2, 7b, 11, 22).

609 Two matters affecting the ordinary letters can help us to identify genres. The first is the simple number of ordinary letters present in the text itself; the second is their size. Certain items in the liturgy tend to be very long: one may cite the readings at Mass and Matins, and especially the Passions during Holy Week. Normally each of these will be introduced with an initial, and thereafter subsequent sentences will begin with a capital, or perhaps an uncoloured large capital. This arrangement can easily be contrasted with the other long texts which may occur, for example in psalms or hymns, where subsequent sentences, or verses, begin with large capitals alternating in colour and regularly spaced throughout the text. Other items are shorter. The differences between prayers and chapters is not great, either in length or in the kinds of capital letters used: both begin with an initial and later use capitals where necessary. Other long or short texts have something distinctive such as repetitive refrains, as in Litanies, or musical chants, as with Prefaces. The musical items themselves are of course obvious in manuscripts which transmit the music: where the chants themselves are omitted, the texts of musical items are distinct because they are conventionally written smaller than the other texts. There are exceptions to this procedure, and in some manuscripts the difference in size is slight enough to be difficult to perceive. Whether provided with music or not, many musical items already mentioned can be distinguished from others by the length and by the arrangement of initials and capitals. It is more difficult to distinguish other musical items when no music is given, but some guides may be given. To anticipate future chapters, we may observe the following. Antiphons, for example, will usually be continued with a brief psalm incipit involving a red abbreviation such as Ps or its rebus ℣ and a subsequent capital or large capital. Introits are continued similarly with a doxology and psalm verse; responsories, on the other hand, like graduals and alleluias, have a fairly long verse with red abbreviation ℣ (here represented by V) and a capital, and later a cue-word for the repetenda, also with a capital.

610 Paleographical matters cannot be dismissed without mentioning the notation of the music, a study of which is not normally a part of the medievalist's training, but one whose lack makes it impossible to examine or describe many liturgical books comprehensively. Distinguishing between obviously different forms of notation is not difficult, and the technical terms present no large task to master.[14] Reading the music itself need not be of primary concern except in detailed study, and if it is needed, presents little difficulty in sources from the later middle ages, at which time square notation on the stave had become more or less universal, except for the Gothic notation of German sources. Both square and Gothic notation can be read with little or no knowledge of music, once the ability to read in various C clefs is mastered.

Music

611 Music, or musica, without which no medieval discipline is complete,[15] often supplies a major part of the evidence about many liturgical and other medieval manuscripts. This evidence is often ignored perhaps because of false assumptions that skills or innate qualities of musicianship are necessary for an examination of plainsong. Such is not the case.

A spiritual and theological meaning may attach to the music, although it seems likely that it attaches to the words rather than to the notes. In any case, we are not concerned with such meanings, which could vary as many times as there are persons explaining them. No one can state what a piece of medieval music means. It may be possible to say what individual symbols mean in the sense that one can give them other names or say what they represent. This substitution of names is a matter of learning some terminology. In every other respect examining a piece of plainsong can be likened to the examination of any set of 'meaningless' symbols: they can only be described. Description can take the form of everyday and commonsense geometric and mensural words, such as 'a black square 3 cm by 2 cm, with a descending tail to the right, sitting on the third line from the bottom of a four-line system of parallel lines, that system having a C-shaped sign on the fourth line up, at the beginning,' or it can take the form of technical language, such as 'a black virga B'. Whichever kind of description is used, and naturally the former will be extremely cumbersome, there is little that can be done with plainsongs except to describe them thus, and to compare them. I have outlined the kind of general styles that plainsongs fall into (**227-30**). There ends what may profitably be said about most isolated chants. Of much more value and importance is the comparative study of chants, either chronologically, comparing a single chant as it develops from the earliest available source, or 'horizontally,' comparing the same chant in numerous contemporaneous sources. Either procedure can be carried out by a simple visual collation, symbol by symbol, and either may be very useful for relating manuscripts to each other, for assigning sources to particular areas or provenances or scriptoria, or possibly for assigning manuscripts to certain clerics (**20**).

612 The musical evidence can be presented, therefore, as a simple matter of comparison, a visual and relatively easy mechanical task involving no musical judgement. Where the procedure becomes more difficult is in the matter of deciding what is a legitimate variant and what is an error, a matter which has been mentioned with regard to the texts. Where we can state certainly that *Omnipotens Deus creatura mundi* or *Qeus qui* are errors because of the false or incomprehensible meaning of the words, we cannot state whether the sequence of musical pitches DCDFGAGA is an error for or an intentional variant of FCDFGAAFGA because the pitches are 'meaningless' in the verbal sense: the common core of the tune is the general movement DFGA. The more material given in exactly the same notation that two chants have in common, the more likely are they to be essentially the same tune, and here we must observe that tunes are often adapted to fit numerous different texts with precisely the kind of variant already exemplified. In the same way as texts, chants too are often composed by rearranging and repositioning standard formulas. Deciding whether chants are the same, or are adaptations, or are essentially different may be made easier if the scholar has musical judgement, but even when made by a musical scholar the result is just as likely to be statistical as musical. Unfortunately, just as it is difficult to link slightly variant texts because their position in alphabetical lists may be widely separated, the indexing of variant tunes such as DCDFGA and FDCFGA suffers from the same difficulty. Liturgical indices, both of texts and chants, must be compiled according to principles which are not based entirely on alphabetical information: no such principles have been formulated and here is not the place to discuss them, but I may mention that indexing by motive or idea or by general shape may be a promising alternative.

Before leaving this topic, and so that the simplest of technical terms may be introduced later in this study, I give here below the minimum information needed for any person to understand square notation, that of plates 4, 7, 22 and others: Gothic notation, found in sources of Eastern Europe, merely substitutes for the square symbols other shapes resembling horseshoe nails, whence its alternative name *hufnagel* notation (plates 3, 15, 17).

Stave (or staff)

613 By the late middle ages this usually consists of four parallel red lines enclosing three spaces. Part of a theoretically infinite system of lines and spaces, it provides, by both its lines and its spaces, the means by which the note symbols may be given particular letter names. In some rare cases where four are not needed, fewer lines may be used, and occasionally drypoint ruling is involved. The normal ruling of the page offers the skeleton onto which the stave is superimposed, although the different systems of positioning the stave have been little investigated: Van Dijk made an admirable start.[16] An archaic feature sometimes appears in conjunction with the stave. Here, the stave consists of red or black and drypoint lines in combination with one red and one yellow line either of which may coincide with one of the lines or one of the spaces of the stave.[17] The red and yellow lines specify the location of the pitches F and C respectively and they thus serve as clefs.

Clefs

614 At the beginning of each stave, and often at new sections within the stave, one of several symbols is placed to specify the pitch which is represented by the line or space on which the clef falls. Each of the clefs is in origin a letter made into a stylized symbol. The following occur in descending order of frequency: 𝄡 𝄢 (or 𝄢) ♭ ♮ D g. These specify the pitches: C, F, B flat, B natural, D, G. The last two do not appear in the plates included here. The frontispiece has examples of all the others: two forms of the F in the right-hand column, the B flat & natural (added later?) in the left-hand column. Other examples are in plates 27a-c and 28a-c (closeups). From the letter name of one line or space given by the clef, the letter names of all the others can be deduced if the repeated series of pitches ABCDEFG ABCDEFG ABC . . . is located in the relevant position. The height of the stave is of course much less than in the exploded diagram; indeed it may even be less than one centimetre. Occasionally, extra lines are added above

———— E
D
𝄡———— C
B
———— A
G
———— F

or less often below in order to extend the stave temporarily, but the same effect can be achieved more easily by moving the clef up or down or changing it as necessary. It is very easy to confuse such a change of clef with some of the symbols for the notes. The two clefs for the note B, flat and natural, simply change the 'colour' of the pitch B and may, in preliminary work, be regarded as optional alternatives varying from source to source. They do not necessarily appear immediately before the symbol to which they refer, even though in modern notation such would indeed be the case.[18]

Note symbols, neumes

615 The symbols, called neumes, which actually stand for the musical pitches are, theoretically, square in the notation under discussion. This may range from the geometric rectangle to the rectangle attenuated in the vertical direction to the square with rounded corners verging on the round note shapes of modern notation. Three symbols are used for single notes:

(*virga*) (*punctum*) (*currentes*).

The last symbol is used only in series and almost always descending from one of the other symbols, except in recited chants such as Prefaces where it may be used in the same way as the others. The *virga* and *punctum* appear also in other music of the period, where they are called *longa* and *brevis*; these have obvious implications of duration in the mensural system of rhythmic music used in the middle ages: in plainsong, however, they appear to have no rhythmic meaning and the use of one symbol rather than the other seems to be quite arbitrary, unrelated to rhythm or to accent or to syllable or to any other ascertainable feature of performance.[19]

Pitches are often joined together in symbols sometimes known as compound neumes. These consist of the original rectangles linked by thin lines or sometimes by oblique bars. Here are some typical forms:

When the pitches are vertically 'coincident,' as in the first of these shapes, the lower pitch is read first. In the case of the oblique shapes, as in the third of these, only the extreme notes are represented. Various combinations of these neumes may occur. They are best referred to in common sense terms as two- or three- or four-note neumes, with a more precise geometrical description if that is necessary. Each shape does have a technical name. It is not clear why compound neumes were used in plainsong, except for the obvious traditional retention of earlier forms, but they have a clear relationship to the text: only one syllable of text may occur on any neume. Where the musical style is largely syllabic, few compound neumes can be used because of this limitation. On the other hand, in highly florid and melismatic chants, may compound forms are possible.

616 To the *virga* and *punctum*, and occasionally to the final symbol of a compound neume, there may be added a short tail, upwards or downwards from the right-hand edge: the long tail of the *virga* in this case is transferred to the left-hand edge. Sometimes this short tail, called the *plica*, is thickened at its end to form a smaller note:

The shapes may be rounded, as in the final ones shown here. The last form seems to be peculiar to English sources (plate 27a, above *Dum*, and 27b to c). Other plicas are in plates 14a, above the C of *Conditor* and above *Con*, and 9. The plica represents a note, generally the pitch between the pitch of the symbol to which it is attached and the pitch of the next symbol, and this note is ornamental in nature. Definitions given in medieval treatises do not allow us to be precise as to its length or to the exact way in which it is sung.[20] Nevertheless, it is clear that the plica is always associated with consonant clusters in which a nasal or liquid consonant usually forms the first element: o*mn*i, vi*nd*icta, exsu*lt*a. Neumes with plicas are called liquescent.

Late medieval manuscripts do not use any other directly musical symbols such as those found in modern chant books: the dots, signs for lengthening or accent to be found in the latter are quite foreign although similar signs may appear in very early chant manuscripts. Only the incise, a small stroke drawn vertically on the stave, is to be found and seems to serve to clarify the position of notes with regard to syllables. As with all such matters, experience enables many pitfalls and ambiguities to be avoided. Comparison of a medieval chant with its version in modern printed books may be of help. The above information, concerned only with the paleographic and visual presentation of plainsong, should enable anyone to describe the appearance of music in most late medieval sources, whether liturgical or not, and to compare melodies with each other. For the liturgical scholar, some knowledge of the melodic modes which apply to plainsongs would also be of use.

The modes

617 Only the minimum of information can be supplied here and more detailed discussions should be sought.[21] The modes are theoretical abstractions by which medieval theorists attempted to classify the musical formulas which recur constantly in most plainsongs. Thus a series of pitches, like a recurrent series of words in a text, may give a number of chants a set of common characteristics. The series DCDABA, for example, together with other formulas, characterizes mode 1, while the series EDGACB characterizes mode 3. Modes can be deduced most securely by means of the formulas which they employ: this procedure, however, demands a knowledge of plainsong more thorough than even musical scholars usually possess, and is the least frequently used. Instead, a set of 'rules of thumb' which are mostly accurate but which can also fail has been worked out. Three criteria are sought, from which the mode can be identified: (1) the pitch on which the melody ends, called the final, (2) the range of the chant with respect to that final, that is, the highest and lowest pitches of the melody, (3) the pitch on which the recitation is sung, likely to be prominent as a repeated note, especially in verses of responsorial chants. Best referred to, for this reason, as the reciting tone, it is sometimes less desirably called the *tuba* or *tenor* or (most undesirably) the dominant. These criteria, the second of which in particular is rather variable, are most easily applied to the central repertory of plainsong, misleadingly called Gregorian,[22] which dates essentially from the 9th century. Chants which originate from earlier periods, such as hymns and Prefaces, and those which are clearly newly-composed in later eras, such as chants for many items of the ordinary of the Mass, seem less susceptible to modal analysis. Chronological distinctions of this kind have not been comprehensively determined. Thus, there are a goodly number of plainsongs whose modes cannot so neatly be circumscribed as figure 6.1 would

FIGURE 6.1
The musical modes and their names

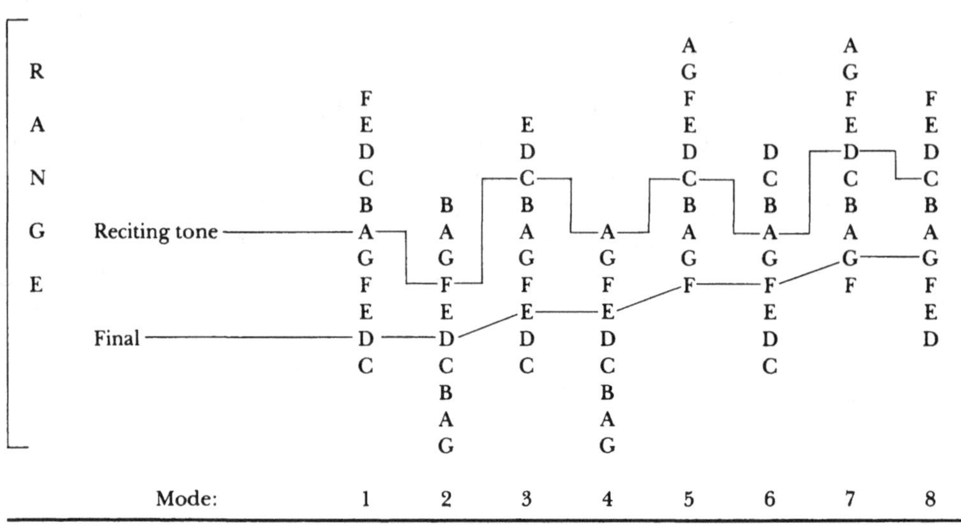

ALTERNATIVE NAMES
Mode 1 or I: Mode I authentic; Dorian; protus authentic.
Mode 2 or II: Mode I plagal; Hypodorian; protus plagal.
Mode 3 or III: Mode II authentic; Phrygian; deuterus authentic.
Mode 4 or IV: Mode II plagal; Hypophrygian; deuterus plagal.
Mode 5 or V: Mode III authentic; Lydian; tritus authentic.
Mode 6 or VI: Mode III plagal; Hypolydian; tritus plagal.
Mode 7 or VII: Mode IV authentic; Mixolydian; tetrardus plagal.
Mode 8 or VIII: Mode IV plagal; Hypomixolydian; tetrardus plagal.

suggest. In fact a ninth irregular mode called the *tonus peregrinus* had to be added to the eight defined in the diagram:[23] this is used only for Ps 113, *In exitu Israel*, and is characterized by a different reciting note for each half of the verse. The terminology and numbering by which the modes are named is not consistent, even in modern practice, and the most common alternatives are shown. The Greek names and numbers should be avoided. (See figure 6.1). It should be observed that, as the alternative names suggest, modes 1 and 2, 3 and 4, etc, have certain features in common: their common final is evident, and they share a number of melodic formulas. Only the really melodic plainsongs, the hymns, antiphons, responsories, invitatories, and the proper and ordinary chants of the Mass, are truly assignable to a particular mode on the basis of the various criteria mentioned: items such as readings and dialogues are not described in modal terms since their music consists largely of repeated notes. Psalms are also recited mostly on a single repeated pitch, which is within the modal framework and whose characteristics are described in the Tonary.

The Tonary, Tonale

618 Psalms are sung on the reciting notes of the modes as shown in the preceding section. Thus, in mode 1 the psalm will be recited on the pitch A: the same psalm may be assigned to any one of the other modes, or to the *tonus peregrinus*, and the correct reciting note will be chosen according to the modal assignation. Psalms are assigned to a particular mode on the basis of the antiphon which accompanies them. The choice of mode for that antiphon has been described. Thus, with an antiphon in mode 7, Ps 118 will be recited on D, with an antiphon in mode 3 it would be sung on the pitch C. In this respect the lesser and greater canticles, and the verses of introits, offertories, communions, and responsories are similar, their reciting note being chosen according to the mode of their refrain. The invitatory follows special principles of its own (**624**).

619 Two points of articulation are needed within the flow of the recited psalm verse (or canticle verse, introit verse, etc), corresponding to the end of the half-verse and the end of the complete verse. Occasionally, where even the half-verse is very long, a subsidiary point of articulation is used. The articulation at the half-verse and the subsidiary articulation, called *mediatio* and *flexa* (mediation and flex) respectively, generally involve the pitch below and above the reciting note to give shape to the verse with a simple musical curlicue: the exact melodic movement differs from mode to mode. The articulation at the end of the verse is more elaborate; its use at the end of every psalm verse, whence the word *terminatio*, stems from the era when the refrain occurred after every verse. Its other function as a terminal articulation ensured its survival at the end of every verse even when the refrain had been eliminated except after the final verse. Since the antiphon, or refrain, could begin with a number of different pitches and formulas, the termination itself had to vary so that a smooth transition could always take place. Each mode therefore has a number of termination formulas and, reflecting this, an alternative name for the *terminatio* is *differentia*, sometimes rendered in English as the *difference* (I shall use differentia). Offertories and communions have lost their verses: responsories and their verses are not interchangeable as psalms and antiphons are. The question of the differentia therefore arises only with psalms, canticles, introit verses, and their refrains, and relates to the link between the end of the psalm verse (or doxology) and the first words and pitches of the antiphon.

Conversely, the last pitches of the antiphon (or its intonation) meet the beginning of the reciting tone. Here too there must be a smooth join, but since the antiphon always finishes with the final of the mode only one linking formula is needed, this being called the *intonatio*. Unlike the differentia, this is sung only when the antiphon is adjacent.

620 The psalm and antiphon are the simplest and most representative pair: in order to sing the psalm properly, the mode must be ascertained from the accompanying antiphon. Once this has been done the correct intonation, flexa, and mediation for that mode can be sought in the Tonary. To my knowledge there are no medieval rules describing the principles by which every psalm verse may be set with correct accentuation and syllabification to the musical formulas of these articulations but there is generally little question if proper accentuation is followed: modern liturgical chant books give a 'pointing' of some kind from which the setting can be realized. The correct termination or differentia has to be chosen according to the opening formula of the antiphon. This opening is called the *variatio*, the variation. All possible variations are listed in a comprehensive Tonary, together with the differentias which fit them: generally a single differentia will serve for a large number of variations. Another means of ascertaining the correct differentia will be described later. Here it may be more useful to complete the description of the Tonary in its best and most comprehensive form.

621 Needless to say, Tonaries vary from use to use according to the musical peculiarities of the Order or rite or era, but the general principles remain the same. Also, the organization of this complicated book is greatly variable: the form below presents the contents logically. Each mode may be presented in turn, and usually after a general description the reciting tone will be given on a musical stave with the proper intonation, flexa, and mediation. Sometimes this is complemented with a short melody called the (p)neuma which is said to represent the essential melodic formulas characteristic of the mode: the neuma is occasionally added, as a textless extension, to certain plainsongs,[24] but it is not precisely the same as the neuma or jubilus added to the alleluia. Within the description of each mode, there should follow a list of the variations of the antiphons, categorized in some way into groups, and each group should be associated with the correct differentia to be used to link the reciting note with each of the variations. The differentia, since it comes at the end of the verse and at the end of the psalm itself, where the join with the antiphon is most crucial, becomes associated with the last words of the doxology and may therefore be represented with a text beneath it. In the Tonary that text is most likely to be *Amen* or *seculorum Amen* or *EVOVAE*, an abstraction based on the vowels of the latter phrase. Some sources, especially those associated with Spain, use *SEVOVAE*. In the Sarum Tonary there are thirty-six variations in the antiphons of mode 1 and nine differentias corresponding to groups of them.[25] Also within each section devoted to a mode, but sometimes in a separate 'chapter' also organized modally, there should be musical examples showing the exact reciting formulas for the major canticles (*super psalmos evangelicos*) and for the introit verses, with a set of differentias as necessary for each of these. Although sung according to the same principles as psalms, the Magnificat, Benedictus, Nunc dimittis, and introit verses have, as befits their liturgical importance, reciting tones and articulations which are slightly more elaborate musically. Example A illustrates some of the features discussed in the previous paragraphs.

622 The intonations, flexas, and mediations of psalm-tones could easily be memorised so that constant reference to the Tonary, in a separate book, was not necessary. The system of variations and differentias, on the other hand, was complex enough that some reminders were convenient to have at hand in the books which actually transmit the music of the antiphons and introits, etc. Antiphonals and Graduals, and the Noted Breviaries and Noted Missals corresponding to them, therefore include the music of the differentia with the antiphon as it occurs within the book. Antiphons are set out as follows: the

EXAMPLE A

The Tonary

This page uses excerpts reproduced from pp i-lxxxvi of W.H. Frere's edition of *The Use of Sarum* (Cambridge University Press 1898), volume 2, by permission of the publisher and of the publisher of the 1979 reprint, Gregg International (an imprint of the Avebury Publishing Company).

Mode 1 To the fourth differentia belong 5 variations

variation 1

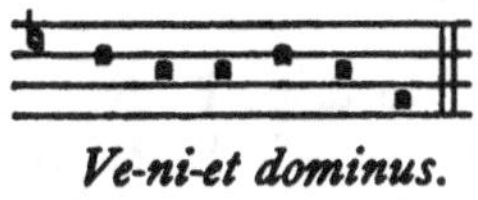

Ve-ni-et dominus.

variation 2

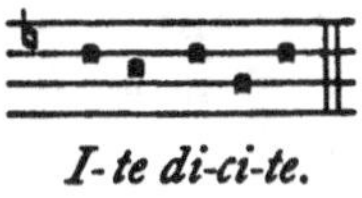

I- te di-ci-te.

variation 3

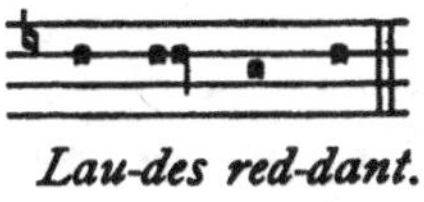

Lau-des red-dant.

variation 4

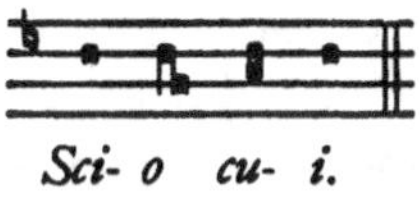

Sci- o cu- i.

variation 5

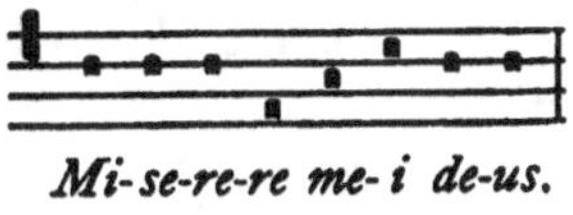

Mi-se-re-re me- i de-us.

fourth differentia *or* termination

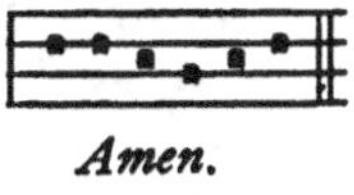

Amen.

neuma of the first mode

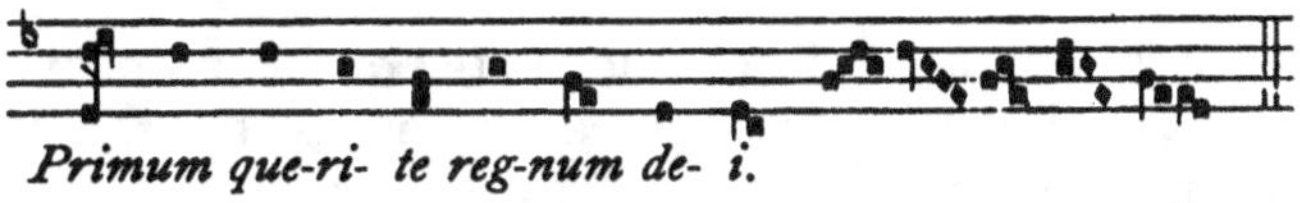

Primum que-ri- te reg-num de- i.

psalm tone

intonation reciting tone mediation reciting tone first differentia

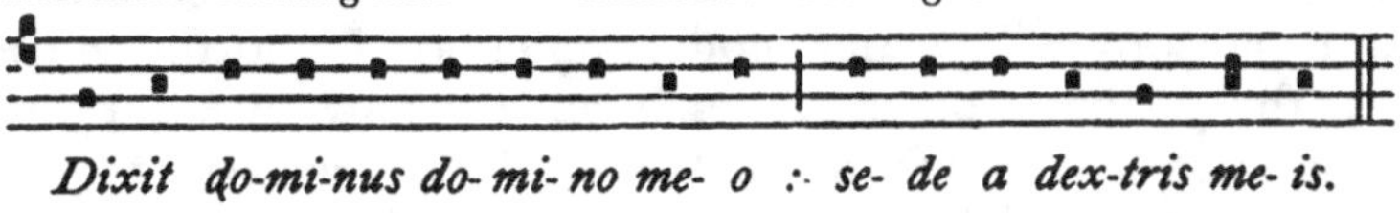

Dixit do-mi-nus do- mi- no me- o :· se- de a dex-tris me- is.

Benedictus tone

unique differentia

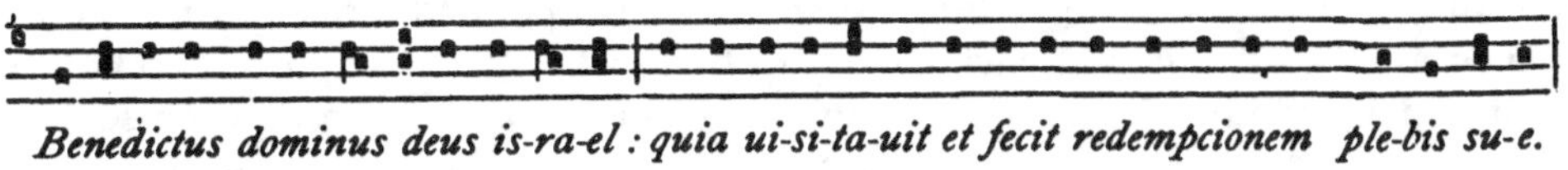

Benedictus dominus deus is-ra-el : quia ui-si-ta-uit et fecit redempcionem ple-bis su-e.

introit tone

second differentia

Beati im-ma-cu-la-ti in ui- a : qui ambulant in le- ge do-mi- ni.

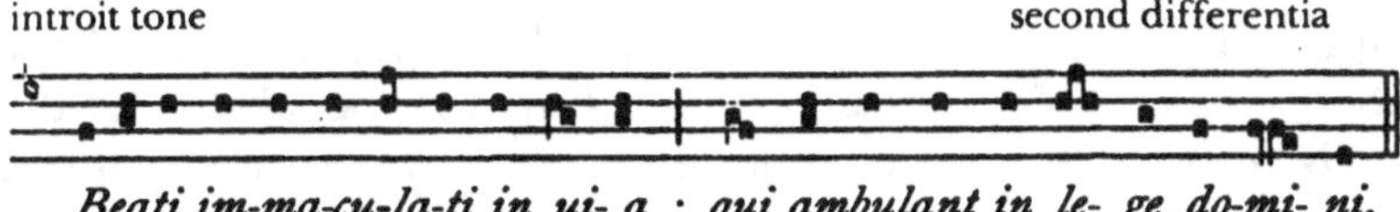

complete chant and text are given, followed by the music of the differentia, separated perhaps by an incise, or by a paraph sign, or by nothing but a new capital in the text below. When the music is run on without a clear separation the exact musical division will have to be worked out. Under the music of the differentia will appear one of the phrases already identified, *Amen, seculorum Amen, EVOVAE*, or the incipit of the psalm text itself: the combining of the incipit of the psalm text with the termination of its musical tone is not uncommon. Whatever the text at this point, the abbreviation Ps or some symbol for it will appear. In one manuscript [26] the incipit of the dialogue which follows the antiphon is written under the differentia music, another example of a format confusing enough to trap the unwary. Plates 14 and 22 show several antiphons with their psalm-incipits or terminations.

623 The responsory verses mentioned earlier but not further described must be recalled. Verses of responsories of the central repertory are clearly based on psalm tones but since they are performed by a soloist the elaboration has become extreme so that the repeated pitch is all but imperceptible amongst ornamental flourishes and melismatic decoration. Nevertheless a central responsory tone to which the decoration is added can be deduced by historical comparison and analysis.[27] In some cases, examples of the responsory tones may be included within a Tonary. Later in the middle ages, newly composed responsory verses appear and the conventional formulas are no longer used as a basis. The verse in this case is set to an independent melody.

The Invitatorium

624 The invitatory psalm is a special case. The characteristics of the psalm and its performance have been described (**618-620**). Divided into five sections, each much longer than the usual psalm verse, the text of Ps 94 is also sung to a reciting tone chosen according to the mode of the invitatory antiphon. The number of articulations is naturally greater and the tone is moderately elaborate, sometimes provided with alternative intonations and mediations. There are no invitatory antiphons in either mode 1 or mode 8 and there are therefore no tones for these modes: on the other hand there are several tones for some of the other modes. Varying from use to use, the number of tones is usually about eight or ten. They are normally presented, complete for the whole psalm, in a Tonary or an Antiphonal. In the latter case they may be given with the first appearance of the invitatory, on Matins of Advent Sunday, or elsewhere in a convenient place. The eight or ten consecutive presentations of the text, all with continuous music and each clearly in five sections, makes for a part of the Antiphonal which is visually very distinctive. The words beginning each section may be recalled from paragraph **218**: the letters beginning those words are V Q Q H Q followed by G for the doxology, also written out in full with its tone. These letters are normally size 1 + 1 initials alternating red and blue. The initial of the first section may be somewhat larger or more elaborate, and that of the doxology somewhat smaller, perhaps calligraphic. All may be placed at the margin or, unusually for initials, run on within the writing area. Plate 12 shows one complete invitatory tone and the beginning of another.

A part of an Antiphonal presenting the invitatory tones separately is sometimes called an Invitatorium.

Further information on the musical aspects of the liturgy must be sought in one of the numerous books on the topic.[28]

Summary

625 Only a few pointers can be cited with regard to the order in which the various elements of a liturgical manuscript were added to the page and how the layout was planned: much detailed study is needed before more can be said. In a manuscript without music, where the initials are within the writing area, the scribe responsible for the text must have worked first, leaving blanks as necessary for the initials. Presumably at the same time he left the spaces necessary for the rubrics and red abbreviations, and also presumably he added these elements immediately after completing the actual text. Even where the initial stands in the margin, the same commonsense approach would seem probable. See my article, "The scribe . . .".

The presence of the music complicates the matter. Not only does the length of texts without music have to be assessed carefully, but also the amount of space needed for the music on the stave, so that unnecessary space is not left over or, worse, so that the space allowed does not run out. One can only admire the skill of the planners: hardly ever in a good manuscsript is there a real miscalculation. In many cases of course a simple measurement taken from an exemplar would provide ready-made formats. When the stave has breaks for initials, or rubrics, or incipits, then surely we can assume that the text was written first, specifying the limits for the ruling of the stave. Numerous sources have, if not throughout at least in certain sections, staves with the proper texts but to which the music has not been added: the reverse situation, of musical notes to which the text has not been written, does not occur. We can conclude, therefore, that in general practice the text was entered before the music. The sequence then seems to be: (1) texts and incipits in black between and below staves and, between items, in the space elsewhere left blank for the stave, (2) addition of the rubrics, (3) ruling of the staves, (4) initials, (5) musical notes. In this order, however, there is a difficulty: to space the text of melismatic plainsongs accurately so that the syllables fall below the correct pitches, precise spacing of the musical notes appears necessary, entailing the order (1) music, (2) text. Measurement from an exemplar, or the skill of an experienced scribe-musician, may enable the reverse order to be adopted. The word 'scribe-musician' has been used because there is little information as to whether the same person wrote both text and music, or whether separate scribes were involved: if the latter, there must have been co-operation.

626 Much more accurate information could be derived from a study of the original manuscripts, where the sequence of events can often be determined by observing where a black descender from the text lies below or above another element, or the colour of a rubric or an initial or stave covers something added previously. For detailed paleographical work, there is no substitute for the original source.

It must also be stressed again that there is no substitute for an ability to read the rubrics and to know the texts themselves. But numerous conventions of scribal format can make the use of liturgical manuscripts much easier: the size, colour, and placing of capitals and initials; the length of the text; the use of certain letters to begin the formulas that conventionally introduce many texts; the size of the ordinary letters; the position of rubrics; the coloured identifying abbreviations. Recurring patterns of prayers, lessons, chants, and versicles tend to produce recurring patterns of notation, script, or layout.

The books

627 The hierarchy of initials and colours by which a manuscript is categorized into sections varies in complexity according to the contents, and the more varied the latter, the more varied and perhaps the more ambiguous will be the hierarchy. The need for and therefore the presence of organized initials arises from the additional complexity of late medieval books caused by the combination into one volume of several previously separate books. The Sacramentary, for example, by and large transmits only prayers, usually the collect, secret, and post-communion for each Mass. The Lectionary contains only the readings, the Cantatorium only the sung items. The combination of all three books into the Missal, which took place in the 11th and 12th centuries and was almost universal by the 13th, creates difficulties of separation for the scholar, although for the contemporary reader, following the items sequentially in the service throughout the year, the problems must have been less taxing. If the Missal results from the combining of three books, the Breviary draws together material from an even larger number. Some, however, such as the Psalter and Hymnal, are often kept in separate sections even though bound within the same volume. And often, a feature which is also true of the Missal, parts of the original books are kept in distinct sections at certain periods of the year. In addition to the Psalter and Hymnal, the Bible, the Lectionary, the Passional, the Homiliary, and the Martyrology may provide material for the readings; the Collectar or Orational provides the prayers; the Antiphonal, or its separate parts, the Diurnal and Nocturnal or Antiphonal and Responsorial, provides the musical items. The origin of the Breviary from these sources and the reason for applying to such a compendium a word implying brevity have been discussed many times.[29]

628 A consistent method of referring to liturgical books needs to be maintained. An excellent categorization, to which little needs to be added and few modifications seem necessary, has been published by Fiala and Irtenkauf.[30] They include the earlier books from which Missal and Breviary were compiled and which had become less important by the 13th century. Although such books (listed below with an asterisk) are not strictly relevant here, it is worth including them to illustrate the essential nature of the Missal and Breviary as compendia. The basic contents are summarized below, with some comments on Fiala's and Irtenkauf's designations. Genre abbreviations precede the descriptions, where appropriate.

BOOKS OF GENERAL USE

Ordinal: this gives incipits with substantial rubrics for the performance of Mass and office throughout the year.

Tonary, Tonale: this gives information about musical matters usually for both Mass and offices, but often excluding the invitatory.

MASS BOOKS

**Sacramentary*: O✠ (collects, secrets, Prefaces, post-communions, and *orationes super populum*)

**Lectionary*: EG (epistles, and gospels) Fiala and Irtenkauf unnecessarily call it a Voll-Lektionar because it combines *Epistle-Book* and *Gospel-Book* (or Evangeliar). They also mention books containing only the incipits of Gospels, calling them Evangelienliste.

Festal Mass-Book: this contains all Mass items, but only for selected feasts of the year. Fiala and Irtenkauf call it Missale festivum or speciale, names for which I know of no medieval documentation. It is perhaps analogous to the Book of Hours.

Ordo Misse: this has all common Mass items. Those with music may be listed separately in the Kyriale.

Kyriale: **KGCSAI** (Kyrie, Gloria, Credo, Sanctus, Agnus, Ite or Benedicamus) Tropes, especially for the Kyrie, may be given.

Gradual: **IGAOC** and where necessary **TH** (introit, gradual, alleluia, offertory, communion, tract, hymnus) Some Graduals include sequences, and in a separate section the Kyriale.

**Cantatorium*: this includes musical items (often only those sung by the soloist rather than by the choir).

**Sequentiary, Troper*: these books contain accretions, the composition of which (but not their use) had become much less common by the 13th century.

Missal: IOE**GA**GO**O**C**O** and where necessary **TH**, and the Ordo including Preface and Canon (introit, oratio [collect], epistle, gradual, alleluia, gospel, offertory, oratio [secret], communion, oratio [post-communion], tract, hymnus) A separate name should be given to the Missal which also transmits the plainsong: I shall use Noted Missal.

OFFICE BOOKS

**Collectar*: OCD□✠ (oratio, chapter, dialogue, preces, benedictions)

**Lectionary*: L (lessons) As with the gospels, some books provide only lists of incipits. Non-scriptural readings such as saints' lives may be in a Legendar, and martyrs' lives in a Passional or Martyrology.

Ordo (or *Pica*): this gives incipits for sections of the year as necessary, and is generally not found as an independent book until the 15th century.

Psalter: this contains only the psalms. It should be distinguished from the

Ferial or *Choir Psalter*, which also contains common items such as antiphons, chapters, canticles, short responsories. A Hymnal is usually appended.

Antiphonal: IARMBN and sometimes H, normally with plainsongs (invitatory, antiphon, responsory, Magnificat- and Benedictus- and Nunc dimittis-antiphons, hymn) The book is sometimes divided into Nocturnal and Diurnal or Antiphonal and Responsorial.

**Benedictional*: ✠ (blessings).

Invitatorium (or *Venitarium*): this gives musical tones for the invitatory. It is generally not found independently.

Breviary: IARMBNOCLD□✠ and often H (as under Antiphonal, with oratio, chapter, lesson, dialogue, preces, benedictions) The Ferial Psalter and Hymnal are usually included. The book is sometimes divided into volumes by season, or into nocturnal and diurnal sections. A separate name should be given to a Breviary which also transmits the plainsong (and therefore also the Invitatorium): I shall used Noted Breviary.

Book of Hours: this is essentially a late 14th- and 15th-century book for private use, excerpting from the Breviary favourite offices, such as to the Virgin and for the Dead, and special psalms.

629 It does not seem necessary to call a normal Missal or Breviary from the 13th century or later a Full missal or Full Breviary (Vollmissale, Vollbrevier), as Fiala and Irtenkauf do. I know of no medieval evidence for the terms *Missale* or *Breviarium plenum*. The terms may be useful in 11th and 12th centuries to indicate final stages in the evolution of the books as earlier ones were merged. It is true that the precise contents of Missals and Breviaries may vary, either in the original layout or through subsequent loss. The order may also vary. Such matters are important. They cannot be encompassed in an adjectival qualification to the name of the book but must be specified more carefully. Many sections of this study will be concerned with elucidating the exact contents and arrangement of the chief books.

630 Breviaries and Missals, with their musical counterparts the Antiphonals and Graduals, will be the main manuscripts for examination and fall into one category of ecclesiastical books. Very broadly, there are two categories. The first includes books which give information about the order and method of performance of the liturgy and which refer to the texts themselves only in abbreviation or by incipit. The second category complements the first by transmitting the texts and in certain cases the music. In the latter category, the information given in the former may be completely absent or may be repeated in considerable detail. There appears to be a trend at the close of the middle ages for as much information to be included as possible, presumably so as to reduce the necessity to refer to a separate book which has no direct place in the church. The inclusion of such rubrical information in books of the second category, if it is to be at all comprehensive, naturally makes the latter much more extensive, bulky, and in some respects more difficult to use. The trend is therefore by no means universal. The amount of overlapping between the two categories is so varied that generalizations can hardly be made successfully. In any case, books of the second category must be rated of primary importance, to be supplemented by reference to the 'information' books where problems occur. In this study, books of the second category are obviously the main consideration, and books of the other type have been little used: frequently they are not available, or, if known at all, have not been 'paired' with other books of the same use, or even catalogued at all. It is probably no exaggeration to state that only for the Sarum use have all the basic medieval books been published in modern editions.

631 Books for the Offices are normally kept separate from those of the Mass, although there seems to be little reason, apart from tradition and the different character of the services themselves, for this dichotomy. Here is a list of the main books relevant to each of the services, aligned so that books of the same general character are paired:

MASS	OFFICES
Main books, giving the propers for the Temporale and for feasts of the saints, and the material common to feasts of the saints (see **745-6, 888**).	
Missal	Breviary
Gradual	Antiphonal (sometimes divided into Diurnal and Nocturnal or Antiphonal and Responsorial)
Books giving the common items for the Temporale.	
Ordo misse	–
Kyriale	Ferial Psalter
–	Hymnal
Subsidiary books: Tonary, Troper or Sequentiar, Processional.	

All of the Mass books may be bound within a single set of covers and called a Missal, in which case the musical elements of the Gradual will be incorporated into the original Missal section, making the whole a Noted Missal. In view of the inconsistency with which the terms are used, a precise specification of the sections included and of the presence of the plainsongs seems advisable. Exactly the same situation applies to the books for the Office, where the name Noted Breviary is sometimes applied.

632 The proper items will most conveniently be arranged in the order they appear in the church year, and Missals, Graduals, Breviaries, and Antiphonals, are so organized. The arrangement of books containing the common items depends to a large extent on the exact nature of the items as common, ferial, seasonal, and so on, as well as on the completeness with which the main book gives the common texts. The hierarchy of initials is therefore likely to be more consistent in the books giving propers. The exact scheme can be worked out in detail for each manuscript studied, although for the experienced user this is usually an unnecessary and profitless chore. Figure 6.2, for example, gives the proper items of Vespers which one may expect to find in the seasons or on the days listed at the left. It is derived from the information summarized in figure 4.9: to make the transition clear, I repeat the details of the beginning of Advent from figure 4.9 with explanation:

Advent Vespers
P f/ A f / C 12s / R 1s / H s / D s / M p / O w

The psalms and antiphons are ferial, part of the common of the Temporale, and will thus not appear in our summary of items which will be found in

FIGURE 6.2
Proper items for Vespers on certain occasions

	Vespers 1 Saturday	Vespers 2 Sunday	ferias
Adv	CRMO	CM	M
Nat	PACRHDMO	PACRHDMO	M
Circ	CMO	M	M
Epi (oct.)	CRHDMO	HM	M
XL 1-2	CRHDMO	RM	CMO
XL 3	CRHMO	RM	MO
XL 4	CRMO	RM	MO
XL 5	CRHDMO	CRM	MO

Vespers at the beginning of this season (if any reference to them does occur, as is frequent, it will normally be in the form of incipits appearing unobtrusively in the running text, without initials). The chapter, however, is proper at both first and second Vespers and will appear in both services with its correct size 2 initial: the chapter for the weekdays, on the other hand, is seasonal, and, if it appears at all, will have no prominent initial. The responsory is proper at first Vespers and thereafter seasonal. The hymn and versicle are seasonal. The antiphon for the Magnificat is proper for both Vespers 1 and 2 and for ferias and will therefore appear in all services with its initial. The oratio, being weekly, will appear only at first Vespers, and has an initial. We could thus list the items of the first week of Advent for which there would be an initial at the margin, as follows:

Vespers 1 Saturday	Vespers 2 Sunday	ferias ii-vi
CRMO	CM	MMMMM

Since each of these items does in fact begin with a size 2 initial, one would expect to find four such initials at first Vespers, two at second Vespers, and only one for each of the weekdays Vespers. In figure 6.2, which lists some other parts of the year, not all items begin with a size 2 initial even when they appear in full in the sources: the relation between size and genre has yet to be examined. Some may begin with a much larger size; most will begin with a large capital. The elaborateness of Christmas, with its proper psalms and antiphons is clear. Figures for many services or seasons would be much more cumbersome, and their usefulness, except to present a clear picture in brief form, may be questioned.

633 Missal and Gradual, Breviary and Antiphonal differ because they are used by different people. The apparent but false distinction is that associating the former of each pair with spoken texts and the latter with music. The Missal and Breviary are essentially for the cleric celebrating the service and give all the material he must say or sing: in all but the smallest churches some of this material may be taken over by one or more ministers. The Gradual and Antiphonal are for use by the choir. Not needing before its eyes the words of the items performed by the celebrant, the choir sees only the musical items in a complete form. The celebrant, however, ought to say or sing everything, including the musical items. Where a choir is present he will read the choral-musical pieces to himself: that the responsibility for them lies elsewhere is reflected in the smaller size of the script used to write them into his books. In churches where no choir exists, or in private recitation of the office, the celebrant must perform even the choral items aloud. This he may do in a spoken voice and no music is required. The need for a Missal or Breviary with the texts of the musical pieces is therefore easy to explain. What is not easy to understand is the need for Noted Missals and Noted Breviaries. To explain the presence of music in these volumes, it has occasionally been suggested that, where a choir is not present, the celebrant might have sung all the music himself.[31] Unless a totally inadequate, and probably ridiculous, performance was frequently the case, I believe that no single person could, in addition to speaking the texts, sing the entire Mass or Office: the range of the musical chants is too great, the length of them is too extended, the difficulty of many of them, especially parts of the elaborate responsorial forms, is too taxing for any but the trained singer. The existence of the Noted books has not yet been explained to my satisfaction, and here is not the place to enter into a documented argument: my own theory is that such books may represent complete, final, reference or master copies from which all questions may be answered and from which standardized rites could be copied. Such compendia appear in the 13th century, along with the *summa* which appears in many other disciplines: these are surely *summe liturgice*. The most famous such final authority is Humbert's Codex, already mentioned in the Introduction, a compilation which contains everything relevant to the Dominican services at the time it was put together. This Codex, however, is really a collection of all the different books bound together, including the constituent elements of both Breviary and Missal. An argument for accepting the Noted book as a reference or master copy is that most of them are in very good condition, suggesting that they were not much used: the manuscript of Humbert's work, and its copy in the British Museum, both certainly used, are also in good condition.

For the moment, then, I shall adopt the theory that Missals are for the celebrant, Breviaries are for all who wish to say the offices, in public or in private, Graduals and Antiphonals are for the choir, either directly or indirectly through the precentor. Certain special Antiphonals and Graduals are for the soloists rather than the choir (**843, 7003**). Noted Missals and Noted Breviaries, on the other hand, are for reference, or are exemplars for the transmission of one rite to another institution. The *Ordo Misse*, Choir or Ferial Psalter, the Tonary, and other such books containing the ordinary or common of Mass or offices are also to be regarded as reference books, since they contain material which either through prior prescription or through constant use was memorized.

7

Mass Books

700 Missals contain all the proper texts, including those given in Graduals: Noted Missals also contain the music. Graduals, on the other hand, supply only the genres performed with melodic plainsongs; all the readings and prayers, and normally all the dialogues, are therefore omitted. With fewer items to organize, the Gradual provides a convenient introduction to the Missal.

GRADUALS

Advent

701 If there is a daily Mass, the services on weekdays normally adopt the texts of the preceding Sunday. Minor variations in the week do not affect the sung texts and are therefore not recorded in the Gradual. There are special Masses for the Ember days of the third week of Advent, and a proper Mass for the Vigil of Christmas. The identification of the end of Advent by searching for Christmas is somewhat complicated by the fact that Christmas Day has three Masses, the last of which is the most important.[1] Preceding the main service of Christmas Day, then, are four Sunday Masses, three ferial Masses in the third week, a Vigil Mass, and the two earlier Christmas Masses. Both Advent Sunday and the main Mass of Christmas are generally distinguished by the very largest initial of a manuscript, easy to identify, and intervening Masses are given the size 2 initial, which may vary in colour. The large and the size 2 initial begin the first item of each Mass, normally the introit. In carefully written sources each of the services, with the frequent exception of Advent Sunday itself, is identified by rubrics, for which there is little variation. There are noticeably different and equally correct rubrics for the Masses of Christmas Day. Ignoring different methods of abbreviation, we may expect to find rubrics such as: *Dominica prima* (*secunda, tertia, quarta,* or *i*[a], *ij*[a], etc) *in adventu* or *adventus Domini*; and for the ferial days of the third week *feria iiij* (*jejunii hiemalis* or *quatuor temporum*) etc. For the Vigil Mass there is the almost invariable *In vigilia nativitatis* (or *natalis*) (*Domini*), and for Christmas some common forms are:

Missa	in gallicantu	in aurora	ad publicam missam
	de nocte	in mane	ad magnam missam
	ad pullorum cantum	in diluculo	missa in die
			ad maiorem missam
	prima missa	missa secunda	ad summam missam

702 Identification of the day or of the service at Christmas can be secured by a combination of the initial and rubric. Unfortunately, the size 2 initial, used for the services other than Advent 1 and the main Mass of Christmas, is also commonly used for the *hymnus trium puerorum* and occasionally also for the tract, on the Saturday fast of the third week. Why these two items should be singled out for visual emphasis I do not know. Otherwise, all items after the introit begin with small initials or large capitals (size 2 – or 1 +).

There is often some form of hierarchy, and colour distinctions are reflected in the various shades of grey on microfilm. Verses sometimes begin with a capital smaller than or different from that of the main text: this is true of the psalm verse for the introit, gradual, alleluia, and offertory (if it has verses), and usually for the verses of the hymnus and tract. The refrain of the last item, and the text identifying the differentia of the introit psalm may have a yet smaller initial, probably size 1, the smallest. Frequently however, verses have a small initial the same size (2 –) as that beginning the parent chant, and in these cases the initial for the verse is likely to be more rather than less elaborate, with tracery and penwork, while the parent letter is plain. Some specific arrangements are described below.

703 Apart from the normal daily repetition of the Sunday Mass, in the nine Masses which precede the main service of Christmas Day very few items are repeated. On the fourth Sunday the gradual and communion are commonly drawn from the Mass on the Wednesday of the third week, an Ember Mass. Occasionally the alleluia for the Vigil, when the latter is on a Sunday, is the alleluia of the fourth Sunday, most items of which are superseded by the propers of the Vigil Mass. Such repetitions are not indicated fully in the sources: in careful manuscripts only the incipit is given, sometimes with the musical incipit and perhaps with a 'page-reference.' References may be in one of several forms. Where a manuscript is foliated a number, usually roman, written above or alongside the incipit may refer to the folio (verso or recto) or to the opening, that is, a facing verso and recto, on which the item occurs fully. These numbers and in many cases the foliation itself have often been added to the manuscript at a later date. Alternatively, a short rubric indicates the location of the item: *require feria quarta ante*.[2] Poor manuscripts such as G1 may omit the repeated item entirely, not giving even an incipit, or may have a rough marginal annotation perhaps scrawled in later as a matter of convenience. It is possible, in the absence of either incipit or reference or rubric, that a true variant is intended: this can be determined only by a comparative study of other books of the same use. Source G2, to be described later, gives two introits for Advent 4, each with a size 2 initial, rather close together because only the incipit of the first introit appears: the second introit, as a rubric makes clear, is for use during the week. A number of Masses in Advent have extra or perhaps alternative verses for the alleluia, and some manuscripts present verses for the offertory. Such verses are given the same class of initial or capital as other verses in the source. The alleluia for Advent 2, for example, often has an additional verse: in source G3 a complete extra alleluia with a different verse is included.[3] An additional alleluia and verse occurs in source G13 on both Advent 2 and 3 with the rubric *infra ebdomadam*, and it is entirely possible that unrubricked additional verses or items are also for use on weekdays in place of the Sunday text. Again this kind of matter can be determined only by a comparative study and an investigation of the relevant Ordinals. The inclusion of offertory verses is uncommon, marking a use as conservative by the 13th century. In the sources examined only G8 and G19 regularly give several verses, and G1 has a verse for the first Mass of Christmas. Ms G8 betrays another conservative feature since many of its communions are followed by a psalm incipit and a textual cue directing a return to a point within the communion chant itself, making the item into a responsorial form. The offertories and verses of source G19 also have similar cues.

704 It is hardly possible to generalize about the sequence and hierarchy of initials and capitals because, although the same principles recur, each manuscript differs from the next in small details. In addition, a manuscript is rarely completely consistent within itself. A few sources have been chosen to exemplify some of the points mentioned above and even in these more detailed descriptions the spirit rather than the letter of the rules by which a manuscript is organized has been singled out. Ms G2, said to be a 14th-century Gradual of Paris, is neatly written, reasonably consistent in its application of initials, capitals, and colours, and uses large initials (2 + 2) for Advent and the main Mass of Christmas: after the Advent initial the second letter is a small initial, after the Christmas initial it is an ordinary letter. There are only three smaller sizes: 2 (or 1 + 1 since this is a chant manuscript), 2 –, and 1. Size 2, following the principles outlined in sections **603-8**, and alternating quite strictly between black and a colour, is used for introits (that is, the beginnings of Masses) and for the hymnus and tracts. The next size of letter has not only a highlight but also some simple internal penwork which makes it more like an initial than a large capital: it has therefore been assigned the size 2 –. The large capital (1 +) appears rarely: the capital, slightly larger than the ordinary letter, has a highlight (size 1). Size 2 – is used for all items and verses except those mentioned and the differentia of the introit psalm, unless the item is given only in incipit. Rubrics begin with either an ordinary letter or a simple capital. We could construct a table such as figure 7.1, where the letters along the top are the abbreviations for the genres. Initials at the margin are shown in heavy brackets and coloured initials in italic heavy brackets. The ‡ denotes items presented only in incipits, the second and third column of the introit are for the psalm verse and differentia, the column following the hymnus is for its refrain. Unless a change is recorded, the arrangement is as on Advent 1. Note that the hymnus has the seventh initial in the manuscript.

FIGURE 7.1
The initials and capitals of Advent
(from a Gradual of Paris, ms G2)

The numerals indicate the size of the letter: initials at the margin are in heavy brackets and when the initial is coloured, in italic brackets. ‡ denotes items presented only in incipit. The second and third columns of the introit are for the psalm-verse and differentia: the column following the hymnus is for the refrain. Unless a change is noted, the arrangement is as on Advent 1. The dots indicate that the genre is not present on that occasion. **III** indicates a large initial.

genre:	**I**	**P-V**		**G**	**V**	**H**	refrain	**H-V**	**T**	**V**	**A**	**V**	**O**	**C**
Adv 1	**III**	2 –	1 +	2 –	2 –	.	.	.	.	.	2 –	2 –	2 –	2 –
2	*[2]*													
3	[2]													
fer. iv	*[2]*													
fer. vi	[2]												‡1 +	
sab.	*[2]*					[2]	1 +	2 –	*[2]*	2 –	.	.	2 –	2 –
Adv 4	‡[2]	.	.	.	.	.	.	.	.	.	.	.	.	.
	[2]			‡	‡									
Vig. Nat	[2]													
Nat I	*[2]*													
Nat II	[2]													
Nat III	**III**													

705 In mss G3 and G4, related sources from Austria, the large initials are black with elaborate coloured tracery, followed in the Advent Mass (plate 15) by an almost equally elaborate size 2 initial for the second letter and, as in the previous source, by an ordinary letter in the Christmas Mass. The initial, size 2, is also black with coloured tracery but coloured initials with tracery appear later in the manuscript, apparently on a more or less haphazard basis. Of the next size, 2 –, used for the beginnings of items and their verses, there seem to be three varieties alternating in a fairly consistent sequence abaca, or bcbcbc: (a) the letter has a black, firm outline with little or no tracery, (b) the letter is black with coloured tracery, (c) it is coloured with coloured tracery. The large capital is black with no tracery; the capital has only a highlight. All of these letters are shown in plates 3a-e. In figure 7.2, based on ms G4, which is more consistent, the small initial, 2 –, is replaced by the relevant letters a, b, c, just defined. It must be said immediately that figure 7.2 is probably inexact, since the shade of the size 2 initials and the difference between the b and c is slight: I suspect that as well as black and red, there are blues which differ little from black on a microfilm. Nevertheless, the difference between b or c and a is clear because it involves the kind of decoration. The four graduals of the Saturday Mass are shown, as they were not in the previous figure; after the seventh initial, the verses of the hymnus alternate small initials c and b. It is interesting to speculate about the absence of an initial of type a between the offertory and communion: elsewhere the b and c initial are not normally juxtaposed. Could this be the result of copying a hierarchy of initials from earlier sources in which the

FIGURE 7.2
The initials and capitals of Advent
(from two Graduals of Austria, mss G3 and G4)

See note to figure 7.1. In this figure, the letters a, b, and c represent different styles and colours of the small initial (size 2 –). See **705**.

genre:	I	P-V	G	V	H	refrain	H-V	T	V	A	V	O	C
Adv 1	III	a 1+	b	a	.	.	.	.	.	c	a	b	c
2	[2]	a 1+	b	a	.	.	.	.	.	b	a	c	b
3	[2]	a 1+	b	a	.	.	.	.	.	c	a	b	c
fer. iv	[2]	a 1+	b	a	.	.	.	.	.	b	a	c	b
fer. vi	[2]	a 1+	b	a	.	.	.	.	.	.	.	c	c
sab.	[2]	a 1+	b	a									
			c	a									
			b	a									
			c	a	*[2]*	1	c/b	b	a	.	.	b	c
Adv 4	[2]	a 1+	‡1+		.	.	.	.	.	c	a	b	‡1+
Vig. Nat	*[2]*	a 1+	b	a	.	.	.	.	.	‡1+		b	c
Nat I	[2]	a 1+	b	a	.	.	.	.	.	c	a	b	c
Nat II	*[2]*	a 1+	b	a	.	.	.	.	.	c	a	b	c
Nat III	III	a 1+	b	a	.	.	.	.	.	c	a	c	c

offertory verse, with an initial of type a, was present? The principles by which these sources are organized are little different from those of the first manuscript, and whatever the details, we can be sure that the verses are here distinguished from their parent chants, in contrast to those in figure 7.1.
706 In ms G13 the verses are also distinguished, in this case by the presence of ornamentation on the otherwise plain small initial (2 –) which begins the item. In this manuscript, too, the Masses on the ferias of the third week are begun

FIGURE 7.3
Initials and capitals of Advent
(from the Gradual, ms G13)

See note to figure 7.1. In this figure, the letters x and y represent the plain and ornamented size 2 – initial respectively. See **706**.

genre:	I	P-V	G	V	H	refrain	H-V	T	V	A	V	O	C
Adv 1	III	y	x	y	.	.	.	.	.	x	y	x	x
2	[2]												
3	[2]												
fer. iv	x												
fer. vi	x									.	.	‡1	
sab.	x				x	1+	1+	x	y	.	.	x	x
Adv 4	[2]		‡1		.	.	.	.	.				‡1
Vig. Nat	[2]		x	y									x

with this lesser initial rather than with the full size 2 letter. Neither the hymnus nor the tract is emphasised by a larger letter. The plain and ornamented size 2 – initial will be represented by x and y respectively. (See figure 7.3)

707 Some Graduals, including G7 and G11, have sequences in their correct positions after the alleluia. Like the hymnus and occasionally the tract, sequences begin with a size 2 initial: subsequent verses adopt the large capital (1+), normally alternating blue and red. When the following item, the offertory, also begins with a large capital, the quick identification of that item may be difficult. Separation of the two, and indeed identification of sequences themselves, is easy in manuscripts with music because the notation, which reflects the musical style, is distinct (**228-9, 615**). Other accretions to the proper chants occur but rarely. Source G2 has a two-'verse' extension to the communion of the second Christmas Mass, the second part of which is called a *prosa*. This *prosa* text reappears in G8 as an offertory verse for the same Mass: the possible relationship between verses and tropes has not been explored. Ms G19 has the incipits of two psalm verses for the introits of most Masses, an addition which may be to allow for a longer procession in the church for which this stational manuscript was used. G20, another stational source, does not have the extra verses. The main Mass for Christmas in G10 has an introductory trope to the introit, *Hodie cantandus est nobis puer* . . ., followed by the apparent rubric *ps[almus]* (although the next text, *Quis est iste*, is not from a psalm) and a verse, *Hic enim* . . . The trope has an initial corresponding to those at the beginning of normal Masses and the verses have large capitals.

708 Also equal to the initials at the beginnings of Masses are those for additional items in source G21. In this manuscript, which has lost most of Advent, the *Liber generationis* of Christmas Eve is given in full with the reading tone and the preceding versicles, introduced with the rubric: '*in nocte nativitatis Domini post nonam lectionem cantetur et postea hunc evangelium in pulpitum legatur* Dominus vobiscum. Et cum spiritu tuo. Sequentia sancti . . . Gloria tibi Domine. Liber generationis . . .' The words *Dominus* and *Liber* begin with size 2 initials; subsequent sentences begin with alternating red and blue large capitals. At the end of the reading a further rubric instructs that '*sacerdos in capa serica incipiat* Te Deum, *quo dicto rector chori incipiat missam*.' This reading, which really falls within Matins, is usually recorded in the Antiphonal or Breviary. The following Mass, the first of Christmas, also has an additional *lectio* after the collect and before the epistle, noted with music at the end of a longer rubric which will be discussed later: '*Duo clerici de secunda forma in capis sericis in pulpito simul cantent lectio* Laudes Deo.' This consists of a series of trope-sentences beginning *Laudes Deo* alternating with a reading from Isaiah: the letter L is a size 2 initial, and each subsequent sentence begins with a large capital. Rather than these large capitals alternating in colour, as is usually the case in this kind of item, the sentences themselves alternate in colour, distinguishing the trope-sentences from those of Isaiah.[4]

709 Five sources combine the Temporale with the feasts of the Sanctorale, a conservative feature (G6, G7, G8, G9, and G19). In none does the feast of St

Andrew occur, nor do any include information about the adjustments necessary when the saint's day falls on one of the Sundays or fasts. Such instructions would presumably be in the Ordinals. The initial hierarchy is no different from that of Temporal Masses and only the rubric preceding the introit, or the initial picture if historiation is present (and of course the texts themselves), identify the feast. G6 has a marginal picture of St Lucy, denoting the only saint's feast included. G6, G8, G9, and G19 include only St Lucy, placing her Mass immediately after Advent 2 even though her feast, 13 December, can fall before or after or on the third Sunday. G19 includes the date as part of the rubric: *natale s. lucie m̅ Dec. d xiii.* G7 is more complicated: after the Mass of Advent 2 the manuscript gives the feasts of Nicholas, the Conception, Lucy, and Thomas the apostle, the first two of which straddle (that is, fall before, after or on) the second Sunday. Lucy straddles the third, and Thomas comes after the third but may fall on the fasting days or the fourth Sunday. The principle of incorporating saints in groups into the Temporale, as though transferred in a group from a Sanctorale, seems in general to outweigh the convenience of placing the feast nearer its place with respect to the Sundays. As is apparent from the arrangement of G7, Thomas the apostle's Mass is placed with those of the other saints even though several Temporal Masses intervene before it would have been sung. In G7, too, the Mass of feria iv is affected by the incorporation of the Conception feast since it includes as extra items two alleluias and their verses and the Conception sequence *Missus Gabriel*: none of these texts is in the main feast of the Conception and presumably they are given here in order to cope with the octave of the Conception, which may fall on feria iv. Without further information it is not possible to identify the exact arrangement, or which of the two alleluias should be used.

710 Finally, we come to the presence of rubrics and incipits other than those already mentioned. Ms G9 refers in the rubric of Advent Sunday to the votive Masses which should be said, specifying that the Sunday rather than the Trinity votive Mass should be done on Sundays, and on ferias iii, v, and vi. Feria ii has the *Missa pro defunctis*, iv *pro familiaribus*, and sabbato the *Rorate* Mass. The last comes from the Saturday fast of Advent: the others must be sought elsewhere, perhaps at the end of the book (**749**).

Sarum sources are usually supplied quite liberally with rubrics, although information about the daily Masses such as that just described does not occur in any of the Graduals studied. The simplest type of additional rubric concerns the non-musical propers and the sung common of each Mass: in the correct position the incipits of the prayers, the epistle and the gospel (*Evangelium*) may be added, and frequently the presence of a Kyrie trope may be specified. Sometimes the latter information, together with facts specifying the yearly use of other common items and their tropes, is quite extensive. In addition there may be useful information about the methods of performance, about those who are to sing the item, what they should wear, and where they should stand. Liturgical adjustments because of coincident Sundays and feasts may be included. Sarum Graduals will be analysed in more detail. The opening pages of the British

Museum ms add 17001, used as replacement pages is the facsimile edition of the Gradual (G14), present Advent Sunday as a model, giving information not only about the musical items and their performance but also about the collects and readings. The following paragraphs summarize the content of the first pages, many sentences being paraphrases of the rubrics themselves: numbers in parentheses refer to the sentences of the transcription given in the note.[5]

711 Preceding the introit are two sentences which are curiously out of place: they refer to the *Benedicamus Domino* or *Ite missa est* at the end of Mass, the former occurring in Advent and from Septuagesima to Maundy Thursday (1), the latter appearing only when the *Gloria in excelsis* occurs (2). A statement (5) that the Gloria is not said during Advent appears after the introit (3) and information about the performance of the introit and doxology have been given (4). From (5) and (2) we can deduce that the Ite is replaced by the Benedicamus during Advent. The rubric then passes to a long statement about the collect, which follows the Gloria when it is said, or else follows the Kyrie directly. This prayer is 'of the day,' *de die*. However, at this point services of previous days, or superseded services of the same day, can be commemorated. The extra collects, which are of course 'of the day' on which they first appear, are called memorials, *memorie*. Sentence 6 indicates that wherever Mass is said the collect *Excita quesumus* occurs: this is the collect of Advent Sunday and its week. Following this, and common till the Vigil of Christmas, is a collect for the Virgin. Neither of these is said on saints' feasts or at the *Salus populi* Mass (7).[6] The general rule (8 & 9) is that there must always be an odd number of prayers here, and the same number that occur at Matins (that is, Lauds), except on Christmas Day and the following week. If there is an even number the prayer for All Saints, *Concede quesumus*, will be added.[7] Sentences 10 and 11 extend these rules, and 12 makes it clear that a feast falling on any of the fasting days or in Lent does not take a memorial of the fast. In this case the Mass of the fast is said separately at the main altar. Sentences 14 almost to the end of the rubric list the collects, three, five, or seven in number, on various occasions, on the ferias of Advent, the octave of St Andrew, after Epiphany, during Lent, after Trinity, and so on. On its first appearance in the rubric, the collect is specified by its incipit.

712 The major divisions of this long, unparagraphed text are indicated in the manuscript by double diagonal strokes. Apart from this there is little to guide the eye to the important material. It is evident that this manuscript contains information not needed by the choir but which could be useful to the precentor. Continuing with similar useful rubrics, it is perhaps more likely to have been used as a reference book than in choir. Following the sentence just analysed, for instance, is another stating that during the last collect before the epistle the subdeacon goes through the middle of the choir to read the epistle. There follow not merely rubrics explaining how the epistle is said, but also examples of the reading tone to which it is sung. The opening and closing and other formulas are illustrated for both the Old and the New Testaments. This source shows both the method of ending the specific text, and a variety of formulas which follow other epistles:

Lectio ysaie prophete. In diebus illis, Locutus est Dominus . . . Item in eodem *Nunquid parum* . . . et sic finiatur *Butirum est mel* . . . *locum*. Et hoc modo finiatur *Dicit Dominus omnipotens*. Vel hoc modo *In Christo Jesu Domino nostro*. Vel hoc modo *Per Jesum Christum Dominum nostrum*.

From *Lectio* to *locum* refers to a single lesson from Isaiah 7.10-15; the remaining formulas are common. Each phrase has the tone supplied.

Continuing the rubrics, we learn that when the epistle is finished two boys in surplices, after bowing to the altar, go through the middle of the choir to the pulpit at the choir-step (*ad gradum chori*) to sing the gradual and its verses. They begin the gradual, whose incipit is given exactly. The rubric then tells us that the choir repeats the incipit and continues, and the incipit is again written, followed by the rest of the chant. This method of singing is observed through the whole year, except when the cantor begins, as in Masses said in copes (*in capo*), in stational processions, and Vespers of Easter Day and week. The repetition of the incipit by the choir is thus specifically required, and the reference to processions and Vespers suggests that the same method must be used for responsories other than those in these particular rituals. After the gradual are the reading tones for the gospel. As with the epistle, various models of the beginnings and ends of the text are given, with variations for sentences which are questions, for passages in Greek and other foreign tongues, for monosyllables, and the like. In this case, the phrase following *Et hoc modo finiantur omnes evangelia per totum annum* . . . is from a specific gospel, and there is no other common closing formula. When the gospel is finished the priest begins the Credo, and the choir continues, not alternating. Although the Credo is one of the ordinary items of the Mass, which appear in the Kyriale, its chant is given here complete since there is only one tune in the Sarum use. The frequent separation of the Credo from the remainder of the sung ordinary will receive comment later (**736-7**). There follows a list of feasts on which the Credo is or is not sung.

713 At this point the facsimile edition of the Gradual breaks off, in favour of the main source chosen for the edition and, since I have analyzed this book because of its availability in facsimile, the remaining rubrics will be cited from the main source, British Museum ms add 12194. In fact, this manuscript begins part of the way through the long rubric after the introit of Advent 1: the text of that rubric may be compared with note 5. There is, however, no information about the epistle and gospel except their incipits, nor about gradual or alleluia except their texts and music. A sequence incipit also occurs. Only the text *[C]redo in u.* appears, and as in the previous manuscript it is followed by a long rubric stating when the item is sung. The offertory and communion are given as in any Gradual, being separated by the brief rubric *Prefatio non dicatur per totum adventum quando de adventu agitur nisi cotidiana*, which is an elliptical way of saying that only the daily Preface is said 'when it is a question of Advent [rather than a feast].' Expressions such as *quando de adventu agitur* must be understood to mean the Temporal services of the season, excluding saints' or other feast days even though occurring in the season. Similarly, *de die* refers to the Temporal service even when a feast falls on the day, and it may refer to a weekday or a Sunday. In its proper place following the communion is a rubric noting the use of

Benedicamus Domino. The Sunday Mass and information about it is now completed, but since the texts of epistle and gospel change on the Wednesday, Friday, and Saturday, their incipits are now listed: in this source, such incipits appear after every Sunday Mass. The next rubric to appear relates to the Wednesday of the third week, the Ember Wednesday. For all of these fasting days the incipits of the additional readings are given, together with instructions as necessary that the collects are said without the preceding liturgical greeting. The readings on the Saturday are all begun with their 'titles': *omnes lectiones cum suis titulis legantur.* Precise instructions for the performance of the hymnus appear: *duo clerici in super pelliceis de secunda forma* [that is, the second bench in the choir stalls] *dicant tractum,* and after the solo refrain the chorus is to repeat it (the refrain) after every solo verse.

We are told that when the Vigil of Christmas falls on the fourth Sunday, the Ember days will be celebrated in the previous week, and otherwise the week before Christmas will be celebrated in full. When the Vigil is a Sunday the normal Mass will be said *in capitulo*[8] and the Vigil Mass at the main altar, with the alleluia. At the first Mass of Christmas, the Gloria is said for the first time in the year and that fact is noted, together with the comment that it is said whenever the Te Deum occurs at Matins, with various exceptions specified. At this Mass, too, there is for the first time a proper Preface whose incipit is given with information about the length of time through which that Preface continues.

714 Somewhat surprisingly, neither of these two Sarum sources gives information about the ordinary of the Mass other than the Kyrie and the occasions on which the Gloria and Credo are sung. For such directions we may turn to other Graduals. The Kyriale of G21 is used for the facsimile edition. The information in question here is not that given in the Kyriale, which will be discussed later, but the additional rubrics of the Temporale. The manuscript lacks much of Advent. Rubrics after the first Mass of Christmas specify a troped Kyrie without indicating the text of the trope: *Kyrie cum suis versibus dicitur.* The Gloria is sung as on a doubles feast. On the other hand the Kyrie is without a trope for the second Mass, and the Gloria, Sanctus, and Agnus are said as on a feast of nine lessons. Ms G16, also Sarum, indicates the trope *Deus creator* for the main Mass of Christmas. The great variety of trope texts makes the failure to specify in all cases somewhat puzzling. The Gradual of Roncton, G17, indicates the Kyrie trope for the first Mass by a marginal addition, and instead of specifying the class of feast from which the various ordinary chants are taken it gives the music with the textual incipit of both Kyrie and Gloria. The York Gradual, G18, refers to *Kyrie cum nota Puerorum caterva* and *Gloria cum nota de Angelis,* distinguishing the different chants by the titles of prominent Masses for which the chant assigned would presumably be well known. This Gradual also refers to the Gloria, Sanctus, and Agnus tropes as in the rubric for the third Mass of Christmas: *Kyrie conditor. Et nota quod in omnibus principalis duplicibus per annum Kyrie, Gloria, Sanctus, et Agnus cum versibus cantentur. In minoribus duplicibus festis sine versibus.* The first occurence of a greater doubles feast gives the opportunity for general rubrics about that and other classes of feast.

715 The presence of information such as this makes English books particularly useful. The more frequent and longer rubrics which are required are immediately visible in the sources, as are the insertions of incipits referring to the non-musical items, when the normal format of a Gradual is understood. There is therefore little need for a complex system of initials, and in the rubrics so far mentioned only the small capital, not distinguished by colour, appears. When the rubrics include references to days, however, as will happen during the period from Christmas to Septuagesima, initials again play a role. Where complete texts and music of certain items are provided, such as the readings with their tones and the Credo with its chant, they are treated like tracts, sequences, and other items not part of what we may call the normal Mass (that is, to reintroduce the abbreviations which will be used: **IKGO EGAG COOSACOI**). In other words, they have size 2 initials corresponding to introits of the beginning of Masses.

Christmas to Lent

716 This period is complicated by several factors. The presence of feasts of fixed date, not only Christmas and Epiphany but usually the feasts of the saints after Christmas also, together with the octaves of those feasts, complicates the adjustments for Sunday or ferial performance. The variable number of Sundays after Epiphany lends additional difficulty, confused by the erratic and often erroneous numbering used in the sources.

The two earliest manuscripts studied, both from the 12th century, already exemplify the problem. One of them, G19, combines the Sanctorale with the Temporale; the additional saints, a large number all presented within a single group, will not be itemized. The sequence of services recorded in these two Graduals is as follows (feasts placed between parentheses are recorded only in rubrics, usually with incipits):

G19	Christmas	G20	Christmas
	St Stephen		St Stephen
	Vigil Mass of St John		(Vigil Mass of St John)
	Main Mass of St John		Main Mass of St John
	Holy Innocents		Holy Innocents
	St Silvester		

After these normal and unsurprising Christmas feasts, G19 has the Mass *Dum medium silentium* (the first words of the introit) for the Sunday within the octave of Christmas, followed directly by the Mass for Epiphany, *Ecce advenit Dominator*. G20 omits *Dum medium* but includes rubrics about the Vigil Mass of Epiphany, which draws all its proper sung items from either the second Mass of Christmas or from *Dum medium*. The omission of the Vigil Mass in G19 is of little concern: custom, habit, or a separate Ordinal will indicate the source of its chants. The omission of *Dum medium* from G20, however, is more difficult to account for since some of its texts are needed for the Vigil Mass, whose rubrics and incipits therefore refer to items which have not appeared. This kind of difficulty is

frequent. We can only note whether the item is given elsewhere farther on in the book, or we may consult other books for instructions. The solution in this manuscript, to be shown shortly, raises other problems.
717 After Epiphany, G19 has these Masses:

Omnis terra for Dominica 1 after Epiphany (Dominica infra octava)
In excelsis throno for Dominica 2 (Dominica 1 post octavam)
Adorate Deum for Dominica 3 (Dominica 2 . . .)

A group of proper Masses for saints now intervenes between these Sundays and Septuagesima, and then the Temporale services up to Lent continue. Here, then, three Masses are provided for the minimum of one to a maximum of six Sundays after Epiphany. No information about the distribution is given in the source, but other manuscripts to be discussed will suggest some examples of how the arrangement might be made.

Ms G20 offers a good example of the confusion and error which can arise. After Epiphany is the *Dum medium* Mass containing the communion needed for the Mass on the Vigil of Epiphany, with the explicit rubric *Dominica prima post nativitatis Domini.* This rubric is correct. But the Mass can never occur after Epiphany. Its position is inexplicable since the manuscript is not misbound. The error is compounded by the rubric for the next Mass, *Omnis terra,* said to be for *Dominica 2 post nativitatis*: the correct rubric should be *Dominica infra octava Epiphanie* or *Dominica 1 post Epiphaniam.*[9] The Mass *In excelsis,* which follows, as in G19, should then be for *Dominica 1 post octavam* or *Dominica 2 post Epiphaniam*: it is in fact assigned to *Dominica 2 post octavas Epiphanie.* The rubric for the third Mass, *Adorate Deum,* is correct: *Dominica 3 post Epiphaniam.* Relying on the rubrics in this source, then, can lead to disaster. Only advance knowledge of what is likely to be the proper situation, by comparison with G19, can help. Let us adopt G19, with its three Masses after Epiphany, as the starting point. These are the standard Masses for the period. In all the other sources studied, however, from at least a century later, their order is changed: *In excelsis* apears first, *Omnis terra* second, and *Adorate Deum* third as before. This reversal of the first two must have increased the chances for confusion, but has the benefit of giving us a possible clue to the dating of sources.
718 Some manuscripts of those studied[10] omit altogether the Christmas saints, Stephen, John, and Innocents, placing them in the relevant place in the Sanctorale. Most manuscripts of this later period include Thomas of Canterbury, at least in rubric, but only two preserve the Vigil Mass for St John.[11] Silvester appears only when Temporale and Sanctorale are combined and in this case there may be other saints at this point: G7 for example gives the Mass for St Gregory after Thomas of Canterbury. If additional saints are present they invariably follow as a group directly after the third Mass of Christmas and the Masses of the normal Christmas saints. Between them and Epiphany there may be five occasions to note: (a) the Sunday within the octave of Christmas always appears, and is *Dum medium.* In Sarum sources it is given under the rubric *sexta die* and G14 makes it clear that the same Mass, with a procession, is used for the

FIGURE 7.4
Masses after Epiphany

Iet: In excelsis throno; Ota: Omnis terra adoret; ADo: Adorate Deum omnis.

Dominica infra octava		1	2	3	4	5	post oct. Epi
Dominica 1		2	3	4	5	6	post Epi
Either as on the day		Iet	Ota	ADo	(rubrics)		
Or:	Iet	Ota	ADo	–	–	–	
On the octave, the Mass is as on the day.							

Sunday (which of course may be the sixth day after Christmas);[12] (b) & (c) Circumcision and the octave of Christmas, which fall on the same day, have Masses which normally adopt items from the Christmas Masses and which may therefore appear only as incipits in rubrics if they are not, as more often, omitted altogether; (d) similarly, the octaves of the saints after Christmas are usually omitted since they repeat the Mass of the feast, but occasionally a rubric indicates how that Mass is to be adapted if the octave falls on the Sunday; (e) as already indicated, the Mass for the Vigil of Epiphany borrows its propers from the Christmas Masses and from *Dum medium*: only rubrics are necessary, and even these are frequently omitted.

719 We come now to the weeks following Epiphany. In the following discussion the rubrics *Dominica post octavam Epiphanie* and *Dominica post Epiphaniam*, although not in fact so, are treated as identical and interchangeable, and erroneous use of one or the other will not be noted.[13] But it may be pointed out that the error usually involves the omission of the word *octava* rather than its incorrect presence. The three Masses already isolated, *In excelsis throno, Omnis terra, Adorate Deum*, are placed within the period in two ways: in figure 7.4 they are reduced to their initial letters. In the first method the repetition of the Epiphany Mass on the Sunday within and on the octave, and the repetition of *Adorate* for Sundays 5 and 6, is stated in rubrics, perhaps because the arrangement is English.[14] Continental sources prefer the second arrangement but do not comment on the repetition of *Adorate*. The printed Roman Missal of 1474 probably belongs in the second group because *In excelsis* is used for the Sunday within the octave: however, it records only two Sundays, 4 and 5, after *Adorate*. The repetition of that Mass for any remaining Sundays is unanimous in all sources which refer to the problem. Only the rubricated Sarum manuscripts give instructions about the procedure when there are insufficient Sundays to sing all three Masses[15]: if the time between Epiphany and Septuagesima is brief, so that the three Masses cannot be sung one to a week, then two or even all three may be sung in the same week. Probably because the arrangement is different from that followed in the rest of Europe, the rubric then reaffirms that *In excelsis* may not be sung before the historia *Domine ne in ira*, that is, the second Sunday after Epiphany, so called from the first responsory at Matins of that day. When the time is long, *Adorate* is sung for two or three Sundays as necessary. This rubric fails to explain what happens when the time is so short that there is no second Sunday on which to sing *In excelsis* itself. For clarification here we must turn to G21 where, following Dominica 1, is a somewhat longer rubric partly identical with the previous one: it says that when no Sunday intervenes between Dominica 1 and Septuagesima, then *In excelsis* must be sung on a feria after the octave of Epiphany, and the other two Masses on subsequent weekdays. Even this, as the reader may work out for himself, does not explain what happens when Epiphany falls on a Thursday, Friday or Saturday and the time is at its shortest (see **518**). Such an occurrence would be rare, and the rubrics are not often, if ever, entirely comprehensive.

720 After the Epiphany Sundays there follow without complexity the Sundays in Septuagesima, Sexagesima and Quinquagesima, in one Sarum source (G16) called *prima, secunda,* and *tertia* in Septuagesima. Tracts replace the alleluias on these Sundays and that substitution continues up to Easter. Apart from these Sundays, and very frequently the Mass for the Holy Innocents, the alleluia is a normal part of the Mass after Christmas. A brief comparison of two sources will serve to illustrate how the arrangement can vary and how the Sanctorate is combined with the Temporale where that conservative principle is adopted.

G8:	Epiphany	Vincent
	Dominica infra oct.	octave of Agnes
	Felix	Purification
	Dominica 2	Agatha
	Marcellus	Valentine
	Prisce	Gregory
	Fabian & Sebastian	Annunciation
	Agnes	LXX
	Dominica 3	LX
		etc.

G19 places all its saints' feasts, including most of those on this list, between Dominica 3 and Septuagesima (LXX). No doubt other arrangements can be found.

721 Sources which have additional items such as sequences, or rubrics with incipits of ordinary chants, continue to include them in the same manner during this season and through the remainder of the year. Occasionally the additional item is the only one to appear in full. For example, on the Sunday within the octave of Christmas all the items normally proper are drawn from the services of Christmas Day, but the sequence may be truly proper and thus given complete. It does not seem necessary to list the additions in detail again and the following summary must suffice as a reminder. The sung items of the ordinary of the Mass, especially when they are troped, and more often the intoned prayers, memorials, and readings are sometimes noted in incipit between the relevant chant propers. Some manuscripts add brief rubrics about such items as the Gloria, not sung on the feast of the Holy Innocents unless it is a Sunday, and not sung at all during Lent.[16] Changes of text in epistle and gospel during the week may be recorded after the Sunday Mass, and sometimes Votive Masses to be performed during the week are mentioned (G9). During this period ms G14 begins to list the incipits of the items in the procession before Mass, and this information is given more fully in Missals. A source with real rubrics, such as this Gradual, also gives brief instructions about the adaptations made for the coincidence of feast days: after Septuagesima, for example, it says that the Sunday Mass is changed only for Purification when the latter falls on a Sunday. In matters such as these, where each use may vary considerably, there can be no reliable generalizations. There is no short cut to careful perusal of the rubrics and of related books.

Initials

722 Although not differing much from those of Advent, initial schemes seem occasionally to be less carefully maintained. Compared with the largest initial of Christmas Mass, all other services of this period which have proper items begin with the initial of size 2, the Mass or introit initial: Epiphany is distinguished by an initial larger than size 2, but generally not as elaborate and as large as those of Advent and Christmas. Sequences, when given, have size 2 initials. As will be obvious from the preceding pages, during this period there is a great deal of repetition, and a number of services have no proper items. In graduals, these services may be omitted completely. Incipits for incidental repetitions are given, with or without reference to their source, as during Advent. It is worth remarking that some items in the services of the Christmas saints are drawn not from the Temporale but from the Common of Saints: if they are not recorded complete in their position after Christmas, the incipit may have a rubric such as *require in communi plurimorum martyrum* with or without a page reference. We must distinguish the rubrics for incidental repetitions, for references, and for instructions from those which refer to complete services on specific days. The latter begin with a reference to the day but may be run on in a continuous rubric devoted to a number of different matters: in this case, such rubrics are usually set off by a capital of a special colour or larger size, or by some other means such as the paraph sign. The letters frequently beginning rubrics announcing days have been specified (**608**). Only one exception to the above procedures was noted, in sources G7 and G9. Here the introit beginning the Mass for St John is provided with an initial of the largest size. The manuscripts may have been for churches of which St John was the patron.

Lent to Advent

723 With the exception of Lent and Easter Week, which will be examined separately in chapter 9, there is little complexity in the remainder of the year, and the hierarchy of initials established in the earlier part of the year is generally continued in the same style. The main outlines can be traced quite easily, but the landmarks denoting the major feasts tend to be widely separated because of the 'un-distinguished' days of Lent and the Sundays of summer time.

After Epiphany, which, as remarked earlier, often has an initial smaller than the largest but larger than the normal Mass initial, there will generally be no initial larger than size 2 until Easter Day, which naturally has the largest size. The weeks after Epiphany and from Septuagesima to Easter, then, since there is a proper Mass for every feria of Lent, present some fifty-five Masses with some fifty-five size 2 initials. There is usually no distinction between the ferial and the Dominical Masses of Lent in this respect.[17] Passion Sunday and more frequently Palm Sunday may have a larger initial. Apart from these fifty-odd size 2 initials, the tracts of Lent normally have this initial. So too do any other items such as the antiphons for the blessing of the ashes on Ash Wednesday (see **915**), the processions of Palm Sunday and the following week (**917, 927-30, 932-3**), and the special services of that week which are sometimes included in Graduals and Missals (chapter 9). A few sources entirely omit the ferial Masses of Lent after Ash Wednesday.[18] Two of these sources are of English use (Sarum and York). It seems very unlikely that the ferias of this season would have repeated the Dominical Mass, and the omission may perhaps be explained by the possible destination of these books for a bishop or archbishop, who may not have celebrated on ferias.

724 The Easter season is bounded by Easter Day and Pentecost, both of which feasts are denoted by initials of the largest size. Within, the ferias of Easter week and the following Sundays have normal size 2 Mass initials.[19] Occasionally, as in G7, the first Sunday after Easter has a somewhat larger initial: Ascension Day, on a Thursday, sometimes has the largest size of initial, sometimes an intermediate size, and occasionally the normal Mass initial. Sequences, and sometimes the alleluias also, usually have size 2 initials, but on the main feasts beginning with larger initials the sequence initials may also be larger.[20] During this season there are a number of possible variants from normal Masses. Graduals are mostly replaced by alleluias, so that there are at least two alleluias per Mass. The verses for these alleluias vary considerably from source to source, the variability suggesting that at some time there was only a stock from which a choice could be made. Indeed, in some sources a list of alleluias with their verses is given as a self-contained section somewhere in the season. Naturally, it is most convenient to have this section near the place where the first choice is to be made, and the list mostly appears before *Quasimodo* Sunday, the first Sunday after Easter.[21] Ms G8, for example, has the following list before the introit *Quasimodo*:

A Pascha usque ad Ascensionem Domini Alleluia in diebus dominicis: primum Alleluia In die resurrectionem, *feria ii* Surrexit Dominus . . . *feria iii* Obtulerunt . . . *feria iv* Benedictus es . . . *feria v* Crucifixus surrexit . . . *feria vi* Dicite . . . *sabbato* In resurrectionem.

In octava Pasche ad missam Resurrexi, *primum Alleluia* In die resurrectionem mee, *secundum* Pascha nostrum.

Ms G21 gives us a similar list after the *Quasimodo* Mass with information about ferias iv and vi:

Sciendum quod in omni festo cum regimine chori ab octava Pasche usque ad Ascensionem Domini secundum Alleluia erit unum de subscriptis quibus dictis dicuntur illa de ebdomada Pascha, viz., de iii, iv, & vi feria per ordinem dicuntur quibus Dominicis reincipiantur subscriptus ut per prius [the list of alleluias and verses follows].

Ms G1 gives only the incipits of alleluias for Easter Masses: presumably the complete items were once to be found in the manuscript somewhere. Ms G13 lists the alleluias for Sundays before the *Quasimodo* introit, and those for ferias are given in the Easter Day Mass itself, after the alleluia for that day: that Mass therefore appears to have seven alleluias. Alternative sequences, or sequences *per ordinem* through the week, may be listed in a similar manner where necessary. An additional confusion may arise from the practice of some sources, such as G21, of listing in Graduals the alleluias for use at Vespers of Easter week (**932-3**). A similar case is that of the Easter week graduals. The gradual refrain is common for the week while its verses change. Before Easter Mass, therefore, ms G6 gives the common refrain, listing only its incipits, together with the proper verse, in the correct place within the Mass.

725 Ms G12, one of those omitting the ferias of Lent, also omits the first, second, third, and fourth Sunday after Easter, although the alleluia verses for them are listed with the information for the performance of the octave of Easter Day. From G16 we may discover the probable reason: all the Sundays of Easter time are said as 'on the day' except for the alleluia verses. The octave of Easter, as may be ascertained from the previous sentences, presents a small problem. Most sources note it in a rubric, stating that the service is that of Easter Sunday, sometimes with special items and a proper sequence which may be given in full. But the octave of Easter falls on the first Sunday after Easter, also provided with its own Mass, *Quasimodo*. Whether both the octave Mass and *Quasimodo* were always said is not possible to ascertain from Graduals, but the latter must be included in the books because, as sources G14 and G21 indicate, it is the *Missa dominicale per ebdomadam*.

The Monday and Tuesday following the fifth Sunday after Easter are the Rogation Days, *in majori letania*, and the Mass provided for the first serves *per duos dies rogationes*. Few sources record more than the Mass at this point, although one of the early Graduals, G19, has numerous antiphons for the Rogation ceremonies. G20, the other early Gradual, omits even the Mass and gives it later, in the Sanctorale. Of the following days, the Vigil and feast of Ascension, there is little to note in Graduals. Mass on the Vigil of Pentecost is noted only in a rubric with incipits, except for the offertory and communion, which are proper.

726 The summer Sundays can be isolated between the initial of Pentecost, of the largest size, and the large initial of the section following the Temporale. Nevertheless, there may be other large initials between the two: Trinity Sunday, like Ascension, may have the largest or an intermediate size initial or occasionally the normal Mass introit initial, and the same is true of Corpus Christi if it occurs. The first Sunday after Trinity or after Pentecost (if Trinity is omitted) begins with the introit *Domine in tua*. Sometimes this and very occasionally the introit for the thirteenth Sunday, *Respice Domine*, have an intermediate size initial. Mostly, then, the summer Sundays and Ember days have the normal Mass initial, also used for sequences and tracts as usual. There are two Ember weeks between Pentecost and the end of the church year. The first comes in the week following Pentecost, except in Sarum use which omits this fast entirely.[22] The weekdays after Pentecost are therefore provided with ferial Masses. The second or September fast, commonly occurs in the fourteenth, fifteenth, or sixteenth week after Trinity.[23] Sarum and York Graduals do not specify the week in which the fast occurs, since they either omit the Masses altogether or list them after the last Sunday of summer.[24] These discrepancies do not, I think, all stem from the uncertainty about numbering to which I have already referred. Of course, the sixteenth week after Pentecost in sources G19 and G20, which lack Trinity, becomes the seventeenth in sources with that feast, although probably called the sixteenth after Trinity. The source of confusion is apparent. It is better to refer not to weeks but to Masses. The order of Sunday Masses during the summer is invariable in all the sources studied, and is presented below. The location of that series one or two weeks after Pentecost depends on the presence of Trinity or the octave of Pentecost: the coincidence of Trinity and that octave creates the same kind of situation as that already described for the octave of Easter. The location of the September fast within the series varies by up to four weeks. Each manuscript must be examined separately.[25] In the list below the number of the Sunday is followed by a letter, corresponding to that assigned by me in appendix II, by which the text can be identified as in that appendix and in the previous note.

Sundays after Pentecost/Trinity

1	A	*Domine in tua*
2	B	*Factus est Dominus*
3	C	*Respice in me*
4	D	*Dominus illuminatio*
5	E	*Exaudi Domine*
6	F	*Dominus fortitudo*
7	G	*Omnes gentes*
8	H	*Suscepimus Deus*
9	I	*Ecce Deus adiuvat*
10	J	*Dum* (or *Cum*) *clamarem*
11	K	*Deus in loco*
12	L	*Deus in adiutorium*
13	M	*Respice Domine in testamentum*
14	N	*Protector noster*
15	O	*Inclina Domine*
16	P	*Miserere mihi*
17	Q	*Justus es Domine*
18	R	*Da pacem*
19	S	*Salus populi*
20	T	*Omnia que*
21	U	*In voluntate tua*
22	V	*Si iniquitates*
23	W	*Dicit Dominus*

Ember day introits

X	*Exultate Deo*
Y	*Letetur cor*
Z	*Venite adoremus*

Any subsequent Sundays which are needed are listed by means of incipits which refer to the *Dicit Dominus* Mass together with a proper alleluia and verse and, in those manuscripts which include such information, incipits referring to the prayers and readings. Only in ms G17 is there any variation in what must be said on these extra Sundays: it specifies *Si iniquitates* for the following two Sundays, if required, then *Dicit Dominus* if yet more Sundays are necessary. The number of Sundays required after Trinity varies, of course, from 22 to 27.

727 If this series of Masses is invariable, the alleluia verse within each Mass is not. In fact, the variability of these verses is one of the standard means by which sources are related to each other and to uses. As with the alleluia verses of Easter time, then, the verses of this period are often omitted or given in incipit only, and a list of alleluias and verses is placed separately, usually at the end of the Temporale. Occasionally the alleluia verse is changed during the ferias following a Sunday. In this case, as in G21, the proper alleluias are noted complete between the Sunday Masses. As is apparent from the previous note, several of these Masses have introits or other items which are listed only with incipits. This abbreviation as usual indicates that the Mass or item is drawn from elsewhere. Incipits, again as usual, do not generally take the size 2 initial and are given a large capital as are the items within the Mass, from which the introit is therefore little distinct. The following list, referring only to the introits, shows the commonest repetitions with their occasions and sources:

Omnes gentes, Trinity 7, drawn from the Vigil of Ascension
Suscepimus Deus, Trinity 8, from the feast of the Purification
Dum clamarem, Trinity 10, from feria v (*caput jejunii*)
Deus in adiutorium, Trinity 12, from feria v (XL 2)
Letetur cor, September fast, from feria v (XL 4)
Salus populi, Trinity 19, from feria v (XL 3)
Omnia que, Trinity 20, from feria v (Passion Sunday week)

It can hardly escape notice that the majority of these are drawn from the Thursdays of Lent. Those days were *vacant*, or lacking Masses, until Gregory II's revisions.[26] Many summer Sundays were similarly vacant: the repetitions from one period to another are thus easy to explain.

728 The combination of Sanctorale with Temporale, when it occurs, does not affect Lent, during which season feasts were severely restricted. After the group of saints following Epiphany, then, no more occur until the end of Easter week at the earliest (G11). Thereafter the Easter Sundays are intact in the few sources studied, with a further group of saints appearing after the fifth Sunday in source G7. Other groups may appear at various places in the sequence of Masses following, the week before Pentecost and immediately before or after Trinity being favoured rather than within the week after Pentecost, probably because of the fast within that week. During the summer, saints may be added at any number of places and the only noteworthy feature is that subsequent Sundays are occasionally numbered after the last saint's feast, for example *Dominica 1 post [festum] S. Laurentii* (source G19).

MISSALS

729 Missals and Noted Missals contain all the texts of the Gradual plus prayers, readings, introductory and closing formulas, and versicles and responses, as well as the texts for many days, especially ferias, which do not appear in Graduals. Moreover, numerous special services other than Mass are often included. It would seem therefore that their format would have to be correspondingly more complex. In fact it is visually simpler. In Graduals, all texts are set to chant and thus appear the same unless the distinctions of musical style are closely observed. In Missals, the sung texts, prayers, readings, and sentences are more obviously distinct because of their length and other features. The chanted texts, those which occur in the Gradual, are normally set off in Missals by the smaller size of their script, and in Noted Missals by the presence of the plainsong. Prayers and readings are often distinct in length, the former being shorter, and the initials which begin them and the rubrics which separate them are thus distributed irregularly.
730 In Missals without chants the hierarchy of initials is much the same as in Graduals, but the size 2 initial cannot be used in the same way to locate the beginnings of Masses. Large and moderately large initials denote the principal feasts, the initial of size 2 denotes the beginnings of Masses and also the beginnings of prayers and readings within Masses. The capital is used for the musical items in conjunction with the smaller script. As in Graduals items such as the hymnus, tracts, sequences, and often processions and hymns of Holy Week, have size 2 initials with large capitals for verses and capitals for internal sentences. Incorporating the size and the letter with which an item commonly begins, then, a table such as figure 7.5 would represent the typical format for a single Mass. Several comments can be made on the scheme shown in this figure. Unless the introit appears only as an incipit, when it begins with a large capital or capital (1+ or 1), it is the only regularly recurring item which combines the large initial (for the principal feasts) or the size 2 initial with the smaller size of script. Tracts and sequences, when they occur, have the same feature but their texts are much longer. On fasting days with numerous readings the series oratio-epistle-gradual (or tract) with its characteristic visual organization will be repeated several times, 2 2 1+ 2 2 1+ with the other criteria, and during Lent the normal presence of the *oratio super populum* also gives the characteristic outline of five size 2 initials, mostly with quite short texts, the central one of which is in smaller script: post-communion, oratio super populum, introit, oratio, epistle.
731 This organization of initials seems to be the conventional and wide-spread practice of the later middle ages. Noted Missals differ only in having the musical stave and notes along with the smaller texts of the chanted items. There are occasionally variations of the scheme. Source NM2, for example, employs a capital for the secret and post-communion which is almost identical in size to the letter used for the musical items: this source often gives the incipit or complete text of the Preface and *Communicantes* prayer after the secret, these two texts

FIGURE 7.5
The texts and initial letters of a typical Mass

In column two, the letter does not stand for a genre, but is the actual letter with which the text commonly begins. The tract and sequence appear only in certain circumstances.

	size of initial or capital	common first letter	size of script	length of text
introit	2 (or larger)		small	short
oratio	2	D, O, P	large	longer
epistle	2	F, K (or C)	large	long
gradual	1+		small	short
alleluia	1+		small	short
tract	2		small	long
sequence	2		small	long
gospel	2	I	large	long
offertory	1+		small	short
secret	2	D, O, P	large	longer
communion	1+		small	short
post-communion	2	D, O, P	large	longer
IN LENT:				
oratio super populum	2	D, O, P	large	longer

taking the size 2 initial. Moreover, tracts and sequences in this manuscript are not distinguished by their initial from the other musical items. Very occasionally, as in NM1 and NM2 the collect rather than the introit takes the larger initial of feasts, the introit keeping its normal initial. Sometimes the collect may have a slightly larger size 2 initial even when the introit does have the larger letter. In M2 this is sometimes the case. In fact, Epiphany in this manuscript is distinguished only by the initial for the collect, and a number of feasts in the Sanctorale with large initials for the introit have larger ones for the prayer. But it is perhaps dangerous to assess minor and slight variations such as these as deliberate: the precise size of letters may have been forgotten during the long time needed for the writing of manuscripts.

732 Let us now examine the other material which is to be found in the Temporale of a Missal or Noted Missal, but not in Graduals except those which are substantially rubricated. Extra days occur. Most items of the Sunday Mass are repeated throughout the week and thus the ferias need not appear in Graduals: often, however, the epistle and gospel change during the week, especially on Wednesday and Friday. In Missals the texts of these readings must be given in full. Between Sunday Masses, therefore, will appear an epistle and a gospel, and then a second epistle and gospel, for Wednesday-Thursday and Friday-Saturday if that is the practice of the use in question. The sequence of initials F I F I, for *Fratres* and *In illo* of epistle and gospel respectively, is easy to isolate. At certain seasons, notably after Epiphany and at the end of the summer Sundays where there are extra weeks which repeat the previous Sunday

Mass, there will be a longer series of such readings separated by a rubric referring to the repetition of the Sunday Mass, that repetition itself having a proper epistle and gospel:

Dom. 24 rubric:	as on Dom. 23	
with this	proper epistle	[F]ratres ...
and this	proper gospel	[I]n illo ...
feria iv:	proper epistle	[F]ratres ...
	proper gospel	[I]n illo ...
feria vi:	proper epistle	[F]ratres ...
	proper gospel	[I]n illo ...
Dom. 25 rubric:	as on Dom. 23	
with this	proper epistle	[F]ratres ...
and this	proper gospel	[I]n illo ...
feria iv:	proper epistle	[F]ratres ...
	proper gospel	[I]n illo ...
feria vi:	proper epistle	[F]ratres ...
	proper gospel	[I]n illo ...

etc

733 Before Sunday Masses and before the Masses of prominent feasts there may be processions. These may consist of chanted items for the procession to a station, readings and prayers at the station, and a chant for the return procession. Readings and prayers may be given in the Missal. The musical items may appear complete (with music in the Noted book) or in incipit, and in the latter case the full text and music must be sought in a Processional since it rarely appears in Graduals. From Missal to Missal there seems to be little consistency about which of the musical items shall be given complete, although generally chants for the processions themselves are recorded only in incipit while chants actually sung at the station are more often given in full. The procession before the Sunday Mass includes the blessing and aspersion of Holy Water. Some or all of the largely common texts and music of this little ceremony, described in section **502**, are often given immediately before Advent Sunday or before Easter Sunday, where a seasonal change occurs.

734 Within each Mass, the rubrics and incipits are normally much more numerous in Missals even than in rubricated Graduals. Common and ordinary texts may be referred to, especially when they are common only to seasons or to particular feasts. The Kyrie and its trope may be noted after the introit, the trope incipit serving to identify which of the Kyrie chants should be used. Similarly the Gloria may be identified at the same point with its musical incipit, or its absence may be noted. After the gospel, there may be a reference to the presence or absence of the Credo, or occasionally of a sermon, the latter in some late medieval sources being required in the vernacular.[27] The Sanctus and Agnus, being part of the Preface and Canon, are more usually described in the Ordo misse, but their absence, as on Good Friday, may be noted in a rubric. Lent, and in particular the triduum, has a number of additional items, as on Ash Wednsday, or even special services, as on Maundy Thursday. The chapter on Lent provides more information about how there are recorded in the various liturgical books. Additional prayers, such as the memorials which follow the daily collect and the *oratio super populum* of Lent, are given in full in many Missals, with a size 2 initial. The omission or replacement of the *Oremus* or liturgical greeting before many prayers in Lent and on other fasts may be observed. Proper Prefaces and proper texts for the *Communicantes* prayer within the Canon may be given in full or in incipit after the secret; their full text is more likely to occur in the Ordo.

General information about the conventional formulas and the sentences which precede prayers and readings and so on is often included in rubrics on Advent Sunday, and occasionally even the musical tones are given. The 'normal' procedure for Mass explained by these instructions, taken in conjunction with the material presented in the Ordo, is followed whenever there is no reference to anything different.

The Kyriale and the Ordo misse

735 The Common of the Time, as the entire repertory of invariable prayers, sentences, formulas, and the texts of ordinary chants may be called, will in theory be presented complete in the Ordo, compiled to contain everything needed by the celebrant(s). The plainsongs of the ordinary chants, however, which render the ordinary items seasonal or proper in other ways, are needed by the choir and are transmitted in a separate section of the plainsong books.

The Kyriale

736 Generally placed towards the end of Graduals and after the Temporale in Noted Missals (**749-51**), the Kyriale may be constituted in several ways. The arrangement whereby all Kyries are noted, then all Glorias, then the Sanctus, then all Agnus chants, as in source G21, is by no means as common as many text-books would suggest and in the sources studied was relatively infrequent. Figure 7.6 summarizes the presentation of the ordinary chants in some of the manuscripts.

Six of the sources keep the items of the ordinary separate, and none includes the Credo. One lists the Ite chants, another the sequences, in their logical postion, the latter separating the section of Kyries and Glorias from Sanctus and Agnus by some fifty pages. In source G11, a 12th-century Gradual, these sections are separated by the remainder of the book; the Kyries and Glorias with their tropes are before the Temporale, the Sanctus and Agnus at the end of the book. A clear distinction between the two sections emerges. Two reasons for the separation seem possible. One is the traditional retention of a scheme acknowledging that, historically, Kyrie and Gloria were later additions occurring

FIGURE 7.6
Common arrangements of Ordinary chants

source	this group of items occurs once	in each column here, the item (or group of items) appears any number of times before the next item (column) appears; groups of items are repeated as groups							
G8		**K**		**G**		**S**	**A**		
G21		**K**		**G**		**S**	**A**		
NM1		**K**		**G**		**S**	**A**	**I**	
NM6		**K**		**G**	Seq	**S**	**A**		
G11		**K**		**G**	(1)	**S**	**A**		
NM2		**K**		**G**		**S**	**A** (2)		
G1		**K** (3)		**G**		**SA**		**I**	**B**
G5			**KG**			**S**	**A**	**I**	
G12			**KG**		**C**	**S**	**A**		
G13			**KG**		**C**	**SA**			
G2		**KGSA**						**I**	**B**
G3		**KGSA**		**KG**		**KSA**	**SA**		
G4		**KGSA**		**KG**	**C**	**KSA**	**SA**		
NM5		**KGSA**		**KGSAI**	**K C**				
G10		**KGSAI**		(4)	**C** Seq	**KSA**			
G9	**KGCSA**	**KGSA**		**KG**	**KGSA**				
G6	**KGCSA**	**KSA**			**KGSA**	**KSA**			

NOTES
(1) Between Kyries and Glorias and Sanctus and Agnus comes the whole of the remainder of the book.
(2) Followed by the Credo text, Apologia, Aspersion, Prefaces, and more Kyries and Glorias.
(3) Each Kyrie ends with a Gloria incipit.
(4) Inserted here is much material concerning the tones for versicles and responses, *Humiliate*, *Levate*, *Flectamus*, etc.

in the Fore-Mass, while Sanctus and Agnus were inherent parts of the Canon and Communion cycle respectively. The second possibility stems from the presence in a use of a large repertory of sequences. The sequence was sung between the Gloria and Sanctus. Sequences, however, are normally proper and their presence in the Kyriale, which includes common texts, is itself an oddity. Sequences, later additions to the liturgy than Kyrie or Gloria, were perhaps added to the books at a place where a new section was already specified by an older tradition. Several sources present either the Kyrie and Gloria or the Sanctus and Agnus, or both pairs, as pairs.[28] G1 goes some way towards the pairing of Kyrie and Gloria by listing the incipits of the latter after each Kyrie. The exact arrangements, and whether the Credo is present, can be deduced from figure 7.6: the pairing is not always strict, however, since several Kyries may accompany each Gloria, and several Agnus each Sanctus, for example **KKKG KG KKG** and **SA SAAA SA**. One or more of each group may be listed only in incipit.

737 Pairs of items are often presented even when more ambitious groupings are the normal practice, as in G3 and G4 and G9: the relationship of G3 to G4 has been mentioned several times, and this analysis provides more evidence. Groupings of complete Masses without the Credo, and sometimes including the Ite, may be noted in seven sources. In three the Credo is recorded separately, in two (G6, G9) it is included in the first group, which thus has every major item of the ordinary. The relationship between G6 and G9 has also been mentioned and is similarly strengthened by this detail. The only other grouping which is prominent is that of **KSA**. This is certainly true for ferial Masses, which omit Gloria and Credo.

In most sources, each item of the ordinary begins with a size 2 initial, and this is generally true even when the item is given only in incipit. Occasionally the *Et in terra* of the Gloria and *patrem omnipotentem* of the Credo, where the choir begins after the solo intonation, and the Benedictus of the Sanctus also have this size of initial, but elsewhere the internal capitals are smaller even for the successive invocations of Kyrie and Agnus. Sometimes, as in G6 and G9, G10, and NM5, the Gloria and Credo have a distinctly larger initial than the Kyrie, and the Sanctus or Agnus texts or both items have smaller letters than the Kyrie. Very occasionally, as in G6, certain words in Gloria and Credo such as *Maria, homo*, etc, are in raised capitals.

The absence of Ite or Benedicamus chants in the majority of sources is puzzling, since the choir needs them for the Deo gratias response. In this respect, we should note that most Kyriales which do include these items give the *Ite* or *Benedicamus* text rather than *Deo gratias*. The explanation of the absence is probably connected with the performance of these formulas by one of the ministers, so that their chants need to be in the Ordo, where indeed they frequently do occur. Most are very short unless troped: the choir would have little difficulty in remembering the tune just sung and adapting it to the words *Deo gratias*. When troped, by the solo singers of the choir, it would have been impossible for the choir to isolate the notes required for the response, and troped versions with the proper indications always appear in the Kyriale. Often the Ite borrows a musical phrase from one of the Kyrie tropes, or from a melisma of an office responsory,[29] and cues to the original chant may be given: *Ite* Deus creator *missa est*, or *Bene* et egrediens *dicamus Domino*.

The Ordo misse

738 Presenting the common texts and, by means of rubrics, referring to the proper items and generally giving many directions for performance, the Ordo transmits this information mostly in the order in which it is required in the service. Designed for the celebrant, the Ordo gives texts, music, and instructions where it is necessary that he should speak, sing, or act. Sections **502-16**, in chapter 5, are essentially a very expanded and comparative Ordo, except that only the incipits of texts are given and that the necessary music is omitted. For this reason, and because sentences which really belong in the Ordo are often placed in the Temporale and have already been discussed, it would be repetitive to follow the Ordo in detail. However, the visual presentation of the section is both distinctive and confusing. A photographic facsimile of a whole Ordo would be excessively long, and finding a typical, perfect, and comprehensive model might have been impossible.[30] I have compromised, therefore, by presenting a typographical facsimile of an ideal Ordo (**741**), in which the actual rubrics are replaced by a running commentary. Line numbers are used for reference. The format is designed to be medieval rather than modern. Such an artificial construction is, of course, only an approximation. The overall characteristics are based on a specific source, ms M5, and the kind of initial and its position are reproduced as far as is possible.

Size 2 initials are shown as [A] and are placed at the margin or within the running text as in the manuscript, and the asterisk fills incomplete lines. Large initials are shown. Capitals, however, have not been distinguished except by comment in the 'rubrics.' The incipits of texts usually given complete in an Ordo are printed in modern capital letters, followed by *etc.* The full texts would occupy several lines in the manuscript rather than part of a single line as here: size 2 initials, then, especially in the Offertory and Communion cycles, are closer together than they would be in fact. Musical staves and notes are shown by dots, mostly under the incipits to which they relate, but also elsewhere to give a more correct visual effect.

739 The Ordo usually appears before Easter Sunday, in Missals and Noted Missals and at least from the Canon onwards is written in a script larger than that in the rest of the book. Texts of antiphons, hymns, and sometimes dialogues may be relatively smaller in script, as is generally the case for musical items in liturgical books: if this smaller script suggests that such pieces were once sung there seems to be no other evidence for that practice. Musical settings for the Prefaces and a few other texts are always provided, even in books which otherwise contain no music, and frequently there are full page pictures before the Canon. The Ordo is thus easy to locate in a Missal.

The most obvious visual divisions, which do not all correspond with the natural divisions of the service, are created by: (a) the pictures and the elaborate T of *Te igitur* (lines 132-55 of section **741**); (b) the three large initial Ps. These Ps are sometimes size 2, but often larger. In each case, and despite the implication of lines 112-14 and the continuity of the musical stave beginning with the P, these are all doxologies concluding the preceding prayers. The contexts are these:

reference to the secret and its conclusion (lines 92-4)

proper Prefaces (lines 98-111, see below)

Per omnia secula . . . Amen. Dominus vobiscum . . .
continuing with the dialogue and the common Preface

Canon prayers, the last concluding with
Per omnia . . . Amen. Oremus. Preceptis . . .
continuing with the Paternoster and ending with the next doxology

Per omnia . . . Amen. Pax Domini . . . Agnus . . .

Here the new sections begin with Dominus, Oremus, and Pax, but these words are presented only with capitals, generally no larger than the line of script, and the musical stave is continuous. Plate 10 shows the *Per . . . Dominus . . .* section, but the staves and chant have not been entered, even though room has been allowed for them. Only the Paternoster may have an initial, as in plate 20.

740 Lesser sections of the Ordo, also separate by visual appearance rather than by inherent logic, are made distinct by the musical staves. Lines 1-42 have no music. Lines 43-55 have numerous short, interrupted staves followed by text without music. Plate 9 illustrates this precise section in a real manuscript. Between 54 and 94 several short pieces of music interrupt a section consisting mostly of rubrics and short dialogues: the Credo chant, however, is occasionally given complete. There are few size 2 initials. Lines 95-111, separating the reference to the secret from its doxology, are distinctive, and the initial E of line 98 is often replaced by the more characteristic ⊕ . This unit, lines 98-111, repeated for each of the proper Prefaces, may be placed elsewhere, as in source NM1, where it appears before the complete Ordo. Lines 112-29 consist mostly of musical stave and text: 130-55 and 183-210 consist entirely of texts, size 2 initials, and rubrics. The sections from 156-68 and 169-78 resemble each other. From line 211 to the end is mostly concerned with music.

The following are a few miscellaneous notes.

Line 1: the aspersion and blessing of Holy Water may appear beforehand.

Lines 1-70 concern the Fore-Mass and are occasionally omitted. If the necessary information does not occur in the Temporale, it will have to be sought in another book such as the Manual.[31] In some cases were the Fore-Mass was omitted, the Oblation section from offertory to secret is also omitted (sources M2, M4, NM6).

Lines 71-2: see section **508**.

Line 141: in one source, M2, *Communicantes* has an internal capital rather than an initial, perhaps because of the true grammatical function of that word as a present participle continuing the preceding prayer.

Lines 162-8: the Embolism.

741 An *Ordo Misse*

The * symbols in the typographical 'facsimile' on pages 151-3 are purely for visual effect and have no meaning. The approximate justifying of the right margins would have been achieved in the original by means of turnovers, abbreviations, and other adjustments of the layout.

Many sources precede the vesting ******
ceremony with apologiae, of which *****
the most common is St Augustine's *****
[S]UMME SACERDOS, etc. ************
Otherwise, the Ordo may begin as ******
follows: **************************
[A]_d missam dicendam dum induit_ *****
se sacerdos, et dicat hunc ympnum: *****
[V]ENI CREATOR, etc. ***************
(subsequent verses with alternate black **
and coloured large capitals), con- ******
tinued with various sentences and ******
[D]EUS CUI, etc. _the prayer, and_ *******
then follows the antiphon Introibo ad **
altare dei _with the psalm:_ ************
[J]UDICA ME DEUS, etc. *************
(subsequent verses alternate black and **
coloured capitals), and afterwards the **
whole antiphon is sung followed by *****
preces: Introibo, etc. Kyriel. Xpel. ***
Kyriel. Pater noster. _Then there is a_ **
rubric about the introit and its doxology, *
the entrance and the censing. Et ne ****
nos inducas in temptationem. ******
Sed libera, etc., Confitemini, etc. ***
Then the priest says the **************
[C]ONFITEOR DEO, etc. _con-_ *********
[M]ISEREATUR, etc. _fession_ **********
prayers and Absolutionem, _and_ ******
a psalm (subsequent *****************
[D]EUS TU, etc. _verses alternately_ ******
black and coloured capitals). Preces ****
and rubrics about the Kyrie _and its_ ****
tropes, and its complete text lead up to ***
[A]UFER A NOBIS, etc. _the prayer_ ******
Aufer, _and rubrics follow about_ *******
censing, the actions of the minister, *****
and the occasions of the Gloria ********
and the Ite. _The reversal of the words_ ***
in the phrase propter magnam tuam *
gloriam _may be mentioned. Then_ ******
follow sixteen intonations, all with *****
music, of the [G]LORIA IN EXCELSIS DEO.
***********......................................
.................................._All of the intona-_
tions begin with a..................................
size 2.................................. _initial, but_
not at the margin........................... _and_
............................._rubrics separate the_
intonations. After ....
the intonations, the remainder *********
of the text, ET IN TERRA, etc. *********
is given, with trope sentences in colour. **
Within the next rubrics the formulas for *
the collect, Dominus vobiscum _and_ ***
Oremus.................................*******
beforehand and PER OMNIA, etc.*******
after, are given........................*******
with their tones. Rubrics then **********
refer to memorials, the epistle, graduals, *
alleluias, tracts, sequences and actions **
concerned with these items, and finally **
the request for the blessing of the reader *
is asked: JUBE DOMNE, etc., **********
with its reply, and instructions for ******
the reading of the gospel. After the *****
gospel, the priest begins **************
[C]REDO IN UNUM DEUM _and the_ ******
.... _choir_ *****
continues PATREM OMNI- ************
POTENTEM, etc. _Here, the_ ***********
unnecessary liturgical greeting, *******
Dominus vobiscum, _and_ Oremus ***
which precede the offertory may be ******
mentioned. The prayers **************
[S]USCIPE, etc. _of the offertory and_ *****
the actions concerned with the *********
preparations at the altar now occur, ****
together with some miscellaneous *******
versicles such as DIRIGATUR, etc. ******
and the prayer MUNDA ME, etc. *******
and IN SPIRITU, etc., _and_ IN *********
NOMINE, etc. _Then the prayer_ ********
[O]RATE FRATRES, etc. SPIRI- ********
TUS SANCTI, etc. _The various_ ********
additions for the Mass of the Dead: *****
HOSTIAS ET PRECES TIBI ************
.... ************
DOMINE OFFERIMUS _with the_ *********
.... _remainder of_ *****

the text, and miscellaneous versicles ****
continuing to a reference to the secret ***
and memorials before it, and the *******
formulas Oremus *and* Per omnia. ****
There may here be a reference to the ****
opening formulas of the common *******
Preface. *************************

[E]TERNE DEUS, etc. *The proper* ******
.... *Prefaces* *****
.... *come next,* ****
perhaps as many as ten, usually *******
.... *each with its* ***
.... *musical tone,* **
interspersed with rubrics, and *********
.... *each perhaps* **
.... *followed by a* **
proper text for the prayers ************
[C]OMMUNICANTES, etc. ************
within the Canon. This section in a ****
[H]ANC IGITUR, etc. *box, then* ********
may be duplicated many times. ********

The common Preface and all
the proper Prefaces begin ***
in this manner: ***********
ER OMNIA SECULA, ********
....
etc. DOMINUS VOBISCUM, etc. ********
....
SURSUM CORDA, etc. *continuing* ******
....
with the tone throughout the common ***
....
introduction, and a short rubric *******
.... *before the*
remainder of the common Preface: *****
[V]ERE DIGNUM, etc. *The tone* ********
....
is given throughout this part also. ******
....
The Sanctus text is then given *********
and, in a rubric, the Marian trope, ****
BENEDICTUS MARIE FILIUS, etc. ******

Pictures before the Canon *********

All the prayers of the *******
Canon are then given, com- *
plete, each after the ********
E IGITUR, etc. *first be-* *****
ginning with a size 2 initial *
[I]N PRIMIS, etc. *at the mar-* *********
[M]EMENTO, etc. *gin, and ru-* ********
[C]OMMUNICANTES, etc. *brics* ********
[H]ANC IGITUR, etc. *often* ***********
[Q]UAM OBLATIONEM, etc. *ap-* *******
[Q]UI PRIDIE, etc. *pearing* ***********
[S]IMIL, etc. *between the* *************
[H]IC EST CALIX, etc. *texts.* **********
[U]NDE EST, etc. *The names of* *******
[S]UPPLICES, etc. *saints or* ***********
[M]EMENTO, etc. *benefactors* *********
[N]OBIS QUOQUE, etc. *are some-* ******
[P]ER QUEM, etc. *times written* ********
in raised capitals, or at **************
least begin with a large, co- ***********
loured capital. At the end, ************
a rubric refers to the Pater. **********
The conclusion of the *******
last prayer, and the fol- *****
lowing versicles, complete ***
ER OMNIA SECULA, etc. ****
....
with their PRECEPTIS, etc. ************
....
musical tones and rubrics as necessary, **
lead to the [P]ATER NOSTER, **********
etc., *also*..
with its complete tone, up to [L]IBERA ***
NOS, etc. [D]A PROPITIUS, etc. *******
This last prayer ends with the formula: **
All of these versicles have the *
tone provided complete, up **
ER OMNIA SECULA, ********
....
etc. PAX DOMINI, etc. ******
....
to the text of the Agnus, *which is* ******

given complete. Sometimes, there is *****
an insertion for Masses celebrated ******
by a bishop, consisting of the verse ******
[H]UMILIATE VOS AD BENE- **********
....
DICTIONEM *with its tone. The* *********
............................*remainder of the Ordo*
[H]EC, etc. *consists of the Com-* *******
[D]OMINE, etc. *munion prayers* *******
[D]EUS, etc. *(see* **514**), *all* ************
[D]OMINE, etc. *of which begin* ********
[C]ORPUS, etc. *at the margin* *********
[A]VE IN ETERNUM, etc. *with a* *******
[Q]UOD ORE, etc. *size 2 initial and* ****
[H]EC NOS COMMUNIO, etc. **********
[G]RATIAS TIBI, etc. *which are* *******
accompanied by rubrics as necessary. ***
There will be a reference to the ********
communion chant and the post- ********
communion prayer. The rubrics end with
[P]LACEAT TIBI, etc. ***************
references to the final versicles, ********
Ite missa *and its alternatives, and* *****
to the various readings such as In ******
principio *which may take place,* *******
[I]N PRINCIPIO, etc. *and to the* ********
preces in prostratione. The many *******
dialogues and versicles making ********
up these preces are generally **********
given in black letters beginning ********
with a large capital, within ***********
the rubric. Then the texts and *********
chants of all the final formulas ********
are given, with their musical **********
chants, and rubrics as necessary: *******
[B]ENEDICAMUS DOMINO, etc. ********
....
Ten or a dozen different chants ********
may appear, beginning with initials ****
or large capitals not necessarily placed **
at the margin. The Ite missa est, ******
or Deo gratias,....................................
or Requiescat in pace *alternatives* ****
....*also appear.*

THE SANCTORALE AND COMMON OF SAINTS

742 These two sections present few complications and the differences between Graduals and Missals, apart from the obvious ones, are few. Each section normally begins with an initial of the largest size, athough the Common of saints is less often distinguished in this way. Within the Sanctorale the usual hierarchy obtains except for a few feasts: in most sources the Marian feasts of Purification, Annunciation, Assumption and Nativity have larger initials, and commonly the feasts of John the Baptist and All Saints. It is possible that some sources use different sizes of the larger initials in order to rank the feasts in more detail. Apart from those mentioned, other saints are singled out for extra prominence when there is special reason to do so. These are mostly saints of local importance: source M3, for example, a Durham Missal, uses a large initial for the feast of St Cuthbert. This same manuscript exhibits an unusual application of the initial hierarchy to the Common of saints. Usually, once the section has been introduced with a large initial only the normal initials are used. Here, however, larger initials denote the different divisions of the Common of saints to be discussed.

743 The contents of the Sanctorale offer no particular problems. Saints' feasts occur in Kalendar order and a few of the more important are provided with information about the Mass within and on the octave of the feast. Only the more important consist entirely of propers, since many items, and frequently all the items, are drawn from the Common. That is to say, the gradual in the Mass for apostle X may be identical with that used in the Mass for apostle Y and apostle Z and other apostles: or the epistle for the virgin martyrs A & B may be identical with the one for virgin martyrs C & D & E. Such items, distributed by the class of saint, appear in the Common of saints and are noted only in incipit in the Proper of saints, the Sanctorale. Some variations on this procedure may occur: the Mass for Thomas of Canterbury, for example, when it appears in the Temporale may or may not give the introit in full. This chant is in fact a common introit for martyrs. If it is given in full in the Temporale it may not occur at all in the Common of saints, and other feasts needing it will refer to the feast of St Thomas. Such a procedure may perhaps be explained partly by the position of Thomas' feast in the Temporale, and other examples of the same sort may be found for the other saints in that location.

744 If few of the saints' feasts are entirely supplied with propers, it follows that the number of incipits, with rubrical page references or with some such statement as *require in communi*, is much greater than in the Temporale. Many feasts of lower rank indeed consist of nothing but incipits. The appearance of the Sanctorale is thus different: complete Masses may be presented in exactly the same way as in the Temporale, but separated by pages consisting of little but incipits, and the occasional proper item. Sometimes, the presence of items in the Common of saints is taken for granted and no proper is listed, so that neither incipit nor rubric appears. An increase in the appearance of rubrics and incipits, or the complete absence of certain items, leads to the distinctive appearance of the Sanctorale. A few other minor differences may be noted. Because of the variable date of Easter some feasts may fall now inside, now outside Easter time. Adjustments such as the addition of optional *Alleluia* terminations noted with a rubric such as *tempore paschali* are common. Furthermore, there may be rubrics giving information about the coincidence of Temporale and Sanctorale feasts or of feasts from the Sanctorale with each other.

745 The Common of saints is different from both the Temporale and the Sanctorale in its appearance. The order of items within each Mass is the same, but there are frequently numerous alternatives: there may be several introits, several graduals, or several different epistles, and so on. The consecutive listing of numerous items of the same kind is frequent in the Common of saints, disregarding for the moment the quite different Kyriale. It results visually in much longer sections of music or smaller script, alternating with much longer sections of text or normal script. In addition, consecutive introits are normally each given the size 2 initial. In graduals, where introit initials are conventionally larger than those of other items, the result is the consecutive appearance of initials which are elsewhere separated by smaller letters such as capitals: in Missals, where the introit initial is also used for the prayers and readings, the distinction is less visible. After the introits there may be graduals and alleluias and tracts and sequences, even though the alleluia and tract are mutually exclusive. This difference in organization stems from the function of the

Common of saints to provide items for many different saints: one of the feasts drawing on the Common may be celebrated during Lent, another during Easter time, one may call for a particular introit, another for a different introit. Alternatives are often introduced with the rubric *aliud* or *alia*. Within these extended series of similar items there is ample opportunity for error in rubrical description. To cite a typical example, the common of saints who are virgins and martyrs has in the Sarum Missal[32] three introits, one collect, three epistles, five graduals, six alleluias, a tract, a sequence, one gospel, four offertories, one secret, five communions, and one post-communion. Moreover, some of the musical items are further 'subdivided' with optional *Alleluia* extensions for Easter time. A first deduction from such an arrangement might be that, because of the six alleluias, there must be at least six virgin martyrs in the Sanctorale. In fact, less than twelve such saints would automatically render proper some of the alleluias for, in order to be common, each alleluia must be sung in at least two feasts. In the Kalendar of this Missal there are indeed twelve virgin martyrs. Whether this kind of mathematical and logical deduction would hold true in many cases is doubtful. Even in this case, some of the alleluias are not strictly common. One virgin martyr, Christine, has no Mass in the Sanctorale, and is represented only by a memorial in the Vigil Mass of St James. The absence of her Mass and the fact that one of the alleluias, *Veni electa*, is common to three saints, causes two other alleluias, *Diffusa* and *Loquebar;* to be in effect proper to the Masses of Wenefred and Katherine respectively. In any case, all these alleluias are fully written out in the Sanctorale every time they appear and are thus unnecessary in the Common. Why they should be thus repeated is puzzling, since other items in the Masses of these saints give only the incipits in the Sanctorale. There may be a long-lived trace of the later addition of alleluias and verses. Alternatively, it is possible (although not likely) that all six alleluias for virgin martyrs were indeed proper at some time, became common with the addition of other saints, and that the corresponding adjustments of the Proper and Common of saints were not carried out. It must have been virtually impossible for the 'editor' of a medieval liturgical book to keep track of all the places where relevant information was to be found. These minor discrepancies should not cause alarm. Consistency cannot be expected, and, as with the rubrics, comprehensive and accurate organization is rare. A careful account of such discrepancies may enable the historian comparing many sources to trace the changes that have occurred in a rite.

746 There remains now only to describe the Common of saints as a whole. Each class of saints has its own Common. The number of classes and subdivisions of each varies considerably from source to source, and the precise qualifications may be used to confirm the presence of certain kinds of saints in the use. For instance, a Common for one Abbot or for one Matron (for example, ms M1) would suggest the presence of such saints in the Kalendar, and might help to identify the provenance if the Kalendar and Sanctorale, from which such information is more readily available, were missing. The order in which classes of saints are presented is conventionally: apostles, evangelists, martyrs, confessors (including doctors, abbots), and virgins. Each may be subdivided, and apostles are frequently provided with a Common for the Vigil. Each class is normally subdivided into the Common for a single saint, followed by the Common for several saints of that kind: beyond this, virgins are usually classed as martyrs or non-martyrs. Confessors and martyrs are often qualified as bishops. Because the Common for a confessor and bishop, for example, may use several items from the Common for 'unqualified' confessors, or because different classes may themselves share some common items, there is frequent reference from one common Mass to another in the usual manner, with incipits and rubrics. A different method of organization is occasionally found, in which the subdivision is made within the Mass for the general category by appending extra introits, say, with a rubric: for example, the Common of one martyr may have several introits, and then one or two more under the rubric *martyr et pontifex*. Where fewer categories are needed some may be combined, as in the Common for one evangelist or apostle. The extent and organization of the Common of saints must depend on the size and complexity of the Sanctorale.

Other sections

747 The Mass for the Dedication of the Church may or may not be distinguished with a large initial. The service commonly appears at the end of the Temporale or after the Common of saints although a more logical place, if the user's convenience were the sole criterion, would be in the Sanctorale at the relevant date. That date is fixed for each church, but variable from place to place. Presumably rather than upset the fixed order of the Sanctorale with a feast which in its position would vary from manuscript to manuscript, tradition and the other *ad hoc* dedication services which conventionally accompany it, dictated its presence as a separate service. The date of its observance should appear in the Kalendar. It is a normal Mass with a full repertory of propers and sometimes an octave, and it may be provided with both an alleluia (and sequence) and a tract depending on the occasion of its performance in or out of Lent or Easter. In Missals or by incipits in Graduals it may be extended with the propers for the Consecration or Reconciliation of a church, or for the Dedication of an Altar. These services are performed only when necessary.

The Mass for the Dead is similarly *ad hoc*, although with certain variations it is commonly used as a votive or commemorative Mass on ferias. The propers of the Gradual are those of the Mass *in corpore presenti*, celebrated at the main altar, as well as those of the commemorative service, which is normally performed *in capitulo*. The prayers and readings, which vary considerably for the commemorative service, are recorded with the necessary rubrics in Missals. The Mass is normal, with graduals and tracts in place of alleluias, but it does have a sequence, *Dies ire*; this is one of the occasions on which a sequence does not have a preceding alleluia. Another peculiarity is that the Mass has preserved the verses to the offertory and communion. The first verse for the former item is begun by the celebrant and its text and music are thus often in the Ordo. The prayers are frequently proper and numerous: collects, secrets, post-communions, and memorials proper to any number of categories are therefore listed after the Mass, for bishops, for brothers and sisters, parents, kings, etc.

748 Votive Masses are generally assigned one to each of the days of the week, including Sunday. A common arrangement is as follows: Sunday, the Mass to the Holy Trinity; for Thursday, Corpus Christi; for Friday, the Holy Cross; for Saturday, the Blessed Virgin. The assignations for Monday, Tuesday, and Wednesday are more variable: Masses for the Holy Ghost, Angels, All Saints, or special Masses such as *Salus populi* or *Rorate celi* may be specified. These are all normal Masses, although not performed at the main altar, and are provided with the usual alternatives for Lent and Easter. The votive Mass to the Virgin may vary from season to season, there often being three Masses supplied, for Advent (*Rorate celi* in Sarum use), from Christmas to Purification (*Vultum tuum*), and from Purification to Advent (*Salve sancta parens*). Following the Marian Masses in most Missals is a series of occasional votive Masses, asking for peace, or rain, or praying for the king, sinners, penitents, the infirm, and so on. The marriage service may be included. Baptism and confirmation rituals may appear during Holy Week, when they take place (**909-10, 930-1**), or amongst these special services. The book usually ends with miscellaneous memorials, single prayers serving the same purposes as some of the votive Masses just mentioned, and prayers of a general character.

Other additions are of a minor nature and may be tucked away in some convenient but unexpected spare leaf of the book. The most frequent are those which relate to the music and are thus most common in Graduals. The tones of the Prefaces and readings, not needed by the choir but perhaps needed by the Precentor in order to train someone, occasionally occur. Information about the tones of the introit psalm and its differentia, also not necessary if the introit is correctly noted within the book but useful for the Precentor, sometimes appears. The tones for the dialogues and other formulas may be added.

GRADUALS AND MISSALS AS COMPLETE BOOKS

749 The contents and order of Graduals and Missals is quite consistent in its overall arrangement, although the placing of less important material frequently differs. The order Temporale, Sanctorale (or the two combined), Common of saints, Votive Masses is rarely changed, and the other sections may intervene at different points. The main sections will be abbreviated **T S C ⊕** in the immediately following pages. Missals always, Graduals almost never have Kalendars (**K**): when present the Kalendar is at the beginning of the book. Graduals usually contain, as a separate section, a Kyriale (**Ø**) presenting the ordinary chants, and Missals have the Ordo (**O**) and in a separate section the texts of the ordinary if they are troped. Noted Missals commonly have both Ordo and ordinary. Other items usually common to both Graduals and Missals are the Masses for the Dedication (**D**) and for the Dead (†). Masses votive to the Virgin (**V**) are normally presented in a separate section, as are sequences (**Seq**). Many other smaller sections such as the Aspersion (~) will be included, especially in Missals. Figure 7.7 gives the structure of most of the manuscript sources studied: numbers refer to intercalations or other material described below.

FIGURE 7.7
Common arrangements of Graduals and Missals

C, Common of saints; D, Dedication feast; K, Kalendar; O, Ordo misse; Ø, Ordinary of the Mass (Kyriale); S, Sanctorale; Seq, Sequentiary; T, Temporale; V, Marian votive Masses; ⊕, other votive Masses; †, Mass for the Dead; ~, Aspersion.

Graduals

G2	K	T D	S	C	Seq			Ø	
G12	K	T V	S	C	⊕		†	Ø (1,2,3)	
G11	Ø	T	S	C	D Seq			Ø	Seq
G13	(7) ~	T	S D	C	⊕	V	†	Ø	Seq
G10		T	S	C		V	†	Ø ~ Credo Seq Ø (5)	
G5		T D	S			V	(5)	Ø	Seq
G16		T D Ø	S	C					
G17		T	S	C	D		†		
G18		T D V Ø	S	C			†		
G20		T	S	C	D				
G21		T D Seq Ø		C		V	† S (6)		
G3		T	S		D		† ⊕ V (4)	Ø	
G4		T	S		D		† ⊕ V ~ (4)	Ø	
G6		T & S D			⊕		†	Ø (3)	Seq
G9		T & S D					† (4)	Ø (3)	Seq
G8		T & S		C			(9)	Ø	

Missals

M3	K		T OØ		O	S	C	⊕ etc † etc D ~ (10)	Seq
NM5	K		T OØ (7)			S D	C	⊕ etc † etc	Seq
M4	K		T	Credo (6)	O	S D	C	⊕ etc † etc ~ (10)	Seq
NM6	K	~	T D	Credo (6)	O	S	C	† etc OØ	
NM1	K O Ø	~	T D		O	S	C	⊕ etc † etc	Seq
M1	K	~	TOT		O D	S	C	⊕ etc † etc	Seq
M5	K		TOT D			S	C	⊕ etc † etc OØ	
NM3			TOT			S D	C	⊕ etc † etc	Seq
NM4			TOT			S	C D	⊕ etc † etc OØ V	
M2	O		T & S	⊕			C	† etc	Seq

NOTES
(1) Quatuor tempora Masses; (2) Mass for Peace; (3) Litany; (4) office antiphons and hymns; (5) alleluias; (6) preces; (7) Liber generationis; (8) reading tones; (9) introit tropes; (10) ceremonies for Purification, Ash Wednesday, Palm Sunday, Maundy Thursday, and Holy Saturday.

Figure 7.7 presents only the general structure, since it ignores later additions and minor differences of content within sections. The ends of manuscripts in particular, and blank folios between sections are frequent points for the insertion of later feasts such as Trinity and Corpus Christi or other miscellanea. Possibly some of the sources studied are now misbound, a condition which could help to explain the odd position of the Sanctorale and sequences in G21.

750 Sources G3 and G4 are clearly related: sources G6 and G9 are almost as clearly so. G3 and G4 are consecutively numbered in the same library, and G6 and G9 also are nowadays in the same library, although one is from an identified *fonds*, the other from an unknown provenance. Such tables may provide some evidence for the establishment of families. In the few Missals examined, the relationships are less clear. NM1, NM6, and M1, which include the Aspersion ceremonies after the Kalendar at Advent Sunday, are from Canterbury (?), Sarum, and York respectively, but their organization differs later in the book. The most obvious grouping seems to be that of the Ordo and Temporale of M1, M5, NM3, and NM4, in the last three of which the Ordo appears before Easter Sunday in the middle of the Temporale, and in the first of which it is between Pentecost and Trinity Sunday. The former position is more common than figure 7.7 suggests.

The information of figure 7.7 needs to be presented more compactly if relations are to be seen easily and if such material is to appear in catalogues. Some of the detail must be eliminated. The main sections must be kept, and the different positions of the Office of the Dead and of the Dedication seem to be significant: the distinction between services votive to the Virgin and other votive services does not seem necessary and both may be included under the symbol ⊕: other sections are of even less importance and may be combined under a symbol for general additions ■. Graduals may now be categorised. In one category, the Dedication service occurs after the Temporale and a subgroup can be isolated according to the position of the Kyriale **Ø**:

751 Category (1) **TDSC** or **TDCS**. The reversal of the **S** and **C**, which appears in one source, is a characteristic which, when enough statistics have been gathered, may make it possible to identify the provenance more exactly (see **890, 893-6**). The subgroups are (**K**) **TD S C■ Ø**, appearing in two sources apparently unrelated,[33] and **TD Ø S C** or **TD Ø C⊕† S**, as in three manuscripts all of English provenance.[34]

In a second category the Dedication feast is after the Sanctorale and into this category fall the two related sources from Austria, G3 and G4, both of which lack the Common, and a source from Holland, G13. Subgroups could probably serve well here: Category (2) **T SD (C) Ø**. The exact contents of the three manuscripts can be drawn from figure 7.7.

Category (3) **T S CD**. Here, the Dedication is after the Common, a position occurring in two 12th-century sources and one 14th-century source.[35]

Other categories, and certainly refinements of these three, will need to be elucidated as more sources are catalogued: a fourth category would include the manuscripts with Temporale and Sanctorale combined.

As for Missals, several categories may be specified on the basis of the position of the feast of the Dedication, as with Graduals, and of the Ordo. The placing of the latter within the Temporale, represented by **TOT**, or after the complete Temporale with or without Dedication (**TO** or **TDO**) may suggest that there are two large families of Missals but the information known about the manuscripts from which these facts were abstracted does not confirm such a division. It is obviously premature to draw conclusions of this kind.

Nevertheless, even these preliminary investigations may give us some hints as to what should be included in a catalogue of liturgical books. Suggestions about what should perhaps be included in such a catalogue are found in appendix VIII.

8

Office Books

800 The daily round of offices, as we have seen, is more complex as well as more extensive than the services of Mass and as a result the books, Antiphonals and Breviaries (both normal and Noted), are larger and more difficult to use. Their structure, however, follows the same general principles as that of Mass books in that an item is given in full only when it is proper, or on its first appearance as a common text. We must distinguish between items which are provided for use throughout the whole year, such as the psalms and ferial antiphons assigned to each weekday, and those which are common only to seasons or to shorter periods such as octaves. Items for the former, the yearly common, are recorded in the Choir Psalter, together usually with other material, and occur in the Temporale only in incipit or are omitted entirely. Items proper to particular periods and common within those periods are usually recorded where necessary in the Temporale. Because of the complexities, most office books give incipits and informative rubrics quite extensively, often repeating them where in theory they are unnecessary but in practice useful and even essential. The presence of an incipit or even a complete text, then, need not necessarily imply that this is the first appearance of an item, and the texts and formulas of the preceding days must be searched thoroughly in order to establish the actual state. To elucidate the precise sequence of texts completely for any occasion would require a minutely detailed examination and inventory of texts and rubrics probably extending from the occasion right back to Advent, and necessitating reference to other books of the use: such a task is hardly ever necessary, unless an authentic re-enactment is proposed,[1] and is probably not worth the effort. It may not even be possible.

The purpose of this book, in any case, is not the minute examination of texts and offices, but the general method of organization of various parts of the year and of the liturgical manuscripts, so that the user can identify the peculiarities of particular sources. Reduction of the complexities to formulas eliminates most of the varying detail, and is essential if an overall view of the structure of the books is to be grasped quickly. I shall therefore employ various schemes to make the order of events more visually immediate, and shall use the accompanying text to fill in details. In particular, individual items and sometimes complete services will be reduced to letters and numbers, as outlined in the list of abbreviations (**4**). Mostly, where the precise contents of an office are diagrammed with letters for individual items, the letter for the office will not be shown: a discrete series of letters beginning with I or ending with B or M clearly isolates Matins or Lauds or Vespers respectively. Even these schemes are too cumbersome for certain cases: for example, if only one of the antiphons or responsories of Matins were noted in incipit form, the full abbreviation would be much longer, for example: Ih A2ad LRLRLR a3d LRLrLR . . . This would carry the algebraic text too far, and such minor variants will normally be disregarded, and a qualification may be mentioned in the text.

ANTIPHONALS

801 As with the Mass books, I shall begin with the books containing only the music of the offices, the Antiphonals. The reason is the same, that there are fewer items with which to contend. Unlike Graduals, however, Antiphonals may vary considerably in their contents, a feature which will be examined in a later section. The term Antiphonal is not as precise as could be desired since it is now conventionally used to denote the book which contains all the musical propers for day and night offices, antiphons, responsories, and invitatories: this meaning is adopted here so that all these items may be expected. Hymns, which are generally proper to seasons, may be given in their correct place within the offices, lending a distinctive appearance to the book, but are more usually placed in a separate section at the end or quite separately in the Psalter or in an independently bound book.

The initials

802 All office books, including Breviaries, depend principally on two items, both musical, for the visual organization. These are the first responsory of Matins and the first antiphon of Lauds, items chosen probably because most are proper: they are therefore rarely omitted. The Benedictus and Magnificat antiphons are intrinsically more important and are omitted even less frequently, but they are denoted with special initials only when the responsory and first antiphon of Lauds are not available, or in a few other circumstances. The responsory and the Lauds antiphon begin with a size 2 initial, and on a few occasions such as Maundy Thursday there is usually a third initial of the same size preceding the one for the responsory. This third initial may occur on a number of different items, according to what is proper on the occasion: on Maundy Thursday the first antiphon of Matins, *Zelus domus*, has it. In other cases it may be one of the antiphons of first Vespers, or the Magnificat antiphon. More important feasts, and indeed sometimes Maundy Thursday itself, have this anticipatory initial, which may be raised to an even larger size, with a larger initial for the responsory. In this case the Lauds antiphon generally has the size 2 initial as usual, and the first item of second Vespers usually also has an initial of that size. Important feasts, therefore, are emphasized by four initials:

size 2 or larger	*large initial*	*size 2*	*size 2*
Vespers A or Vespers M or Matins A etc	Matins first R	Lauds first A	Vespers first A

When they are listed within the services, hymns usually adopt the size 2 initial and in this respect are analogous to the sequences and tracts of Graduals. As in Graduals, too, other specal items are given this size of initial, the series of great O antiphons of Advent being the most prominent example. Very occasionally each of the nocturns may be similarly distinguished, as in source A12, and this Antiphonal uses size 2 initials for the chapters and prayers which are included. As in Graduals, the largest initials denote the major feasts, Advent, Christmas, etc, and there is sometimes the same differentiation from the lesser feasts such as Epiphany, which have elaborate but smaller main initials. As we have noticed before, it is misleading to regard the initial as marking the beginning of a service or of a day: in particular, the largest initial on the first responsory may be preceded by a good deal of material in first Vespers and Compline and at the beginning of Matins, so that the rubric announcing the day may occur some distance beforehand. One source, ms A6, sometimes gives the largest initial to the first item of first Vespers and a less elaborate main initial to the first responsory. The capitals and large capitals are reserved for the subsequent antiphons of services, and for the subsequent responsories, which may begin with the smallest capital used, but which are usually denoted by a large capital. Responsory verses and repetenda, the doxology, and the psalm intonations and evovae formulas which accompany antiphons generally have a normal capital letter no larger than the surrounding text. The variability of this scheme from source to source and within a manuscript is considerable because of the different repertories of proper and common items. In order to illustrate the principles further, I present a few analyses in more detail.

803 In ms A1, a Dominican Antiphonal, the hierarchy is quite complex since there are six kinds of letter, mostly distinct although the difference between adjacent sizes is occasionally difficult to determine:

(i) Large initials, followed by a capital or large capital, denote the first responsory of major feasts,

(ii) Square initials, which we must describe as size 2+, are used generally for the first item of a feast, the first responsory of ordinary days, and the first antiphon of Lauds. They stand at the margin and are distinct from (iii).

(iii) Thin initials, size 2, which do not necessarily stand at the margin, are used for subsequent responsories and the first antiphon of each nocturn. It is difficult to distinguish between the square initial I and the thin I.

(iv) This letter, the large capital (1 +), is sometimes almost as large vertically as the thin initial, but lacks the filigree penwork. It is tempting to call the tallest of these letters small initials (2 –) but the difference between them and the large capital does not seem to be maintained consistently and their calligraphic rather than decorative style supports their description as capitals rather than initials: in a few cases to be mentioned later, manuscripts do include a calligraphic size 2 – initial as well as the large capital. The large capitals in ms A1 are used, anywhere within the writing area, for subsequent antiphons after the first, for responsory verses, and occasionally in rubrics.

(v) The ordinary capital identifies the psalm incipits following antiphons, the cue words specifying the repetenda of responsories, the beginning of dialogues (where these are not provided with music), and rubrics. This size of letter is shown as 1.

(vi) The ordinary letter, with no increase in height, serves for the single-letter abbreviations for genres, when it may have a difference in form (eg R instead of r), and for the word evovae. These letters are represented by 0.

804 There is thus a fairly clear descending hierarchy here, but some additional comments are needed. Where the letter beginning an item is larger than usual, the subsequent sections of that item may also take letters larger than usual. For example, when the first antiphon of an office has a square initial rather than an initial, the beginning of its psalm incipit, often the Magnificat, seems to adopt the large capital rather than the ordinary capital: on the other hand the letter beginning the evovae which follows is not raised from an ordinary letter to a capital. In many manuscripts the raising of a first letter to a higher size does, however, seem to carry with it the principle of raising the size of letters beginning other principal sections of the item. As will be clear from the above remarks, ms A1 gives both the psalm incipit and the evovae formula for the psalm tone: above the former is shown the intonation of the tone, above the latter the terminatio or differentia. The invitatory, not mentioned when the letters were described, is generally treated as a first antiphon, given a thin initial, unless it is the first item of an office to appear. The differentiation in this manuscript and in Dominican sources in general between the first and subsequent antiphons of the nocturns is interesting and not universal. Where more than a genre abbreviation is required, the musical stave ends, rubrics are written, and the musical stave begins again. Rubrical script is normally smaller than the real texts, and four lines of rubrics fill the height otherwise occupied by a single line of text and stave. In this source, the rubrics read downwards. Within the rubric, incipits of real texts are sometimes written in a script a little larger than the rubric and of course in black. After a rubric, the following item may be announced with an abbreviation or a reference to a day written in the normal size adopted throughout: the blocks of script which intervene between the staves, then, may incorporate three different sizes of ordinary letter, and the capitals which go along with those sizes. Versicles and responses are given in this manuscript, normally without music, and are written in rubric size in the space left in the stave between the last antiphon of the nocturn and the next responsory, or between the last responsory and the first antiphon of Lauds. Where it is necessary for the music of these dialogues to appear, as in Holy Week, it is given on a stave of two or three lines rather than the usual four, unnecessary for these simple tones. Two of these staves, with the text beneath each, are fitted into the height of a single line of normal text and its stave. Most of these features, except the last (dialogue-staves) and the first (large initials) are illustrated in plate 26a-c, and described in the caption to that plate (appendix IX). The sequence of initials and capitals could probably be determined from the above information, but it may be useful to summarize the procedures in this source with some examples.

805
Advent Sunday

Magnificat, psalm-incipit and evovae	[2+]	1+ 0
Invitatory and psalm-incipit	2	1+
Nocturn I, only one antiphon, psalm-incipit and evovae	2	1 0
versicle	–	–
first responsory, repetenda, first verse, and cue	[3+3]	0 2– 1
other repetenda, verses, cues		0 1+ 1
all other responsories, etc	2	0 1+ 1

Other nocturns follow the pattern of the first, if the first responsory is removed (the large initial which begins that item is followed immediately by an ordinary script letter). Note also that the first verse of the several which are peculiar to that responsory has a 'raised' initial of a kind which does not appear elsewhere, decorated like the initial, but smaller even than the thin initial denoted by size 2. After the three nocturns, the office continues:

Lauds antiphon, psalm-incipit and evovae	[2+]	1 0

The square initial is followed by an ordinary capital. Because the first antiphon has a 'raised' letter, the second antiphon begins with a square initial rather than with a large capital, which otherwise characterizes subsequent antiphons:

Lauds, second antiphon, psalm-incipit, evovae	2	1 0
other antiphons, etc	1+	1 0
Benedictus antiphon, etc	2	1+ 0
Prime, Terce, Sext, Nones; responsories, repetenda,	2	0
verses, cues	1+	1
Second Vespers, Magnificat, psalm-incipit, evovae	2	1 0

The weekdays then continue the 2 1 0 sequence through their antiphons, for the little hours on feria ii and for Benedictus and Magnificat on every day, up to the second Sunday of Advent. Only a somewhat longer rubric distinguishes the

FIGURE 8.1
Genres, initials, and capitals of a typical Antiphonal (ms A1)

The letters stand for the genres; numerals stand for the size of initial or capital with which each genre (or section of a genre) begins. Substantial rubrics are shown by ≠.

Vig. Epi: I B M N

I	B	M	N
[2+] 1+ ≠	2 1+ ≠	2 1+	2 1+

Epiphany Matins (lacking the invitatory): (A3D R3)3

	A	A	A	D	R	R	R
=	2 1	1+ 1	1+ 1	D	[2+2] 1+ 1	2 1+ 1	2 1+ 1 (● 1+) 1
=	2 1	1+ 1	1+ 1	D	2 1+ 1	2 1+ 1	2 1+ 1 (● 1+) 1
=	2 1 ≠	1+ 1	1+ 1	D	2 1+ 1	2 1+ 1	2 1+ 1 (● 1+) 1

versicles for the *Liber generationis* with music: all 1+

versicle before Lauds

Lauds: A5D B

A	A	A	A	A	D	B
[2+] 1	1+ 1	1+ 1	1+ 1	1+ 1	D	2 1

Little Hours, each with a responsory, in which the cue is sometimes omitted: R / R / R / R

R	R	R	R
2 1+	2 1+ 1	2 1+	2 1+

Second Vespers: M
2 1

beginning of this Sunday: its first responsory, however, has a square initial [2+]. We can therefore establish for this source the normal pattern of 2 1 0 (or 1+ 1 0) for all subsequent antiphons, and 2 0 1+ 1 for all subsequent responsories. Since the 0 here merely represents an ordinary script letter not distinct from its surroundings, it is perhaps simpler to omit it from the formula, and this may be done if the normal conventions for the source have been established.

806 Rather than duplicate this lengthy description for a different day, I shall reduce the matter to the numerals representing the initials and capitals: in figure 8.1 the distinction between the first and other antiphons in each nocturn is included. The letters are the abbreviations for the genres: substantial rubrics with incipits are shown by ≠, and smaller rubrics such as *in primo nocturno* by =.

807 The three main divisions of an important liturgical day emphasized by the hierarchy of initials, then, are: (a) material for the Vigil, (b) Matins, (c)Lauds. On less important days only the last two will be stressed. Within these sections outlined visually, the individual items are not difficult to perceive. It is a little more tricky to isolate the first antiphon of each nocturn where there is no separation between the final responsory of one and the first antiphon of the next. Where there is a rubric, *in primo nocturno*, as in figure 8.1, there is no problem. Some manuscripts have no break, rubric, or other guide at this point: some may place a special sign such as a coloured paraph ¶. An organization such as the following enables the nocturns to be identified very quickly:

in	====================	versicle	====================	in
i°	====================	and	====================	ii°
n°	antiphons	response	responsories	n°

There are of course variants and adaptations of these schemes. The text of the versicle and response, for example, may be written under the tone for the evovae of the preceding antiphon, the psalm incipit and evovae words being omitted (ms A11, fol a^{v}). Only careful observation and a knowledge of what is expected can prevent mistakes in interpretation of this kind of 'irrational' procedure. The place where psalm incipits or evovae words or both should appear is particularly susceptible to confusing format. We have so far assumed the presence of a psalm, either incipit or evovae, for every antiphon: but there may be several psalms 'under' a single antiphon. In this instance the first psalm may be shown conventionally, as described above, and the remainder (which will use the same psalm tone, whose formulas do not therefore need repeating) may be given in incipits in the break in the stave, or below the stave but without notes, or in other ways. In some sources neither psalm incipit nor evovae may appear, and lacking these lesser points of reference the manuscript may employ a simpler scheme of initials. In fact, the one described is rather more complex than is usual. It is also fairly consistent. This relative tidiness may perhaps be attributed to its Dominican provenance.

808 The following section demonstrates some of the variations possible. After the larger initials, source A8 has three distinct initials mostly placed *in* the margin; a square coloured letter (2+) used for Magnificat antiphon, Lauds, and the invitatory; a calligraphic (perhaps coloured, but certainly plain) letter (2) larger than the capital of size 1+ under which category such calligraphic letters are more neatly included, and a small coloured initial (2−). Size 2 is used for hymns and for the first antiphon of Matins, the small initial (2−) for responsories and subsequent antiphons. In a manuscript at Autun (Bibl mun S 173), the large capital (1+) in calligraphic style for use within the musical items has to be distinguished from the large coloured capital, also size 1+ but considerably larger because it stands within some passages where only the text is given, in larger script. In several sources from Switzerland, eg, Fribourg, Chap ms 1 and Solothurn, Zentralbibl ms S III 6, the thin rather than square size 2 initial is either coloured or black, the former marking responsories, the latter their verses and the doxology. I append various schemata of responsories and antiphons other than those involving large initials:

responsories	
[1+] 1 1	(source A11)
1+ 1+ 1	(A13)
2- 1+ 1	(Beaune, Bibl mun ms 26)
2- 1+ 2- 1+	(Sion, Chap ms 1)
2- 1+ 1+ 1	(Autun, Bibl mun ms S 173)
2+ 1 1+ 1	(Trier, Bistumsarchiv ms 480)
2 0 1 0	(A7)
2 1 2- 1	(A16)
2 1 1(+) 1	(A15, and Brno, Univ Lib ms R 17)
2 (col) 1 2(black) 1	(Fribourg, Chap ms 1 and Solothurn, Zentralbibl ms S III 6)

antiphons	
1	(A11, A7)
1 1	(A15)
1+ 1	(A13, and Autun, Bibl mun ms S 173, and Trier, Bistumsarchiv ms 480)
1 1 1	(Autun, Bibl mun ms S 173)
2 1	(Solothurn, Zentralbibl ms S III 6)
2- 1+	(Sion, Chap ms 1)
2- 1+ 0	(Beaune, Bibl mun ms 26)

Finally, it must be emphasized again that these schemata are approximate, and size 2 in one manuscript may not be the same as size 2 in another even though the general description will be the same. Different schemes may appear within one and the same source. Far more comprehensive statistics must be gathered before significant deductions can be made.

Advent

809 In the Antiphonals studied Advent is relatively unencumbered with memorials and services to the Virgin, compared with contemporary Breviaries. Whether this is an indication that the Marian services were recited privately rather than sung in choir or that the Marian chants were so well known as not to need recording cannot be answered here. Few of these Antiphonals include complete hymns in their correct position although many give their incipits, without music. Where the complete hymn is given, only its first verse is normally supplied with music. This arrangement gives a distinctive appearance to the book since there will be several lines of continuous text, without musical staves, only at the points where hymns occur. The few manuscripts which, unnecessarily, repeat the tune for all verses are not distinctive in this respect, but the item can be clearly isolated by its different musical style. As with the sequence, its predominantly syllabic chant results in a layout in which the text runs on continuously, with single note symbols on the staves, and without the separation of syllables by blank spaces or decoration, a separation which is characteristic of the majority of other chants.

In addition to the proper chants, most sources give the relevant dialogues, versicles and responses, which occur after the antiphons of Matins, between Matins and Lauds, and at places in the other services. Normally only the response is provided since the choir does not need the opening sentence and it may be complete, given in incipit, or complete but written with massive abbreviation (as in plates 1e and 2b), for example, *Et nubes pluant justum a t e g s* (Advent 1, ℣$_1$). These brief texts are written in smaller script where the stave breaks off unless, as is occasionally the case on Advent Sunday to provide a model, the tone is given. The abbreviation identifying the versicle is normally V and the response R, but if only the latter appears it may be preceded only by V: the confusion between these items and responsories and verses has been discussed (**436**).

810 On Advent Sunday first Vespers may use ferial antiphons whose incipits may be given, or it may have its own set of propers, and it may or may not have a responsory, according to the use. It always has a proper Magnificat antiphon, which is therefore the only item which appears complete in every source. The dialogue may be recorded. Thus, presented as a formula, this Vespers may appear in one of the following ways, or others: aRM or A5DM or rDM or A4RhdM, or most simply M. Compline does not appear in any of the sources studied and must be sought in the Psalter. Matins is complete with the relevant number of antiphons and responsories, according to its use and its monastic or secular nature, and its precise constitution must be elucidated for each source. Mostly there is one antiphon for each nocturn, common to Advent and thus not appearing in subsequent Matins of the season. A common scheme therefore would be Ih (ADR3)3. It is important to remember that in monastic uses there is never more than a single antiphon for the third nocturn, the antiphon *ad cantica*, however many there are for nocturns one and two. It is also worth recalling that the first responsory of this Sunday has several verses. Following Matins there may be a list of ferial responsories for use during the following week: although such lists occur at other points in some of the sources studied, none has such a list for Advent Sunday and, in the absence of evidence to the contrary, we must assume that in all of these manuscripts the Sunday responsories are distributed in numerical sequence. The *Te Deum* or its absence may be mentioned and one source, the Worcester Antiphonal (A14), gives it in full with its tone. A few sources also note here the dialogue with which Lauds is begun. Lauds, with its five antiphons and ending with the Benedictus, is quite standard in form, differing only in the inclusion of a responsory or in references to its hymn or dialogue: A5DB or A5RhDB may be taken as representative. It is in several sources followed by memorials and occasionally processions to the Virgin, which are given in incipit or fully. The antiphons of Lauds are in most uses repeated as the antiphons for the little hours, in which case nothing normally appears between Lauds and second Vespers: this is the case in sources A5, A7, A11, and A12. In other cases the Lauds antiphons may be recorded as though they were for the little hours: Lauds: AB / Hours: AAAA. In those uses where there is a proper antiphon or a short responsory at the little hours these items must of course appear, and the dialogue may be included, so that the sources vary considerably in what occurs at this point. It may be nothing, or R or RD or A or AD or ARD for each of the little hours. Second Vespers in all sources studied has no proper antiphons, and uses the ferial texts designated in the Psalter: these, or the single antiphon under which all the psalms are performed, are often given in incipit. The responsory, where it is a part of the service, is present and as in first Vespers, the Magnificat antiphon is always proper. Typical formats are therefore M or aM or arM or aRM.

811 Such analyses of the contents of each office are useful only when examination and comparison in detail are required, and to obtain a fluent working acquaintance with the manner in which the books reflect particular uses, and to obtain by similar analyses of later days a general or detailed view of the sequence of proper and common items. It may also serve to signal the unusual case. In the sources studied, two deserve additional comment. Ms A9, which is a Diurnal and thus excludes Matins, exhibits an odd arrangement: it omits the Benedictus antiphon since Lauds may be considered a night office, and the material for Prime, even though the other little hours are provided with proper items. Ms A11 places the material for the little hours after the commemorative items following second Vespers: the scheme for the whole of Advent Sunday in this source is therefore:

M / I(AdR4)3 / A5RB / ✠ / aM / ✠ / Hours: A4.

812 Of the weekdays of the first week of Advent, Monday is singled out since it includes an invitatory and antiphons for the little hours in addition to the antiphons for Benedictus and Magnificat. The general scheme for Monday is I / B / A4 / M. The remaining days of the week are characterized by propers only for the Benedictus and Magnificat antiphons, and can thus be represented simply by the formula BM for each day. On Saturday however, it is more correct to place the Magnificat antiphon, which is proper to first Vespers of the following Sunday, in the scheme for that day, since it will be separated from the Saturday Benedictus antiphon by the rubric announcing Sunday. This separation is even more emphatic when a saint's office intervenes, as it may if the Temporale and Sanctorale are combined. The offices for Nicholas and Lucy could be included before Advent 2, so that the formula for Saturday would become: B (complete saint's office) rubric M. In this case, the proper Magnificat antiphon for the saint's feast will complete the Saturday Vespers. Since the normal ferial arrangement in Antiphonals calls for only Benedictus and Magnificat antiphons, there results a long series of alternating B and M, which may however be identified only as antiphons rather than *ad evangelia, ad benedictus*, or *ad magnificat*. The scheme for this particular week (Advent 1, ferias) would be: I B A4 M / BM / BM / BM / BM / B. A possible alternative in a manuscript not specific in its designations might be: I A15. Oddities inexplicable without further research were observed in ms A5, which lists only twelve antiphons and no invitatory, and in A11, where the Monday Magnificat is omitted.

813 Continuing Advent, we may observe that the remaining Sundays follow the pattern of the first except that the Matins antiphons are omitted, as are the items for the little hours, the former being common throughout the season and the latter being drawn from the antiphons of Lauds. In addition, the Magnificat antiphons for Sundays 3 and 4 are usually omitted since they are drawn from the series of great O antiphons to be discussed. A rubric might indicate *ad magnificat O*. The formula for Advent 3 might therefore be: M / I R9 / A5B / incipit for O. If monastic, the R9 will be R12. After the 9 or the 12 there may be additional responsories for use during the following week: a secular Antiphonal with three ferial responsories might then appear to be monastic: R12. All ferias of the second week adopt the normal scheme, BM. Apart from the *Quatuor tempora* (QT), the Ember days of the third week, all other ferias of weeks 3 and 4 have only the Benedictus antiphon, the Magnificat being drawn from the list of great Os. The Ember days have certain proper items which will appear in diagrams to be shown below. The fourth week never has Saturday services since Saturday must be Christmas Eve, unless the Eve has come earlier in the week.

814 The order in which these items, days, and services occur in the sources is unfortunately not always straightforward. The great O antiphons, which are usually seven in number but which may be as many as twelve, must all be sung every year and, depending on how soon Christmas Day occurs after the fourth Sunday, must begin on different dates each year: if seven in number they begin on the seventh day before Christmas Eve, if twelve on the twelfth. They must therefore be listed together in the order in which they are to be sung, and cannot be given to specific days. The possible days on which they may occur must have the necessary rubric. The O antiphons are normally listed immediately before the services of Christmas Eve. The Ember day services are sometimes recorded separately just before the great Os rather than in the third week. The Antiphonals studied therefore present these four weeks in different ways. Up to the third Sunday they are unanimous in giving the days in the correct order: thence there is considerable variety. In the next few diagrams Ø indicates the great O antiphons.

(1) Adv 3, ferias incl QT / Adv 4 / B5 R Ø8.

This is the simplest method. The Ember days are in their proper place, as is the fourth Sunday and the five Benedictus antiphons for ferias ii-vi of the fourth week. The responsory which follows is the responsory for Vespers for these days. The great Os follow, with a ninth for the Magnificat of the feast of St Thomas, apostle. This method is adopted in the Sarum Antiphonal (A13) which is clear enough from this point, although pages are missing until the third week.

An English monastic source, the Worcester Antiphonal (A14), is only a little different:

(2) Adv 3, ferias incl QT / rubric giving the incipits and a few propers for the ferias of fourth week / Ø7 / Adv 4.

A possible reason for this arrangement is that much of the ferial material for fourth week is drawn from the third.

Both of these English sources give the Lauds services for the third week, which are completely proper for each day, in the correct place. The next two sources, both Dominican (A1, A4), separate the proper items for Lauds, excluding the Benedictus antiphon, and place this material after the ferias of fourth week:

(3) Adv 3 / BM / BM / (QT) I R3 BM / BM / (QT) i R3 BM / (QT) i R3 B /

M and Adv 4 / (BM)5 for ferias ii-vi / (A5)6 Ø7

In place of texts for the Ms here there is normally a rubric to one of the great Os. After the five BMs for the fourth week there are thirty proper antiphons explicitly for Lauds, divided into services for ferias ii-vii: (A5)6. There cannot be six ferias in fourth week, as has been explained, and comparison with other sources indicates that these propers must be for Lauds of the third week. Again appended to the list of great Os is a proper antiphon for St Thomas, apostle.

815 Other sources are even more complex, since they list the propers for the Ember days after the fourth Sunday and often fail to give the material for the fourth week explicitly. Source A7 for example has the following arrangement:

(4) Adv 3 / (BM)6 / Adv 4 / (QT) I R12 / (Lauds: A4)6 Ø12

Benedictus and Magnificat antiphons, or rubrics for Os, are given for the whole of third week. The proper invitatory and twelve proper responsories for the Ember days are listed immediately after the fourth Sunday: distributing the twelve responsories over the three Ember days results in four each day, an apparent oddity since the source is secular and should have only three. This discrepancy cannot be explained from the information in the manuscript but the next arrangement can suggest an answer. Lauds, without the Benedictus antiphon, and proper antiphons for each of the little hours, Lauds A4, are then given for six ferias with some commemorative antiphons for each day. As in the previous arrangement these services must be for third week. Source A8 is similar although more explicit:

(5) Adv 3 / (BM) 6 / Adv 4 / (feria ii) Lauds / (feria iii) Lauds /

(feria iv) R I R3 Lauds / (feria v) i R3 Lauds /(feria vi) R I R3 Lauds /

(feria vii) i R3 Lauds / Ø7

(feria vi is erroneously called iiii in the manuscript)

Again, because of the presence of Saturday (vii), the material after Advent 4 must be for third week. There is a proper invitatory on ferias iv and vi and responsories for first Vespers of those days. Moreover, there are three proper responsories for feria vi, not one of the Ember days: in other words there are twelve proper responsories distributed over the last four days of the week, three for each day. The same practice would explain the twelve responsories in arrangement 4. Another arrangement, somewhat more complex, may be noted, but the source (A6) by itself is not explicit enough to answer some of the questions:

(6) Adv 3 / (feria ii) A2 (feria iii) A2 (feria iv) A2 (feria v) A2 (feria vi) A7 M /

Adv 4 / (feria iv) I R3 Lauds / (feria v) R3 Lauds /

(feria vi) R3 Lauds A4 / (feria vii) R3 Lauds / (ferias) r3 Lauds / Ø11

The antiphons of ferias ii-v are not specified for Benedictus and Magnificat, although the second of each pair is for Vespers. Saturday is not given and the seven antiphons under feria vi are not described. After Advent 4 and without rubrical identification are the propers for the Ember days, and each of the Lauds services includes the Benedictus antiphon. Presumably, the services are for distribution as shown above and the last section, specified only with *feria* and noting only incipits of the responsories, is for use on the other ferias of weeks 3 and 4. Since the Lauds services include the Benedictus, the first of the antiphons for ferias ii-v of week 3 may not be for the Benedictus of those days. Further elucidation can be obtained only by comparative study. One other point about this source is worth noting: feria iv, the Ember Wednesday of the third week, has a rubric indicating the incipits of some proper items for use if the day is the eighth before Christmas Day. A similar situation is in ms A5, where the third week is characterized by pairs of antiphons not specified as Benedictus or Magnificat, and where the Lauds services for six ferias presented after Advent 4 include the Benedictus antiphon. The Ember propers are listed in one undifferentiated section immediately after Advent 4:

(7) Adv 3 / (feria ii) A2 (feria iii) A2 (ferias iv-vii) A9 /

Adv 4 / (QT) I R15 / (Lauds plus B) / Ø12

How the fifteen responsories are distributed over the three (or four) days is not clear.

816 The variability in the placing of the Ember days and the ferias of fourth week may result from some earlier separation of the ferial, fasting, and Sunday repertories, and the problems of conveniently combining them into a single sequence. No doubt, too, numerous other arrangements occur in the sources. The topic will be dealt with briefly again when Breviaries are discussed. At that time, too, when rubrics are more available, I shall give some information about the feast of St Thomas, apostle, some of whose propers have been mentioned in connection with the great Os.

One or two of the Antiphonals studied retain the old-fashioned combination of Temporale and Sanctorale. The following arrangements were observed and where necessary must be used to modify the organization of Temporale material already presented:

Adv 1-4 / Nicholas, Lucy, Lazarus / QT / Øs;
Adv 1 and ferias / Nicholas / 2 and ferias / Lucy / 3 to Christmas;
Adv 1-2 and ferias / Lucy / 3-4 / Thomas, apostle / QT and ferias.

The Vigil and Christmas Day

817 The term vigil encompasses both the whole day preceding Christmas, from its Vespers, and in another proper sense the first Vespers of Christmas Day itself. There is little to note about either of the two days: either may be a Sunday, and rubrics or alternatives for such a contingency are sometimes provided. Apart from the antiphons of Matins and the little hours, often repeating those of earlier days and thus not given or given only in incipit, most of the sung items on Christmas Eve are proper. Almost everything is proper on Christmas Day, often including the antiphon and Nunc dimittis antiphon of Compline. After this service, and indeed at other points such as after Lauds, commemorative antiphons forming part of the suffrages (that is, with a prayer and dialogues not recorded in Antiphonals) are often listed and may be numerous. Additional items to be noticed on this feast are the *prose* frequently included after the last responsory of nocturns one and three. There may be ferial responsories for the octave and perhaps commemorative antiphons for the Virgin, after Matins. At this point, too, the *Liber generationis* may be mentioned and occasionally given complete with its tone and introductory dialogue. The *Te Deum* and *Missa in gallicantu* which follow are normally indicated only in a rubric, although ms A8 gives the musical incipits for the latter. This source also refers to the *Missa in primo diluculo* after the Marian antiphons following Lauds.

Christmas to Lent

818 This period, with its three or four important saints and its frequent commemorations of both the Nativity and the Virgin, is very complex, and because the items proper to the commemorations are very variable from source to source it is difficult to describe in general terms. When the saints' feasts are not in the Temporale, as is the case with Dominican books, the pages between Christmas and Circumcision are taken up with antiphons, often a large number. These are of various different kinds. The Benedictus and Magnificat antiphons are the most important. Two Dominican books studied, mss A1 and A2, give a single Benedictus and a single Magnificat *infra octavam*. Omitting all references to or commemorations of the saint, these two sources include only an extra antiphon for a Benedictus and Magnificat in commemoration of the Virgin. With such Marian antiphons aside, the basic repertory up to Circumcision is a proper Benedictus and Magnificat antiphon. Some sources extend this with a few variants, usually noted in rubrics, for the Sunday when it falls within the octave, and most sources provide in addition commemorations for the Nativity, the Virgin, for the saints, and sometimes processional items, presumably given in an order convenient for the use. Rubrics describing what the chant is for may or may not occur and without further information it may be impossible to reconstruct the services of the period more accurately. When the saints' feasts are present, the distribution of the commemorative items over the days of the octave is more clearly evident.

819 Source A7 may be studied first. The saints are omitted. Immediately after the Magnificat of second Vespers of Christmas there is a commemoration of the Virgin. Again it should be emphasized that these commemorations will be suffrages with a prayer and dialogue. The source then lists fourteen antiphons without description: comparison with other manuscripts and the texts themselves indicate that there are eight antiphons commemorating Christmas and six for the Virgin, distributed X3 ⊕6 X5 (where X is for Xmas and ⊕ for the Virgin). Incipits then indicate the dialogue for the nocturns and before Lauds and at the other hours, presumably for the days within the octave. Thomas of Canterbury is not included in the Sanctorale and the day after Holy Innocents is thus vacant, together with die vi. These two days are often referred to as the two days (*dies* rather than *ferie*) after Innocents. Source A7 now provides the propers for these two days, beginning with a rubric specifying the ferial psalms for the nocturns and giving the incipits of invitatory, hymn, and antiphons. Many of the remaining items are given only in incipit and the days are really distinguished by their proper responsories. After the Vespers of the first day and after Lauds and Vespers of the second, the incipit of a Marian antiphon is noted. Similar commemorations are recorded by incipits after the Vespers of the Sunday within the octave of Christmas, which is shown next, and which consists almost entirely of items repeated from earlier services of the Christmas period, except for the Benedictus antiphon, *Dum medium silentium*, adopting the same text as the introit of the Mass of the day (**716**). Circumcision is next, with commemorations after both first and second Vespers and after Lauds, and with both Magnificat antiphons proper. Rubrics for the performance of the octaves of the saints and for the Vigil of Epiphany if those days fall on a Sunday complete the material preceding Epiphany. In the following scheme most items are given only by incipits. The scheme indicates the arrangement of ms A7, and shows the position of commemorations with X or ⊕ (or x and ⊕ for incipits) as explained above:

day	*service*	*genre*
Nat	Vespers 2	M
		A14 (X & ⊕)
die i post Inn	Matins	
	Lauds	
	Vespers	⊕
die ii	Matins	
	Lauds	⊕
Sunday in octave	Vespers	⊕
	Matins	
	Lauds	B
	Hours	
	Vespers	⊕
Circumcision	Vespers	M ⊕
	Matins	
	Lauds	⊕
	Vespers	M ⊕

820 Source A5 is less complex, even though it includes the saints. Immediately after the Magnificat of Christmas it lists thirteen commemorative antiphons, most of which have the same texts as in the previous source. The Sunday within the octave then follows with only proper Benedictus and Magnificat antiphons. Then, unencumbered with the commemorative antiphons which must be inserted as necessary, the feasts of Stephen, John, Holy Innocents, and Circumcision are recorded and are almost entirely proper. Each saint's feast is followed by several antiphons proper to that saint, presumably for use as commemorative antiphons during or on the octaves of their feasts. The separation of daily and commemorative items in this source is unusual:

Nativity	Vespers 2	M
		A13 (X & ⊕)
Sunday in octave	Lauds	B
	Vespers	M
Stephen		
John	all	
Innocents	services	
Circumcision	proper	

Source A11 is a little more complex and arranges the material in a different order:

Nativity	Vespers 2	M
		A (⊕)
feria proxima post natalem innocentum		R6
		A11 (X)
		A6 (⊕)
		processional antiphon
feria		i(nvitatory)
Stephen		
John		
Innocents		
Sunday		incipits
Circumcision		

The six responsories must surely be for die i and die ii, three for each day, despite the rubric. In the margin of the first responsory the cue *Johannes ev.* appears. As is clear from the marginal cues to the other five responsories, this refers to the biblical source of the text rather than to the nearby feast of St John. Commemorative antiphons for the Nativity are clearly separated from those for the Virgin, and they are followed by an antiphon *ad processionem* and the incipit of the ferial invitatory. Again the daily and commemorative propers are kept separate.

821 It would probably be very difficult to combine the commemorative and daily items in the correct sequence given only the information in the sources just described. We may gain a good idea of the procedure, however, from source A6, in which the services are laid out from Christmas to Epiphany in the order in which they occur, with the saints' feasts included and with the commemorations inserted. There are nine Marian antiphons, five for Christmas, and they occur basically in pairs, X and ⊕, after Vespers and Lauds of the feasts. Following the saints' feasts are die i and die ii, and a third day which must be the Sunday within the octave, and incipits and rubrics for the feast of St Silvester, which is celebrated on the day after die ii. Marian and sometimes Christmas commemorations follow the Lauds and Vespers of each of these four days:

Stephen	M		⊕	Matins	Lauds	X	⊕	Hours	Vespers		
John	M	X	⊕	Matins	Lauds	X	⊕	Hours	Vespers		
Inn.	M	X	⊕	Matins	Lauds	X	⊕	Hours	Vespers	X	⊕
die i				Matins	Lauds		⊕	Hours	Vespers		⊕
die ii				Matins	Lauds		⊕		Vespers		⊕
Sunday				Matins	Lauds	x	⊕	Hours	Vespers	x	⊕
Silvester									Vespers	x	⊕

The regular scheme is quite clear. A rubric states that there are no commemorations of the saints during their octaves. Some uses do include such commemorations, which would follow those of the Nativity and the Virgin. Commemorations on the feast of St John would therefore be: Christmas, Virgin, Stephen; and on the feast of St Thomas of Canterbury they would be: Christmas, Virgin, Stephen, John, Innocents.

822 None of the sources so far studied includes the feast of St Thomas of Canterbury, which takes place on die i post Innocentum. The principle of memorials and the interlinking of saints' feasts is much the same as in the sources studied and the details can easily be observed in the printed Sarum Breviary of 1531[2] or, in an Antiphonal of Sarum use, in source A15. The saints are commemorated in order after the Christmas and Marian memorials, and occasionally there is a commemoration in advance, especially when a proper first Vespers cannot be said. Thus, a commemoration of Thomas of Canterbury is included after the second Vespers of St John and another in the same place in the feast of the Holy Innocents. Both the Breviary and the Antiphonal list numerous Christmas and Marian memorials before the feast of St Stephen, and refer to them thereafter by incipits. Sarum use also has processional responsories to each of the altars of the saints, the procession taking place after the memorials. When no procession is made, an alternative commemoration is provided: two additional musical items, a responsory and an antiphon, therefore appear in such sources. The Breviary and Antiphonal referred to also include an extra 'feast' between the second Vespers of St John and Matins of the Holy Innocents. In addition to the memorials and processions there is a responsory begun by the *eposcopus puerorum*, together with its verses, and an antiphon, dialogue, and episcopal benedictions. In the Antiphonal, all of these items are provided with the relevant chant or tone. This 'office' is the feast of the Boy Bishop.[3]

Between Circumcision and Epiphany the sources give rubrics or incipits showing the proper memorials of the Christmas saints, and rubrics with incipits of the few propers necessary for the Vigil of Epiphany. There is little to note about the propers for Epiphany itself. Most secular sources do not include the invitatory, omitted from the service (**408**). The Genealogy according to Luke, recited after Matins, is sometimes mentioned and the tone for the preceding dialogue (and sometimes for the whole reading itself) may occur. The days through the octave are provided with a varying number of antiphons, sometimes a dozen or more, for Benedictus and Magnificat. These antiphons are written after the second Vespers of Epiphany, except in source A6, where they seem to be listed with Epiphany Lauds. Two Dominican manuscripts, A1 and A4, provide only a single antiphon for each of these canticles throughout the whole octave. The Sunday within the octave and the octave itself occur without complication, providing only a few propers each, mostly the Magnificat antiphons.

823 The first Sunday after the octave, *Domine ne in ira*, is repeated with a few minor proper variants on every Sunday up to Septuagesima: the ninth responsory, for example, may change and its alternative will be given immediately after Matins. In a number of sources, A6, A7, A8, the Magnificat antiphon of second Vespers is not provided and the same is true occasionally for the following ferial services (mss A6, A8): the chants must presumably be sought in the list of antiphons provided after Epiphany itself. Apart from the Magnificat antiphon just mentioned, the ferias of the week following *Domine ne in ira* each have a complete set of services, mostly proper, except for the little hours where the Monday propers are repeated throughout the week. These ferial services are used until Septuagesima. The four possible Sundays remaining, Epiphany 2-5, repeat the items of the first Sunday except for proper Magnificat and Benedictus antiphons, which are here provided. Monastic sources, and also ms A8, give a differing number of proper antiphons for each of these days: three for Epiphany 2, five, six, or seven for Epiphany 3, two, three, or five for Epiphany 4, and two for Epiphany 5, where that Sunday is given at all. It is not clear what the extra antiphons in addition to the Benedictus and Magnificat are. Ms A5 adopts a quite different arrangement for this period:

normal organization			source A5		
day	service	genre	day	service	genre
Epi 1	Vespers Matins Lauds		Epi 1		A3
	Hours Vespers		Epi 2		A4
feria ii	Matins Lauds Hours		Epi 3		A2
	Vespers		Epi 4		A3
feria iii-vii, each	Matins Lauds Vespers		[Epi 1]	Matins Lauds Vespers	
Epi 2-5, each		BM or A2	ferias more or less as normal		

Source A5 specifies the first antiphon of each Sunday as *ad evangelium*. Sources A10 and A11 adopt a similar arrangement.

824 The three Sundays from Septuagesima to the beginning of Lent and the ferias following them, up to Ash Wednesday, are provided with the necessary propers in an uncomplicated order. Most items of the Sundays are proper, except for the Matins antiphons, and the ferias have the usual alternative responsories, noted at Sunday Matins, and proper antiphons for Benedictus and Magnificat (or a series of unspecified antiphons for the same purpose).

FIGURE 8.2
The historie before Lent

Responsories giving the names to the historie are printed in capitals: they and others are shown with a number specifying their position within Matins. The incipits of the Lauds and Benedictus antiphons are also shown.

Septuagesima		Sexagesima		Quinquagesima	
Early					
DOMINE NE IN IRA	(1)	IN PRINCIPIO	(1)	QUADRAGINTA	(1)
				Ponam arcam	(2)
				Per memetipsum	(3)
				Edificavit	(4)
				Locutus est	(5)
				resp. 6-12	
Ecce nomen (Lauds)		Miserere (Lauds)		Secundum mult. (Lauds)	
Simile est (Ben.)		Cum turba (Ben.)		Ecce ascend. (Ben.)	
Monastic					
IN PRINCIPIO	(1)	IN PRINCIPIO	(1)	QUADRAGINTA	(1)
				Ponam arcam	(2)
				Per memetipsum	(3)
				Edificavit	(4)
				Locutus est	(5)
				resp. 6-12	
Miserere (Lauds)		Miserere (Lauds)		Secundum mult. (Lauds)	
Simile est (Ben.)		Cum turba (Ben.)		Ecce ascend. (Ben.)	
Dominican and English					
IN PRINCIPIO	(1)	NOE VIR	(1)	LOCUTUS EST	(1)
		Quadraginta	(2)	resp. 2-8	
		Edificavit	(5)		
		Ponam arcam	(6)		
		Per memetipsum	(7)		
Miserere (Lauds)		Secundum mult. (Lauds)		Averte (Lauds)	
Simile est (Ben.)		Cum turba (Ben.)		Ecce ascend. (Ben.)	

Source A5 is unusual since, as noted earlier, it includes the list of antiphons at the end of Lauds of the Sundays instead of after second Vespers. It is perhaps worth remarking that the actual propers of these weeks, although easy enough to follow in the sources, vary from manuscript to manuscript in an interesting manner. The changes are shown in figure 8.2. Excluding the differences between secular and monastic rites and the minor variations in order which often characterize books even of the same rite, the manuscripts show the following repertories: the oldest source studied, A5, of the 12th century, has no propers for Septuagesima, which repeats the propers of *Domine ne in ira.* Sexagesima has the historia (that is, essentially the services of Matins and Lauds) *In principio*, and Quinquagesima the historia *Quadraginta*, these titles being the incipits of the first responsories. In all later sources *In principio* belongs to Septuagesima and it is repeated for Sexagesima in monastic sources where secular sources bring up the first nocturn of *Quadraginta* with a new first responsory, *Noe vir*. For Quinquagesima, secular manuscripts then use a third historia, *Locutus est*, many of whose items are the same as the later items of monastic historia, *Quadraginta*, for the same Sunday. The early, monastic, and secular repertories agree in their choice of text for the Benedictus antiphon, which in all three cases changes from week to week. The first antiphon of Lauds, however, the other key item by which a historia is identified, is not the same from repertory to repertory. The Dominican sources, A1 and A4, secular in form, are the most regular, together with the Sarum Antiphonal, A13. If there is an evolution at work here, providing for the somewhat indiscriminate and arbitrary Sundays from Septuagesima to Quinquagesima propers of their own, as the liturgy was partially stabilized in the 13th century, the historical movements and the establishment of propers must be examined in more detail before conclusions can be drawn.

Lent to Easter

825 There is little to describe in detail about the presentation of this period in manuscripts, and little variation from source to source in what is proper and common. The ferias of this time, for example, are characterized by a proper antiphon for Benedictus and Magnificat each day at least until Holy Week, when more complete propers for Matins and Lauds are generally supplied. Ash Wednesday and the ferias after Passion Sunday occasionally have proper responsories (mss A7 and A6 & A13 respectively). Mondays usually have a proper invitatory for the week. Although a few sources supply proper antiphons for Lauds during this time, the Vespers antiphons (apart from the Magnificat) seem always to be ferial and therefore drawn from the common repertory in the Psalter. The formula for a typical week excluding Sunday would therefore be:

IBM BM BM BM BM B, or I (BM)5 B, or I A11,

with the Magnificat for the Saturday forming part of first Vespers of the following Sunday, and alternative responsories perhaps listed in Matins of the preceding Sunday.

For Sundays a complete set of propers is usually provided, with the exception of the Vespers and sometimes the Matins antiphons. Propers for Compline on certain Sundays may occur. The formula would thus be:

M [AN] I R9 [ferial R] Lauds Hours M with (AR3)3 a possible alternative to R9.

Easter to Trinity

826 This period and the period from Trinity to Advent are both variable and complex in their organization. The pattern of the services established before Easter may well be quite different during Easter time, especially at Matins, where the number of nocturns is often reduced to only one (although there are

FIGURE 8.3
The nocturns at Matins of Easter time

1 = one secular nocturn with three responsories.
3 = three secular nocturns with nine responsories.
1 = one monastic nocturn with four responsories.
3 = three monastic nocturns with twelve responsories.

ms	PASCHA	Pas 1	2	3	4	5	Asc	Pen	Tri
Monastic sources									
A6	1		*3*	*3*	*3*	*3*	*3*	*1*	*3*
A7	1						*3*	*1*	*3*
A11	1	(a)	*3*		*3*		*3*	*1*	*3*
A14	1		*3*		*3*		*3*	*1*	*3*
A16	*3*		*3*		*3*		*3*	*3*	*3*
Secular sources									
A18	1	3	3				3	3	–
A2, A13	1				1		1	1	3
A17	1						1	1	3

(a) The octave of Easter in this source apparently has three nocturns, and the exact form of Matins on this Sunday and Pascha 2 and 4 is conjectural: the source will be examined in the text.

frequent exceptions) and where monastic offices may adopt secular forms. Moreover, the manner of recording the items, which are frequently common to the period or drawn from the ferial repertory, is often highly abbreviated, so that it is usually difficult to reconstruct the exact contents of the services from a single book. Each source must be studied. Let us first consider Matins only, for the Sundays from Easter to Trinity, and including Ascension. Figure 8.3, compiled from manuscripts whose organization is relatively unambiguous, will give a rough indication of the differences one may expect to find. The absence of a description implies that the texts of the office as well as its form are repeated from the preceding Sunday: figure 8.3 therefore shows where proper texts occur. Even in these manuscripts, whose arrangement seems clear, it is possible that practices so well known as not to need recording may affect the forms. For example, the last responsory, *Dum transisset*, of Easter Matins is often common as the third responsory throughout Easter on Sundays[4] and on these Sundays it may be given in incipit or not at all. In the latter case nocturns may appear to have only two responsories in secular sources, or in monastic sources only three. Such items unspecified even by incipit may change what appears to be a secular into a monastic form: this might account for the long preservation of the secular nocturn in source A7. Study of the corresponding Breviaries, which contain lessons and rubrics, and of Ordines may help to identify the correct arrangement. A good deal more research is required. As far as the figure can be trusted, then, it shows that in monastic uses the Matins items remain proper mostly for two consecutive Sundays, except in mss A6 and A7. Where a secular form is employed it is only for Easter Sunday and its octave. Thereafter the three-nocturn monastic Matins reappears until Pentecost, which has only a single monastic nocturn. Source A16 does not adopt a reduced form of Matins at all. Secular sources, A2 and A13, Dominican and English respectively, show the distribution which becomes increasingly standard for the later middle ages, consisting of a single nocturn until Trinity Sunday, and adopting for the three Sundays following Easter the propers of that day. Source A17, a Bohemian Antiphonal of the late 15th century, keeps the Easter propers for all Sundays of the season. The early 13th-century Dominican book,[5] ms A18, has what I take to be an earlier form in which the Sundays immediately after Easter have their own propers, with three nocturns. Some of these propers are in fact those which occur on the weekdays of these Sundays in other sources, a modification which we shall discuss later.

827 We should now examine the sequence of propers during Easter as a whole so that the actual manuscript arrangements can be understood. The formulas in figure 8.4 show where proper texts occur: they are abstractions which cannot show detail, and which do not represent any one source. The different kinds of Matins services already mentioned can be superimposed in order to complement the information. Five days of the season have almost complete sets of propers for each service: Easter, its octave, Ascension, Pentecost, and Trinity. The three ferias immediately after Easter Day also have fairly complete sets, including the gradual and alleluia verse, sometimes plus a sequence, which makes Vespers of these days and Easter Day itself different from Vespers of the remainder of the year (see chapter 9). Processions and memorials after Lauds and Vespers are also common on these days. Eleven ferias, after the octave of Easter, the fourth Sunday, Pentecost, and Ascension, also have proper responsories and sometimes proper antiphons for the nocturns: here it may be remembered that in secular uses there is a single nocturn for ferias, in monastic there are two nocturns, the second of which has no responsories (**405-6**). The first of these ferias in some cases has a proper invitatory which is then repeated. In every week except that of Ascension, ferias v-vii repeat the responsories of ii-iv in numerical sequence and only the Benedictus and Magnificat antiphons are truly proper. There are therefore some eighty proper responsories, depending on the use of one or three monastic or secular nocturns, some sixty Benedictus antiphons and sixty Magnificat antiphons. The cycles of proper responsories and antiphons *ad evangelia* determine the organization of manuscripts.

Most sources arrange the material generally in the order in which it appears, except for ferial responsories noted on Sunday and for antiphons *ad evangelia,* which are often given in large stocks at various points in the season. Most typically the antiphons may be listed in one group either before or after the

FIGURE 8.4
Office propers for Easter time

Genres in brackets are not always proper: under Hours, the word Hours signifies that the normal genres are proper. →⊕ stands for memorials and processions. Where there is no genre, the previous proper is repeated. Texts for items in brackets appear less frequently and less consistently than for items not so marked.

	Compline	Matins			Lauds			Hours	Vespers	
PASCHA mostly proper										
ii		I	A	R3	[A]	B	[→⊕]	[Hours]	**G A** M	[→⊕]
iii & iv each				R3	[A]	B	[→⊕]	[Hours]	**G A** M	
v-vii = ii-iv										
Pas 1	[N]	I	[A]		[A]	B		Hours	M	
ii		I	A	R3		B		Hours	AM	
iii & iv each			[A]	R3	[A]	B			M	
v-vii = ii-iv										
Pas 2				[R9]		B			M	
ii-vii						B6			M6	
Pas 3						B			M	
ii-vii						B6			M6	
Pas 4				[R9]		B			M	
ii-iv each				R3		B			M	
v-vii = ii-iv										
Pas 5						B			M	
ii-iii each						B			M	
Vig. ASC						B			ARM	
ASCENSION	N	I	A3	R3	A5	B		Hours	ARM	
vi		I	A	R3		B			M	
vii			A	R3		B			M	
Pas 6				[R3]		B			AM	
ii-vi each			[A]			B			M	
vii						B			AM	
PENTECOST	N	I	A3	R3	A5	B		Hours	M	
ii		I	[A]	R3		B			M	
iii-iv each				R3		B			M	
v-vii = ii-iv										
TRINITY	[N]	I	A3	R3	A5	B		Hours	ARM	
ii-vii						B6			M6	

other ferial propers for Easter week, and the second and third weeks. Sources A2 and A3, Dominican, and the Sarum Antiphonal, A13, have the following arrangement:

Pascha, ferias, and Pascha 1 (propers listed in order)
ferial propers for Benedictus and Magnificat
other ferial propers, including invitatory, antiphons, and many responsories

The following weeks, which lack propers other than antiphons for Benedictus and Magnificat, have only groups of such antiphons preceded by rubrics identifying the weeks to which they belong.

828 The number and destination of the items listed in groups is very variable, depending partly on the length of time for which propers are required and the repetitions characteristic of each use. Sometimes there are not sufficient antiphons for each day to have its own propers, and instructions for repetitions from within the groups may occur. We should also note that the number of antiphons provided for the weekdays following the fifth Sunday is usually smaller because there are only two weekdays before the Vigil of Ascension. To illustrate these points further and to stress that each source must be scrupulously examined and inventoried, I shall discuss two difficult manuscripts in more detail. Each manuscript will be presented in a figure which shows its contents from Easter to the fifth Sunday. The source of the items presented only in incipit (lower case letters in the figures) is indicated by a line connecting the incipit to its source as a complete text in another service of the period, where this method is possible without confusing the diagram, or in a footnote proper to the day. Where the text is repeated not from another service but is drawn from one of the stock repertories, this will be shown by means of boxes, circles, etc, surrounding the incipit and the stock. Some texts given only in incipit could not be traced to any service or stock within this section of the book and are perhaps drawn from the ferial repertory in the Psalter: such items are placed between parentheses. It is worth observing that even when an item is presented only in incipit, that incipit may be accompanied with proper alleluias as extensions to be added to the actual antiphon. Even though figures 8.5 and 8.6 represent specific manuscripts, the correspondence may not always be exact: the clear presentation in nutshell form of some fifty days has difficulties which will be immediately evident. Moreover, the sources themselves are sometimes confusing. For example, it is difficult to tell even with an item by item inventory whether rubrics at the end of lines refer to the item on that line or on the following one. Occasionally, processional and commemorative items, which appear mainly after the Benedictus and Magnificat, have been omitted: such items are in any case given in full where they occur and are not drawn from other services or from stocks.

829 Ms A11, a monastic Antiphonal, is presented in figure 8.5. The first eleven days are given in daily order and three stocks of antiphons appear as shown: □○⊔

The remaining ferias of the first two weeks follow but almost entirely use repetitions. Thereafter the season is given only in terms of stocks of antiphons and later, of responsories. The octave of Easter appears twice, as do Sundays 2 and 4, because of the organization of subsequent stocks in genres. Antiphons of all services, not just those for Benedictus and Magnificat, may be drawn from one of the stocks, usually from stocks which are given earlier but sometimes, as with the antiphon for Terce of Pascha 1 and the following feria, from stocks appearing later. Only occasionally are antiphons drawn from other services: notable in this respect are the single antiphons of Lauds of the first week and first Sunday, drawn from the five antiphons of Easter Day in order, beginning again when necessary. The proper antiphons for Benedictus and Magnificat of second week are omitted entirely except on the Sunday, but no indication is provided as to which of the stock texts should be used.

830 Easter Day clearly has only a single secular nocturn. The ferias of first week have two nocturns, corresponding to the ferial nocturns of winter. The octave of Easter at first sight looks very odd: it has three nocturns, the last of which has five antiphons given in incipit and all specified as *ad cantica*. As the figure shows, these five incipits refer to the complete texts found in the five stocks of Sundays 1-5 respectively. We may therefore conclude that the five antiphons must be distributed one each to the five Sundays: the third nocturn therefore corresponds to the normal monastic form with a single antiphon for the canticle. However, no responsories are given: to correspond in this respect, there should be twelve. There is no evidence from the manuscript itself, but the normal practice of repeating the Easter Day responsories on the following Sunday would provide three: the nine propers of the ferias of first week would bring the number up to twelve. Whether this is the solution is not certain. The form of Matins for the following Sunday is equally uncertain, although it is clear that there should be three nocturns. Common practice in other sources (figure 8.4) suggests the use of three monastic nocturns, for which the stocks given after Sundays 2 and 4 would provide sufficient responsories, twelve for Sunday 2, repeated on Sunday 3, leaving two for ferial use, and a similar distribution for Sundays 4 and 5.

831 A similar, even more abbreviated layout is to be observed in source A7, figure 8.6. Here Sundays 1 and 2 are not specified at all. I suspect a rubric for the latter may have been omitted. Instead of three different stocks of antiphons there is a single large stock at the end of Easter Day, and as in the previous manuscript it is used to supply antiphons for all services as necessary. The first problem here arises on feria iv, where ten responsories are given, followed by seven antiphons. Now, the majority of these items are the same as those which appear in stocks for Pascha 2 in the previous source examined. It seems possible that instead of ten consecutive responsories for feria iv, the manuscript should specify a distribution as follows: R3 (for feria iv), *Pascha 2* (rubric omitted), R7. The failure to mention Pascha 1, the octave, can be explained quite normally by the assumption that there are no propers for that day since it repeats the items of the previous Sunday. The ten responsories listed under feria iv, however,

FIGURE 8.5
The Easter weeks: office propers and stocks
(from monastic Antiphonal ms A11)

The complete text of the items given only by incipit (lower case) is shown in one of several ways: a) by a linking arrow where this is possible, b) by a footnote (the numbers in parentheses), c) by an = and a reference to a day specified in the left-hand column, d) by a geometrical figure surrounding the item and the stock from which it is drawn. Incipits between parentheses cannot be traced: incipits without parentheses or geometrical figures are discussed in the footnotes, as stated in b) above.

		Matins				Lauds	Hours	Vespers	stocks
Pascha	AM	I A3 R3	–	–		AAAAAB	AAAA	A2RM	A16
ii		I A R3	A	–		a RB	AAAA	M	A3
iii		a R3	a	–		a B	AAAA	M	A2
iv		a R3	(a)	–		a B	a AA a	M	
v		a r3 = ii	a	–		a B	AAAA	A M	
vi		a r3 = iii	a	–		a B	a AAA	M	
vii		a r3 = iv	a	–		a B	a a a a	a M	(1)
Pascha 1 (the octave)									
		I a	respon-	a	a a a a a	a –	a a a a	(a)M	(2)
ii		I a	sories	a	–	a –	a a a	(a) –	(3)
iii		a	as in	a	–	a –		(a) –	(4)
iv		a	preced-ing week	a	–	a –		(a) –	
v & vi as ii & iii									
vii as iv up to							→	a–	(5)

Pascha 1 (the octave) A8. Versicles of dialogues are recorded for all services.
Pascha 2 A8; *Pascha 3* A8; *Pascha 4* A8; *Pascha 5* A4
Pascha 2 r i [R14] (6); *Pascha 4* r [[R13]] (7)

(1) The antiphon of nocturn 1 is drawn from the nocturn of Easter Day, of Prime from Prime of Easter Day, of Nones from Terce of feria vi, of Vespers 2 from Vespers 1 of Easter Day.
(2) The antiphon of nocturn 1 is drawn from the nocturn of Easter Day and is used for nocturn 1 of Sundays until Ascension. The antiphon of Prime is drawn from Prime of Easter Day, of Nones from Terce of the preceding feria vi.
(3) The antiphon of nocturn 1 is drawn from the Benedictus of Easter Day, of nocturn 2 from Terce of Easter Day, of Lauds from Sext of Easter Day, of Sext from Nones of feria ii after Easter.
(4) The antiphon of nocturn 1 is from Prime of the preceding feria v, of nocturn 2 from the Magnificat of the preceding feria iv or v.
(5) The Vespers antiphon repeats the antiphon of first Vespers of Easter Day.
(6) The responsory is from stock [R14]: the invitatory is from feria ii after Easter.
(7) The responsory is from stock [[R13]].

could be explained quite differently. The fifth, *Gavisi sunt*, and its verse are given only in incipit, or so it appears. This text is the same as that of the antiphon for the second nocturn of feria iv in some sources which, as the table shows, is not given in source A7. It seems just possible that this responsory and

FIGURE 8.6
The Easter weeks: office propers and stocks
(from ms A7)

The complete text of the items given only by incipit (lower case) is shown by a linking arrow where this is possible, or by a geometrical figure surrounding the item and the stock from which it is drawn. Incipits between parentheses cannot be traced.

		Matins		Lauds	Hours	Vespers	stocks	
Pascha	AM	I A3R3		A5RB	AAAA	ARM	[A25]	
ii		I [a]R3	[a]	a rB	AAAA	M		
iii		i [a]R3	(a)	B	AAAA	M		
iv		[a] ———				→	(R10)	[Ev-A7]

Pascha 3 (2 after the octave) Ev-A5
Pascha 4 Ev-A1 R12 A7 (ie, M R12 A7)
Pascha 5 A6 and Ev-A2 for rogation days

verse is incorrectly rubricked in the manuscript and that instead it is an antiphon followed by the versicle of the dialogue. The arrangement in this case would be: R4 AD Pascha 2 (rubric omitted) R5. There are of course problems with this explanation: why are there four instead of three responsories for feria iv, and only five for Pascha 2?

832 Such are the problems of dealing with this season in books isolated from related Ordines, Breviaries, etc. Often the difficulty can only be noted. A general survey of the texts used during this period indicates that each manuscript employs the same texts, but in different services. This is especially true of antiphons and not so characteristic of responsories, which tend to be used more or less in the same order even when their assignation, in groups, to particular Sundays may differ. This characteristic of the period, its dependence on a basic repertory of texts shuffled and distributed differently, makes it very suitable for comparative studies, from which it may be possible to derive some more accurate answers than can be offered here. If some of the questions are difficult to answer now, was the situation any different when the books were in use? Naturally, the users had other books to hand and could consult them, at least before the service, to establish or perhaps to choose the particular items for performance. Nevertheless, the Antiphonals alone would have been extremely difficult and confusing, and the amount of page turning would have been considerable, unless the chants and their order were memorized. Sections laid out in as confusing a manner as is true of this season and to some extent the next, must cause us to ask whether the books were for use or were for reference and rehearsal. It seems generally true to state that as the middle ages progresses towards the 15th century and as reliance on the memory becomes gradually less, the books are organized in a simpler fashion. Tradition, and the absence of any reason to have the books in the actual services, perhaps combined to preserve an arrangement which was not entirely convenient. The preservation of stock groups of items derives, at least in commonly held opinion which I see no reason to question, from the combination of several different books into one. Instead of distributing the items as necessary during the day and season, items from one book were inserted wholesale somewhere near where they were needed, items from another, and from a third, inserted also in groups. The history of this procedure has been examined in general by Salmon and Van Dijk, but the detailed comparison of earlier and later books seems not have been presented in print.[6]

The saints
833 Only a few of the sources studied combine the saints of the Easter season with the Temporale, and as in the seasons already examined the insertions are made in a few large groups rather than piecemeal. The usual place for the first insertion, generally of a small group, is before the propers of Ascension or its Vigil. Here occur the feasts to Philip & James, and for the Invention of the Holy Cross, occasionally preceded by the feast of St Mark, and followed by St Alexander. Also commonly appearing before these saints' feasts are recorded is a small section of the Common of saints which shows how these items common to saints during Easter may be performed: this section is usually called the *Commune sanctorum tempore paschali* (see **888**). The days from Ascension to Pentecost are not interrupted, and Trinity and Corpus Christi follow, also without interruption in those sources written at a time when those feasts had been established. In earlier manuscripts either or both of these feasts may be absent altogether or written later by the same or another scribe. A second group of saints' feasts may be given next, before the Temporale for the summer.

The initials
834 The variety of methods of presenting Easter time in the books results in a similar variety of initial schemes, and each source is unique. A few generalizations, very similar to those given for earlier periods, may be repeated. The largest initials are to be found beginning the first responsory of Easter and Trinity Sundays and usually, but not invariably, of Ascension and Pentecost. Occasionally, however, these two feasts have a somewhat smaller initial which is still elaborate and clearly belonging to the same general category as the largest. This lesser initial may also appear for the first item of first Vespers of these main feasts and in addition for the first responsory of those Easter Sundays which have proper responsories, and often for the first responsory of the three ferias following Easter Day. Corpus Christi, if it is present, seems to adopt this kind of initial. The square (size 2+) initial, as well as its normal function of distinguishing the first item of Lauds and often the first item of Vespers of the main feasts, also marks the first antiphon of the stocks which may appear. The special Kyrie, and the sequence which some sources indicate following the gradual and alleluia of Easter week Vespers, may be distinguished with this

initial. The thin, size 2, initial generally serves for invitatories, the first antiphon of Matins, responsories after the first, and for Benedictus antiphons which occur in their proper place rather than in stocks. The lesser initial, size 2 – , is used for other antiphons, including Magnificat antiphons, and for the verses of responsories.

Trinity to Advent: the summer Sundays

835 The division of the variable number of weeks of the summer into historie must be recalled:

(a) Regum (Kings), *Deus omnium* (R), 5-10 weeks;
(b) Sapientia (Wisdom), *In principio* (R), 4 or 5 weeks;
(c) Job, *Si bona* (R), 2 weeks;
(d) Thobie (Tobias), *Peto Domine* (R), 2 or 3 weeks
 or *Peto Domine*, 1 or 2 weeks, and
 Judith, *Adonay* (R), 1 week
 or *Peto Domine*, 1 week, and *Adonay*, 1 week, and
 Esther, *Domine rex omnipotens* (R), 1 week;
(e) Machabees, *Adaperiat* (R), 3-5 weeks;
(f) Ezechielis (Prophets), *Vidi Dominum* (R), 4 or 5 weeks.

As in Easter time most propers for summer are listed in groups or stocks. Very evident in the summer arrangement is the separation of Old from New Testament material. Presented first and complemented as necessary with miscellaneous proper items are groups of responsories alternating with stocks of memorials and Magnificat antiphons for first Vespers. These are drawn from books of the Old Testament. Only when these items for the whole of the summer have been completed do the manuscripts give the antiphons for Benedictus and Magnificat of Sundays, drawn from the gospels and listed consecutively through the twenty-odd summer weeks. In general each historia has its own propers, repeated until the next historia, for the major services of Matins and Lauds and occasionally for the lesser hours.

836 Responsories characterize all the historie. Usually consisting of a single set of propers for the first Sunday with some propers for the weekdays, they form the most extended and obvious group of items. Often the smaller subdivisions, *Adonay* and *Domine rex*, differ from previous historie only in the presence of new responsories. *Deus omnium*, the longest of the divisions, usually has proper antiphons for Matins and a proper invitatory: in later historie only the invitatory may complement the responsories. *Deus omnium*, too, may have propers for the antiphons of Lauds. Preceding these nocturnal services will be the proper antiphon for the Magnificat of Saturday, first Vespers of Sunday. Antiphons proper to the Magnificats of Saturdays after the first of each historia or for memorials of Sundays on saints' feasts may be listed with this antiphon of first Vespers, or ending the historia in a separate group extending second Vespers.

The former position seems to be characteristic of English sources. Summarizing the overall structure of historie, then, are these skeletons:

historia *Deus omnium*
M / I As and Rs as necessary plus ferial Rs / Lauds / Ms for remaining Saturdays. English manuscripts prefer: Ms for all Saturdays / Matins / Lauds.

later historie
M / Rs / Ms for Saturdays, *or* Ms for all Saturdays / Rs.

Showing this arrangement in a little more detail, but omitting items given only in incipit, are these formulas for several sources:

mss A2 & A3

Deus omnium	M I (A3R3)3 A9
In principio	M R9 A4
Si bona	M R9
Peto Domine	M R9 A2
Adaperiat	M R9 A4
Vidi	M R9 A4

I cannot explain the absence of proper antiphons for the Saturday Magnificats in the historia *Si bona*: otherwise, these Dominican sources are simple and unambiguous.

ms A18

Deus omnium	M I (A3R3)3 Lauds A ferial-R4 A9 I
In principio	M I R9 + R3 A4
Si bona	M I R9 + R3 A5
Peto	M R6
Adonay	R7
Domine rex	R3 A4
Adaperiat	M I R9 + R3 A5
Vidi	R9 + R6 A5

The extra invitatory at the end of *Deus omnium* is for the following Sundays. The absence of the Magnificat for first Vespers of *Vidi* is puzzling: the item is perhaps included erroneously in the previous group of five antiphons. This source, too, is Dominican: a comparison with the formulas just presented indicates that even within this Order considerable differences could arise.

ms A13

Deus omnium	M8 I (A3R3)3 ferial-R3 memorials and rubrics
In principio	M5 R10
Si bona	M2 I R9 (9th is ferial)
Peto	M2 R9 (9th is ferial)
Adonay	M R6 ferial-R
Adaperiat	M5 I R10
Vidi	M4 I R10

A typical English layout combines the Saturday Magnificat antiphons into a single group before the responsories. The tenth responsory, where given, is the ferial item, and otherwise the ninth or specially identified items are used.

837 There are a number of minor modifications of these schemes, none of which need be examined in detail. Some sources, for example mss A6 and A11, have no propers for any of the historie except antiphons and responsories. A number of manuscripts, especially English, give rubrics, often quite lengthy, about the exact duration of each historia and how the items are to be distributed within the available days. The number of Saturday Magnificats provided is fairly consistent from source to source and the number used in any one year will of course depend on the calendar for that year.[7] The naming of the historie is unanimous in the sources studied, except for A17, a 15th-century Bohemian Antiphonal. In this book the following responsories begin the historie: *Deus omnium / Emitte Domine / Si bona / Omni tempore / Nos alium* (for *Adonay*) / *Spem in alium* (for *Domine rex*) / *In hymnis et confessionibus / Laudabilis populus*.

After the historie, the responsories of Matins, the Magnificats of Saturday Vespers, and other miscellaneous propers are completed the manuscripts give the Benedictus and Magnificat antiphons of second Vespers on Sundays. These are proper for each week. The section consists of the twenty-five Sundays of summer presented consecutively. Each Sunday, beginning with the first after Pentecost (sometimes even when Trinity is present) or the first after the octave of Pentecost, or the first after Trinity, has a single antiphon for the Benedictus and another for the Magnificat in most sources, thus: Dominica 1: BM / 2: BM / 3: BM and so on to 25. Some manuscripts give more than two antiphons here, generally four but occasionally two, three, five, or six: Dominica 1: A4 / 2: A4 / . . . 4: A3 / . . . 6: A2 etc. Presumably these are sung in order and then repeated as necessary.

838 Although the separation of responsories and Saturday Magnificats from the Benedictus and other Magnificat antiphons is to be found in most sources, giving rise to two separate sections of the book devoted to the summer season, there are occasional modifications. Source A8 gives the antiphons *ad evangelia* as usual for all the summer Sundays, separately after the historia, except for a group of nineteen antiphons for the Benedictus which are added to the propers of *Deus omnium*: M I R11 M14 B19. Ms A7, a monastic Antiphonal, combines the two sections into a series of smaller sections so that each historia contains within it the antiphons *ad evangelia* and, separately, several antiphons *de historia* whose destination is not clear. In this manuscript the Benedictus for *Deus omnium* Sunday is included within the propers for the day:

Deus omnium M I (R4)3 R4 A3RB A6 A13 de historia
Dominica 2 A5
Dominica 3 A6
Dominica 4 A4
Dominica 5 A4
Dominica 6 A3
Dominica 7 A4
Dominica 8 A1

In prinicipio I R15 A4 A8 de historia
Dominica 9 A4
Dominica 10 A3
Dominica 11 A5
Dominica 12 A1

Si bona and other historie are similar. The material for the Sundays, Dominica 1-12, etc, duplicates the antiphons *ad evangelia* which in other sources appear in the separate second section, the items relevant to a particular historia being placed with that historia, but in fact the distribution is not the same as far as can be determined. The single antiphons *ad evangelia* given under Dominica 8 and 12 are for the Magnificats of first Vespers of the following historia, drawn from the Old Testament. The distinction between Old and New Testament is therefore obscured by this combination of different groupings. As far as can be determined, and much is conjecture, the six antiphons immediately following the Benedictus of *Deus omnium* are the proper antiphons for the Benedictus of the remaining six Sundays of the historia, and similarly with the four antiphons following the responsories of *In principio*. The antiphons *de historia*, judging from their position, would seem to be Magnificat antiphons for second Vespers of the Sundays supplemented with memorials. The first antiphon of Sundays seems from a comparison of the texts to be for the Magnificat of first Vespers: the destination of the remaining antiphons is not known. It is not possible, from a study of the manuscript in isolation, to be certain of the exact distribution. Moreover, a comparison of texts in other sources is not helpful since most uses, adopting a stock repertory of texts for each historia, distribute them between Benedictus, Magnificat, and memorials with little consistency. Only an Ordinal or Incipitarium or Breviary of the same use as this source would provide some clues.

The Saints

839 Few manuscripts, even when they combine Temporale and Sanctorale, interrupt with saints' feasts the sections devoted to the summer weeks. The whole section may be delayed by the complete Sanctorale and Common of saints, indicating the relatively minor importance which was accorded to the summer Temporale, but normally all the historie and the section of antiphons are kept together. The notable exception is ms A8, where each of the historie is separated by pages devoted to saints' feasts. The first insertion includes Corpus Christi as a later addition, a subsequent insertion includes the Dedication feast, and the last historia is separated from the summer Sundays by the remaining saints' feasts and the Common of saints. These arrangements will be obvious when the whole Antiphonal is examined as a complete book (**889, 896-7**).

The initials

The sections requiring visually distinct beginnings are naturally the historie themselves, the summer Sundays, and the groups of antiphons within historie. The most prominent initials are reserved for the first responsories of the historie: *Deus omnium* and *In principio* are often distinguished with larger initials than those of succeeding historie. The first item of the first Sunday of summer is occasionally given such an initial, but more often takes only a initial of the next lower category, the square initial (2+). It is given to the first antiphon of the group within historie, to the first antiphon of the first summer Sunday and occasionally to the first item of each subsequent Sunday.

SPECIAL ANTIPHONALS

840 Unlike Graduals, Antiphonals are of several different and commonly occurring types. In this respect we ignore the secular as opposed to the monastic Antiphonal, which differ only in detail. We can ignore also the frequent division into two volumes, generally split before Easter Sunday and before the feast of Philip & James in the Sanctorale. Many Antiphonals are split into many volumes: the largest number to my knowledge is in the set of 223 books in El Escorial monastery.[8] Such divisions make no essential difference to the contents, although some recurrent material may be repeated for convenience in each volume or at least in as many of them as necessary. Commonly, too, the Antiphonal is divided into a Nocturnal and Diurnal. For these purposes Matins is the only night office, Lauds is in a 'twilight' position which will need further discussion, and all other services belong to the Diurnal. Since the most characteristic and numerous chants of Matins are the responsories, which appear infrequently in the other offices, the Nocturnal becomes closely associated with these items, and the Diurnal with antiphons, so that some books divide the material strictly according to this distinction. A book containing only the responsories (of Matins, and the other offices where they have responsories) is normally called a Responsoriale. A suitable name for the book containing only antiphons has not evolved, although Antiphonale is the logical choice. The use of that term for the book containing all the chants including responsories is perhaps unfortunate but now seems irredeemable. An Antiphonal with only antiphons must be distinguished by some adjectival qualification, and it is difficult to find a reasonable English name. I shall adopt the Latin *Antiphonale* *purum*. In fact, separate books of this kind are rarely completely pure in their contents. A Diurnal, for example, may well contain the Matins services of the major feasts. The division of the books in mid-service, as it were, by presenting antiphons in one and responsories in another again raises questions about the practical use for performance of such volumes. The constant alternation of books in Matins, for example, would have been irritating, one would imagine, and certainly two lecterns for each side of the choir would have been required. As I have commented earlier, here is a major area for research.

841 Two sources studied are Diurnals, or partly so. Source A9 presents the Temporale in the order already established, and with the same kind of material except that all the items from Matins are normally omitted. Only Christmas Day, Easter Day, Pentecost and the feast of the Assumption have the service. The same is true of Lauds, although in practice the antiphons of Lauds do in fact appear. This is because the antiphons of Sunday are used for the little hours of the diurnal round. The key to the statement that Lauds is omitted along with Matins lies in the absence of the Benedictus antiphon which appears only where Matins and Lauds are, exceptionally, given. The arrangement in this manuscript is therefore on the pattern of

Sundays	Vespers	[AR]M
	Lauds	A5
	Hours	D & R as necessary
	Vespers	[AR]M
ferias	succession of M antiphons	

In sources where the little hours are presented in this way, the dialogues, usually preceded by V for *versus* or *versiculus*, and the responsories, if they occur, become the most prominent feature and make these services difficult to recognize: a succession of responsories, verses, and versicles is not likely to bring the little hours immediately to mind.

Source A10 is also a Diurnal, including the Benedictus but presenting the antiphons of Lauds more clearly in connection with the ferias. The manuscript begins in fact by giving basically the Diurnal items only for ferias, although it does include the antiphons for the canticles on Sunday. The basic organization is occasionally:

Sunday	[AR]M AB AAAA M
each feria	BM

but more characteristically is:

Sunday	[AR]M BM
ferias, *ad horas*	Lauds A Hours A4
feria ii	BM
feria iii	BM
etc	

The four antiphons of Prime to Nones are the last four of the Sunday Lauds and their presentation, with the first antiphon, immediately after the Magnificat of second Vespers of the Sunday rather than in their correct position indicates the ambiguous place of Lauds in Diurnals. In periods where Lauds rarely has proper antiphons of its own, virtually the only items to appear in this source are the antiphons for Benedictus and Magnificat. After the Temporale is completed with the antiphons of the historie and of the summer Sundays (the former listing only the Magnificats for first Vespers, the latter only the Benedictus and Magnificat antiphons for Sundays) the manuscript continues with the diurnal propers for Advent Sunday, the Vigil and feast of Christmas, the Vigil and feast of Epiphany, Assumption, and then the Sanctorale. Festal propers generally follow this pattern:

Vespers	[AR]M
Lauds	[A]RB
Hours	AAAA (usually each with the D)
Vespers	A4RM

842 The strict separation of responsories from antiphons seems to be relatively rare, and I have no source to hand which may be studied in more depth. The presence of a Responsoriale in a use implies the presence of an Antiphonale purum to correspond: I know of only one such surviving pair (or what appeared at a preliminary glance to be a pair), in the Biblioteca Central of Barcelona. These are 16th-century volumes of choir-book size. A word about enormous 'chorali' of this kind is in order. It is possible that the division into Nocturnal/Diurnal and into Responsoriale/Antiphonale purum is connected with the trend of the later middle ages, especially in southern countries, to increase the size of the text and notation so that a single copy is large enough for the choir to read from a distance. Staves may extend vertically over nearly an inch of parchment, individual notes may be almost a third of an inch in dimensions, texts almost a half, and the books themselves sometimes as much as three feet in height and correspondingly heavy. The amount of material in each volume must therefore be reduced, and more volumes are needed. Many sets of such volumes, and many individual survivors of sets, are still in existence, mostly in Italy, Spain, and Portugal and although they are by no means completely catalogued (least of all from the liturgical and musical aspects) they are well known and often well described because of the splendour with which their illuminations are frequently carried out, often by renowned artists.[9]

843 Many manuscripts are called Antiphonals for want of a better understanding of their contents. These cannot be discussed here, but a few of the other kinds of manuscripts to which the Antiphonal could apply may be mentioned briefly. A few manuscripts give the texts of the musical items but without the music. Others are true Antiphonals as to the items they contain but do not supply a complete Temporale or Sanctorale, restricting themselves to selected feasts. Such books are sometimes called Officia, and in addition to the items for the offices they may contain the relevant Masses also, or at least the proper alleluia and sequence for the Mass. Mass items may also be included in a normal Antiphonal where later feasts such as Corpus Christi have been added.

The inclusion of complete hymns in their proper places is not uncommon and has been mentioned already: a few Antiphonals give some or most of the prayers, or at least the prayer of the day, and perhaps the chapters. Rather few Antiphonals give rubrics to any extent, with English sources once again providing frequent exceptions. Even so, rubrics are generally in the form of textual incipits rather than descriptive of performance.

I know of only two instances of an Incipitarium.[10] Whether these are true Incipitaria in the sense that they would have been used by the solo singers for learning or for performance, or whether they are in fact more like Ordines I cannot say. Many manuscripts present the material in a very abbreviated form and the precise nature of these and their relation to Ordines (which present only the incipits in order to establish the correct sequence of texts from year to year) needs examination. I have examined almost none of these special Antiphonals and my information derives principally from catalogues and other secondary references or from very brief personal inspection. The assignations in the list which follows must be regarded as very tentative.

DIURNALS
Bamberg, Staatsbibl ms lit 94
Munich, Bayer. Staatsbibl mss Clm 7381, 7600, and 23017?
Einsiedeln, Monastery Lib ms 613
Vatican, Ottoboni 668
Florence, Bibl Medicea-Laurenziana, ms Aedil 148

NOCTURNALS
Modena, Bibl Estense, ms α P.1.8
Vatican, Pal lat 520

RESPONSORIALE
Barcelona, Bibl Central ms 304
Munich, Bayer. Staatsbibl ms Clm 23003
Sion, Chap ms 46

ANTIPHONALE PURUM
Barcelona, Bibl Central ms 305
Monserrat, Monastery Lib ms 837

ANTIPHONALS without music
Lisbon, Bibl Nac ms 5271 and mss 7687-8
Munich, Bayer. Staatsbibl mss Clm 2847, 2992

INCIPITARIA
Freibourg-im-Breisgau, Stadtarchiv, ms 4° H 132
Mainz, Cathedral Lib ms without call number

Abbreviated ANTIPHONALS (Ordines?)
Monserrat, Monastery Lib ms 837?
Mainz, Stadtbibl ms II 273

ANTIPHONAL with prayers
Munich, Bayer. Staatsbibl ms Clm 14926

ANTIPHONAL with chapters
Cambrai, Bibl mun ms A 121

ANTIPHONAL with lessons
Autun, Bibl mun ms S 171.

BREVIARIES AND NOTED BREVIARIES

844 A thorough understanding of the method by which Antiphonals are organized is of immense help with Breviaries since, in the latter, texts which appear also in the Antiphonal are easy to distinguish. As usual, they are conventionally written in smaller script, although sometimes the difference is minimal and not always easy to ascertain. The identification of the musical items, then, by the size of the script or by the presence of the stave in Noted Breviaries enables the user to isolate the other texts, that is, the lessons, chapters and prayers. Furthermore, it is these 'spoken' texts which are graced with the larger initials in Breviaries while the musical items are generally begun by capitals buried within the writing space. In figure 8.7 I tabulate some general principles, citing the genres in alphabetical order and showing initials (at the margin) as size 2 (within heavy brackets) and capitals as size 1 or 1+. As subsequent diagrams will indicate, these principles are extremely fluid. Abbreviations in upper case letters as usual indicate the presence of the complete text, and lower case abbreviations its reduction to an incipit (some genres are so rarely abbreviated that examples could not be found). When thus abbreviated, some genres such as the chapter retain an initial but removed from the margin and placed within the writing area (the initial may still coincidentally appear at the margin). Later verses of hymns and canticles, etc, are normally denoted in manuscripts by large capitals, coloured and square or in decorative frames. First items of complete days or services or sections may as usual take more elaborate initials, and the following letter may be raised, together with the letters at other important points within the item.

The importance of the gospel, and of the canticle in monastic sources, is clearly evident. The major canticles, on the other hand, are rarely emphasized in Breviaries although in Noted Breviaries they are somewhat more prominent, as are most of the musical items, with large capitals at the margin or, in the case of several consecutive items such as antiphons of the nocturns, beginning at the margin and then placed where they occur.

845 Apart from the 'spoken' items and the musical items of the regular offices, Breviaries are almost always made more complex by the inclusion of commemorations, suffragia, preces, votive offices, and rubrics. Commemorations or suffragia take the form of a single prayer in addition to the normal daily texts or are somewhat more extended, consisting of an antiphon or processional responsory, a dialogue, and prayer, sometimes followed by a second musical

FIGURE 8.7
Initials and capitals in Breviaries

This figure shows the initials and capitals generally used for each of the genres. On the left the texts are given complete in the sources; on the right only the incipit appears.

when texts appear complete				incipits	
		Breviary	Noted Breviary		
genre		size of letters		genre	size
A	and psalm incipit/evovae	111	[1+]11	a	1
B		1+ or 1	[1+]	b	?
C		[2]	[2]	c	2
D		1+ or 1	1+ or 1	d	1
G	(the gospel after Matins in monastic uses, or the sentences of the gospel preceding the homily of the final nocturn and upon which the homily is based)	[2+]	[2+]	g	?
H		[2]1+..	[2]1+..	h	1
I		1	1+	i	1
K	(canticles of monastic uses)	[2+]1+..	[2+]1+..	k	1
L		[2]	[2]	l	?
M		1+ or 1	[1+]	m	1 ?
N		1+ or 1	[1+]	n	1 ?
O		[2]	[2]	o	2
P	(rarely appearing in full in the Temporale)	–	–	p	1 or 1 –
preces	(often presented in two columns within the writing area, whether that is a page or is itself a column)	1+ or 1	1+ or 1	preces	1
R	and repetenda	1+1 or 11	[1+]1	r	1
V	and cue	11	11	v	1
✠	(rarely appearing in the Temporale)				

item for the return procession. These additions normally occur immediately after Lauds and second Vespers, perhaps intervening before the final prayer of those services, and concern commemorations of the Lord, of the Cross, or of the Blessed Virgin. Only in complex seasons such as the weeks after Epiphany or the days after Christmas, where there are numerous saints, are commemorations or suffragia to saints included in the Temporale. In other seasons such commemorations would be made as necessary according to the conflict and coincidence of saints' feasts, but the texts do not appear in the Temporale. Preces also occur after Lauds and Compline (but since Compline rarely needs recording in the manuscripts, they seem to come just after second Vespers), and in connection with the little hours. Detailed information about them, and their relevant texts, is often given in the correct place in the first week of Advent, so that numerous extra dialogues and prayers may interrupt the usual presentation of the services. Later in the year incipits and rubrics may appear in similar positions.

846 Votive offices which consist of a complete round of services appear in a few sources interleaved, as it were, with the normal round. Services to the Virgin and for the Dead are the most commonly found. As with the preces they tend to appear in the first week of Advent in their fullest form, and the Temporale services of Advent Sunday may be duplicated or triplicated in substance. The ferial form of these services may also be included so that Advent Sunday may become very confusing to follow. To choose an easily accessible printed source to exemplify such additions, I refer to the Sarum Breviary of 1531. The Advent Sunday services are interrupted with memorials and votive services as follows:

ADV: Vespers
  BVM: ⊕ & Vespers
    Holy Ghost: ⊕
    patron saint: ⊕
    Relics: ⊕
    All Saints: ⊕
    Peace: ⊕
ADV: Compline, preces
  BVM: Compline
ADV: Matins, Lauds
  BVM: ⊕ Matins (Sunday and ferias ii-iv), Lauds, Hours
ADV: Hours, Vespers 2
  BVM: ⊕ Vespers 2

As appears, there is a complete round of services to the Virgin, together with memorials to her after first and second Vespers, and after Lauds. Memorials of other kinds occur after first Vespers. The Matins service to the Virgin is organized to include material for the whole week and, as so often in Breviaries, the presentation is not straightforward. The procedure used will have to be examined several times for certain periods of the year. Here the invitatory and hymn, common to the Sunday and ferias (in fact to the season), are given first, then the antiphons, psalm incipits, and dialogues proper to the Sunday and ferias ii-iv. The exact arrangement is:

Dominica (& the season)	Matins to the Virgin	Ih
Dominica & feria ii	Matins to the Virgin	ApppD
feria iii and iv	Matins to the Virgin	ApppD

A rubric then states that the remaining ferias repeat the same items. The three lessons common to all the services then appear. The principle to be established is that the material proper to the different days is recorded separately from the material common to them. This principle generally means that the texts and services appear in an anti-chronological order: here, for example, the propers for feria iii are given before the lessons of feria ii (and the other ferias) and, in a larger sense, that some material for the Marian services of the ferias of first week appears before the services of Advent Sunday are completed. All of the material is additional to the Temporale services *per se*, but the same principle frequently applies to the Temporale materials themselves. It is usually easy to orient oneself in the sources through the rubrics: if these are not readable, as is often the case on microfilm, a more extensive task of inventorying and comparing must be undertaken. Rubrics are usually quite explicit and often detailed, stating both day or feast as well as the service within the day. In the above case, the doubled Matins services are distinguished by qualification: *Ad matutinas de adventu* and *Ad matutinas de sancta Maria*. Moreover, rubrics will frequently indicate the period for which a certain item is sung, for example, 'this invitatory is sung on all feasts of twelve lessons throughout Lent.'

847 Breviaries, then, because of the variability of memorials and votive offices and the greater or lesser need for extensive rubrics, are more varied in appearance and presentation than other books. The main services themselves do not vary a great deal from book to book, or within a single source, and even where there is considerable difference in appearance because some items are proper at certain times while others are common, a good Breviary will normally include the incipits, with an identifying rubric, of items which are common. Thus, unlike other books, where common items may be tacitly omitted, the Breviary is more likely to include incipits where necessary between the proper items. This is perhaps more true of the little hours and Vespers than of Matins and Lauds. The little hours in particular are the most changeable from source to source and within a single book. No generalizations can be made and usually an item by item examination is necessary to follow the presentation clearly. Since the little hours are less interesting for most purposes, I find it useful to work through the end of Lauds, easily identifiable by the antiphon preceding the incipit Benedictus, and then to locate the antiphon preceding the incipit *Magnificat*. A brief glance at the material between the Benedictus and Magnificat antiphons is usually sufficient to discover whether there is anything peculiar, which is unlikely. The individual hours are normally identified with rubrics.

848 The Magnificat and Benedictus antiphons are useful landmarks, especially for ferias, where they are likely to be the only musical items to appear. However, since they are almost always proper, in many seasons they are presented in stocks rather than in their correct place. When in their correct position they are followed immediately by prayers, whose initial provides an additional means of identification. Examined with caution, the format for Benedictus/Oratio or Magnificat/Oratio can be distinctive:

musical text, smaller or with stave, ending *Bnds* or *Mag*	short text with size 2 initial at the margin

Even more distinctive is the duplication of the pattern, as represented by BOMO . . . , which characterizes many places in the Breviary to be discussed later: only when the prayer is separated from the antiphon by preces is the pattern disturbed.

The major feasts, and Sundays beginning seasons, tend to have more proper items and more rubrics stating how long these items may be used. It is here, too, that stock repertories are placed, stocks of antiphons for the Benedictus and Magnificat with the Magnificat of first or second Vespers, stocks of chapters or prayers in a similar position, stocks of ferial responsories after the responsories of Matins. Such stocks disturb the normal appearance of the services with extended passages whose format is unlike that of the constantly changing appearance of the straightforward presentation. A stock of antiphons or responsories, for example, involves perhaps several columns of smaller text or of musical staves, more extended than occur elsewhere. A stock of chapters or prayers, in all of which the text is quite short, will result in a long series of lines in normal script uninterrupted except by the frequent size 2 initials at the margins which denote the beginning of each text. This format is very distinctive. Plates 2a-b have stocks of chapters, and 14 stocks of prayers. Where such stocks appear, even the ferias become obvious. Proper to ferias in general are the lessons for Matins and the antiphons for Benedictus and Magnificat, occasionally with the following prayers. When the antiphons and prayers are listed in stocks, only the lessons are left. Again, therefore, extended passages of similar format with normal lines of script occur. Similar in this respect to the stocks of chapters and prayers, many consecutive lessons may be distinguished by the length of their texts: lessons are generally considerably longer than either chapters or prayers and the size 2 initial which begins each lesson, as it does each chapter and prayer, is therefore more widely distant from the adjacent one. Ferias, then, may contain only lessons, in the correct chronological position. These lessons appear to be in stocks only because of the removal of all other items into true stocks. In the latter, there may be an element of choice as to which text is drawn from stock. Ferial lessons, however, are listed in groups of three, each group preceded by an identification of the feria on which the three lessons are to be used. Of the ferias, Monday is generally a little more elaborate, often listing a proper invitatory and material for the little hours.

849 Other characteristic formats may be recognized and used as landmarks. Hymns and monastic canticles are distinctive if they are included complete: they are long and have many stanzas or verses. Beginning with a size 2 initial at the margin, they continue with a text longer than a chapter or prayer but distinct from the lesson because each verse, regular in length, begins with a large capital, often coloured and in a frame. The chant of a hymn is supplied in books giving the music, normally for only the first stanza since subsequent stanzas use the same melody.

Matins is not difficult to isolate, especially in a Noted Breviary. The nocturns, consisting of a regular alternation of lessons and responsories, both long items, appear in the manuscripts as a series of nine (or twelve, in monastic sources) repetitions of the pattern

long text, beginning with an initial at the margin	long musical item in smaller script or with a stave

Clearly preceding the first of these patterns, but later obscured as an unobtrusive continuation of the second part of the pattern, is the text or musical stave of the antiphons beginning each nocturn:
A3 LRLRLRA3 LRLRLRA3 LRLRLR.
Where the lessons are consecutive sections of a homily, the first lesson will be preceded by the sentences of the gospel on which the homily is based and at that point there will be two initials at the margin, the first being the I of *In illo tempore* and the second beginning the homily. The actual beginning of the gospel text after its formulaic introduction, *In illo*, may be marked with a large capital. A monastic Breviary will have twelve lessons and responsories, followed by a separate gospel and prayer. Some monastic Breviaries also list the canticles (abbreviation: K) in full before the third nocturn at the beginning of the season to which those canticles are proper. The reader must be careful to observe whether the source is monastic or secular. Plates 1 and 2 show a monastic Breviary: plate 1b, columns 3 and 4 have the canticles; plate 1c, column 2 has the gospel *In illo . . . Nuptie*, followed by a homily by Bede, *Quod Dominus*.

The following sections will be devoted to brief analyses of the various seasons in Breviaries and Noted Breviaries, mostly presenting formulas and initial schemes in order to avoid repetition of basic information already given. Some interesting cases will be examined in more detail.

Initial schemes and formulas for the services

850 Figures 8.8-10 illustrate, in as much detail as seemed desirable and possible, the items which have initials at the margin on Advent Sunday (and sometimes the following ferias). Each column in the figures represents a single manuscript. The choice of manuscripts will be justified below (**851**). In the following pages, each manuscript is described in additional detail, and in particular the precise schemes of initials and capitals are presented in lists: these identify the genres and the normal sequence of initials and capitals which applies to each genre. Thus these lists show the general format of initials and capitals used throughout each of the manuscripts, whereas the figures show only the sequence of initials which stand at the margin in Advent.

In the lists, the normal abbreviations identify the genres, and there follow the numerals representing initials and capitals: initials (and occasionally capitals) occurring at the margin are, as usual, enclosed in heavy brackets. Some genres such as hymns and responsories have more than one numeral: the latter genre, for example, has four numerals, such as 1 + 1 1 + 1, for refrain, repetenda, verse, and cue. Genres not listed have either no capital or the smallest size of capital.

In figures 8.8-10, each column (manuscript) is subdivided. The left-hand part lists the genres occurring on the day identified. The right-hand part shows initials at the margin: the numeral in the column identifies the size of initial which appears with the genre shown at the left. If there is more than one genre at the left, only the first has the initial.[11] Where the genre or group of genres is 'multiplied,' for example (LR)3, then the initial, belonging in this case to the lesson, is similarly repeated. Genres for which there is no numeral on the right begin with a capital not at the margin except accidentally.

In the figures, major offices are separated by a single horizontal line: days are separated by a thick line. The identity of the services may be established also by means of unique genres such as invitatory, Benedictus or Magnificat antiphon.

Psalm incipits are not shown: there may be several after each antiphon. The incipits of Benedictus, Magnificat, Nunc dimittis, and Venite texts are similarly omitted.

851 The sources where chosen to provide a reasonably balanced summary: Breviaries of the two regular Orders, Franciscan and Dominican, may be compared with a Breviary according to the Roman curia and with English, French and Czechoslovakian books (figures 8.8 and 8.9). Three monastic sources, two Benedictine and one Cistercian, are shown in figure 8.10. Figure 8.9 deals with Noted Breviaries, where the presence of the chant complicates the schemes. The sources chosen, however, are not necessarily either typical or desirable models: the Dominican book, for example, is the Breviary section of Humbert's Codex and items which might otherwise have been included in a Breviary are omitted because they appear elsewhere in one of the other sections of that manuscript. Ferial lessons, to cite a specific instance, are referred to only in a rubric, and their texts appear in the Lectionary. The layout of an ordinary Dominican book is presented in note 12 with an explanation of why it appears only as a note.

The sources chosen, and some details of them, are outlined below.

In figure 8.8 section 1, ms B10, a Dominican Breviary, from Humbert's Codex, has the following scheme of initials and capitals:

C, G, H, L, O	[2]
A, B, I, M, R	[2–]
H	[2] 1+ . . .
LR	[2] [2–] 111

The elimination of many of the common items and material such as the ferial lessons, has been mentioned.[12] Greater simplicity and regularity of initial schemes are typical of Dominican books.

In figure 8.8 section 2, ms B11, a Breviary according to Roman use, has the following scheme of initial and capitals:

G	[3]
H	[2] 1+ . . .
L, C, (O?)	[2]
A, B, c, D, I, M, R, =	1+
LR	[2] 1+1+1+1+

In a highly elaborate scheme of initials, the first lesson of each nocturn has a larger initial (size 4), and the gospel is emphasized (size 3). The chapter of first Vespers receives the Advent initial (size 9). Texts of the musical items are not written in smaller script, which makes them difficult to pick out in a black and white reproduction.

852 The material listed is also quite elaborate. Immediately after the versicle and response of each nocturn is the incipit of the Paternoster (a prayer: o), and the text of the absolution, complete on Sunday, given in incipit thereafter (also a prayer: O or o). Before each of the lessons the text of the benediction is given in full. Instead of the usual A3D (LR)3, then, the nocturn has A3DoO (✠ LR)3. The ferial lessons, listed in one section on feria ii, are divided not into ferias but into the biblical chapters (Isaiah 2-8) with a rubric specifying their distribution up to Christmas: 'There are three lessons daily, where proper lessons are not assigned, and they are distributed so that the whole is read before Christmas, because the lessons of Christmas (sc. *Primo tempore*) are written immediately after the text indicated below.'[13] The biblical chapters each begin with size 2 initials and some are subdivided by the abbreviation *lc.* written in the margin but without a noticeable break in the text. Advent Sundays thereafter lack the lessons of nocturn 1, which must be drawn from this 'stock.' The Franciscan manuscript, NB5 of figure 8.9, should be compared.

In figure 8.8 section 3, ms B12, an English Breviary, has the following scheme of initials and capitals:

C, G, H, L, O	[2]
(B?), M	1+
A, R	1
LR	[2] 1111

As usual with English sources, this manuscript is lavishly supplied with rubrics and incipits, and has memorials and votive offices separating the Advent services. The formulas shown in figure 8.8 are highly condensed; the ferias are extremely complicated and are too long to list; the memorials and votive offices are omitted in the table, but occur exactly as is shown in section **846**, with a scheme of initials which is the same as that of the main offices. The printed Sarum Breviary is identical in its general arrangement.

FIGURE 8.8
Initials at the margin: Advent Sunday and ferias (Dominican, Roman, and English Breviaries)

The figure is explained in paragraph **850**: genres are in the left-hand column, size of initials in the right; items in circles are stocks; rubrics are shown thus = ; preces thus □.

	ms B10 (OP)		ms B11 (Rom.)		ms B12 (Eng.)	
Advent Sunday						
Vespers 1	ap		=	2	=	9
	Cr	2	Cd	9	CR	2
	HDM	2	HDM	3	HDMd	2
	O	2	O	5	O	2
			=		=	
Compline					A	
					C	2
					HDN	2
					□	
					O	2
Matins					o	
	I		I	1+	DI	2
	H	2	H	2	H	2
i	AD		A3Do		a3D	
			O✠	2		
			L	4	L	5
	(LR)3	2	R	2	R	2
			(✠LR)2	2	(LR)2	2
ii	AD		A3DoO✠		a3D	
			LR	4		
	(LR)3	2	(✠LR)2	2	(LR)3	2
iii	AD		A3DoO✠		a3D	
	G	2	G	3	G	2
			LR	4		
	(LR)3	2	(✠LR)2	2	(LR)3	2
			R5		R2	
Lauds					D	
			A	1+	A	1+
	A5c		A4c		A4	
					C	2
	HDB	2	HDBo	2	HDBo	2
Hours					Ha	2
					=	2
					C3R	2
					□	1+
	R				O5	2
	cRD		RcRD		HaRDo	2
	(CRD)2	2	(CRD)2	2	HaCRD	2
					Ha	2
					CRD	2
					□	

continued overleaf

	ms B10 (OP)		ms B11 (Rom.)		ms B12 (Eng.)
Vespers 2	M		achDMo		a5cRhdMo
feria ii					
Matins	Id =		I = Do		ferias not
	r3				listed here
			L	3	
			(L6)	2	
Lauds	B		ChDBo		
Hours	A4		a =		
			C4	2	
Vespers			a		
	M		ChdM	2	
ferias iii-vii	(dBM)2		doBM		
	(BM)2		DoBM		
		(BM)2			
	B		B		

853 Figure 8.9 shows the formulas employed in Noted Breviaries, where sometimes the musical items have marginal initials, as the spoken items do. This increase in marginal initials makes it necessary to eliminate the ferias from the figure, and only Advent Sunday is shown. Size 2 initials for the musical items, as in ms NB2, are usually physically as large as the size 3 initials of the spoken texts because the stave is roughly equivalent to two lines of text. Where the responsories as well as the lessons have marginal initials, the normal formula (LR)3 with a size 2 initial for the lesson is expanded to (L.R)3 and 2.2 for the initials.

In figure 8.9 section 1, ms NB2, a French Noted Breviary, has the following scheme of initials and capitals:

C, G, H, L, O	[3]
A	[2−] or 1+
R	2− or 1+
B, M, N	2−
LR	[3] 1+1 1+1

The Advent initials occur on the chapter of first Vespers, and on the first lesson and its responsory: the Lauds antiphon also has a larger initial. The hymns are often provided with alternative chants for different seasons.

FIGURE 8.9
Initials at the margin: Advent Sunday
(Noted Breviaries of France, Hereford, Czechoslovakia, and Franciscan)

The figure is explained in paragraphs 850 and 853: genres are in the left-hand sub-column, size of initials in the right; rubrics are shown thus =; preces thus □.

	ms NB2		ms NB3		ms NB4		ms NB5	
Advent Sunday								
Vespers 1	=	1+					=	2
	A =	2	A	2				
	A4		A4					
	C	11	CR	2	(missing)		C	2
	R	2						
	HdM	2	HdM	2			HD	2
							M	2–
	O	2	O	2			O	2
Compline	A	2–	A					
	H	2	C	2				
	CN	3	HN	2				
	□		□					
	O	3	O	2				
Matins	I =	2	I		I	2	I	2–
	H	2	H	2	h		H	2+
i	A3D		A3d		ADo		A3do	2–
							O	2
	L	10	L	3	L	8	L	3
	R	8	R	4	R	2	R	2
	(LR)2	3	(LR)2	2	(L.R)2	2.2	(L.R)2	2.2–
ii	A3D		A3d		ADo	2	A3DoO	2–
	(LR)3	3	(LR)3	2	(L.R)3	2.2	(L.R)3	2.2–
iii	A3D		A3d		AD		A3DO	2–
					O	2		
	G	3	G	2	G	2	G	2
			LR	1+				
	(LR)3	3	(LR)2	2	(L.R)3	2.2	(L.R)3	2.2–
	=							
Lauds	d		d		D			
	A	3	A	3	A	2	A	2–
	A4		A4		A4		A4c	
	C	3	C	2	Ch		HD	2
	HB	2	HB	2	Boao	2	Bo	2–

continued overleaf

	ms NB2		ms NB3		ms NB4		ms NB5	
Hours	H =	2	ha2		h		h = p	
					AC	2	Cd	2
	CRd	3	CRd	2	Rd	2	R	2–
	□		□		□		□ =	
	O3	3	Od	2				
			OD	2				
			O	2				
	HcRdo	2	HacRd		h			
					AcRdo	2	RDo	2–
	Ha	2	HaCRd		h		hp	
					A	2		
	CRD	3			C	2	C	2
					RD	2	RD	1+
	Ha	2	ha		h		hp	
					A	2		
	CRd	3	CRd	2	C	2	C	2
					RD	2	RD	2–
Vespers 2			A	2	ahd		achdr	
			A4					
	crhdM		cRdhM		M	2	Mo	2–

In figure 8.9 section 2, ms NB3, a Hereford Noted Breviary, has the following scheme of initials and capitals:

C, G, H, L, O [2]
A, B, D, I, M, R, □ 1 or 1+
LR [2] 1+1 1+1

The largest Advent initial is on the first responsory. The initial of the first lesson and the Lauds antiphon are larger than normal. On the other hand, the initial of the homily following the gospel is smaller than usual.

In figure 8.9 section 3, ms NB4, a Czechoslovakian Noted Breviary, has the following scheme of initials and capitals:

G, L [2]
A, B, C, I, M, R 2 or [2]
LR [2] [2] 01+1 or [2] 201+1

The Advent initial is on the first lesson. The normal initial of lessons and responsories alternates between (a) coloured in a black penwork frame and (b) black in a coloured penwork frame (responsory and lesson, respectively).

In figure 8.9 section 4, ms NB5, a Franciscan Noted Breviary, has the following scheme of initials and capitals:

C, G, H, L, O	[2]
A, B, I, M, R	[2–]
O	1+
D	1
LR	[2] [2–] 111

Because ferias are not listed in the figure, I display the arrangement here, so that they can be compared with the ferias of the manuscript of Roman use (figure 8.8 section 2, ms B11): the lessons are distributed between the ferias, with incipits of other items and the Benedictus and Magnificat antiphons, so that the general format is L3BM.

854 Figure 8.10 shows monastic sources. In section 1, ms B4, a monastic (Benedictine) Breviary (nocturnal), has the following scheme of initials and capitals:

G	[2]
C, K, L, O	[1+]
o	1+
A, B, I, M	1
CR, LR	[1+] 1111

Since this manuscript is a Nocturnal, the day hours are not included. The ferial formula of L3BM may be noted in the figure.

In Figure 8.10 section 2, ms B7, a monastic (Benedictine) Breviary, has the following scheme of initials and capitals:

K	[3]
G	[3] or [2]
H, L, O	[2]
C	1+
A, B, I, M	1
LR	[2] 1111

The ferial lessons are collected in a separate section of the book, which may have been prefixed to the manuscript later.

In Figure 8.10 section 3, ms B9, a monastic (Cistercian) Breviary, has the following scheme of initials and capitals:

G	[3]
C, O	[2] or [1+]
c, o, R	1+
L	[2]
A, B, I, M	1
LR	[2] 1+111

The ferial formula L3BM may be noted in figure 8.10.

FIGURE 8.10
Initials at the margin: Advent Sunday and ferias (monastic Breviaries)

The figure is explained in paragraphs **850** and **854**: genres are in the left-hand column, size of initials in the right; items in circles are stocks; preces are shown thus □.

		ms B4		ms B7		ms B9	
Advent Sunday							
Vespers 1				CR	3		
				H	2		
				dM			
				O	2		
Matins		Ih		I		(missing)	
				H	2		
	i	ad		ad			
		LR	5			R	3
		(LR)3	1+	(LR)8	2	(LR)3	2
	ii	ad		ad		ad	
		(LR)4	1+	(LR)8	2	(LR)4	2
	iii	a		A		ad	
		K	1+	K3	3		
		G	2	G	3	G	3
				LR	1+		
		(LR)4	1+	(LR)3	2	(LR)4	2
		G	2	Go	2	Go	3
		O	1+				
Lauds		a		A	2	a	
				A4cR		CRBo	2
		CRhdB	1+	H	2		
		O	1+	dBo			
Hours				ac		a	
				aco		Cdo	1+
				aCd		cd	
				O	2	O	1+
				aCd		Cd	1+
				O	2	O	1+
Vespers 2				aCRhMo		cRdMo	
feria ii				*(all ferias)*			
Matins		Ihad		Ihrh		Id	
		L	2			L3	2
		L2	1+			aCd	2
		a				O	2
		Cd	1+				
		O	1+				
Lauds		A				AcRBo	1+
		CRBo	1+	(BM)5			

	ms B4		ms B7		ms B9	
Hours			M		AA	
					Cd	2
			c2		O	2
			C14	2	A	
					Cd	2
			□		O	2
					A	
					Cd	2
			O3	2	O	2
Vespers			□		crMo	
ferias iii-vii	L3BM	1+	c3		L3BM	2
	L3BM	1+	C8	2	L3BM	2
	L3BM	1+			L3BM	2
	L3BM	1+			L3BM	2
	B				B	

Advent to Christmas

855 There are few comments to be made about the organization and presentation of the Advent season: the above figures indicate its variability. Fairly standard is the ferial format of L3BM, repeated six times except for the Magnificat omitted (or, more correctly, delayed) on the Saturday. Monday and occasionally Saturday sometimes have a few other items such as the invitatory and items for the little hours. More complicated arrangements do occur. Source B3 separates the lessons as follows:

(first week) ID (L3)6 incipits BM r (BM)4 B and (second week) (L3)6 (BM)5 B.

Source NB2, continuing from figure 8.9, has:

(first week) (L3)3 B preces incipits OCM (BM)4 B and

(second week) L14 (BM)5 B.

Later weeks follow much the same kind of pattern except where the Magnificat antiphon is omitted because the great Os have begun. The Ember days, too, have some special items. Despite the practice in Antiphonals, in the Breviaries studied, these days are invariably listed in their correct position in third week.

Few sources employ stock lists for Advent, except for the great Os. Two positions are used for these antiphons, immediately preceding either Advent 4 or Christmas Eve. Source B1 lists all the chapters for Advent, followed by all the prayers, in stocks after second Vespers of Advent Sunday: source B7 has a similar list preceding Advent 2, as figure 8.10 shows. Both of these are monastic manuscripts. The dialogues for the season are listed together in ms B2 (Dominican) and B3 has a stock of responsories preceding the Ember Wednesday of week three for use on the six days leading to Christmas Eve.

Christmas to Epiphany

856 In the monastic Breviary, B1, this entire period is placed at the beginning of the Sanctorale, rather than in the Temporale. This procedure must have been adopted because of the number of prominent saints: instead of retaining them in the Temporale, or separating them for inclusion in the Sanctorale, the unusual but logical transfer of the entire material to the Sanctorale was carried out. I know of no other source using this method.

Of the services of Christmas and saints Stephen, John, Innocents, and Thomas of Canterbury, there is little to record except the presence of the Genealogy after Matins of Christmas Day. Preceded with the liturgical greeting, it is provided with the tone in the sources studied. As in Antiphonals, antiphons for commemorations and for Magnificats are listed after second Vespers of Christmas and, frequently with processions, after second Vespers of the saints' feasts. Source B7 lists chapters and prayers in the former position. All of these feasts are lavishly supplied with rubrics and incipits. Following saints' feasts, the principal items to be given are the lessons, three for ferias, and six or occasionally nine (eight or twelve plus the gospel for monastic sources) for the Sunday within the octave. The order in which these are presented is very variable and no generalizations can be made. Often, the nine lessons for the feast of St Silvester, and occasionally lessons for other saints, are incorporated in a suitable position. Circumcision, or the octave of Christmas, is distinguished only by its proper items, nearly all of Matins being listed. Thereafter, some manuscripts provide six or three lessons for the octaves of the saints.

Epiphany to Septuagesima

857 The Genealogy is present after Matins of Epiphany except in monastic sources, where it occurs after Matins of the octave of Epiphany. The organization of the following weeks is complex, most sources preferring to collect at least the antiphons *ad evangelia* into lists, which appear either after second Vespers of Epiphany, or close to the beginning of the following feria. Two monastic manuscripts, B1 and B7, complement the list with collections of chapters and prayers. The same two sources and a third monastic Breviary, ms B4, have a second list of antiphons, generally containing only two or three items before, in, or at the end of the first Sunday after the octave (the Sunday *Domine ne in ira*). These are the antiphons for the Saturdays (first Vespers of the Sundays) remaining in the period. Similar groups of two or three antiphons for use *per ebdomadam* occur at the end of Sundays 2 and 3 after the octave.

The first Sunday, *Domine ne in ira*, is lavishly supplied with proper items, as are the following ferias, which have propers for Matins, Lauds, and second Vespers, and frequently numerous propers for the little hours. In particular, each feria has proper hymns, normally listed complete. The order of presentation up to the Saturday after *Domine ne in ira* is therefore not difficult to follow. Thereafter, the Sundays are distinguished by a proper prayer and proper lessons, and by antiphons for Benedictus and Magnificat when these are not listed in stock. The typical pattern of Sundays after the first, then, is O L9 BM or in monastic sources L12 GO BM. The three lessons for each feria of the later weeks are sometimes listed in the proper order after each of the Sundays (mss B4 and B6), or are not given at all (mss B1, B7, NB2, NB3). Source NB1 gives lessons only for ferias ii and vi, an odd arrangement for which I can offer no immediate explanation except that the manuscript does also include proper lessons (which may supersede ferial texts) for some saints' feasts occurring in the period.

858 One manuscript presents an arrangement which is intricately complex. It is the Breviary of Philippe le Bon (ms B3). The order of presentation is:

1	EPI	propers	
2	die ii	I	L3BM
3	die iii		L3BM
4	die iv		L3BM
5	Dom. 1 infra oct		L9BOM
6	die vi		L3 BM M
7	EPI OCT	MO	L9 A5BM
8	EPI 2 (*Domine ne*)		A5CM AN
9	ferias, each		L3
10	EPI 2		L6
11	EPI 3		L6
12	EPI 2	IH	(A3R3)3 ACH Hours A5CH N
13	EPI 2		L3BOM
14	EPI 3		L3BOM
15	EPI 4		L3BOM
16	EPI 5		L3BOM
17	ultima die ante LXX		O
18	ferias after the oct	I	A6R3 DA5B A5M each for ferias ii-iv

Dispersed into the eighteen sections numbered above, the arrangement is so confusing that one wonders how the book was used, and what planning, if any, was devoted to this period. Sections 1-7, from Epiphany to its octave, present no problem. Epiphany 2, however, must be assembled from section 8 (first Vespers and Compline) and 12 (which gives the following services: Matins, plus lessons from sections 10 and 13; Lauds, plus Benedictus and prayer from section 13; second Vespers, plus Magnificat from section 13; Compline). Propers for Epiphany 3 are to be found in sections 11 and 14 and other proper material must be drawn from Epiphany 2, section 12. The final section, 18, presents the propers for ferias ii-iv (repeated on v-vii) following the octave, but no lessons are provided. A complete set of nine lessons can be assembled for Sundays 2 and 3 (from sections 10 & 13, and 11 & 14 respectively) and the separation of the first six from the last three is on the basis of their source: a rubric states that the first three are to be drawn *de psalmodia*, presumably the Old Testament, while the last three are *de expositione*. The three lessons of the second nocturn are gospels. The first six are thus from the Bible, the last three are commentaries and are specifically indicated in the source as lessons seven to nine. Fortunately few manuscripts are as confusing as this.

Septuagesima to Lent

859 Few sources have proper antiphons for Matins of any of the Sundays of the period, even though many other items are proper. Source B6 lists the antiphons *ad evangelia* after the three lessons of feria ii in each week, but most manuscripts give them in groups after second Vespers of Septuagesima and before first Vespers of the other Sundays. Groups of ferial responsories sometimes occur, mostly not in the usual position after the Matins responsories (as in ms B3) but after second Vespers with the stocks of antiphons. Inconsistently, however, ms NB3 lists the responsories for ferias separately in a group preceding feria ii:

feria ii R6 L3BM / feria iii L3BM

Because the antiphons *ad evangelia* are listed in stocks, the ferias of Septuagesima to Quinquagesima are provided with only their three proper lessons. Although this had been the normal procedure in ms NB3, after Septuagesima feria ii there is only a single long text *per ebdomadam*, from which the necessary lessons are drawn, presumably according to choice.

The two ferias between Quinquagesima and Ash Wednesday usually have their Benedictus and Magnificat antiphons in the correct position after the Matins lessons rather than in stock: L3BM.

Lent to Easter Day

860 As during the other seasons most of the Sunday items except the antiphons of Matins and Vespers are proper. In monastic sources the canticle antiphon is sometimes proper, but other proper antiphons for these services do not appear until Passion Sunday, and then only in a few sources. Apart from the more elaborate Mondays, ferias up to Maundy Thursday agree in format with the ferias of other periods, plus a proper prayer following each of the antiphons. The typical pattern is thus: L3BOMO. Ms NB3 shows the repeated sequence L3B; the prayers and Magnificat antiphon are presumably in stocks elsewhere. Additional prayers such as these, and chapters which are more frequently proper, result in the presence in some sources of stocks of chapters and prayers at various positions in the season. As we have observed earlier, monastic sources seem to make use of such stocks more readily than do secular sources. Ms B1, for example, has a stock of chapters before the Magnificat of Ash Wednesday, that is to say, where the chapter of Vespers normally appears there are seven chapters. Preceding the proper items for Ash Wednesday, source B7 has seventeen chapters and fifteen prayers, followed by preces and many other prayers associated with them. Numerous chapters and prayers *per totum quadragesimam* occur after second Vespers of the first Sunday of Lent (ms B1), and a stock of chapters after the same service on Passion Sunday (B7). Memorials, especially for the penitents, and preces such as the preces *in prostratione*, are frequent during Lent and result in the appearance of additional prayers and antiphons.

861 Passion Sunday and Palm Sunday are distinguished only by the increasing number of propers, especially chapters and prayers, and items for the little hours. Essentially, however, the Sunday and ferial services through Lent remain consistent until Holy Week, where ferias ii-iv have proper responsories with their lessons in a single nocturn, and proper antiphons for Lauds, proper prayers and antiphons for the canticles: (LR)3 A5BOMO. The remaining three days of Holy Week are very consistent from source to source, even in monastic manuscripts. They have a) three secular nocturns and b) Lauds and Vespers with complete sets of musical propers: the complete form of each day would in this case be (A3 (LR)3)3 A5B A5M. Lauds is proper each day whereas the Vespers of Maundy Thursday, beginning with the antiphon *Calicem salutaris* and ending with the Magnificat antiphon *Cenantibus autem*, is repeated on Good Friday. Vespers of Holy Saturday, the Vigil of Easter, about which time the resurrection takes place, is proper according to the pattern of the Easter period. Between Lauds and Vespers each day the little hours are quite abbreviated, some of their normal items being omitted, and preces appear prominently. They are often said privately. Very few sources note proper prayers for these three days.

Easter to Trinity

862 First Vespers, Matins, and Lauds of Easter Sunday are provided with complete sets of propers, but Compline rarely appears, and only hymns, various prayers and chapters are proper in the little hours, and the Magnificat antiphon at second Vespers. The form of Matins is most frequently that of the single secular nocturn, and where monastic sources use this form there is no gospel and prayer afterwards. Two of the monastic sources studied preserve the monastic form of three nocturns with the gospel and prayer. A few sources indicate the items of a *Visitatio sepulchri* in connection with Matins. Peculiar to this Sunday and to the ferias which follow it is the presence in many sources of a Kyrie, gradual (common to the week with a proper verse for each day), alleluia, and sometimes a sequence in second Vespers before the Magnificat, or distributed in some way over the little hours, second Vespers, and occasionally Compline (source B6). Processions and commemorations are common on Easter Sunday and the following ferias. The octave of Easter in most sources adopts the propers of Easter but has its own lessons, with a gospel and prayer if monastic and preserving the monastic form, and has proper antiphons for Benedictus and Magnificat. It also has its own proper prayer. It thus resembles most ferias: O L3BM. Compline is often provided with some propers for this Sunday, which last thereafter until Ascension. The responsories and antiphons of Matins, Lauds, and Vespers are very rarely proper.

863 There are in almost every manuscript weekly stocks of antiphons for Benedictus and Magnificat, normally placed after second Vespers. Other stocks, including some stocks of chapters and prayers, contain the repertory either for the following ferias or for the whole of Easter time. Stocks of chapters and prayers are commonly found only in monastic sources where, as usual, stocks are more common. Sources of Dominican use, such as B10 and B2, include

FIGURE 8.11
Pascha 1 (the octave)

Manuscript references are on the left. Stocks appear within circles. The minor variants in order seen in NB3 at Lauds and in B7 at second Vespers may be errors in the original or in my own interpretation of the manuscript. Ms NB2 includes the aspersion ~ after Terce.

ms	Vespers	Compline	Matins
B10	aCHdMO ⊕	acRHdN	IH L3
NB2	Mo	H N	iH (Lr)2 LR
NB3	MO ⊕	Ac H N	IH Ad(LR)2 Lr
NB4	mo	Cr dnO	*sicut in die*
NB5	MO ⊕		iH Ad (LR)3 AD L3 AD L3
B7	MO		ih ad (Lr)4 (Lr)4 (Lr)4 Go

	Lauds	Prime	Terce	Sext	Nones
B10	d c HdBo ⊕	Rd	crd	CRd	CRd
NB2	da c H	hacr □	hacRdo	aCRd	aCRd
NB3	A HcBo ⊕	hacRd	hAcRdo	haCRd	HACRdo
NB4	c dbo ⊕	h cRdoo	h R o	h CR	h CRd
NB5	A3c HDbo ⊕	hAcRD□	AcRD	ACRD	ACRD
B7	a crhdBo	a	ac do	ac do	ac dO

	Vespers
B10	a M (BM)
NB2	Hdmo *prosa*
NB3	a cHdM ⊕
NB4	a hdm
NB5	A c dMo *
B7	acrdhMo (M4) (B12)

stocks of ferial psalms for the whole season, listed by incipits according to day. Source NB2 is unusual in that it has a stock of antiphons for Matins and Vespers placed after second Vespers of Pascha 2, so that the stock of antiphons *ad evangelia* normally placed here has to be placed after first Vespers. These and other features of the organization of Easter time will be displayed by means of figures comparing the contents and order of several manuscripts. In order to illustrate the way in which Breviaries tend to include incipits even where they are not strictly necessary, these figures are minutely detailed. Although a few minor and unimportant licences have been taken (such as the ≠ where rubrics and incipits are too extensive to be easily summarized), the figures represent the manuscripts accurately with the exception of the incipits of psalms, which have been omitted, and some of the longer commemorations, also omitted. Figure 8.11 deals with the octave of Easter.

864 Feria ii of the octave of Easter is also complex. In figure 8.12 the list of ferial psalms at the beginning of source B10 is omitted.

When the spaces caused by the layout of figure 8.12 are eliminated, the four

FIGURE 8.12
Pascha 1, feria ii

ms	Matins	Lauds	Hours	Vespers
B10	(LR)3		A A A A	a
NB2	Ih A (Lr)3	daChdBO ⊕	c o C C	A5c dMo ⊕
NB3	Ih Ad(LR)3	dAChdBo ⊕	Ar ACr ACR ACr	A ChdM ⊕
NB4	i ad L3	AC BO ⊕	A A AC AC	A5Chd M7
NB5	I L3	Ch B21	c C C	A c M A5
B7				

antiphons of B10, written immediately consecutively in the manuscript, may appear to be a stock. Other patterns, such as the cC2 or coC2 of the little hours, may be similarly obscured by the spacing. Ms B7, a monastic source, gives the lessons in stocks before Advent, and otherwise has no items recorded until feria vi (is this an error for feria ii or iii?): on that day there are stocks of antiphons, chapters, and prayers, with an *ordo* to be discussed in the next paragraph. Only ms NB3 of those listed in figure 8.12 persists in showing the incipits of the invitatory, hymn, antiphon, and dialogue of Matins for the later days of the week (figure 8.13).

FIGURE 8.13
Pascha 1, ferias iii-v

ms	feria iii	feria iv	feria v
B10	(LR)3	R3	
NB2	L3 Bo A8	L3 A5	L3 A5
NB3	ih ad(LR)3 B	ih ad(LR)3	ih ad(LR)3
NB4	ad L9 cC2 A5mo	ad A5m	ad m
NB5	Ad L3 A	Ad L3 A	Ad L3 A

865 The three responsories prescribed for feria iv in the Dominican ms B10 are confirmed in another Dominican source, B2: it is not clear from the information available how they are to be distributed over the remaining days. The eight antiphons with which feria iii ends in ms NB2 are described as *ad evangelia*, as are some of the other stocks shown in these tables. Ms NB4 shows nine lessons in stock on feria iii for distribution over feria iii, iv, and v: feria vi is entirely occupied with the propers for the feast of the Holy Lance, omitted in figure 8.14. Between the first stock of antiphons and the stock of chapters in ms B7, fol. 134v-135, is a long list of incipits referring to the lesser hours of the ferias of Easter time. This list is organized exactly as is an *ordo*, although it is only for ferias of one season, and is perhaps not as comprehensive as a full *ordo* would

FIGURE 8.14
Pascha 1, ferias vi, vii

ms	vi and vii
B10	–
NB2	L3 A5 L3
NB3	ih ad(Lr)3 L3
NB4	L3
NB5	A L3 A AL3
B7	(A4) (C11) (O14)

be. The following excerpt will give some idea of how this section, and a standard *ordo*, appears in a manuscript:

Iste ordo tenendus est per totam resurrectionem privatis diebus feria ii. In j° N°. ant. Alleluia.*ut*.postulavi. *Ps.* Exultate iusti. *In ii° N°. ā.* Alleluia.*ut*.angelis.*Ps.*Dixi custodiam. *In l.ā.* Alleluia.*ut*.pre timore. *Ad iii.de evangelia. Ad vi.ā.* Alleluia.*ut*.erat autem. *Ad ix.ā.* Alleluia.*ut*.Et respicientes. *Ad vesperas super Ps.ā.* Alleluia.*ut*.Jesum quoniam nostris.*feria iii. In j° N°.ā.* Alleluia *sabbato sicut feria iii.ad. vesperas.ā.* Alleluia.*ut*.vespere. *Sciendum quod iste ant. nunquam dicantur donec ipsum.evangelia.legatur. . .*

This rubric gives us the opportunity to introduce the alleluiatic antiphons. These are antiphons for the lesser hours of Easter ferias whose texts consist solely of the word 'alleluia': their chants, however, are those of other antiphons whose incipits appear after the *ut*, and those antiphons appear elsewhere in one of the more important services of the period. The *ut*, in ms B7 at least, is not written completely in red, as it should be since it is part of the rubric, and has only a red highlight on one stroke of the *u*. The dots, in any case, separate text from rubric.

866 The second Sunday of Easter is generally somewhat simpler in its format than the first, although the little hours are frequently burdened in their presentation with repetition of the incipits (figure 8.15). As figure 8.15 shows, Prime does not appear in any of the sources, but as in the previous weekdays the pattern of c(o)C2 typifies the other little hours in some sources. The ferias of the following week are characterized in most sources only by lessons, sometimes distributed as necessary over the days (the last three ferias of the week sometimes repeating the lessons of the first three), or else in one large block of text (source NB5) from which the proper sections may be chosen. Ms B7 as usual has no ferial material at this point in the book. Only ms NB4 differs. It has no material after first Vespers of the Sunday because all is repeated from previous Sunday. Stocks for the ferias and other items such as the weekly prayer therefore appear on feria ii together with the proper lessons and chapters. Later

FIGURE 8.15
Pascha 2

ms	Vespers		Matins				Lauds
B10	m	O	A (Lr)3				B
NB2	C hd (M4)	O	Ih a (LR)3			(R12)	ac hdB
NB3	aCrhdM	O	(Lr)3				dac hdBo
NB4	acRhdM	o	*ut supra*				
NB5	AC hdM	O	(LR)3	(LR)3	(LR)3	(R3)	c bo
B7	acrhdM	O	ih ad(LR)4	(LR)4	(LR)4	Go	acrhdBo

ms	Terce	Sext	Nones	Vespers
B10				M (BM)
NB2	c o	C	C	achdMo (A5)
NB3	cr o	C	C	ac M (A4)
NB4				
NB5	c	C	C	c Mo (A5)
B7	aac do	acdo	acdo	ac dMo (A3)

ferias are also characterized by the presence of more incipits than in other sources:

feria ii (ms NB4)	(Lr)3 aCBO C2 (M7) (R15)
ferias iii & iv (each)	ad(Lr)3 aa
ferias v & vi (each)	ad(Lr)3 a A5m
sabbato	ad L3

867 Figures similar to those of figures 8.11 and 8.15 could be constructed for the remaining Sundays of Easter time: those for the third and fifth would differ principally in the omission of the proper responsories which appear in Sundays 2 and 4. The ms NB4 gives only first Vespers in every case and would therefore repeat the format of figure 8.15 quite closely each time. Stocks of responsories and antiphons and other items occur in the same kinds of position. Weekdays following the third and fourth Sundays duplicate in general those following the second Sunday, and again ms NB4 has the approximate format shown in the preceding paragraph. The three ferias following the fifth Sunday are a little more elaborate since they are the Rogation Days and the Vigil of Ascension.

Ascension Day itself, and Pentecost, Trinity Sunday, and Corpus Christi (where the last occurs) are all typified by a predominance of proper items with the exception of the antiphons for second Vespers. Trinity and even more the feast of Corpus Christi have almost nothing given in incipits (apart from the psalms) except these Vespers texts, a characteristic which may have arisen because the feasts were later additions to the Temporale and their precise textual organization was perhaps at first unfamiliar. We have observed the same feature in Antiphonals, where these feasts often have material in addition to

FIGURE 8.16
Ascension Day to Sunday

	Vespers	Compline	Matins
B10	a Cr HDMo	N	Ih A3 (LR)3
NB2	a C Hd Mo	N	IH A3d(LR)3 (R8)
NB3	A CR HdMo	aHdN	Ih A3d(LR)3
NB4	a5 hdM	N	I A3 (LR)3
NB5	a C HDMO		IH A3D(IR) 3 A3 (LR)3 A3 (LR)3 (R)
B7	a Cr HdMO		IH A6d(LR)4 A6d(LR)4 A kd(LR)4 GO

	Lauds	Prime	Terce	Sext	Nones	Vespers	Compline
B10	DA5cHDBO	r	cR	CR	C R	a M	
NB2	d A5c HdBO	h	aCRdo	aCRd	C2Rd	A crhdMo	
NB3	d A5chd BO	haR	hacRdo	haCRd		a5 crhdM	
NB4	A5C BO	hCRdo	h Rd	h Crd	hC rd	a3AacrhdM	ChdnO
NB5	A5chd Bo	crd	cRd	Crd	C rd	a hdMo	
B7	A5crHdBo	a	ac do	aC do	aC do	a crhdMo	

	feria vi					sabbato	
B10	I A d(LR)3		(BM)			A d(LR)3	
NB2	A3d L3	a	B	M (A4)		A3 L3	
NB3	Ih A3d(LR)2 Lr	achdBo		achdM		ih A3d(LR)3 aB	
NB4	i A3d(LR)3	a	B	a M		i A3d(LR)3 B	
NB5	(L) ⟶					⟶	
B7	I	a R b		a a rdMo	(coC3c)	(O2o5O)	

	Sunday within the octave						
B10		L3		a bo		⊕	⊕
NB2		L3		BO		Mo	
NB3	aCr dMO	L3		C Bo	cC2	a M	
NB4	a Mo	L3		aC BO	C2	a rhdM	
NB5	C hdMO						
B7	crhd Mo	I (adL4r)3	GO	acdhBo	a acdo aa	acrhdMo (A3)	

what is normally recorded. Moreover, these newer feasts may have the proper Mass included even in the Breviary. The ferias after these spring feasts and Sundays follow the normal pattern of three lessons after a common invitatory, with their canticle antiphons given in stocks. Sundays within the octaves and the octaves themselves usually have three nocturns of the type which is in use. The stocks may occur after second Vespers of Ascension, for the following ferias and Sunday, and the occasional source has a stock after the same service on Pentecost. Figure 8.16 shows organization of the feast of Ascension, the following two ferias, and the Sunday within the octave.

868 From figures 8.11-16 we can see immediately that not one of the six sources summarized is identical with any other. The texts and music actually sung may be identical, but the number of reminders in the form of incipits and the exact arrangement of items in stocks or distributed over the proper days may differ. Whether such detailed comparisons would enable sources to be related to each other it is not possible to say, but it seems not unlikely that a manuscript copied directly from another source may well exhibit exactly the same format, the same number of incipits, and the same placement of stocks. There are always passages which appear inexplicable in the abbreviated form necessary for such figures: the unusual reduction of the lessons to incipits in ms NB5 for Matins of Ascension Day cannot easily be explained within the figure, and footnotes are necessary. In this case, the lessons are repeated from Easter Day, as far as can be determined. There are many errors in the originals: the six antiphons of the first monastic nocturn in ms B7, Ascension Day, are erroneously called antiphona *in evangelia*. I had considered the idea of trying to indicate in these figures the items which begin with initials or large initials at the margin. In many cases this could have been done, at some expense of clarity, by printing the relevant items in bold type. Chapters, prayers, lessons, and hymns would have been so marked in the Breviaries, to which the first antiphons of services, the first responsories of nocturns, and antiphons for Magnificat and Benedictus would have been added in Noted Breviaries. The complexity and length would then have been considerably increased, as when only the first responsory has an initial: in place of (LR)3, the figure would need **LR LR LR** or some similar expansion. It seems doubtful whether the inclusion of such information would be worth the difficulty: once a scheme of intials and capitals related to the items they serve has been worked out, it remains more or less consistent throughout the source and the scheme can be superimposed as necessary on the formulas for particular services. The schemes for the six sources just presented in figures 8.11 to 8.15 have been presented in paragraphs **851-5**, figures 8.8 to 8.10.
869 The figures above give a general idea of the way in which the material is presented for the Easter season. There are unusual manuscripts. Source B3, in which the weeks after Epiphany were organized in a peculiar fashion (**858**), also presents Easter Sunday in a seemingly unnecessarily complex manner, dispersed into several sections. The 'inventory' below shows only the main items, ignoring many incidental incipits and rubrics. Frequent rechecking of this manuscript eventually forced me to list the folio numbers more than would normally be necessary: section 1, f.180; 2, f.184; 3, f.194; 4, f.194v; 5, f.199v; 6, f.201; 7, f.202v; 8, f.204; 9, f.204; 10, f.204v; 11, f.205; 12, f.205v; 13, f.208; 14, f.212; 15, f.215; 16, f.216.

1	PASCHA	mostly proper
2	feria ii	(LR)3 BOMO⊕
	ferias iii-iv	L3 BOMO⊕ each
3	PASCHA 1	as Pascha, plus L3 O
4	feria ii	numerous propers and commemorations
5	ferias iii-vii	L3 each with some C, H, o
6	ferias ii-vii of Pascha 2	L3 each
7	ferias ii-vii of Pascha 3	L3 each
8	ferias ii & v	R3
9	ferias iii & vi	R3
10	ferias iv & vii	R3
11	rubric about Lauds and Vespers	
12	A31 antiphons *ad evangelia* for ferias to Ascension	
13	Pascha 2, 3, 4	L3 BOM or (LR)3 BOM each followed by rubrics for ferias
14	ferias ii-vii of Pascha 4	L3 or (LR)3 each; feria vii also has M
15	Pascha 5	L3 BOM
16	ferias ii-iii	L3 BOM each

The anti-chronological arrangement is clear: the ferias of Pascha 2 and 3 appear before the items for the Sundays themselves, and the lessons for the ferias of Pascha 3 are separate from the proper responsories for the week. The antiphons for the canticles on ferias up to Ascension are listed in stock after the ferias of Pascha 3. Ferias of Pascha 4 are separated from ferias of the preceding weeks by the presentation of items for the Sundays. The correct distribution of the material can be ascertained, but the reason for the difficult presentation is unknown.

The summer weeks

870 As in Antiphonals, material for these weeks is normally in two large sections presented consecutively in the manuscripts, the first of which lists the Old Testament lessons for first and second nocturns of Sundays and the ferial lessons, together with the Magnificat antiphons for first Vespers. Under the general heading of *Expositio(nes) evangelii* the second section gives the gospel sentences and homilies which constitute the lessons for the third nocturn of Sundays, with the Benedictus antiphons and the antiphons for the Magnificat of second Vespers, and the prayer proper to each week. The antiphons for Benedictus and Magnificat are common to the ferias following each Sunday, and sometimes a choice is presented. Illustrating the two sections in the most concise form possible, the following shows the arrangement, to which some refinement will be added:

(section 1)
Dominica 1 and ferias M L6 (L3)6 – repeated to Dominica 25
monastic M L8 (L4)6

(section 2, secular)
Dominica 1 L3 BOM *or* O L3 BM – repeated to Dominica 25

Section 2 in monastic sources is slightly different since the last nocturn is completed by the addition of a gospel and prayer:

(section 2, monastic)
Dominica 1 L4 GO BOM *or* O L4 GO BM – repeated to Dominica 25

The format of these sections can be identified quite easily, consisting as it does of long passages devoted to lessons and a prayer (each beginning with a size 2 initial at the margin) and containing two musical items, consecutive or close to each other, written in smaller script or with a musical stave.

871 Some refinements to section 1 may now be introduced. The twenty-five Sundays are divided into the historie which have already been discussed (**107, 835-8**). Each historia has additional proper items, principally the responsories, according to the first of which the historia is named. Each may have a proper invitatory and hymn, and may also have some responsories proper to the following ferias. English sources usually have proper antiphons for Matins of the first Sunday of each historia. The first Sunday of each historia, then, with numerous musical texts, is easy to identify within the sequence of Sundays in the first section. Frequently, a larger initial denotes it. The second refinement to be made concerns the Magnificat antiphons for first Vespers of each Sunday. All of these are collected into stocks either before or after the propers for the first Sunday of each historia. Thus, the musical items appear only in connection with this first Sunday, and the intervening material consists only of lessons. The pattern for the first Sunday of a historia may therefore be:

M [IHA] (LR)6 R3 (ferial Rs)(Ms for Vespers 1)
(LR)8 R4

or (Ms for Vespers 1) [IHA] (LR)6 R3 (ferial Rs)
(LR)8 R4

After the first Sunday, there is a variable number of Sundays depending on the length of time for which the historia is used. Later Sundays include only the six or eight lessons. Thus we have the format:

M (Ms) [IHA] (LR)6 R3 (ferial Rs) L18 L6 L18
(LR)8 R4 L24 L8 L24

or M [IHA] (LR)6 R3 (ferial Rs) (Ms) L18 L6 L18
(LR)8 R4 L24 L8 L24

The final groups of lessons (from L6 or L8 above) are repeated as necessary up to the next historia. English sources, as observed earlier, often present only a single long text each week from which the ferial lessons are drawn. Other sources do not include a proper lesson for every feria: source NB2, for instance, has nine lessons for ferias ii-iv, repeated for v-vii, or occasionally only six for distribution in some unspecified fashion. The monastic sources studied all lack ferial lessons at this point in the manuscripts, although mss B1 and B4 have several ferias, each with three lessons, after the final historia.

872 The second section needs no refinement, but we should notice again that there are often more than two antiphons for Benedictus and Magnificat, giving some choice for the following ferias.

Two sources identify the position for the Ember days during this period. Since they are ferias, the logical place for them is in the first section in their proper calendar sequence, and this is the method adopted in ms B3. They appear in this source after Dominica 15, an assignation which may be incorrect because of the faulty numbering of Sundays. The days are distinguished only by the addition of a proper prayer to the ferial lessons. Source B6 notes these days in the second section, between Sundays 17 and 18: no special items are added to the three ferial lessons and only their position amongst the Sundays of the second section distinguishes them from the other ferias.

One source organizes this period quite differently, presenting the material in a single section arranged in calendar order. The first Sunday of each historia, in this monastic manuscript (B7), has the following format:

O / 3 monastic nocturns / Go BoMo / stock antiphons

No ferias are given, and the beginnings of historia are separated only by the ordinary Sundays of the period, for which the following pattern is typical:

O L12 (often only L4) BoMo

After the twenty-fifth Sunday a different hand has added what appear to be stocks of Magnificat antiphons for the ferias.

The schemes of initials need little comment. Those items normally adopting initials at the margin continue to do so, and larger initials sometimes emphasize the beginnings of historie. If the counting of initials is used as a method of orientation, it is worth noting that in section 2, the *Expositiones evangelii*, the first lesson may have two initials, the first opening the gospel sentences, the second the homily itself. Thus, the formula L3 BOM will have five initials:
[G][L][L][L] B **[O]** M.

THE PSALTER AND HYMNAL

The Psalter

873 Leroquais' admirable description in the introduction to his catalogue of

Psalters in French libraries cannot be repeated in full.[14] I repeat only essential information.

Of the three early translations of the Bible, only two are significant for the Psalter. The first translation, made from the Greek Septuagint in 384 and usually thought, incorrectly, to be by Jerome, produced the version known as the Roman text: it was used everywhere except northern Italy and Spain until the 9th century and in St Peter's, Rome, until the time of Pius V, 1566-72. Texts drawn from the Roman version are still in use in the older parts of the Breviary and Missal. In the 9th century, the Roman translation was superseded by Jerome's translation of the Hexapla, made in 389. This version, taken up in the reforms of Charlemagne, is known as the Gallican. It was intended not for liturgical use but as a working reference copy. As far as the Psalter is concerned it is inferior to the Roman version because of contamination caused by memory of earlier Psalters. Numerous revisions of the Gallican translation were made through the middle ages and renaissance. The final translation, made by Jerome in 393 directly from the Hebrew, eventually came to replace all the others as the Hebrew version or the Vulgate, except for the psalms, which were not translated and were retained in their Roman or Gallican forms.

The Itala Psalter, designated thus by St Augustine, is not a separate version but refers only to the Vulgate, Jerome's Hebrew translation; with respect to the invitatory psalm, however, it is often used to refer to the older Roman psalter (**218**).

874 Of more significance for our purposes are the various traditional and practical divisions of the Psalter. They are as follows:

(1) fivefold, or biblical. This is a division into five books, each ending with something like a doxology-psalm stressing the text *Benedictus Dominus* in its final verses. The division is said to be rare in France. Beginning the five books are Ps 1 *Beatus vir*, 41 *Quemadmodum*, 72 *Quam bonus*, 89 *Domine refugium*, 106 *Confitemini Domino quoniam bonus*;

(2) eightfold, or liturgical. This is a division according to the secular distribution of the psalms in Matins for the seven days of the week, with an eighth section devoted to Vespers, and is presumably the one also called the Roman division.[15] Psalms for Lauds and the other hours are interspersed numerically according to the cursus of the particular use. Beginning the sections are Ps 1 *Beatus vir*, 26 *Dominus illuminatio mea*, 38 *Dixi custodiam*, 52 *Dixit insipiens*, 68 *Salvum me fac*, 80 *Exultate Deo*, 97 *Cantate Domino*, 109 *Dixit Dominus Domino*;

(3) threefold. Said to be of Irish origin, this arrangement is rare in France, more common in Germany. It divides the Psalter into three equal sections and has no relation to the arrangement of psalms within the services: Ps 1 *Beatus vir*, 51 *Quid gloriaris*, 101 *Domine exaudi*;

(4) tenfold. This appears later in France, and combines the threefold and eightfold (Ps 1 is common to both, reducing the sum to ten). Ps 1 *Beatus vir*, 26 *Dominus illuminatio*, 38 *Dixi custodiam*, 51 *Quid gloriaris*, 52 *Dixit insipiens*, 68 *Salvum me fac*, 80 *Exultate Deo*, 97 *Cantate Domino*, 101 *Domine exaudi*, 109 *Dixit Dominus Domino*.

Leroquais identifies various kinds of Psalter according to what is contained other than the psalms themselves. Although useful, his more precise titles have not acquired a firm place in the literature, and one may suspect that the contents of Psalters are sufficiently varied and inconsistent for even his nine or ten qualifications to be inadequate. For our purposes the contents will certainly have to be specified: Leroquais' names will be mentioned where suitable. Leroquais also refers to the largely universal nature of Psalters, finding them for that reason difficult to localize. My own experience, minimal compared with his, demonstrated in the following pages, suggests that when sufficient factors are taken into consideration, and especially when the format and organization are precisely compared in a manner similar to that attempted for the Easter season of Breviaries (**862-8**), families of Psalters may be discernible, making a localization much easier.

The Choir Psalter

875 The Choir or ferial or liturgical Psalter differs from its biblical counterpart since it provides material for the performance of the daily services apart from the psalms themselves. It serves, in fact, as the complement to the Temporale of office books in the same way as the Ordo does for Mass books or the Common of saints for the Sanctorale. The additional material it supplies and the order in which that material is presented can differ widely from source to source, though the number of items and their texts which are in fact common to all daily services does not differ as much from use to use as the variety of presentations would suggest. The discrepancy arises from the willingness or reluctance of the scribe to include here material which is only seasonally or partly common. Texts which vary from season to season may find a more suitable place in the Temporale on the day of their first occurrence. The psalms themselves, which form the core of the ferial psalter, may appear not in biblical order but in an order more convenient to the cursus in use, or they may appear in biblical order with variations in accompanying material or rubrics to suggest their correct liturgical position.

876 In this complicated matter it may be as well to start by outlining the chief divisions of the Psalter which are made clear by the initials. As usual, the size 2 initial at the margin is the standard size for beginning texts, and larger or smaller divisions are denoted by larger or smaller letters. Individual verses are given size 1 or 1+ capitals, normally run on from the end of the previous verse and alternating between red and blue. Of the manuscripts studied, four conventionally begin even the verses with size 1 capitals at the left-hand margin, leaving the right-hand edge of the column ragged: apart from the fact that three of them are of English provenance (the fourth is from Normandy), there seems little in common between these manuscripts.[16] The size 2 initial, as stated, is used for the beginning of psalms and of other items such as the Lauds antiphons and hymns and the chapter for some of the other hours. Occasionally, too, prayers have this initial. Just as the capitals tend to alternate in colour, so do the initials, but seemingly in a less consistent manner: verses are short enough for the previous capital and colour to be visible and within memory, whereas a complete psalm may begin on a previous folio and long enough beforehand for the colour of its initial to have been forgotten. The larger initials, in the size of which there rarely seems to be an internal hierarchy, define the major divisions.

of the book described earlier (**874**), and the number of divisions employed will be examined below. The major initials are generally at least four text lines in depth, and usually many more, thirteen or fourteen being not uncommon. The exact size may vary within the same source, and there seems to be no significance to these minor differences. Indeed, it appears quite likely that the scribes forgot what sizes and schemes were in use so that inconsistencies in style and organization are not uncommon. The large initials are usually historiated or flourished. Some monastic Psalters, transmitting a different cursus of psalms, display a more extended system of large initials which, although expanding it, coincides with the secular system at most but not all points. The two systems, which may be taken as typical for the two kinds of rite, are collated in figure 8.17.

877 The eightfold or liturgical division at Pss 1, 26, 38, 52, 68, 80, 97, and 109 is universal to all secular sources and is marked with large initials. All except the divisions at Pss 80 and 97 are found also in monastic books, although they do not represent the beginnings of the same services in monastic ritual: initials at 80 and 97 may appear even though they do not begin any monastic service. This figure should be compared with the secular and monastic cursus as set out earlier (**402**). A few discrepancies other than the differences between monastic and secular rites should be observed: many may be merely unique practices or errors of the sources considered. (1) There is no initial for the second nocturn of Friday in the monastic source B13, where Ps 95 should be emphasized. Instead, the invitatory psalm, Ps 94, has the large initial. I am inclined to suspect an error here since no other source singles out the invitatory psalm in this way, although it would not seem odd to do so. (2) Secular sources usually emphasize no psalms beyond Ps 109. Monastic Vespers for the weekdays are emphasized in ms B13, with initials on Pss 113, 129, 134, 138, 141, 144. In the same source Pss 118 and 119 are similarly emphasized: they belong not to Vespers but to Sunday Prime and Tuesday Terce respectively. Why these two, and not Ps 117 (Sunday Prime), 122 (Tuesday Sext), 125 (Tuesday Nones) and others for the little hours, should be emphasized is not clear. Mss B15 and C1, monastic and regular respectively, emphasize only Ps 119 here, although the latter treats Pss 131 and 143 (regular Thursday and Saturday Vespers) in the same way. It would seem more logical to emphasize Pss 117 and 118 rather than 118 and 119. Unfortunately, few comparisons could be made since the other monastic sources available displayed a different pattern from that of B13. (3) The other manuscript which emphasizes Vespers, although Tuesday and Wednesday Vespers are inexplicably omitted, is NB6, a Franciscan Noted Breviary. Another regular (Augustinian ?) Breviary, C1, mentioned above, emphasizes Ps 119 and only Thursday and Saturday Vespers. The Dominican Humbert's Codex, B10,

FIGURE 8.17
Initials in Psalters

Psalm number with large initial	Secular services	sources		Psalm number with large initial	Monastic services		sources	
1	Sun ℳ	all		1	Sun 𝒫		all	
				20	Sun ℳ	noct 1		B13
				26		noct 2	all	
	Sun ℒ				Sun ℒ			
26	Mon ℳ	all		32	Mon ℳ	noct 1		B13
				38		noct 2	all	
	Mon ℒ				Mon ℒ			
38	Tue ℳ	all		45	Tue ℳ	noct 1		B13
51			P1	51			all exc	B13
				52		noct 2	all	
	Tue ℒ				Tue ℒ			
52	Wed ℳ	all		59	Wed ℳ	noct 1		B13
				68		noct 2	all	
	Wed ℒ				Wed ℒ			
68	Thu ℳ	all		73	Thu ℳ	noct 1		B13
				79		noct 2		B13
	Thu ℒ				Thu ℒ			
80	Fri ℳ	all		80	–		all exc	B13
				85	Fri ℳ	noct 1		B13
				94	–			B13
				95		noct 2	–	–
	Fri ℒ				Fri ℒ			
97	Sat ℳ	all		97	–		all exc	B13
101			P1, C1, NB1	101	Sat ℳ	noct 1	all	
				105		noct 2		B13
	Sat ℒ				Sat ℒ			
109	Sun 𝒱	all		109	Sun 𝒱		all	
				113	Mon 𝒱			B13
114	Mon 𝒱		NB6					
118	–		NB7	118	Sun 𝒫			B13
119	–		P1, C1	119	Tue 𝒯			B13, B15
				129	Tue 𝒱			B13
131	Thu 𝒱		C1, NB6					
				134	Wed 𝒱			B13
137	Fri 𝒱		NB6					
				138	Thu 𝒱			B13
				141	Fri 𝒱			B13
143	Sat 𝒱		C1, NB6					
				144	Sat 𝒱			B13

emphasizes no psalms after 109. Ms NB7, a secular manuscript lacking most of its Psalter and most large initials (through mutilation) even where the Psalter is present, gives a large initial to Ps 118, the only secular source to do so. Ps 119 is perhaps emphasized because it is the first of the Gradual psalms.[17]

878 Apart from this irregular and inconsistent singling out of the psalms within the Vespers sequence, there are a few sources which display large initials at other points within Pss 1-108. Three monastic sources and one other, probably secular, all of English provenance,[18] have a large initial for Ps 51, followed immediately by the one conventionally appearing for Ps 52. The secular source, which is a normal Choir Psalter, also has a similar initial on Ps 101: so do the monastic manuscripts just cited, because that psalm begins the first nocturn of Saturday. The emphasis on Pss 51 and 101 in the secular Psalter and on Ps 51 (and 101 coincidentally) in monastic Psalters must be a proclamation of the threefold division said to be of Irish origin and here appearing consistently in English sources. On the other hand, three secular sources from England have neither 51 nor 101 specially marked[19] and another has 101 so emphasized but not 51.[20]

The hierarchy of large initials therefore appears to be an irrational and inconsistent mixture, perhaps partly the result of tradition and of liturgical divisions, one secular, the other monastic, with a regular, Franciscan and perhaps Roman division, and with a threefold division not of liturgical origin. A statistical and comparative study of the practices in this respect may well reveal some clues to the provenance and perhaps to the date.

879 The psalms for Lauds and the little hours occur at different places within the main sequence, and the position for inserting other items needed for the common of those services can differ. Lauds of each day normally appears in both secular and monastic sources immediately after the psalms for the nocturns of each day (see figure 8.17), and the additional texts common to Vespers are given immediately after the psalms for daily Vespers. Items for the little hours are in most sources to be found separated in two positions: some of the material for Prime occurs with Pss 21-25 in secular manuscripts, and with 1-19 in monastic, while the rest of the items for that service and all the items for Terce, Sext, and Nones occur with Pss 117 and 118 (secular) or 117-127 (monastic). This splitting of the material for the little hours into two places is partly due to a desire not to move the psalms themselves out of numerical order. On the other hand, that very procedure does occur: a few sources[21] place all the items for all the little hours, including psalms later in the sequence such as 117 and 118, with Pss 21-25. One source deals with Prime when Pss 21-25 appear, and material for Terce, Sext, and Nones appears after Ps 113: this odd arrangement is perhaps due to a desire not to disturb the psalms for Monday Vespers.[22] Common items for Compline, when they appear at all in the Psalter, seem to occur in different positions, all of them justifiable somehow. Only three of the secular manuscripts consulted had items for Compline: one places them after Sunday Vespers between Pss 113 and 114, another at the very end of the psalms, after Ps 150, a third places these common items after Ps 93 and omits the rest.[23] Figure 8.18 summarizes the various positions where items can occur.

880 Where psalms such as 117 and 118 are required within the other Prime psalms 21-25, only their incipits normally appear and the complete text occurs in the correct numerical sequence. Occasionally there may be a rubric, as in the Printed Sarum Breviary of 1531, stating *non dicitur ad (nocturnos* or *vesperas)*: in a few sources, however, the whole text is given where it is needed, in the proper

FIGURE 8.18
The organization of the Choir Psalter

The numerals are psalm numbers. Where there is no psalm number at the left, material for other offices is interpolated, as shown (sometimes these offices use the psalms in sequence). The material for Prime is interpolated in two sections, near the beginning of the Psalter and around Psalms 117 and 118. The material for other offices is interpolated at various places: alternative positions are shown in italics. Compare figure 4.2.

Secular		Monastic	
1-20	Sunday Matins		1-19 Prime, completed below
	Sunday Lauds	20-31	Sunday Matins
	21-25 Prime, completed below		Sunday Lauds
	occasionally also	32-44	Monday Matins
	Terce, Sext, Nones		Monday Lauds
26-37	Monday Matins	45-58	Tuesday Matins
	Monday Lauds		Tuesday Lauds
38-51	Tuesday Matins	59-72	Wednesday Matins
	Tuesday Lauds		Wednesday Lauds
52-67	Wednesday Matins	73-84	Thursday Matins
	Wednesday Lauds		Thursday Lauds
68-79	Thursday Matins	85-100	Friday Matins
	Thursday Lauds		Friday Lauds
80-89	Friday Matins begun	101-108	Saturday Matins
	90 *Compline* (in ms B17)		Saturday Lauds
90-96	Friday Matins completed		Compline
	Friday Lauds	109-112	Sunday Vespers
97-108	Saturday Matins	113-116	Monday Vespers begun
	Saturday Lauds		117-127 Prime completed,
	Terce, Sext, Nones (in		Terce, Sext, Nones
	ms B 17)	128	Monday Vespers completed
109-113	Sunday Vespers	129-132	Tuesday Vespers
	Compline (in ms B18)	133-137	Wednesday Vespers
114-116	Monday Vespers begun	138-140	Thursday Vespers
	117-118 Prime completed,	141-144	Friday Vespers
	Terce, Sext, Nones	145-147	Saturday Vespers
119-120	Monday Vespers completed	148-150	Lauds
121-125	Tuesday Vespers		
126-130	Wednesday Vespers		
131-136	Thursday Vespers		
137-141	Friday Vespers		
142-147	Saturday Vespers		
148-150	Lauds		
	Compline (in ms B16)		

position within the Prime psalms beginning with Ps 21, and the text is not given in the proper numerical sequence. Nothing indicates the absence of a psalm, in most cases. Sources B16 and B17 apply the latter procedure quite consistently.

With the discrepancies as marked, these two manuscripts omit the following psalms from their proper numerical position:

4 (ms B16 only), 5 (ms B16 only), 42, 50, 53, 62, 64, 66, 89-92, 99 (ms B16 only), 117-118, 133, 142

The reader may perhaps wish to work out for himself from figures already presented which of the hours other than Matins and Vespers these psalms occur in (I know of no reason for the omission of Ps 99 from ms B16). The omission of Ps 50 causes one peculiar situation: it is omitted in order to occur in Lauds of Tuesday, which material follows Ps 51. Because there is little other material to be supplied here, the sequence of psalms involves only an inversion of order which may seem to be merely erroneous: Ps 49, 51 [Lauds, Ps 50 . . .]. Other places where omission may seem to occur may be caused by the division, *divisio* (or *phares* in ms B13), of one psalm into several parts, each of which is supplied with a size 2 initial as though it were a new psalm, or by the opposite, the combining of psalms into one text without a separation by initial. The most common psalms for these practices are 118, divided into eleven or twenty-two sections (given Hebrew letters in ms B13), and 148-50, normally regarded as a single psalm. Some manuscripts seem to omit the occasional psalm: two fail to include Ps 64; two others omit Ps 42.[24] Why only these should be omitted I cannot say.

Now let us observe the details of what items are added throughout the Psalter, either with psalms in normal numerical order or with misplaced psalms. The following items which are not psalms may be considered normal additions to the Choir Psalter: doxologies, antiphons, invitatories, hymns, versicles, major and minor canticles. Each is a daily or ferial or common text, and such a qualification may be added to the noun, as in ferial antiphon. A Litany usually appears towards the end of the Psalter. Other items which may occur are preces, common chapters and prayers, and very occasionally the ferial lessons and responsories (source P2). Where necessary the plainsongs are given in sources which transmit the music, but this applies only to melodic items such as antiphons: the reciting tones of the psalms do not appear unless there is a section specifically devoted to the Tonary. The reason for this is obvious: the psalm may be sung to any one of the eight different tones, the choice depending on the mode of the antiphon which accompanies it. The only exception is Ps 113, sung to a very special and characteristic tone, the *tonus peregrinus* (**617**): this tone is occasionally given complete with the psalm, as in source A19. The dialogue-tone for the versicles and responses is sometimes given in musical sources, and similarly the tune for the Te Deum may appear. When not supplied with the music, the texts of musical items are as usual smaller in size.

Ferial antiphons, versicles (dialogues), and doxologies

881 These occur in all the hours and therefore appear throughout the Psalter in both the normal sequence and in the additions. There are two principal methods of recording them. In the first and less common method the complete antiphon is given only after the psalm or psalms which it covers. More usual is for the incipit of the antiphon to appear before the psalm or psalms covered and the complete text to appear afterwards. There may be more than one antiphon in either of the above cases. In the latter procedure a characteristic sequence of texts is set up. Before Ps 1, or any other place where a new sequence begins, will be the incipit(s) of the antiphon(s): at the end of the psalm or psalms covered will be the complete antiphon(s), followed immediately by the incipit(s) of the next antiphon(s). Thus, at Matins, where each group of psalms is covered by a single antiphon, the Psalter may open as follows (incipits are shown as usual with lower case letters, and psalms by their numbers):

Nocturn 1	Nocturn 2
a 1-6 Aa 7-10 Aa 11-14 A	D a 15 Aa 16 Aa 17 Aa . . .

In this arrangement the versicle preceding the second nocturn is included in its correct position. Where the ferial antiphon changes from season to season, all the alternatives may appear at the same place in the Psalter. The organization of incipits and complete texts is thus:

aaa 1-6 AAAaaa 7-10 AAAaaa 11-14 . . .

Plates 4a-c show the end of Ps 16, the two antiphons *Inclina Domine* and *Pectora nostra* followed by the incipits of the two antiphons *Dominus* and *Tu populum.* The complete texts and chants for these occur after the intervening Ps 17. In this source the evovae formula appears only with the incipit. A few sources have this very odd and not very practical arrangement:

aaa 1-6 AaAaAa 7-10 AaAaAa 11-14 . . .

Source A19 and Humbert's Codex, B10, adopt this format. Rubrics may be present to explain the seasonal variation. The correct numerical placing of psalms which are said at other services can cause dislocation of a consistent pattern: in the ferial Matins, for example, where each antiphon normally covers two psalms the appearance of three psalms, before the antiphon text is given complete, alerts the reader to the presence of material not needed here:

feria iii (Matins): a 38, 39 Aa 40, 41 Aa 42, 43, 44 Aa 45, 46 Aa . . . (42 *non dicitur ad nocturnos*).

Doxologies appear inconsistently in most sources, and are normally indicated only by the incipit, *Gloria* or *Gloria patri.* The presence or absence of the indication cannot be taken to mean anything unless the source is very carefully presented. The Sarum Breviary of 1531 is such a source.

When we examine the way in which Lauds and the other hours are presented we shall find some minor modifications of this arrangement: nevertheless, this is the style in which the bulk of the Psalter is organized. At the relevant places, other material for Matins appears. Before each day, that is, before Pss 1, 26, 38, 52, 68, 80, and 97 and after any material for Lauds which may occur, the ferial invitatory will appear together with the relevant hymn or its incipit: several seasonal alternatives for the latter may be given. At the end of nocturn 3 of Sunday, that is, after Ps 20 and its antiphon(s), the Te Deum may appear:[25] more commonly, however, this hymn is to be found with the canticles at the end of the Psalter.

Lauds

882 The ferial antiphons, versicles, chapters, hymns, and other items which appear occasionally are listed in the daily position described in section **879** and in figure 8.17. The basic outline of such items, excluding psalms and canticles, is: D A5 CHDB preces O. The appearance of the versicles, chapter, hymn, preces, and prayer is inconsistent, and any or all may be given only in incipit: alternatives may occur for the hymn. The Benedictus antiphon does not usually appear in Sunday Lauds since there is almost always a proper text. The text of this canticle itself is usually presented at the end of the Psalter (in source BS it is at the end of Sunday Lauds). The ferial antiphons, which occasionally differ in number, are set out in a manner similar to the ferial antiphons already discussed with the necessary modifications caused by the presence or absence of the relevant psalm texts or incipits. Whether or not the complete psalms are included with this material, many sources tend to include the proper minor canticle text complete here, although it too may occur only in incipit, the complete text appearing at the end of the Psalter. Several different arrangements are thus possible, of which these are some:

D A5 CH (*or* ch) [B]

As in sources NB2 and B19, where this arrangement occurs, the antiphons are accompanied by either the differentia, to identify the termination of the psalm tone, or the incipit of the psalm or canticle. Source P2 has this scheme:

A (incipits of Pss 92, 65, 62)
A (canticle complete)
A (incipit of Ps 148)   Chd   BO

Sources A19 and NB7 have:

D A3
  a (canticle complete)
  A2   Ch   B preces

Sources such as the Sarum Breviary (BS) and ms B17, which provide complete psalm texts, have the following schemes for Sunday, where texts common to all of the days of the week, such as Pss 148-50, appear:

BS: D A5 (Pss 92, 99, 62, 66, canticle, 148-50) CHd B
B17: a 92, Aa 99 Aa 62 66 Aa (canticle) Aa 148-50 A Hd

On subsequent ferias only the proper canticle and psalm texts are shown:

B17: Aa 42 Aa (canticle) AA HdB

In the single manuscript from which monastic Lauds was studied, very little ferial material was given: the versicle, one or two ferial antiphons, often with marginal incipits referring to the relevant psalm and canticle texts, a short responsory, chapter, hymn, and Benedictus antiphon appeared irregularly and often only in incipit.

It should be remembered here that the first Lauds antiphon and often the hymn are emphasized with a size 2 initial.

Vespers

883 No psalm or canticle texts have to be sought from other parts of the Psalter, except for the Magnificat canticle, usually occurring at the end of the book. The arrangement of the service is thus relatively simple. The ferial antiphons are distributed with the relevant psalms in one of the manners already described, one antiphon covering a single psalm. After the last psalm and antiphon for each day the chapter, hymn, versicle, occasionally a short responsory, and the Magnificat antiphon (except on Sunday, when there is a proper text) may appear, but often only the incipits are given, especially later in the week when repeats are used:

ms B16: a 137 Aa 138 Aa 139 Aa 140 Aa 141 A CHdM

The little hours

884 Exactly the same principles apply and are complicated only by the presence or absence of the necessary psalm texts, and by the presence of the text for the Athanasian creed, *Quicunque*. The division of Ps 118 into numerous sections may also be remembered. Numerous prayers and preces frequently occur after the items of Prime have been presented and may take up a good deal of space in the Psalter. Four different secular arrangements will be shown. Most common is the format in which the hymn of Prime appears with Pss 21-25, while the remainder of the service and all of the other little hours are with Pss 117 and 118:

ms B6

Matins	. . . 20
Lauds	A5 Hd
Prime	H 21-25 . . . 53 . . . 117
	118^{1-2}
Terce	H 118^{3-5}
Sext	AH 118^{6-8}
Nones	AH 118^{9-11}

Here, the psalms between 25 and 117 are in their correct order, and *Quicunque* is presented at the end of the Psalter.

ms A19	
Matins	. . . 20
Lauds	D A5 CHH
Prime	21-25 . . . 53 . . . 117
	H (numerous alternatives)
	a 118^{1-2} A *Quicunque*
	H5 A5 C3 R4
	preces O (numerous)
Terce	H4 A2 118^{3-5}
	ACRd plus alternatives

Sext and Nones follow with a similar arrangement. The presence of many alternatives may be noted.

ms B17	
Matins	. . . 20
Lauds	92 A 99 A 62 66 A K A 148-50 A Ha
Prime	H 21-25 53 Aa 117
	118^{1-2} Aa *Quicunque*
	A CRO . . . 113
Terce	H 118^{3-5}
	ACRd
Sext	H 118^{6-8}
	ACRd
Nones	H 118^{9-11}
	ACR

All the material for Prime is together; all the material for Terce, Sext, and Nones, is after Ps 113.

BS	
Matins	. . . 20
Lauds	D A5 92 99 62 66 K 148-50 CHD (with alternatives)
Prime	H 21-25 53 117
	118^{1-2} A3 *Quicunque*
	A5 C3 R3
	D preces Os, etc

Terce, Sext, and Nones follow, each with H 118^{x-x} ACRd and alternatives.

The little hours in the monastic source (B13) are presented as follows:

Prime (ferias ii-vii) Pss 1-19 . . . 117
Prime (Sunday) $118^{1\text{-}4}$ *Quicunque* DO
Terce $118^{5\text{-}7}$ Aco
Sext $118^{8\text{-}10}$ ACoR
Nones $118^{11\text{-}13}$ Acdo

Ps 118 continues to the twenty-second section at Terce, Sext and Nones of Monday, then through Pss 119-127, without antiphons, chapters, or hymns, for the remainder of the week.

Compline
885 As stated, the common for Compline is rarely presented and the psalms are generally given in sequence. Exceptions have been described (**879** and figure 8.18).

Other material
After Ps 150 and distinguished with size 2 initials just like those of the psalms, the major and minor canticles are normally given, together with the texts of the Te Deum and the Athanasian creed. Although the minor canticles will be together, as will the major canticles, the order in which most of this material appears will differ from source to source, and it is possible that specific arrangements could provide another means of identifying the family, provenance, and date of the manuscript.

The Litany usually follows. Its structure of repeated petitions, *Ora* (or *Orate*) *pro nobis*, following a recital of the name(s) of the saint(s) to whom the petition is addressed, is very distinctive. The list of names on the left, and the repeated petitions usually abbreviated to *or.* on the right, naturally make the item fall into two columns subdividing the page or, more usually, subdividing each of the two columns already present. Prayers follow, and the Psalter may be completed with votive offices, the daily office to the Dead, and the daily office to the Virgin, and perhaps with offices to important saints. Various commemorations, especially for newly added feasts, and perhaps the benedictions for Matins lessons, may occur here. Even the Preface and Canon of Mass sometimes appears, especially in monastic books, and this is thought to be an indication that the Breviary was for use by clergy outside the monastery where the usual books may have been difficult to obtain.

The Hymnal
886 Where the complete texts of hymns do not appear in the Temporale, Sanctorale, or Psalter, they would normally be included in a separate section of the Breviary, often in a separately bound book; when bound in with the other

sections, the Hymnal frequently occurs immediately after the Psalter. The presentation of the hymns individually is exactly as it would be for the presentation of a hymn within the Temporale or elsewhere: the text begins with a size 2 initial and subsequent stanzas are listed after the first, alternating colour on the capitals with which they begin. Only the first stanza is normally provided with music, if the chant is noted at all. Within the Hymnal are sections, not usually marked with any larger initial, devoted to the Temporale texts, those for the saints, and those for the Common of saints. Common or seasonal hymns for the Temporale seem less frequently to be included and will presumably be listed where they occur in the Temporale, or in the Psalter itself.

SANCTORALE AND COMMON OF SAINTS

887 Just as in Missals, the presence of a saint's feast in the Sanctorale of a Breviary or Antiphonal is determined by his presence in the Kalendar of the institution for which the manuscript was destined. Furthermore, the feast's rank, usually specified in the Kalendar, determines the character of the offices presented in the Sanctorale. Feasts of major importance have elaborate services typified by a large number of proper texts and proper chants and by solemn ceremonial. The most important feasts may have proper antiphons even for the lesser hours and even proper psalms. Each of these will be recorded, the psalms by means of incipits. Normally, however, the psalms are ferial according to the day on which the feast falls in a particular year. Antiphons are frequently ferial, too, especially for the less important hours.

The repertory of propers, then, presented in the Sanctorale, can range from virtually every item to just the prayer. Some propers such as hymns may be recorded in their own special section, in this case the Hymnal, if that is the practice of the source, with only an incipit in the Sanctorale. Where no propers are given, rubrics usually indicate whether the text is to be drawn from the Common of saints or from the ferial items for the day. The little hours are more likely to be drawn from the Common. On the other hand, the Matins lessons are usually proper and are frequently not Biblical or written by an early Church Father, but are more recent narratives relating to the feast. This is especially true of saints and feasts of relatively late date. Frequently the lessons of nocturn 3 are drawn, by means of rubrics, from specified homilies: *tres ultime lectiones de expositione evangelii.* Even lesser feasts normally have the proper prayer and at least three lessons, O L3, with rubrics such as *cetera de communi.* The least important feasts have only a proper prayer, used for memorials.

At some place in the Breviary there will be a section devoted to prayers for general and special occasions, for peace, for benefactors, for kings, bishops, popes, etc. Such proper commemorations may occur at the end of the Psalter or within the office of the Dead, or within some feast of the Sanctorale such as All Saints or All Souls.

888 The Common of saints provides those texts proper to classes of saints which, with a suitable name inserted, become proper to an individual within the class. Thus, there are prayers for martyred bishops used for all such saints not given a proper of their own: rubrics within the Sanctorale will there specify *cetera* (or *oratio* or *responsoria*, etc) *de communi* (*unius confessoris et pontificis* or *unius virginis non martyris*, etc). Within the Common of saints there is frequent reference from one class to another class, especially within basic categories such as confessors: confessors and bishops may have a certain item in common with confessors not bishops, etc. Rubrics identify such cross-references.

One section of the Common of saints deals specially with the common of feasts during Easter time, *paschalis temporis*, giving the alternative common items for that period: different terminations such as *Alleluia* will still be recorded as necessary in the Temporale. This part of the Common is mostly inserted into the middle of the Sanctorale, at the end of the spring feasts: when the Sanctorale is split between two books giving winter and summer respectively, the section devoted to the Common of Easter time appears, misleadingly, at the beginning of the summer Sanctorale. Sometimes, the Easter Common is attached to the Common of saints itself.

BREVIARIES AND ANTIPHONALS AS COMPLETE BOOKS

889 The order in which the different sections of Breviaries and Antiphonals are bound or written into a single volume is quite variable. Three main arrangements are evident, and begin to associate themselves with provenances and uses. To be certain that a particular order is correct, it would be necessary to examine each manuscript 'in the flesh' to ascertain whether leaves, fascicles or even whole sections had not been lost. This has not been possible with most of the manuscripts used here, since collation is not usually possible from microfilm. Thus, most sources can be discussed only in general terms.

We need to observe only the main sections in order to begin. For Breviaries, we may record five; the Kalendar, Temporale, Psalter, Sanctorale, and Common of saints (henceforth in this discussion **KTPSC**) and for Antiphonals only three (**TSC**). The different orders in which these sections appear is occasionally quite sufficient for a family assignment to be clear. Nevertheless, in order to include more detail, we may also record some sections of lesser importance: for Breviaries, the Ordo, the offices of the Dedication, of the Dead, and to the Virgin, the Hymnal, the section giving benedictions, and the section with the great rubric (see appendix V) (**OD† VH✠** and **R** respectively); for Antiphonals, the Tonary and Invitatorium may be added (⊥ and **I**). Miscellaneous additions will be shown as ■. For both Breviaries and Antiphonals, the position of the Common of saints for Easter time is probably an extra detail to be observed. As stated in paragraphs **833, 888**, it may occur adjacent to the Common of saints or within the Sanctorale at the correct seasonal point. Even though sources from a single use are mainly consistent in their arrangement, the smaller sections are more peripatetic than the main ones: mostly placed between the main sections, they may move from one slot to another. A few, such as the offices of the Dead and of the Dedication, may be recorded within the Sanctorale rather than between sections. In the following pages I have used only books which are complete, containing all the main sections outlined above. Many other books could probably have been included with little risk. For example, provided it is not misbound a Breviary having the following order, **KPTS**, could be considered as belonging to the category **KPTSC**. In this case the Common of saints may have been lost or it may never have been added. Similarly, a book lacking leaves as follows, **T□PSC**, could fairly safely be included within the category **TKPSC**. Occasionally such books have been considered. Although some sources may be incorrectly categorized in the following descriptions because misbinding is not apparent from film or from general notes, the overall principles outlined cannot be challenged.

Breviaries

890 Three categories of Breviary emerge very quickly: (1) **KPTSC**, (2) **KTPSC**, and (3) **TKPSC** or **TKPCS**. The first is certainly the most widespread, occurring about three times as often as category 2. A statistical comparison of categories 1 and 2 against 3 is not valid because I made a special attempt comprehensively to collect Breviaries of the kind which happen to fall into category 3. The reversal of the Sanctorale and Common noted in category 3 as an equally frequent order is also to be found in the other categories, but rarely. Apart from the last category, which consists almost exclusively of British sources, there is little significantly in common between the sources of the other two categories: specified provenances, uses or orders, as far as the assignation of these can be trusted from the available catalogues, are distributed haphazardly and irrationally between them. Some details are given below. In fact, what we are aiming for is to be able to deduce the family, provenance, use, or order from the arrangement, not to work in the other direction. The failure of obvious relationships to emerge is probably due to an insufficiency of detail, and to the inconsistency with which details have been recorded.

Manuscripts of the Roman curia or of the Franciscan order seem to fall into either category 1 or 2 almost equally and I can detect no geographical or chronological preference. No further reference will be made to manuscripts of this type, unless they are special in some way. I have no worthwhile statistics about Dominican sources: the four for which I have the information all fall into category 1.[26]

Category 1

891 KPTSC The most that can be said at the moment is that numerous manuscripts of French and Iberian provenance use this order.[27] Insertions other than Easter tables and sometimes an Ordo almost never occur after the Kalendar but are very common between the Psalter and Temporale, where the Hymnal and offices to the Dead and to the Virgin may be given. After either the Temporale or the Sanctorale the office of the Dedication may be presented, and no geographical preferences can be observed for the choice of one or the other place.[28] The Common of saints, being the last section, is often followed by all sorts of later additions, but in the same hand and as an intended continuation there are frequently the offices to the Dead and to the Virgin, and the benedictions, where these are not given at the end of the Psalter.

Some precise schemes follow. **KP† HV TSD C**: this order, in a Hungarian Cistercian Breviary of 1481, may be compared with that of a Czechoslovakian book of 1353:[29] **KP†H■ TD SC■**. After the Psalter of the latter there are miscellaneous additions other than those shown here, and before the Temporale begins there are sections devoted to chapters (with some incipits of other items) and prayers: the Common of saints in Easter time is within the Sanctorale. Somewhat simpler is a Noted Breviary of Verdun, from 1302:[30] **KP† TSDI C(✱)**. The benedictions are in a later hand. Some Spanish sources have these arrangements:

■ KPHV† T■SD C■ (ms B20, preceded by tables, has benedictions and miscellaneous rubrics. Between the Temporale and Sanctorale are some lessons for the latter. After the Dedication the manuscript dissolves into fragmented, although apparently continuous, parts)
KP T S (ms B22)
KPH† T■SD C (ms B24)

Three manuscripts of the use of Braga, Portugal, have

K■PH TV■ SD CV✱ (ms B26)
K PH†V■TS CV (ms B23)
K PH TV S C† (ms B21)
After the Kalendar of the first of these is the Vita and Passion of St Alexis; between the Temporale and Sanctorale are miscellaneous services, the new feast of Corpus Christi, the *novum officium* of the Virgin, and others.

892 The alternative order, in which Sanctorale and Common are reversed, occurs in three manuscripts known to me; one is an Italian Franciscan book, another is of the use of Paris, the third is a Noted Breviary, 1262, of Chartres. **K■PH T CDV† ■S**: in the Franciscan manuscript,[31] except for the major feasts, the Temporale and Sanctorale have only the diurnal services with a format ranging from just the prayer to the full offices, and represented typically by ABMOC. The Common has complete offices. Just before the Sanctorale is a section giving all the Benedictus and Magnificat antiphons and prayers for the summer Sundays. The Common for Easter time follows the Sanctorale. The Paris Breviary[32] has **KO P TCS**. The office of the Dead is included within the Sanctorale, after the feast of All Saints. Following the Kalendar is an Ordo or pica beginning *In anno* ... (see appendix V). The Noted Breviary of Chartres[33] has **KPV■ TC†■ S■**. Here, the Ordo *In anno* ... is included within the Temporale.

Category 2

893 KTPSC Sources from Tuscany [34] seem to favour this order but it is distributed also outside Italy; no Iberian representatives of this category have come to light. There is less tendency to insert material between the sections. Only at the end of the Psalter are the Hymnal, the offices to the Dead and to the Virgin; an Ordo occasionally follows the Temporale. Most additions are made right at the end of the manuscripts, following the Common of saints.

There follow some specific arrangements. **KTI PSCDV†**: this Breviary [35] of about 1500 made by Flemish scribes for Eleanor, Queen of Portugal, follows a Franciscan rite. Its beautiful illuminations and clear denoting of the liturgical season with shoulderheads reflect the clarity of its order. Another Franciscan Breviary, from Italy, also has a very clear order of presentation:[36] **KTPSCDVO**. The office of the Dead is within the Psalter, and at the end is the Ordo *In anno*, already noted in some manuscripts of the previous category. The office of the Dead is attached to the Common of saints in several sources of this class, as in the following three: **KTO PH SC†** (ms B66, according to the Roman curia), **KTO P SC†✱■V** (ms B67, according to the Roman curia), **KOTO PH SD C†** (ms B68, Italian monastic).

894 The uncommon alternative order in which the Sanctorale and Common of saints are reversed occurs in two manuscripts known to me. A Roman Breviary of ca 1511, written and illuminated at Rodez for Guy de Castelnau, abbot of the Cistercian abbey of Bonneval,[37] adopts the order **KTPH CDV S†**. A summer Breviary of St Aubin d'Angers with the order **K■✱TPCS** is described more fully in Leroquais' catalogue.[38] No doubt an analysis of this feature of Breviaries in Leroquais' book would reveal other manuscripts with this reversal.

Three English manuscripts, one of them monastic, take the main order described under category 2, although some are not complete. **KTPDO SC**: this is in a book specified as *secundum . . . Sarum* (fol 7) with the immediate qualification *anglicane*, unique to my knowledge.[39] Some incorrect spellings of English saints (such as Wlestane, Damstane) occur. These features, together with the order, unusual for English books, make one suspect that the manuscript was not written in England. **KTD ⊥ PS[]**: this is in a Noted Breviary for Norwich, which is specified in the Dedication feast of the Kalendar.[40] **K■V TPV† SD C**: preceded by stocks of lessons and prayers, this monastic Breviary has an index of saints and incipits following the Kalendar.[41]

Category 3

895 TKPCS or **TKPSC** Almost all sources with this arrangement are of British provenance. At the moment I can say little about the preference for one form or the other except that all the Irish manuscripts use the former:[42] Sarum manuscripts use either form apparently indiscriminately, as do sources whose provenance in Britain is not certainly known; York sources favour the second form by two to one; single sources of Hereford, Norwich, and Lichfield all use the former arrangement, as do four Benedictine manuscripts.[43] On the other hand a Worcester Breviary and the Benedictine Breviary of Battle Abbey, the latter said to be modelled on a French prototype,[44] use the second arrangement. The arrangement of British Antiphonals, shown in the following pages, should be compared.

Insertions between the main sections are most common after the Temporale, where the Dedication is conventionally placed, with the benedictions and lists of Sarum feasts. Here too may be offices to the Virgin, material for Masses, an Ordo (peculiar to York sources), or the Tonary of noted sources. After the Psalter the Hymnal, Tonary, or the offices of the Dead and to the Virgin may occur. The office of the Dead, however, is more often at the end of or within the

Sanctorale. Insertions at other points are rare. Here is the arrangement of noted manuscripts from each of the principal British uses:

Sarum:	TD KI P ⊥ SC	(ms NB11)
York:	TDVO K P CS† ⊥	(ms NB12)
Hereford:	TD H K P SC†I ⊥	(ms NB3)

Manuscripts without the plainsongs are similarly arranged.

Several sources of English provenance or destination do not show the typical reversal of Temporale and Kalendar and use either category 1[45] or category 2.[46] Conversely, there are a handful of European sources, mostly from the north of France or Flanders, which adopt the English arrangement, placing the Kalendar after the Temporale. I have observed two manuscripts from Paris, one each from Troyes, Cambrai, Flanders, and one from Spain.[47] In the last two the Common of saints precedes the Sanctorale. There is also a single source from Italy.[48]

Antiphonals

896 The standard arrangement is **TSC**. British Antiphonals, however, are mostly distinct from their European counterparts since the majority of them have the same sections and insertions in exactly the same order(s) as do Breviaries from Britain. Of about twenty British Antiphonals complete enough for accurate observation, sixteen include the Kalendar after the Temporale and twelve the Psalter after the Kalendar, and the same variability in the order of Sanctorale and Common is present: **TK(P) SC** or **CS**. The manuscripts in which the Common precedes the Sanctorale are from Ireland, two from Norwich, and one each from London and the Midlands.[49] A Benedictine Antiphonal from Gloucester combines the Temporale and Sanctorale in a format which is highly abbreviated and in which the nocturnal offices are often omitted, but which includes processions and Masses (see appendix VII). Two manuscripts from York and an Augustinian source follow the simpler continental form:

TD S C†	(ms A25)
TD S† [?]	(ms A26)
TV S CH	(ms A27)

The outline of the continental form, **TSC**, rarely varies, and lesser sections are mostly before the Temporale or after the Common rather than between sections. Four manuscripts may be cited:

T S CD†I ⊥ H	(ms A28, now in Madrid)
S CD†I ⊥ H	(ms A29, from Lorvão, Portugal)
I T SV C	(ms A30, now in Trier)
T SD C I H	(ms A31, from the Cistercian abbey of Himerode)

Dominican sources frequently place the Tonary first.

I know of only one continental manuscript which includes either the Kalendar or the Psalter:[50] **K PB T SC†**. Many Antiphonals, however, do not contain even the three main sections. Presumably because of the size and length caused by the inclusion of the music, the Temporale is often separated from the Sanctorale and Common of saints so that two or more volumes result. Both may have the Tonary or the Invitatorium, and the relevant part of the Hymnal.

Temporale and Sanctorale combined

897 The combination of Temporale and Sanctorale in Breviaries and Antiphonals is not common. Several sources may be compared:

ms C5 (monastic, Gloucester)	ms A22 (Roman curia)	ms B60 (German, monastic)
	Adv 1-3	Adv 1
Adv 1	Nicholas, Lucy	Barbara
Andrew	Adv 4	Nicholas
Adv 2	Christmas	Adv 2
Nicholas	saints to Silvester	Conception
Conception	Epi to XL	Lucy
Adv 3	Marcellus and	Adv 3
Thomas apostle	others	Thomas apostle
Adv 4	Palm Sunday to	Adv 4
Christmas	Pascha 4	Christmas
saints	Common of saints in	saints
Epi	Easter time	Epi
BVM	Mark	Sebastian to
LXX-L	Rogation	Annunciation
Sebastian to the	Philip & James to	LXX to
Conv of Paul	Pancras	Pascha 4
LX-XL 2	Asc to	Common of saints
Cath Peter	Pente 1	in Easter time
XL 3	Petronilla and others	Philip & James to
Annunciation		John at the Latin Gate
Palm	Sundays	
Ambrose	saints	Asc to
feria ii	Sundays	Corpus Christi
Pascha to Advent	saints, and Nat BVM	John the Baptist to
	Sundays, and Dedication	Andrew
remaining sants	saints	Common of saints and
		Dedication
		Summer Sundays

Certain places within the year are favoured, such as after Christmas and after the fourth Sunday of Easter, and the tendency is for saints to be inserted in groups at these points. In Advent, saints are often inserted between each of the Sundays, as in C5 and B60 above. In C5 the period from Easter to Advent is uninterrupted, and so is the section devoted to the saints from St George,

23 April, and Philip & James, 1 May, to Saturnine, 29 November. The mixing of smaller sections throughout the year is much more evident in the Roman source, A22: some saints' offices here have only the responsories and Lauds antiphons, occasionally only the canticle antiphons. The German-Bohemian monastic source, B60, like the first source, has several large sections of uninterrupted Temporale and Sanctorale. Two of these sources are monastic and it seems reasonable to suggest that the combination of Temporale and Sanctorale was preserved longer in the cloistered tradition than in the secular rites.

9

Lent and Easter Week

900 Two ritual matters other than praise of the Lord are of concern during Lent. Both require the presence of additional services and both are related to Mass since the ability to take communion is in question. The one matter is the exclusion of penitents from Mass until their reconciliation; the other is the exclusion of the catechumens until their baptism. During Holy Week there are a number of other services, some of which are also related to Mass either because they originally took place as part of a Mass which disappeared by the later middle ages or because they involve, for example, the 'burial' of Christ's body symbolized by a Host consecrated at Mass. After Christ's death, consecration of the Host cannot take place, and a different kind of Mass must be said until the resurrection is symbolized by his return at a new consecration on the Vigil of Easter. This service is called the Mass of the Presanctified.

901 Most of the texts and chants for these ceremonies would therefore appear most naturally in Missals or Graduals rather than in office books, and even where there is no direct or obvious connection between the special ceremony and Mass, the 'gravitational attraction' of the latter will cause the former normally to appear in Mass books. On the other hand the offices are characterized, at least during Holy Week, by omissions rather than additions and are therefore less difficult to understand. It is generally thought, and there seems no reason to doubt the matter, that the omissions are of items which were added to the services only later in their history, so that the structure as it occurs during Holy Week, and especially the last three days of the week, represents more closely the original or oldest ascertainable form of the office. Typically omitted, for example, are the hymn, doxologies for introits and responsories, versicles, and chapters. It has seemed preferable in this chapter, therefore, to describe the services according to their appearance *in ecclesia* rather than *in libro*, and the combination of Mass with office services which occurs in some cases makes this procedure more economical. Nevertheless, since this study is aimed at an understanding of how the books are organized, a careful account of what appears where and how it is presented will be necessary. Selecting only what is required for understanding the services, I present much of the following as an abbreviated paraphrase of two splendid studies by other authors: Tyrer's book, which is a historical and comparative survey of Holy Week, and Hardison's essays on Lent and Easter week.[1] The latter, in particular, gives an extremely valuable view of the whole period. Neither author, however, deals specifically with the late middle ages, and Hardison is concerned mainly with the periods prior to the 9th and 10th century. Many other texts are devoted to this important time of the year. As even a casual comparison of this chapter with Tyrer or Hardison will reveal, it is impossible to generalize and at the same time to refer to specific sources: Hardison excels at the first, Tyrer becomes too involved with detailed comparisons in a running text. Since the content of specific sources is of more importance to my purpose, I propose first to summarize the liturgical movement of the weeks in question, and to follow this with annotated comparative tables. The order and often the content of many of the additional ceremonies is frequently quite variable, and many of them celebrated in the Carolingian era described in Hardison's book were no longer needed later and fell out of use: certain relics of them are occasionally to be found, and their inclusion in the preliminary generalizations is therefore justified.

902 The extending of Lent from the Sunday back to Ash Wednesday and later to Septuagesima,[2] need not concern us except to offer an explanation for anomalies from Septuagesima to Ash Wednesday which may not be consistent with Lenten practices. With the beginning of Lent, the alienation of man from heavenly Jerusalem is symbolized by the omission of the angelic hymns, Gloria and Te Deum, and of the expressions of joy in the alleluia. The last may be replaced with a gradual or tract (**506**): the Ite missa est is replaced with the Benedicamus Domino. The doxologies remain.[3]

Before describing the services related to penitents and catechumens, it may be of use to dispense with the other additional matters, which would otherwise have to be referred to twice.

Holy Week miscellanea

903 Additions and changes occur in Holy Week, and are caused by the requirements of the events being remembered. First, more items disappear: the doxologies after introit and responsories and elsewhere are omitted, and the gospels at Mass are begun without introductory formulas. The closing formulas, as well as other versicles, the invitatory, hymns, chapters, and benedictions before readings also disappear on Maundy Thursday, Good Friday, and Holy Saturday. On Good Friday even the liturgical greeting is omitted. Originally the Monday, Tuesday, and Wednesday were *vacant*, having no Masses at all, although no sign of this is normally evident in the late middle ages: the gospels of Palm Sunday, Tuesday, and Wednesday are the Passions according to Matthew, Mark, and Luke respectively. The John Passion is said during the Fore-Mass ritual on Good Friday. The reciting tone used for the Passions is quite special, and thus may be included even in a manuscript which otherwise does not transmit music. The layout of the tone implies that three singers are required for three different pitches according to a distinction by speaker (Evangelist, Christ, and all others), but this performance *à trois* has been questioned by Karl Young, who asserts that the distinctions are ones of voice production by a single singer:[4] the musical implications of this assertion have not been considered, and there remain severe problems concerned with performance which cannot be discussed here.[5] Monastic sources adopt the same procedures at Mass: after Matins of the ferias of Holy Week there is of course no gospel, and most manuscripts follow the secular form of Matins with three nocturns for the last three days of the week. This reduction to the secular form was questioned at times, on the basis that St Benedict makes no reference to such shortening, and there were movements to reinstitute the monastic form including, as it should, invitatory, hymn, and versicles, and doxologies where Benedict prescribed them for normal days.[6]

904 No consecration of the Eucharist was allowed between Christ's death and the Vigil Mass of Easter, a fact which accounts for the erstwhile omission of Masses on Monday, Tuesday, and Wednesday, for the special kind of Mass celebrated on Good Friday, and the absence of Mass on Holy Saturday before the Vigil. Maundy Thursday, the day of the Last Supper which Mass commemorates, was exempt from the prohibition of consecration, and had three Masses in the 9th and 10th centuries. The first, the Mass of Remission, concerned the reconciliation of the penitents, and although the Mass disappeared, the ceremonies relating to that procedure survived: the third, associated with the Mandatum ceremony, also seems to have fallen into disuse in the later middle ages. The Mandatum itself remained. Only the main Mass, the Missa Chrismalis, need concern us. Some features distinguish this Mass from all others. During it the three kinds of oil, for the sick, for the catechumens, and the chrism for baptism, are consecrated. These consecrations can be performed only by a bishop and the Mass is therefore a pontificial ceremony whose texts will be found in the Pontifical.[7] Nevertheless, they are also included in most standard Missals. By exception in Lent, the Gloria is sung. The second unique feature is the reservation ceremony. No consecration can take place on Good Friday. Despite this, it was customary for certain persons, especially if cloistered, to communicate daily and in order to provide the Host for Friday some of the Thursday Host had to be reserved. Mass on Good Friday was called the Mass of the Presanctified.

Processions and Depositions

905 Taking advantage of that other feature so much emphasized during Holy Week, that is, the processions which arose out of the practice in Jerusalem of re-enacting the events in their historical locations,[8] the reservation ceremony of Maundy Thursday often continues with a procession to the sepulchre to 'bury' the Corpus. Reversing this action before the Mass of the Presanctified, a procession brought the Corpus back (an unsuitably early 'resurrection') on Good Friday: it was 'buried' again after Mass along with the cross in a ceremony of Deposition. The raising of the cross took place sometime early on Easter morning in an Elevation, and the Host was returned unobtrusively to the altar for the Vigil Mass.[9]

The other major procession of Holy Week is that of Palm Sunday: after the palms are blessed and sprinkled and distributed with the proper prayers and versicles, the procession moves in a tour geographically suitable to the location, but certainly out of the church, to the accompaniment of numerous hymns, antiphons, and responsories. Apart from those already mentioned for the burial of the Corpus and the cross and incidental small processions within services, the other important processions are to and from the font on Holy Saturday and in services commemorative of baptism at Vespers of Easter week, and processions with the Paschal Candle.

Tenebrae, the Paschal Candle, and the Mandatum

906 On the triduum, or in some places on Maundy Thursday, the candles of the church are extinguished one by one with each antiphon of Matins and Lauds, which are of course nocturnal offices sung when there is otherwise no illumination. Reversing this procedure[10] is the ceremony of igniting the New Fire after Lauds on Holy Saturday, the blessing and lighting of the enormous Paschal Candle, and the illumination of the remainder of the church. Carried out with a real consecration prayer and the performance of the Exultet hymn, which resembles a Preface,[11] this ceremony is observed by those awaiting baptism: the New Fire, symbolizing the light of Christ, will be 'buried' in the water with which the baptism is carried out. No provision is made in the liturgical books for a procession here, but after the Prophetic lessons (**929**) the Candle is carried at the head of the procession to the font and during the octave to stational churches if there are any.

Before the renewal of Holy Saturday and the desolation of Good Friday, the altars were stripped, and the church cleaned and washed on Maundy Thursday. This action takes place after the Missa Chrismalis and Vespers service and is associated with the evening service of the Mandatum. Water is blessed, and to the accompaniment of several responsories, versicles, and prayers, perhaps votive to the saints of the various altars, the washing and stripping is carried out. Afterwards, the Mandatum occurred. During this ceremony, while antiphons are sung, the priest washes the feet of twelve pilgrims or poor men.[12] The antiphons vary considerably from use to use.

Solemn prayers, Adorations, and Reproaches

907 These special rituals occur on Good Friday, although the solemn prayers may be anticipated on Wednesday. The prayers occur after the recital of lessons and tracts for the catechumens (**925**) and consist of petitions for divine aid and mercy of all kinds, especially for the catechumens, and for the church's enemies. A typical series of nine, the usual number according to Tyrer,[13] is: for the whole church; the Pope; Christians; the Sovereign; catechumens; the world; heretics and schismatics; Jews; the heathen. Each begins with an extended version of the *Oremus* formula with itself begins and ends with *Oremus*, and from the initial Os of which derives the distinctive appearance of these prayers in the manuscripts (plate 18a-b). After this invocation, the Deacon says *Flectamus genua: Levate* before each prayer except the one for the Jews.[14] A considerable interval between these prayers and the Reproaches and Adoration seems to have been a frequent, although not by the later middle ages universal, practice. Sometimes indeed, when the later ritual took place in the evening, the prayers were repeated beforehand.[15]

It seems to have been the general theory that the Improperia, or Reproaches, should be completed before the Adoration but in practice items of the Adoration are sung as the cross was exposed and elevated during the Reproaches. The latter consist of the refrain *Popule meus* preceding Christ's sentences, to each of which the priest replies in Greek *Agios o Theos*, and the choir in Latin *Sanctus Deus* (plate 18b). After each Reproach, the cross is advanced and after the third its shroud is removed. When it is elevated a hymn or antiphon may be sung, interrupting the Reproaches, or reserved till afterwards. The texts used are variable, expecially in order: *Ecce lignum, Crucem tuam*, and *Dum fabricator*.[16] The hymn *Pange lingua* usually ends the ceremony, and the Mass of the Presanctified follows after the procession to fetch the Corpus from its place of reservation or burial.

The penitents and catechumens

908 We can now examine the services which are of particular concern to the penitents and catechumens. For the former, we must return to Ash Wednesday.

Ash Wednesday is characterized by the initial arraignment of sinners, who are forbidden to enter the church again until the Maundy Thursday rite of reconciliation. Dressed in sackcloth, between Terce and Sext they are publicly expelled from communion and, in a ceremony of prayers and antiphons during which they are marked with ashes, they are dismissed.[17] Until the service of reconciliation no additional ceremony is to be noted in the liturgical books. On Maundy Thursday, the absolution and reconciliation was in the earlier middle ages performed before the first Mass of the day, the Mass of Remission. With the disappearance of this Mass the ceremony was delayed later and later into the day, and was carried out before the main Mass, the Missa Chrismalis. The ritual is one of suspense, the penitents assembled outside the church until the priest has recited the penitential psalms and a Litany in the vestry. Then, with prayers, exhortations, prostrations, and chants, the sinners are reconciled by means of blessings, censing, and aspersion.

909 Contrasting with the extreme penitential nature of the dimissal of Ash Wednesday is the preparation of the catechumens, more joyful in that it emphasizes redemption. No special ceremonies occur on Ash Wednesday itself, but there were, usually, seven 'scrutinies' incorporated into Lenten Masses or taking place between Terce and Sext of Wednesdays and Saturdays after the third Sunday of Lent. These took the form of public exorcism and exhortation to progress towards baptism in the form of prayers, lessons, and sermons, directed at the catechumens in the Fore-Mass. We have already examined the presence of such extra lessons on Wednesdays and Saturdays (**519-22**).[18] These additional readings remain, even though the theme of redemption became much less important after the 10th century. As Hardison expresses it: 'the increasing importance of monastic churches, the decrease in adult converts, widespread infant baptism ... conspired to reduce the importance of the catechumens.'[19] Of the seven scrutinies, the third and the seventh were the most important, and some elements of these remain in the liturgies of the later middle ages. The third, performed usually on the Wednesday of *Letare* Sunday (XL 4), the Day of Great Scrutiny (**916**), is significant because it continues with the exposure of the catechumens to the gospels, with the word *ephpheta*, 'be thou opened,' whereupon passages from each gospel were read and explained. Thereafter occurs the *traditio*, or transmission of the Paternoster and creed, also with explanations, to the catechumens.[20] Scrutinies and exorcisms continue, without extra ceremonies needing to be written into the books, until the seventh and final scrutiny, which takes place on Holy Saturday.[21] In the earlier middle ages, this was after Terce and before Mass. By the later era, however, the scrutiny was considered more as part of the Vigil service and its precise time of occurrence is not always certain (**916, 930-1**).[22] The ceremony consists in the exposure to the gospels as already explained, if this had not taken place earlier, followed by the *redditio*, or return of the Paternoster and creed, recited aloud by the catechumens. They are then ready for baptism, and are temporarily dismissed. Baptism is delayed by the kindling of the New Fire and the Paschal Candle, and the illumination of the church. The blessing of the Paschal Candle takes place to the chanting of the Exultet hymn in which 'the two Lenten themes of baptism and penance are linked to the victory of the Resurrection. Baptism is introduced through allusions to the deliverance of Adam and the passage of the Hebrews through the Red Sea.'[23]

The Paschal Vigil

910 The Vigil of Easter now begins and, as in earlier scrutinies, the catechumens listen to lessons and prayers and chants of the Old Testament, except that these are performed before rather than within the Vigil Mass (**521-2**). The number of lessons and chants differs. The readings, from the Prophets, are in historical and chronological order, describing, for example, the Creation, the Flood, Abraham's sacrifice of Isaac, and the passage through the Red Sea (just noticed as a typological reference to baptism).[24] The lessons are separated by prayers and tracts as shown in paragraph **929**. The last tract, *Sicut cervus*, from whose text comes the imagery of the stag frequently to be found on fonts,[25] accompanies the procession to the font, which was often in a separate building, the Baptistery.

Baptism is begun and ended and often interrupted by Litanies, the first usually sevenfold, the second fivefold, and the third threefold. The last may be replaced with the metrical processional litany-hymn, *Rex sanctorum*.[26] The baptism ceremony consists of exorcising and blessing the water and the font, the 'burying' in the water of the lighted taper symbolizing the reborn Christ, and the pouring of the chrism onto the water. Chrism is an oil which was consecrated on Maundy Thursday in the Missa Chrismalis already mentioned. Aspersion, baptism, and confirmation conclude the rites, and the final Litany leads, because of the omission of the introit, directly into the Kyrie of the vigil mass. As Hardison puts it, 'baptism is an integral part of the sequence that reaches its climax during the vigil Mass.'[27]

911 The vigil Mass should begin, and certainly used to begin, just after midnight so that the resurrection symbolized in the service, traditionally at the commingling of bread and wine, took place at about the historically correct hour. The performance of the whole vigil ceremony and Mass took place earlier and earlier on Holy Saturday until the Mass itself occurred even as early as the morning, so that coincidence between service and history was dislocated.[28] As well as the introit, the Mass lacks offertory, Credo, the Kiss of peace, Agnus, and communion antiphon, but it includes the Gloria to signify a healing of the breach between man and heaven, and an alleluia, even though they occur before the actual rebirth of Christ on the altar. Because the newly baptized were communicating the normal communion chant was perhaps not long enough. Rather than extra verses after the chant, a shortened form of Vespers was sung simultaneously with the communion ceremony. This office consisted only of Ps 116 with a triple Alleluia antiphon, and the Magnificat with its antiphon *Vespere autem*. The prayer with which both Mass and Vespers end, normally the same in any case, served as simultaneous oratio and post-communion, and the services closed with the dismissal formula *Ite missa est* (which, like the *Gloria in excelsis*, returns) and with a benediction.

Easter week

912 When the prolonged vigil service, baptism, and Mass were performed at the proper time, ending well after midnight, Easter Matins proved too long and it was consequently shortened from three nocturns to a single one, an abbreviation which continued throughout the Easter season. The details of this process are obscure.[29] The Mass on Easter morning is unexceptional, returning as it does to the normal form with introit, Gloria, two lessons, gradual, alleluia, and the remainder of the ordinary and proper items. Its texts through Easter week, however, contain repeated allusions to the neophytes, *infantes*, and of course to rebirth through baptism, and to 'union with Christ.'[30] More clearly commemorating the resurrection and baptism, however, is the Vespers service of Easter week. It is particularly elaborate in Roman practice, including a procession to the font with psalms and antiphons and items from Easter Mass.[31] This special Vespers service is the only part of the Lenten and Easter week ceremonies to occur, as normal with Vespers offices, in Breviaries rather than in Mass books. In place of chapter, responsory (if there is one), hymn, and versicle there will be a gradual and alleluia whose verses are likely to be proper each day of the week. The opening antiphon(s) of the service may be preceded by a proper Kyrie. Instead of A(5) C(R)HDMO there may be **K** A **GA** MO: later in the week, when the antiphon is no longer proper, the presentation may be reduced to **KGA** MO. Some sources include a sequence after the alleluia,[32] and some include certain of the Mass items within the little hours.[33]

913 To summarize this complicated series of events, not presented in chronological order, I include a 'calendar' of the period, figure 9.1, showing where the separate services occur, and tracing the sections relevant to the main themes and actions. First, I should perhaps summarize the latter.

Adorations: Good Friday
Aspersions: usually after blessings
Blessings: see Consecrations
Burials: Maundy Thursday
Consecrations: Palm Sunday (palms), Maundy Thursday (oils), Holy Saturday (Candle, water, font, catechumens)
Deposition (cf Burials): Good Friday
Improperia (Reproaches): Good Friday
Lessons for the instruction of catechumens: at the scrutinies, and on Good Friday and Holy Saturday
Light: extinguishing (Tenebrae, Matins and Lauds of the triduum)
Mandatum: Maundy Thursday
Processions: Palm Sunday, Maundy Thursday and Good Friday (the burial of the Corpus); Maundy Thursday (washing of the altars), Holy Saturday and Easter week (to and from the font)
Redditio: Holy Saturday
Reproaches: see *Improperia*
Reservations: Maundy Thursday, for Friday
Solemn prayers: Good Friday (sometimes also the preceding Wednesday)
Tenebrae: see Light

The themes and actions of the season as presented in figure 9.1 are distinguished by an alignment in columns, and braces link some separate but related actions. Of the items presented in the figure, all are to be found in the Missal except Tenebrae, Easter Matins, and Vespers of Easter week, and the Vespers elements of the Masses on Maundy Thursday, Good Friday, and Holy Saturday. Some of the others, such as the lesser scrutines and the reservation, burial, and retrieval processions on Maundy Thursday, Good Friday, and the Vigil may not appear at all if the action is carried out without much ceremony or is not performed: still others, such as the washing of the altars, procession, and Mandatum on Maundy Thursday, the Deposition and procession on Good Friday, and the kindling, procession, and blessing on Holy Saturday, may be so continuous in performance that there is little or no separation between them in liturgical books. The processions aligned under the third 'indentation' may be written down in the Processional, whose contents are often largely devoted to Holy Week and Easter week, but they will usually appear as necessary in the Missal and Gradual.

FIGURE 9.1
The themes of Lent and Easter week

Ash Wednesday	DISMISSAL OF PENITENTS (before Mass)
XL 3 iv & vii	EXORCISM AND SCRUTINY OF CATECHUMENS
XL 4 iv	Day of Great Scrutiny. *Traditio*
XL 4 vii	Scrutiny
XL 5 iv & vii	Scrutinies
PALM SUNDAY	PROCESSION
	MASS (Matthew Passion)
feria iii	MASS (Mark Passion)
iv	Solemn prayers
	MASS (Luke Passion)
Maundy Thursday	TENEBRAE
	Prime, Terce, Sext, Nones
	RECONCILIATION OF PENITENTS
	MISSA CHRISMALIS and VESPERS (oil for the sick, catechumens, and chrism)
	Reservation of Host
	PROCESSION (Burial of Host)
	Washing and stripping altars
	PROCESSION
	Mandatum
Good Friday	TENEBRAE
	Prime, Terce, Sext, Nones
	Fore-Mass (with John Passion)
	Solemn prayers
	Reproaches and Adoration
	PROCESSION to fetch Host for the
	MASS OF THE PRE-SANCTIFIED
	Vespers privately
	Reservation of Host
	PROCESSION (Burial of Host and Deposition of the cross) ~
Holy Saturday	TENEBRAE
	Prime, Terce
	Scrutiny and *Redditio*
	Sext, Nones
The Vigil	KINDLING OF NEW FIRE (outside the church)
The Vigil	PROCESSION carrying the New Fire to the Candle
The Vigil	Blessing of the Paschal Candle
The Vigil	EXULTET and illumination
The Vigil	Twelve Prophets and tracts
The Vigil	PROCESSION with Litanies, to the font
The Vigil	Blessing font, Baptism, Litanies
	PROCESSION
	MASS and VESPERS
EASTER DAY	~ PROCESSION to fetch cross, Elevation of cross
	MATINS (shortened) Aspersion and
	PROCESSION, Harrowing of Hell, *Visitacio sepulchri*
	MASS VESPERS with Mass items
	PROCESSION to the font
Easter octave	VESPERS and PROCESSION as on Easter Day

914 Let us now examine the structure of these services more closely, setting out the texts as they occur in the Roman and Sarum Missals, with important variants recorded in footnotes and with commentaries as needed. The prayers, which often begin with conventional formulas, will be abbreviated, as often in the sources, to the initials of the incipits: the expansion of these abbreviations, which soon become obvious, is given below.

CqoD	Concede quesumus omnipotens Deus
D	Deus (*occasionally* Dominus)
Da qDD	Da quesumus Domine Deus
DJXq	Domine Jesu Christe qui
Dq	Deus qui
EqD	Excita quesumus Deus
OD(q)	Omnipotens Deus (qui)
OsDq	Omnipotens sempiterns Deus qui
Pq	Presta quesumus
qD	quesumus Domine

In the lists of texts in the following pages, letters between square brackets are merely references or identification letters as opposed to the abbreviations for genres, which appear next. When the latter are lower case letters, they represent spoken or recited items not usually present in Graduals: capital letters represent items which are sung and which in Missals may appear without music, or only in incipit. Thus, in the immediately following list, the first item, identified by [A], is sung and is an antiphon, A: the second item, identified by [a], is spoken and consists of the liturgical greeting and a benediction, *D*✠. The letters of identification are used in the notes and in the parallel comparisons between Roman and Sarum uses instead of repeating the whole text.

Ash Wednesday

915 The service blessing the ashes normally includes three sung items given in the Gradual, the antiphons *Exaudi nos Domine, Juxta vestibulum,* and *Immutemur* (not necessarily in that order): these appear before the introit for Wednesday and may occasionally have a capital rather than an initial, making them somewhat difficult to identify. In a few sources,[34] these antiphons may be reduced in number or are omitted entirely. When included, there is ample opportunity for the rubricator to err: sources A5 and A6, for example, misplace the rubric *officium* for the introit, and *graduale* for the gradual, as though these antiphons were the first proper items in the following Mass. Rubricated manuscripts normally give additional instructions here. For the service blessing the ashes, the Roman and Sarum Missals have:

MR I 46-48		MS cols 123-135	
ante missam		post sextam	
[A] A	*Exaudi nos* and Ps 68	[g] A	*Ne reminiscaris* (spoken over the seven penitential
[a] *D*✠	*OsD parce metuentibus*	[h] P	psalms)[36]
[b] ✠	*Dq non mortem*	[i] D	preces
[c] ✠	*Dq humiliatione*	[j] *DO*	*EqD preces nostras*
[d] ✠	*OsDq immutis*[35] blessing of ashes ends, imposition of ashes begins	[k] O	*Adsit qD famulis*
[B] A	*Immutemur*	[l] O	*Da qDD*
[C] A	*Juxta vestibulum*	[m] O	*Preveniat hos famulos*
[D] R	*Emendemus*	[n] O	*Adesto Domine supplicationibus*
[e] O	*Memento homo quia pulvis*	[o] O	*Domine D noster qui offensionem*
[f] *DO*	*Concede nobis Domine presidis*	[p] O	*D cuius indulgentia*
	Mass	[q] O	*Absolvimus vos vice*
		[r] ✠	*OsDq miseris omnium* blessing, aspersion, and distribution of ashes, then items
		[be] Ps 68 [CBf] and the ejection of penitents	
			Mass

The quite wide difference between these two major uses of the late middle ages and the further differences to be observed in the other sources studied[37] make the appearance of sources also considerably different. Other uses are usually more or less clearly related to either Roman or Sarum forms.

Scrutinies, *traditio*, and *redditio*

916 Of the special services for the catechumens and of the delivery and recital of the Paternoster and creed, no trace survives in Missals of the late middle ages except for the extra lesson in the Day of Great Scrutiny (XL 4 iv) and the extra lessons on Holy Saturday. These have already been described. The disappearance of the scrutinies is explained by the replacement of adult baptism with infant baptism. In the latter circumstance, examination, memorization, and recital of the Paternoster and creed were hardly possible, and as a result a different form of service had to evolve. The new service took place during the baptism on Holy Saturday and will be examined in that section.

The Palm Sunday processions

917 As with the service of Ash Wednesday, the practices of Rome and Salisbury are quite different, and other sources follow one or the other or vary yet again.[38] The procession at Salisbury is more elaborate and involves at least four stations, at the first of which the gospel [c] is read. The second and third come before the processional items [L] and [M], and the fourth is at an altar in the church itself.[39]

MR I 128-134		MS cols 253-262	
[A] A	*Osanna filio David*	[b]	
[a] *DO*	*D quem diligere*	[o] ✠ L	(John) *Turba multa*
[b] L	(Exodus) *Venerunt filii*		blessing
[B] R	*Collegerunt* . . . V *Unus*	[p] O	*Exorcizo te creatura florum*
	or	[q] O	*OsDq in diluvii*
[C] R	*In monte Oliveti* . . .	[r] O	*D cuius Filius*
	V *Vigilate*		
[c] ✠ L	(Matt) *Cum appro-*	[h]	
	pinquasset Jesus		
	blessing		sprinkling, censing, blessing
[d] ✠*DO*	*Auge fidem*	[s] *D*✠	*DJX Fili*
[e] *DD*	Preface. *Nos tibi*		distribution, then items
	semper et ubique	[DE]	then a procession
[f]	*Sanctus*	[N] A	*Prima autem*
[g] O	*Petimus Domine*	[FGH]	
[h] O	*Dq dispersa*	[O]A	*Ante sex dies passionis*
[i] O	*Dq miro ordine*		first station, then item
[j] O✠	*Dq per olive*	[c]	
[k] ✠	*Benedic qD hos*	[P] H	*En rex venit*
[l] S	*Asperges* (not sung)	[Q] A	*Dignus es Domine*
[m] *DO*	*Dq Filium*	[I] A	*Occurrunt turbe*
	distribution of palms	[R] R	*Dominus Jesus* . . . V *Convenerunt*
[D] A	*Pueri Hebreorum por-*	[S] R	*Cogitaverunt* . . . V *Testimonium*
	tantes (or *tollentes*)		second station, then items
[E] A	*Pueri Hebreorum vesti-*	[LB]	third station, [M]
	menta	[T] A	*Ave rex noster*
[n] *DO*	*OsDq Dominum*	[U] R	*Circumdederunt me* . . . V *Eripe me*
	procession	[o] O	*OsDq humano generi*
[F] A	*Cum appropinquaret*		
[G] A	*Cum audisset*		
[H] A	*Ante sex dies solem-*		
	nitatis		
[I] A	*Occurrerunt turbe*		
[J] A	*Cum angelis*[40]		
[K] A	*Turba multa*[41]		
[L] H	*Gloria laus* (refrain		
	and verses)		
[M] R	*Ingrediente* . . . *Cumque*		
	audisset[42]		

Masses on Sunday, Tuesday, and Wednesday

918 Masses on these days are distinguished only because of the Passion which, as stated, may be provided with its tone even in books which do not supply any other music. The three tones representing the three different 'speakers' are distinguished in the sources by such symbols as ✠, for Christ, or by the letters a, m, and b, for *alta*, *media*, and *bassa voce*. The relative pitches of the three reciting tones are thus specified.

Tenebrae

919 The Matins and Lauds services called Tenebrae are different from normal Matins and Lauds of this week only by virtue of the gradual extinction of the candles.

Maundy Thursday

The Reconciliation of the penitents

920 Neither the printed Roman Missal of 1474 nor the manuscript Roman Missal which was available, NM4, transmit this ceremony and I have not been able to find the precise form it took in the late middle ages in Roman use. Pontificals of Rome probably contain it, but none was available. Sarum Missals preserve the ceremony even in the late middle ages, as follows:

MS cols 295-300

After Nones, the celebrant and two deacons proceed to the west door of the church, where (if the celebrant is a bishop) one deacon reads the lesson –

[a] L *Adesto o venerabilis*

[A] A (bishop) *Venite, venite*

(interrupted by the deacon opposite the bishop) *Flectamus genua*

(deacon with the bishop) *Levate*

Again: *Venite, venite. Flectamus genua. Levate*

Then: *Venite, venite, filii, audite me . . .*, with Ps 33.

The penitents are led into the church, where all prostrate themselves while the seven penitential psalms are said, under the spoken antiphon *Ne reminiscaris* (see, for example, the service of Ash Wednesday, items [g] and [h]).

[b] A *Ne reminiscaris* (spoken over the seven

[c] P penitential psalms)

[d] D preces (cf Ash Wednesday, item [i])

[e] *DO* *Adesto Domine supplicationibus* (cf Ash Wednesday, item [n])

[f] O *Deus humani generis*

[g] O *Domine sancte pater*

[h] O *Absolvimus vos vice* (cf Ash Wednesday, item [q])

All rise, and the bishop blesses them.

Only the Missal M5 gives the text of the last item, the benediction, *Benedictio Dei Patris*. The recapitulation of some of the Ash Wednesday texts should be noted: presumably Roman use also incorporates some of the earlier service.[43]

Mass and reservation

921 The Missa Chrismalis, at which the oils are blessed and after which the reservation and its procession occur, differs from a normal Mass. It is a pontifical service sometimes involving a special hymn for the consecration of the oils and is combined with Vespers at the end. As a pontifical service it normally occurs in Pontificals, but also in Missals and Graduals. Doxologies, Gloria in excelsis, Ite missa est, and special blessings are included. All sources adopt the same structure and texts up to the secret: **I● KG** OL **G** L **O** O. If there are proper sentences within the Canon, these may be noted next, either in incipit or in full, as in sources M3, M4, NM2, and the MR 1474. If it is to be performed at all, usually just before the consecration,[44] the hymn *O redemptor sume carnem* will appear, with its verses unless it is given only in incipit. The hymn often is introduced in the middle of rubrics explaining the Preface and consecration rituals. These rituals, being episcopal as far as the oils are concerned, do not generally appear in Sarum Missals and are to be found in Pontificals. No particular ceremony is attached to the reservation itself, and it may be announced only in a rubric such as that before the secret in Sarum Missals: 'A subdeacon places three Hosts to be consecrated, of which two may be reserved for the following day, one to be taken by the priest: the others to be placed with the cross in the sepulchre.'[45] In the Durham monastic Missal, M3, the reservation is described in a rubric which precedes the communion chant *Dominus Jesus postquam cenavit* (called postcommunio, terminologically incorrect, although chronologically correct):

> . . . *vadat ad locum constitutum decentissime preparatum ibique reponat corpus domini incensato ipso loco ante reposicionem et post antequam locum lumen continue ardeat. Episcopo vero vel sacerdote ad altare redeunte et postcommunionem percantat, videlicet,* Dominus Jesus postquam . . . *pulsetur tabula ad vesperas* . . .[46]

922 Once the communion chant has been sung, Vespers begins immediately, without introductory versicles. Of this office only the five antiphons with their psalms and the Magnificat with its antiphon are sung. There are very few differences between sources. Graduals only rarely include these office items complete or even in incipit and some Missals, including the Roman Missal of 1474, omit them. Most Missals, however, give at least the incipits. The incipits are:

MS cols 304-8
Calicem salutaris with Ps 115
Cum his qui with Ps 119
Ab hominibus with Ps 139
Custodi me with Ps 140
Considerabam with Ps 141
and the Magnificat antiphon
Cenantibus autem with the Magnificat.

Only one difference from these items was observed.[47] As in the Durham Missal, M3, a monastic source, there may be preces before the post-communion prayer and the Ite missa est with which the service closes.

Washing and stripping of the altars

923 The water may be blessed first. In the Roman Missal of 1474 the washing takes place to the accompaniment of a single antiphon, *Diviserunt vestimenta*, with Ps 21: in the Sarum Missal the ten responsories, including the ferial alternative, of the historia *In Monte Oliveti* from Matins of the day are specified, with as many repetitions as necessary and an obligatory repeat of the second responsory, *Circumdederunt*, at the end.[48] In addition, the rubrics specify a versicle and prayer to the saint whose altar is being stripped, but those texts, which must vary from church to church, are not listed. As with the preceding Vespers service, Graduals tend not to include material for this ceremony: between the two extremes, however, Missals may include incipits or rubrics but not the complete texts, which have appeared in the Breviary or Antiphonal at Matins (Tenebrae). Variants occur in some sources.[49]

The Mandatum

924 After entering the Chapter house the participants may hear the gospel of the Mass of the day repeated with a sermon, before the footwashing ceremony, or pedilavium, begins. All the actions are carried out while psalms and antiphons are sung, and there are no readings or prayers until the very end. The whole 'office' is thus chanted. The texts of the chants are variable both in order and in liturgical source, except for the first antiphon, from whose incipit the title of the service derives.[50] Roman and Sarum practice is compared.[51] Material between parentheses is explained in the text.

MR I 159-61

[A] *Mandatum novum* (Ps 118)[52]
[B] *Postquam surrexit* (Ps 47)
[C] *Dominus Jesus postquam* (-)
[D] *In diebus illis* (Ps 84)
[E] *Maria ergo unxit* (Ps 6)
[F] *Vos vocatis me* (?) *Exemplum enim*
[G] *Diligamus nos* (Ps 83)
[H] *Ubi est caritas* (Ps 66)
[I] *Congregavit nos* (?) *Mulier erat*
[J] *Domine tu mihi* (?) *Quod facio tu*
[K] *Si ego Dominus* (-)
[L] *In hoc cognoscent* (-)
[M] *Maneant in vobis* (-)
[N] *Nunc autem manent* (-)
[O] *Benedicta sit sancta Trinitas* (?) *Benedicamus Patrem*
[P] *Ubi caritas et amor*: refrain with numerous verses

MS cols 311-16

[A] (with Ps 66)
[G] (Ps 132)
[D] (Ps 50)
[E] (Ps 118)
[B] (Ps 48)
and, if necessary, these items:
[F K]
[Q] *Ante diem*
[R] *Venit ad Petrum*
The service ends with:
[a] D *Suscepimus* . . . and preces
[b] O *Adest qD officio*
[c] L (John) *Amen amen dico*

The Roman service, characterized by the final antiphon, *Ubi caritas*, which must not be omitted, is much more difficult to describe than the Sarum service. In the latter each item is an antiphon with its psalm or psalm verse. The same texts occur in the Sarum rite, but in a different order and with different psalms, and two additional ones are provided. The last, *Venit ad Petrum*, is perhaps the most characteristic.[53] Whereas the Roman Missal prescribes only a single verse to each antiphon, the Sarum book states that the antiphon is to be repeated after each verse of the psalm,[54] and there are fewer items. In Roman use it is hardly possible, unless the chant is given, to say which are antiphons, which are true psalm verses, and which are independent verses sung to true melodies. Some of the antiphons (to retain that term until a more accurate one emerges) have no verses (-), some verses are clearly drawn from psalms, others are of unknown origin (?) and their incipit is shown. The antiphons themselves are occasionally drawn from obvious sources: item [C] is the communion chant of Mass of the day, associated with the reservation; item [O] and its verse originate from the feast of Trinity Sunday. The chants do not appear in the Roman Missal and the abbreviations preceding each item are inconsistent and often misleading. In the above list, for example, item [D], called a psalm, seems to be the verse for item [C], and [E] the psalm verse for *Benedixisti*, Ps 84, which appears to be the psalm verse for [D]. The layout of the above list is derived mainly with the help of the Noted Missal of Roman use, manuscript NM4, where the chants are given. Even that source is not devoid of problems. As the list and the character of the chants makes clear, some antiphons do not have verses: *Ubi caritas*, however, has very many, with the antiphon appearing as a refrain after every two or three. In modern practice, cues to the beginning of the antiphon are given after the verses, as though some kind of responsorial practice were intended:[55] there is no such cue in any of the medieval sources studied. The difficulties of categorization just explained, which require a good deal of research, make it rather problematic to list variants. Even though the Roman Missal does not indicate them, the final preces, prayer, and gospel are surely said, as in the Sarum rite.

The chants for the service do not appear in Graduals and are only rarely given in Noted Missals: Processionals are the most likely source for the music.

Good Friday

Fore-Mass and solemn prayers

925 The Fore-Mass, with its four lessons and two tracts, is arranged thus: LTO LT L L. The first two lessons are from the Old Testament (Hosea and Exodus), the last two are gospels; the Passion according to St John, followed by another part of his gospel. Except for the occasional reduction of some of these items to incipits, there is hardly any variation from source to source. Sometimes the prayer precedes the first lesson and another prayer appears in its place.[56] Also consistent from manuscript to manuscript are the nine solemn prayers. Each preceded with its own special formula emphasizing *Oremus*, and each beginning with *Omnipotens semipterne Deus*, they are the same in Roman and

Sarum Missals with the exception of the word *rege* in the latter for *imperatore* in the former:[57]

Oremus et pro beatissimo papa nostro N. ut Deus et Dominus noster qui elegit eum in ordine episcopatus salvum atque in columem custodiet ecclesie sue sancte ad regendum populum sanctum Dei. Oremus.

Between the invocation and the prayer are the commands *Flectamus genua: Levate*, except for the eighth prayer, to the Jews.

Reproaches and adoration (Improperia)

926 The elements common to both Roman and Sarum uses are the elevation and discovery (in the literal sense of removal of covers) of the cross, for which the short antiphon *Ecce lignum* is appointed, and the adoration, during which the Improperia are sung. In the Roman rite the discovery and elevation seems to take place before the adoration and Improperia, in the Sarum rite it takes place during the Improperia as part of the adorations. Obviously the two musical items cannot be sung simultaneously, but there is less difference between the Roman and Sarum practices than the reversal would suggest:

MR I 170-3		MS cols 328-31	
[A]	*Ecce lignum . . .*	[B]	with two verses, after which *Agyos* rather than *Popule* is repeated as a refrain
	partial discovery and elevation		
[A]	repeated, then complete discovery and elevation	[A]	sung once
[A]	repeated		
[B]	*Popule meus . . .* *Quia eduxi te . . .* *Agyos o theos. Sanctus Deus* *Agyos ischiros. Sanctus fortis* *Agyos athanatos eleyson ymas. Sanctus et immortalis, miserere nobis* several verses, with choir repeating *Popule meus . . .* as a refrain		

Rome and Salisbury differ in the performance of the Improperia ([B] above) not only in the choice of material for the refrain, but in that alternating choirs sing the Greek and Latin formulas in Rome, and two deacons alternating with choir in Salisbury. Thereafter the uses agree with each other in prescribing first the antiphon *Crucem tuam* (or *Tuam crucem*) with Ps 66 and then the hymn *Pange lingua*, to which the two sections of the 'hymn' or antiphon *Crux fidelis* act as alternating refrains sung after each verse (Rome) or the whole text as an unchanging refrain (Salisbury):

[C] A *Crucem tuam* (Ps 66)
[D] *Crux fidelis . . . Dulce lignum . . .* acting as refrain for the verses of
[E] H *Pange lingua*

Sarum use then provides a long responsory, called an antiphon, during the singing of which the cross is carried through the church for adoration:

Sarum: [F] R *Dum fabricator* . . . V *O admirabile* . . .

Of these six items all except [F], the additional responsory for the procession, are normally found in Graduals and Missals.[58]

Procession

927 This procession to fetch the reserved Corpus is not of common occurrence and is not in any of the sources studied. In the Roman Missal the reserved sacrament is retrieved during the performance of *Crux fidelis* and *Pange lingua*, [D] and [E] of the previous ceremony. There is no reference in the Sarum Missal. In a York Missal and the monastic Durham Missal,[59] before Mass there are processional items connected in other sources with the Deposition of the cross and reservation of the sacrament after the Mass of the Presanctified. Unless this reversal is simply an error, it seems possible that some of those items may be used for both the retrieval before, and second reservation after the Mass.[60] See section **934**.

Mass of the Presanctified

Involving no sung items of the Mass, this service occurs only in Missals:

MR I 173-4		MS cols 331-2	
preparation of the Host and wine for communion, *omissa confessione consueta*		[g]	*Confiteor/Misereatur/ Absolutionem*
[a]	*Incensum illud* . . .	[h]	preces
[b] O	*In spiritu humilitatis*	[i]	*Aufer a nobis*
[c]	*Oremus preceptis salutaribus*	[bcd]	
			No Pax, Agnus, or Kiss
[d]	*Paternoster* and preces No Pax, Agnus, or Kiss	[j]	*Corpus Domini* . . . *Corpus et sanguinis*
[e]	*Domine Jesu Christe Fili*	[k] O	*Respice qD*
[f]	*Quod ore sumpsimus*		No *Ite* or *Benedicamus*
	No *Corpus tuum* or *Placeat tibi*		
rubric for Vespers			

There is considerable variety in the order, and in the number of these items that are actually written into Missals.[61]

Deposition and reservation

928 There is no evidence of any additional texts or processional items for these ceremonies in Roman use. In the Sarum rite, however, two processional responsories and three antiphons are provided for deposition, reservation, and for the censing of the sepulchre:

MS cols 332-3
[A] R *Estimatus sum . . .* V *Posuerunt . . .*
[B] R *Sepulto Domini . . .* V *Ne forte . . .*
[C] A *In pace in idipsum*
[D] A *In pace factus est*
[E] A *Caro mea*
a choice of other prayers

The chants are to be found in some Graduals, and in Processionals.[62] (See **934**.)

Holy Saturday

Kindling, procession, and blessing of the Paschal candle
929 For the scrutiny and *redditio*, see the section above (**916**), and the description of the ceremony of baptism (**930-1**).

MR I 174-7	MS cols 334-43
kindling	kindling and procession
[a] *DO Dq per Filium tuum*	[d] Ps 26 (spoken)
no processional items	[bc]
[b] ✠O *Domine Deus noster Pater omnipotens lumen*	[e] O *Celesti lumine*
	[f] ✠O *Exorcizo te immundissime spiritus*
[c] O *Domine sancte Pater omnipotens eterne*	[g] ✠O *Eternam ac justissimam*
[A] ✠ *EXULTET*	[h] ✠O *Descendat benedictio tua*
	procession returns
	[B] H *Inventor rutili*
	[A] ✠ *EXULTET*

The absence of processional items in the Roman Missal does not necessarily mean that there were no processions: since the book was designed for all churches following that use, whereas the Sarum book is more strictly for use at Salisbury (although followed in many dioceses), it could not take into account the geography of every church. Processions would be arranged as necessary, their texts and chants drawn from a Processional. Of the above items, the Exultet is often but not always found in Graduals as well as Missals. There are a number of variants from use to use.[63]

Twelve Prophets

MR I 177-93		MS cols 343-8		
[a] L	*In principio*	[a]		
[b] O	*Dq mirabiliter*	[b]		
[c] L	*Noe vero*			
[d] O	*Deus incommutabilis*			
[e] L	*Temptavit Deus*			
[f] O	*Deus fidelium*			
[g] L	*Factum est in vigilia*	[g]		
[A] **T**	*Cantemus Domino*	[A]		
[h] O	*Deus cuius antique*	[h]		
[i] L	*Hec est hereditas*			
[j] O	*OsD multiplica*			
[k] L	*Audi Israel mandata*			
[l] O	*Dq ecclesiam*			
[m] L	*Facta est super*			
[n] O	*Dq nos ad*			
[o] L	*Apprehendet septem*	[o]		
[B] **T**	*Vinea facta*	[B]		
[p] O	*Dq in omnibus ecclesie*	[n]		
[q] L	*Dixit Dominus ad Moysen*			
[r] O	*OsDq in omnium*			
[s] L	*Factum est verbum*			
[t] O	*Dq diversitatem*			
[u] L	*Scripsit Moyses*	[u]		
[C] **T**	*Attende celum*	[C]		
[v] O	*Deus celsitudo humilium*	[l]		
[x] L	*Nabuchodonosor rex*			
[y] O	*OsD spes unica*			
	procession to the font			
[D] **T**	*Sicut cervus*	[D]		
		[α] O	*Concede qoD ut qui festa Paschalia*	
[z] *DO*	*OsD respice propitius*	[z]		

The Sarum ceremony here is obviously much shorter, with only four lessons [a g o u]. There is a further difference in the timing of the procession to the font: taking place during the tract *Sicut cervus* [D] in Roman use it is delayed until after the prayer [z] at Salisbury. Where there is no font, according to the Roman rubric the ceremony ends with the prayer *Omnipotens sempiterne Deus spes unica* [y]. The presence of the four tracts in Graduals is complemented by the frequent appearance of incipits referring to the lessons, and occasionally even the complete text. The Graduals G6, G7, and G13, for example, have the lesson *Factum est* [g], probably because its text in the Bible immediately precedes that of the tract *Cantemus Domino* [A]. Missals present the complete texts, and there is relatively little variation from source to source.[64]

The ceremony preceding the blessing of the font on the vigil of Pentecost is similar in format, although shorter. The texts of lessons and prayers may be different.[65]

Procession to the font, blessing the font, and baptism

930 As just explained, the procession to the font in Roman use has already occurred, during the tract *Sicut cervus*. The blessing of the font(s) in both Roman and Sarum Missals is referred to only in rubrics. The texts and rituals, however, are given in the notes accompanying the editions:

MR II 89-92	MS cols 347-54
[a] *DO OsD adesto magne*	[A] sevenfold Litany accompanies the procession
[b] *DD* (Preface) *Nos tibi semper . . .*	[B] fivefold Litany
Qui hanc aquam . . .	
Sit hec sancta . . .	[ab]
Unde benedico te . . .	
Qui te de paradisi . . .	
Hec nobis precepta . . .	
Descendat in hanc . . .	
[c] sprinkling	

When a baptism is to take place, it begins with what remains of the seventh scrutiny and the *redditio*. The formulas for baptism are normally to be found in a separate place in Missals, for example, amongst the votive Masses towards the end of the book, rather than in the correct position on Holy Saturday. Since the rubrics beginning the ceremony do not, in the sources studied, indicate when it is carried out, it is difficult to state precisely when the last scrutiny occurred. If, as the rubrics seem to indicate by failure to state otherwise, there is no gap between the scrutiny and the actual baptism, then the former takes place between the blessing of the candle and the blessing of the font just described, rather than after Terce. Hardison refers to such a shift of the service from earlier in the day to a place within the vigil.[66]

In any case, the blessing of the font occurs in the middle of the ceremony described under *Ordo ad catechuminum faciendum* or *Ordo baptizandi*. This blessing, as recorded in the sources, may be identical with the one just described, as in the Sarum books, or different, as in the Roman. In the former case the blessing is surely not to be repeated: it will be performed once during the service of baptism if that occurs, or otherwise in its place in the Missal under Holy Saturday. The same must also be true of the Roman use, and the 'blessing' texts provided within the baptism service must be additional items: how the real blessing, which naturally involves a Preface as shown above, fits in with these additional texts is not clear. If baptism is to take place the priest mixes the chrism with the water to the formula *Sanctificetur et fecundetur*, or *Coniunctio olei*, [c+ and r+] below.

931 We must move backwards in time, therefore, to the scrutiny and *redditio*, after which we shall observe the blessing of the font again and the actual baptism. Using the letter N. in place of the Christian name, the scrutiny begins outside the church with an interrogation:

MR II 315-8		MS (Legg ed) 123-31	
[d]	*Quis vocaris?* *N.* *Quid petis ab ecclesia Dei?* *Fidem.* etc	later in the service, at several points, as between [p+] and [o], below	

There follow injunctions [e g], exorcisms [f], the sign of the cross on the forehead and breast [i j]. and prayers [k l m]:

[e]	*Si vis habere*		
[f]	*Exi ab eo immunde spiritus*		
[g]	*N. accipe spiritum sanctum*		
[h] D	*Pax tibi . . . Et cum spiritu . . .*		
[i]	*N. signum salvatoris*		
[j]	*N. accipe signum*	[ijmkl]	(note the change in the order of these items)
[k] O	*Preces nostras*		
[l] O	*Dq humani generis*		
[m] O	*OsD Pater Domini nostri*		
blessing of the salt:			
[n] ✠	*Benedic oD hanc creaturam*	[p+] ✠	*Exorcizo te creatura salis* rubric: *sacerdos interrogat nomen*
[o]	*Accipe sal*		
[p] O	*[Os] D patrum nostrorum*		
over male children:		then items [o-v]	
[q] O	*Deus Abraham . . . Dq Moysi . . .* *Ergo maledicte . . .*		
[r] O	*Deus immortalem . . .* [67] *Audi maledicte . . .*		
[s] O	*Exorcizo te immunde spiritus in nomine . . .* *Ergo maledicte . . .*		
over female children:		over male and female children:	
[t] O	*Deus celi Deus terre . . .* *Ergo maledicte . . .*	[q+] O	*Eternam ac mitissime . . .*
[u] O	*Deus Abraham . . . Dq tribus . . .* *Ergo maledicte . . .*		
[v] O	*Exorcizo te immunde spiritus per Patrem . . .* *Ergo maledicte . . .*		
		[zαx]	these three items precede the entry into the church at Salisbury

The catechumens are led into the church:
[w] *Ingredere in sanctam ecclesiam*
Because the baptism would be of an infant in the late middle ages, the *redditio* of the catechumen has been changed into a recital by the Godparents. The Roman Missal has the rubric:

Tunc patrinus vel patrina illius
ponat eum super pavimento et
dicat Paternoster et Credo.

[x] *Paternoster* and *Credo*
[y] L (Matthew) *Oblati sunt Jesu*
[z] *Nec te lateat Sathana*
[α] *Ephpheta . . . Tu autem effugere*
Here the blessing of the font is carried out in preparation for baptism. The Sarum books merely repeat the prayer and Preface already given above (items [a] and [b]). Roman use adds the following:
[a+] O *Exaudi nos oD et in*
[b+] O *Exorcizo te creatura aque*
the chrism is mixed with the water:

[c+] ✠	*Sanctificetur et fecundetur*	[r+] [c+]	*Coniunctio olei*

Then there are further interrogations, enquiring whether the postulant renounces evil and about his beliefs:

[d+]	*Abrenuncias Satane . . . ?* *Abrenuncio.*		
[e+]	*Et omnibus pompis eis?* *Abrenuncio.*	[d+f+e+g+]	(an inversion in order for these items)
[f+]	*Et omnis operibus eis?* *Abrenuncio.*		
[g+]	*Et ego te lineo oleo*		
[h+]	*Credis in Deum . . . ?* *Credo.*	[h+i+] [j+]	mingled with the first interrogation [d]
[i+]	*Credis et in Jesum . . . ?* *Credo.*		
[j+]	*Credis et in spiritum . . . ?* *Credo.*		
[k+]	*Vis baptizari?* *Volo.*	[k+l+m+n+o+]	
[l+]	*Et ego te baptizo . . .*	[s+]	*Corpus et sanguinis*[68]
[m+] O	*Deus omnipotens Pater* *Domini nostri . . .*	[t+] O	*OsDq regenerare*
[n+] O	*Accipe vestem candidam*		
[o+] O	*Accipe lampadem*		

The Litanies [A B] and the Preface [b], the only items which are sung, may appear in Graduals, although infrequently.[69] Item [a], the prayer which goes with the blessing of the fonts, will appear with [b] (and [A] and [B] if given) in Missals, but only the Norwich Missal, M5, and some other versions of the Sarum Missal referred to in the edition by

Legg[70] include the baptism service in Holy Saturday. Apart from the differences between Roman and Sarum use, other variants are minor.

The procession to Mass, Mass, and Vespers

932 The procession is accomplished in Roman and some other uses by a normal Litany.[71] At Sarum and Norwich[72] the metrical Litany *Rex sanctorum* is used.[73] Replacing the introit, the Litany leads directly into the Kyrie, and up to the gospel the Mass is otherwise normal, including the Gloria and a single alleluia followed by a tract between the epistle and gospel. Thereafter, the consecration is made, without Credo or offertory, Agnus or Pax. As on Thursday and Friday, Vespers intervenes. On this day there is a single alleluia-antiphon on Ps 116 and the Magnificat with its antiphon *Vespere autem sabbati* before the combined services end with a final prayer and *Ite missa est* with an alleluia termination. The proper items for this Mass-Vespers are given complete in Missals, with incipits for ordinary material which is reappearing: the text of the Preface may be given. Graduals also tend to record the service quite fully, but the non-musical items are given only in incipit.

Easter day and Easter week

Procession and elevation of the cross: Matins

933 None of the sources studied has any special items for the procession retrieving the cross. Matins is distinguished only by the presence of a single nocturn in those uses, the majority, which abbreviate the service for Easter time: this practice has been described (**405-6**).

Easter Vespers and the processions to the font

The addition of the Kyrie, gradual, and alleluia, and sometimes even a sequence, to Vespers in place of the chapter and responsory has already been mentioned and needs no further examination (**912**). The procession to the font which occurs after the Magnificat may consist of one or more processional antiphons (some of which have verses, either independent or drawn from psalms) or processional responsories, together with versicles, the prayer which normally ends Vespers, and other memorials as usual. The procession to and from the font, apart from the presence of a musical item at least for outward and return procession, therefore takes on the character of the normal memorial.

Summary

934 The first part of this chapter, summarized from Hardison's essays, essentially stated the services which formed part of the seasons of Lent and Holy Week in 9th and 10th centuries. The middle section compared liturgical books from 13th to 16th. Let us now summarize what the latter contained and how it differs from the earlier arrangement. Few changes are to be observed. There is no sign in later books of the scrutinies and *traditio* of Lent: the final scrutiny and *redditio* of Holy Saturday occur as part of the baptism rather than earlier in the day, and the *redditio* is made by the Godparents rather than by the infant catechumen. The blessing of the font(s) finds its place in the Temporale of secular books, whereas the scrutiny and baptism themselves usually occur later in the book, where the items for the blessing of the font are repeated again between them. Only two sources, a Norwich Missal and on Sarum Missal,[74] transmitted the baptism in the Temporale. The Durham monastic Missal[75] includes neither baptism nor blessing for obvious reasons. In this manuscript, too, the service of reconciliation of the penitents, and the kindling and blessing of the New Fire and Paschal candle are excluded from the Temporale, to appear later in the book.

Of the actual consecration of the oils there is no trace in Missals, and the prayers must be sought in Pontificals. It is clear in several sources[76] that the reservation ceremony is carried out to the accompaniment of a chant which in other sources is simply the communion antiphon. The action and procession therefore take place before the Vespers service begins. Even though there is no reference to the reservation on Good Friday, we may assume that it was done in the same way. The washing ceremony, since its chants are drawn from Matins, does not need to be recorded except in a rubric, although sometimes incipits of each item are given. The Mandatum service, however, is not borrowed from other services: despite this, neither Graduals nor ordinary Missals usually contain it, and it may be found in Noted Missals or Processionals. One other significant change needs to be mentioned: where the deposition of the cross on Good Friday is recorded, in some half of the sources examined it occurs *after* the Mass of the Presanctified and is therefore unexceptional. In a York source and in the monastic Missal[77] it is *before* the Mass. The latter arrangement is not unsuitable, since the altar is deprived of any sign of Christ during the Mass, emphasizing the inability to consecrate. In addition, it is practical. After depositing the cross in the sepulchre, the clergy can retrieve the Corpus to be used at Mass, probably from the same place.

935 From these variations in arrangement and from a comparison of the actual texts used and their order, some conclusions can probably be drawn about relations among the manuscripts used. Such conclusions are not the purpose of this book, and the necessary detail has not been presented for results to be more than hints. Indeed, we shall probably not be able to do more here than confirm what was already known from more accessible and easily perceived features of the manuscripts. Nevertheless, we should not ignore what can be said. It is clear that source NM4 is essentially a Roman book. On the other hand M5, NM1, and NM6 are Sarum. Sources M1, M3, NM2, NM3, NM5, and NM6 cannot be grouped together, although all of them are more like the Sarum version than the Roman as far as the Twelve Prophets service is concerned: in addition, NM3 resembles NM6 (Sarum) in the layout of the baptismal service. What makes comparisons of this sort especially difficult is the tendency, even with sources which are otherwise 'identical' for minor inversions or omissions to occur. For example, items [A] and [B] of the Reproaches, probably performed more or less in an interlocking fashion, are sometimes written [AB], sometimes [BA]. This is perhaps not significant as far as the order of service is concerned, and may reveal only relations between scribal habits rather than between rites. In the baptismal service, the sentences [i] and [j] or [d+], [e+], and [f+] often appear in changed orders. Similarly insignificant but troublesome to consider are variants such as *Omnipotens Deus* in place of *Omnipotens sempiterne Deus.*

936 The visual appearance of Holy Week in the manuscripts is naturally distinctive, more from the unusual sequence of items rather than from any peculiarity in their initials or layout. In fact, the scheme of initials and capitals and the position of rubrics and identifying abbreviations is just the same as elsewhere. The size 2 initial or 1+1 for an item with plainsong is the normal, standing at the margin and serving prayers, lessons, chapters, tracts, hymns, and often the first of a number of musical items, except where any of these is referred to only by an incipit. The musical items, apart from those just mentioned, are usually begun with a capital, large or ordinary (1+ or 1), and are therefore run on within the text rather than beginning a new line. Their texts, in otherwise non-musical books, are as usual written in smaller script. The size 2 initial appears in some very characteristic positions in Holy Week. The Good Friday Fore-Mass, consisting entirely of prayers, lessons, and tracts, has only this initial for many pages, and is followed by the nine solemn prayers, whose eighteen initial Os are unmistakable.[78] Similar is the service of the Twelve Prophets on Holy Saturday, followed by the immediately identifiable Litanies. Within both of these sequences, isolated prayers or lessons are occasionally drawn from other services: only in these few cases will a smaller initial or even a plain capital be used. One confusing situation must be noticed. The subsequent verses of hymns and the subsequent sections and refrains of the Reproaches and even occasionally the verses of graduals and tracts may sometimes have size 2 initials, making it very difficult to determine where a new piece begins unless the text is known. Most such sentences or verses begin with an ordinary capital. So normally do all incipits, even where they are provided with music, and the musical items of the Missa Chrismalis and the refrain sentences of the Reproaches may have capitals. The large capital is less frequent, and less consistently used: it may appear at the beginning of isolated sentences such as the interrogations for the baptismal ceremony, for preces, or for special sentences such as the *Sanctificetur* (item [c+]) in the blessing of the font.

937 As has already been made clear, except in Noted Missals musical items which do not normally appear in Mass are mostly given in incipits. Thus, the processional items, the antiphons for the Mandatum and for the deposition, often have to be sought elsewhere. On the other hand, even those volumes which do not otherwise supply the music tend to give it for certain material. (a) The Passions; the tone is often included, at least for certain important passages of the text. (b) The beginnings and ends of certain prayers may have the relevant tones; the Norwich Missal, M5, for example, gives these passages of music for the liturgical greetings and for several prayers on Ash Wednesday, Palm Sunday, the Reconciliation, and other services. (c) The special versicles in the pontifical Missa Chrismalis may be completely supplied with music, for example, *Humiliatione vos, ad benedictionem,* the sentence sung by the deacon before the bishop's blessing. (d) The Vespers items, not normally appearing in Mass books, may have music.[79] (e) Items such as the Kyrie, Gloria, and Ite, which have not been performed in the preceding Masses of Lent, may have their incipits provided with music for their revival on Maundy Thursday and Holy Saturday. (f) The Exultet is normally and the Litanies often supplied with the chants as necessary; that is, complete for the former and one or two invocations for the latter.

Especially during the last three days of Holy Week, the distinctions between office and Mass are blurred, the function of the bishop rather than of a simple priest becomes important, and the requirements of individual churches define the number and type of processions. Not only are the services unusual, then, but they are also quite varied from source to source. Their representation within single books is similarly varied, and their distribution between Mass books, office books, Pontificals, Processionals, and Manuals makes study of these three important days more difficult than usual.

APPENDICES

NOTES

BIBLIOGRAPHY

SOURCES

INDICES

Appendix I

The Kalendar, Feasts, and the Sanctorale

1000 Kalendars generally occupy a separate fascicle of a manuscript, with one month to a page so that a ternion, or fascicle of three bifolia, six leaves, twelve pages, would seem sufficient. A quaternion, more usual elsewhere in the manuscript, would be filled out with Easter tables and similar material.
1001 The purpose of several features of Kalendars is not immediately obvious to the modern reader. It is necessary to examine only a small part of one month for the most important characteristics of the whole year to be explained, and I take the opportunity to introduce a brief consideration of colour and the Kalendar. Black, red, and blue are the basic colours, as usual; others are rare and are used only for the most important saints and for saints of great local significance. Saints and feasts of lesser importance, generally with a feast of only three lessons, are written in black script; others, the most solemn, with full services of nine lessons (or twelve, monastically), may be written in red script, from which practice derives the phrase 'red letter day.' Red normal letters in the Kalendar below are printed in italic; the number of lessons is placed at the right-hand edge, and sometimes the rank of the feast is expressed in the same place.

Several ranks of feast occur in every use, ranging from the principal doubles to the lesser simple feast, and different ranks are characterized by the solemnity of the ceremonial, the number of processions, the elaborateness of text and chant and vestment, and by certain special methods of performance practice.[1] The choir may be ruled, *cum regimine chori*, when certain soloists were singled out for the more elaborate performance of some items. The invitatory, for example, may be simplex, duplex, or triplex, according to whether it is sung by one, two, or three singers, or the canticle antiphons may be doubled, that is, sung complete before and after the canticle. The different combinations of these variables and the variation from use to use are beyond the scope of this book, and the topic needs more investigation. In Kalendars, information relating to rank and performance often appears at the right.
1002 The letter with which the saint or feast begins is usually a large capital and an alternation of blue and red occurs. However, strict alternation is broken

FIGURE I.1
The Kalendar (January)

		KL		Ⓘ *anuarius* (habet dies xxxi. Luna xxx)		
iii	Ⓐ			Ⓒ *ircumcisio domini duplex festum*		1
	b	*iiii*	N	Oct. sci Stephani protomartiris (invitatorium duplex) cum regimine chori	iii lc	2
xi	c	*iii*	*N*	Ⓞ *ct. sci Johannis apostoli* (invitatorium duplex) *cum regimine chori*	*iii lc*	3
	d	*ii*	N	Oct. scorum Innocentum (invitatorium duplex) cum regimine chori	iii lc	4
xix	e	N		Ⓞ ct. sci Thome memoria (tantum). *Sci Edwardi regis et confessoris memoria quando vigilia duplex festum*		5
viii	f	*viii*	iduum	Ⓔ *piphania domini duplex festum*		6
	g	*vii*	*iduum*			7
xvi	Ⓐ	*vi*	iduum	Sci Luciani sociorumque eius martyrum memoria		8
v	b	*v*	*iduum*			9
	c	*iv*	iduum			10
xiii	d	*iii*	*iduum*			11
ii	e	*ii*	iduum			12
-	f	IDUS		Ⓞ *ct. Epiphanie*. Sci Hillarii episcopi et confessoris	*ix lc*	13
x	g	*xix*	KL	Ⓕ *ebruarii*. Sci Felicis episcopi et martyris	iii lc	14
	Ⓐ	*xviii*		Sci Mauri abbatis et confessoris	iii lc	15
. . . . .	. . . . .	. . . . .				. . . . .
xiv	b	*iii*	KL	Sce Batildis regine	iii lc	30
iii	c	*ii*				31

when a red capital would introduce a red letter feast: in this case, blue is repeated. The criterion seems to be that the capital shall be a different colour from the following script, and the strict alternation is subordinate. In the Kalendar section printed here (figure I.1), the blue capitals are printed in circles: other capitals are red. The Roman numerals, to be explained below, are red (italic); lower case letters in the second column are black; material in the fourth column alternates black and red, as shown. Transcribed is part of January, taken from the ms B40. To the Kalendar as it appears in this source I have added some extra information taken from the Kalendar of the Sarum Breviary of 1531: this is printed between parentheses. There are some differences between the two Breviaries in their ranks and descriptions. The modern date, not included in the original, is in the far right-hand column.

The symbols in the first four columns now remain to be explained. Columns 3 and 4 give the date according to Roman practice. 13 January, for example, is the Ides of January and 6 to 12 January are the eighth to the second (*viii-ii* or pridie) before the Ides; similarly 5 January is the Nones of January preceded by the pridie (*ii*), and third and fourth before Nones (*iii, iiii*), and the first of January is the Kalends of the month. After the Ides follow the nineteenth, eighteenth, . . . day before the Kalends of February.

1003 Columns 1 and 2 are the Golden number and Dominical letter respectively. From these two 'figures,' which continue throughout the year, the date of Easter can be determined according to a formula. The mathematics and history of this formula is not relevant here, and now that we have comprehensive chronological tables such as Capelli's[2] even the formula itself is hardly necessary.

The Golden number
Each year has a number and the location of this number in the Kalendar indicates the full moons through the year (the actual lunar full moons may not coincide). Thus, the apparently irrational series of numbers in the first column, spaced in various ways, repeat themselves every 29 or 30 days. In January, the cycle begins again, with *iii*, on the 31st of the month. The number of days in the month and the number of days separating the full moons may be specified at the beginning of each month. In Kalendars, the number denoting the Paschal full moon may be written in black rather than red. To find the Golden number for any given year x, take x + 1 and divide it by 19: the remainder is the number. If the remainder is zero, the number is 19 (*xix*). Thus, for 1236, the equation is 1237 ÷ 19 = 64, remainder 1. The number is 1 (or *i* in the Kalendar).

The Dominical letter
Each weekday throughout the year is assigned a letter, and 1 January is always A in Kalendars. In normal years the same letter represents the same day. Kalendars always represent common years. In practical reckoning, the extra day in leap years causes letters after the 29 February to be delayed:

	M	T	W	Th	F	S	Sun	M	
February	26	27	28	29	1	2	3	4	March
	A	b	c	d	d	e	f	g	
					e	f	g	A	

	A	b	c	–	d	e	f	g	
February	26	27	28	–	1	2	3	4	March

To explain this in discussions of the Kalendar, leap years are given two Dominical letters for each day of the week: in the above example, Monday would have g and A. This complexity is relevant only in calculating the date of Easter. Ascertaining the Dominical letter, that is, the letter which in a particular year represents Sunday, is as follows: from the year 0 to 1582 (5 October),[3] the year is added to a quarter of itself, ignoring remainders, and the result divided by seven. The remainder from this operation is then subtracted from three, or, if that produces zero or is impossible, from ten. Thus, for 1374, the equations are:

(a) 1374 ÷ 4 = 343, remainder 2
(b) 1374 + 343 = 1717
(c) 1717 ÷ 7 = 245, remainder 2
(d) 3 − 2 = 1

FIGURE I.2
Golden numbers and Dominical letters

March			*April*			
1	*iii*	d	1		g	Year 804: GN *vii* : letter f.
2		e	2	*xi*	A	
3	*xi*	f	3		b	GN *vii* occurs on 17 March.
4		g	4	*xix*	c	Fourteenth day is the 30th.
5	*xix*	A	5	*viii*	d	31st is next date with the letter f.
6	*viii*	b	6	*xvi*	e	Easter Day: 31 March.
7		c	7	*v*	f	
8	*xvi*	d	8		g	
9	*v*	e	9	*xiii*	A	
10		f	10	*ii*	b	
11	*xiii*	g	11		c	Year 1274: GN *ii* : letter g.
12	*ii*	A	12	*x*	d	
13		b	13		e	GN *ii* occurs on 12 March and 10 April.
14	*x*	c	14	*xviii*	f	Fourteenth day is either 25 March or 23 April.
15		d	15	*vii*	g	The next dates with the letter g are 1 April
16	*xviii*	e	16		A	and another date after the last possible day
17	*vii*	f	17	*xv*	b	for Easter. Easter Day: 1 April.
18		g	18	*iv*	c	
19	*xv*	A	19		d	
20	*iv*	b	20	*xii*	e	
21		c	21	*i*	f	
22	*xii*	d	22		g	
23	*i*	e	23	*ix*	A	
24		f	24		b	
25	*ix*	g	25	*xvii*	c	
26		A				
27	*xvii*	b				
28	*vi*	c				
29		d				
30	*xiv*	e				
31	*iii*	f				

The letter indicated by the remainder is A, according to this correspondence:

A	b	c	d	e	f	g
1	2	3	4	5	6	7

In 1374 the Dominical letter is A. Everywhere A occurs is therefore a Sunday; in leap years it is the Sunday letter only after February.

Finding Easter
1004 Locate the Golden number of the year between 1 March and 12 April. The same number may appear twice, but only one will produce a date between the extremes for Easter. Count from the number, including it, fourteen days onward. The next appearance of the Dominical letter is Easter Day. If there is any choice, Easter must fall between **22 March and 25 April** inclusive. The

Golden number and Dominical letter from 1 March, to 25 April are given in figure I.2, with some examples.

Miscellanea

Other material or information included with the Kalendar generally appears at the foot of the page, or within the blank space where there are no feasts, or in the margins. It is often emphasized with blue paraph signs. Here may appear lists of the most prominent feasts of the month, references to the length of day and night, astrological information, and sometimes poems whose meanings are usually either obscure or quite incomprehensible.[4]

The Sanctorale

1005 In examining the Sanctorale of liturgical books it is useful to have in memory the order of the chief saints and feasts of the yearly round. The appearance of a known feast can help in identification of the precise location within the Sanctorale, or within the Temporale if the saints are included in that section. The unwary, perceiving the saint's name in rubrics such as the following, can easily believe that all occur on the date of the saint's feast: 'memorial to St Gregory,' 'homily by St Gregory,' 'octave of St Gregory,' 'feast of St Gregory,' etc. Even though this seems a mistake too elementary to mention, it may be as well to remind the reader that saints' names can appear at many places other than that of the relevant feast, in both Temporale and Sanctorale. Church fathers or other prominent saints who wrote or were later credited with writing homilies, and the apostles who wrote gospels or epistles, may be identified as the authors of these readings.

It is evidently impossible to list all saints and feasts. The two most basic Kalendars, to which later additions were made, are the Gelasian, a Frankish compilation of the 8th century, and the so-called Gregorian of 791.[5] Rather few of the saints on either of these Kalendars, however, are provided with full and prominent offices in manuscripts of the later middle ages. I append below a list of the saints and feasts whose dates I have found it most useful to memorize.

NOVEMBER

30 Andrew

DECEMBER

13 Lucy
25 Nativity
26 Stephen Protomartyr
27 John the Evangelist
28 Holy Innocents

JANUARY

6 Epiphany
20 Fabian & Sebastian
21 Agnes, Vincent
25 Conversion of Paul

FEBRUARY

2 Purification
5 Agatha

MARCH
12 Gregory
25 Annunciation

MAY
1 Philip & James
3 Invention of the Holy Cross
6 John at the Lateran Gate

JUNE
24 John Baptist
26 John & Paul
29 Peter the Apostle

JULY
11 Benedict
25 James the Apostle

AUGUST
1 Peter in Chains
2 Stephen, Pope & Martyr
3 Invention of Stephen, Protomartyr
10 Laurence
15 Assumption of the BVM

SEPTEMBER
8 Nativity of the BVM
29 Michael

NOVEMBER
11 Martin of Tours
22 Cecilia

KALENDAR DATES

For the major, universal feastdays, that are generally the oldest celebrations of the liturgical year, dictionaries generally agree as to their dates. For less well-established saints and feasts, the disagreement on feastdates among the various standard reference works is often quite remarkable. There are numerous reasons for these apparent conflicts and although error cannot be ruled out it is not usually the explanation. The same feast, with or without qualification such as 'translation' or 'ordination,' may occur on many different dates, mostly depending on locality or ecclesiastical order.

It does not seem to have been adequately observed, however, that every standard reference work – likely to be called a Dictionary of Saints, or an Encyclopedia of some kind – has as its principal concern the biography and history and social setting of the saint, and for the most part will have as its sources historical documents, chronicles, and other records of a general nature. Rarely is liturgical function considered, and only very rarely are liturgical documents consulted.

It has become increasingly apparent, in the compilation of a comprehensive liturgical Kalendar, that the *only* reliable source of the liturgical date is a manuscript liturgical Kalendar *for the area and years in question.* The date in a Kalendar for Rome may differ from that in a Kalendar for Hereford, and those two dates from the date in every other Kalendar. When manuscripts are not available, a printed reference work may be the sole recourse, but the possibility of legitimate variants must be remembered. The full extent of this difficulty cannot be described here. More details will be in the subsequent volume of my *LMLO,* to appear in 1995.

Appendix II

Historie, Responsories, Introits, Antiphons, and Psalms

2000 The first responsory of Matins, the first antiphon of Lauds, the introit of Mass, and certain of the psalms are emphasized with large initials or normal initials: in Breviaries without plainsong the initial of the first responsory is placed instead on the immediately preceding first lesson but the corresponding respnsory can still be located easily. If the incipits of these items are memorized, preliminary work with liturgical books is made immeasurably easier. Apart from the psalms, which will not vary, a collation of these items in numerous sources can sometimes enable a tentative family for individual manuscripts to be identified fairly quickly. Leroquais suggested this approach, citing only the responsories of Advent,[1] and the method has been comprehensively applied by Hesbert in his *Corpus antiphonalium officii*. A uniform method for 'notating' variants in this kind of matter is needed: any system requires a large amount of space in order to record even the basic information. The length of the figures below is some indication. If information of this kind is to be included in catalogue descriptions, some form of abbreviation is evidently needed. What is required is a standard table with some convenient reference symbol for each item, against which all sources can be compared by means of repetition or variation in the symbol. The figure below includes such symbols, placed against the incipits of the relevant items of the Breviary and Missal, and these symbols are used below to collate some sources. Hesbert uses a numerical system, more cumbersome than mine but more flexible. I use an alphabetical system, dividing the year into five periods, each with its own alphabet. Since they will rarely be needed together, the Mass items and office items are also provided with separate alphabets: in the case of combined Missals and Breviaries, the two can still be kept separate in descriptions provided some general comment is added. Despite this apparently complicated system, the procedures and tables below are really self-explanatory.

Finally, in order to make really complete the comparisons based on these principles, the responsories beyond the first must be included, as Hesbert does, a massive task more properly suited to a specific study such as his, and the plainsongs must be compared in those sources which transmit them. Since

FIGURE II.1
Advent to Epiphany
The letters are for identification only, and do not stand for genres.

Adv		Responsory and Lauds antiphon		Introit	other names
1	A	Aspiciens a longe	A	Ad te levavi	
	B	In illa die			
2	C	Jerusalem cito	B	Populus Sion	
	D	Ecce in nubibus			
3	E	Ecce apparebit	C	Gaudete in Domino	Gaudete
	F	Veniet Dominus			
4	G	Canite tuba	D	Memento nostri	
	H	Canite tuba		*or*	
			K	Rorate celi	
VN	I	Sanctificamini hodie	E	Hodie scietis	
	J	Judea et Jerusalem			
Nat	K	Hodie nobis	F	Dominus dixit ad me	
	L	Quem vidistis	G	Lux fulgebit	
		or	H	Puer natus	
	O	Natus est nobis			
die vi *or* Sunday within the octave			I	Dum medium silentium	
Cir	M	In principio erat	J	as H	
	N	O admirabile commercium			

mechanisms for the comparison of melodies are very cumbersome, difficult in application, not always accurate to the last detail, and are not widely accepted, the counsel of perfection here may perhaps be tempered by practicality. Comparisons of the plainsongs may be postponed for more specialized studies. It would be a relief to have liturgical manuscripts catalogued at all.

Advent to Epiphany

2001 (figure II.1) The standard sequences in this season may be written as A-N (offices) and A-J (Mass), where the hyphen stands for all the intervening letters of the alphabet: the two variants noted above may be written in full as A-KOMN (offices) and A-CKE-J (Mass)[2]. Other variants may be specified by noting that 'H is . . . ' etc, or less specifically by replacing H with x ('differs'), or m ('missing,' for instance, in a mutilated manuscript), or o ('omitted,' which in many cases implies a repetition of the previous item or items). Where an item is omitted in these tables, as for *die vi* above, repetition is to be assumed as normal practice, and does not need specifying.

FIGURE II.2
Epiphany to Lent
The letters are for identification only, and do not stand for genres

		Responsory and Lauds antiphon		Introit	other names
Epi	A	Hodie in Jordane	A	Ecce advenit	
		or			
	K	Illuminare illuminare Jerusalem			
	B	Ante luciferum			
1 (Sunday within the octave)			B	In excelso	
2	C	Domine ne in ira	C	Omnis terra	Domine ne
	D	Regnavit Dominus			
		or			
	L	Ecce nomen			
3, 4, 5, and 6			D	Adorate Deum	
LXX	E	In principio fecit	E	Circumdederunt	
	F	Miserere mei			
LX	G	Noe vir	F	Exurge quare	
	H	Secundum multitudinem			
L	I	Locutus est Dominus ad Abraham	G	Esto mihi	
		or			
	M	Quadraginta dies et			
	J	Averte Domine			

Epiphany to Lent

2002 (figure II.2) If necessary preceded by the numeral 2 for the second period of the year, the standard sequences are A-J and A-G and the principal variants shown above can be recorded as was done for Advent. The shuffling of order in responsories and antiphons which was described in sections **823-4** would result in the following formulas: A-DC-FMH (early sources), A-FEFMH (later monastic sources), and A-J (later secular sources). The similar shuffling and delaying of introits described in sections **716-19** would result in these arrangements: ACBD-G (early), AA-G (English), and A-G (continental). In offices and Mass, items are repeated as necessary to fill in the extra Sundays, Epiphany 3-6.

Lent to Easter
2003

FIGURE II.3
Lent to Easter
The letters are for identification only, and do not stand for genres

		Responsory and Lauds antiphon		Introit	other names
XL 1	A	Ecce nunc tempus	A	Invocavit me	In albis[3]
	B	Cor mundum			
2	C	Tolle arma tua	B	Reminiscere	
	D	Domine labia mea			
3	E	Videntes autem	C	Oculi mei	
	F	Fac benigne			
4	G	Locutus est Dominus ad Moysen	D	Letare Jerusalem	Letare
	H	Tunc acceptabis			
5	I	Isti sunt dies	E	Judica me Deus	Passion
	J	Vide Domine afflictionem			
6	K	In die qua	F	Domine ne longe	Palm
	L	Domine Deus auxiliator			
MTh		(Matins antiphon)			
	M	Zelus domus tue	G	Nos autem gloriari	
	N	In monte Oliveti			
	O	Justificeris Domine			
GFri	P	Omnes amici mei			
	Q	Proprio Filio			
HSat	R	Sepulto Domino			
	S	O mors ero			
		(Vespers antiphon)			
	T	Vespere autem			

Common variants are not recorded.

[3] This is note 3 of this Appendix.

FIGURE II.4
Easter to Corpus Christi
The letters are for identification only, and do not stand for genres

		Responsory and Lauds antiphon		Introit	other names
Pascha	A	Angelus Domini descendit	A	Resurrexi	
	B	Angelus autem			
1	C	as A	B	Quasimodo	Quasimodo *or*
	D	as B			In albis (depositis)
2	E	Dignus es Domine	C	Misericordia	
	F	as B			
3	G	as E	D	Jubilate Deo	
	H	as B			
4	I	Si oblitus fuero	E	Cantate Domino	
	J	as B			
5	K	as I	F	Vocem jocunditatis	
	L	as B			
Asc	M	Post passionem	G	Viri Galilei	
	N	Viri Galilei			
6	O	Tempus est	H	Exaudi Domine vocem	Dominica
	P	as N			expectationis
Pen	Q	Dum complerentur	I	Spiritus Domini	
	R	Dum complerentur			
Tri	S	Benedicat nos Deus	J	Benedicta sit sancta	
	T	O beata et benedicta			
CX	U	Immolabit hedum	K	Cibavit eos	
	V	Sapientia edificavit			

Easter to Corpus Christi

2004 (figure II.4) The only major variant in this period is the repetition of the introit A on all the Sundays before Ascension, whose full formula AAAAAAG-K we may abbreviate to A & G-K or as necessary. When A is repeated, introits B-F are usually performed at a second Mass on the Sunday or on feria ii in a Dominical Mass for the week: this could be shown as A(B-F)G-K.

FIGURE II.5

The summer

The letters are for identification only, and do not stand for genres

For the dates associated with these historie, see **107**.

	historia	Responsory		Introit	name
A	Regum (Kings)	Deus omnium	A	Domine in tua	Domine in tua
B	Sapientia (Wisdom)	In principio	B	Factus est Dominus	
C	Job	Si bona	C	Respice in me	
D	Thobias	Peto Domine	D	Dominus illuminatio	
E	Judith	Adonay	E	Exaudi Domine	
F	Machabees	Adaperiat	F	Dominus fortitudo	
G	Ezechiel	Vidi Dominum	G	Omnes gentes	
H†	Esther	Domine rex omnipotens	H	Suscepimus Deus	
			I	Ecce Deus adjuvat	
			J	Dum (*or* Cum) clamarem	
			K	Deus in loco	
			L	Deus in adjutorium	
			M	Respice Domine	
			N	Protector noster	
			O	Inclina Domine	
			P	Miserere mihi	
			Q	Justus es Domine	
			R	Da pacem	
			S	Salus populi	
			T	Omnia que fecisti	
			U	In voluntate tua	
			V	Si iniquitates	
			W	Dicit Dominus ego	
				Ember day introits:	
			X	Exultate Deo	
			Y	Letetur cor	
			Z	Venite adoremus	

† After E in some sources.

The Summer

2005 (figure II.5) Here the historie (offices) and introits must be listed separately. The Lauds antiphon is ferial and will no longer be recorded. Names of periods are also listed separately. In this case the sequence A-H (offices) will indicate that the unusual historia Esther is included in its correct position between Judith and Machabees. The introits for the Ember days, however, will occur in the source exactly where it is listed in the formula. The summer Sundays, A-W, may be after Pentecost, or after its octave or Trinity Sunday: the notation of the Easter introits must be observed, and a note added if necessary. The formulas A-I for period 4 followed by A-W for the summer period (5) should indicate that neither Trinity nor Corpus Christi is in the manuscript, but this is better specified explicitly: A-Ioo/A-W.

Also useful to remember, but hardly necessary to include in any variants, are the responsory and Lauds antiphon, and the introit, for the Dedication and for the office for the Dead:

Dedication	*In dedicatione* *Domum tuam Domine*	*Terribilis est locus*
Dead	(Vespers antiphon: *Placebo*) (Matins antiphon: *Dirige*) *Credo quod* *Exultabunt*	 *Requiem eternam*

2006 Three Graduals will be descpibed according to the principles extablished here:

(G1)	A-Ix	A-G	A-G	mB-Jo	A-QXYZR-W
(G12)	A-CKE-J	A-G	A-G	A & F-K	A-W
(G18)	mC-J	AoB-G	A-G	A-K	A-W

The variant (x) in the first can be recorded: (variant: J is *Vultum tuum*). The similarities and differences are apparent. A comparison of more sources quickly reveals that the K-variant of period 1 (A-CKE-J) occurs in two Graduals, G2 and G12, both of French origin, and in the Noted Missal, NM4, now in Toulouse and already identified (**935**) as Roman in character: other French Graduals, G7 and G22, have the normal introit (D) in Advent. Nearly all other sources, in fact, adopt the D introit. The collation of other information in connection with that introit reveals a subgroup which may be defined by virtue of a different psalm-verse which accompanies the introit, but I have inventoried too few members of that subgroup for reliable conclusions to be possible. A somewhat larger subgroup based on the psalm-verse of the C introit of Advent 3 may be isolated and is more clearly German-Austrain-Roman in orientation (G1, G5, G8, G10, G15, G17, G19). The variant *Vultum tuum* for J recorded with source G1 above also occurs in the Cluniac Breviary and Missal, C4.

In the second group of introits the alternative forms AA-G (or AoB-G), where B is delayed until the third place, and A-G denote the differences already noted in sections **716-19**, and represent English[4] and continental practices respectively. Introits of the third group, representing Lent, do not vary. Apart from the presence or absence of Trinity (J) or Corpus Christi (K), introits of Easter vary only in the repetition of the Easter Day introit as in source G12 above, where it is (unusually?) superseded on the fifth Sunday (F) instead of the sixth (G). Variations in the fifth period, the summer, mainly concern the placing of X-Z, the Ember Masses. Although in most cases there are as yet too few statistics for conclusions to be valid with respect to the manuscripts studied, two sources may be fairly safely related because of their common variants in periods 3, 4, and 5 (many other variants apart from those in introits also occur in

FIGURE II.6
Main divisions in the Psalter

	Liturgical, or eightfold	Fivefold	Threefold
Ps 1	Beatus vir	Beatus vir	Beatus vir
Ps 26	Dominus illuminatio		
Ps 38	Dixi custodiam		
Ps 41		Quemadmodum	
Ps 51			Quid gloriaris
Ps 52	Dixit insipiens		
Ps 68	Salvum me fac		
Ps 72		Quam bonus	
Ps 80	Exultate Deo		
Ps 89		Domine refugium	
Ps 97	Cantate Domino		
Ps 101			Domine exaudi
Ps 106		Confitemini Domino quoniam bonus quoniam	
Ps 109	Dixit Dominus Domino		

common but are not recorded here):

(G1 and G20) ACBD-G A-DFEGHIoo A-PXYZQ-W.

2007 A similar comparison of office books, a much larger undertaking, must be postponed. One Antiphonal, one Breviary, and one combined Missal-Breviary may be 'inventoried':

(A6) A-KxxN A-CxEFEFMH A-GmJ-T ABooE-L [saints inserted] MxxoQ-Sm A-G
(variants, in order: L is *Genuit puerpera*; M is *Quem vidistis*; D is *Alleluia*; N is *Videntibus illis*; O = M). Monastic, of Salzburg

(BS 1531) A-N KB-J A-T A-V A-G
Sarum

(C4) A-KOxN A-CxEFEFMH A-T A-NMPQRmT (oo ?) A-G
(variants: M is *Hic qui advenit*; D is *Alleluia*). Cluniac, English

Psalms

2008 Only the three main divisions of the Psalter need be shown (figure II.6). For the purposes of manuscript description it would seem satisfactory to note some such statement as: Psalter (3-fold division) or Psalter (3 + 5-fold) or Psalter (8-fold plus Ps 118). Such a presentation would of course need explanation: it could be abbreviated further – P (3) or P (3 + 5) or P (3 + 5, 118).

Appendix III

Purification

3000 Similar to those services of the Temporale which involve processions, blessings, and distributions is the feast of the Purification of the Blessed Virgin, celebrated on 2 February and normally included in the Sanctorale. The feast marks the end of a 'season' for some items of the liturgy which are common *usque ad Purificationem* and which change *post Purificationem*. The doxology of certain hymns, the items in the memorials to the Virgin after Lauds and at Mass may be cited.[1] Immediately preceding Mass on the feast, the ceremony of blessing, lighting, and distributing the candles occurs. The ceremony is much the same from source to source, except for the processional items which intervene before Mass: according to the geography of different churches the number and length of processions will vary. The presence of a Preface, often with the tone, the additional prayers, and the processional chants make this service very distinct since it is the only service in the Sanctorale of Mass books with such items in large number. I shall compare the Roman and Sarum uses:

MR I 313-16		MS cols 696-703	
[a] O	*Domine sancte pater eterne*	[g] ✠	*Benedic Domine JX hanc creaturam cerei*
[b] O	*OsDq hodierna*		
[c] O	*Domine JX lux vera*	[ab]	
[d] O	*OsDq per Moysen*	[h] ✠	(Preface) *Fons et origo*
[e] O	*Domine JXq hodierna*	[i] O	*Domine sancte pater omnipotens*
		[j] O	*OsDq unigenitum*
	sprinkling, censing, and distribution of the candles		sprinkling, censing, and distribution of the candles
[A] A	*Lumen ad revelationem* with *Nunc dimittis*	[A]	
[B] A	*Exurge Domine adjuva* with Ps 43		
[f] O	*Exaudi quesumus Domine plebem*		
[C] A	*Ave gratia plena*		
[D] A	*Adorna thalamum*		

[E] A *Responsum accepit Simeon*[2]
[F] R *Obtulerunt* . . . V *Postquam*
Mass

Processions for churches adopting the Sarum use will presumably draw the necessary items from the Processional: the Durham monastic Missal, source M3, includes processions for use within the Galilee chapel of Durham cathedral as well as material for use in other churches.

Appendix IV

Colour

4000 I have studied a few sources specifically from the aspect of colour and present below details of schemes in some manuscripts and of several feasts in others, together with what general observations seem possible. Carelessly written manuscripts are of course less reliable, and I have tried to choose well-prepared sources. Most described here are Antiphonals, Breviaries, and Noted Breviaries, but no doubt the principles which emerge are applicable to Mass books in much the same way. Fewer Missals have been described.

Each source differs as to minute details, and as usual manuscripts do not seem to be entirely consistent within themselves. I present the material in two ways. First, I shall give the schemes of initals and capitals applicable to certain sources, as in sections **805-6, 850-5**.

The first source is a York Antiphonal (A26). Large initials normally spanning two staves and their lines of script identify the first responsory in feasts earlier in the book, and the first item, usually the first antiphon of Vespers 1, later in the book. These initials are predominantly gold with blue and red foliage and marginal descenders and ascenders: a capital highlighted with red follows. Ordinary initials, size 1 + 1 for musical items and size 2 for non-musical items, are blue with red penwork when they stand at the margin, and otherwise black with black penwork. The former are more important, denoting the first musical items of services or main sections of the services. Thus the first antiphon of Vespers or Lauds or of complete historie or the first responsory of Matins usually has this kind of initial, followed by a capital with a red highlight (size 1 +). Hymns, tropes, the great O antiphons, the first antiphon of Maundy Thursday (*Zelus domus*), and other special items such as the Liber Generationis have similar blue marginal initials. The first antiphon of nocturn 1 adopts this style when the feast begins with a larger initial. Prayers and chapters, which are included in this Antiphonal, conventionally have blue initials. Other musical items and the verses of responsories have the standard black initial, not necessarily at the margin, followed sometimes by an unhighlighted capital. Large blue capitals (1+) denote rubrics specifying Sundays, and blue paraph signs mark important points within rubrics. Psalm incipits, evovae formulas, incipits or texts within rubrics, have a simple black capital, sometimes highlighted with red: new sentences within rubrics have a simple red capital. Alternately blue and red capitals (1 or 1 + 1) begin the verses of hymns and the sentences of items such as the Liber Generationis.

4001 On the basis of these characteristics and their reasonably consistent use, it seems quite clear that both the Ranworth and Wollaton Antiphonals (A19 and A24), although they exhibit minor variations, must originate from the same workshop as this York Antiphonal: the similarities between the York and Ranworth books are, however, greater than between those and the Wollaton book. The only common variation from the above schemes is that initials (size 2 or 1 + 1, at the margin), instead of being blue with red penwork, alternate fairly consistently between blue and red with penwork of the other colour. Some examples of this will be presented later. Of the British group, Irish Antiphonals adopt the alternating procedure (A20 and A35). The cumbersome nature of the above description of the York book obviously precludes its presence in a catalogue entry, and later I shall devote some thought to a shorter presentation.

The application of these principles in the York book seems quite consistent. Much the same kind of colour scheme applies to the Noted Sarum Breviary (NB17), and a few variants, some caused by the fact that it is a Breviary rather than an Antiphonal, may be recorded. Blue initials do not alternate with red. In addition to marking the same items as in the previous source, blue initials also begin lessons, occasionally the rubrics specifying Sundays, and the beginnings of psalms in the Psalter (psalm verses, like hymn verses, begin with the conventional capital, alternating blue and red). As in the York source, too, the blue initial is used for the great O antiphons, but the O antiphon to the apostle Thomas is excluded. Rather than blue paraphs marking important points in rubrics, blue capitals denote ferias, services, and miscellaneous texts such as versicles, where they occur. In normal Breviaries, the schemes are simpler because the hierarchies of initials and capitals are simpler. Blue initials are used for the chapters, prayers, and lessons, and where those items are given only in incipit the size is reduced to that of a large blue capital. Musical items take only a black capital, as in source B40, or a large blue capital, source B54. Other distinctions are in the use of blue paraphs or blue capitals in rubrics, or the denoting of a major rubric with a blue inital (B40) as opposed to a blue capital (B54).

4002 In Litanies the petitions each begin with the letter S, for *Sancte*, etc; after each group of a single class of saints the summarizing petition begins with O:

Sancte Thoma	ora pro nobis
Sancte Sixte	ora pro nobis
...	
Sancte Petre	ora pro nobis
...	
Omnes sancti martyres	orate pro nobis

The first letter of each of these petitions and the first letter of each of the sentences following Litanies and of preces in general are usually large capitals alternating blue and red, and the remaining text is usually black. Occasionally, the name of a very prominent saint or feast of local importance may, as in Kalendars, be written in red script with a gold initial of more elaborate type. Between the saint's name and the *ora* the parchment may be blank or may be filled with a decorative ornament usually of the same colour as the S or O. The presence or absence of the filler may be another clue to the grouping of sources.

In a French Missal, source M6, the large initials are red and blue followed by a capital with a red highlight. The ordinary initial, used for all the spoken items and for the introits of Sundays, alternates quite strictly between red and blue with tracery of the other colour: the sequence of alternation may be interrupted or changed by the appearance of a larger initial. Musical items, apart from the introits, incipits of spoken texts, and divisions within the Preface, begin with a large capital at the margin where the alternation of blue and red is much less strict, perhaps because these letters are more widely spaced by the long texts of readings and prayers. The capitals of offertory and communion chants are quite consistently red and blue respectively: gradual and alleluia adopt the marginal capital only after the opening pages in which they seem by error to have been given a lower status. Their verses, the gradual and alleluia themselves in the opening pages, the incipits of psalms, and sentences within the readings begin with a normal black capital highlighted with red and not necessarily at the margin. The principle of giving an incipit an opening letter one degree smaller than the item would normally receive is very clearly in operation, and the items of f.12v may be cited.

Whereas the manuscripts examined above seem to be quite consistent, others appear deliberately to avoid consistency in some respects. I present below the schemes of several manuscripts and the details of initials and large capitals in a number of feasts. None of the sources is English: all are Antiphonals. In the following diagrams red will be denoted by x, blue by o: both represent size 2 initials at the margin unless otherwise stated. Black initials not at the margin are not marked, although the items they begin are included.

4003 A 15th-century Roman Antiphonal (A34) has the following scheme:

large initials: elaborate and coloured, usually on the first item of an office.
[1 + 1]: blue or red alternating, on I M B R and the first A.
1 + 1: black with red highlight, mostly for verses of responsories and for subsequent antiphons.
1: black with red highlight, for psalm incipits, repetenda, etc.

In this manuscript, the feast of Ascension has the following arrangement:

ASCENSION DAY

```
Vespers     Compline  Matins
A     M     A         I AAARVRVRV  AAARVRVRV  AAARVRVRV
[2+2] x     o         x o  x o x   o  x o x   x  o x o
                                          └───┘

Lauds    Vespers
AAAAAB   M
x    o   x
```

There is strict alternation except between second and third nocturn: I cannot now ascertain whether there is a page turn or some other 'interruption' at this point. The feast of Pentecost has the same arrangement. Corpus Christi is not as strict:

CORPUS CHRISTI

Vespers					Matins		
A	AAAA	RV●	M	I	AAARVRVRV	AAARVRVRV	AAARVRVRV
[2+2]		x	x	x	o x o x	o x x o	x x o x

Lauds	Vespers	
AAAAAB	RV	M
x o	x	o

The variation in colour for the responsories of the three nocturns, xox – xxo – xox, is not at all rare in this source and in the other continental sources described below. In this Antiphonal, one break in sequence may indicate a deliberate attempt to use colour informatively. In the stock of canticle antiphons for the historia Regum, the initals alternate strictly red and blue until the last antiphon, which has a black initial: this antiphon is probably not a canticle antiphon but for Matins of the next historia.

4004 A 13th-century Antiphonal, source A25, has these initials and capitals:

large initial: elaborate and coloured, followed by large capitals highlighted in red or yellow with pale tracery; usually on the first responsory.
[1 + 1]: blue or red with tracery of the other colour, followed by a capital with a highlight: A I M B R H.
1 + ½: blue or red; verses of responsories (major hours).
1 + ½: black; verses of responsories (little hours).
1 + : black with highlight; for psalm incipits, dialogues, repetenda.
0: normal letter with highlight; for evovae.

INVENTION OF THE HOLY CROSS

Vespers		Matins		
HM	⊕	I A RVRVRV	A RVRVRV	A RVRVRV
x o	x	o x []o x o x o	x o x o x o x	o x o x o x o

Lauds	Prime	Terce	Sext	Nones	Vespers
AHB ⊕	A	ARV	ARV	ARV	AHM
x o x o	o	ox	ox	ox	o x o

The inclusion of verses of the Matins responsories in the colour scheme causes a reversal of the pattern from nocturn to nocturn, and the large initial on the first responsory interrupts a strict alternation:

[] oxoxo
oxoxox
xoxoxo

On the other hand, the omission of verses in the little hours from the scheme causes the responsories in those hours all to begin with the same colour. The antiphon of Prime causes the only inexplicable break in an otherwise strict alternation. Other feasts are different:

JOHN the BAPTIST

Vespers	Matins
M	I AAA RVRVRV AAARVRVRV AAARVRVRV
x	o xox []oxoxo xoxxoxoxo xoxoxoxox

Lauds	Terce	Sext	Nones	Vespers
AAAAAB	RV	RV	RV	M
oxoxox	o	x	o	x

4005 If colour schemes are to be used as a tool for analysis and comparison, some form of 'notation' suitable for index cards or computers if not for running text, must be evolved. Henceforth, then, I shall use shorter forms. To represent red, blue, gold, and yellow we may perhaps accept x o g and y: where it is possible to distinguish only between black and grey, as on a black and white microfilm, the letter c for 'colour' may represent grey. A sign for black will probaly be necessary at some time, although normally its omission may be simpler: the letter b will be suitable. Equality of colours can be expressed as follows: gxo; subordination of one or more in the form of tracery as g+xo or g+x+o; alternation as x/o. Highlighting, an extreme form of subordination, may be shown as b(x).

The next source, an Italian Dominican Antiphonal (A33), includes the doxology of responsories in the colour scheme, as well as the verses of the responsories in the little hours:

large initial: gxo; first R
[1 + 1] or [2]: gxo; first items and B
1 + ½: x+o/o+x; A M I R V●
1 + : b(x); P and repetenda.

The services of Trinity Sunday have this arrangement:

TRINITY SUNDAY

Vespers		Matins				
A	M	I AAA	R	VRVRV●	AAARVRVRV●	AAARVRVRV●
[2]	o	x oxo	[2+2]	oxooxx	ox xo o xxoxo	xo xoxo xo ox

Lauds		Terce	Sext	Nones	Vespers
A	AAAA B	RV	RV	RV	M
[x]	o x o x [2]	ox	ox	ox	o

The pattern of each nocturn is different, perhaps deliberately so. The careful reversal from (x)oxo through ooxx to oxox for the first two responsories of each nocturn seems designed:

A	R	R	R
oxo	[]o	xo	xoo
oxx	oo	xx	oxo
xox	ox	ox	oox

The nocturns of the historia Regum are similar but not so carefully executed:

xox	[]o	xx	oxx
oxo	ox	ox	oxo
xox	ox	xo	xox

Obviously, before comparisons can be made and conclusions drawn, a method of recording such information in accurate and condensed form has to be evolved and accepted, and many sources have to be collated. It may be that the investigation of these minute differences and similarities will prove to be of limited use, revealing relationships which can be perceived more easily by other means. Nevertheless, there will always remain instances where conventional methods of comparison are insufficient. The expert liturgist should have many different tools available, even if some are used only as a last resort.

Appendix V

Rubrics, Ordines, Picas

5000 In Mass books the relatively simple instructions for the performance, repetition, and omission of Masses in the difficult periods of the year, after Epiphany and after Trinity Sunday, may appear in fairly short rubrics appended to individual items as necessary and general instructions will appear in the ordo, in the first week of Advent, and wherever they are needed elsewhere in the books. Such rubrics in some Mass books have been described. Office books, being a great deal more complex, require longer and more detailed instructions. As well as the general short rubrics appearing here and there and the more extended descriptions in Advent, there is normally one major rubric, called the *rubrica magna* or *generalis*, placed after Trinity. A much shorter version follows Epiphany. In addition, some manuscripts present a tabulated form of similar information at various points in a distinct section called the pica. Whereas the rubric is written in normal prose mostly without reference to specific items, the pica appears as a series of days, feasts, and services interspersed with the relevant textual incipits. Very occasionally, as in a York Breviary,[1] the intonations of the plainsongs are given in an otherwise non-musical book, to supplement the textual incipits. Antiphonals, being subordinate to Breviaries in matters of year by year adjustment, and their contents being less affected, do not normally include rubrics or picas of the kind discussed here. The combination of all the picas of a Breviary into a single volume creates the Ordinal: derivation of the pica by incorporating sections of a 'dismembered' Ordinal does not seem to have been the practice. In other words, Ordinals were abstractions from Breviaries and tend to be later, chronologically. The topic needs investigation.

In this appendix it seems suitable to describe the information which might appear in the *rubrica magna*, and to give examples of part of picas and other sections devoted to adjustments. The general rubric is fairly consistent in its subject-matter and the following is a paraphrase of its most important statements, which may of course appear in different order.[2]

5001 From Trinity to Advent, Saturdays in many uses are devoted to the full offices of the Virgin, except for the Ember Saturday and when a feast coincides.

In these cases the Marian services are said on another convenient day, and rules for first Vespers are given in case that service conflicts with another feast on the previous day. Such an adjustment will often consist in the reduction of Vespers to a memorial, and rules for memorials in general are given. Sarum practice was to omit memorials in the summer unless two feasts ranking at least three lessons fell on the same day. Thus on the feast of St Mary Magdalene, 22 July, a feast of nine lessons with a tripled invitatory, there was a memorial to St Wandragesillus. Information of this kind may also be given in the Kalendar.[3] Rules for the coincidence of feasts and Sundays are cited and during the summer the former are more important, delaying even the first Sunday of a historia, which is *differtur*, 'deferred,' to the first free feria or, if the historia lasts more than a week, to the following Sunday. When the historia lasts only a week, the Sunday services must be sung on the middle three ferias of the week, and of the ferial homilies and responsories only one of the latter is used, on the third day in place of the ninth responsory. Whereas offices may be moved from one Sunday to another or to a weekday, Mass may be moved only if the time is long or if the Sunday is also a feast of major importance such as the Assumption or Nativity of the Virgin, or the feast of the Dedication. The precise length of the historia *Deus omnium* needs to be stated, and the presentation gives some idea of the difficulty in conveying information about dates before the era of printed yearly calendars. Whenever it begins, *Deus omnium* is said until the first Sunday after the fifth day before the Kalends of August, but the first Sunday of August 'does not always begin in August.'[4] This can be explained more simply as follows:

Deus omnium is said until the first Sunday (Dominica) after the fifth day before the Kalends of August:

July		August	July		August
Dominica		ii iii iv-vii	Dominica		ii iii iv v-vii
	iv	iii ii Kalends		v	iv iii ii Kalends

The second line here shows the Sunday and following ferias, ii-vii: the third line shows the number of days before the Kalends, the Kalends being counted as i. In the first case the Sunday is considered to be first Sunday of August, on which the new historia would begin; in the latter case it is the last of July, only one day farther from the beginning of August but still part of the historia *Deus omnium*.

Appended to the rubric, or part of it, there may be useful lists. A Sarum Breviary[5] gives the feasts in which the invitatory is performed by three soloists and a list of feasts of nine lessons in which the usual homily is not present in lessons 7 to 9 (it may, for instance, be replaced by a continuation of the vita or passion of the saint). Such lists of feasts in Sarum books, however, often follow the Kalendar or Temporale, as described earlier (**895**). Naturally, the general rubrics of individual manuscripts will have to be read for specific information, but the organization and matters for discussion appear to be similar from source to source.

5002 More precise about the adjustments necessary from year to year are the instructions given within the ordo-like passages, of which the commonest begins with the text *In anno* . . . (plate 6), or within the tabulations of the pica. In order to cope with all possible situations, the 'ordo' for controlling Advent, for example, will be divided into seven sections, each of which begins with a simple description of the season, such as 'When Christmas Day falls on Monday, there are three weeks and one day in Advent. The Ember days are in the third week. The feasts of St Lucy, etc, fall on . . . The great O antiphons begin on . . . ' Here is one complete section, and sentences of others:[6]

In anno quo Nativitatis Domini die dominica evenerit sunt in adventu quatuor septimane et in tertia sunt jejunia quatuor temporum, quarta, sc., et sexta feria et sabbato. Feria tertia festum Sancte Lucie. Feria secunda ad Benedictus A. *Ite dicte Johannis*; ad vesperas ad memoriam adventus A. *Beatam me*; In crastino ad matutinas ad memoriam adventus A. *Prophete predicaverunt*; ad vesperas ad memoriam adventus A. *Spiritus Domini*. Quatuor feria legatur omelia R. *Missus est Gabriel*, incipiuntur R. *Clama in fortitudine*, in laudibus A. *Amplius lava*, A. *Te decet*, A. *Melior*, A. *Exaltavit*, A. *Celi celorum*; ad Ben. A. *Missus est Gabriel*; ad vesperas incipitur O. Feria quinta R. *Precursor*.

In anno quo Nativitatis Domini secunda feria evenerit sunt in adventu tamen tres septimane et una [die] . . .

In anno . . . quinta feria evenerit sunt tres septimane et quatuor dies et in tertiam fiunt jejunia quatuor temporum, et in secunda vii (sc. sabbato) festum Sancte Lucie . . .

With more emphasis on the later weeks of the season, each day of Advent is specified as necessary; the presence of memorials is noted, and incipits of relevant items recorded. The seven sections modify the format to suit the information. Each section will probably begin with a size 2 initial for *In anno* and sometimes also for *Dominica*,[7] and each feria described may be emphasized by means of paraph signs or a prominent capital. Each section may be called a *tabula*[8] so that the initials fall on the words *Prima, Secunda* . . . In one Benedictine manuscript[9] the general introductory description of the season is presented as a running text, giving details of the calendar and matters of performance such as information about the presence or absence of a doxology with the responsories. Below this, in the left-hand column of a two-column format, are the specified services, and in the right-hand column the textual incipits. Another common name for rules of this kind is the very word *Regula*, in which the R may receive the prominent initial. Frequently involved in these passages, too, are the Dominical letters, and if the information is organized by means of these letters the sections are often known as picas, pyes, or pies, modern names which perhaps derive from the size of type used for these sections in early printed Breviaries. Despite this possible origin, I shall retain the term for the use with manuscripts. In picas, the prominent initial may be L for *Littera dominicalis*, and the Dominical letter itself may be emphasized.[10] Picas may occur in rubrical or tabulated form.

5003 The pica is even more detailed than the rubrics and tabule just discussed, and it therefore occurs more frequently, dealing with smaller periods. In the Sarum Breviary, for example, in its printed form of 1531, there is a pica before each single week of Advent and of Septuagesima to Trinity Sunday, and before each historia of the summer, and there is one after Epiphany. The organization and contents are much the same, although more detailed, as has already been discussed. The picas of the summer and other complex weeks may therefore be quite long: for each historia there are seven major sections of the pica, listed according to the Dominical letter, and each subdivided into as many sections as there are Sundays within the historia. Later subsections, however, frequently refer to previous sections where repetitions occur. Moreover, from Epiphany to the historia *Deus omnium* each Dominical letter itself has five different sections devoted to it, to cope with the thirty-five possible dates of Easter (seven Dominical letters with five variants).

The vast increase in length caused by the inclusion of such detail must have made it less desirable to present the material within the Breviary. As a consequence, from the 15th century at least, separate books containing only rubrics, ordines, and picas being to appear. Some such books may date even from the 13th century or earlier. They are known under various titles such as Ordinals, Directories, and the like.

Appendix VI

Doxologies and Terminations

6000 Because its text varies, especially from season to season, the doxology of a hymn, equivalent to its final verse, is often specified clearly when the hymn first appears or when a change is necessary, or the variants are set out in the Psalter or Hymnal. The presence of a doxology after a psalm, a series of psalms, or ending a responsory, is not so evident. No doubt there is a comprehensive rurbic in some book, although I have been unable to find an example: the sentences incorporated into the Sarum Ordinal,[1] which deal mostly with responsories, do not give a general practice. There seems little reason to doubt the inclusion of a doxology at the end of every psalm, or group of psalms sung as a single text. The almost universal presence of the evovae formula with antiphons or introits and similar items is the most obvious indirect evidence. The prescription of the doxology after the psalms as they occur in the Psalter is, as already stated (**881**), haphazard.

At the moment, too, I can discuss the doxology of responsories only from the indirect evidence of the Breviary and Antiphonal. In the latter, the doxology must sometimes be given in full because the tone of the responsory verse, which the doxology traditionally repeats, may need to be adapted if there is a different number of syllables. In Breviaries, only the word *Gloria* may appear, and given common knowledge of everyday practice even that incipit may be left out. Many statistics are needed, as with so many other features of the liturgy, and here, wishing to point to discrepancies within a single use, I draw information from the Sarum books again. In the Breviary of 1531, the first, third, sixth, and ninth responsories of Advent Matins have the *Gloria* indicated. Nowhere is it given in full, and there is no reference to the fact that, for responsories, it consists of only the first verse, ending with the word *sancto*. The fourth responsory also has the *Gloria* incipit with the rubric that the doxology is sung only *quando dicitur*,[2] an instruction which is of little help in determining when the *quando* is. To dispense with this matter first: the first responsory of Sunday is not used on ferias, and the second therefore becomes the first and the fourth the third. In its ferial position as the last responsory of the nocturn the fourth responsory of Advent Sunday would require the doxology. The text is given not on the ferial appearance of the item (which is by incipit only) but on its complete appearance on the Sunday, so that the arrangement of verse, doxology, and repetenda can be shown. In the Breviary, then, Advent Sunday has a doxology on first, third, sixth, and ninth responsories. This agrees exactly with the indications in the Antiphonal,[3] but not with the passage in the Ordinal,[4] where only the sixth and ninth are provided with – while the first and third are lacking – the doxology.

Whatever the true Sarum use and the explanation for this discrepancy, the traditional practice seems to be the presence of a doxology with the last responsories of each nocturn, and with especially elaborate responsories such as the first of Advent.

Terminations

The terminations proper to prayers of the Sarum rite are set out in a long rubric in the Ordinal,[5] which contains various mnemonic verses summarizing the principles. These brief verses are repeated in even shorter form in the Psalter[6] and may be given here:

Versus de conclusione orationum sive collectarum.
Per Dominum *dicas: si Patrem presbyter oras.*
Si Christum memores: per eundem *dicere debes.*
Si loqueris Christo: qui vivis, *scire memento.*
Qui tecum, *si sit collecte finis in ipso.*

As these lines partly indicate, the termination depends on the mention of the Father, Son, or Holy Ghost, or of the Trinity, and the position of such references near the beginning or end of the prayer.

Appendix VII

Breviary-Missals and Other Books

7000 The combination of Breviary and Missal is most common in monastic manuscripts, perhaps because such a compendium was most useful to the monk away from his monastery. I exclude from consideration here those compendia designed as *summe*, as master reference works from which universal copies could be made. Humbert's Codex, source B10, is one of this type.

Amongst the compendia used for this study there are several different methods of organization, and in only one of the manuscripts is the arrangement at all confusing, partly because of the mutilated state of the book itself. In some sources, Mass is worked into the office services in correct chronological order. Where the little hours have sufficient propers of incipits for them to exist at all in the Breviary, Mass will intervene between Terce and Sext, or between other hours as called for (**115-16**). When, as so often happens later in seasons, the little hours do not appear at all, Mass intervenes between Lauds and second Vespers. Thus, on Thursday of the third week of Lent in source C2, a Cluniac book, to the usual sequence, L3 BoMo, Mass with its extra prayer *super populum* is added: L3 Bo (**IOEGGOOCOO**) Mo. Where possible, in the same manuscript, the gospel immediately following Matins is indicated only by means of an incipit or a rubric referring to the gospel in Mass, *require evangelium in missa*. The presence of Mass, therefore, apart from disturbing the normal order can result in the apparent omission of items elsewhere, and the consequent interruption of the usual sequence of initials and texts.

7001 If Mass is not present in its correct position, the alternative presentation involves a separate section of the book so that nothing in the normal order of the Breviary is upset. In the Premonstratensian manuscript of Guisborough, for example,[1] the sections are as follows, where T stands for Temporale, etc:

Antiphonal and hymns	Missal		Brev.	Ant.	Lectionary	Processional
TV⊥	TSC	K	PV†I	S	TSC	T

In the Benedictine Breviary of Ely, the complete Missal intervenes between the Temporale and Sanctorale of the Breviary. The Benedictine Antiphonal of Gloucester/Hereford[3] presents mostly the day hours, with processions and Masses, and since many of the items are ferial and given only by means of incipits, this source resembles an ordo. Nevertheless, all truly proper items appear in full. Not only are Masses included in their proper chronological order, but the Temporale and Sanctorale are combined, creating a very rare format for which the cumbersome title Diurnal Breviary-Missal-Processional would be reasonably appropriate. In fact, the manuscript also includes tropes for the ordinary of Mass, given in their correct position within the service. The following is the format at the beginning of Advent:

Advent 1
Vespers
a4 RHdM (rubric, and stock of eleven antiphons for memorials, etc)

Prime	Terce	
hA	RA	(Mass rubrics and incipits) two processional responsories

Sext	Nones	Vespers
Ad	Ad	a4 RhdM (rubric and pica, relating to St. Andrew and Mass)

Feast of St Andrew

For the feast of Thomas of Canterbury the Mass includes the Kyrie, Sanctus, and Agnus tropes and two sequences, all written in full between Prime and second Vespers:

IK-trope **EGA** sequence **O** S-trope A-trope C

(a second sequence and incipits of offertory and communion follow).
7002 Resulting in more complex organization, the position of Mass within the Cluniac Breviary-Missal of Wenlock[4] is erratic and seems inconsistent: the absence of certain leaves and the possible misbinding of some sections makes the manuscript difficult to assess. An accurate collation is required. Nevertheless, the following features seem to be correct. The book begins as a Breviary, giving only the offices in Advent. Masses for Advent Sundays, Christmas Eve, the *missa de nocte* of Christmas Day and, presumably (since leaves are missing here and the service does not occur elsewhere), the *missa de aurora* of Christmas Day appear all together, as they would in a Missal, after the Psalter. The main Mass of Christmas is recorded after Terce of Christmas in the section which began as a Breviary. Thereafter, Mass for all services up to the second Sunday of Lent is given in 'hourly' sequence after Terce. No ferial Masses for Lent appear and from the second Sunday of Lent Mass is delayed until after second Vespers of the Sundays. As we have seen (**115-16**), Mass is later in the day in Lent, but usually after Nones: a position after second Vespers would surely be unlikely, even in monastic communities. Easter Mass reverts to its position after Terce. During Easter time the service is written after second Vespers or after the stocks of Benedictus antiphons and before the stocks of daily lessons:

Pas 2: crhdmo ihad (LR)12 GO B5 **I**oE(**GAgOOCO**) (L3)4

Because of the stocks which occur on or around the Rogation days the Masses, given complete, are more in evidence than elsewhere but this emphasis changes immediately the spring feasts begin. On the summer Sundays, which are here worked into the sequence of historie, the Mass occurs after second Vespers on

the first Sunday of a historia, or after the stock of Benedictus antiphons on other Sundays. The placing of Mass within the sequence of offices is therefore after Terce, Nones, or second Vespers, or after Lauds or stocks for Lauds because no material for the little hours occurs. With the relevant differences, the same is true of the placing of Mass within the Sanctorale.
7003 Mass is usually announced by means of a second rubric referring to the day in question. Thus, in the example cited above, showing the order on the second Sunday of Easter, the preceding rubric is *Dominica prima post octavam pasche cap.* and the chapter incipit of first Vespers follows. This rubric begins with a large capital, either blue or black. Immediately before Mass the rubric, capitalized in the same way, is repeated, with *officium* for *cap.* The normal size 2 initial for the introit follows.

Incipitaria
Source G12, essentially a Gradual followed by an Antiphonal, gives only those parts of chants which are sung by soloists: all the items, together with the schemes of initials and capitals, are present as in a normal book, but only the solo sections, such as gradual and alleluia verses and tracts are given complete. Everything else is indicated only by its incipit, or more correctly by its intonation. A source such as this can be very helpful to the musical scholar, since it is often difficult to decide just how far the solo intonations of chants should be taken. A similar problem occurs with the alleluia, where the exact length and final note of the repetition of the alleluia *sine neuma* after the verse may be obscure.[5] The first verse of the sequences included in this manuscript must also have been intoned by a soloist, a point of performance not usually stated or known. The inclusion of the whole *hymnus trium puerorum* suggests an entirely solo performance of verses and refrain: rubrical information already presented clearly indicates the alternation of soloist and choir in Sarum use (**221**).

Some other special books have been mentioned (**840-3**), but of those available none is sufficiently complex to need further description.

Appendix VIII

Catalogues, Inventories, and Editions

8000 The failure of many libraries properly or adequately to catalogue liturgical books has often been lamented. I hope some of the material presented in this book will make it possible for librarians and other scholars more easily to identify the chief sources of the late medieval liturgy. Even to be sure that the single entry 'Breviary' in a catalogue is correct would save much time and fruitless ordering of microfilm. Unfortunately the reasonable desire of librarians and scholars to be complete as well as accurate in their descriptions hinders the appearance of any description at all. When the principles explained in this book are understood, it is easy to distinguish the various categories. In the case of books for the offices it is easy to add the qualification 'monastic' when necessary. Much of the other basic information for an adequate catalogue is a matter of simple geography, counting, and measurement: the location by city, library, and fonds requires no research; the counting and measuring of folios needs little learning; qualifications such as 'illuminated,' 'long-line,' 'two-column,' or 'incomplete' need little perceptive ability. To incorporate information about various subsections such as Psalter or Sanctorale requires a somewhat more careful perusal of the book and of earlier pages in this study. Collation of the source, a technique not described here but easily learnt from any number of convenient handbooks, adds little to the basic description needed for a catalogue and is normally needed only for detailed studies.

None of the above criteria for what I consider to be an adequate catalogue is difficult or very time-consuming to do. When complemented by a list of the introits or responsories as described in appendix II and by a general specification of the schemes of initials and capitals, two pieces of information more difficult and lengthy to achieve, the catalogue begins to include many useful facts.

Omitted from the description so far are the date and provenance. Unless information about these two facts is quickly evident from a statement such as an explicit, not always trustworthy, much long research may be necessary. And the results may be inconclusive. I believe it is the frequent difficulty of deciding on these two pieces of information which makes scholars unwilling to commit themselves to published descriptions. The date, at least, has become an essential part of preliminary work without which all later research is tentative. This is an attitude which, for liturgical books, must be changed. Liturgical scripts and schemes of initials are sufficiently traditional and conservative in the later middle ages that it may well be possible to make errors of many decades on the basis of such evidence alone. As for provenance, not enough evidence about the distribution and ranking of feasts and saints in Europe is known for safe deductions to be made when there is no quickly obvious choice. The same is true of archival evidence about local secular benefactors who may be mentioned in obits or commemorations.

8001 Most of the information about distribution and importance of feasts in the later middle ages can come only from the liturgical books themselves. One begins to sense a circular difficulty. What is necessary to define date and provenance can be studied only in sources whose date and provenance have already been established. My own special research into rhymed offices[1] has forced me to include, even in the briefest of descriptions of manuscripts, a preliminary inventory of the Sanctorale. When sufficient information is accumulated, a statistical plotting of occurrences should, with other known facts, allow families, groups, and schools of manuscripts to emerge more clearly. A detailed textual comparison of specific offices, such as I am undertaking with some 300 sources of the rhymed offices to St Thomas Becket, will certainly allow some conclusions about descent and chronology to be made. In comparisons of this kind, the plainsong must not be ignored. Troublesome to consider in the comparison of such texts, and multiplied geometrically in difficulty for the plainsong, are the variants which make it impossible to compile a normal sort of inventory of textual incipits. Texts which are identical except for a legitimate variant, or an error, within the first words will appear in different places in an alphabetical list. Moreover, one can rarely be sure whether an error has occurred or whether there is a variant which may help to place the source within a family. Methods of accurate comparison have yet to be developed for both text and music and the topic is too complex to be continued here. On the basis of working with plainsong, it seems that an alphabetization by formula rather than strictly by letter (or musical pitch) may be a possible solution. The difficulties, however, make it no less necessary to begin this kind of work if the dissemination and character of the late medieval liturgy is ever to be fully understood.

8002 To summarize the problems of cataloguing, then, it is my belief that scholars should not hesitate to compile, and journals should not hesitate to publish, provisional inventories in which some important information may be missing. The precise order of a catalogue description is perhaps not too significant. It is probably a dream to hope for consistency. My own format, with items listed in the order most convenient for the kind of work I have been involved in recently, is shown below. The amount of information usually depends on the ease with which it can be acquired. Items often left unrecorded are given in brackets.

[Country], City, Library, Fonds, ms number, [previous numbers]
Kind of book (eg, Gradual), [monastic, easy to ascertain only with office books], [provenance], sections (eg, KTSC), [date]
Folios: number, size (height by width, in cm), where and how numbered, [collation]
Miscellaneous basic appearance (eg, two-column, long-line, illuminated, etc)
Musical notation
Explicits, or other obvious references to date, provenance, or Order, etc, with folio numbers
Saints [and obits] in Kalendar, proper offices in Sanctorale, [saints in Litanies, proper names in various commemorative items especially the *Communicantes* and *Memento* prayers (**512**)]
Lists of responsories and Lauds antiphons (for office books) or introits (for Mass books) in comparison with 'standard' lists such as those in appendix II
Initial schemes and colours as suggested in appendix IV
Temporale [folio numbers of main divisions], presence and folio numbers of Trinity Sunday and Corpus Christi, [presence or absence of saints after Christmas]
Other information as time and ease allow.

8003 It may be useful to summarize some of the other methods by which books may be related or in which they may differ. The list below includes references to the section of this study where the matter is discussed in more detail.

(a) the naming of Sundays: by simple chronology, by action, by introit, or by responsory;
(b) R instead of Gr for gradual: officium for introit;
(c) the variability and repetition of versicles and responses (**410, 435-6**), of responsories and refrains and verses in Easter time (**421**);
(d) the variability and repetition of items within stocks, such as canticle antiphons after Christmas (**818-21**) and Easter (**827-32**);
(e) the variability of alleluia verses of Easter time (**724**) and especially after Pentecost (**727**);
(f) the placing of the summer Ember days (**872, 2005-6**);
(g) specific subdivisions of the Common of saints (**746**), and the order of sections in general (**749-50, 889-97**);
(h) the main divisions of the Psalter (**874, 2008**) and the order of the canticles (**885**).

No doubt many other points for comparative study could be assembled, and no doubt some points are more likely to produce quick results than others. Before leaving this topic it remains only to ask the question 'Whence come these variants?' Such an enquiry will probably separate into many different questions such as 'Is this variant common to a use, an Order, a diocese, or is it unique?' and 'Who was responsible for unique, purely local, or more widespread variants? How much discretion did the scribe and the illuminator have? Who was responsible for the planning and format of a liturgical book?' Few of these questions seem to have been asked. The evidence has not been assembled, at least in print. Few answers are therefore available.

Editions

8004 Here is not the place to present a complete theory of editing liturgical books. And having no experience in that specific task I hesitate to make more than a few tentative suggestions. Consistent principles certainly need to be evolved. The appearance of a modern edition and the ease with which a neophyte may use the publication are clearly factors in the reluctance or willingness of researchers to work in liturgical matters.

To be considered is the question as to how far the modern edition will reproduce the format of the original. Those aspects of the original which cause difficulty and confusion should obviously be discarded: those which help to clarify the presentation may be kept. Thus it seems futile to place turn-overs in awkward positions at the end of the next line of text and to separate with a rubric the syllables of a single word. The continuously run-on lines of the manuscript may by clarified for the modern reader with paragraphs and indentations. But it would seem proper to run on items which naturally belong together such as the antiphon and its psalm incipit, or the incipits of chapter, hymn, responsory, and dialogue at the little hours: separate lines for each of the antiphons in the Matins nocturn would probably be overly fussy. Where a judicious use of different sizes of type can allow the editor not to separate items, that principle should probably be followed. Different type styles and in inclusion of larger capital letters can serve to distinguish rubrics from text, for example, and can allow the editor to preserve marginal and internal landmarks much as in the original. It does not seem necessary to keep the two-column format although to do so makes the edition more like the original.

Running heads giving, on the left-hand page, the section of the manuscript and, on the right hand page, the liturgical day or feast make it very easy for the user to orient himself in the book:

COMMON OF SAINTS   BISHOPS NOT MARTYRS

or

PSALTER: WEDNESDAY   LAUDS: Pss 63-4

Calendar rubrics denoting Sundays or major feasts should be centred on the page in prominent, large type either after a substantial space or even beginning a new page. Rubrics denoting ferias may be in bold capitals after a space, and services within the day may be stated by means of bold letters at the margin. But each category should be distinct. Large initials and initials of size 2 should be kept at the margin, and larger capitals should be used, as in the manuscripts, to articulate the text within the page. Rubrics should be in italic type, and, also as in the original, texts set to music should be smaller in size. None of these suggestions is surprising, and all may be modified as necessary. The main principle is that some consistent hierarchy should appear. To suggest procedures in technical matters of this kind is perhaps to encroach on the province of the designer of the edition, but unless he has a clear understanding of the hierarchy of the material to be printed he can advise only on esthetic and typographical appearance. Liturgical clarity is perhaps more important.

8005 Two other matters must be mentioned. They concern editorial additions and editorial omissions. Where the source is inconsistent in showing rubrics of identification, for example, the editor should add them in some way. Where the editor adds text or text within a rubric the device of brackets [ ] is useful: it seems clumsy where only a single letter is involved [A]. I see no objection to such additions being made tacitly, without editorial fuss, just as most abbreviations may be realized without typographical differentiation. Of more concern is editorial omission. Where the manuscript merely duplicates a long standard text, such as a gospel, many editors merely list the incipit. A note showing where the complete text may be found is sometimes added. In view of the ubiquitous abbreviation to be found in the originals themselves, it seems absolutely necessary in some way to distinguish between editorial and manuscript shortening. Furthermore, it is surely important, if comparisons are to be made, to note where the source differs even from a truly standard text such as a gospel. The editorial abbreviation, reference to a source of the complete text, and the recording of variants and errors could perhaps be included in a footnote.

Many of these devices are of course already in use. Perhaps more than in most similar areas of editing it is the responsibility of the editor to indicate clearly to the publisher what is necessary regarding typographical styles, formats, punctuation, and similar matters. Many of the editions in the noted series published by the Henry Bradshaw Society demonstrate both good and bad features mentioned above, and all should be studied. Different kinds of sources no doubt call for different methods of editing, but there are surely some respects in which all editions should or could agree.

Appendix IX: Facsimiles

9000 The plates have been arranged so that manuscripts of different types follow one another. The reader can then detect, without constant reference to the headings, where a succession of leaves from one source ends and leaves of another begin. The headings are intended only to identify the source as briefly as possible; where appropriate, detailed descriptions of what the leaves show follow each heading.

The plates are not meant to be read in detail, although it is possible in many cases to do so, even with the naked eye. Rubrics, in particular, may be illegible, either because the paint in the original manuscript has disappeared, or because it was not possible to obtain better reproductions (in order to bring the grey rubrics to a darker image, the long exposure would have caused the black text to bleed, blurring the script). In any case, more important are the general appearance of the page, the relationship between grey and black, between initial and capital, large and small script, long and short texts.

Following are descriptions and, where possible, inventories of the leaves, using the abbreviations adopted for this book (see pages xv–xix).

FRONTISPIECE

Sarum (Ranworth) Antiphonal, source A19, f 1

Reproduced by permission of the Vicar, Churchwardens, and the Parochial Church Council of St Helen's, Ranworth

Advent Sunday, beginning with general rubrics including the tone for the dialogue, *Deus in adiutorium*, and later for the Vespers chapter, *Erit in*. Between the two tones are instructions for performing psalms and antiphons, and at the end of the leaf for performing the responsory at Vespers. The Advent Vespers responsory, *Ecce dies*, ends the leaf. The leaf therefore deals with Vespers in general, and Advent Vespers in particular.

The distinction between size 2 coloured and calligraphic letters is clear: apart from the large initial, the only other capital is the normal size 0 internal capital letter. The notation is standard square, but uses more diamond-shaped notes than are usual in true plainsongs because these are reciting tones. The w-shaped sign at the end of staves is the *custos* or direct which indicates the next pitch on the following stave. On this leaf, there are C, F, and B flat clefs, and some B natural signs.

Compare plate 14a

PLATE 1

Monastic English Breviary, source B7, ff 75v-81
Oxford, Bodleian Lib ms Univ College 101, reproduced by permission of the Master and Fellows of University College, Oxford

1a 75v column 2 Dominica 2 after Ephiphany (here called *Theophania*) CHdMO I
76 H(App)3 LR L (other material added at foot of leaf)
1b 76v R(LR)2 (nocturn 2 at foot of column 1) (App)3d (LR)2 L
77 RLR AK2
1c 77v Kd GLRL
78 R(LR)2 G
1d 78v (Lauds two-thirds down column 1) ApppAApAp CRH
79 dB oHHaCdoHahCdO
1e 79v HaCdO (Ap)4 cRHdMo A2 (these are canticle antiphons for the week) H
80 H (alternative hymn for Compline) d □ O
1f 80v □ O (feria ii) I H App(Ap)3d (LR)2 L
81 R (L *in estate* and R *breve*) d (App)3 CO (column 2, Lauds) (Ap)4 CRH

The size 2 initials clearly alternate colour, as to the size 1+ capitals of the hymn and canticle verses and in the preces. Highlights can be detected in the ordinary capitals of normal internal sentences. The distinction in size between spoken and sung text is very clear.

1a

1b

1c

1d

1e

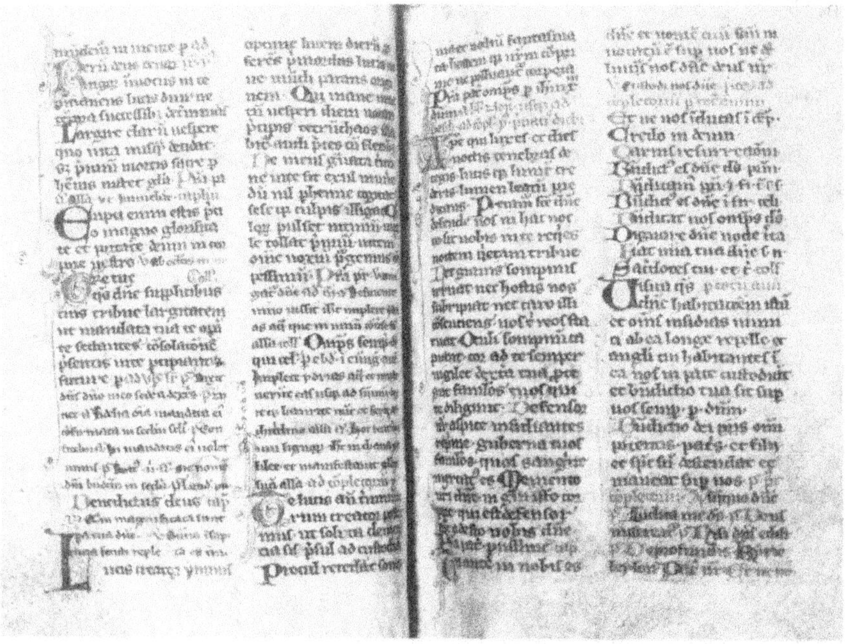

1f

PLATE 2

Monastic English Breviary, source B7, ff 35v-7
Oxford, Bodleian Library ms Univ College 101, reproduced by permission of the Master and Fellows of University College, Oxford

2a 35v (Lauds begins on previous page) (Ap)4 crHdBo acacd (column 2) oaCdOaCdO acRhMo (feria ii) Ih
Note the rubric at the foot of the leaf directing the user to find the ferial lessons at the beginning of the book.
36 (Lauds) ahBM (feria iii) BM (feria iiij) BM (feria v) BM (feria vj) BM (sabb) D c C8

2b 36v C6 (various rubrics attached to this stock of chapters) □
37 O3 □ O3

The alternating styles and colours of the initials and capitals are as in plate 1. The nearly complete column of smaller script in 2a signals the occurrence of a stock of items, in this case, antiphons for ferial Benedictus and Magnificat. The regular and equally-spaced appearance of size 2 initials in 2a, column 4, and 2b, column 1, signals the appearance of stocks of texts, in this case, the ferial chapters.

2a

2b

PLATE 3

Cistercian Gradual, source G4, ff 4v-6v
Graz, Univ Lib ms IV 9, reproduced by permission of the University Library, Graz

3a 4v (end of offertory)**C** (sabb) **IV● GV**
3b 5 (**GV**)3
3c 5v **H** with refrain, *Et laudabilis*, eight verses, and doxology
3d 6 compare plate 7b (end of **H**) **TVV**
3e 6v **OC** (Dominica iiii) **IV● G**

Compare plate 15.
The musical notation is standard *hufnagel* or Gothic, using both C and F clefs simultaneously. Several B flats and naturals occur, and some might be a later additions. The incises through the stave are presumably performance marks, indicating where the solo intonation ends, or where breaks for breathing may be made. At the end of each stave, just in the margin, is the direct, or *custos*, which indicates the first pitch of the following stave. The distinction between the size 2 initial of *Veni* and the size 1+ capitals elsewhere is clear, as is the difference between the size 1+ capitals themselves, by either colour or ornamental style.

3a

3b

3c

3d

3e

PLATE 4

French Noted Breviary, source NB2, ff 7v-10
Paris, Bibl de l'Arsenal ms 279, reproduced by permission of Phot. Bibl nat, Paris

These folios are from the Psalter.

4a–c 7v-10 (end of Ps 16) A2a2 (Ps 17) A2a2 (Ps 18) A2a2 (Ps 19) A2a2 ()s 20) A2 D (Ap)5 chd (Ps 21)

The evovae formula or the incipit of the psalm with the relevant tone is usually present after each antiphon or group of antiphons. The noticeably longer section with chants on 4c, with the prominent size 2 initial a short distance after the section begins, denotes the appearance of Lauds, whose five ferial antiphons are emphasized, as in the Temporale, by the initial.

4a

4b

4c

PLATE 5

French Noted Breviary, source NB2, ff 52v-3
Paris, Bibl de l'Arsenal ms 279, reproduced by permission of Phot. Bibl nat, Paris

The opening shows the Litany, with decorative filler between the saint's name and *ora*. Dialogues and prayers follow.

5

PLATE 6

Italian Breviary, source B73, f 13
Chicago, Newberry Lib ms 71, courtesy of the Newberry Library, Chicago

This shows the end of the *rubrica generalis* and beginning of the pica, with general instructions and references to days occupying the whole column, then the service on the left and incipits on the right of the subdivided column. Here Christmas Day is on Sunday, and the second column ends with feria iii of the fourth week. The paraph symbol appears several times, although its colour does not seem to be different. In the pica, it denotes the beginnings of days.

6

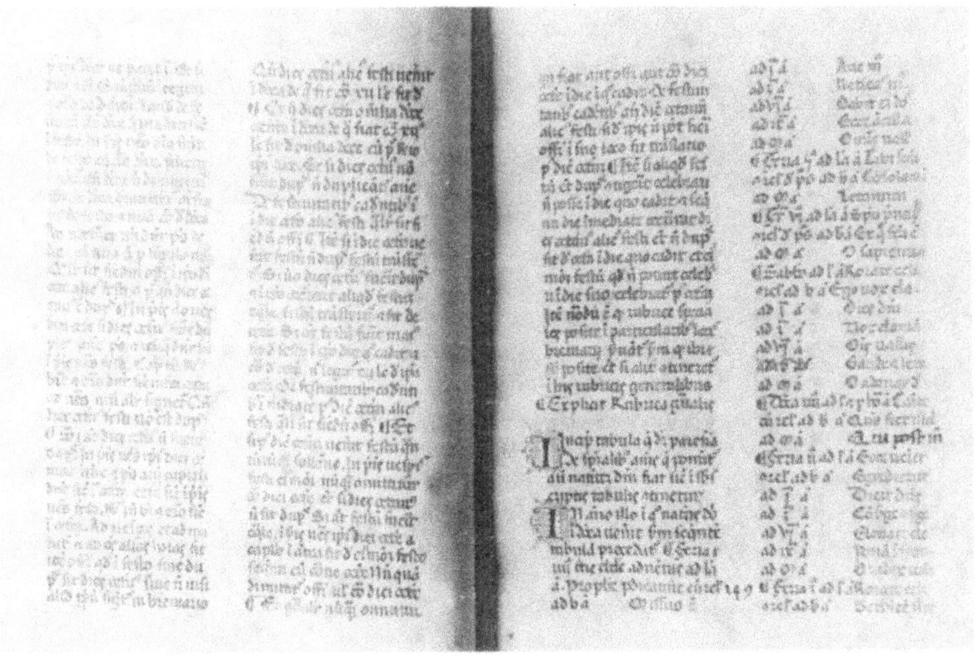

PLATE 7

Sarum Gradual, source G16, ff5v-6, 2v-3, and 22v-3
London, British Lib ms Cotton Nero E VIII, reproduced by permission of the British Library

7a 5v (end of a sequence, whose last versicle is said three times, according to the rubric) **OC** (each with an ending for Easter time) (Holy Innocents) **IV k** (with incipit of trope text) l **gav** sequence
6 (end of sequence) **oC** (Thomas of Canterbury rubric erased) **IV k** (with incipit of trope text l **gav** sequence

Note the alternating colour of the capitals in the sequences, and the distinctively regular notation of the syllabically set sequences, especially compared with the irregular and melismatic offertory in column 1.

7b 2v compare plates 3d and e
(end of **H**) **TVV OV** (n.b. the offertory verse, not present in plate 3e) C (Dominica iiij) **IV**
3 **lg AV** sequence **Oc** (rubric *ut supra in quarta feria proxima precdent* (Christmas Eve) **I** = ***ll*G**

Note the prominent capital I for *In vigilia.*

7c 22v-3 (end of **G** and its **V**) **A** (with two verses, the second for use at Easter Vespers) seq **OC** (feria ii) **I**

7a

7b

7c

PLATE 8

Monastic English Missal, source M3, ff 74v-5
London, British Library ms Harley 5289, reproduced by permission of the British Library

The gospel ends, followed by **OOCO** (Dominica ii) **IOET**, demonstrating the five closely spaced size 2 initials, the middle one introducing smaller script. In this case, the script is minimally smaller, and the distinction is perhaps more of lateral compression.

8

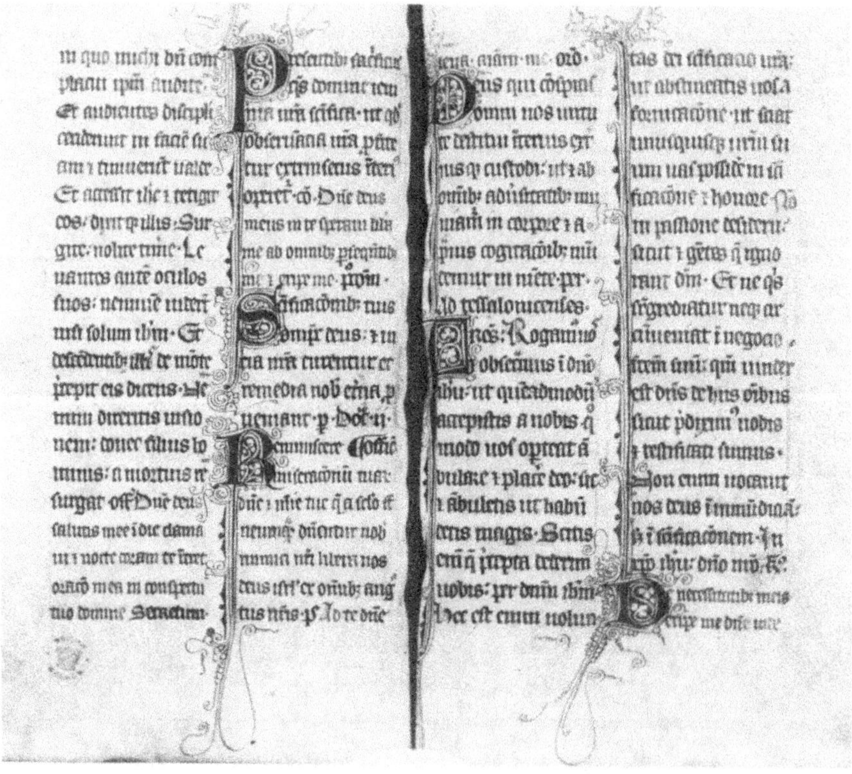

PLATE 9

Norwich Missal, source M5, ff 102v-3
London, British Library ms add 25588, reproduced by permission of the British Library

This shows the part of the Ordo listing the Gloria incipits with their music: the remainder of the text is in column 4. In column 1 is the common prayer, *Aufer a nobis*.

9

PLATE 10

French Missal, source M6, opening clxvi
Manchester, John Rylands Univ Lib ms L 151, reproduced by permission of the John Rylands University Library of Manchester

This shows the part of the Ordo preceding the Preface, *Vere dignum*, with the large initial P for the *Per omnia* concluding the offertory cycle. That concluding formula, the immediately following liturgical greeting (*Dominus vobiscum*), and the other versicles and responses, and the Preface itself are normally supplied with the proper musical tones, for which space has been left but not filled in this source.

10

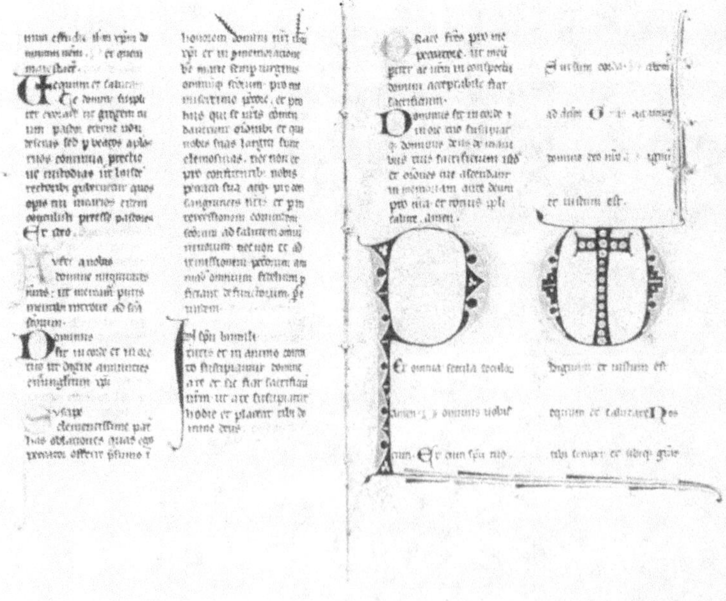

PLATE 11

Sarum Breviary, source B12, ff 8v-9
London, British Library ms Harley 512, reproduced by permission of the British Library

This shows the end of Advent Sunday, with numerous rubrics including text incipits. The rubrics are paragraphed by clearly evident paraph signs. Feria ii begins at the top of column 3. After more rubrics and incipits there are three lessons, and the leaf ends with preces in continuous line rather than in subdivided columns: the small capitals of alternating colour make the preces distinct, especially when compared with the internal capitals of the lessons in column 3.

11

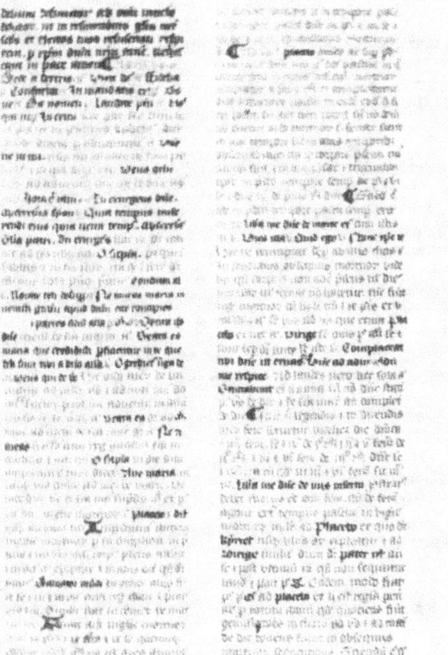

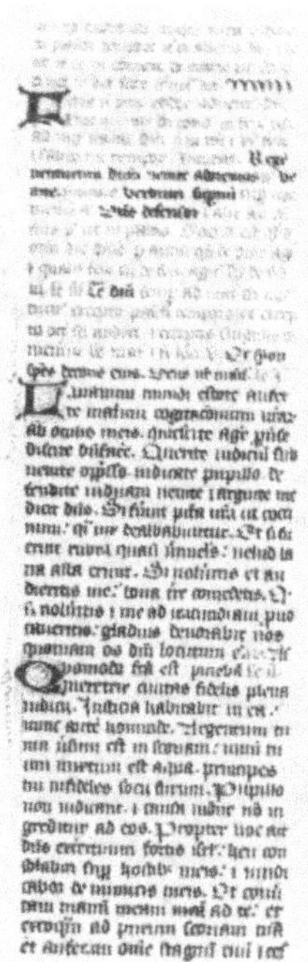

PLATE 12

Czech Noted Breviary, source NB4, ff 2v-3
Breviarium Olomucense seu Libri horarum, mss of the Benedictine Monastery at Rajhrad, sign. R 625, 626, now in the holdings of the University Library in Brno

This shows the end of an invitatory tone, a complete invitatory tone (note the initials VQQHQG), and most of a third. There are musical scribbles in the lower margin.

Compare plate 17.

12

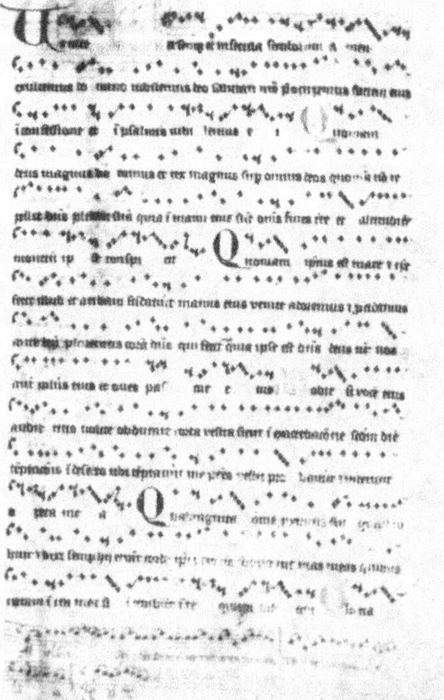

PLATE 13

French Missal, source M6, opening vi
Manchester, John Rylands Univ Lib ms L 151, reproduced by permission of the John Rylands University Library of Manchester

This shows the repeated pattern **OLG** or **OLT**: (end of lesson) **G** (**OLT**)2 Gospel. The gradual and tracts have the usual verses.

13

PLATE 14

French Noted Breviary, source NB2, ff 54-60
Paris, Bibl de l'Arsenal ms 279, reprinted by permission of Phot. Bibl nat, Paris

14a 54 compare the frontispiece
First Vespers of the first Sunday of Advent
Ap (note the psalm incipit is shown as *Ipsum*, indicating the same text as that of the antiphon) = (Ap)4 CRH (only the first stanza of the hymn has the chant)

14b 55v-56 The first Sunday of Advent, the word *fideles* ending the second antiphon of nocturn 1. Then: p4+ Ap4+ DL and the first R with rubrics and three verses continuing on
56 (LR)2 (the second of these Rs has an alternative ferial verse). At the foot of the column is the beginning of the first antiphon of nocturn 2, *Nature.*

14c 56v (Ap)3 D (LR)2
57 LR (Ap)3 D G LR

14d 57v-58 (LR)2 (incipits for the ferial responsory, and rubrics about the Te Deum, and Gloria and Ite missa est) d (Ap)5
58 CHdB = h H (four different chants are given for this hymn, to subsequent stanzas, with rubrics specifying the occasions for each)

14e 58v-59 rubrics and incipits for Prime of Advent Sunday, then CR●
followed by preces in subdivided columns
59 more rubrics and incipits, then 94 = H

14f 59v (several chants for the preceding hymn) appp● c R● ro = H appp● O R●
60 DH appp C R● dpcrhdM (feria ii) Ihapd LL

Apart from the large initials, there are several sizes of letter: the size 2 initial takes up three lines when it precedes text, and one line and the stave when it comes before a musical item. Within the textual items, internal sentences use capitals of size 0. Musical items after the first of a group use size 1+ calligraphic capitals: internal sections within the musical items, such as psalm incipits or the repetenda of responsories, take a smaller capital. The notation is standard square. There are no directs.

14a

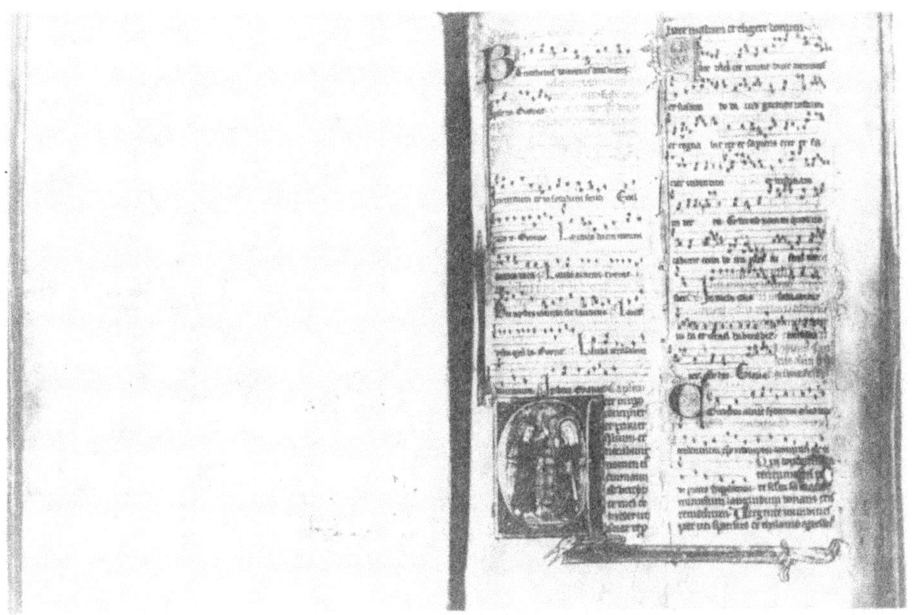

14b

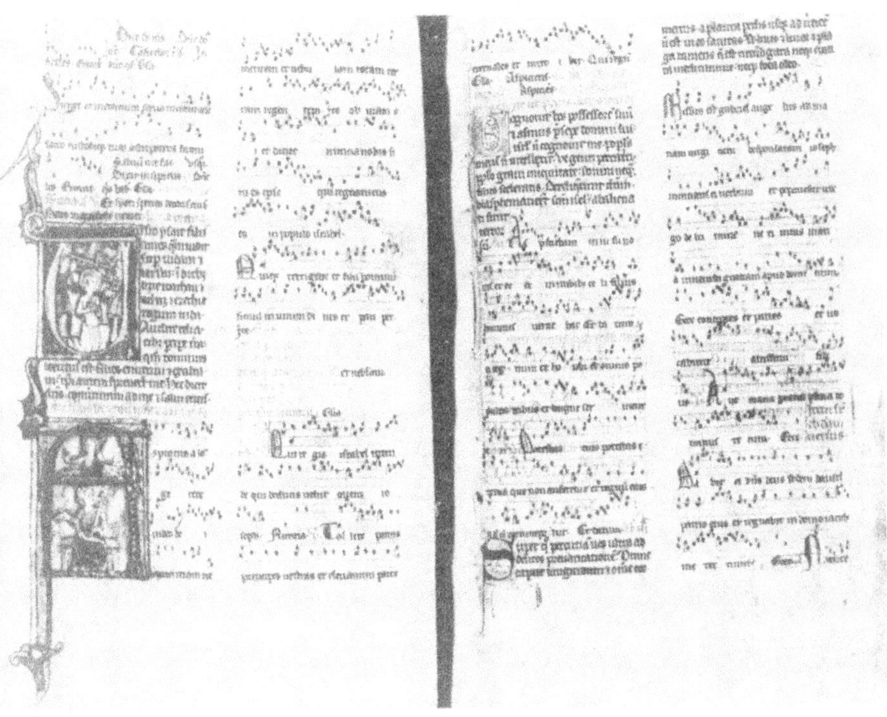

14c

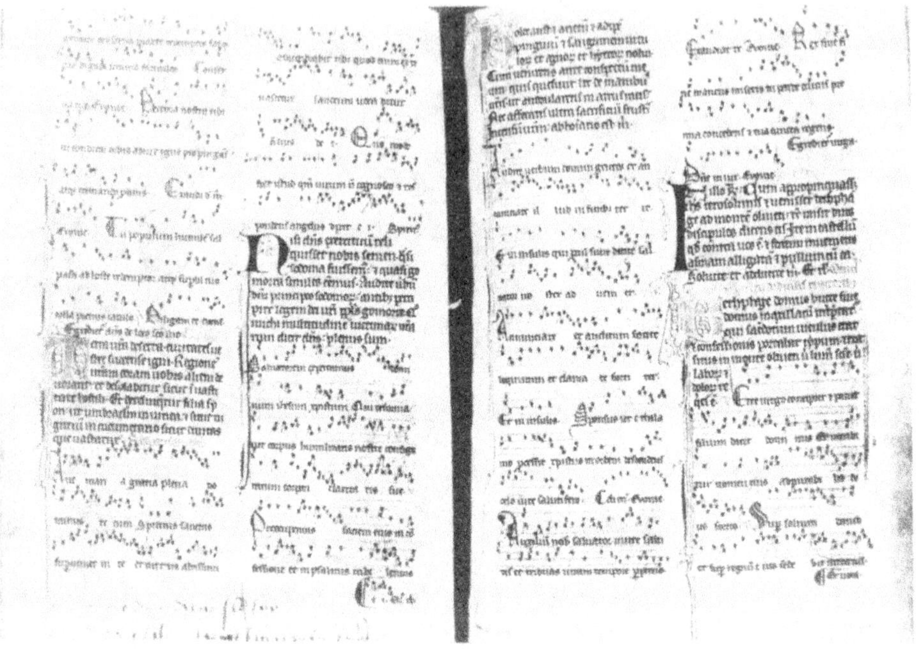

14d

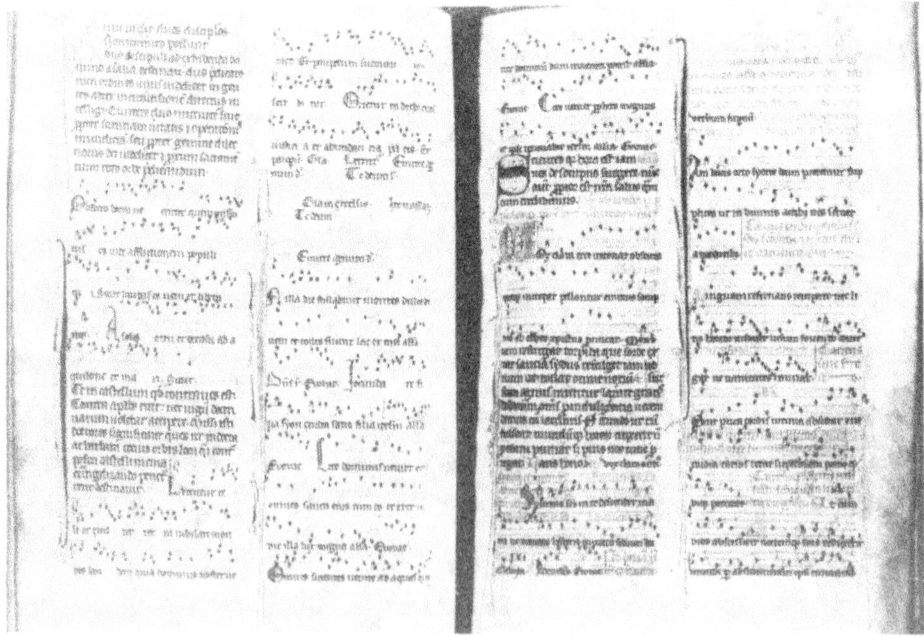

14e

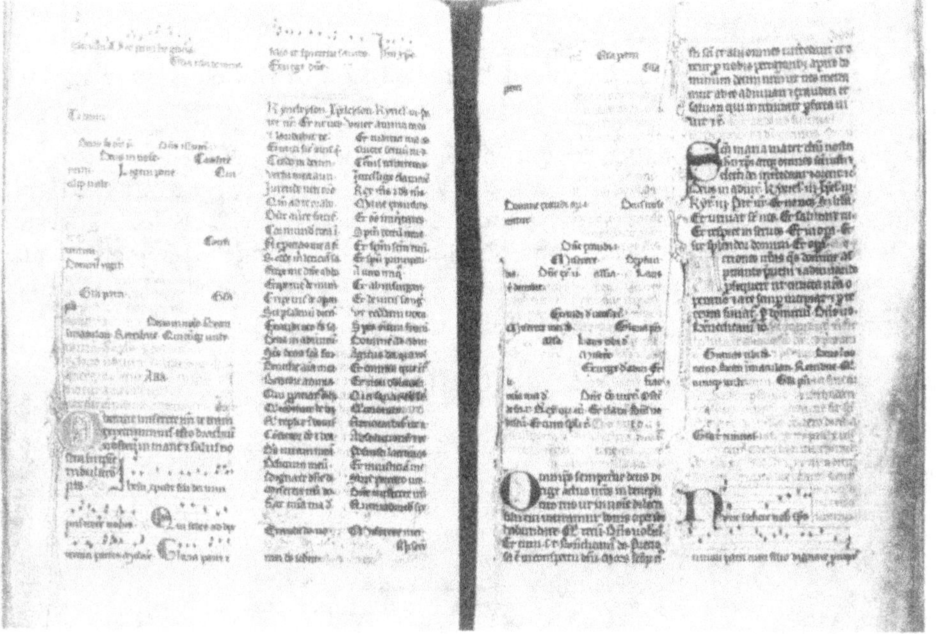

14f

PLATE 15

Cistercian Gradual, source G4, f 2
Graz, Univ Lib ms IV 9, reproduced by permission of the University Library, Graz

This shows the initial of the Advent introit, with a size 2 initial for the second letter. The items of the leaf are **IV● GV AV**.

The notation is described under plate 3. In stave nine the C clef is changed to a different line, and the scribe has highlighted the change with incises: such changes of clef, if not emphasized in some way, can be difficult to notice. The introit chant appears in square notation in plate 24.

15

PLATE 16

French Noted Missal, source NM3, ff 15v-16
Rouen, Bibl mun ms 227 (Y50), reproduced with permission

This shows the repeated pattern OLG (the gradual here preceded by R for responsorium): **G** (OL**G**)2 OL.

The notation is standard square, using only C clefs on these leaves: in column 2 between the words *facias* and *nos* the C clef changes without special emphasis and could easily be mistaken for a ligature.

There are no directs.

16

PLATE 17

Czech Noted Breviary, source NB4, ff 5v-6
Breviarum Olomucense seu Libri horarum, mss of the Benedictine Monastery at Rajhrad, sign. R 625, 626, now in the holdings of the University of Brno

Advent 1 (Lauds) (Ap)5 ChdB oao hApCRDo hApcRDo hApCRD hACRD aphdM = (feria ii) IhadL

The notation seems to be a simplified form of Gothic. Both C and F clefs appears on these leaves. There are no directs. As in columns 1 and 2, the size 2 initial for chapters sometimes appears within the writing area rather than at the margin.

PLATE 18

French Noted Missal, source NM3, ff 135-7
Rouen, Bibl mun ms 227 (Y5O), reproduced by permission

These leaves transmit the solemn O prayers of Good Friday, followed by the reproaches, *Agios o Theos*, and the adoration of the Cross, with the items *Ecce lignum* and *Crucem tuam*.

17

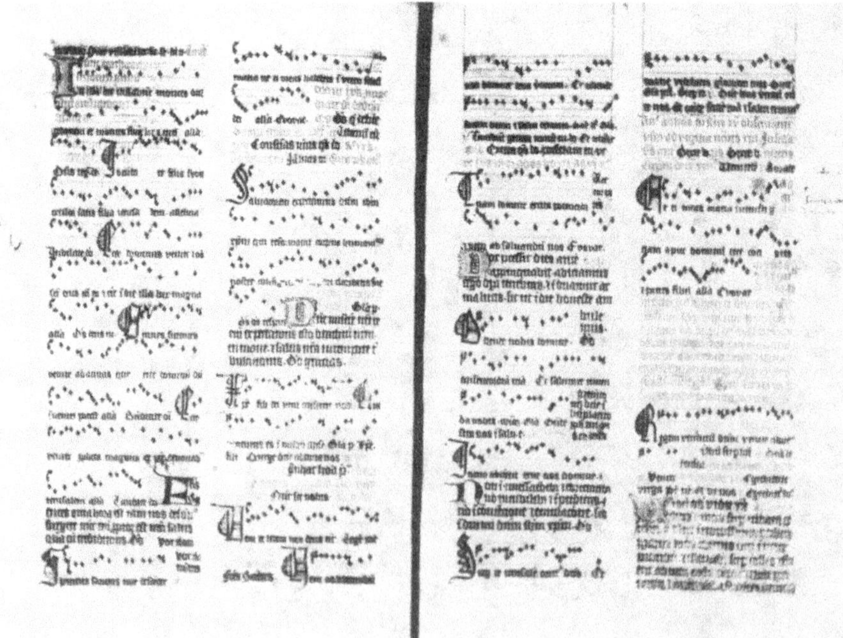

18a

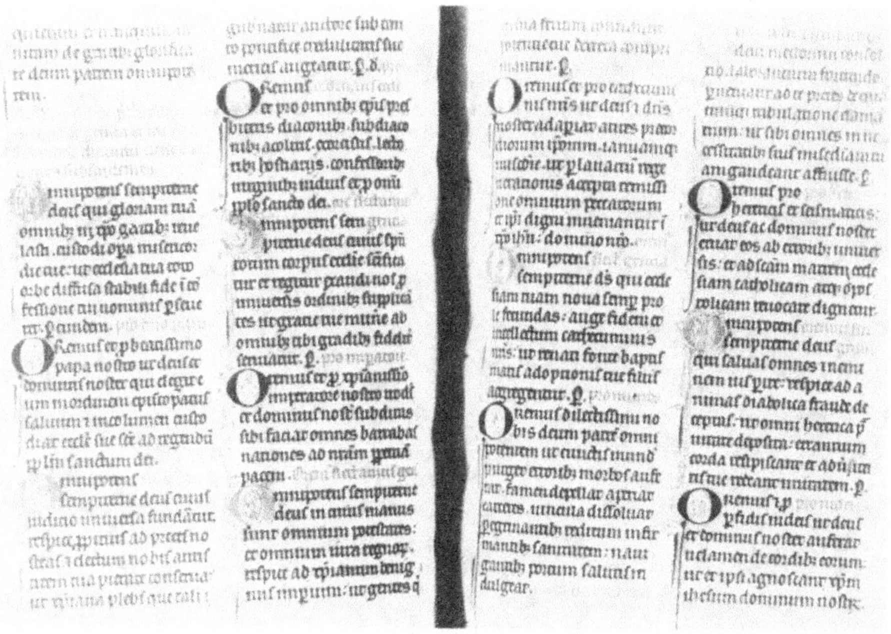

18b

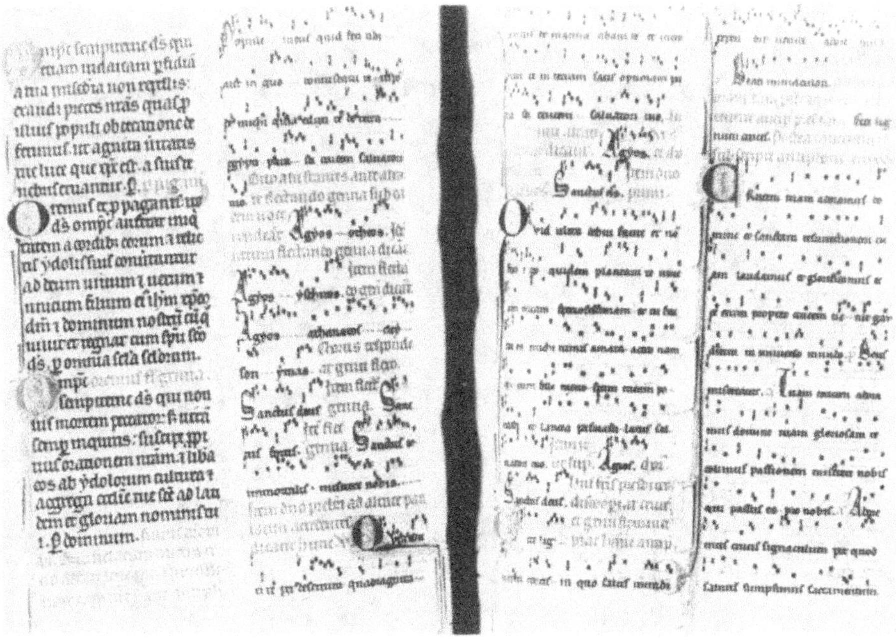

PLATE 19

Augustinian Missal, source M2, ff 16v-17
London, Brit Lib ms add 24198, reproduced by permission of the British Library

This shows the prayer, *Communicantes*, with the saints' names highlighted, followed by the next two prayers of the Canon, *Hanc igitur* and *Quam oblationem*.

19

PLATE 20

York Missal, source M1, folios not numbered
Cambridge, Sidney Sussex College ms 33, reproduced by permission of the Master and Fellows of Sidney Sussex College, Cambridge

This shows part of the Ordo: the *Per omnia* formula concluding the Canon, and the beginning of the Embolism, *Preceptis*, with the *Pater noster*. The notation is standard square, using rather more diamond-shaped notes than true plainsong, because the text is intoned rather than sung.

20

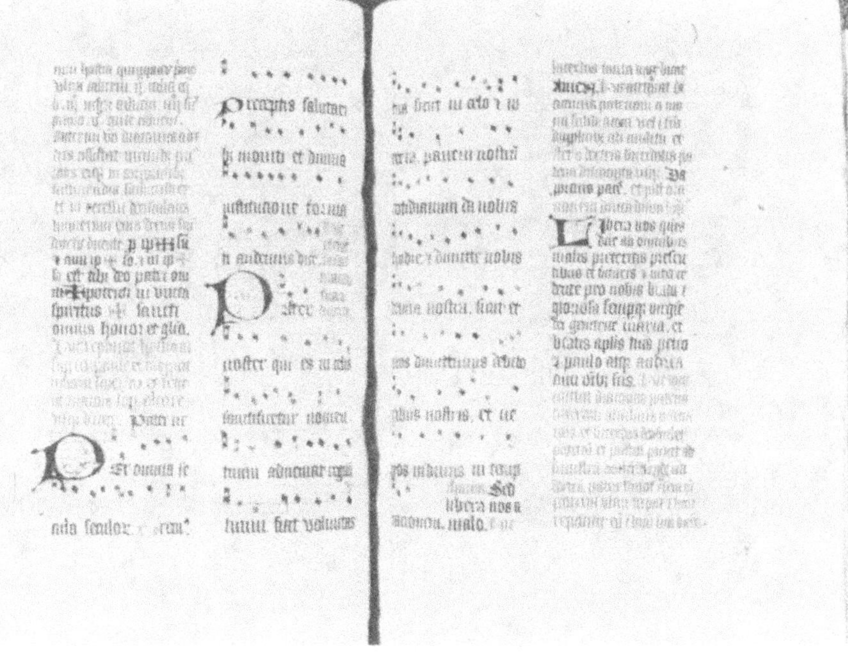

PLATE 21

French Missal, source M6, opening cxxvii
Manchester, John Rylands Univ Lib ms L 151, reproduced by permission of the John Rylands University Library of Manchester

The first three words conclude the previous alleluia. Then:
G OOCO (feria iii) **IV** O L **AVAV** G **O**

This shows the pattern of five closely adjacent size 2 initials, in which the third begins script of smaller size. In this case, the character of the fifth initial as a size 2 letter is obscured because, being on the bottom line of the column, it is bent around underneath the text. Two other normal Is occur. Beginning the internal sentences of the gospels are size 1 capital letters, which can be seen to have highlights.

21

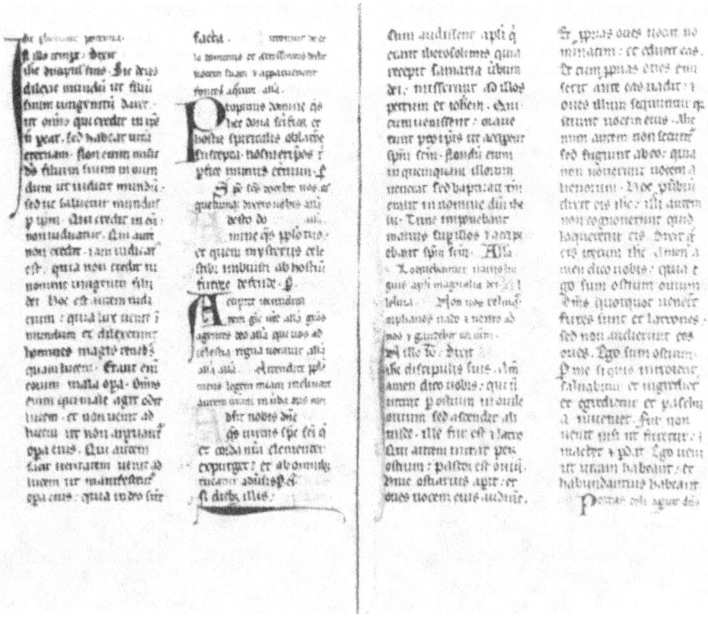

PLATE 22

Sarum (Ranworth) Antiphonal, source A19, ff 52v-61
Reproduced by permission of the Vicar, Churchwardens, and the Parochial Church Council of St Helen's, Ranworth

This is a rubricated Antiphonal which also often gives the complete texts of some non-musical items.

22a 52v (Dominica ii post oct. Epi) ap (psalm incipit is *Ipsum*, see plate 14) O lg BM (Dominica iii) O lg BM (Dominica iiij) O lg BM (Dominica v) O lg BM
53 (Dominica in LXX) A ap CrhdMO = ih ap l R3 ap l R3
22b 53v-54 apd gl R3 = (R2 for ferias) d Ap (the whole psalm verse is given with its tone) (Ap)4
22c 54v chdrBo = Appp ApCRd ApCR
55 d apchdM = A8 (stock of ferial antiphons for B and M)
22d 55v (Dominica in LX) ap CrhdMO I h apd l R3 apd l R3 apd gl R3
22e 56v d (Ap)5 chdBo Ap Apc ApC ApC
57 apchdMo A4 (stock) of ferial antiphons for B and M) (Dominica in L) apCrhdMO ih ap l R3
22f 57v ap d l R3 ap d gl R3 (R2 for ferias) d (Ap) 4
22g 58v Ap chdBo Ap Apc ApC ApC apchdMo (feria ii) B (feria iii) M (feria iv in capite jejunii) R3 d CBO AdO crdMO Ado
22h 59v = (feria v) dcBO chdmO (feria vi) dcBO cHdMO (sabb) iH ap dd apc H
60 d BO (Dominica i XL) apCHdrMO ApcRH

The difference between the coloured size 2 initial and the calligraphic size 1 + 1 capital is clear. There is a noticeable difference between the size 2 initial for textual items, and the coloured 1 + 1 initial for musical items: the latter is much larger. Within the rubrics the coloured size 1 + capitals stand out: they are mostly Ds or Fs for Dominica or feria.

22a

22b

22c

22d

22e

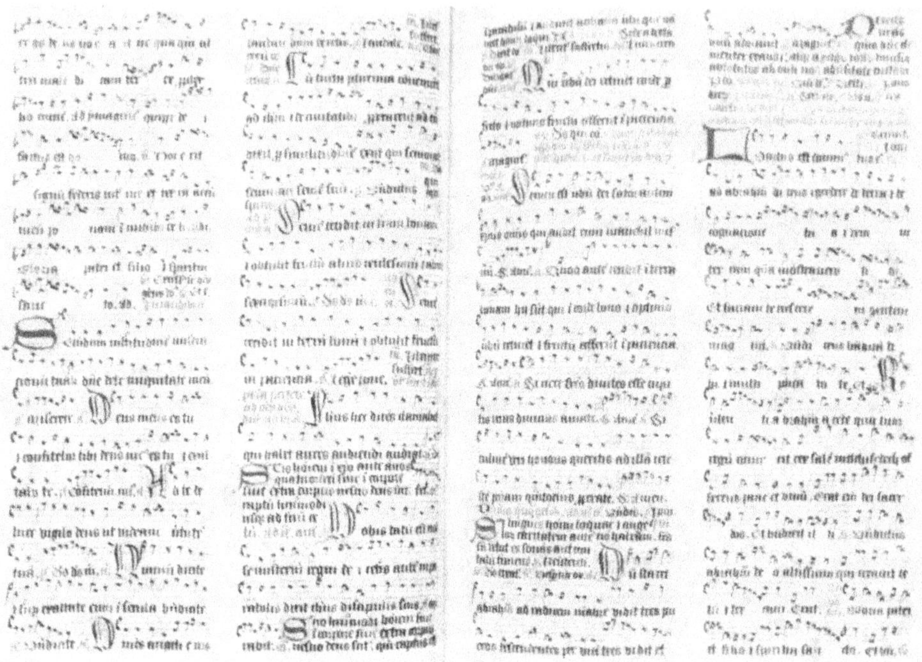

22f

22g

22h

PLATE 23

Missal, Tournai, Bibl centrale, ms 13/10, ff 44v-5
Reproduced by permission of the Librarian

This shows the end of one Preface, with the word *dicentes* followed by the Sanctus, at the foot of the left-hand page. On the right-hand page is the proper Preface for Christmas and its week: the *Vere dignum* symbol is here combined with the E for *Eterne*. The notation is Gothic, using C and F clefs.

23

PLATE 24

Sarum Noted Missal, source NM1, ff 15v-16
Manchester, John Rylands Univ Lib ms L 24, reproduced by permission of the John Rylands University Library of Manchester

This opening shows the two variants for the aspersion before Mass, *Asperges me*, and for Easter time, *Vidi aquam*, followed by a dialogue, *Ostende nobis* . . . , and the prayer, *Exaudi nos*. The item which follows, *Missus est*, is a long and elaborate processional antiphon. Various rubrics with incipits follow, including references to the Benedicamus Domino, Gloria, and Ite missa est. The Advent Mass then begins: **IV g** O2 L.

The notation is standard square, with no directs, using only C clefs on these leaves: several B flats appear, and the C clef is changed on several occasions within the stave (eg, column 2, staves 1, 3, 4, 8, and 9). The verse of the introit, beginning *Vias tuas*, has the introit tone characterized by more repetition of a single pitch (C in this case, aligning with the clef) than in the introit itself.

24

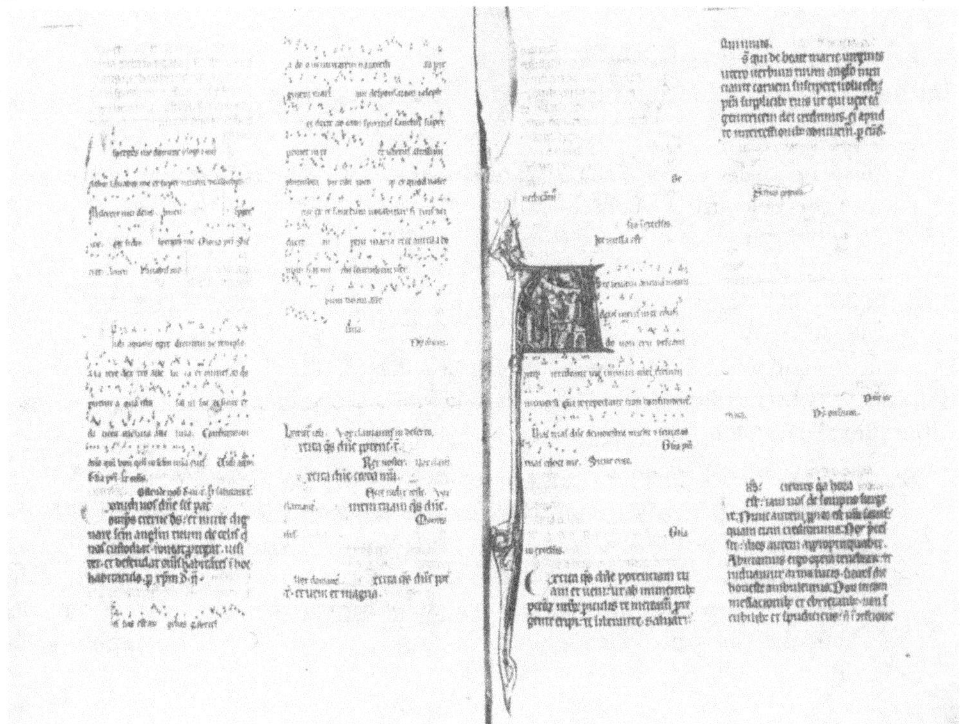

25

PLATE 25

Franciscan Breviary, source B73, ff 9v-10
Chicago, Newberry Lib ms 71, reproduced courtesy of the Newberry Library, Chicago

9v (end of lesson 4) RV (D [*Jube domne* . . . ✠] RV(2 (nocturn 3) Ap = G and the beginning of the homily

PLATE 26

Dominican Antiphonal, source A1, ff 19v-20, 22v-3, 52v-3
Bruxelles, Bibl royale Albert Ier, ms 6429-30, copyright Bibliothèque royale Albert Ier, Bruxelles

26a 19v (Dominica 3 of Advent, end of Matins) RVRV (Lauds) ApA3
Note the thin size 1 + 1 initials for the responsories compared with the 'square' 1 + 1 initial V for the first antiphon of Lauds. Subsequent Lauds antiphons have only a 1 + capital, as do the responsory verses: psalm incipits have a capital distinctly smaller, but larger than the letter with which the responsory repetenda begins. The evovae has no capital letter at all.

26b 22v-3 (ferias iv to vi of Advent 3) RV BM BM (vi) i R
The rubric for feria v is omitted.

26c 52v-3 Br (Epi) D M AN (Ap)3 D R
The rubric on f 52v reads *Ad vesperas R. In columbe. V Reges tharsis et insule munera offerent Reges arabum et saba dona adducent.* This is not a responsory and verse, as it appears: the presence of a complete verse text with a responsory incipit would be very unlikely. Rather it is the responsory incipit followed by the complete dialogue (also given before the first responsory of Matins on f 53)

This Dominican manuscript illustrates the considerable care for informative details and layout that characterizes most sources of Dominican origin. The Magnificat, Benedictus; and Nunc dimittis canticles are preceded by the abbreviation *can* rather than the strictly incorrect *ps*; the incises in the musical stave demonstrate a care for the correct placement of the words in performance, and the double incises show where the solo incipit ends. In general the layout has been anticipated, so that staves are broken where rubrics will be added later. On the other hand, at the top fo f 53, between *thus* and *deferentes*, there seems to have been a miscalculation; at the beginning of the responsory there is a similar overestimate of the space required for the music.

26a

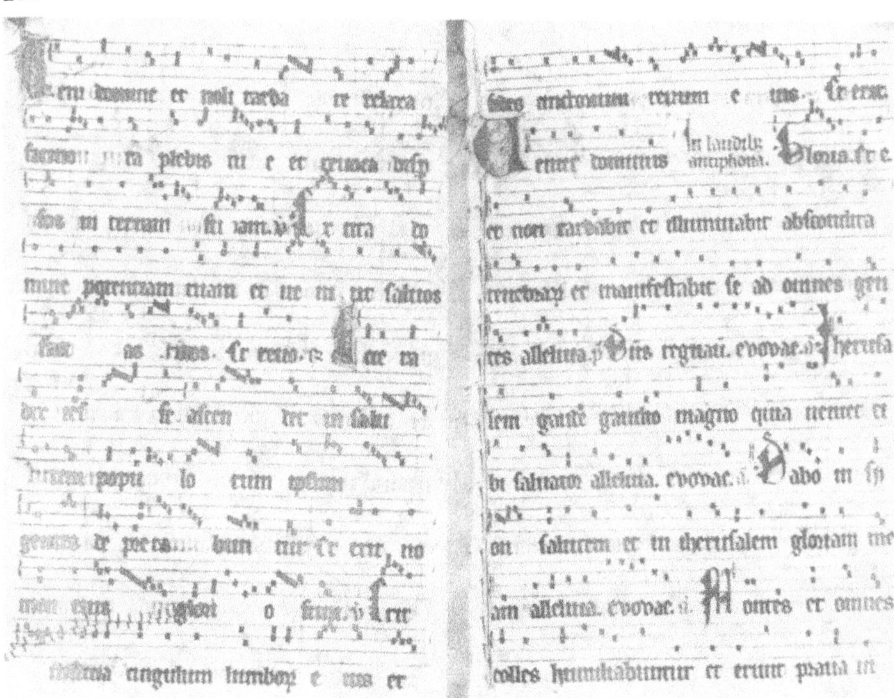

26b

26c

PLATE 27

Details of plate 22d, 22e (pages 345-6)

27a

27b

27c

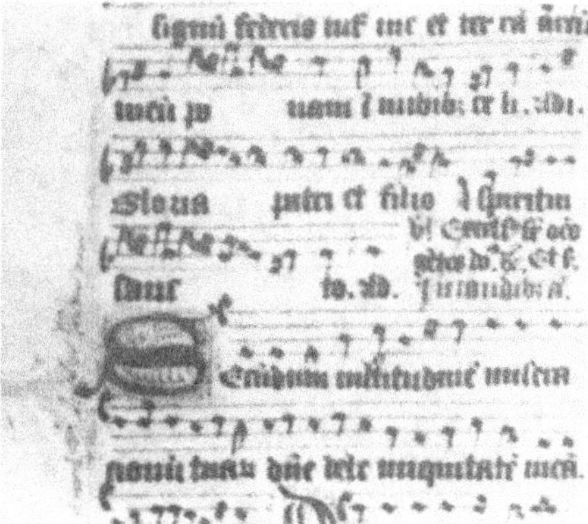

PLATE 28

Details of plate 17 (page 338)

28a

28b

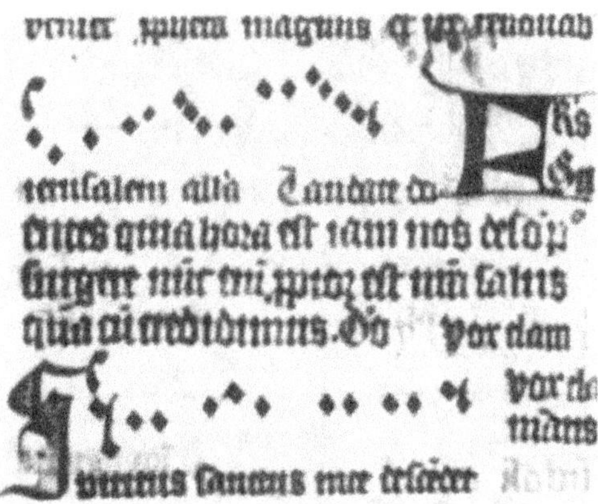

28c

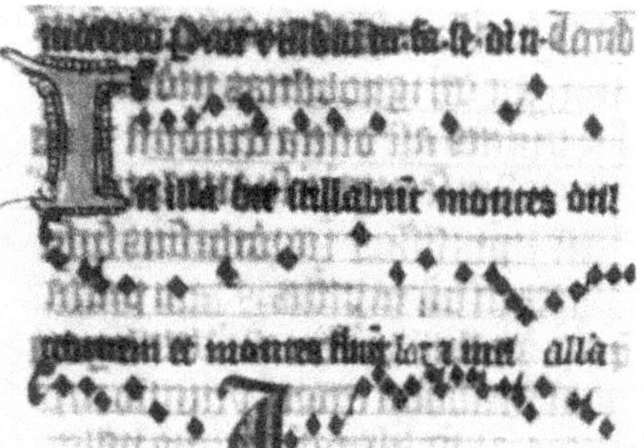

28d

Notes

INTRODUCTION

1 Van Dijk (1957) 14
2 Poole 2
3 Van Dijk (1957) 13; also J. Van der Veen 'Les Aspects musicaux des chansons de geste' *Neophilogus* 41 (1957) 82-100
4 Vogel 9
5 Ibid x
6 When referring to the liturgical organization or to the written-down 'table' in which it is codified, I prefer to spell the word with a K: this not only distinguishes it from the secular version but also allows the initial to be used in abbreviations, where C would be confused with Compline, chapter, etc.
7 Apel (1958) 28
8 BS 1531 and MS, occasionally BS 1555 and MS (Legg)
9 MR
10 Bailey ix-x
11 Tolhurst
12 Van Dijk (1960 and 1963)
13 Bonniwell, passim; Boyle 367-75
14 Eg AS (source A13), and GS (source G14)
15 Eg Loriquet
16 Bukofzer 217-310
17 References omitted
18 Bonta 87
19 Hughes (1968)
20 F. Ll. Harrison 'Music for the Sarum Rite' *Annales Musicologiques 6 (1958/63) 109*
21 *domne* spelt thus: see chapter 2, n64; Wagner (1931) 49; and Harrison (1958) 118
22 L. Treitler ' "Centonate" chant: *Übles Flickwerk* or *E pluribus unus?' Journal of the American Musicological Society* 28 (1975) 1-23
23 Andrew Hughes 'Monarchs, Music, and Manuscripts: the medieval English Coronation,' typescript (1974) as yet unpublished
24 Van Dijk (1960 and 1963) passim
25 Van Dijk (1960) 214

26 The original manuscript is source B10; see n13. The Master-general's copy is British Library ms add 23935; see Hughes (1976)
27 King (1955 and 1959)
28 Apel (1956); for a summary and bibliography of the topic see items 605-31 in Hughes (1974)

CHAPTER 1

1 Irtenkauf
2 Alternative methods of numbering these Sundays, not dependent on Trinity Sunday, will be mentioned later.
3 The Ordo Romanus XV, compiled ca 750-80, has a list of rules governing the church year which begins with Advent (Lechner and Eisenhofer 26). But early Sacramentaries begin with Christmas (Van Dijk [1960] 1972). 25 March was also used, and, in Rome, 1 January since the civil year began on that day (Cabrol I ii 3226, and Eisenhofer I 473-4). In Liège, New Year's Day was on 6 January until at least 1303. The precise day of the New Year varies in the middle ages according to the locality, but in the church Kalendar was always 1 January (Mâle 68-9). Advent was regarded as an anticipation and contemplation, to some extent penitential, of Christ's coming: Rupert of Deutz says *contemplationem adventus domini* (PL 170 col 55; Cabrol s.v. *Avent*).
4 The frequently used ablative case of this and other forms (eg *sabbato sancto*) is probably because of an understood *in* preceding the terms. Hardison 109 claims that the triduum is Friday, Saturday, and Sunday; cf Lechner and Eisenhofer 147-54
5 The Roman method of counting included both beginning and end.
6 Sundays will henceforth be numbered with Arabic numerals, and weekdays with small Roman numerals, after a clearly recognizable abbreviation for the day after which they are numbered.
7 Procter and Wordsworth, in the BS of 1531, vol II xiii, give 22 December and 18 January as the limits for the saints which are included in the Temporale, but the main concern was evidently with those whose feasts fall between Christmas and Epiphany.
8 Books are sometimes assigned to these Orders partly according to whether or not saints' feasts are in the Temporale and a circular argument is clearly a danger here. The evidence seems to indicate the following: Dominicans and Cistercians place the saints in the Sanctorale: I have found several exceptions in Cistercian books (source C6; *Bamberg, Staatsbibl* ms lit 31; *Aarau, Kantonsbibl* mss Muri 6 and 8). The Franciscans and the Roman curia, whose usage is based on that of the Franciscans, place saints in the Temporale. Benedictine books are inconsistent (*Montserrat*, ms 36; *Munich, Bayerische Staatsbibl* ms 15502; *Würzburg, Universitätsbibl* ms M ch f 286; *Florence, Bibl Medicea-Laurenziana* ms conv sop 461; saints in the Temporale/ *Florence, Bibl Medicea-Laurenziana* ms conv sop 90; source B13; *Würzburg, Universitätsbibl* ms M ch f 287; saints in the Sanctorale). Books for secular uses normally place the saints in the Temporale, although exceptions can be found.
9 For Gradual of Monza see Hesbert (1935) 117-69; cf Hesbert's preface x-xi, and Apel (1958) 51-60. For other early Breviaries see Salmon (1967) 70, 72-3.
10 The first contemporary saint to be celebrated, according to the New Catholic

Encyclopedia 12, 1045. Occasionally his feast is to be found in the Sanctorale even when the other sants after Christmas are in the Temporale, as in source B58; Madrid, Bibl nac ms A 174; Trier, Bistumsarchiv, ms 480

11 BS 1531, I ccclix-ccclx, citing *Crede michi* of 1495-7.

12 Sources NB2, G21

13 Indicating the day on which the catechumens first don the white robes they will wear until the Saturday after Easter. The Sunday following that Saturday is also known as *in albis (depositis)*. See n15.

14 Fortescue (1934) 364

15 See n13: on this Sunday the newly baptized catechumens have put off their white robes. *Quasimodo* is the first word of the introit.

16 It was a popular feast from the 8th to 10th centuries, and the Gelasian and Gregorian Sacramentaries list it as one of the Sundays after Pentecost. Stephen, bishop of Liège 930-20, composed an office for the feast. This office was widely circulated and from the 10th century in the Netherlands, England, Germany, and France Trinity was regarded as a proper feast. Pope John XXII authorized its universal use in 1334 (Lechner and Eisenhofer 165-6).

17 Lechner and Eisenhofer 166

18 Frere (1898) II sviii. See **418**.

19 If the historia *Adonay* begins early enough in the month an extra historia is added in some uses: *Domine rex omnipotens* (R), 'Esther'

20 Ferias will be referred to with small roman numerals.

21 The Concise Oxford English Dictionary, presumably based on current but loose and incorrect use, defines Sabbath only as the Christian Sunday, overlooking its liturgical meaning.

22 *Sabbatum* is normally found in the ablative, *sabbato*, presumably dependent on the understood preposition *in*.

23 Frere (1898) I 133-4: *si aliquod festum novem lectionum in Quadragesima fiat in aliqua feria* . . .

24 See BS 1531 I cclxi (asterisk footnote)

25 Apel (1958) 12 is misleading as to the week of the summer fast. With respect to the Advent fast, it is difficult to know what to make of the statement in the Sarum Breviary (BS 1531 I clxiv), which clearly says that if Christmas Eve falls on a Saturday, the fast is not in the same week (ie, the fourth) but in the preceding week (the third): *Si hec Vigilia Nativitatis Domini in Sabbato contigerit, jejunia Quattuor temporum non in ipsa ebdomada sed in precedenti erunt.*

26 Tolhurst VI 107-29

27 Harrison (1958) 76; BS 1531 III lxx-lxxx

28 There is considerable disagreement amongst modern scholars as to the derivation of the services from Jewish practices. The question is not important here, but a summary of the points of view may be useful. Van Dijk (1960) 15 evades the issue: Eisenhofer II 482-3 and Klauser (1969) 6 attribute both morning and evening prayer as well as the three day hours to Jewish practice: Werner 2 and Oesterley 125 assign morning, afternoon, and evening prayer to Jewish practice and do not mention the private hours: Dugmore 11-25, on the other hand, denies the origin of the little hours

in Jewish practice while agreeing to the three public services. See also Idelsohn xviii and 257-9.

29 Much of what follows is based on Batiffol and other authors who deal in general with the divine office.

30 Dendy 147-8; Eisenhofer II 538-9

31 Batiffol 27; Bäumer I 144-5

32 St Benedict was apparently the first to call the evening service part of the day office: Eisenhofer II 539

33 There are numerous editions of the Rule; see bibliography under Benedict. A recent critical edition is that of Rudolf Hanslick; McCann provides a useful English translation; that of de Vogüé and Neufville is a compendium of linguistic, textual, liturgical, and historical data pertinent to the rule, and includes a French translation. Subsequent citations refer to chapters and paragraphs of the rule.

34 Divine office is sometimes used to include Mass as well as the hours.

35 The *Regularis concordia* of ca 980 says *temperius*, 'punctually' (Symons, trans, 22 n2); Knowles 449, 451

36 *Regula Benedicti* 17.7, 41.8, passim. Vespers is not exactly the *lucernarium* any more than Matins is exactly the *vigilia*. Up to the time of St Benedict, Vespers had been a night office or a preliminary to it designated as *prima vigilia*. Benedict wished that it take place early enough so that lights were not needed for the evening meal which followed, and that both would be ended by dark. By the time of Amalarius, Vespers was customarily celebrated in the evening. See H. Leclercq,'Vêpres' in *DACL* 15 ii, 2943-4

37 *Regularis concordia* 22

38 Ibid 13

39 The chronological implications of 'later' may be questioned. The earliest occurence of these terms has not been researched since the matter is not material to the issues of this book. The names were surely adopted gradually, at different times in different places. Etheria (trans. Pétré) ch 24.4-7 pp 190-4

40 *Regula Benedicti* 41.8; see footnote 36. Matins was occasionally sung in the evening immediately after Vespers and Compline, but Lauds was never moved from the daybreak hour: Harrison (1958) 55; Frere (1898) I 221

41 BS 1531 III lxv

42 Jungmann I 247-9

43 Instructions for Sarum use state that Mass is after Terce, even on ferias, except in Advent when it was after Sext on ferias and in Lent when it was after Nones; Frere (1898) I 99-100, 105, 134, 141 and II 21. See the *Regularis concordia* 19, 21, 32-3, 39, 48, 54; Dalton I 17, 40, 294, 305; and Hautcoeur 24, 36, 53, 69 for varying times for the Mass. In large establishments Mass was celebrated several or many times a day, according to the number of chantries. Lincoln, for example, had thirty-eight Masses daily in 1506; Harrison (1958) 56 n5

44 Frere (1898) II 148

45 *privatim*: probably just in a low voice. For *secreto* with the same meaning, see Jungmann II 91 n7 and 42 n4

46 Frere (1898) II xxiv, 229

47 Frere (1898) I 18; see also H. Leclercq 'Chapitre monastique' in *DACL* III i, 508 and J. Baudot 'Capitula' in *DACL* II ii, 209, n2 (citing the *Ordo Romanus* VI)

48 Although usually called *in capitulo*, the Mass can hardly have been performed in the Chapter House; see Dickinson vii, where it is suggested that the Mass took place behind the main altar in what the French call the *chevet* (etymologically derived from *capitulum*), an apse with radiating side chapels.

49 Hautcoeur 26

50 Batiffol 96, n4

51 So called from the incipit of the first antiphon to be sung; see **924**.

CHAPTER 2

1 Although there was a rule of silence during the Canon, it was frequently violated. The congregation was advised to pray quietly, or to utter short ejaculatory prayers at the Elevation; Jungmann II 214-6

2 The collect is called the *oratio prima* in the Roman Mass, *collecta* in the Gallican; Jungmann I 360. If a distinction is to be made, it should perhaps be on the basis that the collect is more specific than the oratio and is always preceded by the liturgical greeting, *Dominus vobiscum*. The oratio is a simple petition. A phrase which may occur, in modern sources, in this respect is 'relative predication,' referring to a prayer on days of special solemnity which normally begins *Deus qui* and incorporates the thought of the feast into the petition; Jungmann I 375.

3 Especially when the biographies involved not only the lessons but also the sung items for the hours: usually in the later middle ages the latter items were rhymed. See Jonsson.

4 This term is used, as in the Oxford English Dictionary and normal speech, to mean the performance of any 'psalms, hymns, anthems, etc' in liturgical services: strictly, of course, it refers only to items whose texts are drawn from the Book of Psalms.

5 The different numbering of the psalms will be discussed in section **401**. Vulgate numbering will be used here.

6 Leroquais (1940) I xvi

7 Werner 161. The complete text is: *Gloria Patri et Filio et Spiritui Sancto. Sicut erat in principio, et nunc et semper, et in secula seculorum. Amen.*

8 Werner 131. Performance methods and styles of the early period in general are described by H. Avenary in 'Formal structure of psalms and canticles in early Jewish and Christian chant' *Musica Disciplin* 7 (1953) 1-13

9 Batiffol 4 n5

10 See T.H. Connolly 'The *Graduale* of S. Cecilia in Trastevere and the Old Roman tradition' *Journal of the American Musicological Society* 28 (1975) 413-58

11 Marbach 60

12 Batiffol 80

13 I have seen a doxology including the second half of the text, in some newly composed responsories of the later middle ages. This practice is highly exceptional.

14 Batiffol 80 cites Amalarius, a 9th-century authority, stating that the whole refrain was

first sung by the soloist, then repeated by the choir: this double performance does not seem to survive. See n20 below and **712**.

15 Source A13 and BS 1531 I xxi, respectively

16 It sometimes sits during the verses; Frere (1898) I 16-7

17 Wagner (1911) I 136

18 Apel (1958) 95-6, 182

19 For possible exceptions see Apel (1958) 183-4

20 Source G23 fol iii; *Dum episcopus legitur duo pueri in superpellicis facta inclinacione ad altare ad gradum chori in pulpitum per medium chori ad Graduale incipiendum et suum versum cantandum se preparent et sic incipiatur: Gr.* Universi. *Chorus idem repetat et prosequatur totum Graduale usque in finem quod per totum annum observetur . . . Gr.* Universi . . . edoce *chorus ultimam dictionem cum neuma dicat* me. *Repetatur Graduale ab illis pueris et percantetur a choro. Notandum est quod per totum annum repetatur Graduale post versum.* Compare source G14. Wagner (1911) I 88-9; Apel (1958) 196-7. In the polyphonic settings of graduals by composers of the Notre Dame school (late 12th and early 13th centuries), where only the words sung by soloists are set in part music, the last word of the verse is not included. Choral usurpation of this part the verse was therefore the practice in Paris at that time.

21 Wagner (1911) I 88-9

22 Jungmann says the refrain was repeated even in the 13th century and later (I 427-8).

23 Wagner (1911) I 88 n6

24 Apel (1958) 89

25 Ibid 378

26 Literature on the sequence abounds; see Hughes (1974) items 752-83. For articles seriously questioning the accepted theories about the origin of the sequence, see R.L. Crocker 'The Repertory of Proses at St Martial de Limoges in the 10th century' *Journal of the American Musicological Society* 11 (1958) 149-64 and P. Dronke 'The beginnings of the sequence' *Beiträge zur Geschichte der deutschen Sprache und Literatur* (Tübingen) 87 (1965) 43-73.

27 Batiffol 19-20

28 Werner 131

29 Apel (1969) 703. Even the *Liber Usualis* is not clear, although the implication is that choirs alternate every half-verse (p xxxii, and the discussion of the asterisk on p xiv).

30 Frere (1898) I 36, 253-4

31 Van Dijk (1952)

32 Apel (1958) 187; Frere (1898) I 253-4

33 Frere (1898) I 53: *cantor incipiat antiphonas et versus psalmi intonat solus, et post unumquemque versum solus cantor incipiat predictam antiphonam . . .*

34 Bailey, passim; Harrison (1958) 90 n2

35 Frere (1898) I 37, 39, 212-3: BS 1531 I xvii-xviii

36 Apel (1958) 188 and n4. The text of the invitatory psalm, Ps 94, is usually said to derive from the *Itala*, said to be a Latin translation earlier than Jerome's: Leroquais cites recent research which indicates that the term *Itala* as used by Augustine refers to Jerome's translation, usually called the Vulgate (*Les Psautiers* . . . I xxv). See section

873. The invitatory is rarely called the *victatorium*, as in source B18 (Leroquais, *Les Bréviaires . . .*)
37 See n33
38 Frere (1898) I 53 and II 148, 230: Harrison (1958) 58
39 MR I xxvii
40 Jungmann (II 28-9) says that offertory and communion were originally antiphonal, then responsorial, then the verses were dropped. Apel (1958) 189-96
41 Jungmann I 320-4; Wagner (1911) I 66-7. The early association between the introit and the litany have been explored in numerous publications; see Wagner (1911) I 58, 71.
42 Wagner (1911) I 66; Apel (1958) 190-1
43 Wagner (1911) I 67-8
44 Apel (1958) 198
45 Wagner (1911) I 67
46 Jungmann II 28-9; Apel (1958) 192-3; for the verses of offertories see Ott (1935) and Ruth Steiner 'Some questions about the Gregorian offertories and their verses' *Journal of the American Musicological Society* 19 (1966) 162-81
47 *Tractum* is sometimes found, and so occasionally are the terms *benedictio(nes)* and *canticum*, but these two are erroneous designations stemming from the confusion between tracts and the hymnus to be described below. Ferretti 148-51; Apel (1958) 184
48 Source G23 fol ix; Frere (1898) I 72, 92, 151
49 Source G23 fol xxxiv-xxxiv^{v}; printed sources as in previous footnote.
50 Apel (1958) 315
51 More recent use adopts only the first two, run together as a single text and repeated on all three of the Saturdays.
52 The arrangements cited here are those of source G23 (*Benedictus es in firmamento*, fos xxxvi-vii; *Benedictus es Domine*, fos viii^{v}-ix; *Omnipotens semper*, fos cvi^{v}-cvii). For the last, another Sarum Gradual (G14, plate 172) has $R^{1a\text{-}1b}$ throughout, and ends with a cue to V_{1b}: for *Benedictus in firmamento* (plates 44-6) the instructions are unclear.
53 Batiffol 7-8
54 Connelly xxii; F.V.E. Raby, *A History of Christian-Latin Poetry from the Beginnings to the Close of the Middle Ages* (Oxford, 2nd ed 1953), 20-8
55 There is indirect evidence for the latter practice in the polyphonic setting of hymns from the 15th and 16th centuries, where alternate stanzas are set to part-music; see Mother Thomas More 'The Practice of alternatim' *Journal of Ecclesiastical History* 18 (1967) 15-32
56 Jungmann I 265, 346
57 BS 1531 I xvii
58 In Sarum use antiphonal performance of the Gloria is specifically prohibited (Frere 1898 I 66): there are no similar instructions for the Te Deum.
59 Connelly xv
60 See Jungmann I 470-4; Owens; Tixeront
61 At one time antiphonal performance seems to have been the case but was eventually

objected to (Jungmann I 473); often the instructions *non alternando* are given (GS plate C; Frere (1898) I 75).

62 Jungmann II 136-7; A. Gastoué 'Le Sanctus et le Benedictus' *Revue du chant grégorien* 38 (1934) 163-8; 39 (1935) 12-7, 35-9

63 Jungmann I 361-6

64 Jungmann (I 454-5 n94) refers to the use of *domne* as distinct from *Domine*, but he gives no references (plate 25 clearly has the abbreviation *dōne*; Hautcoeur 254; Frere (1898) I 119. See Introduction, n21

65 Frere (1898) I 16-8

66 *Enarrationes in Psalmos*, 99.4, ad versum 2 (*Corpus Christianoum* 39 [Turnhout 1956] 1394): 'Qui iubilat, non verba dicit, sed sonus quidam est laetitiae sine vergis; vox est enim anime diffusi laetitia, quantum protest, exprimentis affectum, non sensum comprehendentis. Gaudens homo in exsultatione sua, ex cerbis quibus dam quae non possunt dici et intellegi, erumpit in vocem quamdam exsultationis sine verbis; ita ut appareat eum ipsa voce gaudere quidem, sed quasi epletum nimio gaudio, non posse verbis explicare quod gaudet.'

67 Jungmann I 357-9

68 The Sanctus is supposed to end before the actual consecration but as we have seen the Benedictus itself was oten delayed until the Elevation. The position of the Agnus with regard to the priest's communion was also variable. The actual conclusion of the consecration and the beginning of communion occurs at different points in different times; see **513**.

CHAPTER 3

1 This chapter may appear to some to be needlessly complex. The worshipper need be aware of only the broadest differences: most scholars will not require the detailed specification and minute qualifications described. My purpose is to define how terms are going to be used, and to suggest methods of precise analysis of the way rites vary, so that comparative studies may also take into account the *minutiae* of the service.

2 'Bi-weekly' is ambiguous, and ought to mean twice a week. 'Fortnightly' is possible.

3 What these terms represent can be shown (perhaps more clearly for some) 'algebraically,' as follows:

1a	abcdefg	abcdefg	abcdefg
1b & 5	Xbcdefg	Ybcdefg	Zbcdefg
2	Xbcdefg	Xhijklm	Xnopqrs
3	Xbcdefg (through Advent) Ybcdefg (through Lent)		
4a	aaaaaaa	bbbbbbb	
4b	Xaaaaaa	Yaaaaaa *or* Xaaaaaa Ybbbbbb Zcccccc	
4c	aaaaaaaaXaaaaYaaaaaaaZa		
5	see 1b		

4 The Gloria has two variants: (a) . . . *peccata mundi (miserere nobis. Qui tollis peccata mundi* may be omitted) *suscipe deprecationem* (for Sundays) and (b) *propter gloriam tuam magnam* (for doubles). See Legg (1916) 6-7 and King (1955) for Cistercians and Gilbertines. The Credo varies by only a single word, in the Carthusian rite: *et vitam futuri seculi*. See King (1955) 45, 140, 402.

CHAPTER 4

1 *Regula Benedicti* 18.22-3
2 Ibid 18.16-7
3 Deduced from ibid 18.2-11. Hebrew letters for the sections occur in source B13 (see **880**)
4 Frere (1898)II x-xi. See n16
5 Ibid I 111, 119, 251
6 Ibid II 208
7 Ibid I 251
8 BS 1531 II 28
9 Salmon (1967) 34 describing Matins, with Amalarius as a source (9th century), does not mention a hymn. The sections in Amalarius are II 442, III 19-22. See n20
10 Although this statement is true by and large, there are exceptions, and in the liturgical books there appear to be exceptions which are in fact not so: the situation well exemplifies the problems of discriminating between actual practice and the method of recording that practice in a minimum of space. See **6000**
11 Apel (1958) 22 n5; M. Huglo 'L'Office du dimanche de Pâques dans les monastères bénédictins' *Revue grégorienne* 30 (1951) 193 n2. Also Frere (1898) II 10: *Non dicitur* Te Deum laudamus *per adventum, sed reincipiatur ultimum responsorium. Eodem modo fiat in festis novem lectionum que in adventu evenerit.* See also ibid I 21, 122, 250; source B74 fol 108. I know of no reference to the omission of the last responsory in the late middle ages.
12 Tolhurst VI. Also *Regula Benedicti* 9
13 Tolhurst VI 221-4
14 BS 1531 II 1-4
15 The words in parentheses are not in the Breviary (BS 1531 I xvii) and occur only in the Ordinal (Frere 1898 II 208; cf 216).
16 See **403** and notes 4-8. According to Batiffol 76 n3 Amalarius does not have the dialogue before Matins. See also Salmon (1967) 116. St Benedict and monastic mss of the 11th and 12th centuries do not include it (ibid 96): Roman offices of the same period include it (ibid 158). See BS 1531 III xxix. The Ordinal of Lille (Hautcoeur 43, 51) implies that it was used before Matins.
17 Source B4 includes the incipits on these days, perhaps by error.
18 A monastic source which omits it is B7: a secular source which includes it is NB3. The invitatory psalm, Ps 94, was sometimes sung at the beginning of the third nocturn of Epiphany (Ferretti 215, n1 & 216 n1)
19 Tolhurst VI 193-5
20 See n9: Salmon (1967) 24, 96, 116, 159; Batiffol 76; *Regula Benedicti* 9.4
21 Epiphany has a hymn in sources B3 and NB3: the monastic Breviary B7 has a hymn during Easter week.
22 Connelly xviii-xxi
23 A rubric such as the one which appears in BS 1531 I vi and implying no variation at any time is misleading since it fails to state 'unless a proper text appears': *Eodem modo respondeatur ad omnes versus post hymnum tam ad matutinas quam ad vesperas, et*

completorium per totum annum, nisi in tribus feriis ante pascha et in servitio mortuorum; ita tamen quod in tempore paschali finiantur cum Alleluya *Et sub silentio.*

24 For secular uses secondary literature fails to mention the versicle after the Matins or the Vespers hymn (BS 1531 III xxix, xxxiii) although one is mentioned for the hymn of Lauds (xxxi). The Breviary itself, however, is very clear: the rubric is quoted in 23. Since the versicle for Matins is the same as that for Vespers, it will not be written down again in the Matins service, nor in other services where its repetition is understood from the rubric or from general knowledge. Thus, the Matins hymn appears to lack a versicle even though it has one. It is tempting to believe the same is true of monastic sources, even though once again secondary literature fails to refer to such a versicle (Tolhurst VI 8, 181): the Lauds and Vespers hymn do have the versicle (at least where the rest of the office is proper – Tolhurst VI 10, 11, 156, 197). Is the versicle at Vespers repeated for Matins, as in secular uses? Attractive though this hypothesis is, it seems to be denied by Benedict himself, who specifies the versicle for Vespers and Lauds (*Regula Benedicti* 12.4, 17.8) but fails to mention it at Matins (*Regula Benedicti* 9). Is this simply an error of Benedict's? Original manuscript Breviaries of monastic use have not yet yielded any evidence to doubt Benedict's intentions, or at least the correct implementation of his perhaps erroneous statements.

25 Sources P1, P2

26 Psalter in source NB2

27 Psalter in source B13

28 Batiffol 77-8

29 BS 1531 I xiv, dcclxxv; Frere (1898) II 216; BS 1531 III xxx n

30 BS 1531 I dcclxxv

31 Batiffol 77-8

32 BS 1531 I li

33 In recent Roman use Ecclesiastes was used. In manuscripts the biblical source varies: Sarum and Edinburgh use Ecclesiasticus; Hyde and Hereford use Proverbs, Wisdom, Ecclesiastes, and Ecclesiasticus; Franciscan and Lateran Breviaries use Proverbs, Ecclesiastes, Wisdom, and Ecclesiasticus.

34 Jungmann I 405-6 n11. See sections **34, 226**. Batiffol 78 says the choir responds *Amen* to the benediction.

35 BS 1531 I (unnumbered pages following 32) and Frere (1898) I 232-40, right-hand columns (the left-hand columns present a similar list with a greater choice but do not indicate how the choice is to be made).

36 Note how the intrusion of Corpus Christi causes an awkward dislocation in the original arrangement.

37 Source B13 fol 397v. Cf Tolhurst VI 8-9

38 In the monastic Breviary of Hyde Abbey (Tolhurst I 11v-12v) the patterns of the weeks after Adv 1 (which is itself specially treated) can be inferred only from the week with Ember days, where feria iv has propers of its own, which are given, and feria v

then has incipits which are those of the 10th, 11th, and 12th of Sunday. This would imply a distribution as follows for normal weeks:

Sunday	1	2	3	4	5	6	7	8	9	10	11	12
ii	1	2	3									
iii				4	5	6						
iv							7	8	9			
v										10	11	12
vi	1	2	3									
vii				4	5	6						

On the other hand, in the days after Easter (Tolhurst II 99^{v}-104^{v}) the twelve Sunday responsories are distributed as follows:

Sunday	1	2	3	4	5	6	7	8	9	10	11	12
ii	1	2	3									
iii					5	6	7					
iv									9	10	11	
v-vii	as ii-iv											

39 Source B13 fol 155. Cf Cistercian practice, which is the same, in source B9 fos 24-32.

40 Tolhurst I 1^{v}-8^{r}

41 BS 1531 I dcccvii-dccccclv; Frere (1904) I 325-71; Source B74 fos 222v-47

42 Cf BS 1531 I dccclxix and dcccxcvii: should the ferias of the third week be opq / rst / umn / *or* mno / pqr / stu *or* nom / qrp / tus?

43 BS 1531 II 1 says that the Paternoster is said especially after Matins.

44 One of the mss cited by Van Dijk (1960) 450 adds *nisi in festis novem lectionum* to the prohibition during Advent and Lent: on the other hand the Te Deum is not said on feasts of three lessons (ibid 480). The Sarum Customary (Frere 18989 I 250) says the Te Deum is not said during Advent or Lent and is said only on certain double feasts. See also Batiffol 83, 310-1; M. Huglo 'Te Deum' *New Catholic Encyclopedia*, 13, 954-8

45 Harrison (1958) 56

46 *Regula Benedicti* 11.10

47 BS 1531 I xxx says *loco nec habitu mutato* for the priest saying the versicle before Lauds. Lauds may sometimes still be referred to as *matutinas* or included with Matins under that term: *ad matutinas et ad vesperas super psalmos Benedictus et Magnificat* (Frere 1898 II 88). Cf Batiffol 83

48 BS 1531 I xcii, dxcvi, passim

49 BS 1531 II, 1

50 They are:

Sundays:	Canticle of Daniel, *Benedicite omnia opera* (Dan 3.56-8)
Lent:	Canticle of the Three Children, *Benedictus es Domine Deus patrum* (Dan 3.52-7)
Mondays:	Canticle of David, *Benedictus es Dominus Deus Israel* (I Chron 29.10-13)
Lent:	Canticle of Isaiah, *Confitebor tibi Domine* (Is 12.1-6)
Tuesdays:	Canticle of Tobias, *Magnus es Domine* (Tob 13.1-10)
Lent:	Canticle of Ezechias, *Ego dixi* (Is 38.10-20)
Wednesdays:	Canticle of Judith, *Hymnum cantemus Domino* (Jud 16.15-21)
Lent:	Canticle of Anna, *Exultavit cor meum* (I Sam 2.1-10)

Thursdays:	Canticle of Jeremiah, *Audite verbum* (Jer 31.10-14)
Lent:	Canticle of Moses, *Cantemus Domino* (Ex 15.1-19)
Fridays:	Canticle of Isaiah, *Vere tu es* (Is 45.15-26)
Lent:	Canticle of Habacuc, *Domine audivi* (Hab 3.1-19)
Saturdays:	Canticle of Ecclesiastes: *Miserere nostri* (Eccl 36.1-16)
Lent:	Canticle of Moses, *Audite celi* (Deut 32.1-43)

51 BS 1531 I mclxxix

52 Batiffol 84; Bäumer II 135

53 Batiffol (73 n4) implies that it is omitted in some medieval Breviaries too. He cites Amalarius (*De Eccl Off* 4.7, Hanssens II 434): *Audivi olim responsorios cantari apud quosdam post lectionem vespertinalem, qui continentur in aliquibus antiphonariis; sed apud nonnullos modo ac pene omnes, post lectionem sequitur conjunctim versus.* Batiffol concludes that the presence of a responsory here in monastic rites (see *Regula Benedicti* 17.8) may represent ancient Roman use which had fallen into disuse. So many secular and regular Breviaries of the later middle ages have the responsory after the chapter that its presence or absence canot be used as a distinguishing feature.

54 The original number was probably seven, and all others are thought to be accretions. The texts are all borrowed from the Old Testament, and their order is *O Sapientia, O Adonai, O radix, O clavis, O oriens, O rex, O Emmanuel.* See Huglo 'O Antiphons' *New Cath Encycl* 10, 587-8 and the anonymous article 'Les grandes Antiennes' *Rev Ben* 2 (1885-6) 512-6; Cabaniss; Van Dijk (1960) 116, 355

55 BS 1531 I cliv, xcix (earliest Adv 3), cxxv (latest Adv 3 vi)

56 BS 1531 I dcccxvii: *incipiant Vesperas . . . cum* Kyrie eleyson *super cantum de* Lux et origo

57 BS 1531 I dcccxvii-viii

58 BS 1531 II 221-2

59 BS 1531 I dcliii-iv. The first text is *Media vita in morte*, the second is *O rex gloriose inter sanctos.*

60 BS 1531 I mix

61 BS 1531 I dcxcv

62 BS 1531 I dccxv: *hac die tantum dicitur*

63 BS 1531 I ccxciv (Circumcision)

64 For the summer and the weeks after Epiphany: *Dominus regit me* (𝒫), *Laus et perennis* (𝒯), *Gloria laudis resonet* (𝒮), *Ex quo omnia* (𝒩): BS 1531 I ccccxvi-vii

65 Advent to Vigil of the Nativity:

𝒫	*Veni et libera nos*	
𝒯	*Tuam Domine excita*	from the Psalter,
𝒮	*In tuo adventu*	BS 1531 II 46, 60, 65, 68
𝒩	*Veni Domine*	

Domine ne in ira (Epi 2) to XL
Deus omnium (Tri 1) to Adv

𝒫	*Deus exaudi orationem*	
𝒯	*Veniant mihi*	from the Psalter,
𝒮	*Non confundas me*	BS 1531 II 46, 60, 64, 68
𝒩	*Juxta eloquium*	

XL 1 to XL 5
𝒫 *Vivo ergo*
𝒯 *Per arma justitie* BS 1531 I dlxxxix-dxci
𝒮 *Commendemus nosmetipsos*
𝒩 *Advenerunt nobis*

XL 5 to XL 6 iv
𝒫 *Anime impiorum*
𝒯 *Judicasti Domine* BS 1531 I dccxxxiv-v
𝒮 *Popule meus*
𝒩 *Nunquid redditur*

Pas 2 to Pen (excluding Asc and its octave)
𝒫 𝒯 𝒮 𝒩 *Alleluia, alleluia*

66 BS 1531 I xxxix-xl
67 Frere (1898) I 89, passim
68 BS 1531 II 50-1
69 The proper version is not mentioned in the Old Ordinal (Frere 1898 II 13) but is in the New Ordinal (ibid II 222-3)
70 BS 1531 I xl-xli
71 BS 1531 I ccccxxii
72 BS 1531 I dlxxxic
73 BS 1531 I dccclxv
74 In the Psalter, BS 1531 II 54-5
75 A *profestum* is a lower category of simple feast: the name is not used elsewhere in the Sarum Breviary or Psalter. See BS 1531 III index of feasts (p. xl), and II 54-5. See Harrison (1958) 53.
76 The choir was ruled by one or more of the senior singers responsible for intoning certain items: when it was not ruled, a singer from the senior stalls performed the function (Harrison 1958, 65). Whether the choir was ruled or not seems to have depended on the rank of the day, but I have not been able to find much information on the topic. See Harrison (1958) passim; other information in Craig Wright, 'Performance practices at the Cathedral of Cambrai 1475-1550,' *Musical Quarterly*, 64 (1978) 295-328.
77 Frere (1898) I 15, 227

CHAPTER 5

1 J.A. Jungmann *The Mass of the Roman Rite*
2 Ibid I 170-5
3 Jurgmann (ibid, I 170) notes the term as early as the 5th century. According to Apel (1958) 26 *missa* up to about 1300 refers only to the proper, and the eventual inclusion of the ordinary is caused by the 14th-century introduction of polyphonic settings of the ordinary. It seems unlikely that a rather numerically unimportant new musical preference should affect liturgical terminology.
4 MR I 27, 35
5 Jungmann I 261

6 In the Ordinal of Lille *Vidi aquam* is replaced by the antiphon *Pascha nostrum*: Hautcoeur 52
7 Jungmann I 269
8 Ibid I 369
9 Ibid I 274
10 Ibid I 300
11 Ibid I 295
12 Ibid I 309 and Frere (1898) I 62: *Cantata vero tercia et officio misse inchoato, dum post officium Gloria Patri inchoetur, executor officii cum suis ministris ordinate presbiterium intrent et ad altare accedant.*
13 Jungmann I 266-7
14 Ibid I 270, 324
15 At Antioch it was placed at the end of the Fore-Mass (ibid I 334-5)
16 See **932**. MR I 238: (vig Pen) *Pervento autem ad Kyrieleyson letanarium Kyrieleyson pro missa solemniter incipitur.*
17 Jungmann I 265, 346
18 Ibid I 359-61
19 Ibid I 388. Kantorowitz; Ian Bent 'The English Chapel Royal before 1300' *Proceedings of the Royal Musical Association* 90 (1963/4) 77-95 passim
20 See chapter 3 n4 for a proper alteration to the Gloria
21 Frere (1898) II 157: 'when a bishop celebrates.' The Maundy Thursday Mass is pontifical; see **921**.
22 MR I 196: 'whenever the Te Deum is said, and on Maundy Thursday and Holy Saturday.' I suspect that a corresponding Breviary would comment about the Te Deum 'Whenever the Gloria is said.' The Gloria is omitted on Rogation Monday (and Tuesday?) in the Roman Missal (MR I 231).
23 Jungmann comments on an antiphon *post Evangelium*, I 425 n33
24 Eg, G5 (= source G14) plates 124, 127 passim
25 Jungmann I 440-2
26 Eg, the conductus, as in the Compostella ms (see Introduction, n21 and Wagner 1931, 49-51)
27 Frere (1898) I 266; source M5
28 Jungmann I 456-61
29 More precise details in Frere (1898) II 150 and MR I 196-7. For a specifically proper Credo see chapter 3, n4.
30 Borella 107
31 MS 593; Jungmann I 480; apart from the *oratio communis*, there were often prayers for peace, against plague, or *prières du prône*, etc (ibid I 487).
32 The preparation sometimes extends right back to the gradual and alleluia (Jungmann I 441).
33 Jungmann II 52-90
34 Ibid II 90-100
35 Ibid I 200-1
36 MS cols 593-6
37 Martimort 412. See **739-41**.
38 I 204-5
39 Martimort 389

40 Jungmann II 121. The MS has a *cotidiana* text for ferias and Sundays; the MR has one for double feasts and Sundays, another for simple feasts and ferias.
41 This original chant is now the one known as Sanctus XVIII (Jungmann II 128)
42 Jungmann II 128-9
43 Ibid II 136
44 Ibid II 216-17
45 Ibid II 101
46 Ibid II 340
47 Ibid II 340
48 Ibid II 359-67
49 Ibid II 394-5
50 Ibid II 398
51 Ibid II 398
52 Ibid II 400
53 Ibid II 430; BS 1531 I dlviii; Fortescue says the prayer came into mass from Vespers (1937, 390-1); Baumstark disagrees (27).
54 MR I 211
55 Frere (1898) I 100, section 36 (ferias); cf ibid I 62 (Adv Sunday)
56 Ibid I 101, section 37
57 Ibid I 105, end of section 40
58 Ibid I 90, section 43
59 Ibid II 150
60 Dalton I 336. The introduction of Trinity Sunday theoretically forced the original Mass of that day onto the following feria, so that the sequence of subsequent Sundays was not disturbed.
61 Jungmann II 292-3
62 Dalton I 297
63 Apel (1958) 28. Ferias ii, iv, and vi of each week have the tract *Domine non secundum* or *De necessitatibus* after the **GT** or **G-**, repetitions which are often specified only by a rubric on the first appearance of the tract. The absence of even an incipit thereafter can be very misleading. On the Friday Ember day of Lent, for example, only one Missal (NM5) out of fifteen Mass books studied had the incipit of the tract immediately after the gradual; one Gradual (G8) had a second gradual. The MR I 49 and MS cols 136-7, 142, 150, 156, 162, etc are explicit. An alleluia is often given for Christmas Eve in the manuscripts, with or without the rubric that it is for use only when the day is a Sunday. Cf n64: of the same fifteen Mass books on this day only two (M5, NM5) showed the incipit of the tract after the two graduals.
64 This seems to be the practice of the MR. In the Sarum Missal the words *Flectamus genua: Levate* are used only during Lent, if the phrase *Oremus tantum* for all other days means precisely what it says: the interpretation 'Only the *Oremus* [*Flectamus genua, Levate*, and not the *Dominus vobiscum*]' is perhaps intended: MS cols 33-4, 444, 543
65 Apel (1958) 30; Hesbert xl; the *Ordo Romanum* IX (PL 78, 1008) has: *XII lectiones propter XII lectores dicuntur, non propter XII varietates sententiarum.*
66 MR I 237-8. Compare the somewhat different arrangement in the Sarum ceremonies for Holy Saturday (**929**).
67 MR I 237-8 and this chapter, n16

CHAPTER 6

1 Source G5
2 The typographical presentation of modern editions needs to be regularized. In this example, for instance, the format ought to make any editorial abbreviation of the lesson (here expressed by . . .) distinct from the abbreviation, present in the original, of the communion text (here expressed by *etc*).
3 Source NM5 fol 28
4 Source G13 fol xv and xvii^{v}
5 Source B1 fol 15
6 Van Dijk's article of 1956 makes a useful start; also Van Dijk (1960) 216, 330.
7 A highlighted letter has a flash of colour added to the black penwork: sometimes a complete word will be highlighted with a coloured line drawn right through the word making it appear, on a black-and-white film, as though the word were crossed through.
8 Eg, source G13
9 Two manuscripts from Switzerland (Fribourg, Univ Libr L 125 and L 40) have letter Is drawn square within the writing area, and Ps and Ls have no descenders or ascenders.
10 Source M3 f.23
11 Source M21 fos 22, 29, 30
12 Source G13
13 Source B1 fos 94v-5
14 The most exhaustive compendium of early plainsong notation by Suñol. Wolf has excellent material on later notations. For more specialized studies, see Hughes (1974), items 136-67.
15 The 'sine musica nulla disciplina potest esse perfecta' sentiment crops up throughout the middle ages, from Isidore of Seville at least until the 13th century.
16 Van Dijk (1956) 59-64; idem (1960) 216
17 There are coloured diagrams in Smits van Waesberghe.
18 This very complicated topic is dealt with in Hughes (1972).
19 A study in depth is required. For theories about the rhythmic performance of earlier plainsong, a very controversial topic, see Hughes (1974) items 546-59, of which 546 presents an excellent summary of the various opinions. The Dominican theorist, Jerome of Moravia, seems to suggest in the 13th century that the rhythmic practices of that time were applied to plainsong (see Cserba 179-80). In the late 15th century, plainsongs were sometimes written explicitly in rhythmic notation.
20 For more specialized information, see Hughes (1974) items 166 and 167.
21 The best discussions in English are in Apel (1958) 133-78 and Gustave Reese, *Music in the Middle Ages* (New York 1940) 149-64. For others, see Hughes (1974) items 193-212.
22 Apel (1956) clearly reviews the issues. See Hughes (1974) 89-93.
23 See Apel (1958) 35-6, 212-14
24 Harrison (1958) 59, 63, 67, 74 and passim
25 Frere (1898) II i-lxxxvi (following p 236). In this Tonary the variations are

categorized according to the differentias rather than the more logical reverse.

26 Source A11 fol a[v]

27 Frere, *Antiphonale Sarisburiense*, introduction 3-61

28 Eg Apel (1958); Harrison (1958); Wagner (1911)

29 Especially in the standard histories of the Breviary, eg Bäumer II 425-8, Batiffol 156-7, Leroquais (1934) I vi, Salmon (1967) 67-9, Van Dijk (1960) 29-44

30 Fiala and Irtenkauf (1963). See also Gy.

31 Jungmann I 209 refers to John of Avranches' *De officiis ecclesiasticis* 1.13, published in PL 147: 32.

CHAPTER 7

1 Source G7 has only two Masses, the first of which is called *missa in aurora*

2 Source G14, Adv 4

3 A third alleluia and verse at the foot of the page seems to be an afterthought.

4 Harrison (1958) 71

5 Source G14 (facsimile in Frere 1894, plates A-D). The rubric begins: (1) *adventus et a lxx usque ad cenam domini missa cum* Benedicamus Domino. (2) [*Sciendum quod ad missam* ?] *dominicam generalis habetur regula quod semper quando ad missam* Gloria in excelsis *dicitur ipsa missa semper cum* Ite ... *finiatur.* [D]*ominica prima adventus domini.* (3) *Ad missam Officium* Ad te ... *ps.* Vias ... (4) *Repetatur officium et postea dicitur* Gloria Patri *et* sicut . . . *Tertio dicitur officium. Et hoc per totum annum observetur tam in dominica quam in festis sanctorum et in octavis et infra quando chorus regitur et in omnibus missis de sancta Maria per totum annum nisi a dominica passionis domini. Scilicet. ad missam de temporali.* (5) *Per totum adventum non dicitur* Gloria in excelsis. (6) *De quocunque dicitur missa oratio* Excita quesumus domine, *memoria de sancta Maria, oratio* Deus qui de beata Maria. *de quocunque dicitur missa semper fiat memoria de sancta Maria cum supradicta oratio ne usque ad vigiliam nativitatis Domini.* (7) *Cum vero dicitur missa de aliquo sancto licet duplex festum fuerit vel missa* Salus populi *nihil de adventu et de s. Maria fiat memoria.* (8) *Nondum quod in omnibus dominicis et in festis cum regimine chori per totum annum generaliter observetur ut ad missam tot dicitur collecte quot ad matutinas nisi in die nativitatis Domini.* (9) *Ita tam quod ad missam semper impar numerus custodiatur nisi in ebdomadam nativitatis Domini. Nam si due orationes habeantur vel quatuor tunc erit tertia vel quinta oratio de omnibus sanctis, scil.* Concede quesumus . . . (10) *ut in temporale. Per totum annum tam per adventum quam in tempore paschali tum quando in die festo dicitur missa in crastino si fuerit de aliquo sancto memorie habeantur de ceteris festis ad eandem missam dicuntur.* (11) *In dominica vero et in festis cum regimine chori a paschali usque ad ascensionem Domini dominicis diebus diebus contingentibus nulla fiet memoria de dominica ad missam.* (12) *Postea in omnibus festis novem lectionum que in jejuniis quatuor tempora vel in vigilia sanctorum seu per totum xlm evenerit nulla fiet memoria de jejunio ad missam de festo, dicitur solemnis missa de jejunio utroque ad principale altare.* (13) *Si vero fuerit dominicalis missa memoria de trinitate fiat et relique memorie ad magnam missam dicuntur.* (14) *In ferialibus diebus per adventum quinque dicuntur orationes quarum prima de die, ii de sancta Maria, oratio* Deus qui de beata Maria, *iii de omnibus sanctis, oratio* Concede quesumus . . ., *iv per universali ecclesia, oratio* Ecclesie tue, *v pro pace, oratio* Deus a . . . (15) *In octava sancti Andree et quando dicitur missa*

Salus populi *tunc erit ii oratio de adventu, iii de sancta Maria, iv de omnibus sanctis, v pro pace.*

6 *Salus populi* is a Mass for the safety of the realm and of the Christian community. Harrison (1958) 80

7 The Roman Missal of 1474 allows one or more additional prayers here during Epiphany week and from the Wednesday after Easter to Ascension (MR I 32, 217, 224). See also the Sarum Ordinal (Frere 1898 II 150).

8 See chapter 1, n48

9 Source G7 calls Epi 1 the first Sunday after the octave of Christmas, correct but confusing.

10 Sources G2, G3, G4, G11, G12

11 Sources G7, G8

12 Source G14 (Frere 1894 plate 18); cf G16, G21

13 Sources G3 and G4 (related) have Epi 2 and Epi 3 later changed to 3 and 4, suggesting a confusion between *post Epiphaniam* and *post octavam Epiphanie.*

14 Sources G14, G16, G18, G21

15 Source G14 (Frere 1894 plate 21)

16 Except for Maundy Thursday (see **921**)

17 Source G13 is an exception.

18 Source G12, G16, G18

19 As in n17, source G13 provides an exception; the letters for the ferias of Easter week are smaller.

20 Source G7

21 Souces G8, G12, G13, G16

22 Source G16

23 Sources G10, G17, (fourteenth week); source G5 (fifteenth week); sources G12, G19, G20 (sixteenth week)

24 Sources G14, G21

25 The precise details of each manuscript used for this book are too complex to enumerate here, but the following facts relevant to the list in the text may be added:
Source G1: the series begins with *Dom 1 post oct Pen* and introits 8, 10, 19, 20 appear only in incipit.
Source G2: the series begins with *Dom 1 post Pen* and introit 19 appears only in incipit.
Source G3: the numbering proceeds 1 2 3 5 and 6 changed to 5.
Source G4: introits 7, 10, 12, 19, 20 and *Letetur* are given only in incipit.
Source G5: the Ember days are after 15.
Source G6: the series begins with Dom 2 and continues to 24.
Source G10: the Ember days are after 14, and after 10 are incipits for *Dispersit dedit* and *Confessio* (I do not know what these incipits are).
Source G12: Ember days are after 16.
Source G19: Ember days are after 16, and after 4 is a group of saints' Masses.
Source G20: Ember days are after 16.

26 GS xvii

27 As in the Flaunden Missal (Rare Book Room, University of Illinois)

28 Sources G1, G3, G4, G5, G12, G13

29 Harrison (1958) 74-6 and his plate VII

30 Dickinson's edition of the Sarum Missal, cols 577-638, presents the Ordo well but ignores the hierarchy of initials.
31 Collins (Sarum Manual) 74-8; Cooke (Directory for priests) passim
32 Dickinson 718*
33 Sources G2, G5
34 Sources G16 and G21 (Sarum), G18 (York)
35 Sources G20 and G11 (12th century), G17 (14th)

CHAPTER 8

1 Several years ago I was involved in an authentic re-enactment of a medieval coronation ceremony at the University of Toronto and can speak with some confidence about the effort and difficulty. In addition, I have heard of or seen other re-enactments, such as a Sarum marriage service (apparently still valid in New York!), some of which certainly ran into insoluble problems.
2 BS 1531 I cxcvii-cclxxxiii
3 See M.N. Maltman 'Boy Bishop' *New Catholic Encyclopedia* 2, 741; E.K. Chambers *The Medieval Stage* (Oxford) I 336-71; Karl Young *The Drama of the Medieval Church* (Oxford 1933) I 106-10; J.M.J. Fletcher *The Boy Bishop at Salisbury and Elsewhere* (Salisbury 1921); E.F. Rimbault *The Festival of the Boy Bishop in England, Camden Miscellany* VII (Camden Society, ns14, 1875).
4 Eg, BS 1531 I dcccxiv
5 According to Van Dijk (1951)
6 Salmon (1967); Van Dijk (1960) and (1963)
7 The following table presents some comparative statistics, without the detail needed for a completely accurate description. Where the number appears as 1 + 2, for example, the Saturday Magnificat for the first Sunday of the historia is given at first Vespers, Magnificats for the other Saturdays are in a stock with the Magnificat of second Vespers. The six columns refer respectively to the historie (1) Deus Omnium, (2) In principio, (3) Si bona, (4) Peto, (5) Adaperiat, (6) Vidi: sources are indentified at the left.

B1 (monastic)	12	6	2	3	3	3
B2 (Dominican)	1+8 or 9	1+4	1	1+2	1+4	1+4
B3	5+4	4	?	2+1	4	3
B5	9	1+4	2	1+2	1+4	1+4
B6 (Premonstratensian)	9	5	3	1+2	4	5
B7 (monastic)	10	4+1	1+1	1+2	1+4	1+4
NB1 (Sarum)	9	1+4	2	2	5	4
NB2	10	4	3	1	4	4
NB3 (Hereford)	8	5	2	1	5	5
A2	1+9	1+4	1	1+2	1+4	1+4
A7 (monastic)	1+6	1+4	1+3	1+3	1+4	1+3
A8	1+33 (!)	1+6	1+6	1+3	1+6	1+4
A9	1+8	5	5	?	5	5
A10	10	5	2	3	4	5
A11 (monastic)	14	8	5	3+2	3	5
A13 (Sarum)	8	5	2	2	5	4
A14 (monastic)	9	5	2	4	4	3

8 P. Vincent Rabanal, *Los Cantorales de El Escorial* (Monastery of El Escorial 1947)
9 Diringer 311-2, plate VI 19-22
10 Huglo (1971) 371; Georg Paul Köllner 'Eine Mainzer Choralhandschrift des 15. Jahrhunderts als Quelle zum *Crucifixum in carne*' *Archiv für Musikwissenschaft* 19/20 (1962-3) 208-12.
11 A few exceptions occur, eg, (✱ LR)3 [2], where the size 2 initial belongs to the lesson rather than the benediction. Exceptions can be ascertained through a careful comparison of the schemes of initals (presented in the tables) with the representation of them in the columns.
12 An ordinary Dominican Breviary in manuscript was not available to me when this chapter was prepared. Before I knew precisely what information would be required here, I had studied the Dominican book B2: reconstructed on the basis of notes, it has for Advent Sunday the following scheme:

(G ?)	[3]	H	[2] 1 + . . .	C,L,O	[2]
R	1+	LR	[2] 1 + 111	A, B, I, M	

The chapter of first Vespers has the Advent initial (size 10). Advent has the following items: aCRHDMO / IH (AD (LR)3)3 Te Deum / Rs for Sundays / DA5 cHBD / RcRRC / DM = / ferias: ID ≠ r3 / B / A4 / M // (BM)4 B. Compare source B3.
13 Source B11 for 15v: *Tres lectiones . . . cotidie ubi proprie lectiones non assignantur, et ita distribuantur quod tantum sit lectum ante nativitatem, quia lectiones de nativitate, s.* Primo tempore *scribuntur imediate post textum his infra designatum.*
14 Leroquais (1940) I v-lxxxv
15 Van Dijk, 'Some manuscripts of the earliest Franciscan liturgy' *Franciscan studies* 16 (1956) 62-3. The divisions of the Psalter seemed at first to be so much a part of common knowledge that I did not think it necessary to keep references. In fact, this is another area in which information of the most elementary kind is difficult to find. That the liturgical division into eight sections is also the Roman division is only an inference based on common sense and the statement in Van Dijk that it appears in a Franciscan Breviary. The three-part division discussed below this note I have seen referred to only in Leroquais (1940) I xcii.
16 Sources C1, B7, B14, NB2
17 The gradual psalms are 119-33 inclusive. See Tolhurst VI 64-8; Van Dijk (1960) 272-4. They are said to be distinguished in many English Psalters of the 10-11th centuries; see Tolhurst VI 64-5.
18 Sources B7, B14, B15 (all monastic) and P1 (secular)
19 Sources A19, NB7 (Ps 51 is missing), BS 1531
20 Source NB1
21 Sources B16, BS 1531
22 Source B17
23 Sources B18, B16, B17 respectively
24 Sources B6 & B18, NB2 & B15 respectively
25 Sources B16, BS 1531
26 Sources B33-36
27 Sources B20-32, NB8, NB9

28 TD is observed in B29 (Paris), B39 (Hyde Abbey), B6 (Czechoslovakia; SD is in B24 (Toledo), B26 (Braga), B37 (English Cluniac), B38 (German), B40 (Hungarian Cistercian), NB9 (Verdun).
29 Sources B40, B6 respectively
30 Source NB9
31 Source B41
32 Source B42
33 Source NB10
34 Sources B61-3
35 Source B64
36 Source B65
37 Source B69
38 Source B70
39 Source B52
40 Source NB14
41 Source B7
42 Sources B43-6
43 *Sarum sources*: SC B8, B40; London, British Libr mss Harley 2946, Royal 2 A XIV; Salisbury Cathedral ms 152; Oxford, Bodleian Libr ms University College E 22; Oxford, St John's College ms 179; Stonyhurst College ms 40; Edinburgh, National Libr ms 18. 2. 13B; Edinburgh University Libr ms 26; New York, Pierpont Morgan Libr ms 329.
CS B44, B54; London, British Libr ms Harl 2785; London, Lambeth Palace ms 69; Oxford, Bodleian Libr mss Hatton 63, laud misc 299, Rawl C 73; Worcester Cathedral Libr ms Q 10.
York sources: SC York Minster Libr mss XVI O 9, XVI O 23; Dublin, Trinity College ms 85.
CS B71, NB7, NB12; York Minster Libr ms add 70; London, British Libr add 30511; London, Sion College ms Arc L 40. 2/L 1.
Hereford sources: NB3. Cf the same layout in the incomplete Worcester Cathedral Libr ms Q 86, which has TKPS[].
Norwich source: London, British Libr ms Stowe 12
Lichfield: London, Southwark Cathedral ms 1
Benedictine: B14, B47, B50, B51
44 Sources B48 (Worcester), B49 (Battle). See Tolhurst VI xiii
45 Sources B52 (Sarum), NB13 (Sarum, Scottish), NB14 (Norwich)
46 Sources B54 (Sarum; the K is now missing but surely came at the beginning), BS 1555 (Sarum; the Pynson print), B53 (Norwich; split into two volumes and lacking the Psalter)
47 Sources B55, NB15 (Paris); NB16 (Troyes), B56 (Cambrai), B57 (Flanders); B58 (La Peña, Spain)
48 Source B59
49 Sources A20, A21 (Irish); A15, A19 (Norwich); A23 (London); A24 (Midlands)
50 Source A32

CHAPTER 9

1 J.W. Tyrer, *Historical Survey of Holy Week* (London 1932); O.B. Hardison, *Christian Rite . . .* (Baltimore 1965)
2 Hardison 87, 97
3 Ibid 89-90
4 Karl Young, 'Observations on the origin of the mediaeval passion play' *Publications of the Modern Language Association of America* 25 (1910); 309-54; Hardison 115
5 Frank Ll. Harrison, ed *The Eton Choirbook* Musica Britannica 12 (London 1961) vol III 170; Hughes (1968) 175-6
6 Tolhurst VI 207-8
7 John Brückmann 'Latin manuscript Pontificals and Benedictionals in England and Wales' *Traditio* 29 (1973) 391-458; Michel Andrieu, *Le Pontifical romain au moyen-âge* 4 vols (Vatican City 1938-41) describes Pontificals in general.
8 Hardison 86
9 Ibid 137-8
10 Ibid 139; Hardison calls these reversals *peripateia.*
11 A. Strittmatter 'Exsultet iam angelica turba' *New Catholic Encyclopedia* 5, 765-6; R. Hammerstein 'Tuba intonet salutaris' *Acta Musicologica* 31 (1959) 109-29
12 Hardison 127
13 Tyrer 124
14 Tyrer 124 cites a typical formula: *Oremus et pro omnibus episcopis, prebyteris, diaconibus subdiaconibus, acolytis, exorcistis, lectoribus, ostiariis, confessoribus, virginibus, viduis, et pro omni populo sancto Dei. Oremus. Flectamus genua. Levate.* Cf Hardison 130, 115-6.
15 Hardison 130-1
16 Ibid 130-4
17 Ibid 98-100
18 Ibid 94-5
19 Ibid 95
20 Tyrer 47; this was Roman practice. In Gaul and Spain the *traditio* was on Palm Sunday.
21 Tyrer 84: in Gaul the *redditio* about to be described takes place on Maundy Thursday.
22 Hardison 143 note
23 Ibid 148
24 Ibid 151-3; Tyrer 156
25 Hardison 153
26 Ibid 153, 156; Tyrer 161
27 Hardison 157
28 Ibid 141
29 Ibid 170
30 Ibid 168-9
31 Ibid 173-4
32 Sources B2, A2, A9
33 Sources NB1, NB2
34 Sources A7, A18, A19, NB1
35 Not as printed in the Missal.

36 The texts of the penitential psalms are given in full at this point in the source cited. The penitential psalms are Ps 6 *Domine ne in furore*, 31 *Beati quorum*, 37 *Domine ne in furore*, 50 *Miserere mei deus*, 101 *Domine exaudi*, 124 *De profundis*, 142 *Domine exaudi*; see Tolhurst VI 57-64, 68-9

37 Many of these sources refer to musical items only by their incipits unless they are Noted Missals, and to preces only as incipits within rubrics. After the source number, the letters of identification will be given: numerals (which do not appear in the main text) refer to items which do not occur in the two sources used in the main text. The incipits of those items are listed, after the same identification number, at the end of the note.

M1 [1 bri 1 o 2 3 jmn 4 5 Ac 6 D 7 8 i]
M3 (listed at the end of the book, fol 483v): begins with
a short prayer, not given, then [ghijmnopq 9 10 abcdeBi 11]
NM4: [AabcdBCD 12 ef]
NM2: [13 eB]
NM1: [g-r be ACB sf 7 5 D]
M5 and NM6: [g-r be ACB sf]
NM3: begins with Nones and a sermon, then [ghi j(varied) mnoqrfe BCA 14 15 Gi 16-20 A]

On the basis of these comparisons, it is easy to see that sources NM1, M5, and NM6 resemble each other and the Sarum Missal of the main text: source NM4 resembles the Roman Missal. Items not in either the Sarum or Roman Missal used in the main text are: [1] *D*: the liturgical greeting [2] O: *Dq juste* [3] O: *Presta populo* [4] O: *DsJXq dixit* [5] O: confession and absolution [6] R: *In sudore* [7] R: *Scindite* [8] R: *Ecce Adam* [9] O: *ODq dixit* [10] D: *Adjutorium* [11] O: *Memor esto qD* [12] 12 A (called a V): *Adjuva nos* [13] O: *OsDq primo homine* [14] L: *Vox sanguinis* [15] A: *Ne irascaris* [16] O: *Dq proprium* [17] O: *Pretende Domine* [18] O: *Ecclesie tue* [19] O: *Deus a quo* [20] O: *Animabus qD*.

38 Bailey 15-7; Harrison (1958) 91-2; Hughes (1968) ix-x

39 Since there are many processional and musical items here, Graduals have been included: textual items in such books will probably appear only in incipit. Otherwise the method of presentation in this note will be as in n37.

G14, G15, NM1, NM6 are identical with the Sarum Missal
M5: as Sarum up to [E] (remainder is probably in a Processional)
G13: [(bopqrhs?) ABDEFGH 1 TLM 2 t]
G1: [(bopqrhs?) BHGFLDE 1 3 I]
G8: [FBHGL]
G10: [BFGHL]
G5: [HBFG 4 5 E]
G3: [DEIBTL]
G9: [DEIBTLM]
G18: [DEAHNTS 6 GQFBLMT]
G19: [DEIL]
G20: [ACDEILM]
NM4: as the Roman Missal up to [FIJKLM]
NM5: [abBcrk 7 8 IFHGEDT 9 L 2 MT]

NM2: [10 DEFG (patronal responsory here) T 11 (memorial prayers) B 12 LM]
NM3: [HO 13 14 U chej DEGF 15 GNFPQA 2 16 6 LMSBT 17 U 17]
M1: [bor 19 DEA 20 H(or O?) NGFRSBG 21 LMTU t Q]
The astonishing variety of arrangements here allows only a few sources to be related: the often inaccurate designation of items in the manuscripts (see notes 40-2), and the confusion between inadequate incipits (as with items [H] and [O]), makes a comparison such as this useful only in the broadest sense.
Items not in either Sarum or Roman Missals are:
[1] *Fulgens palmis* [2] A: *Ceperunt omnes* [3] *Scriptum est* [4] *Redemire nos* [5] *Omnes collaudant* [6] R: *Cum audisset turba* [7] O: *Osd mundi* [8] ✠ DO: *Mundi conditor* [9] A: *O crux ave* [10] ✠O: *Os redemptor qui* [11] A: *Salvator mundi* [12] A: *Ante quinque dies* [13] O: *Actiones nostras* [14] L: *Dicite filii* (Is) [15] A: *Fratres hoc enim* [16] A: *Domine J* [17] A: *Multa turba* [18] A: *Quoniam principes* [19] DO: *OD mundi creator* [20] DO: *OsDq dum nostrum* [21]: *Si dimittimus.*

40 This and the following item, allegedly antiphons in the MR, are perhaps verses to a responsory whose refrain is item [I]. There are no repetenda cues to confirm this possibility. The MR designations are very unreliable. See n42.

41 See n40.

42 Not two antiphons, as in MR

43 Of Graduals, only the Sarum Gradual, G14, which is lavishly rubricated, includes the service, giving incipits of [abd], the complete texts of [A] and [c], and rubrics for the remainder.
NM1, NM6: as Sarum; M5 as Sarum, beginning with [b] and adding the benediction at the end
M1: as Sarum but adds prayers as follows: [aAbcde 1 fg 2 3 4 h]
M3: (the Temporale (f.161v) has a reference to *in processionario*, but gives the service at the end of the book, f.488v. The service should not be confused with the Reconciliation of a Church or Altar, also in the book) [bcde 1 f 5 2 3 4 h]
M4: [cde 1 6 7 h]
NM3: [bcd 5 e 1 2 4 h 8]
Additional items are: [1] O: *Presta qD famulis* [2] O: *Deus misericors* [3] O: *Majestate tuam* [4] O: *DJXq discipulis* [5] O: *Propitiare Domine* [6] O: *Exaudi Domine preces nostras* [7] O: *Preveniat hos famulos* [8] O: *Absolutionem et remissionem.*

44 Source NM6 gives it at the end of the service.

45 Ms 303

46 Source M3 f.166-166v

47 Source G20 has *Accepto panem* for the Magnificat antiphon.

48 MR I 158; MS cols 308-11

49 Of the Missals available which mention the ceremony at all, source NM5, from Germany, seems identical with Sarum practice except that as well as a versicle and prayer for each saint at his altar, there is an antiphon, making the 'services' before the altars into true memorials. The Noted Missal NM3 mentions the incipits of three responsories (*Circumdederunt . . .* , *Eram quasi agnus . . .* , *Dominus Jesus . . .*) within a long rubric about the ceremony.

50 In source NM5 (German), this antiphon does not appear first: see next note.

51 NM1, NM5: as Sarum
NM4: basically as Roman Missal to item [L]
NM5: [CBKFALDJGQP b] (all musical items with various verses)
52 Only one verse of each psalm occurs.
53 It is used as the source for a cantus firmus in three very important polyphonic Masses of the 15th century, all of which are described in Manfred Bukofzer, *Studies in Medieval and Renaissance Music* (New York 1950) 217-310. Bukofzer's information about the mass said to be by Dufay has been radically changed in more recent publications: see Thomas Walker, 'A Severed head: notes on a lost English *Caput* Mass' *Abstracts of papers read at the thirty-fifth annual meeting of the American Musicological Society, Saint Louis*, December 27-29, 1969, pp14-5 and Alejandro E. Planchart, 'Guillaume Dufay's Masses: Notes and Revisions' *Musical Quarterly* 58 (1972) 1-23
54 MS col 311
55 Liber Usualis 671-7
56 Sources M3, M4, MW
57 MR I 167-70; MS cols 325-8
58 In all the sources studied, including NM4 (which has in earlier notes been related to the Roman Missal), item [B] precedes item [A], as in the Sarum Missal. Other items appearing in several sources in various later positions are: *Adoramus crucem, Vexilla regis, Super omnia ligna.*
59 Sources M1, M3
60 See next note.
61 M1: (Mass of the Presanctified, placed after the Deposition ceremony) [gibcdf]
M3: [(Mass placed as in M1) 1 2 gcd (Vespers incipits) k]
M5: [ghibcdj (Vespers incipits) k]
NM1: [bcdjk]
The additional items in M3 are: [1] *Hoc corpus quod* [2] O: *DJX propitius esto.*
62 G14: [rubric & CDE]
G16: [rubric & A-E] (as Sarum)
M5, NM1, NM6: [A-E]
63 As in previous comparisons, M5 (with one addition), G14, G18, NM1, and NM6 agree with the Sarum version, and NM4 (with one additional prayer) agrees with the Roman version. G2 has a Litany in place of [B].
64 Many Graduals omit the tract [C], eg G2, G4, G5, G8, G9, G15, G17. As in previous notes, the Missals group themselves similarly: M5 and NM4 (the latter incomplete) are in agreement with the Roman arrangement. Six other Missals adopt slight rearrangements of the Sarum version:
M1: [abg A ho B nu C 1 i D α]
NM1, NM6: [abg A ho B nu C 1 - D α z]
NM2: [abg A ho B ni C 1 - D α]
M3: [abg A ho B ni C 1 k D - z]
MW: [abg A ho B pu C v k D - z]
65 MR I 236-7; MS cols 418-22
66 Hardison 141-4
67 MR here has the prayer [q] again, surely in error.

68 Said by the bishop if anyone wishes to communicate after having been baptized and confirmed.
69 G14, G16, G18
70 MS (Legg) 123
71 Source G18
72 MS col 348 and M5
73 NM3 has the *letania sancte sanctorum* then *Accendite* (incipit with music)
74 M5 and NM1
75 M3
76 M3, NM1, NM4
77 M1 and M3
78 In source NM5 there are nine size 3 initials each followed by a capital.
79 Source M1

APPENDIX I

1 Harrison (1958) 53-4
2 A. Cappelli, *Cronologia, Cronografia e Calendario Perpetuo* (Milan 1930)
3 On this date was made the change from the Julian to the Gregorian calendar: thereafter, new rules apply. See Colin Alistair Ronan 'Calendar' *Encyclopedia Britannica* (15th ed 1973) *Macropedia* 3, 601-3
4 Eg Francis Wormald, ed, *English Kalendars before A.D.1100* Henry Bradshaw Society 72 (London 1934); idem, ed, *English Benedictine Kalendars after A.D.1100* 2 vols Henry Bradshaw Society 77, 81 (London 1934, 1946)
5 Leroquais (1934) cxxx-cxxxii

APPENDIX II

1 Leroquais (1934) I lxxx-lxxxi
2 Adv 4 was originally *vacat*, as in sources A19 and A20 (12th century), probably accounting for the variants.
3 Here the catechumens take up the white robe, which they relinquish on the Saturday after Easter: the title *In albis* can be confused with the title for that Saturday, *In albis (depositis)*.
4 The Gradual of Rouen, G22, also has AoB-. The rites of Rouen are close to some of those in England: see Bishop 276-300

APPENDIX III

1 BS 1531 II 6 and I cccxxxi; MS col 5
2 Item [E] is variously an antiphon or a responsory, the latter with the verse *Hodie beata virgo*, as in sources NM4 and NM2 respectively.

APPENDIX V

1 Source B71 f.157
2 The paraphrase is based on the rubric in the BS 1531 I mclxxxiv-mcci, which seems to be typical.
3 BS 1531 I Kalendar
4 Ibid I mcc
5 Source B72 fol 187
6 Source NB10 fol 76: abbreviations realized and errors tacitly corrected.
7 Source NB18
8 Source A36
9 Source B73
10 Source B72 f.187v

APPENDIX VI

1 Frere (1898) I 19, 48, 62, 90, 143, 182, 256
2 BS 1531 I xxiv
3 AS plates 10-13
4 Frere (1898) II 9, but cf I 48 and II 218
5 Ibid I 240-2
6 BS 1531 II 363

APPENDIX VII

1 Source C1
2 Source C3
3 Source C5
4 Source C4
5 Hughes (1968) 187-9

APPENDIX VIII

1 I should like to thank the Guggenheim Foundation, the Canada Council, and the Connaught committee of the University of Toronto for making this research possible. The project produced, among other lists, an alphabetical index to all the items of the rhymed offices so far known, using as a basis the texts printed in Analecta Hymnica and numerous other ms sources: a complete word-concordance (including thousands of the chants) could now be produced, if funds were available. The whole repertory can now be searched for individual words and phrases.

Bibliography

Abate, Giuseppe 'Il primitivo breviario francescano (1224-1227)' *Miscellanea Francescana* 60 (1960) 47-240

Abbott, T.K. *Catalogue of the manuscripts in the Library of Trinity College, Dublin* (Dublin 1900)

Amalarius, see Hanssens

Antiphonaire monastique, XIIIe siècle, Codex F. 160 de la Bibliothèque de la Cathédrale de Worcester Paléographie musicale sér I: 12 (Tournai 1922)

Apel, Willi 'The Central Problem of Gregorian Chant' *Journal of the Americal Musicological Society* 9 (1956) 118-27

– *Gregorian Chant* (Bloomington, Indiana 1958)

– ed *Harvard Dictionary of Music* (2nd ed Cambridge, Massachusetts 1969)

AS *Antiphonale Sarisburiense* see Frere

Augustine, see Finaert

Austin, Gerard 'Liturgical Manuscripts in the United States and Canada' *Scriptorium* 28 (1974) 92-100

Bäumer, Suitbert *Histoire du bréviaire*, transl and revd by Réginald Biron, 2 vols (Paris 1905 repr 1967)

Bailey, Terence W. *The Processions of Sarum and the Western Church*, Pontifical Institute of Mediaeval Studies: Studies and Texts 21 (Toronto 1971)

Batiffol, Pierre *History of the Roman Breviary* transl from the third French edition, 1911, by Atwell M.Y. Baylay (London 1912)

Baudot, Jules L. *The Lectionary: its sources and history*, transl from the French by Ambrose Cator (London 1910)

– *Le Missel romain. Ses origines, son histoire* 2 vols (Paris 1912)

– *The Breviary: its history and contents* transl from the French by the Benedictines of Stanbrook, Catholic Library of Religious Knowledge 4 (London 1909)

Baumstark, Anton *Comparative Liturgy* revised by Bernard Botte, transl from the third French edition, 1953, by F.L. Cross (Westminster, Maryland 1958)

Benedict, see de Vogüé, Hanslik, McCann

Benton, Rita ed *Directory of Music Research Libraries* 3 vols International Association of Music Libraries: Commission of Research Libraries (Iowa City 1967, 1970, 1972)

Bishop, Edmund *Liturgica Historica: Papers on the Liturgy and Religious Life of the Western Church* (Oxford 1918)

Bonniwell, William R. *A History of the Dominican Liturgy* (New York 1944)

Bonta, Stephen 'Liturgical Problems in Monteverdi's Marian Vespers' *Journal of the American Musicological Society* 20 (1967) 87-106

Borella, Pietro *Il rito Ambrosiano* Biblioteca di Scienza Religiosa ser 3 La liturgia (Brescia 1964)

Boyle, Leonard 'Dominican Lectionaries and Leo of Ostia's *Translatio S. Clementis*' *Archivum fratrum praedicatorum* 28 (1958) 362-94

BS 1531 *Breviarium . . . Sarum*, see Procter

Bukofzer, Manfred *Studies in Medieval and Renaissance Music* (New York 1950)

Cabaniss, J.A. 'A Note on the Date of the Great Advent Antiphons' *Speculum* 22 (1947) 440-2

Cabrol, Fernand, H. Leclercq and H. Marrou, eds *Dictionnaire d'Archéologie chrétienne et de Liturgie* 15 vols each in two fascicles (Paris 1907-53)

Cappelli, Adriano, ed *Cronologia, Cronografia e Calendario Perpetuo* (3rd ed Milan 1969)

Chevalier, Cyr Ulysse J. ed *Ordinaires de l'Eglise Cathédrale de Laon, XIIe et XIIIe siècles, suivis de deux mystères liturgiques* Bibliothèque liturgique 6 (Paris 1897)

Collins, A. Jefferies, ed *Manuale ad usum percelebris ecclesie Sarisburiensis* Henry Bradshaw Society 91 (Chichester 1960)

Connelly, Joseph ed *Hymns of the Roman Liturgy* (Westminster, Maryland 1957)

Cooke, William and C. Wordsworth, eds *Ordinale Sarum sive Directorium Sacerdotum* 2 vols Henry Bradshaw Society 20, 22 (London 1901, 1902)

Corbin, Solange, *Essai sur la musique religieuse portugaise au moyen âge, 1100-1385* Collection portugaise 8 (Paris 1952)

Crocker, Richard L. 'The Repertory of Proses at Saint Martial de Limoges in the 10th Century' *Journal of the American Musicological Society* 11 (1958) 149-64

Cross, Frank L. amd E.A. Livingston eds *The Oxford Dictionary of the Christian Church* (2nd ed Oxford 1974)

Cserba, Simon M. ed *Hieronymus de Moravia, O.P. Tractatus de Musica* Freiburger Studien zur Musikwissenschaft 2 Veröffentlichungen des Musikwissenschaftlichen Instituts der Universität Freiburg (Schweiz) 2 (Regensburg 1935)

DACL, see Cabrol

Dalton, John N. and G.H. Doble eds *Ordinale Exon.* 4 vols Henry Bradshaw Society 37, 38, 63, 79 (London 1909, 1909, 1926, 1940)

Davies, John G. ed *A Dictionary of Liturgy and Worship* (London 1972)

Delaissé, L.M.J. 'A la recherche des origines de l'office du Corpus Christi dans les manuscrits liturgiques' *Scriptorium* 4 (1950) 220-39

Delaporte, Yves ed *L'Ordinaire chartrain du XIIIe siècle* Société archéologique d'Eure-et-Loir Mémoires, 19 (Chartres 1953)

Dendy, David R. *The Use of Lights in Christian Worship* Alcuin Club Collections 41 (London 1959)

De Vogüé, Adalbert trans and Jean Neufville, *La Règle de Saint Benôit* Sources chrétiennes 181-6, Série des textes monastiques d'occident 34-9, 6 vols (Paris 1971-72)

Dickinson, Francis H. ed *Missale ad usum insignis et praeclarae ecclesiae Sarum* 2 vols (Burntisland 1861-83)

Diringer, David *The Illuminated Book: its history and production* (revd ed New York 1967)

Dix, Gregory *The Shape of the Liturgy* 2nd ed London 1945; repr 1954)

Dokoupil, Vladislav *Soupis Rukopisů Knihovny Benediktinů v Rajhradě. Catalogus codicum manu scriptorum Bibliothecae Monasterii Ordinis S. Benedicti Rajhradensis*, Soupisy Rukopisných Fondů Universitní Knihovny v Brně. Catalogi Codicum Manu Scriptorum in Bibliotheca Universitatis Brunensis Asservatorum 4 (Prague 1966)

Dugmore, Clifford W. *The Influence of the Synagogue upon the Divine Office* Alcuin Club Collections 45 (London 1944; repr Westminster 1964)

Egeria, see Pétré and Wilkinson

Eisenhofer, Ludwig *Handbuch der katholischen Liturgik* 2 vols (Freiburg 1932-3; repr 1941). This work is based on the book of the same title by Valentin Thalhofer, 2 vols (Freiburg 1883-90; 2nd ed 1894; revd by Eisenhofer 1912)

Etheria, see Pétré and Wilkinson

Ferretti, Paolo *Esthétique grégorienne* transl from the Italian by A. Agaësse (Paris 1938)

Fiala, V. and W. Irtenkauf 'Versuch einer liturgischen Nomenklatur' *Zur katalogisierung mittelalterlicher und neuerer Handschriften*, Zeitschrift für Bibliothekswesen und Bibliographie Sonderheft (Frankfurt a.M. 1963) 105-37

Finaert, Guy and F.-J. Thonnard eds *Oeuvres de Saint Augustin* (Paris 1947)

Fortescue, Adrian and J.B. O'Connell *The Ceremonies of the Roman Rite Described* (5th ed London 1934)

– *The Mass: A Study of the Roman Liturgy* (London 1937)

Frere, Walter H. ed *Graduale Sarisburiense* (GS) Plainsong and Mediaeval Music Society (London 1894; repr 1966)

– ed *The Use of Sarum* 2 vols (Cambridge 1898, 1901; repr 1969)

– ed *Antiphonale Sarisburiense* (AS) Plainsong and Mediaeval Music Society (London 1901-25; repr 1966)

– ed *Bibliotheca Musico-Liturgica. A descriptive handlist of the musical and Latin-liturgical MSS. of the Middle Ages preserved in the libraries of Great Britain and Ireland* Plainsong and Mediaeval Music Society (London 1901, 1932; repr 1967)

Frere, Walter H. and L.E.G. Brown eds *The Herefored Breviary* 3 vols Henry Bradshaw Society 26, 40, 46 (London 1904, 1911, 1915)

Gamber, Klaus *Codices latini liturgici antiquiores* (Freibourg, 2nd ed, 1968)

Gastoué, Amédée *Les Origines du chant romain: l'antiphonaire grégorien* (Paris 1907)

– *Le Graduel et l'Antiphonaire romains: histoire et description* (Lyon 1913)

– 'Le Sanctus et le Benedictus' *Revue du chant grégorien* 38 (1934) 163-8; 39 (1935) 12-17, 35-9

Geering, Arnold *Die Organa und mehrstimmigen Conductus in den Handschriften des deutschen Sprachgebietes vom 13. bis 16. Jahrhundert* Publikationen der Schweizerischen Musikforschenden Gesellschaft ser 2, 1 (Bern 1952)

Gordon, Cosmo A. 'Manuscript Missals: The English Uses' The Sandars Readership in Bibliography: Lectures delivered at Cambridge, 13 and 20 November 1936, typescript and autograph of the lectures and supplementary lists of the Alleluia verses for the Sunday after Pentecost in British Library ms add 44920-1

Gottwald, Clytus *Die Musikhandschriften der Universitätsbibliothek München* Die Handschriften der Universitätsbibliothek München 2 (Wiesbaden 1968)

Gradual *Le Graduel romain* ed by the monks of Solesmes, vol II: *Les Sources* (Solesmes 1957)

GS *Graduale Sarisburiense*, see Frere

Gy, P.-M. 'Typologie et ecclésiologie des livres liturgiques médiévaux' *La Maison-Dieu* 121 (1975) 7-21

Hanslik, Rudolph ed *Benedicti Regula* Corpus Scriptorum Ecclesiasticorum Latinorum 75 (Vienna 1960)

Hanssens, Jean Michel ed *Amalarii Episcopi Opera Liturgica Omnia* 3 vols Studi e Testi 138-40 (Vatican City 1948-50)

Hardison, Osborne B. *Christian Rite and Christian Drama in the Middle Ages* (Baltimore 1965)

Harrison, Frank Ll. 'The Eton Choirbook, its Background and Contents' *Annales musicologiques, Moyen-Age et Renaissance* 1 (1953) 151-75

– *Music in Medieval Britain* (London 1958)

Hautcoeur, Edouard ed *Documents liturgiques et nécrologiques de l'église collégiale de Saint-Pierre de Lille* Société d'études de la province de Cambrai, Mémoires 3 (Lille-Paris 1895)

HBS Henry Bradshaw Society an extensive series of editions of liturgical books, published in London since 1891

Hesbert, René-Jean ed *Antiphonale Missarum Sextuplex* (Brussels 1935)

– *Corpus antiphonalium officii* I: *Manuscripti 'Cursus romanus'* II: *Manuscripti 'Cursus monasticus'* III: *Invitatoria et Antiphonae* IV: *Responsoria, Versus, Hymni et Varia* V: *Fontes earumque prima ordinatio* Rerum Ecclesiasticarum Documenta, ser major, Fontes 7, 8, 9, 10, 11 (Rome 1963, 1965, 1968, 1970, 1975)

Hill, Arthur Du Boulay 'The Wollaton Antiphonal' *Transactions of the Thoroton Society* (1924): a pamphlet issued by the conservation committee of the parish

Hughes, Andrew ed *Fifteenth-century Liturgical Music: I Antiphons and Music for Holy Week and Easter* Early English Church Music 8 (London 1968)

– *Manuscript Accidentals: ficta in focus 1350-1450* Musicological Studies and Documents 27 (American Musicological Society 1972)

– *Medieval Music: The Sixth Liberal Art* Toronto Medieval Bibliographies 4 (Toronto 1974; repr 1980)

– 'Medieval Liturgical Books at Arouca, Braga, Evora, Lisbon, and Porto: Some Provisional Inventories' *Tradition* 31 (1975) 369-84

– 'Forty-seven Medieval Office Manuscripts in the British Museum: A Provisional Inventory of Antiphonals and Breviaries' typescript (1976), on deposit in the Students' Room, British Library

Huglo, Michel 'O Antiphons' *New Catholic Encyclopedia* (New York 1967) 10, 587-8

– 'Règlement du XIIIe siècle pour la transcription des livres notés' *Festschrift Bruno Stäblein zum 70. Geburtstag* ed Martin Ruhnke (Kassel 1967) 121-33

– 'Te Deum' *New Catholic Encyclopedia* (New York 1967) 13, 954-5

– *Les Tonaires: inventaire, analyse, comparaison* Publications de la Société française de musicologie, 3 sér, 2 (Paris 1971)

Idelsohn, Abraham Z. *Jewish Liturgy and its Development* (New York 1967)

IRHT Institut de Recherches et d'Histoire des Textes (Paris)

Irtenkauf, W. 'Der *Computus ecclesiasticus* in der Einstimmigkeit des Mittelalters' *Archiv für Musikwissenschaft* 14 (1957) 1-15

James, Montague R. *A Descriptive Catalogue of the Latin Manuscripts in John Rylands Library at Manchester* 2 vols (Manchester 1921)

Janini, José, J. Serrano and A.M. Mundó *Manuscritos litúrgicos de la Biblioteca Nacional* (Madrid 1969)

– *Manuscritos Liturgicos de las Bibliotecas de Espana* I: *Castilla y Navarra* Publicaciones de la Facultad Teologica del Norte de Espana Sede de Burgos 38 (Burgos 1977)

Jonsson, Ritva *Historia: Etudes sur la genèse des offices versifiés* Acta Universitatis Stockholmiensis Studia Latina Stockholmiensia 15 (Stockholm 1968)

Jungmann, Josef A. *The Mass of the Roman Rite* transl by F.A. Brunner 2 vols (New York 1951-55)

Kantorowitz, Ernst H. *Laudes Regiae: A Study in Liturgical Acclamations and Medieval Ruler Worship* University of California Publications in History 33 (Berkeley 1946; repr 1974)

Kellner, Altman *Musikgeschichte des Stiftes Kremsmünster* (Kassel 1956)

Kennedy, V.L. 'The Franciscan *Ordo Missae* in the Thirteenth Century' *Medieval Studies* 2 (1940) 204-22

King, Archdale A. *Liturgies of the Religious Orders* Rites of Western Christendom 2 (London 1955)

– *Liturgies of the Past* Rites of Western Christendom 4 (London 1959)

Klausner, Theodor 'Repertorium liturgicum und liturgischer Spezialkatalog. Vorschläge zum Problem der liturgischen Handschriften' *Zentralblatt für Bibliothekswesen* 53 (1936) 2-16

– *A Short History of the Western Liturgy* transl from the 5th German edition by John Halliburton (London 1969)

Knowles, David *The Religious Houses of Medieval England* (London 1940)

– *The Religious Orders in England* 3 vols (Cambridge 1948-59)

– *Great Historical Enterprises; Problems in Monastic History* (London 1963)

– *The Monastic Order in England: A History of its Development from the Times of St Dunstan to the Fourth Lateran Council, 940-1216* (2nd ed Cambridge 1964)

– and R. Neville Hadcock *Medieval Religious Houses: England and Wales* (rev ed London 1971)

Kristeller, Paul O. *Latin Manuscript Books before 1600: A List of the Printed Catalogues and Unpublished Inventories of Extant Collections* (3rd ed New York 1965)

Lawley, Stephen W. ed *Breviarium ad usum insignis ecclesie Eboracensis* 2 vols Surtees Society 71, 75 (Durham 1880, 1882)

Le Carou, P.A. *L'Office divin chez les Frères Mineurs au xiii*[e] *siècle* (Paris 1928)

Lechner, Josef and Ludwig Eisenhofer *Liturgik des römischen Ritus* (6th ed Freiburg 1953)

Leclercq, H. 'Vêpres' DACL 15.2 (Paris 1953) 2939-45

Legg, John Wickham ed *Missale ad usum ecclesie Westmonasteriensis* 3 vols Henry Bradshaw Society 1, 5, 12 (London 1891, 1893, 1897)

– ed *The Sarum Missal* (Oxford 1916; repr 1969)

Leitschuh, Friedrich *Katalog der Handschriften der königlichen Bibliothek zu Bamberg* I: 1: *Liturgische Handschriften* (Bamberg 1898; repr 1966)

Leroquais, Victor *Les Sacramentaires et les Missels manuscrits des bibliothèques publiques de France* 4 vols (Paris 1924)

– *Les Manuscrits liturgiques latins du haut moyen âge à la Renaissance* (Paris 1931)

– *Les Bréviaires manuscrits des bibliothèques publiques de France* 6 vols (Paris 1934)
– *Le Bréviaire-Missel du prieuré clunisien de Lewes (collection Georges Moreau)* (Paris 1935)
– *Les Psautiers manuscrits latins des bibliothèques publiques de France* 3 vols (Maçon 1940-41)
Liber Usualis *Liber Usualis missae et officii pro dominicis et festis* ed by the monks of Solesmes (Paris 1953)
Lippe, Robert ed *Missale Romanum Mediolani, 1474* 2 vols Henry Bradshaw Society 17, 33 (London 1899, 1907)
Loriquet, Henri, J. Pothier and A. Collette eds *Le Graduel de l'église cathédrale de Rouen au XIIIe siècle* 2 vols (Rouen 1907)
Mâle, Emile *The Gothic Image* transl from the third French edition by Dora Nussey (New York 1958)
Marbach, Carolus ed *Carmina Scripturarum* (Strassburg 1907; repr 1963)
Martimort, Aimé-Georges *L'Eglise en prière: Introduction à la liturgie* (Paris 1961)
McCann, Justin ed and transl *The Rule of Saint Benedict* (London 1952)
Migne, Jacques P. ed *Patrologia latina* 221 vols (Paris 1844-64)
MMML The Monastic Manuscript Microfilm Library (now the Hill Monastic Manuscript Library) at Saint John's University, Collegeville, Minnesota
MR *Missale Romanum* see Lippe
MS *Missale Sarisburiense* (or *Sarum Missal*) see Legg (1916) and Dickinson
MW *Missale Westmonasteriense* see Legg (1891-97)
Oesterley, W.O.E. *The Jewish Background of the Christian Liturgy* (Oxford 1925; repr Gloucester, Mass 1965)
Ott, Carolus ed *Offertoriale sive versus offertoriorum* (Paris 1935)
Owens, G. 'Athanasian Creed' *New Catholic Encyclopedia* (New York 1967) 1, 995-6
Paecht, Otto and J.J.G. Alexander *Illuminated Manuscripts in the Bodleian Library, Oxford* 3 vols (Oxford 1966, 1970, 1973)
Pétré, Hélène, ed and trans *Ethérie: Journal de Voyage* (Paris 1948)
Phillips, Charles S. *Canterbury Cathedral in the Middle Ages* (London 1949)
PL *Patrologia Latina*, see Migne
Plocek, Václav *Catalogus codicum notis musicis instructorum qui in Bibliotheca publica rei publicae Bohemicae socialistae in Bibliotheca universitatis Pragensis servantur* (Prague 1973)
Plummer, John *Liturgical Manuscripts for the Mass and the Divine Office* (New York 1964)
Poole, Reginald L. *Illustrations of the History of Medieval Thought and Learning* (2nd ed London 1920; repr 1960)
Procter, Francis and C. Wordsworth eds *Breviarium ad usum insignis ecclesiae Sarum* 3 vols (Cambridge 1879, 1882, 1886)
Procter, Francis and W.H. Frere *A New History of the Book of Common Prayer* (London 1902)
Rabanal, Vicente *Los Cantorales de El Escorial* (El Escorial 1947)
Regula Benedicti see de Vogüé, Hanslik, McCann
Regularis Concordia see Symons
RGG *Die Religion in Geschichte und Gegenwart. Handwörterbuch für Theologie und Religionswissenschaft* 7 vols (3rd ed Tübingen 1957-65)
RISM *Répertoire International des Sources Musicales* (Munich 1960-)
Rock, Daniel *The Church of Our Fathers* eds G.W. Hart and W.H. Frere 4 vols (London 1903-4)

Salmon, Pierre *L'Office divin au moyen âge* Lex Orandi 43 (Paris 1967)

– ed *Les Manuscrits liturgiques latins de la Bibliothèque Vaticane* I: *Psautiers, Antiphonaires, Hymnaires, Collectaires, Bréviaires* Studi e Testi 251 (Vatican City 1968); II: *Sacramentaires, Epistoliers, Evangéliaires, Graduels, Missels* Studi e Testi 253 (Vatican City 1969)

Sheppard, Lancelot C. *The Liturgical Books* Twentieth Century Encyclopedia of Catholicism 109 (New York 1962)

Smits Van Waesberghe, J. 'The Musical Notation of Guido of Arezzo' *Musica Disciplina* 5 (1951) 15-53

Suñol, Grégoire M. *Introduction à la paléographie musicale grégorienne* transl from the Catalan by André Mocquereau (Paris 1935)

Symons, Thomas ed and transl *Regularis Concordia Anglicae Nationis Monachorum Sanctimonialiumque* (London 1953)

Taylor, Frank. *Supplementary Hand-List of Western Manuscripts in the John Rylands Library* (Manchester 1937)

Tixeront, J. 'Athanase (Symbole de saint)' *Dictionnaire de Théologie Catholique* 1.2 (Paris 1923) 2178-87

Tolhurst, John B.L. ed *The Monastic Breviary of Hyde Abbey, Winchester* 6 vols Henry Bradshaw Society 69, 70, 76, 78, 71, 80 (London 1932, 1933, 1938, 1939, 1934, 1942)

Tyrer, John W. *Historical Survey of Holy Week, its Services and Ceremonial* Alcuin Club Collections 29 (London 1932)

Van Dijk, Stephen J.P. 'Saint Bernard and the *Instituta Patrum* of Saint Gall' *Musica Disciplina* 4 (1950) 99-109

– 'Handlist of the Latin Liturgical Manuscripts in the Bodleian Library, Oxford' typescript (1951) on deposit in the Bodleian Library

– 'Medieval Terminology and Methods of Psalm Singing' *Musica Disciplina* 6 (1952) 7-26

– 'An Advertisement Sheet of an Early Fourteenth-Century Writing Master at Oxford' *Scriptorium* 10 (1956) 47-64

– and Joan Hazelden Walker *The Myth of the Aumbry: Notes on Medieval Reservation Practice and Eucharistic Devotion* (London 1957)

– *The Origins of the Modern Roman Liturgy: the Liturgy of the Papal Court and the Franciscan Order in the Thirteenth Century* (London 1960)

– *Sources of the Modern Roman Liturgy: The Ordinals of Haymo of Faversham and Related Documents, 1243-1307* 2 vols Studia et Documenta Franciscana 1-2 (Leiden 1963)

Vogel, Cyrille *Introduction aux sources de l'histoire du culte chrétien au moyen âge* Biblioteca degli Studi Medievali 1 (Spoleto 1966)

Volk, Paulus ed *Der Liber ordinarius des Lütticher St. Jakobs-Kloster* (Münster in Westf 1923)

Wagner, Peter *Einführung in die gregorianischen Melodien* 3 vols (Leipzig vol I 3rd ed 1911, II 2nd ed 1912, III 1921; repr 1962): translated in a revised and enlarged second edition by Agnes Orme and E.G.P. Wyatt as *Introduction to the Gregorian Melodies* Plainsong and Mediaeval Music Society (London 1901; repr *Caecilia* 84-6, 1957-59)

– ed *Das Graduale der St Thomaskirche zu Leipzig* 2 vols Publikationen Älterer Musik 5, 7 (Leipzig 1930, 1932; repr 1967)

– ed *Die Gesänge der Jakobusliturgie zu Santiago de Compostela aus dem sog. Codex Calixtinus* Collectanea Friburgensia 29 Veröffentlichungen der Universität Freiburg (Schweiz) N.F. 20 (Freiburg 1931)

Weiser, Francis X. *Handbook of Christian Feasts and Customs: The Year of the Lord in Liturgy and Folklore* (New York 1958)

Werner, Eric *The Sacred Bridge: The Interdependence of Liturgy and Music in Synagogue and Church during the First Millenium* (London 1959)

Wilkinson, John trans *Egeria's Travels* (London 1971)

Wolf, Johannes *Handbuch der Notationskunde* 2 vols (Leipzig 1913, 1919; repr 1963)

Wordsworth, Christopher ed *The Tracts of Clement Maydeston with the Remains of Caxton's Ordinale* Henry Bradshaw Society 7 (London 1894)

Zimmerman, Benedict ed *Ordinaire de l'Ordre de Notre Dame du Mont Carmel par Sibert de Beka (vers 1312)* Bibliothèque Liturgique 13 (Paris 1910)

Supplement to the Paperback Edition

Bailey, Terence, and Paul Merkley *The Antiphons of the Ambrosian Office* Musicological Studies 50/1 (Ottawa 1989)

Boyle, Leonard, OP *Medieval Latin Paleography: A Bibliographical Introduction* Toronto Medieval Bibliographies 8 ed John Leyerle (Toronto 1984)

Dreves, Guido M., Clemens Blume, and Henry Bannister eds *Analecta Hymnica* 55 vols (Leipzig 1886-1922)

Harper, John *The Forms and Orders of Western Liturgy from the Tenth to the Eighteenth Century* (Oxford 1991)

Hiley, David *Western Plainchant: A Handbook* (Oxford 1993)

The Hours of the Divine Office in English and Latin 3 vols (Collegeville, Minn. 1963)

Hughes, Andrew 'Chantword Indexes: A Tool for Plainsong Research' in *Words and Music* ed Paul Laird, *Acta* 17 (Binghamton 1993) 31-50

– *Late Medieval Liturgical Offices: Resources for Electronic Research: Texts* Subsidia Medievalia 23 (Toronto 1994) *[LMLO]*

Hughes, Andrew 'The Scribe and the Late Medieval Liturgical Manuscript: Page Layout and Order of Work' in *The Centre and Its Compass: Studies in Medieval Literature in Honor of Professor John Leyerle* ed Robert A. Taylor and others (Kalamazoo 1993) 151-224

Kelly, Thomas Forest *The Beneventan Chant* Cambridge Studies in Music ed John Stevens and Peter le Huray (Cambridge 1989)

Pfaff, Richard *Medieval Latin Liturgy: A Select Bibliography* Toronto Medieval Bibliographies 9 ed John Leyerle (Toronto 1982)

Strayer, Joseph R., ed *Dictionary of the Middle Ages* 13 vols and index (New York 1982-5)

Vogel, Cyrille *Medieval Liturgy: An Introduction to the Sources* [Introduction aux sources de l'histoire du culte chrétien au moyen âge] Centro Italiano di studi sull'alto medioevo, Spoleto; trans and rev by William G. Storey and Niels Krogh Rasmussen, OP (Washington, D.C. 1986)

Sources

This is a list of sources, not a catalogue of the kind described in appendix VIII. It includes sources which I refer to frequently or in detail: during the ten or twelve years during which the research was carried out, hundreds more were consulted, mostly in the original libraries, some on microfilm.

In fact, the information included is as brief as possible. The use, provenance, and date of the sources were rarely relevant and each of these may take months to determine for a difficult book. The inadequacy of many early liturgical catalogues is well known, and in many cases even the basic information is hard to ascertain or is unreliable. I have included what facts were easy to come by, and those which seemed trustworthy. It did seem useful and was mostly possible to include an inventory of the books by sections, to complement discussions in chapters 7 and 8: here, however, less important material and other interpolations are usually omitted so as not to obscure the main sections. The folio number, or sometimes the number of the opening, is given where it is known: often the sources are not foliated, or lightly pencilled numbers are invisible on film. Where the number is not known or is doubtful, a '?' has been used. The 'Sunday number', as in XL 1, must be distinguished from the folio number, eg XL 1 50. General catalogues can be traced easily through the publications of Kristeller and Benton, listed in the Bibliography. When known to me (and I have made no attempt to be comprehensive) the number of a microfilm reproduction in the Hill Monastic Manuscript Library of St John's University, Minnesota (HMML), or in the Institut de Recherche et d'Histoire des Textes (IRHT) in Paris is given.

Several methods of ordering the list of manuscripts could claim priority, for example, by city, by religious order, by date, etc. Within the overall division into office books and Mass books, with and without plainsong, I finally decided to preserve the quite arbitrary arrangement which followed from the addition of a source to the list as it came into my hands or was used. In a book already so full of letter and number abbreviations the wholesale changing of the manuscript sigla, already assigned, raised frightful potential for error. The Index lists sources according to city, provenance, use, and other criteria.

ANTIPHONALS

A1 *Belgium, Brussels, Bibl royale*, ms 6429-30
- Dominican, of Marienthal?, 13c, 297ff
- Delaissé 221; Huglo (1971) 369
- winter
  T 3v (Nat 38v, LX 89)
  S 163 (Annunc BVM 229)
  C 234v
  H 273v
  D 287
  † 293v

A2 *Belgium, Bibl royale* ms 3585-6
- Dominican, of Marienthal?, 13/14c, 207ff, ca 545x380
- Delaissé 221, Huglo (1971) 369
- summer
  T 5 (Trin 48)
  D 93v
  S 100 (Assump BVM 170v, All Saints 208, † 215v)
  C 241
  H 285, incipits & ordo 298
  memorials 277v
  Katharine 297v, 300v, Elisabeth 307

A3 *Belgium, Bibl royale* ms 223-4
- Dominican, of Marienthal?, 13/14c, 276ff, ca 440x320
- Delaissé 221; Huglo (1971) 369
- summer
  T 5v (Trin 43v)
  D 84v
  S 92? (Annunc BVM 92?, Assump BVM 157, All Saints 192, † 199)
  C 222v
  memorials 254v
  sequences 262
  H 263 (incomplete)

A4 *France, Paris, Bibl du Conservatoire national*, ms Res 1531
- Dominican, of Paris, 13c, 416ff
- Huglo (1971) 369; *RISM* B3.1 87-8
- winter
  T 6v (Nat 55v, LXX 117)
  S 232 (Annunc BVM 324v)
  C334
  memorials 382
  H 394

A5 *France, Paris, Bibl nat, ms nouv acq lat 1236*
- of Nevers, 12c, 180ff, ca 270x186
- T and S combined (Vigil Nat 33v, Annunc BVM 103v, LXX 108v)

A6 *Austria, Salzburg, Nonnberg Abbey*, ms without call-number
- monastic, 15c, 359ff
- MMML 10971
- T and S combined (Nat 29, Annunc BVM 103, Easter 162, Trin 200, Assump BVM 225, All Saints 258v)
  D 292v
  C 299
  T cont 329

A7 *Austria, Graz, Univ-bibl*, ms III 29-30
- St Mary's Church, 13c, 382ff ? (29), 345ff ? (30)
- Anton Kern, *Die Handschriften des Universitätsbibliothek Graz* (Leipzig, 1942) I, 11-12
- ms 29
  T 1 (Nat 37, LXX 92)
  S 199v (Annunc BVM 299)
  C 308v
  H 379
- ms 30
  T lv (Easter lv, Trin 43)
  D 130
  S 122v (Assumpt BVM 228, All Saints 287v)

A8 *Netherlands, Utrecht, Rijksuniversiteit, Bibl*, ms 406 (olim 3 J 7)
- 15c, 256 + ff
- Huglo (1971) 205; *RISM* B 3.1 137-9
- T and S combined (Nat 20v, LXX 61v, Annunc BVM 60, Easter 97, Trin 119, Assumpt BVM 159, D 176, All Saints 189v)
  T cont 222v
  tonary 228
  S cont 234 (Transfig 238 & 248, Visitation 243)

A9 *Poland, Wrocław, Bibl Uniwersytecka*, ms I F 391
- 16c, 223 + ff
- T lv (Nat 15, LXX 39, Easter 56v, Trin 80v)
  D 90v
  S 99 (Assumpt BVM 131v, All Saints 161v, Annunc BVM 192)
  C 195
  polyphony 219v
  S cont (Transfig 223)

A10 *Switzerland, Bern, Burgerbibl*, ms c 50
- 14c with 15c additions, 237ff
- *RISM* B 4.2 55-7
- T 1 (Nat 8, LXX 28, Vigil Easter 50v, Dom 1 Adv 81)

S ? (Annunc BVM 87v, Assumpt BVM 96, Andrew 141v)
D 143
C 147v?
† 165
H 173

A11 *Germany, Karlsruhe, Badische Landesbibl,* ms Aug LX
- monastic, of Peterhausen, 12/13c (palimpsest), 236ff plus insertion of 40ff at f.103
- Huglo (1971) 243, 255, 398
- T and S combined (Nat 16v, Annunc BVM 56v, LXX 58v, Vigil of Easter 91v, Assumpt BVM 137, All Saints 155v)
C 166v
D, 182 Trin 184v
† 219v

A12 *England, London, British Lib,* ms add 28598
- of Sarum/Ely, 14c, 170ff, ca 186x290
- Hughes (1976)
- T (begins incomplete: Vigil Nat 13, XL 1 50, Easter 65)
D 83
S 86
C 157
† 169

A13 The *Antiphonale Sarisburiense,* a facsimile edition (see Frere *AS*) of a deficient manuscript from Salisbury complemented, very confusingly, from other sources. There is a collation in Hughes (1974) no. 505. The main manuscript is a Noted Breviary, NB11 of this list: the other chief source is an Antiphonal, A27 below.

A14 *England, Worcester, Cathedral Chapter Lib,* ms f 160, the 'Worcester Antiphonal'. This 13c monastic manuscript is published in facsimile: see Bibliography under Antiphonaire monastique.

A15 *England, London, British Lib,* ms Lansdowne 463
- of Norwich, 15c, 202ff, 346x498, incomplete
- Hughes (1976)
- T 1 (Vigil Nat 8, Easter 61, Trin 76)
tonary 96v
D 94
K 98
P 104
litany 130
† 131
C 134
S 149 (Annunc BVM 167v, Assumpt BVM 192)

A16 *Germany, Mainz, Stadtbibl,* ms II 138
- Antiphonar des Weissfrauenklosters, for Mainz?, 13c, 265 + ff
- Geering 13
- summer
T (Vigil Easter 2, Trin 27v)
S 75 (Philip & James 75, Assumpt BVM 135v, All Saints 168)
C 191

A17 *Austria, Vienna, Österreichische Nationalbibl,* ms 15502
- of Caslav, post 1472, 223 + ff
- T (Nat 1, LXX 29v, Easter 62, Vigil Pen 83v)
S 117 (Annunc BVM 139v, Assumpt BVM 200)

A18 *England, Oxford, Bodleian Lib,* ms lat lit c 1
- Italian, 13c, 269ff, 343x255
- Van Dijk (1951) II 141
- T and S combined (Nat 21, Annunc BVM 80, Easter 134, Assumpt BVM 203, Trin 248)
C 147v & 231
D 229

A19 *England, Norfolk, Ranworth church,* Antiphonal ca 1460-78, 284ff, ca 520x390
- Frere *AS* I 79
- T 1 (Nat 20v, LXX 53, Easter 85v, Trin 104v)
D 128v
tonary 133v
K 135
P & H 141
litany 171v
C 175
S 193v (Annunc BVM 217, Assumpt BVM 249v, All Saints 266v,
† 269v)

A20 *Eire, Dublin, Trinity College,* ms 79 (olim B.1.4)
- Irish (St John Evangelist, Dublin), 15c, 230ff, 464x306
- Frere (1901) II 62 and *AS* I 80-81, Abbott 10
- T 1 (Nat 16v, LXX 52)
K 81
P 87
† 119v
C 123
S 135 (Annunc BVM 162v, Assumpt BVM 195)

A21 *Eire, Dublin, Trinity College,* ms 80 (olim B.1.5)
- Irish, 15c, 180ff, 432x270

- Frere (1901) II 63 and *AS* I 80, Abbott 10
- T 1 (LXX-Dedic)
  K 65 (May-Aug)
  P 66
  C 85
  S 99 (to Assumpt BVM)

A22 *England, London, British Lib*, ms add 29988
- Spanish or Roman? 13c, 154ff, 201x290
- Hughes (1976)
- T and S combined (Nat 21v, Easter 72, Pen 92v, Assumpt BVM 117, D 128, All Saints 133v, Trin 152v)
  K 110v (Aug-Sept), 121 (Sept), 130v (Oct)
  C 87 & 143v
  † 153v

A23 *England, Oxford, Bodleian Lib*, ms Bodley 948
- London, 15c, 344ff, 457x337
- Van Dijk (1951) II 232
- T 1 (Vigil Nat 23v, Easter 111, Trin 137v)
  K 173
  P 177
  H 201
  C 215
  S 242v (Annunc BVM 267v, Assumpt BVM 302v, All Saints 323, † 328v)

A24 *England, Nottingham, Univ Lib*, Wollaton Antiphonal
- for York, ca 1460, 414ff?
- Frere *AS* I 82a; Hill
- T 1 (Nat 34, LXX 82v, Easter 133, Trin 165)
  D 200v
  K 207
  P 213
  C 267
  S 303 (Annunc BVM 330v, Assump BVM 368v, All Saints 393)

A25 *England, Manchester, Rylands Lib*, ms L 74
- 13c, 268ff, 485x330
- James 149; Frere (1901) II 37
- T 1 (Easter 1, Vigil Trin 91)
  D 99
  S 116v (Assumpt BVM 156, All Saints 200v)
  C 220
  † 260

A26 *England, Sussex, Arundel Castle, Library of the Duke of Norfolk*, Antiphonal
- York, Collegiate Chapel of St Mary and Holy Angels, 15c, 257ff, ca 410x280
- includes prayers and chapters
- T 3 (XL 81, Easter 98, Vigil Trin 126)
  D 151
  S 156 (Assumpt BVM 219V, † 245v)

A27 *England, Cambridge, Univ Lib*, ms Mm ii 9
- of Barnwell?, 13c, 291ff, 340x240
- This is part of the facsimile edition of the *Antiphonale Sarisburiense*. Frere, (1901) II 79 and *AS* I v, 76-77
- T 1
  later hymns to BVM 122
  S 123
  C 267
  H 265

A28 *Spain, Madrid, Bibl nacional*, ms M 1322 (olim a 1)
- 14c, 203 ff, 430x320
- Janini (1969) 282-3
- summer
  T 1 (Trin 25v)
  S 61 (Annunc BVM 64v, Vigil Assumpt BVM 102, All Saints 125)
  D 171
  † 176v
  H 188

A29 *Portugal, Lisbon, Arquivo nacional da Torre do Tombo*, ms 19
- of Lorvão, 1451 *in era* (ie 1413)
- Hughes (1975) 381; Corbin 186, 192a, 277
- S (begins incomplete: Stephen 1, Annunc BVM 30, Nat BVM 64v)
  C 89v
  D 114v
  † 119
  H 130

A30 *Germany, Trier, Stadtbibl*, ms 1683 (olim 395b)
- 16c, 485 + ff
- summer
  T (Easter 2, Trin 22)
  S 50 (Assumpt BVM 76, All Saints 100v)
  D 121v
  C 128
  H 161

A32 *France, Autun, Bibl mun*, ms S 171
- of Autun, 15c, 465ff, 255x342
- this includes lessons
- P 1 (Litany 75v)
  T 83 (Vigil Easter 257, Asc 293v)
  S 304 (Purif 366v, Annunc BVM 383, D 401)
  C 430
  † 458

A33 *England, Manchester, Rylands Lib*, ms L 171
- Dominican, of Northern Italy, 14c, 210ff, 580x405
- James 294
- summer
  T (Vigil Trin 1)
  S 59? (Assumpt BVM 186)

A34 *England, Manchester, Rylands Lib*, ms L 439
- Roman, 15c, 204ff, 405x305
- Taylor 19
- summer
  T (Easter 1, Vigil Trin 42v)
  S 95? (Assumpt BVM 142, All Saints 172v)
  D 200
  C 206

A35 *Eire, Dublin, Trinity College* ms 77 (olim B.1.1)
- of Armagh, 15c, 126ff, 510x336
- Frere (1901) II 63, Abbott
- T 1 (Vigil Trin 18v)
  K 50
  P 55

A36 *Germany, Munich, University Lib*, ms 2° 176
- Benedictine, from Tegernsee, 1443, 309ff, 570x400
- Gottwald 37-38
- winter
  T 1
  S 189
  C 260

A37 *Germany, Karlsruhe, Badische Landesbibl*, ms Licht 15
- monastic, 83 ff
- S only (Annunc BVM 62v)

BREVIARIES

Noted Breviaries are listed after Breviaries

Printed Breviaries

BS 1531: the printed Sarum Breviary of 1531 (Chevallon, printed in Paris), edited 1879-86. See under BS in the Bibliography.

BS 1555: printed Sarum Breviary of 1555 (Richard Pynson, printed in London), said to be another edition of the print of 1508. The winter volume used is now in *Manchester, Rylands Lib* 13774.

Manuscript Breviaries

B1 *France, Laon, Bibl mun*, ms 255
- Abbey of Bec, 14/15c (after 1388), 586ff, 145x106
- Leroquais (1934) II 143-46; IRHT 5432-34
- K 1
  T 7 (LXX 41, Easter 101v, Trin 143)
  P 217
  litany 277
  S 282 (begins with Vigil Nat, Blasius 344, Maria Magd 416v)
  D 527
  C 541
  † 578

B2 *France, Provins, Bibl mun*, ms 9
- Dominican, German?, 15c (post 1461), 340ff, 161x122
- Leroquais (1934) iv 52-54; IRHT 6176-77
- K 4
  P 11
  litany 69
  T 73 (Nat 84v, LXX 109, Easter 139v, Trin 160)
  D 194
  S 203 (Blasius 235, Assumpt BVM 285v)
  C 323v

B3 *Belgium, Brussels, Bibl royale*, mss 9511 and 9026
- the Breviary of Philippe le Bon, 15c, 525 + and 400 + ff
- ms 9511 winter
  ordo 1
  T 15 (Nat 43v, LXX 89v, Easter 180, Vigil Pen 229v)
  K 244v
  P 252
  C 364
  S 398 (Vigil Annunc BVM 499)
- ms 9026 summer

B4 *Germany, Bamberg, Königl Bibl,* ms lit 84
- monastic, Cistercian, of Langheim, 14c, 467ff ?, 166x130
- Leitschuh (1966) I 231-32
- K and Easter tables 2v
  T 16 (Vigil Nat 39v, LXX 83, Easter 140v, Trin 173v)
  S 245v (Annunc, BVM 289, Assumpt BVM 336v, All Saints 366v)
  C 381
  D 413
  H 418
  litany 467

B5 *Germany, Bamberg, Königl Bibl,* ms lit 93
- Dominican, of Groh? Nurnberg?, 16c, 223ff, 170x117.5
- Leitschuh (1966) I 240
- summer
  T 1 (Easter 8, Trin 14)
  D 38 preces, etc 42
  S 83 (Assumpt BVM 138, All Saints 164)
  C 184
  P 215

B6 *Czechoslovakia, Prague, University Lib,* ms VII F 23
- Premonstratensian, of Chotěšoviense, 1353, 827ff (not foliated), 185x130
- Ploček I No 72
- K 1
  P 2
  † ?
  H 178
  T 269
  D ?
  S ?
  C 790

B7 *England, Oxford, Bodleian Lib,* ms University College 101
- monastic, of Pontefract Priory, later Monkbretton, 13c, 385 + ff?
- Frere (1901) I 1-8; Van Dijk (1951) II 266
- T 1 (lessons for ferias, etc)
  K 25
  T 33 (Nat 47v, LXX 91, Vigil Easter 124v, Vigil Trin 152)
  P 178
  litany 227
  † 234v
  S 237? (Annunc BVM 261v, Assumpt BVM 305v, All Saints 327)
  D 342
  C 345

B8 *England, London, British Library,* ms Sloane 1909
- Sarum, 14c, 490ff, ca 157x103
- Hughes (1976)
- T 1 (Nat 15, LXX 66v, Easter 124, Vigil Trin 164)
  D 232
  K 244
  P 248
  litanies 301v
  S 306 (Annunc BVM 346v, Assumpt BVM 396, All Saints 432 v)
  C 458
  † 484v

B9 *Czechoslovakia, Brno, Universty Lib,* ms R 598 (olim B/K I α 26)
- monastic, Cistercian, of Sedlecensis (?), 1308, 287ff, 195x150
- Dokoupil 308-09
- winter
  K 18
  T 24 (Nat 57v, LXX 118)
  S 179v (Annunc BVM 229)
  C 235
  H 253v

B10 *Italy, Rome, Santa Sabina, Archives of the Dominican Order,* ms XIV L 1 (Humbert's Codex)
- ca 1250, 997pp, 480x320
- This consists of fourteen independent books bound together to form the complete reference work for all Dominican services. The sixth book is the Breviary, ff 87-141v. Bonniwell 85-97; Boyle 368-74; cf the copy in London, British Library, ms add 23935 described in Hughes (1976)
- litany 85
  T 87 (Easter 104)
  C 133

B11 *Italy, Florence, Bibl Medicea-Laurenziana,* ms Aedil 118
- Roman (for S. Salvatore in Florence), 15c, 523ff, 255x358
- K 3
  T 10 (Vigil Nat 28v, Pen 156)
  P 210
  S 265
  D 458v
  C 478

B12 *England, London, British Library*, ms Harley 512
- 15c, 197ff, ca 460x310
- Hughes (1976)
- T 3 (Nat 25v, LXX 73v, Easter 122, Vigil Trin 148v)
  D 190v

B13 *Vatican, Bibl Apostolica Vaticana*, ms Rossi 81
- monastic, of Erfurt and Bursfeld, 14c, 412ff, 145x103
- Salmon (1968-69) I 154-55.
- K lv
  P 20
  T 151 (Nat 168, LXX 189, Easter 227v, Vigil Trin 252)
  C 279
  D 300v
  S 305 (Annunc BVM 340, Assumpt BVM 363v, All Saints 383)
  † 398v

B14 *England, London, British Library*, ms Harley 4664
- monastic, of Coldyngham Priory, 13/14c, 333ff, ca 245x165
- Tolhurst I vi and VI 238; Hughes (1976)
- T 9 (Vigil Nat 21, LXX 48v, Vigil Easter 80v, Trin 102)
  K 126
  P 133
  litany 175
  H 181
  S 190
  C 3v

B15 *England, London, British Library*, ms add 49363 (= C4 below)
- monastic, Cluniac, of Wenlock Priory, ca 1300, 384ff (misbound?), 152x98
- Hughes (1976)
- T 1 (Nat 16v, LXX 66, Vigil Easter 113, mid-Trin 200)
  mid-P 145
  mid-S 239 (Assumpt BVM 293, All Saints 332v)
  C 363
  D 360
  litany 374v

B16 *Vatican, Bibl Apostolica Vaticana*, ms Ottoboni 672
- of Besançon, 1452-53, 353ff, 102x70
- Salmon (1968-69) I 138
- K 1
  P 8
  T 94 (Nat 108v, LXX 137v, Easter 169v, Vigil Pen 189)
  S 227 (Annunc BVM 253, Assumpt BVM 292v)
  † 319
  C 339

B17 *Vatican, Bibl Apostolica Vaticana*, ms lat 8247
- of Zagreb, 1460, 314ff, 189x135
- Salmon (1968-69) I 188
- K 2
  P 8
  T 55 (Nat 67, LXX 91v, Easter 129, Vigil Trin 145)
  S 177v (Assumpt BVM 245)
  C 291v
  D 308v
  † 311v

B18 *Vatican, Bibl Apostolica Vaticana*, ms Barb lat 408
- of Laon, 15c, 337ff, 159x118
- Salmon (1968-69) I 108
- K 1
  P 7
  H 98
  T and S combined 101 (Nat 118v, LXX 151v, Easter 187v, Annunc BVM 233v, Pen 251v, Assumpt BVM 286, All Saints 301v)
  C 311
  D 328

B19 *France, Paris, Bibl de l'Arsénal*, ms 595
- of St-Etienne, Châlons-sur-Marne, 14c, 460ff
- Huglo (1971) 418; Leroquais (1934) II 342
- K 1
  P 6
  litany 33
  T 39
  S 254v (Annunc BVM 301v, Assumpt BVM 357, D 396v, All Saints 403)
  C 417v

B20 *England, Cambridge, University Lib*, ms add 4500
- Sarum, 15c, 546ff, 180x122
- Frere (1901) II 77
  T 4 (Nat 40v, LXX 101v, Easter 156, Vigil Trin 188)
  D 243v
  K 270
  P 276
  C 337
  S 362 (Annunc BVM 402v, Assumpt BVM 463v)

B21 *England, Oxford, Bodleian Lib*, ms lat lit e 12
- of Braga (written in Portugal), 15c, 596ff, 228x165
- Van Dijk (1951) II 255
- K 3
  P 9
  H 101
  T 135 (Nat 163v, Easter 254v, Trin 285v)
  S 345 (Assumpt BVM 474v)
  C 567
  † 585v

B22 *Spain, El Escorial*, ms P III 14
- of Saragossa, 13c, 314ff, 202x137
- Janini (1977) 106
- K 1
  P 8
  T62 (Vigil Nat 75v)
  S 169
  C 275

B23 *Spain, El Escorial*, ms E IV 10
- of Braga (written in Portugal), 15c, 492ff, 185x125
- Janini (1977) 87
  K 1
  P ?
  H75
  † 89
  T 103
  S 281
  C 464

B24 *Spain, Madrid, Bibl nacional*, ms 9694 (olim Ff 147)
- of Toledo (written in Castille), 15c, 653ff, 137x187
- Janini (1969) 115-16
- K 1
  P 7
  † 89v
  T 98 (Vigil Pen 230)
  S 287 (All Saints 562)
  D 588
  C 633

B25 *Spain, Madrid, Bibl. nacional*, ms res 186 (olim A 169)
- 1463, 485ff, 141x191
- Janini (1969) 211-12
- K 1
  P 1 (new foliation)
  T 45 (XL 3 128)
  S 248
  C 394

B26 *Portugal, Braga, Bibl pública*, ms 657
- of Braga (Breviary of Manuel Fernandes Sorito), 14c, 323ff, 202x250
- Hughes (1975) 379-80; Corbin 277
- K 1
  P 8
  T 64 (Nat 76v, Vigil Trin 135v)
  S 177 (Concep BVM 168v)
  D 304v
  C 305

B27 *England, London, British Lib*, ms add 35311
- of Burgundy, 14/15c, 438, 242x176
- Hughes (1976)
- winter
  K 1
  P 7
  T 121 (Nat 157v, LXX 252)
  S 341 (Annunc BVM 383v)
  C 389v
  P cont 414
  † 435

B28 *England, London, British Lib*, ms Harley 2927
- of Paris, ca 1420, 518ff, 116x164
- Hughes (1976)
- K 3
  P 9
  litany 105v
  T 132 (Nat 161, Easter 290, Vigil Pen 330)
  S 341
  C 476

B29 *England, Manchester, Rylands Lib*, ms L 136
- of Paris (Notre Dame), 15c, 47ff, 185x133
- James 238
- K 1
  P 7
  T 90 (Vigil Trin 90)
  D 166v
  S 175
  C 386

B30 *England, Oxford, Bodleain Lib*, ms Can lit 171
- Franciscan, written in Italy (post 1234), used in France or N. Spain (15c), 287ff, 165x120
- Van Dijk (1951) II 283; Van Dijk (1960) passim
- K 1
  P 7
  H 108v
  T 125
  S 224v

B31 *USA, New York, Pierpont Morgan Lib*, ms 909
- of Chalon-sur-Saône, ca 1440, 525ff, 235x165
- K 3
  P 9
  T 129 (Easter 129, Trin 196)
  S 293 (Assumpt BVM 384v, All Saints 460)
  C 493
  † 514

B32 *Spain, El Escorial*, ms P III 13
- of Quimper (Paris use), 15c, 834ff, 205x140
- Janini (1977) 105-06
- K 1
  P 13
  ordo 109
  T 137 (Vigil Nat 163)
  S 411 (Annunc BVM 513v, Assumpt BVM 667, All Saints 769)
  C 811

B33 *Wales, Aberystwyth, National Lib of Wales*, ms 495B
- Dominican-Premonstratensian, of St Mary de Parco (Louvain), 15c, 331ff ?
- K 2
  P 9
  T 61 (Nat 75)
  S 225 (Purif BVM 244v)
  C 317v

B34 *Italy, Florence, Bibl Medicea-Laurenziana*, ms conv sop 389
- Dominican, of Ss John and Paul convent (Venice), 1473, 325ff, 105x148
- Del Furia II 139
- K 1
  P 7v
  T 62v
  S 171
  C 297

B35 *Vatican, Bibl Apostolica Vaticana*, ms Barb 400
- Dominican, of Rieti, 14c, 436ff, 149x96
- Salmon (1968-9) I 107-8

B36 *Eire, Dublin, Trinity College*, ms 84 (olim B.3.12)
- Augustinian, of county Meath (monast B. Mariae de Trin), 15c, 254ff, 211x145
- Frere (1901) II 64, Abbott 11
- summer
  K 1
  P 7
  S 83 (Assumpt BVM 158, All Saints 207)
  C 232v

B37 *Eire, Dublin, Trinity College*, ms 85 (olim B.3.9)
- of York, 15c, 377, 231x149
- Frere (1901) II 64, Abbott 11
- T 1 (Nat 16v, LXX 50v, Easter 89, Vigil Trin 113)
  K 160
  P 166
  S 233 (Annunc BVM 265, Assumpt BVM 316v, All Saints 356)
  C 376

B38 *England, Oxford, Bodleian Lib*, ms Can lit 286
- Augustinian nuns, of Marienthal-Niesing, 1463/4, 324ff, 178x130
- Van Dijk (1951) II 278
- K 2
  P 8v
  H 64
  T 74 (Nat 86v, Easter 144, Trin 163)
  S 191
  D 293v
  C 296

B39 *England, Oxford, Bodleian Lib*, mss Rawl lit e 1 and Gough lit 8
- Sarum, monastic, of Hyde Abbey (Winchester), ca 1300, 286ff ? (Rawl) and 72ff (Gough), 145x85
- Van Dijk (1951) II 265; Tolhurst (edition) I vii-xi
- (Gough)
  K 4
  P 12
- (Rawl)
  T 1 (Vigil Nat 16, Easter 98v, Trin 129v)
  S 189

B40 *England, Blackburn. Stonyhurst College*, ms 44
- Sarum, of Ashridge, ca 1380, 469 + ff
- Frere (1901) II 31
- summer
  T 1 (Vigil Trin 11)
  D 94
  K 120
  P 127
  † 222v
  S 224 (Assumpt BVM 331v)
  C 469v

B41 *England, Manchester, Rylands Lib*, ms L 346
- Franciscan, Italian, 15c, 429ff, 105x78
- This is essentially a diurnal. Frere (1901) II 29
- K
  P 2
  H 129
  T 145 (Vigil Nat 153, LXX 176, Easter 242, Vigil Trin 259v)
  C 278v
  D 311
  † 321v
  S 336v (Annunc BVM 352v, Assumpt BVM 396v, All Saints 412v)

B42 *USA, Washington (D.C.), Library of Congress*, ms 75
- of Paris, 15c, 563, 190x120
- K 2
  P 18
  T 88 (Vigil Nat 108, LXX 139v, Easter 197, Vigil Trin 233
  C 306
  S 328 (All Saints 476)

B43 *England, Cambridge, Emmanuel College*, ms 64 (olim I. 3. 11)
- Sarum, of Dublin, 14c, 523ff, 197x119
- Frere (1901) II 128
- T 1 (Nat 30v, LXX 90v, Easter 145, Trin 179)
  D 239
  K 253
  P 260
  C 317
  S 346 (Annunc BVM 390, Assumpt BVM 455v, All Saints 497v)

B44 *England, Oxford, Bodleian Lib*, ms Can lit 215
- Sarum, of county Down?, 15c, 410ff, 147x100
- Van Dijk (1951) II 300
- T (Vigil Nat 24, Vigil Easter 98v, Trin 124)
  D 161v
  K 176
  P 182
  C 244
  S 269

B45 *Eire, Dublin, Trinity College*, ms 86 (olim B.3.10)
- Carmelite, of Kilcormick, 1489, 349ff, 232x157
- Frere (1901) II 65
- T 5 (Nat 16v, LXX 40v, Easter 68, Vigil Trin 87)
  K 115
  P 121
  C 165
  S 180 (Annunc BVM 202)

B46 *Eire, Dublin, Trinity College*, ms 88 (olim B.3.13)
- Sarum, of Dublin, 15c, 464ff, 201x128
- Frere (1901) II 64
- T 2 (Nat 37, Easter 130v, Trin 161)
  D 211
  K 220
  P 227
  C 288
  S 308

B47 *England, London, British Library*, ms add 43405/6
- monastic, of Muchelney, 14c, 301ff (405) and 351ff (406), 156x255
- Hughes (1976); Tolhurst I vi, VI 239
- ms 405
  T 1 (Vigil Nat 21v, Trin 212v)
- ms 406
  K 1
  P 7
  † 91v
  S 98
  C 285

B48 *England, London, British Library*, ms Harley 587
- Sarum, of Worcester, 15c, 432ff (2 vols), 182x123
- Hughes (1976)
- T 1 (Nat 25, LXX 67v, Easter 114, Vigil Trin 134)
  K 185
  P 191
  C 269
  S 289 (Annunc BVM 320, Assumpt BVM 373)
  † 428v

B49 *England, Cambridge, Trinity College*, ms 1359 (olim O. 7. 31)
- monastic, of Battle Abbey, 15c, 206ff
- Tolhurst I vi, VI 238
- T 1 (Vigil Nat 12v, Trin 81v)
  C 103
  S 119
  D 194

B50 *England, Canterbury, Cathedral Lib*, ms add 6 (The Burnt Breviary)
- monastic, of Canterbury, 1373-83

- C.S. Phillips, *Canterbury Cathedral in the Middle Ages* (London 1949) 19
- folder 1 T 1-80
  folder 2 K 83
  folder 3 P 1
  S 60
  C 301v
  S cont 345?

B51 *England, Oxford, Bodleian Lib*, ms Barlow 41
- monastic, Benedictine, of Evesham (Flemish, for English use), 13c, 358ff, 175x107
- Van Dijk (1951) II 264; Tolhurst VI 239
- winter
  T 4 (Vigil Nat 30, LXX 91)
  K 158
  P 164
  † 242
  H 245v
  S 262v
  C 319

B52 *England, London, British Library* ms Royal 2 A. XII
- Sarum, 15c, 637ff, 187x130
- Hughes (1976)
- K 1
  T 7 (Nat 47v)
  P 275
  D 366
  S 387
  C 605

B53 *England, Cambridge, University Lib*, ms add 3474/75
- of St George's (Norwich)?, 14c, 257ff (74) & 171ff (75), 144x101 (74), 144x105 (75)
- Frere (1901) II 76
- ms 3474
  K 1
  T 7 (Nat 55, LXX 119, Easter 168, Vigil Trin 201v)
- ms 3475
  K 258
  C 272
  S 297 (Annunc BVM 325v, Assumpt BVM 376, All Saints 470v)

B54 *England, Blackburn, Stonyhurst College*, ms 52
- Sarum, 14c, 488ff ?
- Frere (1901) II 31
- T 1 (Vigil Nat 22v, LXX 74, Trin 151)
  D 202
  P 210
  C 279
  S 303 (All Saints 441)

B55 *France, Paris, Bibl nationale*, ms lat 745
- of Paris, 15c, 459ff (foliation incorrect), 255x175
- Leroquais (1934) II 421-3
- ordo 1
  T 1
  K 177
  P 185
  S 245
  C 431

B56 *France, Cambrai, Bibl mun*, ms A 97 (olim 98)
- of Cambrai, 15c, 375ff, 219x156
- Leroquais (1934) I 186-9
- T 1
  K 148
  P 154
  S 254

B57 *USA, Washington (D.C.), Library of Congress*, ms 73
- Flanders, 15c, 405ff, 130x100
- summer
  T 4 (Vigil Trin 4)
  D 88v
  K 100
  P 107
  C 219
  S 251

B58 *Spain, El Escorial*, ms G IV 29
- monastic, Benedictine, of La Peña (Aragon), 14c, 449ff, 165x115
- Janini (1977) 88-9
- T 2 (Vigil Nat 16v)
  K 161
  P 179
  H 233
  C 260v
  S 280
  D 437
  † 441v

B59 *Vatican, Bibl Apostolica Vaticana*, ms lat 10,000
- Franciscan, of Otricoli, 14c, 474ff, 171x117
- Salmon (1968-9) I 191-2

B60 *Vatican, Bibl Apostolica Vaticana*, ms Borgia lat 209
- monastic, of Germany/Bohemia, 14c, 275ff, 158x118
- Salmon (1968-9) I 114
- P ?
  H 8

T and S combined (Nat 87, Annunc BVM 124v, LXX 127, Vigil Easter 158, Trin 187, Assumpt BVM 214v)
C 244

B61 *Vatican, Bibl Apostolica Vaticana,* ms Urbin. 111
- of Tuscany, 15c, 534ff, 356x249
- Salmon (1968-9) I 166

B62 *Vatican, Bibl Apostolica Vaticana,* ms Urbin. 599
- Camaldolese, of Florence (Santa Maria de Angelis), 15c, 510ff, 138x98
- Salmon (1968-9) I 168

B63 *Vatican, Bibl Apostolica Vaticana,* ms Barb. 409
- Franciscan, of Tuscay, 15c, 516ff, 160x117
- Salmon (1968-9) I 109

B64 *USA, New York, Pierpont Morgan Lib,* ms 52
- Franciscan, made in Ghent or Bruges for Eleanor, Queen of Portugal, before 1525, 593ff, ca 230x170
- K 2
T 9 (Nat 32v, LXX 86v, Easter 146v, Trin 189v)
P 233v
S 345v (Annunc. BVM 388v, Assumpt BVM 478v, All Saints 532v)
C 558v
D 578v

B65 *USA, Washington (D.C.), Library of Congress,* ms 47
- Italian, 15c, 328ff, 110x70
- K i
T 1 (LXX 41, Easter 76v, Vigil Trin 92v)
P 111
† 170
S 191 (Assumpt BVM 233)
C 255v
D 287v

B66 *Italy, Florence, Bibl Medicea-Laurenziana,* ms Aedil 116
- Roman, 15c, 441ff, 242x330
- K 1
T 7 (Vigil Pen 148v)
P 207
H 255
S 265
C 403
† 426

B67 *Italy, Florence, Bibl Medicea-Laurenziana,* ms Aedil 117
- Roman, 14c, 429ff, 230x333
- K 1
T 7 (Pen 135)
P 183
S 245
C 362v
† 386

B68 *Italy, Florence, Bibl Medicea-Laurenziana, Bibl nazionale centrale,* ms Magl XXXVI, 6
- monastic, for S. Salvatore in Florence, 535ff, 140x199
- K
T 1
P 237
S 329
D 459
C 468
† 520

B69 *USA, New York, Pierpont Morgan Lib,* ms 8
- written and illuminated at Rodez for Guy de Castlenau-Bretenoux, abbot of the Cistercian abbey of Bonneval, ca 1511, 420ff, ca 220x150
- K
T 16 (Easter 108v)
P 190
H 263
C 274
S ? (Assumpt BVM 377v)
D 291
† 417v

B70 *France, Angers, Bibl mun,* ms 116
- of St Aubin-d'Angers, 15c, 399ff, 125x89
- Leroquais (1934) I 27-8
- summer
K 1
T 5
P 84
C 196
S 237

B71 *England, Oxford, Bodleian Lib,* ms Laud misc 84
- of York, 15c, 389ff, 260x175
- Huglo (1971) 22; Van Dijk II 254
- T 1 (Vigil Nat 15v, LXX 48, Easter 84v, Trin 110)
D 152v
K 163
P 170
C 220
S 242

B72 *England, Cambridge, Kings College*, ms 30
- Sarum, 14/15c, 522ff, 190x140
- Frere (1901) II 144
- T 6 (Nat 27, LXX 65, Easter 102v, Vigil Trin 130v)
  D 182
  K 193
  P 199
  S 256 (Annunc BVM 287, Assumpt BVM 339, All Saints 374v)
  † 378
  C 397

B73 *USA, Chicago, Newberry Lib*, ms 71
- Italian, 15c

B74 *Vatican, Bibl Apostolica Vaticana*, ms lat 4751
- of Krakow, 15c, 425ff, 210x155
- Salmon (1968-9) I 172
  K 1
  P 7
  H 93
  T 106 (Nat 125, Easter 222v, Vigil Trin 259)
  D 292
  S 294v (Assumpt BVM 365)
  C 407

NOTED BREVIARIES

NB1 *England, Oxford, Bodleian Lib*, ms E Mus 2
- Sarum, of Bedwin, 14c, 1008pp
- Van Dijk II 221
- T 1 (Nat 29, LXX 167, Easter 338, Trin 389)
  D 500
  K 517
  P 534
  S 635 (Annunc BVM 736, Assumpt BVM 849)

NB2 *France, Paris, Bibl de l'Arsenal*, ms 279
- of Caen (for Cathedral at Bayeux, used at St-Sépulchre), 13c, 598ff
- Leroquais (1934) II 334-8
- K f.A
  P 4
  T 54 (Nat 81, LXX 136v, Vigil Easter 199v, Trin 245v)
  S 324 (Annunc BVM 381v, Assumpt BVM 447v)
  C 528
  D 557
  S cont 570

NB3 *England, Hereford, Cathedral Lib*, ms P 9 VII
- of Hereford, ca 1270, 365 ff, 274x190
- Frere (1904) III lv-lxi
- T 1 (Vigil Nat 19, LXX 63, Vigil Easter 112, Trin 141)
  D 175v
  K 183
  P 188
  S 223 (Annunc BVM 253v, Assumpt BVM 291, All Saints 314v)
  C 334
  † 356v

NB4 *Czechoslovakia, Brno, University Lib*, ms R 625/626 (olim Rajhrad F/K.I.a.1 & 2)
- of Olomouc, ca 1395-7, 345 and 325ff, 615x430
- Dokoupil 316-9
- ms 625, winter
  K
  T 2 (Nat 35, LXX 96v, Easter 172)
  S 212 (Annunc BVM 265, Assumpt BVM 150, All Saints 247v)
  C 287
- ms 626 summer
  K
  T 1 (Vigil Trin 1)
  D 70v
  S 76v
  C 286

NB5 *Vatican, Bibl Apostolica Vaticana*, ms reg lat 2050/2051
- Franciscan, of Ascoli Piceno, 13/14c, 341 and 232ff, 295x207
- Salmon (1968-9) I 152; Van Dijk (1960) 219
- ms 2050
  K 1
  T 5 (Nat 45, LXX 125v, Easter 219)
- ms 2051
  S 1 (Annunc BVM 38v, Assumpt BVM 113v, All Saints 159)
  C 182v
  D 227v

NB6 *USA, Chicago, Newberry Lib*, ms 24
- Franciscan, of Perugia?, post 1232, 266ff, 200x140
- Van Dijk (1960) passim
- T 34
  S 164

NB7 *England, Oxford, Bodleian Lib*, ms Gough lit 1
- York, 14c, 200ff, many leaves missing
- Van Dijk (1951) II 229
- P 1 (begins incomplete)
  C 31 (begins incomplete)
  S 54 (Annunc BVM 92, Assumpt BVM 143, All Saints 184, † 187)

NB8 *England, London, British Library*, ms add 37399
- of Paris, ca 1300, 459ff, 183x132
- Hughes (1976)
- winter
  K
  P 2
  T 80 (Vigil Nat 109v, Vigil Easter 235, Vigil Pen 273v)
  S 282v (Annunc BVM 360v, All Saints 454)

NB9 *England, London, British Library*, ms Yates Thompson 8
- of Renaud de Bar (Verdun), 1302, 360ff, 292x207
- Hughes (1976)
- winter
  K 1
  P 7
  † 86
  T 91v (Nat 122v, LXX 174)
  S 249
  D 316
  C 330

NB10 *Vatican, Bibl. Apostolica Vaticana*, ms lat 4756
- of Chartres, 13c (1262), 362ff, 140x105
- Salmon (1968-9) I 173-4
- winter
  K 1
  P 4
  T 53 (Nat 86, LXX 144v, Vigil Easter 192, Trin 248v)
  C 253
  † 263v
  S 269 (Annunc BVM 327)

NB11 *England, Salisbury, Cathedral Lib*, ms 152
- of Arlingham, Gloucester, ca 1460, 385ff, 508x327
- Frere (1901) II 20. See *AS*.
- T 2 (Vigil Nat 23v, LXX 57, Easter 92v, Trin 121)
  D 153v
  K 160
  P 166
  S 215 (Annunc BVM 251, Assumpt BVM 296, All Saints 325v
  C 343v

NB12 *England, York, Minster Lib*, ms add 69
- 15c, 356ff ?
- T 1 (Nat 14v, LXX 45, Easter 82, Vigil Trin 106v)
  D 136v
  K 150
  P 156
  C 180
  S 202 (Annunc BVM 242, Assumpt BVM 295, All Saints 332v, † 336)

NB13 *Scotland, Edinburgh, University Lib*, ms 27
- of Lincoln?, later of Scotland, 14c, 484ff, 190x122
- Frere (1901) II 55; C.R. Boland, *A Descriptive Catalogue of the Western Medieval Manuscripts in Edinburgh University Library* (Edinburgh 1916) 39.
- K
  T 7
  P 233
  S 289
  C 444

NB14 *England, London, British Library*, ms add 17002
- Norwich, 15c, 176ff (incomplete), 268x404
- Frere *AS* I 80; Hughes (1976)
- winter
  K 1
  T 8 (Nat 8v, LXX 34, Easter 67v, Trin 84v)
  D 107v
  P 114
  S 144 (Annunc BVM 168v)

NB15 *France, Paris, Bibl Nationale*, ms lat 1263
- Paris, 15c, 519ff, 185x125
- Leroquais (1934) III 90
- ordo 1
  T 9
  † 167v
  K 172
  P 178
  S 263
  C 500?

NB16 *France, Troyes, Bibl mun*, ms 109
- of Moutier-la-Celle, 13/14c, 372ff, 227x313
- Leroquais (1934) IV 212-4
- winter
  T 1
  K 156
  P 165
  S 217 (Annunc BVM 312v)
  C 319

NB17 *England, London, British Library* ms add 32427
- Sarum, of Worcester? Gloucester?, 15c, 306ff, 560x451
- Hughes (1976)
- T lv (Nat 19v, LXX 49, Easter 82, Vigil Trin 105)
  D 136
  K 142
  P 148
  S 175 (Annunc BVM 205, Assumpt BVM 247, All Saints 269v)
  C 289

NB18 *France, Paris, Bibl nationale*, ms lat 1028
- of Sens, 13c, 342ff, 200x130
- Leroquais (1934) III 3-5
- K
  P 7
  S 143v

COMBINED BREVIARY-MISSALS

See ms B10, Humbert's Codex, for the Dominican order. Many of the following are discussed in appendix VII.

C1 *England, London, British Library*, ms add 35285
- This combines Antiphonal, Missal, Lectionary, and Processional, for the Augustinian Priory of Guisborough, 1246-1322, 347ff, 175x245
- Hughes (1976); Huglo (1971) 343, 350
- Breviary
  T 1 (Vigil Nat 27, LXX 51, Vigil Easter 78, Trin 92)
- Missal
  T 107 (Epiphany 110v, Vigil Easter 119v)
  S 138 (All Saints 151v)
  C 154
  K 168
  P 176
  † 212
- Antiphonal
  S 221v? (Annunc BVM 237v, Assumpt BVM 256v, All Saints 272)
  C 281
- Lectionary 295
- Processional 343

C2 *England, Cambridge, Fitzwilliam Museum*, ms 369
- monastic, Cluniac, of the Priory of Lewes, 13/14c, 517ff, 190x130
- Leroquais (1935)
- winter
  K 8
  P 14
  T 75 (Vigil Nat 89, Vigil Easter 203v, Trin 240v)
  Canon 295v
  S 308 (Vigil Assumpt 394, Vigil All Saints 435)
  D 461 v
  C 464v
  † 502

C3 *England, Cambridge, Fitzwilliam Museum*, ms Ii iv 20
- monastic, Benedictine, for the cathedral priory of Ely, 13c, 318ff, 204x148
- Frere (1901) II 83
- Breviary
  T 2 (LXX 59, Easter 92, Vigil Trin 113)
  S 194 (Annunc BVM 224v, Assumpt BVM 257, All Saints 278v)
  C 281
- Missal
  T 137 (Dom 1 Adv 139, Easter 147v, Pen 149v)
  † 165
  S 172v (All Saints 195)
  C 198

C4 *England, London, British Library*, ms add 49363 (= B15 above)
- monastic, Cluniac, of Wenlock Priory, ca 1300, 384ff (misbound?), 152x98
- Hughes (1976)
- because it is now apparently disordered, the book is too complex to inventory briefly

C5 *England, Oxford, Bodleian Lib*, ms Jesus College 10
- monastic, Benedictine, Antiphonal with Masses and processions, for St Peter's, Gloucester, and St Guthlac's, Hereford, 13c, 192ff, 200x140
- Van Dijk (1951) II 136
- K 1

T and S combined 7 (Vigil Nat 28, LXX 49, Annunc BVM 68v, Easter 92v, Trin 101, Assumpt BVM 127v)
C 152
H 155

C6 *USA, New York, Pierpont Morgan Lib*, ms Glazier 7
- monastic, Cistercian, of Hungary (the Liechtenstein-Kalmancsehi Codex), 1481, 335ff, ca 250x190
- Breviary
K 1
P 7
† 41
H 43v
T 57 (Nat 67v, LXX 84v, Easter 104v, Trin 116v)
S 136 (Annunc BVM 152v, Assumpt BVM 176v)
D 199v
C 202
- Missal
Canon 216
T 222 (Vigil Nat 226, Easter 248v, Trin 261)
S 246 (Assumpt BVM 292v, All Saints 299v)
C 301
D ?

GRADUALS

G1 *Germany, Munich, Bayerische Staatsbibl*, ms clm 11764
- of Polling, 14c, about 115ff
- *RISM* B 4.2 80-1; Geering 11
- T & S 1 (Vigil Nat 6v, Purif 23, XL 1 27, Easter 63v, Pen 76, John Baptist 88, Trin 90)
Ø 106

G2 *France, Paris, Bibl de l'Arsenal*, ms 110
- of Paris, 14c, 276ff, 242x155
- winter
K 9
T 1 (Vigil Nat 21v, Epi 26, Pascha 78v, Pen 91)
S 116v (Stephen 116v, Purif 121, All Saints 138)
C 141
Seq 165
Ø 261

G3 *Austria, Graz, University Lib*, ms IV 10
- of Neuberg, 15c
- *RISM* B 4.3 73-4; Geering 17

G4 *Austria, Graz, University Lib*, ms IV 9, as G3.

G5 *East Germany, Stralsund Stadtbibl*, ms without call-number
- church of St Nicholas, 14c
- *RISM* B 4.2 86; Geering 11
- winter
T 1 (Nat 7v, Passion 33, Vigil Easter 49v, Vigil Pen 60V)
D 76v
S 78 (John Baptist 92v)
Ø 108
Seq 113

G6 *Germany, Karlsruhe, Badische Landesbibl*, ms UH 1
- Cistercian, of Wonnental, 14c, 259ff
- *RISM* B 4.3 347.
- after some leaves which are foliated, the manuscript has roman figures for openings:
T + S ii (Adv 1 ii, Vigil Nat xiii, Pascha lxxxviii, Pen cxvi, Purif cli, Benedict clix, Assumpt BVM cxci)
† ccx
Ø ccxiii, Litany ccxxix
Seq ccxxxii

G7 *France, Limoges, Bibl mun* ms 2
- Gradual of Eleanor of Fontévrault, 13c, 304ff, 183x264
- *RISM* B 4.1 270-2
- T + S (begins incomplete at 5, Nat 19v, Agatha 64v, Palm 100v, Philip and James 131, Pen 143, Vigil of John Baptist 153v)
(remainder of ms not filmed)

G8 *Germany, Munich, Bayerische Staatsbibl* ms clm 6419
- of Freising, 14c, 111ff
- *RISM* B 4.2 79
- T + S (Adv 1 1, Nat 9, Purif 23v, Palm 52v, Easter 63v, Pen 76, John Baptist 80, All Saints 88)
Seq 103v
Ø 104

G9 *Germany, Karlsruhe, Badische Landesbibl* ms Wonn 1
- 15c, about 160ff
- *RISM* B 4.2 72

T (Adv 1 i, Vigil Nat ix, Epi xvi, Palm lvi, Easter lxxi, Trin lxxxvii)
S (Silvester lxxxxix, John Baptist cxviii)
D cxxxii
† cxxxiii
H 134
Ø 141
Seq 149

G10 *Austria, Salzburg, Benediktiner-Erzabtei St Peter* ms a VII 20
- 14c. The manuscript is in very bad condition, and the microfilm worse.
- *RISM* B 4.2 335-6
- T ? (Nat viiii, Easter 118, Trin 149)
  S ? (John Baptist 178)
  D 207
  C ?
  † 259
  Ø ?

G11 *England, London, British Lib* ms Royal 2 B IV
- troper and gradual of St Albans, 12c

G12 *France, Lille, Bibl mun* ms 26 (olim 599)
- incipitarium of St Pierre (Lille), 14c. The manuscript also includes incipits for the offices.
- Huglo (1971) 417; appendix VII
- Gradual
  K ?
  T ? (Vigil Nat vi, Easter xxxiiii, Trin liii)
  S lxxi (Andrew lxxi, Vigil Assumpt BVM cxvii)
  † clxiiii
- Antiphonal
  T i (Adv 1 i, Nat vi, Palm xviii, Trin xxvi)
  S xxxv (Andrew xxxv, John Baptist lvi)
  D lxxxii
- Invitatories and tonary lxxxxii

G13 *Netherlands, Haarlem, Bisschoppelijk Museum* ms 21
- of northern Holland (Utrecht), 15/16c
- *RISM* B 4.3 1112-13.
- T4 (Nat xi, LXX xx, Easter lxxi, Pen lxxxvii)
  S cvii (Andrew cvii, Nat BVM cxx)
  D cxxv
  C cxxviij
  † cliiii
  Ø clvi
  Seq 170

G14 The *Graduale Sarisburiense*, a facsimile edition (see Frere *GS*) largely based on the British Library mss add 12194 (Sarum, 13c) and Lansdowne 462 (see G21 and G23 below).

G15 The Gradual of St Thomaskirche (Leipzig), edited in facsimile (see Wagner 1930).

G16 *England, London, British Lib* ms Cotton Nero E VIII
- 15c, 83ff, 420x310
- T (begins incomplete at Adv 3 lv, Vigil Nat 3, Easter 22, Pen 31, Trin 34)
  D 47
  Ø 49
  S 56 (Andrew 56, Purif 59, Assumpt BVM 69, All Saints 75)
  C 77

G17 *England, London, British Lib* ms Harley 622
- of Roncton, 14c

G18 *England, Oxford, Bodleian Lib*, ms lat lit b 5
- East Drayton (York), 15c, 139ff, 410x280
- Van Dijk I 97
- T (begins incomplete with f.2)
  D 70
  Ø 79v
  S 90v
  C 118
  † 133

G19 *Vatican, Bibl. Apostolica Vaticana*, ms. lat. 5319
- Old Roman, of St Peters (Rome), 11/12c, 157ff
- Salmon (1968-69) II 88
- T + S (begins incomplete with Adv 2 i, Vigil Nat x, Fabian and Sebastian xxviii, Easter lxxxiiii, Philip and James ciii, Pen cvii)
  D cxxxvi
  Ø 145v

G20 *Vatican, Bibl Apostolica Vaticana*, ms St Peters F 22
- Old Roman, 12/13c, 104ff
- Salmon (1968-69) II 75-76
- T (begins incomplete in Adv, Nat 6v, LXX 16, Easter 53v, Asc 61)
  S 74v (Purif 75, John Baptist 80, Andrew 85)
  C 86
  D 100v

G21 *England, London, British Lib,* ms Lansdowne 462
- Sarum, 14c, 152ff, 495x330
- *RISM* B 4.3 607-12
- T (begins incomplete in Adv, John 6, Epi 10, Easter 50v, Trin 69)
  D 86
  Ø 89
  C 98v
  S 124v (Purif 128v, John Baptist 134v, All Saints 148v)

G22 The Gradual of Rouen, 13c. This is a facsimile edition of the ms *Paris, Bibl nat* lat 904 (see Loriquet 1907).

G23 *England, London, British Lib,* ms add 17001
- Sarum 15c, 175ff, 405x280, rubricated
- T i (Nat xv, XL 3 xli, Palm li[v])
  Prefaces lxiv[v]
  T cont (Easter lxix, Asc lxxxii, Trin xc[v])
  D cvii[v]
  Ø cxi
  † cxxvii[v]
  C cxx[v]
  S cxlv (Annunc cli[v], Assumpt BVM clxii)

MISSALS

Noted Missals are listed after Missals.

Printed Missals

MR The Roman Missal, printed 1474 in Milan. See Bibliography, under Lippe.

MS The Sarum Missal, a collation of numerous sources, edited by Francis Dickinson, 1861-83. See Bibliography.

MS (Legg) Another edition of the Sarum Missal, made basically from NM1 compared with NM6 and others. See Bibliography, under Legg (1916).

MW The Missal of Westminster, edited by J. Wickham Legg. See Bibliography under Legg (1891).

Manuscript Missals

M1 *England, Cambridge, Sidney Sussex College* ms 33
- of York, 15c, 250x162
- the order in this mostly unfoliated manuscript is K T Prefaces I D S C †

M2 *England, London, British Lib,* ms add 24198
- of St Thomas the Martyr (Dublin), 14c, 133ff, 325x225
- this manuscript contains only the feasts, benedictions, ⊕, Litany, Preface, Canon T & S (Nat 22, Purif 38v, Easter 43v, Asc 47v, Trin 53v, Laurence 67v, All Saints 80)
  C 89
  † 105

M3 *England, London, British Lib,* ms Harley 5289
- of Durham (cathedral), 14c, 496ff, 260x160
- K 2
  T 9 (Nat 26v, Easter 188v, Asc 209v, Trin 228)
  Ø 274
  Canon 282
  S 290 (Purif 304, John Baptist 320, All Saints 374)
  C 302v
  ⊕V
  † 461
  D 474v

M4 *England, London, British Lib,* ms add 34662
- of St Valéry (northern France), 14c, 269ff, 220x135
- K 11
  T (begins incomplete at 17, Adv 3 18, Vigil Easter 85, Corpus Christi 106v)
  Prefaces, etc 129v
  S (begins incomplete at 138, All Saints 171)
  D 176
  C 178v
  Baptism, ⊕V etc
  Seq 238

M5 *England, London, British Lib,* ms add 25588
- of Norwich, 15c

M6 *England, Manchester, Rylands Lib* ms L 151
- of France, 13c
- James 258-9

NOTED MISSALS

NM1 *England, Manchester, Rylands Lib* ms L 24
- 13c
- See MS (Legg) above

NM2 *France, Douai, Bibl mun* ms 90
- of Abbey of Anchin, 12c, 2 vols 179ff, 188ff
- Leroquais (1924) I 350-4
- vol 1
  K 1
  Ø 7
  Asperges 10, Preface 11, ⊕V
  † 22v
  D 27
  T 29 (Nat 42, Epi 48v)
  Canon 59
  T cont (LXX 64, Vigil Easter 141)
  S 150 (Purif 167)
- vol 2
  K 1
  Ø ?
  Prefaces, ⊕ etc
  † 23
  D 28
  T 29v (Easter 29v, Pen 46v)
  Canon 98
  S 94 (James 130, Assumpt BVM 138, All Saints 158)
  C 165
  Seq 175

NM3 *France, Rouen, Bibl mun* ms 277 (olim Y 50)
- of Rouen, 13c, 408ff, 220x155
- Leroquais (1924) II 70-1
- T 7 (Vigil Nat 23v, Palm 107v, Prefaces 151)
  Canon 159
  T cont (Pascha 167, Pen 194)
  S 249 (John Baptist 272v)
  D 306v, ⊕ 339v
  † 357
  Seq 367

NM4 *France, Toulouse, Bibl mun* ms 94
- 14c
- Leroquais (1924) II 225
- T 2 (Nat 15, Palm 98)
  Prefaces, Canon
  T cont (Pascha 158, Pen 182)
  S 227 (Purif 238, John Baptist 232)
  C 276v
  † 329v
  Ø 334

NM5 *Germany, Bamberg, Königl Bibl* ms lit 41
- Teutonic Knights, 14c, 315ff
- Geering 11
- K 2
  T (Nat 16v, Palm 72v, Easter 107v, Pen 124v)
  Ø 154
  S 161
  C 206v
  Trin 230v, ⊕V 233v
  † 249v
  Seq 257v

NM6 *France, Paris, Bibl de l'Arsenal*, ms 135
- 13c, 317ff, 180x120
- See MS (Legg) above; Leroquais (1924) II 132-5
- K 1
  T 7v (Palm 72, Asc 108v, Trin 117v)
  D 144v
  Preface 147
  Canon (begins incomplete at 150)
  S 153 (John Baptist 164v, All Saints 180)
  C 186v
  Trin 224
  Ø and sequences 228
- a Noted Breviary section begins on 292

PSALTERS

P1 *England, Oxford, Magdalen College* ms 100
- of Worcester, 13c
- Frere (1901) I 151

P2 *Vatican, Bibl Apostolica Vaticana* ms Barb lat 530
- of Umbria (Todi?), 14c
- Salmon (1968-9) I

Figures

Indices

All references are to section numbers. Multiple references within sections are not noted.

The linking of section numbers does not necessarily indicate continuous treatment of the subject.

References between square brackets refer to discussion of the physical representation of the subject in the manuscript sources, rather than general descriptions.

The user should always cross-refer to the sub-headings as main headings.

References to the frontispiece and to the plates will lead the user in fact to Appendix IX.

Index of Sources and Other Manuscripts

The present location of the sources is given in the Index of manuscripts by location, pp 415–17. See also the List of Sources, pp 390–407.

Antiphonals

Breviaries

Missals

Noted Missals

Psalters

Index of Manuscripts by Location

Index of Incipits

Dq stands for *Deus qui*; OsDq stands for *Omnipotens sempiterne Deus qui*

General Index

www.ingramcontent.com/pod-product-compliance
Lightning Source LLC
Chambersburg PA
CBHW081729130726
48089CB00018B/281

* 9 7 8 0 8 0 2 0 7 6 6 9 4 *